Florida Founder William P. DuVal

Florida Founder
William P. DuVal

Frontier Bon Vivant

James M. Denham

The University of South Carolina Press

© 2015 University of South Carolina

Published by the University of South Carolina Press
Columbia, South Carolina 29208

www.sc.edu/uscpress

Manufactured in the United States of America

24 23 22 21 20 19 18 17 16 15   10 9 8 7 6 5 4 3 2 1

Library of Congress Cataloging-in-Publication Data can be found at http://catalog.loc.gov/.

ISBN: 978-1-61117-466-3 (cloth)

ISBN: 978-1-61117-467-0 (ebook)

This book was printed on a recycled paper with 30 percent postconsumer waste content.

Contents

Illustrations vii
Preface ix

1. Scion of the Old Dominion 1
2. Soldier and War Hawk Politician 19
3. Judge and Governor 39
4. Founder of the Florida Territory 55
5. Neamathla and a New Territorial Capital 74
6. A "Corrupt Bargain" and a New Home in Florida 90
7. Trials, Tribulations, and "Left-Handed Justice" 106
8. "I have health, activity, good spirits, and a small share of *Perserverity*" 126
9. "Harassed by the persecution of their neighbors" 141
10. Storm Clouds on the Horizon 155
11. "I intend to examine . . . Your relation to the President" 173
12. Nullifying an Election 185
13. "I shall return very poor to Kentucky" 202
14. "Do all you can for Texas" 224
15. Canals, Banks, and a Constitutional Convention 240
16. Faith Bonds, Division, Depression, and a Plague 263
17. "Tyler Too," Washington Intrigue, and St. Augustine 284
18. State of Texas—State of Florida 304
19. "I will not be the cause of disunion in our ranks" 321

20. Gone to Texas—Gone to Washington 340
    Epilogue 353

Abbreviations in Notes 357
Notes 357
Bibliography 417
Index 441

Illustrations

Maps

Wilderness Road to Kentucky Settlements, c. 1800   8
Kentucky, Indiana, and Illinois Territories during the War of 1812   24
William Pope DuVal's Florida Territory, ca. 1834   187

Illustrations

Henry Clay, ca. 1810   12
Washington Irving, ca. 1820   30
General Andrew Jackson in uniform   36
John C. Calhoun, ca. 1820   37
President James Monroe   45
James Gadsden, ca. 1820   65
Neamathla, ca. 1830s   71
Samuel Southard, ca. 1820s   81
Tallahassee Plan, 1824   100
Tuko-see-Mathla   116
Legislative Council Meeting House, Tallahassee, ca. 1826   128
John Gratton Gamble   130
Thomas Brown, ca. 1820s   131
Achille Murat, ca. 1820s   149
William Wirt   150
President Andrew Jackson   158
John Quincy Adams, ca. 1830s   167
William Pope DuVal, ca. 1830s   174
The Capitol, Washington, D.C. West from City Hall, 1832   204
Lewis Cass, ca. 1833   210

City of Washington from beyond the Navy Yard, 1834   221
Louisville, Kentucky, Street Scene, ca. 1834   225
John Eaton, ca. 1834   228
Tallahassee Street Scene, ca. 1836   229
John P. DuVal   247
Samuel Parkhill and his brother John   256
Robert Raymond Reid   259
Martin Van Buren, ca. 1840   265
Richard Keith Call, ca. 1840   270
Washington Irving, ca. 1840   279
John Tyler, ca. 1840   285
William P. DuVal, ca. 1840   288
Thomas Douglas, 1840   289
St. Augustine Plaza, ca. 1840   294
David Levy Yulee   318
Edward Carrington Cabell, ca. 1848   335
Thomas Brown   338
John C. Calhoun, ca. 1850   342
Washington—Capitol, ca. 1848   349

Preface

BORN ONE YEAR AFTER the American Revolution in Richmond, Virginia, and dying six years before the Civil War, William Pope DuVal lived a life full of excitement, adventure, triumph, tragedies, and disappointments. Son of a well-to-do Richmond lawyer, Revolutionary War hero, and scion of a prominent Huguenot family, the fifteen-year-old DuVal and his older brother joined thousands of other Virginians heading west to Kentucky in 1800. The DuVal brothers' purpose in traveling to the "dark and bloody ground" of Kentucky was to patent thousands of acres of Kentucky land their father had acquired from his service in the American Revolution. While the dangers of migration were real enough, the DuVal brothers had advantages that other migrants to Kentucky lacked—cash and connections. With a loan from his father and land warrants in his saddlebags, DuVal found relatives and his father's business associates who eased the transition from urbane Richmond to the Kentucky frontier.

Reading law in the Bardstown area, DuVal achieved notoriety as a lawyer and politician. In 1812 he was elected to Congress, but before going to Washington, D.C., he volunteered for service in the War of 1812. DuVal's service in the Indiana Territory during the War of 1812 was brief and inauspicious, but he did meet numerous persons with whom he would associate in later years, such as William Henry Harrison, Zachary Taylor, Ninian Edwards, Duff Green, and Lewis Cass. As a "War Hawk" congressman representing Kentucky's Tenth District in the Thirteenth Congress, DuVal debated legislation on the controversial issues of the day, including the embargo, conscription, and the National Bank. And in the fall of 1814, he was among the members of the Thirteenth Congress who arrived to find the capital in ashes after the British attack. DuVal met many men who would have a significant impact on his future career in politics. Among these was his lifelong mentor, John C. Calhoun. Returning to Kentucky after one term, he practiced law but fell on hard times during the Panic of 1819. Relief came in 1821, when Calhoun, James Monroe's secretary of war, used his influence to have DuVal appointed judge in the newly created Florida Territory. The next year, also thanks to Calhoun's influence, Monroe appointed DuVal the territory's second governor, succeeding Andrew Jackson's brief three-month tenure. DuVal served three consecutive terms, remaining territorial governor until 1834. In those years he presided over the first civil territorial government of Florida and the founding of the capital at Tallahassee.

As territorial governor DuVal labored under extreme hardships. When he arrived in the territory, in 1822, Florida contained only a few thousand white inhabitants who were clustered around two Spanish towns, Pensacola and St. Augustine, separated by almost five hundred miles of wilderness. Also in Florida were roughly five thousand Indians, many of them refugee Creeks, recently arrived from conflicts in Alabama. They joined other Creeks of varying linguistic and cultural backgrounds, collectively referred to as Seminoles. In the Peninsula some bands lived alongside their black allies in towns. Other Creeks, who had allied themselves with Andrew Jackson during the First Seminole War, lived on reservations along the Apalachicola River. Still other bands lived in "Middle Florida," the region that would form the focal point of white settlements in the years following the founding of Tallahassee. As ex officio superintendent of Indian affairs, DuVal worked closely with Washington officials and oversaw the initial negotiations with the Seminole Indians. Careful examination of DuVal's correspondence offers a mixed picture of his attitudes regarding Florida's Native Americans. Some of his writings reflect compassion, while others reflect frustration and anger. One close student of the Seminole Wars summarizes these conflicting emotions well: "One can assume the double burden of governorship and superintendency had frayed his nerves. After all, he was under steady attack from all quarters. The tender-minded assailed him for having used force" in various agreements with the Indians (which he denied); "the economy-minded criticized him for spending money to feed the Indians (yet if he had not done so, they would have starved); while day in and day out the slaveholders carped at him for every move."[1] Though tension existed between DuVal and Seminole leaders, the majority trusted him, and the fact that there was no major rebellion until he left office is a tribute to his skill.

As a political appointee DuVal was closely linked to national politics from the 1820s through the 1840s. During his tenure as governor and throughout his life DuVal maintained close political ties to Kentucky, Washington, and the Virginia Dynasty. A Jeffersonian Democratic-Republican politician turned Jacksonian Democrat, DuVal, though a Kentuckian, counted Henry Clay among his enemies throughout his life. Even before the "Corrupt Bargain" episode, DuVal was convinced that Jackson's elevation to the White House was inevitable. Joining his Kentucky associates in earnest, DuVal worked hard for Old Hickory's election in 1824 and 1828. He and his friend Richard Keith Call visited the Hermitage often during those years. Not long after the election, however, DuVal was one of the many casualties of the Peggy Eaton Affair and the Nullification Crisis. The Jackson-Calhoun split was catastrophic for DuVal's political fortunes. The fallout soured DuVal and Jackson's cordial relationship, and the result was that John Eaton himself supplanted DuVal as territorial governor of Florida in 1834. The break also wrecked John C. Calhoun's presidential aspirations, elevating Martin Van Buren to the presidency in 1836. Not surprisingly, DuVal and his friend Call were lukewarm on Van Buren and eventually broke with his administration. Both supported William Henry Harrison (DuVal's old War of 1812 comrade) and the Whig Party in the election of 1840. DuVal eventually returned to the Democrats, but the temporary departure from party orthodoxy damaged his standing in the party, both nationally and later in Florida.

After DuVal left the governor's chair, he returned briefly to Kentucky, where he lent his efforts to the cause of Texas independence. Two of his sons participated in that conflict: Burr, his oldest, was killed in the Goliad Massacre, while another son, John C., was one of its few survivors. In 1836 DuVal was appointed an honorary brigadier general by the Republic of Texas and traveled widely raising men and supplies. Returning to Florida, DuVal was elected to the Florida State Constitutional Convention (1838) and the Florida Senate (1839), becoming its president in 1841. After his wife's death that year, he resigned from the Florida Senate and moved with his daughter and son-in-law to St. Augustine. From that time until his quixotic run for Congress in 1848 as a Democrat, DuVal dabbled in law and sought unsuccessfully to obtain other federal offices.

The next year he migrated to Galveston and then Austin, Texas, joining his son Thomas's law practice and playing the role of elder statesman. In his later years, DuVal despaired of the future of the Union. By that time DuVal had renewed his correspondence with John C. Calhoun, writing the aging statesman on pressing issues of the day such as the annexation of Texas, the growing fissures between the North and the South, and his sentiments regarding the inevitable breakup of the Union. More than just the ramblings of a bitter, disenchanted, and frustrated man, DuVal's sentiments are emblematic of an older "War Hawk" generation, whose ideas and leadership had been cast aside as obsolete. DuVal eventually set up shop in Washington, where, as a kind of Washington "insider," he represented claimants before Congress, and in this he was well known and successful. In 1854 he died there.

While these broad outlines of DuVal's career in politics are interesting and eventful, these facts do not tell us much about the man, his personality, or what made him so compelling. At an early age DuVal cultivated the art of oratory and storytelling while witnessing and participating in courtroom and political battles in the West. Traveling often on stages, sloops, and steamboats between Kentucky, Washington, and Florida, DuVal was a convivial companion. DuVal delighted in telling stories, jokes, and personal anecdotes. His charismatic, jovial personality captivated his listeners, even as it antagonized his opponents. He also drank—sometimes to excess. According to one observer, DuVal was a "manly, vigorous speaker," and his speeches were "characterized by exalted sentiments and a fervid patriotism." He possessed "unswerving integrity and all the genial graces that mark the perfect gentleman." Later in life he was described as a "short, fleshy, heavy-set man, not over five feet six inches high, flabby cheeks, and an inveterate tobacco chewer." DuVal, the man continued, was a "man of rare gifts, known more for rare colloquial powers, than for professional labors and ability."[2]

One observer who often witnessed DuVal's antics on the Florida frontier noted that the governor had an "inexhaustible store of anecdotes with which he could amuse an audience for hours. His style of rehearsing them would provoke an outburst of mirth under any circumstances." DuVal's facial expressions and body language contributed to his magnetism on the stump. "While his listeners would be convulsed with laughter, not a muscle of his face would be moved." His face "seemed a mixture of earnestness, distress, and complacency with a sort of devil-may-care expression. . . . And whenever the humor came over him the very appearance of the manner was comical indeed. With all," the commentator remembered, "I don't think any man was steel enough to be able to restrain" himself from laughter. "He sometimes made little blunders, but always had a way of making a plausible escape, and frequently added to the ludicrousness of the scenes he was describing, for he was full of information."[3]

Another observer noted that DuVal's imagination was "vivid and brilliant and his style of delivery as a public speaker easy, fluent, and forcible." As a social companion DuVal knew few equals. Whether traveling or at the fireside DuVal also sang an "admirable song" and "strikes upon the productions of Bobby Burns. Who has passed an evening in his life-inspiring company, and has not heard him sing 'My Boy Tommy,' or 'Tam O'Shanter!' . . . As a man in whom dwells a superabundance of 'milk and human kindness,'" the observer continued, "as a social companion, ever mirthful and enlivening, I know not his equal."[4]

It is in this vein as a flamboyant stump speaker, singer, and tall-tale teller that DuVal became the model for the main character in Washington Irving's "The Early Experiences of Ralph Ringwood." The stories DuVal narrated to Irving first appeared in the *Knickerbocker or New-York Monthly Magazine* in 1840.[5] DuVal's precise relationship to the famous writer is obscure, but they may have become acquainted as early as 1807, when the New Yorker visited Richmond as a newspaper correspondent reporting on Aaron Burr's treason trial. As a young man, Irving's friend Martin Van Buren also visited Richmond often, taking in the town's urbane conviviality and hospitality. DuVal's father's house in Richmond was a focal point in the community, and his hospitality was legendary. The town was crowded during the exciting trial, and it is plausible that DuVal—though living in Kentucky at the time—was also in town.

Another meeting might have occurred in 1814, when DuVal was a member of Congress. That year Irving, his brother (who had been appointed to Congress), and their brother-in-law James Kirke Paulding, also an aspiring writer, came to the capital together. The Irving brothers and Paulding were popular, especially among younger members of Congress. One can almost envision DuVal regaling the Irving brothers and Paulding with the songs, stories, and ribaldry of the wild realms of the Kentucky frontier.[6] Paulding, like Irving, would go on to write many books, including *The Lion of the West*, which also appeared as a play. DuVal's antics and storytelling may have inspired Paulding's hero Nimrod Wildfire. Paulding went on to be a mainstay in Washington. By 1815 Paulding had a job as secretary of the Board of Navy Commissioners and continued this employment through 1823.[7]

Irving's "Ralph Ringwood Tales," while embellished, form a kind of fictional autobiography of DuVal as narrated to Irving. Irving quotes Ringwood, and when he does we can reasonably believe that it is DuVal himself sharing his memories with Irving. Every attempt has been made in this study to use the historical record to separate fact from fiction. The "Ralph Ringwood Tales" offer us a window into DuVal's life and times or at least the image that he hoped to convey to his friends, enemies, and the public at large. Irving's stories lived on in future writing about the family. Betty Paschal O'Conner, DuVal's granddaughter, herself an accomplished author, essentially repeats Irving's sketch of the governor in her *My Beloved South*, (1913), a fanciful "moon-light and magnolia" image of the South in which she uses her family as the backdrop. Though she never met her grandfather, she uses Irving's stories and familial oral tradition to paint a picture of the son of a well-to-do Virginia aristocrat who strikes out for the "dark and bloody ground" of Kentucky, lives by hunting, and then settles down to read law and take a wife. Redeeming his promise not to return to Virginia until elected a member of Congress, the hero eventually became territorial governor of Florida, where he tames hostile Indians and civilizes the frontier.

Many elements of America's early national and antebellum history can be brought to light through DuVal's life. For example, DuVal, the son of a well-to-do Virginian of the Revolutionary generation, disagreed with his father's growing ambivalence about slavery. DuVal's father emancipated his slaves, and, like many of his fellow Virginians in the early nineteenth century, he favored colonization of freedmen to Africa. The son himself never was a large slaveholder. But he was certain that the future settlement, development, and prosperity of the Old Southwest were directly linked to maintaining the "Peculiar Institution." During his early years as governor of the Florida Territory and throughout his life, this political calculus dominated his thinking and action. Even so, these strongly held sentiments did not prevent his forming a close personal relationship with Toney and George Proctor, a free black father and son whom DuVal befriended and assisted in St. Augustine and Tallahassee.

An examination of DuVal's political career can also tell us a great deal more about Southern history. Living a long life, DuVal was forced to alter his beliefs in response to changing political and economic realities. He was often accused of inconsistency or, in modern-day parlance, "flip-flopping" as he adjusted to new realities. His stance on banking is only one case in point. Although not a major figure in Southern history, DuVal was intimately associated with many of those who were, such as Calhoun, Jackson, and John Tyler. Moreover, a study of the challenges DuVal faced during his life offers a window of understanding to the process by which antebellum America extended civil government and settlement west from Virginia to Kentucky, south to Florida, and then finally to Texas.

One of the most daunting challenges facing any DuVal biographer is the absence of a large cache of personal papers in any one spot. (It is possible that as an old man DuVal destroyed his papers, as few personal papers written to him survive.) Also, his constant movement and travel, much of it in a moist, humid climate, made it difficult for him to save things. Even so, his official correspondence as governor (1822–1834) is filed in the various departments of the federal government. Finding the documents is a challenge, but they do offer a clear picture of his trials and tribulations and a window into the first and second party systems. As a functionary of the federal government dependent upon and answerable to the whims of political patronage, DuVal wrote hundreds of letters to congressmen, senators, friends, and associates who had political influence. These missives survive today in the extensive manuscript collections of Andrew Jackson, John C. Calhoun, John Crittenden, Samuel Southard, and many other political leaders of the time. The portrait that emerges from these letters is that of a passionate, volatile, and mercurial personality.

One very important source for this study comes from the compilation of documents relevant to DuVal collected over a number of years by the late professor Frank Snyder, formerly associated with Clearwater Christian College. Mr. Snyder's collection consists of thousands of copied items from, to, or about DuVal developed from numerous trips to archives and courthouses in Florida, Kentucky, and Texas. There are legal documents, newspapers, and copies of government papers dealing with DuVal's various terms as governor, Indian negotiator, and frontier politician. The entire collection extends for between ten and fifteen linear feet and is located at the special collections department at the University of South Florida Library.

While DuVal's greatest talent was in oral communication, he was a clear and effective writer. His prose was smooth, but his punctuation was haphazard. One peculiarity in his punctuation was that he never used periods. He ended sentences with a dash, a comma, or no punctuation at all. He capitalized words for emphasis and often underlined statements. His spelling was also a perplexing mix. He often used archaic spelling such as "controul," "labour," or "honour." Sometimes he even spelled the same word differently at different points in the same letter (e.g., "school" and "scool"). DuVal often wrote under extremely trying circumstances. Bad lighting and exhaustion affected the punctuation and uniformity of his writing. Even so, his penmanship is quite legible and identifiable. When quoting DuVal's correspondence, I have retained these characteristics. The strange spellings have been retained without using [*sic*], and the capitalization of words has been retained. Some punctuation (mainly periods) has been silently added. Finally, DuVal always signed his name with the "V" in his name capitalized, that is, "DuVal" rather than "Duval." Thus, even though newspapers, official government documents, and some correspondents wrote his name variously as "Duval" or "Duvall," I have spelled his name as he himself wrote it.

Over the nearly twenty years of the research and writing of this book I have accumulated a number of debts, and now it gives me pleasure to acknowledge the various individuals and institutions that have assisted me along the way. For reading, criticizing, and offering suggestions on all or parts of this book, I thank Margaret Clark, Canter Brown, Walter Manley, Joe Akerman, Keith Huneycutt, Claudia Slate, Joe Knetsch, Richard Adicks, Donald Pharr, and Chuck DuVal. I also thank David J. Coles, who in the initial stages of this project was archivist at the Florida State Archives. David's vast knowledge of Florida's archival past was put to use again and again. Now chair of the Longwood University History Department in Farmville, Virginia, David J. Coles has remained a constant friend. I will always cherish the week we spent together in 2008 in Richmond, William P. DuVal's hometown. I also want to thank Joe Knetsch, whose vast knowledge of Florida's land records is unparalleled. Joe's kindness in sharing documents relevant to DuVal's governorship was unflagging. I'll never forget the summer afternoon we spent tracing out the likely parameters of DuVal's original homestead in Tallahassee's wooded Myer's Park neighborhood adjacent to the Florida state capital.

I would like to thank those whose special friendship offered me support along the way: my mentor at Florida State University, William W. Rogers, was always ready to offer advice about DuVal and any number of other subjects; the late preeminent Florida historian Samuel Proctor constantly encouraged the project forward in long conversations on the University of Florida campus. I also thank several other scholars who have served as an inspiration and great supporters of my work: Bertram and Anne Wyatt Brown, David and Jeanne Heidler, Larry E. Rivers, Randolph Roth, Robert V. Remini, Kathryn Holland Braund, H. W. Brands, Vernon Burton, Stephen D. Engle, Perry Jamieson, the late Ernest Dibble, Frank Schubert, Edward Baptist, Jane Landers, Daniel L. Schafer, Tracy Jean Revels, Paul Ortiz, and Glenn McNair. Also I thank Leland Hawes, the Honorable

E. J. Salcines, the Honorable Susan Roberts, Carolyn Stoia, Risdon Slate, Claudia Slate, Tom Brennan, David Clarke, Gordon Grove, Dale Jacobs, Tom Corcoran, Skip Perez, Jim Rogers, Frank Hodges, Nick Steneck, John Santosuosso, Bruce Darby, Bruce Anderson, and LuAnn Mims.

I acknowledge the assistance and encouragement from superiors at Florida Southern College: Deans Ben Wade, Nancy Aumann, Susan Conner, and Jim Byrd and Presidents Thomas Reuschling and Anne Kerr. Also I want to thank Randall MacDonald and his fine staff at the Roux Library on the campus of Florida Southern College, who always cheerfully responded to my various requests: Eridan Thompson, Ann Rogers, Lisa Lapointe, Mary Flekke, and especially Nora Galbraith, who never ceased to deliver the obscurest of interlibrary loan requests.

Writing is a lonely, solitary enterprise, but one of the joys of the journey is visiting numerous archives and libraries that hold the treasures necessary to undertake the enterprise. I want to thank the Virginia Historical Society for providing a Mellon Research fellowship in 2008. Nelson Lankford and his staff (especially Frances Pollard and Katherine Wilkins) were wonderful hosts and provided me with great assistance in my quest for information on DuVal's early life. I also want to thank the following individuals with whom I have spent countless hours at their respective archives and libraries: Jim Cusick and Carl Van Ness, P. K. Yonge Library at the University of Florida; Boyd Murphree, Gerard Clark, Jody Norman, and Joan Morris, Florida State Archives; Burt Altman, Robert Manning Strozier Library at Florida State University; Paul Camp, Mark Greenberg, and Andy Huse, Special Collections, University of South Florida Library; Margaret Hrabe, Albert and Shirley Small Special Collections, University of Virginia Library; Walter Bowman and David Kirkpatrick, Kentucky State Archives; Sally Bown, Library of the Kentucky Historical Society; Tom Hambright, Key West Public Library; Sandra Treadway, Library of Virginia; Susan Parker and Charles Tingley, St. Augustine Historical Society; Daniel Feller, Jackson Papers Project, University of Tennessee; Clarissa Chavira, San Antonio Public Library; Barry Hayman, Congressional Cemetery in Washington, D.C. I want to thank Sam Maclin of San Antonio, Texas, for sharing DuVal family materials with me.

Finally I want to thank my wife, Patty, and our children, Maggie and Jim, for putting up with me in this seemingly never ending project. They endured much, particularly my tendency to turn family vacations to Washington, D.C., Tennessee, Kentucky, Texas, and other places into yet another search for DuVal documents.

CHAPTER I

Scion of the Old Dominion

In 1848 William Pope DuVal was in the political battle of his life. His decision to run for Congress in his adopted state of Florida as a Democrat put him in the unenviable position of defending a long political career that had seen him often change political positions. The sixty-four-year-old candidate had represented Kentucky in the Thirteenth Congress, and now, thirty-two years later, he was running against fellow Richmond, Virginia, native Edward Cabell for Florida's lone congressional seat. DuVal's long career in Florida had begun in 1821 with his appointment as U.S. judge of the Eastern Judicial District, but a year later he had succeeded Andrew Jackson as territorial governor. DuVal had served three consecutive terms as Florida's territorial governor, until 1834, holding appointments from the Monroe, Adams, and Jackson administrations. Since leaving the governor's chair, DuVal had remained involved—at least peripherally—in political affairs. He had participated in the state's constitutional convention in 1838 and had served as leader of the Florida Senate several years later.

In the spring of 1848, one of Florida's leading Whig newspapers called for DuVal to make "necessary explanations" of the contrary positions he had taken through a long career. Accordingly, the paper, as well as other critics, charged that he was a Federalist in 1815 and a supporter of the National Bank but later became a Democrat and changed his position once Andrew Jackson called for the institution's demise. "He was for Van Buren in 1836—for Harrison in 1840—Tyler in 1841—for Polk in 1844—for Taylor six months ago, and is for Cass now. In 1840 we heard him advocating for Tippecanoe and Tyler Too on the stump, and that he should accept no office under that administration—but one or two months after, he repented and took the office of the United States Law Agent in East Florida. [As governor] he founded the Union Bank and now is opposed to that monster." The Whig press excoriated DuVal as a joker, a trickster, and a hack politician who changed course whenever he thought it would benefit his career.

"We think it is clear that Gov. DuVal has been *dodging about,* not a little all his life, discharging his *blunderbuss.*"[1]

Throughout the campaign the "hero" in Washington Irving's "Ralph Ringwood Tales" faced charges that he was a broken-down politician in pursuit of one last political plum.[2] In a mock depiction of Florida's 1848 Democratic nominating convention, delegates deplore the lack of electable candidates; when a man from Tallahassee puts DuVal's name in nomination, "hisses from several parts of the house" are heard and a voice cries out, "he is an old turn-coat!" But as the man explains, the issue is

> not whom we will have but whom we can elect. I know of no other Individual whom we can elect. And you yourselves gentlemen can't mention one. Now, I will tell you what my reasons are for thinking that we can elect ex-governor DuVal. In the first place—though he has been hitherto a little somewhat erratic in his course, "I think he is now a good and sound democrat. He goes in for the Mexican War tooth and toenail and is in favor of all the other good old Jeffersonian measures. And fellow members, you all know his powers at stumping. You all know his felicity at telling an anecdote. I tell you gentlemen, Cabell will be no where before him. The old governor will be able to upset every thing he can say, with one good laughable story. But, gentlemen, these matters are but trifles compared with what I am going to mention to you—it is that upon which I base my preference for him as an available candidate. Fellow Democrats! Did any of you ever meet with a tale by Washington Irving called Ralph Ringwood? The hero of the story is said to be old Governor DuVal—the tale is one of Irving's masterpieces. He has brought all the powers of his splendid imagination to bear upon it. You know what favorites he always makes his heroes. That story, gentleman, will be irresistible. We ourselves know that most of it came out of Irving's head—but what of it? The people don't know it—they will believe it true as the gospel. It will take mightily with the Whigs of West Florida, and with the romance loving Creoles of Pensacola. As to the Democrats, gentlemen, it will make no difference to them who we nominate—they will vote for the nominee of the convention let it be who it will. All we want to do is, to gain over a few of the Whig votes. And, gentlemen, is it my opinion, that we will be certain to do that with the help of Washington Irving and a few of the old governor's anecdotes.
>
> A stir among the members.
>
> Cries of Capital!! Capital from all sides.
>
> The West Florida Member: 'Well, I will declare! Who would have thought of that? Why the old man won't be so bad after all. Three cheers, gentlemen, for governor Duval (three tremendous cheers). Now three cheers for Washington Irving (Cheers)' . . . Governor DuVal was unanimously elected.[3]

Since the publication of the stories in the *Knickerbocker Magazine* in 1840, DuVal had nurtured the "Ralph Ringwood Myth" when it served his purposes. But in the 1848 campaign the notoriety backfired. It seemed only to confirm DuVal's shifty stances on issues, his playing fast and loose with the facts, and his exaggeration of his own record. According to the "Ringwood Myth," DuVal left his Richmond home as a young lad after an argument with his father, promising never to return to Virginia unless as a member of Congress from Kentucky. Migrating to Kentucky, DuVal hunted in the woods, survived by his own resources, and eventually read law. After thirteen years in the wilderness DuVal had married his sweetheart, become a successful lawyer, been elected to Congress, and returned home on his way to Washington to redeem his promise. DuVal had told this story so often to friends, assembled gatherings, and, of course, Irving himself that the myth took on a life of its own, even before the writer's publication of the "Ralph Ringwood Tales." Like most myths the story carried some elements of truth, but most of the facts of DuVal's past were quite at variance with this tale.

William Pope Duval descended from Daniel DuVal, a French Huguenot, who landed on the York River on March 5, 1701. Duval's great-grandfather and his wife, Philadelphia, came to Virginia by way of England, on board the ship *Le Nasseau*. Eventually settling in Gloucester City, Ware Parish, Daniel Duval was an architect and joiner. Daniel and Philadelphia had four sons, including Samuel (William P. Duval's grandfather), who was born in 1714, and two daughters. Samuel followed his father's profession and in 1752 became prosperous enough to acquire a four-hundred-acre plantation, Mount Comfort, just north of Richmond. By that time he had married Lucy Claiborne, and the two were on their way toward building a large family of eight children. Their first son, William (William P. DuVal's father), was born in 1748. Samuel built, farmed, and took an active part in his community, serving as justice of the peace, county coroner, and vestryman in St. Johns Church.[4]

Five years younger than Thomas Jefferson, Samuel DuVal's son William also attended William and Mary College, where he studied law under George Wythe. Both men came to idolize Wythe. DuVal practiced law and in 1772 married Anne Pope, a distant relative of George Washington. In 1775 and 1776, as the Revolutionary War began, he represented Henrico County in the Virginia House of Burgesses. He was a member of the Committee of Safety and the Virginia Convention of 1774. DuVal's home was familiar to the well-to-do who visited the Richmond area. On March 24, 1774, George Washington recorded in his diary that he "spent the evening & lodged at Mr. Saml. Duvals."[5] DuVal took an active part in the growing controversies between the colonials and the mother country. In 1775 the twenty-seven-year-old lawyer enlisted as a lieutenant in a unit formed by the Committee of Safety under Patrick Henry's command. As the war progressed he served off and on in Virginia as emergencies arose. When Benedict Arnold's raid up the James River threatened Richmond in December 1781, DuVal answered Governor Thomas Jefferson's call for volunteers. He served in the various battles leading up to Cornwallis's surrender at Yorktown on October 19, 1781.[6] By the end of the war DuVal had attained the rank of major, a title he enjoyed for the rest of his days, and near the end of his life DuVal was granted a pension for his service.

But the most significant outcome of the war for William DuVal and his descendants, including his two sons, Samuel, born in 1775, and William Pope, born in 1784, were the Kentucky land grants the state of Virginia gave to its soldiers. DuVal and his brothers, Samuel, Daniel, Philip, and Claiborne, who later migrated to Danville, Kentucky, received vast tracts of Kentucky land for their Revolutionary War service. Among DuVal's brothers, Daniel's service was perhaps the most distinguished. Eventually reaching the rank of colonel, he served under Lafayette and Von Steuben, fighting in the Battle of Monmouth and leading a light infantry regiment at Yorktown. The Popes also received large tracts of land in Kentucky, and various branches of Anne Pope's family were already in Kentucky by the end of the American Revolution. Among the most distinguished of the Popes to migrate from Virginia to Kentucky was John Pope.[7] In the next two decades Kentucky lands—and the profits to be gained through speculating on these lands—consumed the attention of the DuVals as they did that of other well-rewarded Virginia veterans.

The year after the Peace of Paris, William DuVal's father died, and his second son, William Pope, was born. William and Anne would eventually produce five children, but in 1784 their household contained only nine-year-old Samuel and the infant William. After the war DuVal resumed his law practice and also developed planting and mercantile interests in Henrico and Louisa Counties. Not long after the war, Major DuVal had moved into his father's Mount Comfort estate just north of Richmond. Then, in 1791, the year his son John Pope was born, DuVal moved into town, where he lived diagonally across the street from "Chancellor" George Wythe. One year later DuVal's wife, Anne, died suddenly.[8]

Even without his consort DuVal's "double-winged, triple porticoed frame house" on Grace Street was a focal point for Richmond's most fashionable citizens. "One of the last of the cocked hats, satin shorts, and bag wigs," DuVal entertained visiting dignitaries often.[9] According to one account the house was "large and commodious . . . situated on the healthiest and most agreeable part of the city of Richmond on Shockoe-Hill; it contains five large rooms . . . with a kitchen, garden, and all the necessary out houses."[10] Major DuVal remained one of the most prominent citizens in Richmond, serving various posts in city government, including mayor in 1805.[11] As a Richmond lawyer DuVal associated with many of the important lawyers and statesmen of the time, including Thomas Jefferson, John Marshall, and George Wythe and his young assistant Henry Clay, who joined the chancellor in 1793.[12] DuVal also bought and sold land continually. DuVal's lands north of Richmond on which the Mount Comfort plantation sat would eventually be plotted out for sale and annexed to the city as "DuVal's Addition."[13] DuVal also acquired tracts in outlying areas. In 1792, for example, he wrote to his friend Thomas Jefferson in Paris that he had several tracts of Virginia land that he would be glad to exchange for "goods as will answer our market here."[14]

While DuVal and his fellow veterans struggled to rebuild their communities, resume the normal pursuits of life, and establish a more permanent form of government under the Constitution, thousands of the less well-to-do Virginians chose to migrate west into Kentucky immediately following the Peace of Paris. Hardy pioneers had entered the "dark and bloody ground" as early as 1775, establishing "stations" to protect themselves from Indian attacks. The campaigns of George Rogers Clark during the American Revolution introduced Virginians to the entire breadth of Kentucky. By war's end soldiers had crossed the Ohio River and were in possession of the distant outposts of Kaskaskia and Vincennes, in what would later become the Indiana and Illinois territories. Within a few years after the peace, the rush into the fertile lands of Kentucky became a flood. Individuals and their families made up most of the settlers.[15] But those representing huge grantees also patented large tracts. From 1782 to 1792 the Commonwealth of Virginia issued just over 9,500 grants in Kentucky, primarily in consideration for military service in the French and Indian War and in the American Revolution. Before Kentucky became a state, in 1792, Virginia had reserved for its soldiers the lands in Kentucky south of the Green River. Records show that Major DuVal was granted approximately fifty-seven thousand acres of land, surveyed for the first time in Jefferson, Nelson, Mason, and Bourbon Counties from 1784 to 1788.[16] DuVal's acquisition and release of land continued in the new state. Court of appeals records show that from 1794 to 1825 Major DuVal was a grantee of approximately 160,000 acres of Kentucky lands, and from 1793 to1807 he was the grantor of approximately 83,000 acres of lands.[17]

After the Revolution warrants for land surveyed or unsurveyed, patented or unpatented, and deeds in various forms of execution changed hands constantly. Surveys were unclear, of uncertain quality, and often fraudulent. Adding more confusion was the fact that, as one scholar has noted regarding Green River pioneers, "migrants traded debts just as they exchanged land certificates and surveys. Promises to pay passed from hand to hand, with a new assignation scribbled on the back as the note passed to a new owner. In the absence of banks, these petit capitalists created their own money, which functioned as a medium of exchange, and the legal system's role in making debtors pay kept the economic system afloat."[18]

Thomas Abernethy has noted that of the "rank and file of the planters and yeomen, there were few who were secure in the titles to their lands. . . . Furthermore, unlike the inhabitants of the older-settled areas, many lived on lands to which they had no titles at all."[19] Henry Clay's biographer Robert Remini noted that for Clay, who migrated there in 1797, and other lawyers, Kentucky was the land of opportunity. "Land titles were in constant dispute because of earlier Virginia laws that allowed recorded entries in claims to a single tract of land. As a consequence, lawsuits abounded, providing handsome fees for a veritable army of lawyers who had begun to descend on Kentucky."[20] Much of the land by the late 1790s had not yet been surveyed, entered, or patented. The field offered potential wealth for lawyers, especially those skilled at litigating land titles.

By 1800 Kentucky's population neared 221,000 persons. Most of its inhabitants hailed from the Old Dominion, but some migrants came from Pennsylvania, the Carolinas, or other eastern states. Migrants from Virginia traveled southwest along the Great Valley of the Shenandoah and entered Kentucky at the Cumberland Gap, then headed northwest on the Wilderness Road, reached the Falls of the Ohio via Bardstown, or jutted directly north to Lexington. According to one source, "The portion of Road from Kingsport, Tennessee, to the Bluegrass regions of Kentucky, which gave the road its name, was no more than a narrow, difficult, hazardous trail winding over mountains, across streams, through marshes and canebrakes, and penetrating dark forests where hostile Indians and wild animals lurked. From 1775 to 1796 this segment was only a horse path. No wagon passed over it during that period when more than 200,000 people made their way into Kentucky and beyond."[21]

Major Duval's buying and selling of lands linked him with other distinguished Virginia veterans on the make. On July 31, 1799, from Mount Vernon, only five months before he died, George Washington wrote to a business associate thanking him for the information "respecting the removal of Mr. Duval to Kentucky." Washington enclosed a deed for land on Rough Creek, "recommending them to the care of Mr. Duval" for delivery to an associate in Kentucky.[22]

It is not known when William's first son, Samuel, first visited Kentucky, but it is certain that he had taken frequent visits before 1799. He certainly had relatives in the area, and his father's many business contacts would have welcomed him there. For a time Samuel lived with his Aunt Catherine and her well-to-do husband, Christopher Greenup, in Danville, Kentucky. His uncle Claiborne also resided nearby, moving to lands he had acquired in 1794. Records show that Samuel had been granted approximately sixty thousand acres of land. Also, in 1799 he represented Mercer County in the Kentucky state legislature.[23] Kentucky offered excitement, opportunity, and adventure to Samuel's fifteen-year-old younger brother, William. With their father's good name, land warrants, and financial backing from Richmond commercial interests, the DuVal brothers had a number of advantages that a majority of other migrants lacked. Not the least of these advantages was cash and a vast family network to draw from.

The circumstances under which the DuVal brothers migrated to Kentucky in 1799 can be gleaned through a series of court cases that were adjudicated in future decades. These court cases, as discovered and analyzed by the historian Frank Snyder in the Nelson County Court, tell the story of a spendthrift older brother who borrowed money to establish a store on Rough Creek in Ohio County, Kentucky, and later died, leaving his father and younger brother holding the bag.[24] The basic facts are these. In May 1800 William secured his son Samuel approximately $4,000 in cash and bonds for goods he acquired in Richmond from a merchant.[25] In return Samuel mortgaged land, houses, and city lots in Danville and Harrodsburg and ten slaves. Samuel also agreed that he would serve as the legal guardian of fifteen-year-old William. As guardian, Samuel was also custodian of William's property. In an agreement made between the brothers, Samuel agreed to lease from his younger brother a wagon, two horses, and the labor of three slaves.[26]

Once the brothers entered Kentucky Samuel divided the goods at two stores in Bardstown and Hartford, where William resided temporarily. Within weeks after arriving in Kentucky, Samuel sold William's horses, wagon, and slaves. He also converted to his own use the bonds and some of his father's lands.[27] When his father discovered his son's transgressions, Samuel begged forgiveness and mortgaged his remaining Kentucky lands to him. But by October 1802 Samuel was dead and his affairs were in chaos. Even though he was only eighteen years of age at the time, the court named young William the administrator of Samuel's estate on November 8, 1802. It was a trying time for the young man. According to a legal brief William filed some years later, "Samuel left his papers so deranged and scattered that it is impossible to ascertain the quantity of lands" or their status at his death. The situation was further clouded by the fact that, as the brother recalled, Samuel "had no permanent place of residence in this state, or during his life. . . . Samuel was sometimes in Frankfort sometimes in Danville sometimes in Shelbyville, Bardstown, Louisville, and Hartford in Ohio County."[28]

Through his attorney, Henry Broadnax, who had relocated permanently to Bardstown, Major DuVal sold many of his own lands in Kentucky in an attempt to liquidate his son's debts. This raised some money, but Samuel's debts were too extensive. Rather than settle Samuel's affairs with his creditors as an heir under law, DuVal decided to allow Samuel's mortgages to go unpaid and let the creditors divide up the remaining real estate among themselves. This strategy never worked. These obligations would haunt William and his father for many years to come. Litigation against Samuel's estate continued into the 1820s.[29]

When his brother died unexpectedly, in 1802, William may have thought of returning to Virginia. Given the lad's bad luck in Kentucky, it might have seemed

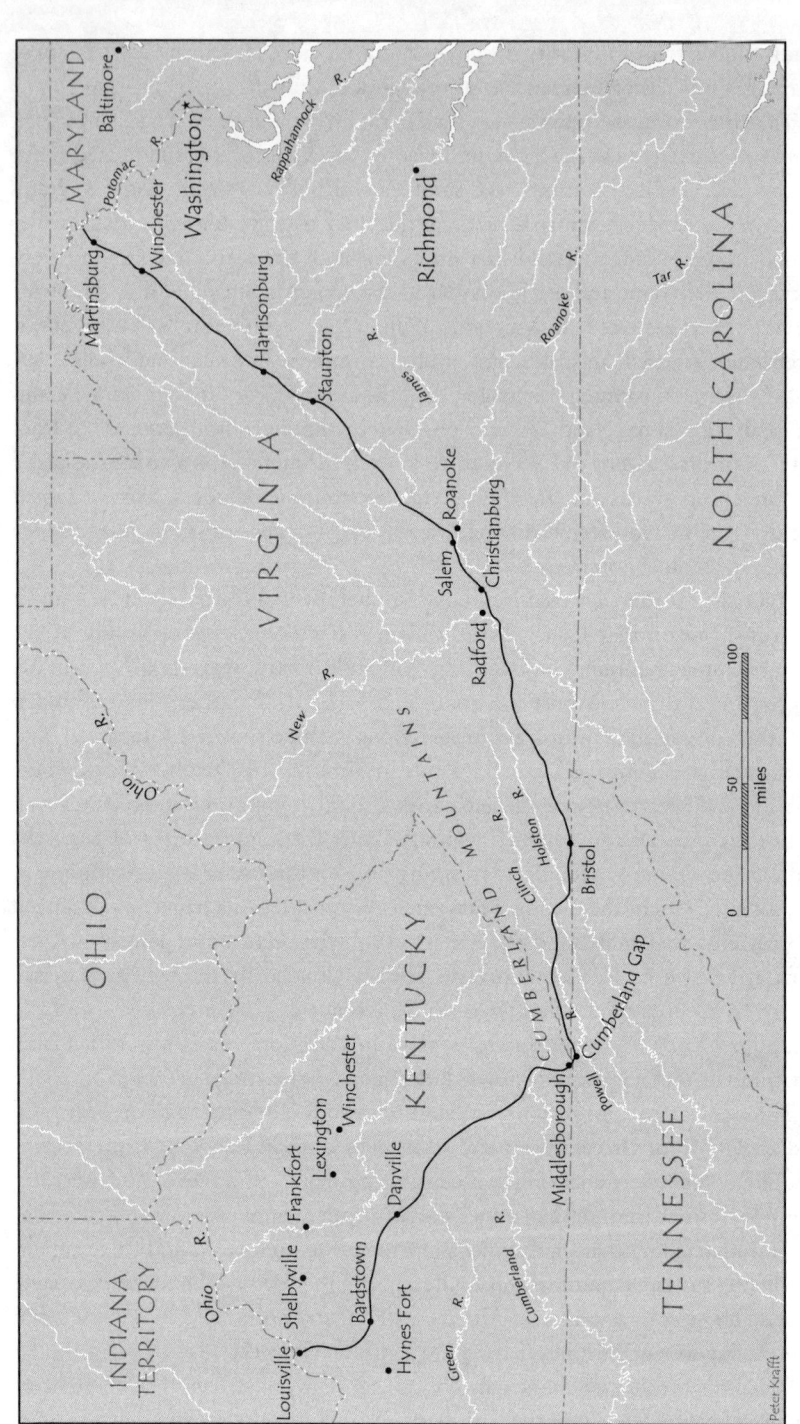

Wilderness Road to Kentucky Settlements, ca. 1800. Map by Peter Krafft.

natural for William to return to Richmond, where his father's wealth and influence might have accorded him the best education available in the young republic. His father offered this opportunity. Instead of studying at William and Mary, William chose to stay in Bardstown. DuVal had taken a liking to the area and no doubt reasoned that his future was bright. Yet another reason necessitated him staying in Bardstown. By that time he had become infatuated with a young woman named Nancy Hynes, the daughter of Andrew Hynes, a prominent Bardstown merchant and one of Kentucky's first settlers. Family lore states the William first took notice of Nancy through the window of a tavern in Bardstown. Immediately smitten, he stole a kiss, and the romance proceeded swiftly.[30]

Meanwhile, on January 27, 1803, in Richmond, Major DuVal gave his attorney, Henry Broadnax, and William power of attorney to sell his lands in Kentucky and to dispose of his deceased son's land in the settlement of his estate.[31] Duval had known Broadnax from his earlier days in Richmond, and the lawyer not only attended to Major Duval's interests as well as he could but also took the eighteen-year-old William on as an apprentice. It was at the Nelson County seat that William read the law under Broadnax.

In 1800 Lexington and Bardstown were focal points of settlement for Kentucky. The Nelson County seat was also home to some of the best legal talent in the West, many of whom had done their legal training in Virginia. It was, according to one old settler, "a mart of trade, and a social educational, political, and legal center." In 1808 the Catholic Church established a diocese in Bardstown, and the founding of St. Josephs College was soon to follow.[32] Bardstown offered many opportunities for a young ambitious man like William P. DuVal. Here he could observe and assist master lawyers at work on complex cases. Also beginning their careers in the area were a number of young men who would go on to flourishing careers in the law and in politics, such as Duval's relative John Pope, as well as Charles A. Wickliffe, Ninian Edwards, Benjamin Hardin, Thomas Speed, George W. Bibb, and Felix Grundy.

Under Broadnax's tutelage, DuVal dedicated himself to the study of the law. According to one authority on legal training in Kentucky at the time, "students usually followed the suggestion of Blackstone, and made notes of reading, and regaled themselves therewith in the intervals of study. The more ambitious digested these notes in books—a laborious but helpful exercise." Students served a kind of apprenticeship, working in the office, copying documents, and going to court under the supervision of the master. At some point the student sat for oral examinations before a committee of members of the bar and judges in the county, receiving a license that could also be recognized in other counties. The study of law was a grueling ordeal. DuVal himself recounted his regimen in later years: "I read and read for sixteen hours of the twenty and four; but the more I read the more I became aware of my deficiencies. It seemed as if the wilderness of knowledge expanded and grew more perplexing as I advanced. Every height gained only revealed a wider region to be traversed, and nearly filled me with despair. I grew moody, silent, and unsocial, but studied on doggedly and incessantly."[33] Despite his difficulties, DuVal was ready for his examination, and he passed. On September 10, 1804, he presented his license to the Nelson County Court and was admitted to practice.[34] DuVal's prospects were bright. A career in the law and politics beckoned. Also that year, his uncle Christopher Greenup was elected Kentucky's third governor, and his uncle's mentorship would draw William into the Kentucky political scene.[35]

Not quite one month after his admission to the bar DuVal married Nancy Hynes, the daughter of Andrew and Elizabeth Hynes.[36] As both of her parents were recently deceased, Nancy's guardian, Dr. Burr Harrison, her older sister's husband, likely officiated at the ceremony on October 3.

Nancy Hynes was the third daughter born to Andrew and Elizabeth Hynes in 1784. Andrew Hynes was the son of a Scots-Irish couple, William and Hanna, who immigrated together to America in 1744. Born in 1750 near Hagerstown, Maryland, Hynes married Elizabeth Warford two years before the outbreak of the American Revolution. Hynes joined an infantry company in the fall of 1776 and fought in many of the important battles in the first years of the American Revolution. Eventually reaching the rank of captain, he endured the winter at Valley Forge and also fought at Brandywine, Germantown, and Monmouth. He and his brother William likely first came to Kentucky as a part of George Rogers Clark's expedition to the Illinois country. In 1780 Andrew Hynes, Thomas Helm, and Samuel Haycraft with their families established the Hynes, Helm, and Haycraft stations in what would later become Elizabethtown, likely named for Nancy's mother. The stations were located about a mile apart and formed a triangle. Theirs was the only settlement between the Green River and the Falls of the Ohio. Here, Andrew Hynes and his brother Thomas formed a mercantile establishment eventually known as Hynes & Company. Andrew Hynes took an active part in public affairs, representing Nelson County in the 1786, 1787, and 1788 Virginia legislatures. He was the chief militia officer in Nelson County and in May 1785 served in Kentucky's first state constitutional assembly, in Danville. Though he owned slaves, Andrew Hynes was ambivalent about the institution, and he voted against slavery in the convention.[37]

When he died in 1800, at the age of fifty, Andrew Hynes had many holdings, debts, and obligations. He also had a large family with many dependents. When Elizabeth died, three years later, the parentless household contained Alfred (5), Abner (11), Polly (17), Nancy (17), and Thomas (21). The two oldest daughters had already married: Sarah (who died the same year as her father) had married Armistead Churchill, and Elizabeth (age 20) had married Dr. Burr Harrison.[38]

Nancy's uncle Thomas Hynes died in 1796, but his sons William and Andrew remained close by for many years and continued their involvement in the mercantile enterprise in which they no doubt had some ownership interest. With her father gone, the mercantile enterprise fell under the management of her cousins William and Andrew.[39] At first relations between DuVal and his wife's in-laws were cordial. But as time went on, numerous disputes regarding the enterprise developed. Unfortunately, the firm foundered, the obligations of Andrew Hynes's will went unmet, and legal battles ensued between Nancy's cousin William and her father's heirs. Taking up these legal battles in the name of Nancy and her sisters were Nancy's brother-in-law Dr. Burr Harrison and her new husband, William P. DuVal.[40]

William Pope DuVal pursued the practice of law with vigor. He also worked to patent and put up land for sale. In 1804, for example, he advertised 3,200 acres on Rough Creek for sale.[41] He kept an active social life and with Hardin, Grundy, Pope, Wickliffe, John Rowan, John Hayes, Ben Chapeze, and six other lawyers formed the Pleiades Club, a debating society that examined all fields of philosophical inquiry, including legal, political, literary, and scientific.[42] DuVal fondly remembered the public gatherings. As he recounted to Washington Irving, who gave his stories voice in "Ralph Ringwood Tales," DuVal noted that "Men of talents, engaged in other pursuits, joined it, and thus diversified our subjects, and put me on various tracks of inquiry. Ladies, too, attended some of our discussions, and this gave them a polite tone, and had an influence on the manners of the debaters."[43]

While the subjects debated during these gatherings were diverse, it is certain that politics and political philosophy entered the discussions. Almost to a man, Kentuckians wholeheartedly supported Thomas Jefferson's Democratic-Republican movement. On national issues, Kentuckians applauded the Pinckney Treaty (1795) opening the Mississippi, railed against the Alien and Sedition Acts (1798), rejoiced in the Kentucky and Virginia Resolutions, celebrated the election of Thomas Jefferson in 1800, and jubilantly hailed his purchase of Louisiana three years later. Jefferson himself had authored the Kentucky Resolutions, boldly declaring that states as sovereign entities had the power and the duty to protect their citizens against unconstitutional federal laws. Indeed, throughout his life DuVal proudly stood for the "Principles of '98." Both before and after DuVal arrived in the new state, Kentuckians argued over the scope and shape of their internal political arrangements. There was indeed much to argue about. Two political groupings styling themselves Conservatives and Radicals emerged. The Conservatives, representing the slaveholders from Virginia, according to Thomas Abernethy, "preferred to hold fast to the Institutions of the Old Dominion, with a property qualification for voters, a legislature made up of two chambers and a bill of rights." The Radicals favored "manhood suffrage and the division of counties into precincts where the voting should be by ballot instead of at the county seat by the viva-voce method. It also stood for representation apportioned among the counties according to population, one-chambered legislature, and popular election of

Henry Clay, ca. 1810.
Courtesy of State Archives
of Florida.

all local and most state officials."[44] Their general goal was to take government away from the aristocrats and lawyers and give it to the farmers.

The Kentucky state constitution of 1792 incorporated some of these ingredients, but in 1798 there was a call to revise the document in favor of adopting more radical measures. There was even serious discussion of ending slavery in the state by gradual emancipation. That year Henry Clay burst on the political scene, arguing that very point. He also made a name for himself denouncing the Alien and Sedition Acts.[45] As time went on political factions developed. They were mostly dominated by politics, but personalities and family connections also played an important role. Two factions emerged, one dominated by Felix Grundy from Bardstown and another dominated by Henry Clay of Lexington. In a series of complicated maneuvers in the state legislature from 1803 to 1805, Clay wrested control of the body from Grundy. By 1807 Clay had thrashed Grundy so completely that the former powerhouse politician chose to immigrate to Nashville.[46]

Just exactly where DuVal stood in this controversy is unrecorded. But it is known that DuVal was not in the Clay faction. Perhaps DuVal had taken Felix Grundy's side in his political combat with Clay from 1804 through 1807, but, whatever the cause, DuVal's writings betray a life-long antipathy for Harry of the

West. There is a certain irony in this because in many ways they were much alike. Though different in physical stature—Clay tall and angular, DuVal short and heavy as he aged—both hailed from the Richmond area. Clay and DuVal's father were on cordial terms. While Clay was far more skilled in intricacies of the law, both were great orators, with an ability to sway jurors and voters. Both had gregarious personalities, attracting a large retinue of onlookers wherever they went. Both excelled at telling stories, joking, drinking, gambling, and playing cards. Both loved music and dancing. Clay played the fiddle; DuVal sang.

One of the most significant institutions in Kentucky as well as in the rest of the country in the years following the Revolution on down to the Civil War era was the militia. The proximity of the British, who still occupied land south of the Great Lakes, caused concern, as did their friendly relations with Indians. The specter of slave uprisings (perhaps more imagined than real) also motivated citizens and officials to remain at the ready. All men were expected to participate. According to one student of the institution, a state law passed in 1806 "was the first concerted effort to build a strong militia." Under the law, the governors could lay off districts and raise troops as he saw fit. Regimental musters occurred in October of each year; battalion musters were held in May. Militia musters were as much social and political gatherings as they were military. Officers' ranks were elective, and aspiring politicians often saw the militia as a stepping stone to political office. Perhaps DuVal was thinking of this on September 11, 1806, when he was commissioned lieutenant in the Rifle Company of the Second Regiment of the Nelson County Militia.[47] DuVal took an active part in his community in other ways. Also in 1806 he was elected to the Board of Trustees of Nelson County, which thereupon ordered him to draw up a set of laws for Bardstown's government.[48]

An ever-present reality in Kentucky, as it was on other southern frontiers, was violence. On numerous occasions DuVal's family was touched by violence. In 1808 DuVal's neighbor and cousin Nathaniel Pope DuVal was killed in a duel with a man named Wilcox. The shocking affair no doubt rocked the community.[49] Throughout his life, William P. DuVal opposed the institution with all the energy he could summon. While he had many political adversaries, he never took part in a duel as a principal or a second. In 1811 DuVal's own house became a scene of violence of another sort. Details are vague, but the bloodshed occurred in DuVal's kitchen when a slave named Reubin murdered DuVal's uncle Claiborne's slave Isaac. In a subsequent trial the bondsman was found guilty.[50]

From 1806 to 1807 DuVal traveled to Richmond to visit his father on at least one occasion. No doubt his father would have taken pride in his son's accomplishments, and the rising young attorney would have renewed and strengthened his contacts in his home town. At that time Richmond was one of the most fashionable towns in the nation. Its docks and business district were booming because of the flourishing trade with the West Indies and other parts of the world. The

Virginia capital was also home to many rising stars in commerce, the law, and politics with whom DuVal would associate throughout his life.

The Gambles, Cabells, Brockenbroughs, Randolphs, and Ritchies were the fashionable set. This was a society that a young Martin Van Buren would find delightful when courting Thomas Jefferson's granddaughter.[51] One of the most significant men in Richmond at the time was William Wirt, who by 1806 was already showing signs that he would become one of the most distinguished lawyers in the United States. Wirt was born into humble circumstances in Maryland and by 1799 (the same year DuVal entered Kentucky) had migrated to Richmond and was soon admitted to the bar. By 1806 Wirt's law career was flourishing and he had married Elizabeth Gamble, daughter of the well-to-do Richmond merchant Robert Gamble. Wirt wrote, practiced law, and eventually prospered enough to purchase Major DuVal's grand house on Grace Street, which made a comfortable home for his wife and three daughters.[52] Wirt divided his time among Richmond, Baltimore, and Washington, D.C., after his appointment as attorney general in 1819. By this time Samuel Southard, a New Jersey native, may also have been among DuVal's circle of friends in the Richmond area. Roughly the same age as DuVal, Southard, a recent graduate of Princeton, was engaged as a tutor in Fredericksburg in 1805, read law, and was admitted to the Virginia bar in 1809.

While William was in Richmond he and his father would have strategized over claims against Samuel's estate. They also would have also consulted over the Major's various land holdings in Kentucky. Records show that the father transferred a 4,200-acre tract in Nelson County to his son. In 1807 the Major also gifted his three sons, Nathaniel, William Pope, and John Pope, 8,122 acres of land in Ohio County near Green River. In subsequent years, while practicing as an attorney, John Pope made numerous attempts to sell these Kentucky lands.[53]

Father and son may also have discussed and corresponded about an incident that scandalized Richmond when George Wythe and his mulatto housekeeper, Lydia Broadnax, and her son were poisoned by Wythe's grandnephew George Sweeney, who also lived in the house. Major DuVal himself, who lived directly across the street from Wythe, was one of the first to notify President Jefferson of the killing. DuVal, who also acted as their mentor's attorney, explained to Jefferson that on May 25, 1806, Wythe and his family became very ill. "Yellow arsenic was found in Sweeney's room & many other strong circumstances concurred to induce a belief he had poisoned the whole Family."[54] It turned out that Sweeney's motive was to beat the housekeeper and her son out of Wythe's will. Once the facts of the case emerged, many assumed that Lydia Broadnax was Wythe's concubine and that he may also have shared parentage of the son. As Wythe's personal attorney and eventually executor of Wythe's estate, DuVal kept Jefferson constantly updated on matters regarding Wythe's estate and Sweeney's trial.[55] William P. DuVal would have taken a keen interest in the case as well. The precise relationship of Lydia Broadnax to William's law teacher is unknown, but the name would likely have brought back memories of his childhood in Richmond and his first legal training under Broadnax in Bardstown.

Like others of his generation Major DuVal was ambivalent about slavery, and the circumstances surrounding Wythe's murder may have further convinced him to begin emancipating his own slaves. Many Virginia slaveholders had used Kentucky as a convenient receptacle for this activity. Either personally or through his son Major DuVal emancipated nine slaves on July 10, 1807, in Bardstown, after they had cleared DuVal's land in Nelson County. By 1821, as he wrote to Henry Clay, he had emancipated all his slaves.[56]

In 1807 Major DuVal's long period as a widower came to an end when he married Susan Brown Christian of Buckingham County.[57] William and Nancy may have attended the wedding. It is also likely that the Major, his new bride, and his son John, who had recently graduated from Washington College, visited William's family in Bardstown. By the end of the year the Major began selling off his Richmond property, and he his new wife moved to a plantation west of Richmond in Buckingham County, near the Appomattox River.[58] He adjusted well to his new surroundings, and his neighbors urged him to run for Congress.[59] Major DuVal's plantation was known as Powhatan and later as Mount Comfort, after his father's original plantation near Richmond. William DuVal's fifty-nine-year-old father and his new wife shared a long life together, producing three daughters, Sarah (born in 1808), Susan Elizabeth (1810), and Frances.[60]

Also that year Richmond was the scene of one of the most exciting spectacles of the time, when it hosted the trial of Aaron Burr. Federal authorities charged the sitting vice president, who had killed Alexander Hamilton in a duel, with treason for his scheme to detach the western from the eastern states. Burr had made trips to Kentucky in 1805 and 1806, and his machinations had caused quite a stir. His presence in Frankfort, Lexington, and Louisville drew the attention of U.S. District Attorney Joseph Daveiss. Especially alarming was his interest in obtaining gunboats.[61]

But now Burr was in custody on a charge of treason. On March 27, 1807, the *Richmond Virginia Argus* reported that "we stop the press to mention the unexpected arrival in this city of Col. AARON BURR. He was conducted by Captain Perkins of the federal army, the officer appointed to this important duty, with a guard of seven men. They stopped for the night at the Eagle Tavern."[62] Over the next several days, Burr's attorneys argued for his release, to no avail. Bail was set at $10,000, and Burr stayed in Richmond planning his case. The "trial of the century," presided over by John Marshall, began on May 22. (William Wirt participated in Burr's prosecution.) According to one account, the "city was crowded beyond its capacity. The inns and taverns could not accommodate all the visitors, so hundreds camped under trees along the river."[63] From the opening of the trial, in May, until Marshall's acquittal of the defendant on August 31, hundreds descended on the town, including a young reporter named Washington Irving, who spent two months in Richmond during the trial. Irving reveled in the scene and soaked up the sights, scenes, and personalities in his first visit to the South. Irving wrote eloquently of the exotic scene. Writing to a lady friend, he represented the South as a land "famous for grog drinking, horse racing and cockfighting; where every man is a colonel or a captain or a Negro, the first title conferred on every man who has killed a rattlesnake." He reacquainted himself with Richmond native Joseph Cabell, a friend with whom he had traveled in Europe.[64] Once in the Virginia capital Irving wrote to his brother William, also an enthusiastic Burr advocate, who edited a pro-Burr newspaper in New York. In these missives Irving speculated on Burr's fate. But he also wrote glowing accounts of the hospitality of Richmond society. "I have been treated . . . in the most polite and hospitable manner by the most distinguished persons of the place," he wrote to James Paulding. "I am absolutely enchanted with Richmond, and like it more and more every day. The society is polished, sociable, and extremely hospitable, and there is a great variety of distinguished characters assembled on this occasion, which give a strong degree of interest to passing incidents."[65] It is not difficult to imagine that during Irving's two-month stay in Richmond he may have enjoyed Major DuVal's hospitality or that he met the Major's son, William P. DuVal.

In 1810 Kentucky was the seventh largest state in the Union, totaling slightly more than 406,000 inhabitants. Slightly more than 82,000 of that total were blacks, the vast majority of them (80,561) slaves. Since 1800 the overall population had increased by 84 percent, and the number of slaves had increased by 99.5 percent.[66] In 1810 the census taker recorded that the twenty-six-year-old DuVal and his wife, Nancy, had eight people (five males and three females) living in their household. From the age distributions noted it can be extrapolated that these included William and Nancy's first two children, Burr Harrison (born the year before and named for his uncle), the infant Marcia, and another unknown boy under the age of ten. Nancy's brothers, Abner (18) and Alfred (12), and her sister Polly (24) may also have resided in the household. DuVal also owned ten slaves, and the following year the Nelson County tax rolls listed him as owning more than twenty-six thousand acres of land in Ohio, Nelson, Casey, and Mason Counties.[67]

In 1810, Nelson County's population stood at nearly fourteen thousand, and less than a third of that total was composed of slaves.[68] Most of the citizens existed by farming. By all accounts Bardstown's social life flourished in the 1810s. One of the most popular events was the "Buck Suppers," held once or twice a month and attended by lawyers, merchants, planters, and other "gentlemen." Venison was the "chief item of the spread." According to one source, "None but gentlemen were admitted on these occasions, who were charged a fixed price per head for their fare. The entertainment embraced eating, drinking, and gaming. Well nigh everybody attended, from the dignified and wealthy lawyer, with superfluous funds, to the hard-working mechanic who subsisted on his income from daily labor."[69] Samuel Haycraft, an old-time resident, writing in 1869, recalled that DuVal's "house in Bardstown was the seat of hospitality." And of its host, he noted that DuVal was the "very life of the social company, always humorous and pleasant, and was a good parlor singer. He was in fact, one of the most generous hearted, liberal men that I ever knew."[70]

While he was an adequate practitioner of the law, DuVal found that his main talents in these early years and in his later life rested in his oratorical skills. By all accounts he was an orator of the first rank. But most of all he was a joker, singer, and teller of tall tales, possessing a winning personality. These were assets in great demand on the frontier in the law and politics. People were naturally drawn to him. As Ben Hardin's daughter recalled, "I remember Governor Duval. He was fond of singing and sang well himself. I recall the old song, 'John Brown's two little Indian boys,' as rendered by him for my amusement in my childhood. He was a most charming man socially." Another man remembered: "I knew Governor Duval and saw him frequently at Hartford. I never knew a more charming conversationalist. It is impossible to exaggerate his powers in this respect. If he emerged from his lodgings, the public seemed to have its eye upon him. The moment he paused, an admiring company would gather around. He did all the talking, and his hearers never wearied." Another man observed that "Duval's charm was in graphic narrative and vivid description. I once made the journey of several hours in a stagecoach from Bardstown to Springfield. . . . Duval was my companion, and so completely was I fascinated by his uninterrupted conversation that I was startled when the journey ended, so entirely had I been oblivious of time, distance and surroundings."[71]

As a lawyer practicing in those days DuVal rode circuit with judges and other fellow members of the bar. Lucius Little describes the scene: "The judge of a district, as he traveled from county to county, was accompanied by a retinue of attorneys, composed of members of various bars. They sat when the court sat and rose when the court rose. The usual mode of travel in that day was on horseback. Saddlebags contained the wardrobe and such books as their itinerants carried with them," Little continued. "The arrival of this cavalcade on the Sabbath preceding the opening of the court produced a sensation in the county towns. The 'great men' on such occasions, unbent themselves in familiar discourse with each other, and each contributed his quota of anecdote, or incident, or learned homily, to the edification of attentive listeners of the laity."[72] Samuel Haycraft remembered seeing DuVal in 1810, 1811, and 1812, while attending court in Elizabethtown. DuVal, his cousin Worden Pope, and a number of other lawyers boarded at Ben Helm's tavern. "I was then a lad," Haycraft recalled, "acting under Major

Ben Helm as deputy clerk, and sat at the same table, and it was a feast to listen to their pleasant conversation and sallies of wit."[73]

DuVal's winning ways and popularity paid dividends in the courtroom. He soon acquired clients. Judges also took notice of his talents. In the early days of the Kentucky circuit courts, judges appointed county attorneys and on an annual basis DuVal filled this position for Nelson County for a number of years, until Ben Hardin wrestled the position from him. Even under the best of circumstances, given the heated and continual forensic struggles and the proximity of rival lawyers as they rode circuit, lawyers often developed conflicts and rivalries. DuVal was not immune from such conflict, and there are echoes in memories of those who experienced those times. A view of DuVal emerged, even in those early years, as a trickster, a manipulator, even a deceiver, under the mask of "hail-fellow-well-met." Ben Hardin's daughter remembered that her father thought DuVal "deceitful."[74] This belief may have stemmed from riding circuit with him or observing DuVal in the courtroom or from attempts to wrest the county attorney position away from DuVal.

By 1810, William P. DuVal had developed a prosperous law practice. He had many friends and a growing family. He could look forward to many productive years in law and politics. In 1812 he was elected to Congress. But that year war clouds were on the horizon, a war that would change his life and offer many new opportunities to meet men who would shape his future.

CHAPTER 2

Soldier and War Hawk Politician

The third federal census (1810) granted Kentucky four new House seats. In August 1812 William P. DuVal ran for the newly created Tenth District seat. DuVal's district bordered the Ohio River to the north and included Nelson, Hardin, Greene, and Washington Counties. Other Kentuckians elected to the thirteenth session of Congress were Henry Clay, Richard M. Johnson, Joseph Desha, Samuel Hopkins, Solomon P. Sharp, Samuel McKee, James Clark, Stephen Ornsby, and Thomas Montgomery.[1] But politics was not the most important thing on the minds of DuVal and other Kentuckians. Two months before the election, on June 18, 1812, Congress declared war on Great Britain. Before they could take their seats on May 24, 1813, Duval, Hopkins, Johnson, McKee, and Montgomery would find themselves engaged in combat.

By 1812 relations between the United States and Great Britain had reached a breaking point. Thomas Jefferson's embargo (1807–1808) had done little to prevent U.S.-British conflicts on the high seas. By 1809 Britain's war with France was at fever pitch, and it began seizing American ships on the high seas, claiming that they were headed for ports controlled by Napoleon Bonaparte. While New England bore the brunt of ship seizures, war sentiment was primarily centered in the West, where evidence of Britain's support for Tecumseh's Confederacy, as well as encroachments on U.S. territory from Canada and Spanish Florida, angered Westerners. Kentucky politicians advocated seizing Canada and driving the British out as a way of securing the northern frontier against Indian attacks. There were also similar calls to drive out the Spanish in Florida. Western congressmen like Henry Clay (selected speaker in 1811), John C. Calhoun of South Carolina, Felix Grundy (now living in Tennessee), and other western congressmen known as the War Hawks called for war. By the time of President Madison's war message in June 1812, Henry Clay had brought all but one of Kentucky's congressional delegation into line for war. (Senator John Pope, DuVal's relative, was the lone holdout.)[2]

The Battle of Tippecanoe, fought on November 7, 1811, between settlers led by Indiana Territorial Governor William Henry Harrison on the one side, and the The Shawnee Prophet, Tecumseh's lieutenant on the other, was a harbinger for the future. After the battle Harrison torched Indian villages in the area, and refugees dispersed. Some joined their leader in Canada. The battle intensified alarm on the frontier and practically ensured conflict between Kentuckians and Indians in the months to come.[3] One month after Tippecanoe, Kentucky governor Charles Scott in his annual message warned the legislature of the approaching danger. "We live, Gentleman, in times of no ordinary import: all our wisdom and virtue may be required for our preservation. A crisis, portentous of events [that] intimately affect us, seems to have arrived. It becomes us to examine it with calmness, and be prepared for consequences. War seems to lower over our horizon." The governor continued, "Our exterior relations have never borne a worse aspect since our revolution."[4]

In May Governor Scott moved to fulfill Kentucky's quota of volunteers. Meanwhile, information from nearby Indiana Territory was ominous. Settlers from there had been so alarmed that the men were building forts and blockhouses. And "apprehensions were so much entertained . . . that some citizens were about to send their wives and children into Kentucky and Ohio." Governor Harrison "apprehends serious danger from nearly all the tribes" and "called on the militia of that territory to be in readiness to march when called upon—to pursue the Indians who may make any incursions into the territory. . . . British presents and British hostility are the cause of all this."[5]

Kentuckians greeted the declaration of war with enthusiasm. According to James Hammack, "The excitement touched off in Kentucky . . . approached pandemonium. . . . Throughout the state, towns, and villages were 'illuminated' on the occasion, as cheering crowds gathered to pledge their support for the war effort. At Lexington, Frankfort, and in numerous other communities, public celebrations, accompanied by the incessant firing of cannons and muskets, lasted late into the evening."[6]

In August Isaac Shelby, Kentucky's first governor and hero of the Battle of Kings Mountain, succeeded Scott as governor.[7] Congressional elections were also held that month. With the war uppermost in people's minds, there seems to have been no campaigning. Newspapers noted that Clay, Johnson, McKee, Desha, and DuVal (who ran for the new seat) faced no opposition.[8] The congressmen-elect, like other Kentuckians, were swept up in the war hysteria, and nearly all immediately volunteered for military service. By late August volunteer units were already formed. A local newspaper described the scene as the Fifth Regiment of the

Kentucky Volunteers marched through Lexington "amidst the cheers and acclamations of a vast concourse of their grateful fellow citizens." An estimated twenty thousand spectators turned out to greet the troops and solemnly assembled to listen to Henry Clay's address on the causes of the war.[9]

Among the units assembling for battle was the Eighth Regiment of volunteers. Serving as captain of the "Yellow Jackets" was Kentucky Congressman-elect William P. DuVal.[10] The Eighth Regiment eventually fell under the overall command of General Samuel Hopkins. The fifty-nine-year-old general had also been elected to Congress in 1812, no doubt because of his military background. A native of Albemarle County, Virginia, Hopkins served on George Washington's staff in the American Revolution, and he eventually attained the rank of Lieutenant Colonel of the Tenth Virginia Regiment. Migrating to Kentucky in 1796, he practiced law and served in various judicial and elected offices, including a stint in the state senate from 1809 to 1813. In 1812, about the time of his election to Congress, he was appointed major general of the western frontier.[11]

Despite the ardor and patriotism of the Kentucky volunteers, American forces suffered serious reverses in the first campaigns on the Canadian frontier. With William Hull's surrender of Detroit in August, the entire northwest lay open to the British as far south as Vincennes. At Governor Shelby's urging, Washington authorities put Governor William Henry Harrison in charge of the Northwestern Army on September 17.[12] As Harrison marched his army north, General Hopkins assembled two thousand troops for an expedition against the Indians on the Wabash River. Under Governor Shelby's authorization the volunteers would serve a thirty-day enlistment and supply their own horses, weapons, and blankets. Even so, Governor Shelby represented the volunteers as among the most "influential and eloquent & respectable characters. . . . I have never seen such a body of men in the western country or anywhere else."[13] The war exposed Captain DuVal to men who would distinguish themselves in later years. Harrison, Lewis Cass, and Illinois territorial governor Ninian Edwards, only slightly older than DuVal, were in leadership positions. So was John J. Crittenden, who served on Hopkins's staff. Roughly DuVal's age was Captain Zachary Taylor, who defended Fort Harrison. Also joining DuVal's regiment was a twenty-one-year-old school teacher from Elizabethtown named Duff Green.[14]

Hopkins's force made its way from Louisville and reached Vincennes by late September.[15] On the twenty-ninth of that month, as Hopkins was preparing to move his whole body to Fort Harrison, the general explained his mission to Governor Shelby as he understood it: "My present intention is to attack every settlement on the Wabash, and destroy their property, then fall upon the Illinois; and I trust in all the next month to perform much of it. Serious opposition I hardly apprehend, although I intend to be prepared for it." The *Niles Register*, published Hopkins's letter and predicted that Hopkins's expedition would "probably *clear out* all the Indian tribes within the great scope he has marked out for his operation." Such a course was necessary because of "the *detestable* influence [of England] that compels the extirpation of the greater portion of this unfortunate race of men, within our territories."[16] The plan also contemplated that Hopkins's force would link up with Illinois forces at Peoria.[17]

As DuVal and his troops moved north, they learned that Fort Harrison, their ultimate destination before heading to the Wabash towns, was under siege. On September 6 Indians had attacked the isolated post, hurling murderous musket fire and setting it ablaze. Somehow twenty-seven-year-old Captain Zachary Taylor managed to extinguish the flames and build barricades to protect the beleaguered fort. For the next ten days Kentucky relief columns tried with little success to break through the Indian barriers.[18] Among those participating in the relief attempts was DuVal's regiment. As DuVal told the story to Washington Irving many years later, his unit was among nine hundred men that General Hopkins ordered to march in relief of the fort. The idea was to get a scouting party through the Indian lines and "apprise the fort that relief was coming." A half-dozen men disguised themselves as Indians and proceeded to within a mile of the fort, but they were discovered and attacked on all sides. Several were killed, but one man managed to make it back to the main force. The survivor reported that the fort "had a part of it burnt and fears were entertained that it had been taken and the people massacred." Though some hope remained for those inside, "The garrison must be in a deplorable condition," they reasoned. Calls for another volunteer "to send comforting assurances of success" went out. "To my surprise," DuVal said, "my brother-in-law [Thomas Hynes] stepped forth & volunteered. A young man, admirably formed." Afterward Hynes came to DuVal's tent, and the captain asked him "what could induce him to go on such a desperate errand which was almost certain death! He said he thought he could succeed. He could imitate the Indian well. He retired dressed & painted himself & when he reentered my tent I did not know him [because of] all his armaments for war & he was completely Indian. He mounted his horse and departed." Hynes's disguise succeeded, and he was admitted to the fort.[19]

The Kentuckians eventually reached the fort after a larger force from Illinois under the command of Colonel William Russell lifted the siege on September 16. As DuVal described the scene, "the garrison had action very thick for three days when we arrived. We had pushed on through a hot prairie of high grass, thirty miles away. Our men fell out of exhaustion in the heat we had nearly 8 days of provisions on our backs. When we could we shared our provisions with the garrison." While waiting for the main force to arrive, DuVal and his men participated in raids launched against Indian villages in the area, and, as he related to Washington Irving some years later, we were "caught by hard fighting, our party returned to fort 5 dead." Meanwhile food supplies were extremely low. "One small ear of hard northern corn a man was a meagre allowance. We became so feeble that we staggered as we walked. At length provisions arrived," he continued, "fresh greens which the men ate so quickly that they were attacked with diarrhea. Many sickened and died. In the march through the prairies our men who had summer overshoes had them all cut to pieces by the tall grass and green briars."[20]

Hopkins's first expedition against the Indians on the Wabash, which began on October 14, was short, unsuccessful, and by most accounts a fiasco. In truth the failure of the campaign was not entirely Hopkins's fault. Crippled by a lack of food and supplies and the thirty-day enlistment of most of his men, the mission was perhaps doomed from the start. By the time Hopkins's main force reached Fort Harrison, there was already dissension in the ranks. Even so, Colonels Wilcox (DuVal's immediate superior), Philip Barbour, and Nicholas Miller and their officers urged the men on from Fort Harrison, toward the Kickapoo and Peoria Indian towns 120 miles to the north. Hopkins marched the men thirty miles a day, but the force soon lost its way. Food ran out, Indians set fire to the prairie, and four days out of Fort Harrison terms of enlistment ran out. Within two days the men mutinied, and despite Hopkins's and his officers' pleading, they absolutely refused to go any further. At that point Hopkins had no choice but to follow his men back to Fort Harrison. Once he returned Hopkins dismissed those mutinous volunteers whose terms of enlistment had run out, glumly wrote his report of the debacle, and regrouped for another effort.[21]

Marching out again on November 11, the better-supplied force led by Colonels Barbour, Miller, and Wilcox and a small company of regulars under the command of Captain Zachary Taylor reached the Prophet's town by the nineteenth. They torched the deserted town as well as the Winnebago and Kickapoo villages in the area. Up in flames went more than 160 houses and all of the Indians' stores for the winter. The damage done, the troops then fanned out through the countryside in search of Indians. On the twenty-first DuVal's unit came under fire. Only one Kentuckian, a man named Dunn, was killed. The skirmish left eighteen Indians killed or wounded. That night the weather turned bitterly cold. The next day, as they attempted to recover the body of their slain comrade, the soldiers rode into an ambush. The result was sixteen killed and three wounded. The main body reached the site of the ambush on November 24, but by that time severe cold forced their body to return to Fort Harrison.[22]

With rivers icing and snow reaching a blizzard stage, the return trip back to Fort Harrison was extremely difficult. DuVal remembered that as the troops headed back south along the Wabash they put the "sick & survivors in boats; soldiers keeping on shore to protect them." Both dead soldiers and the sick were placed in boats and propped up "back to back supporting each other. . . . In all our maladies, however, we didn't complain. My heart ached when I first went among the sick for they were my neighbors. Every man this flower of the cavalry

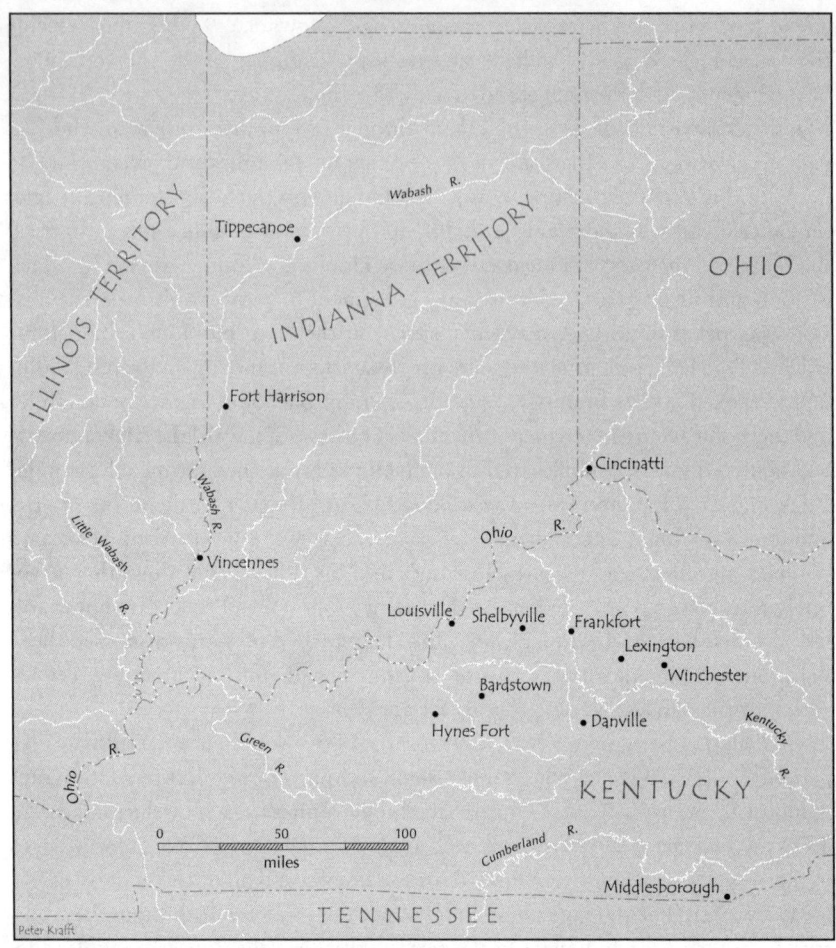

Kentucky, Indiana, and Illinois Territories during the War of 1812: Kentuckians along the Wabash, September–December 1812. Map by Peter Krafft.

I knew their parents. They made no complaints and [took] their hardships like soldiers."[23] Indeed, according to an Indiana soldier named la Plante, DuVal and his fellow Kentuckians were in a desperate condition. "We suffered very much, but I pitied most the poor Kentuckians. They were almost naked and barefoot—[in] only their linen hunting shirts—the ground covered with snow and the Wabash freezing up."[24]

As DuVal recounted to Irving, "If a poor fellow died by the way we cut a hole in the frozen earth with our hatchets—wrapped his body in his blanket" and "hastily . . . proceeded. I found my heart had grown hard. Our men were so exhausted to the cold without clothing—they made surcoats of the rawhides after animals was killed." On their way back to Kentucky "almost naked," they discovered their supplies of clothing. "When I saw my men," recalled DuVal, "clad in their cloth uniforms and boots I thought I had never seen so brave a looking set of fellows." Yet all of DuVal's troopers had to admit that their expedition had come to naught. As one member of Hopkins's force explained to Nancy DuVal's cousin Andrew Hynes in Nashville, "Both expeditions were unsuccessful. We sought the enemy but could not find them, and altho' on the eve of battle, we were disappointed."[25]

Even before the weary Kentuckians trekked home to their families, Hopkins defended himself from attacks and recriminations stemming from the failed campaign. On January 12 he answered an attack by "dirty and malignant scoundrels" who had published false information in two Bardstown papers. He added that he looked forward to defending himself at a court of inquiry investigating the campaign and invited those who were maligning him to attend and make their case. Though his military career was clearly over, Hopkins was eventually exonerated of all wrongdoing.[26]

Whether or not DuVal participated in any of these proceedings is unknown, but it can be assumed that Nancy breathed a sigh of relief when he returned to Bardstown. While he emerged from the campaign physically unscathed, memories of misery, suffering, and death stayed with him his entire life. As he recalled in later years, "by degrees I grew accustomed to sights of death. . . . [I] felt as if I should not have to die myself."[27] At home at last DuVal had three months to rest, recuperate, and arrange his business affairs before he had to set out for Washington to attend the opening of Congress on May 24, 1813.

Not long after DuVal returned home it was discovered that Nancy was carrying another child, and the family ventured to DuVal's father's plantation in Buckingham County, Virginia. The extended visit allowed Major DuVal and his wife, Susan, to assist Nancy in her pregnancy and help care for the children. The family, including three-year-old Burr and one-year-old Marcia, made its way four hundred miles east into Virginia. In November Nancy gave birth to their second son, Thomas Howard.[28]

With his family safely under the care of his father, DuVal made his way to Washington in the spring of 1813. The war was not going well for the United States. Despite several morale-boosting naval victories against the British navy, the war on land, especially in the Northwest, went badly. American attempts to seize Canada had failed miserably. The Battles of Frenchtown and subsequent massacres of their troops in January at the River Raison angered Kentuckians. Also that winter Kentucky troops were bogged down at Fort Meigs, overlooking the Maumee River Rapids.[29] Meanwhile, in the Mississippi Territory, conflicts among the Creek peoples were spilling over into isolated white settlements. An

American force in New Orleans watched warily for British activity on the Gulf. From January to March Nancy's cousin Andrew Hynes (by that time a prosperous Nashville merchant) had joined militia general Andrew Jackson's force of two thousand troops on a march from Nashville to Natchez, only to be ordered back to Nashville without incident.[30] Elsewhere DuVal's twenty-two-year-old brother John had enlisted as a lieutenant in the regular army and was fighting on the Canadian border.

With the enemy on its borders and nearly eleven thousand of their state's citizens under arms, Kentuckians expected their congressmen to support legislation aimed at assisting the war effort. Among the domestic programs they expected to assist both the war and their own economic well-being was the embargo. Thomas Jefferson's embargo (1807–1808) had stimulated nascent manufacturing in the Lexington area, and the war pushed it ahead as well. Before the war most Kentuckians opposed the building of a strong navy and the rechartering of the Bank of the United States. They favored internal improvements and protective tariffs, a sentiment that evolved into support for a renewed embargo against British goods once the war began. Supporters of a new embargo argued that the measure was needed because illicit trade with the British in Canada continued even after war was declared. But sentiment in Kentucky was divided on the subject. Rural areas opposed the embargo, while manufacturing areas favored it. DuVal's stand against the embargo made him unpopular. Near the end of DuVal's first session in Congress the Senate blocked Madison's request for an embargo, only to pass the measure in the first several days of the next session in December.[31]

When William P. DuVal traveled the 120 miles from Buckingham County, Virginia, to Washington in the spring of 1813, the American capital was still a work in progress. By that time the seat of government had been on the banks of the Potomac for only thirteen years. Stumps still obstructed dirt streets, buildings were unfinished, and the artificial community resembled a construction site more than it did the grand vision Pierre L'Enfant, who planned the capital city, originally intended. Most visitors to Washington in those days spoke of the vast barrenness between the White House and Capitol Hill. One observer who visited Washington about that time noted that "There is perhaps no city in the world of the same population, in which the distances to be traversed in the ordinary intercourse of society are so large. The most glaring want in Washington is that of compactness and consistency. The houses are scattered in straggling groups." Indeed, the mile and a half that separated Congress and the seat of the presidency seemed a huge distance. Boardinghouses and taverns serving congressmen clustered around the Capitol, while on the other end of Pennsylvania Avenue were concentrated structures that supported the executive branch. Streets filled with dust when it was hot and with mud when it rained. People at the time often observed that Washington was a kind of artificial city, unlike the rest of America.

Though it contained roughly eight thousand inhabitants it had practically no commerce of any kind, other than what might serve itinerant legislators and executive branch officials—a total in the 1810s that amounted to only approximately three hundred persons. Indeed, according to one observer, "The greatest and most respectable business that is done in Washington is keeping boarding houses."[32] The turnover rate in those years was roughly 50 percent per Congress, so DuVal could count himself among the half of the city's residents who were beginning their congressional careers.

Congressmen stayed in boardinghouses, and social life revolved around the various "messes" that served them. Boardinghouse groups included as many as thirty and tended to associate by regions of the country. Young and old, congressmen and senators, farmers and lawyers mixed together in these messes. But, as one student of the subject has noted, "most members sought provincial companionship, setting themselves apart from men different in their places of origin and differently acculturated. They transformed a national institution into a series of sectional conclaves." These boardinghouses served as a kind of fraternity in which members argued together, debated together, discussed legislation together, and tended to vote together.[33] They also ate, drank, gambled, and told stories ad infinitum. And in the latter activity DuVal excelled. DuVal boarded with fellow Kentuckians James Clark (of Winchester), Samuel McKee (of Lancaster), and fifteen other congressmen at Davis's Hotel on Pennsylvania Avenue.[34]

On Monday, May 24, the first day of the session, DuVal was among 148 other House members who answered the roll call. DuVal's fellow Kentuckian Henry Clay was once again selected speaker. Not long after, members listened to President Madison's message, which "accused the British of inhumanity in the savagery unleashed against the western frontier." The war, Madison reminded members, was going badly: "The treasury was depleted, the country was living off loans, and additional taxes were necessary to prosecute the war. Recruiting was at a standstill."[35] One of the first matters of business was taxes, and on June 30 the Ways and Means Committee took up the subject of taxes on licenses for whiskey distilleries. In his first appearance on the floor "Mr. Duvall" argued against passage of the tax bill on the grounds that it discriminated against the West. "Mr. Chairman, I rise with reluctance to address you on this subject. But the interests of the nation, and particularly the Western States are deeply concerned in the subject now under consideration. . . . I admire the book learning that has been displayed by several gentlemen on this subject; but let me assure you that common sense and practical knowledge of the operation of this tax, are worth all the learned theories and disquisitions which we can have on this subject." DuVal asked rhetorically, "who are to pay the tax on stills?" The people of the West, DuVal asserted, were to pay the taxes and do all the fighting. "Will the people of the South, East and a great portion of the North pay this tax? No. It will be paid by Western people, men without capital, farmers, whose distance from the seaboard compels them to distill the product of their farms, in order to take it to distant markets in the only shape that can reward them for their labors."[36]

The tax would be more than farmers could pay. Not only was the tax unfair; it was unequally distributed. It would also have no chance of raising the revenue calculated by its advocates. Members who advocated approval of the tax "must have been lately been reading some extravagant fairy tale," DuVal continued; "perhaps Aladdin and his wonderful Lamp has engaged the gentleman's fancy and has led his imagination captive through hills of gold and valleys of diamonds; or, perchance he has been dreaming of the philosophers stone, whose magic touch changes everything to gold; or how else can we account for this confined and extravagant calculation?" Some of his fellow legislators, while eager to vote for the war, seemed afraid to ask their constituents to pay for it. "Taxation will endanger their popularity; the very idea of taxing their constituents is appalling; already they feel their seats trembling under them, and another election may tumble them from their elevation."[37] Debate on the bill went on for days.

In his first session in Congress DuVal met men who would influence his life for years to come. Among them was John C. Calhoun, the brilliant, stern, taciturn, and inflexible South Carolinian, who was only beginning his second session of Congress. Though only thirty-one years old (two years older than DuVal), the "cast iron man" seemed much older. He was already a respected leader among the War Hawk faction. Calhoun's intelligence and leadership skills drew men naturally to him. Though Calhoun and DuVal's personalities differed, they agreed on issues, starting with their opposition to President Madison's request for an embargo. On July 21 Calhoun, DuVal, and three others took the floor in opposition to the measure. In DuVal's stand against the embargo he broke with Speaker Henry Clay and the majority of the rest of the Kentucky delegation. (Only McKee and Montgomery also opposed the measure.) The measure failed of passage in the first session but passed in the next.[38]

The embargo was popular in Kentucky, and DuVal, McKee, and Montgomery felt compelled to justify their vote and did so in a pamphlet entitled *Reflections on the Law of 1813, for Laying an Embargo on all Ships and Vessels in the Ports and Harbors of the United States* (1814). "We offer the following reflections," they wrote, "to the candid, honest, and dispassionate citizens of the congressional districts which we have the honor to represent, with a view to the justification for having voted against the passage of the embargo bill; and we cherish a lively hope that a very large majority of the citizens of our respective districts will be disposed to give our remarks an attentive perusal . . . which they intrinsically merit; and we trust too, that upon taking such a course, our fellow citizens will be convinced, that we voted correctly, or that the measure is one so problematical in its nature, that men equally wise and honest might differ on it in their votes."³⁹ The tightly argued treatise utilized all the familiar arguments against a banning of trade, including the premise that the ban on trade would be more harmful to the United States than to Britain. Illegal trade with Britain was overstated, and its offenders would not be restrained by a law at any rate. Britain with its fleets and wealth could supply itself from France, Russia, the Baltic countries, and just about everywhere anyway. The embargo would prevent the United States from obtaining specie, DuVal and his Kentucky colleagues argued.

Five million dollars in revenue would be lost to the United States at the very time that taxes were being raised, DuVal and his colleagues maintained. Also by implementing an embargo the United States would be depriving itself of items in short supply, such as salt. These restrictions would inspire lawbreaking and profiteering and have a *"demoralizing effect* upon the commercial part of the nation." The coastal trade would be entirely cut off, the writers asserted, and sailors would be thrown out of work. Finally, they claimed, the law gave the president too many powers, and opponents speculated that mischief would be done by loose phraseology in a law that allowed seizure of wagons and boats on suspicion that they were trading with the enemy. Despite the well-reasoned arguments, the pamphlet was not well received in Kentucky. DuVal and his two colleagues were subjected to "lavish abuse." Only McKee of the three succeeded in retaining his seat in the next election.⁴⁰

About a month after the end of the first session of Congress the war entered a new phase. On August 30 Upper Creeks allied with Britain attacked Fort Mims, an isolated outpost just north of Mobile, massacring an estimated 250 white, black, Creek, and mixed-blood men, women, and children. Within weeks alarms reached Tennessee, and authorities once again summoned militia general Andrew Jackson. The Creek War was on. Nearly a month later news reached Kentuckians and those in the East of the American victory at the Battle of the Thames. Kentucky volunteers under Richard M. Johnson enjoyed a prominent role in the October 5 battle, which resulted in Tecumseh's death. The victory also ended the viable possibility of a British-backed Indian confederacy directed against the Americans.⁴¹

The second session of the Thirteenth Congress began on December 6 and continued through April 18 of the next year. DuVal was present for only the first two weeks of the session. By December 21 he was back in Bardstown, but he returned to his desk after the first of the year. Midway through the second session, in January 1814, New Yorker William Irving, elected to fill a seat vacated after a resignation, arrived to take a seat. New York merchants also sent his writer brother to lobby their cause to Congress. Washington Irving and his literary collaborator and brother-in-law James Kirke Paulding joined the new congressman in Washington. They made the rounds and were popular, especially among the younger congressman. According to one account, Paulding was irresistibly funny;

Washington Irving ca. 1820. Courtesy of Library of Congress.

his "grave hawk-nosed countenance gave no clue to the dry humor of his conversation which delighted his friends." Perhaps DuVal reacquainted himself with Washington Irving while striking up a new friendship with his fellow congressman and his brother-in-law. One can envision DuVal regaling the Irving brothers and Paulding with the songs, stories, and ribaldry of the wild realms of the Kentucky frontier.[42]

Back in Bardstown for the congressional recess during the summer of 1814, DuVal learned the shocking news that Washington had been attacked and burned on August 24. British forces entered the Chesapeake Bay on August 21 with twenty warships and thirty transports and ranged through the Chesapeake at will, brushing aside weak American resistance and wreaking havoc wherever they went. The carnage was most humiliating in Washington itself. With refugees, including James and Dolley Madison, running for their lives, British commanders ordered their soldiers to torch the city. Up in flames were the Capitol, including the Senate chamber, the chamber of the House of Representatives, as well as the U.S. Treasury, the War Office, and the White House. The scholar Frederick C. Drake has summarized the carnage wreaked in the Chesapeake: "In ten days, British light troops marched 100 miles, won one battle and two skirmishes, destroyed the Chesapeake gunboat flotilla, burned the public buildings of Washington, humiliated the administration, and rejoined their supporting vessels, with a loss of less than 300 men."[43]

The scene that presented itself to congressmen when they convened in special session on September 19 was one of utter devastation. Overseeing the payment of his volunteer company on September 15 at Georgetown, Kentucky, DuVal did not arrive in the capital until three days after the opening of the session on September 22.[44] Boarding at McKeowin's Hotel on Pennsylvania Avenue, DuVal witnessed the carnage firsthand.[45] In addition to the casualties of the English raid already mentioned, the offices of the *National Intelligencer*, the Library of Congress, the navy yard, and the arsenal were also destroyed. The only public buildings unharmed were the patent office and the Post Office, and there the House met in a room so small that, according to one observer, "every spot up to the fireplace and windows was occupied."[46] Not only were congressmen stunned by their physical surroundings; yet another setback on the battlefield had unsettling psychological effects as well. Support for continuing the war was at low ebb. Some even questioned the future of the Union as well. One observer wrote after a few days in Washington, "The appearance of our public buildings is enough to make one cut his throat, if that were a remedy—The dissolution of the Union is the item of almost every private conversation. . . . There is great contrariety of opinion concerning the probability of the event."[47] Indeed, the situation was ominous. The calamity in Washington served only to strengthen elements in New England calling for an end to "Mr. Madison's War."

Congressman DuVal provided Governor Shelby with an appraisal of the mood of Congress. Though Southern Federalists had pledged themselves to vote for taxes to support the war, "the federals from New Hampshire, Massachusetts and Connecticut have refused all support to the government. The New England Congressmen, I fear, threaten the safety of the Union."[48]

Outlooks on Washington's fate differed in the West. When he learned of the capital's fate at the hands of the British, General Andrew Jackson, fresh from his victory against the Creeks at the Battle of Horseshoe Bend, wrote to Nancy DuVal's cousin. "I have this moment recd. The news that the capital is Burnt," Jackson wrote to Andrew Hynes from Mobile, Alabama. "Was it not for the national disgrace I am glad of it—It will unite america, and learn the rulers of our nation, to prepare for defense before it is too late. . . . It will Teach them, not to count their pence but prepare the means, to save our country. It will learn the heads of departments, to listen to information, transmitted, that ought to put them on their guard, and prepare for energetic defense before the enemy reaches the interior." Jackson closed by stating that his troops had given the British a "drubbing . . . in true american stile" at Mobile Point on September 15. Had his troops been present in Washington, Jackson insisted, the "capital would have been defended—and saved."[49]

In October 1814 DuVal once again bucked the general sentiment in Kentucky when he took the floor in the House of Representatives in support of rechartering the Bank of the United States. Madison, an early opponent of the National Bank, now asked Congress to recharter the bank to stabilize the foundering American financial situation. The president also urged Congress to pass a protective tariff to encourage manufacturing and to provide for internal improvements to encourage westward expansion.[50] Following Calhoun's lead, DuVal argued that these were extraordinary times and that Congress needed to do what they could to support the president. He challenged the view that the bank was unconstitutional, arguing that the Constitution prohibited states from coining money and issuing bills of credit, which "negation of power implied the power in Congress. If Congress had not the power under the Constitution to establish a bank," he argued, "nearly all the states had violated their own State Constitutions as well as the Constitution of the United States in authorizing the circulation of bank notes, which call them what you will, are 'bills of credit.'" The measure failed by a vote of 80–81. DuVal thereupon was successful in calling for the bill's reconsideration in order to "save the sinking credit of the country." Once again the bank bill wended its way through various versions, but the final version passed was eventually vetoed by Madison.[51]

Also that session, DuVal consulted with the Illinois territorial delegate seeking more volunteers for the Illinois and Lake Michigan region for renewed campaigns in the spring. That November DuVal joined fellow Kentucky legislators in an offer to raise such a regiment of a thousand mounted volunteers.[52] Also that month DuVal felt compelled to speak in favor of a provision of a volunteer bill, exempting volunteers from being called out for the militia once they had served for two years. After faithfully serving his country for two years, why should a soldier be told that "his patriotism was not worth a rush because it had not carried him to the end of the war?" Using his own experiences as an example, DuVal argued that volunteers had borne every hardship: "In the campaign on the Wabash, in the depth of Winter, they had marched barefoot without complaining . . . how many had returned who were not frost-bitten? Justice and equity of sacrifice argued against submitting volunteers to more than two years of service." DuVal had made his point but his position lost in the final vote.[53]

On December 9 the House debated a bill authorizing the president to draft eighty thousand men. DuVal rose to defend the bill as necessary: "The rejection of the measure would be to disarm the nation, and increase the calamities of the war." DuVal charged that those who opposed the bill were driven by party spirit. DuVal warned that "a powerful and ambitious enemy, who is collecting all the deluge of war to pour on this devoted land, with a Treasury exhausted, and a gallant army reduced in number but not in spirit. I, indeed, had hoped that gentlemen in the opposition (under these circumstances) would have stood forward to defend their soil and sovereignty." DuVal admitted that while some of the "Federal Party" had supported the country in its time of need, the majority had not. "This is the duty of every American; they owe it to themselves and their country. I ask no gentlemen to sacrifice their principles. Surely, when their aid is demanded to preserve our rights, let them expose the errors of the Administration; let them expose the policy which has been pursued by the dominant party; let them endeavor to convince the people that their confidence has been misplaced and abused; nay, let them exert all their powers to change the rulers of the nation, and call other men and measures into action. But, in the name of our common country, I call on them to prepare to meet an enemy as implacable as he is powerful."[54]

DuVal went on to charge that the true purpose of the measure's opponents was to cause friction among the sections. "There is a class of politicians in this country who have for years, with the most unwearied industry and artifice, endeavored to make the Eastern and Northern sections of the Union believe that the Southern and Western states are jealous of their increasing wealth and commercial importance. This opinion has been supported and encouraged by demagogues for base and perfidious purposes. The good sense of the nation (it is the hope of every American) will soon correct so fatal an opinion." DuVal went on to say that all sections, on the contrary, are linked by mutual self-interest. He warned against those plotting disunion. "I tell them they are treading over a volcano that may burst upon them in dreadful ruin. Do they propose to better their conditions or the condition of the country by such dangerous and mad contention? If so, let me drive from them their fatal delusion." DuVal likened the coming storm to that experienced in the French Revolution. "Deceive not yourselves and friends with the vain and foolish hope that you can 'mount the whirlwind and direct the storm,' for you will be scattered before it 'like chaff before the wind of heaven.'" The debate was long and acrimonious, lasting from December 8 through December 12. In the end DuVal and Calhoun won the day by a vote of 84–72.[55]

Only three days after the vote, it was in this spirit as well as under the shadow of disunion that the Hartford Convention met. One observer in Washington wrote to Governor Shelby that "we have the most awful consequence to apprehend.... We are all anxiety here for the fate of New Orleans.... Without more energy in the republicans in Congress—I should not be surprised that each state was acting for itself in less than nine months. This is a painful subject—It is intended for confidential friends only."[56]

Just when things looked darkest, the entire mood of the capital changed on February 3 when DuVal and the rest of the Washington learned of Andrew Jackson's defeat of the British at the Battle of New Orleans. About that time a treaty ending the war had arrived in Washington. On February 16 the Senate ratified both the Peace of Ghent and Old Hickory's Treaty of Fort Jackson, dispossessing the Creeks of most of their lands in Alabama. DuVal may have attended the formal signing ceremony of the Peace of Ghent, hosted by President Madison.[57]

With the war over, Congress adjourned on March 3. As DuVal packed up his things for the trek home to Kentucky, he could take pride in his service to his country as a soldier and as a member of Congress. He was glad to return home to rejoin Nancy and the children. His family was growing. That year Nancy gave birth to their fourth child, Elizabeth Ann, and the next year John Crittenden was born. When he returned to Bardstown DuVal no doubt listened to constituents who both agreed and disagreed with his actions in Congress. Whether or not DuVal ran for re-election to his seat in August is unknown. (Records are unavailable.) But it is known that his old rival Benjamin Hardin took his place in Washington. It is likely that if he did campaign at all, his failure to retain his seat was not distressing to him. (He had been away from his family and his law practice too often over the previous three years.) On September 13, writing from Bardstown, he cheerfully recommended the brother of the "mem-elect for this district" for a judgeship in the Illinois Territory.[58] Nor is it likely that DuVal participated in the unsuccessful campaign of his relative John Pope's attempt to unseat Henry Clay.[59]

In the years immediately following the Peace of Ghent Kentucky experienced an economic boom brought on by postwar nationalism and growing demand for foodstuffs. Kentucky manufacturing had also benefited from the war, and prices for goods remained high for a time. The prosperity encouraged speculation in lands and shaky business ventures. Adding fuel to the fire, in 1818 the state chartered forty-six banking institutions that extended credit on such easy terms that a collapse was almost inevitable. As one source has noted, "almost every town of any size had a bank. The Second Bank of the United States established branches in Louisville and Lexington, but it soon aroused opposition because of a kind of fiscal policing of the state banks. A state that a few years earlier had to rely heavily on barter because of the lack of currency was suddenly awash in banknotes. This easy credit accelerated the speculative boom." The reckoning would soon come. In November 1818 Kentucky banks suspended specie payments. On December 6, Governor Gabriel Slaughter recommended that directors and stockholders of banks be made individually liable for redemption of their notes. Two months later all independent bank charters were repealed.[60]

The crash known as the "Panic of 1819" brought the entire country to its knees. But its devastation was most acutely felt in the West.[61] The political fallout over the economic catastrophe was particularly disruptive in Kentucky, as the state's Republican Party divided into relief and antirelief wings, a conflict that eventually evolved into an Old Court–New Court battle over the structure of the state's courts.[62] Precisely where William P. DuVal stood in this conflict is unclear, but it can be assumed that his personal economic situation was precarious. It is often said that bank crashes make great work for lawyers, but DuVal had several unresolved cases of his own to take care of. Not only did DuVal face the still unresolved legal cases stemming from his brother's estate, but also Nancy and her brother's claim against their father's estate was still unresolved. In June 1814, Nancy's cousin William had sold out his entire stock of goods in the store. How the proceeds were divided is uncertain.[63] A land deal gone sour between DuVal and Felix Grundy was also in litigation.[64] Combined with his economic woes were DuVal's increasing family obligations. In 1819 and 1820 Nancy gave birth to two more daughters, Mary and Laura Harrison. The Census of 1820 recorded twenty persons in his household: nine white and eleven black.[65]

Even though he did not return to Congress in 1816, DuVal continued to stay in touch with friends and political acquaintances in Washington. In the summer of 1818 he visited President James Monroe and met Secretary of State John Quincy Adams for the first time.[66] He also called on his friend John C. Calhoun, who became Monroe's secretary of war. As long as Virginians held the White House those with familial and political ties to the Old Dominion had significant advantages. Territorial expansion of the United States brought with it many opportunities for political appointments, and the field for those opportunities was about to expand.

In 1817 clashes on the southern border between Alabama and Georgia settlers and Creeks residing in Spanish Florida prompted a military response from General Andrew Jackson. In the First Seminole War, fought from March 15 through June 1818, Old Hickory invaded Spanish Florida, captured St. Marks, attacked Bowlegs Town on the Suwannee River, executed two British subjects (one a soldier and another a Scottish trader), and captured Pensacola, holding it temporarily before returning to Tennessee. Critics called the raid "unauthorized" and demanded an explanation. The incident caused consternation among Monroe and his cabinet and in the House of Representatives, where Speaker Henry Clay denounced Jackson's unsanctioned invasion and launched investigations of his conduct. Monroe dissembled, refusing to back Jackson's action with vigor. But the electorate applauded Jackson's military strike, and the upshot was that while the majority of Monroe's cabinet (including Calhoun) voted secretly to censure the General, Secretary John Quincy Adams manipulated the diplomatic crisis with Spain to his own advantage. On February 22, 1819, Adams and Don Luis de Onís signed the treaty that transferred the Floridas to the United States.[67]

Meanwhile, William P. DuVal had renewed his correspondence with his friend John C. Calhoun, whose influence in the administration was strong. Expressing sympathy for the "reverse of fortune that you had made known to me in your last two letters," the South Carolinian wrote, "I brought your case before [the president]: and I can venture to say that he feels a lively interest in your favour of which the first suitable occurrence he will give substantial proofs. He fully confides in

General Andrew Jackson ca. 1818. Courtesy of State Archives of Florida.

your talents and integrity and feels that your claims are increased by your reverses. In the mean time he is not aware of any vacancy to the West, which would suit you; and desires me to say to you that he desires you, should any vacancy occur, which would suit you, to communicate your wish in relation to it." Calhoun continued, "You are young and with an excellent constitution; and with your talents and experiences, will readily with proper exertion reclaim your affairs. You must not therefore dispair; or permit yourself to take any hasty resolution. Continue vigorously the persuit in which you are engaged till a favorable opportunity offers. . . . It is said to be easy to advise those in misfortune, but I am sure you will not set down my suggestions to a cold and lecturing morality, but to a sincere desire to see you prosper."[68]

DuVal had many influential friends ready to write to Washington authorities in his favor. According to Illinois governor Ninian Edwards, DuVal's personality particularly suited him to occupy any important federal post on America's growing frontier. "Of his private worth," Edwards wrote to John Quincy Adams, "it would be difficult to use language more than adequate to do him justice. Joined to a spritely imagination, he possesses great benevolence & generosity & to borrow

John C. Calhoun, ca. 1820. Courtesy of Library of Congress.

the expression his head out flowing with the 'milk of human kindness.' Of his uncorruptable integrity I have no doubt."[69]

In January 1821 DuVal wrote to Calhoun from Bardstown that he had read in the papers that Spain had ratified the Adams-Onis Treaty. "If this news be true, I suppose the immediate possession of that country will be assumed by our Government—If a judge is to be appointed with a comitent Salary for this new country I will accept it or any appointment there in which I can be of service to my Country—I would indeed prefer a situation nearer, Kentucky—but I know of none." When Calhoun received DuVal's letter he enclosed it to Secretary of State Adams, noting that DuVal was the man of whom he had spoken to the secretary "last evening. He is a very worthy man and is very competent to fill the place of judge or District Attorney. I would be much gratified with his appointment." President Monroe appointed DuVal judge of the Eastern Judicial District on May 18 and directed him to reside in St. Augustine. DuVal was notified of his appointment on June 27 and accepted it on July 28.[70]

By the time DuVal accepted his appointment Congress had authorized the creation of the Territory of Florida, and President Monroe appointed federal officials to administer the new province. One of his first acts was to appoint General Andrew Jackson, perhaps the man most responsible for the acquisition of Florida, its first governor. Arriving in Florida in July 1821, Jackson, his wife, Rachel, and several of his lieutenants oversaw the transfer of flags in Pensacola on July 17. More than four hundred miles away, Jackson's protégé, Robert Butler, had presided over a similar ceremony in St. Augustine ten days earlier. After Butler received the formal transfer of flags he informed Secretary of State Adams of the fact and added, "not one of the civil officers appointed by the President has yet arrived except the Marshal." Butler's orders were to leave a captain in charge and to strike out for Pensacola. As no reliable road linked the two settlements, he would have to travel "by Darien & through the Creek nation—The climate and season of the year will render it a long, and fatiguing journey," he wrote to Adams.[71] DuVal's journey from Kentucky to the new Florida Territory was also a long one. When he arrived on November 1821 to assume his official duties in St. Augustine, he must have arrived with some trepidation. Most likely, though, he had no idea that he would be inextricably tied to Florida for the rest of his life.

CHAPTER 3

Judge and Governor

In the fall of 1821, when William P. DuVal arrived in St. Augustine to assume his official duties as judge of the Eastern Judicial District, the territory had been officially in U.S. hands for approximately six months. The most important official business had taken place in Pensacola, where Andrew Jackson resided. No one expected Old Hickory to remain in the territory for long. In fact, on August 4 Jackson confided to President Monroe that "the objects which induced my acceptance are nearly completed. The country has been received[. T]he Government is organized and in complete operation." He was ready to return to Tennessee. Jackson scarcely concealed his frustration that more of his own trusted advisers who had followed him to Florida had not been favored with official appointments. Those he had in mind were men who had fought with him in the Creek Campaign, the War of 1812, and the First Seminole War—men like Richard Keith Call, James Gadsden, and Dr. John Bronough. Of those Monroe appointed Jackson noted that he knew none of them except Judges Fromentin and DuVal, and those "very slightly." Jackson felt compelled to reveal "the opinions expressed here of the characters you had appointed as Judges—It is understood here that Mr. DuVal is of good character, but of very moderate capacity as a lawyer."[1]

Jackson's first priority was to access the whereabouts and condition of the Native Americans in Florida. In his first official instructions, Secretary of War John C. Calhoun directed Jackson and his subagent to make immediate contact with Indians and acquaint them "with their new relations to the U. States and impress on them an assurance of being protected provided they demean themselves peaceably." Calhoun anticipated that with the "the first pressure of emigration" of whites into the "portion of Florida which may be claimed by the Indians, it is to be feared that some collision may take place between them and our citizens. . . . Situated as they are and surrounded as they must in a short time with the white population, it will probably become desirable both to them and us to make hereafter a new Disposition of them either by concentrating them at some one point in Florida, or by giving them a new home in some other part of the U. States. You shall sound them on this point when your residence among them has been sufficiently long to enable you to do it with prudence."[2] Jackson needed no prompting on the subject of removal. Soon after he arrived in the territory his communication with Washington authorities and theirs to him took that tenor.

The first step toward removal was concentration, and concentration would not be easy. At the time the Floridas passed to the United States the number of Native Americans was approximately five thousand. Though they were scattered throughout the peninsula, three broad groups can be differentiated. The Seminole (Upper Creeks, Muskogee Speakers) lived in the middle peninsula on the Alachua prairie and had been in the peninsula since the 1700s. Also in the peninsula were Miccosukee (Hitichi Speakers). The most threatening to the whites were Upper Creeks (Red Sticks), who lived in scattered towns primarily between the Apalachicola and Tampa Bay. These folk were the most recent to come to Florida. Led by Peter McQueen, the Redsticks had allied with the British during the War of 1812. After their defeat by Jackson in the Creek War, many had migrated to "Negro Fort" on the Apalachicola River and then moved eastward toward the Suwannee River and further into the peninsula after American forces destroyed that bastion, composed of Indians and their African allies, in 1816. As one scholar has estimated, roughly "twenty-nine independent bands were scattered throughout the peninsula from the Georgia border to Tampa Bay. . . . Situated near the larger bands were villages of former slaves who paid a tribute of horses, cattle, and produce to the Seminole leaders who had extended protection to them."[3]

While many of the refugees had filtered down into the peninsula by the time of Jackson's raid, the redoubtable Miccosukee chief Neamathla had not. Determining that the Peace of Ghent had invalidated the Treaty of Fort Jackson, Neamathla established a series of Hitchiti Fowl Towns just below the international boundary and only fifteen miles from Fort Scott, just north of the Georgia-Florida border. Neamathla had felt the brunt of Jackson's raid into Florida only three years earlier. Moving his people into the Tallahassee "Old Fields" (the site of the abandoned center of the Spanish Apalachee missions), Neamathla brooded. According to Leitch Wright, even now he was "determined to retain his culture, clan, and way of life."[4]

Perhaps the most vexing problem confronting American officials, vis-à-vis the Indians, was the presence of blacks among them. In the decades before Florida became an American territory, blacks had found sanctuary in Spanish Florida. Maroon settlements had flourished and in some instances had contact with the British on the Gulf and Atlantic coasts in the decades before the transfer. The Spanish policy of augmenting its small military presence with African "militias" in defense against the English began as early as the 1700s and reached its peak during the Patriot War (1812–1813), when Georgians invaded East Florida in an attempt to conquer the province. Emancipation for service rendered created a path to freedom for blacks that was not available to bondsmen in the American states, and numerous blacks lived in freedom in Pensacola and St. Augustine at the time of the transfer.[5] One man that fit this description in St. Augustine, a person who would eventually serve DuVal and the United States as an interpreter, was Antonio Proctor.

Slaveholding among the Indians had evolved into a kind of vassalage relationship, a relationship recognized by the Spanish but one that conflicted sharply with the American system of chattel slavery. The vassalage relationship was unclear, misunderstood, and eventually unacceptable to Americans who considered any deviation from the chattel principle a serious threat to their own Peculiar Institution. Because ownership of slaves could not be proven (and, even if it could, U.S. courts would not recognize property rights of Indians), the presence of blacks among the Indians became a sticking point from the very beginning. It was also true that long before the United States obtained possession of Florida, escaped slaves from plantations had found sanctuary in Florida. Thus to Americans—even though this was not the case—every African in Florida who lived with the Indians was an escaped slave. Finally, making these circumstances even more complicated was the fact that since the early eighteenth century there had been considerable racial mixing among the Africans and the Seminoles.[6]

The presence of blacks living in a state of freedom on the frontier was something Americans would not tolerate. Moreover, the value of slaves in Georgia and Alabama induced renegade whites to cross the boundary and kidnap blacks and sell them into slavery. Such activity had been taking place for decades. (In fact, that was one of the motivations for earlier American incursions into Florida.) Various bands of Indians had also participated in the process. In June, the same month that Jackson arrived in Pensacola, a band of Cowetas sacked black settlements in the Tampa Bay and captured as many blacks as they could and sold them into slavery in Georgia and Alabama. Not long afterward, traumatized Indians began arriving in St. Augustine seeking protection.[7] Jackson was certain that "McQueen and his adherents" were still in the peninsula and likely to give further trouble, and he asked for permission to move against them but was denied. He continued to press the issue. "One thing is certain. As long as they are permitted to remain in Florida, it will be a receptacle for rogues, murderers, and runaway negroes."[8]

Jackson's main preoccupation during his brief tenure in Florida was the Indians. He was convinced that all the Indians, but especially the Red Sticks, must be removed North "within the limits of the country assigned to the Creek nation (of which the Seminoles are a part)." Upon this the "security of the Southern border" depended. "The Government cannot turn the torrent of emigration to the Floridas without great expense; good policy and the safety of the frontier, in my opinion, require that the government should promote emigration to this country, and hasten its admission as a State into the Union." In his view those Redsticks who had "fled from the Creek Nation, and kept up an exterminating war on our frontier until crushed by the arm of our government in 1818," had no right to expect that they could make a treaty to remain in Florida.

But Jackson soon discovered unsettling facts in East Florida that would jeopardize his plans. "Self-made Indian agents" Edward Wanton and Horatio Dexter, he learned, were attempting "to impress on the minds of the Indians, *Their absolute right to the country.*" Jackson immediately ordered the territorial secretary, William Worthington, who was in St. Augustine, to seize these men and detain them until the instructions of the government could be had. These reports "prove the necessity of Congress taking the subject up, and by law prescribing bounds to the Seminoles." Calhoun agreed with Jackson that Wanton and Dexter were "unprincipled men who ought to be removed from the Indian Country. Your letter with its enclosures leaves no doubts as to the correctness of this impression," the secretary of war wrote to Jackson.[9]

On September 18–20 Jackson held talks with John Blount, Neamathla, and the Mulatto King in Pensacola. Blount had been an ally of Jackson's in his previous campaigns, but Neamathla had been hostile, and the General was determined to force the recalcitrant warrior to submit to American will. Jackson reviewed the previous eight years, admonishing Neamathla to reject the British, McQueen, and other false prophets and either return to the "your old nation" or some other specific location. The Indians would not be permitted to "settle all over the Floridas, and on her sea coast. Your white brethren must be settled there, to keep you from the bad men and bad talks." Neamathla named fifteen towns scattered in the peninsula and estimated that there were two thousand Indians in Florida. Jackson wrote to John C. Calhoun of his talks and recommended that the Indians be concentrated along the Apalachicola River adjoining the southern boundary of Alabama and Georgia. "There a white settlement would be interposed between them and the sea shore." He recommended that "from the smallness of their numbers, and the shape of the Floridas that it would be much better policy to move them all up, and amply provide for them by annuity." In order to finalize the agreements Jackson recommended that Neamathla and the other chiefs be invited to Washington.[10] There the matter stood when Old Hickory left Florida, never to return, on October 8. Not long after Jackson reached Nashville he resigned. Florida would be acting Governor William Worthington's problem.[11]

Meanwhile conditions in St. Augustine were also confused. When Colonel Robert Butler arrived in the town in May he reported that "Indians are frequent here, parading the streets in a drunken, riotous manner—There is almost a total absence of legal Government at this time."[12] This situation improved somewhat once the formal transfer was made and territorial secretary William Worthington arrived in August, but by then, as the official reported to Old Hickory, yellow fever was taking its toll. "The vile Black vomit plays sad work among us." A judge, the Indian agent, and "about a half dozen other of my friends already sleep in a watery grave about two feet and a half below the Surface of this Peninsula." The dying continued. In November Worthington wrote that Judge DuVal had not yet arrived. This was fortunate because sickness "rages here still beyond anything I ever saw or heard of." Dexter and Wanton were offering their services as negotiators with the Indians, stating that "the Chiefs have vested in us the power to make for them a Treaty. This duty," they insisted, "we will discharge alone or in concert." Temporary organization of the town, under the leadership of prominent Creoles (Joseph Hernandez, Francis Fatio, Francis P. Sanchez, and Joseph S. Sanchez) offered the prospect of stability.[13]

William P. DuVal arrived in St. Augustine to assume his official duties in the last week of November. DuVal chose not to travel directly to the Ancient City by boat. Instead he (along with his twenty-three-year-old brother-in-law Alfred Hynes) determined to explore the entire length of the St. Johns, before arriving in St. Augustine's back door. Entering the mouth of the St. Johns, DuVal and Hynes paddled past the future site of Jacksonville, Picolata (the stopping off point for those heading to St. Augustine), and Lake George and continued all the way to Volusia. Returning to Picolata and then traveling on horseback the twenty or so miles to St. Augustine, DuVal took a look around town and reported his observations to Secretary of State John Quincy Adams. DuVal reported that he had been "much about in E. Florida since my arrival, and hope in a few days to send you a chart of St. Johns River from its mouth to Volusia." DuVal promised to "add remarks which may serve to give you some little information as to the soil and products of the St. Johns River."[14]

DuVal noted that the disease in St. Augustine had "happily subsided" (even though the district attorney died less than two weeks later).[15] DuVal found "considerable confusion . . . among the several officers of government as to their powers" and added that "nothing less than the timely interposition of Congress can restore harmony and order in this place." DuVal also asked permission to appropriate some part of the public buildings here for the court and Clerk's office" and asked whether President Monroe had "fixed on the allowance intended for the U.S. judge of E. Florida." Finally, DuVal closed his correspondence with the request that he be allowed to appoint a fellow Kentuckian, Greenbury A. Gaither, "now residing in this place," a clerk of his court. Gaither, a "gentleman of excellent legal knowledge from Kentucky," spoke the "French language and reads the Spanish with fluency," and he would be competent to decide on the land titles of E. Florida. Without fully appreciating it, DuVal had hit upon the most vexing problem confronting American officials in the Florida Territory.[16]

The terms of the Adams-Onis Treaty stipulated that the United States would recognize lands granted to subjects of the Spanish king before January 24, 1818. The task of any claimant was to prove that his grants were established before that date, and to do that archival records were indispensable. Boards of commissioners in St. Augustine and Pensacola were appointed and in operation by July 1822, but long before they began their deliberations conflicts over control of records in Pensacola and St. Augustine were rampant.[17] Sometime before DuVal arrived, Colonel Robert Butler warned authorities in Washington that "abuses ... are going on with regard to land titles. I am informed that the authorities here, having possession of those titles, are determined to ship them at all hazards, alleging as a reason *that all the United States would find it in her interest to destroy them* but if my information is correct, the reason is founded on their having mutilated them by *ante-dating tearing out and inserting leaves,* so as to make grants for much larger tracts of land than were originally given."[18] Controversy over the grants went on for decades and was further complicated by the fact that, despite Jackson's vociferous protests, Spanish officials succeeded in carrying off many of the land records to Cuba.[19]

When DuVal arrived in St. Augustine, he moved quickly to hold the first session of court in the new territory. Addressing the grand jury on December 5, DuVal proclaimed to his listeners that "the acquisition of the Floridas [was] a demonstration of the power of our great and growing empire." The meeting of the court witnesses "on this occasion, the interesting spectacle of its highest judicial tribunal ready for the distribution of justice, without regard to religious faith, rank, or nation. . . . Every good citizen of the United States looks with confidence and triumph to the Constitution and Laws of the Union for equal protection of his life, liberty, and property. The humblest individual in society claims and enjoys all rights and privileges in our Courts of Justice in our political institutions, in common with the wealthy and powerful. The despot governs by his will and the highest and the dearest rights of community sink before his interests and ambition. Our government is that of the laws; none are above their influence and power. To you, Gentlemen of the Grand Jury and to the citizens of our country, we look for their execution."[20]

The work of the court was minimal, and DuVal left St. Augustine for Washington on December 23, leaving behind his brother-in-law Alfred Hynes, who served as a clerk to Worthington, the acting governor.[21] Before he departed, however, he had the opportunity to meet most of the town's inhabitants. He no doubt made a favorable impression. A number of those in town solicited him to serve as an unofficial delegate for the territory in Congress.[22] When he arrived in Washington on January 14, the Seventeenth Congress was midway through its first session, and DuVal's friend Philip Barbour was speaker. Congressmen and senators solicited Judge DuVal's advice, and of course, the issue of Jackson's replacement was

President James Monroe. Courtesy of State Archives of Florida.

paramount in the discussions. Despite his knowledge of Spanish and his "very considerable" legal and literary attainments, Worthington's advanced age seemed to rule out the Marylander's selection. DuVal no doubt sensed this and began lining up support for his selection as governor. Securing the support of the entire Kentucky delegation for his appointment as governor, DuVal also drew support from both Illinois's and Indiana's senators, as well as senators from Virginia, Delaware, and Ohio. Congressmen from Pennsylvania, Massachusetts, and Maryland added their support.[23] One of DuVal's supporters suggested that Jackson's short tenure as governor had caused a "sort of irritability in the Territory and a restive, suspicion & uneasy feeling within it." Writing directly to President Monroe, the man suggested that DuVal's easy temperament would "harmonize discordant elements."[24] Simultaneously with his efforts in Congress, a petition arrived supporting DuVal's cause from the inhabitants of East Florida that noted that no other "choice would be so gratifying or acceptable to the people of East Florida as Judge DuVal." Among the prominent citizens signing the petition were Francis and Joseph Sanchez, John Geiger, F. M. Arredondo, Bernardo Sequi, Jose Ximenez, and John M. Fontane.[25]

DuVal may have understood at the time that a patronage battle in Monroe's Cabinet between his friend Calhoun and Treasury Secretary William H. Crawford was under way and that Crawford favored former North Carolina governor John Branch, while Calhoun favored elevating DuVal to the post. Monroe eventually appointed both men on the same day (April 17, 1822): DuVal as governor and Branch as judge of the Western Judicial District. Branch rejected the president's offer, accepting instead a seat in the U.S. Senate courtesy of the North Carolina legislature.[26] (In fact, one of Branch's friends was reputed to have told Monroe's secretary that he might tell "the President to take the judge's commission and put it in his pocket or in hell.")[27] Secretary of State Adams interpreted DuVal's appointment as a victory for Calhoun and an insult to Crawford. Adams recorded in his diary that the North Carolinians' indignation was so great that the president "considered himself personally insulted by them."[28] Also recommended for governor was Joseph L. Smith of Connecticut. Smith eventually accepted appointment to DuVal's post as judge of East Florida.

Meanwhile Congress moved to formally establish the territory, passing legislation that specified the guidelines for territorial government. The legislation provided that there would be *one* territory instead of *two*, discontinuing the Spanish and English precedent. (In January DuVal and others had called for consolidation of the territory as essential and suggested that the governor or special commissioners select a more "central point" for the meeting of the legislature.) The legislation stipulated that the president would appoint governors, U.S. attorneys, judges, and marshals with the advice and consent of the Senate. Governors would reside in the territory and serve three-year terms, "unless sooner removed by the President." Governors served as commanders in chief of the militia and ex-officio superintendent of Indian affairs. Governors could grant pardons for offenses against the territory and had the power to appoint and commission all civil and militia officers. The president retained the power to appoint members of the legislative council, which would meet annually (by 1826 these positions became elective). As with the governing of all territories, the Senate, largely because of its confirmation power, retained significant oversight in the governing of the territories. Its Committee on the Territories launched investigations and held hearings as the need arose.[29]

That winter and spring, President Monroe received numerous solicitations for Florida appointments. One day before his official appointment was registered, DuVal, writing from Washington, recommended to Monroe an entire slate of legislative council delegates. DuVal noted that East Florida should have the "majority of the council as there are eight thousand souls in East, and but five thousand in West Florida." DuVal recommended "to your consideration such gentlemen as I personally know, all of whom are intelligent and well informed and possess in a high degree the respect and confidence of the People of East Florida. . . . All these gentlemen . . . have resided in East Florida, since our Government received possessions of the country. Most of those . . . are natives of the country—and have great influence which I believe they justly deserve." President Monroe accepted several of DuVal's suggested appointees, including the Creoles Joseph Hernandez and Bernardo Sequi, but was moved to appoint a number of other men with prominent backgrounds and significant family affiliations. Henry M. Brackenridge of Pennsylvania was a distinguished jurist and man of letters; the Virginian Edgar Macon was James Madison's nephew. John C. Bronough, Richard Keith Call, and James R. Hanham were Jackson men. Joseph M. White, a Kentucky lawyer and the son-in-law of Kentucky governor John Adair, was also appointed. Practicing law in Frankfort at the time the territory was organized, the thirty-nine-year-old White wrote to Monroe that he understood that Senator Richard M. Johnson had recommended him for a position in the territorial legislature. Because of his wife's illness, he was willing to "abandon a lucrative Office and extensive practice in this State to locate myself in Florida." DuVal knew White. In 1819 he had recommended him for U.S. attorney in Alabama or Mississippi.[30]

From April to June 1822 (when he arrived in Pensacola to assume his official duties as governor) DuVal remained in Virginia or Kentucky. His appointment secured, DuVal traveled to Bardstown to see his family and to attend to several pending law cases. On the way he visited his father's family in Buckingham County. By 1822 Major DuVal had lived fourteen years on his plantation with his second wife, Susan Brown Christian, and DuVal's two half-sisters, Sarah Catherine (14) and Susan Elizabeth (15). At seventy-two, Major DuVal lived a comfortable life. As he had told Henry Clay the year before, "If you would call on me I should be happy to see you. . . . I am in my 73rd year. I emancipated my Slaves 20 Years ago—I work from 5 to 8 Hours a day & have one among the neatest Farms in the County. Three Lads & tradman of mine work it. I have paid including interest & Cost more than Two hundred Thousand Dollars by Securityships and the failures of others, but I was never happier. I walk frequently Seven Miles to & from Meeting. We make a plenty to eat & some thing to spare." The old man attributed his happiness and long life to his commitment "To fear God & keep his Commandments."[31] DuVal's visit with his father would have been pleasant, but, having been absent from his own family for six months, he was determined to reach home as soon as he could.

The ten days DuVal spent in Bardstown were filled with joy at seeing Nancy and his large family of seven children, which included DuVal's oldest son Burr (13), Marcia (11), Thomas Howard (9), Elizabeth (7), John Crittenden (6), Mary (3), and Laura (2).

No doubt the couple's precarious financial situation was a topic of conversation. The governor's annual salary would be $2,500. It is uncertain what other income the family could generate. Perhaps he could supplement his salary practicing law in the new territory, but that was uncertain. DuVal may also have attended to several legal cases he had pending during his brief stay. The ongoing Grundy dispute was one of those cases, but also unsettled were those involving his brother and the Hynes family's estate.³² By early June, the new governor bid farewell to his family and left Bardstown, heading south toward Pensacola (the site of the first meeting of the legislative council). Traveling in company with Joseph White and his young, beautiful bride, Ellen Adair "Florida" White, the party likely traveled down the Ohio and Mississippi, reaching New Orleans and then going on to Pensacola, arriving there on June 20 in the "same conveyance."³³

Pensacola was a village of poorly constructed, irregularly built buildings, with a diverse population of between two and three thousand. According to one visitor Pensacola had "perhaps a greater diversity of character, color, and physiognomy, and withal a greater variety and confusion of tongues than any place of the same magnitude could boast since the ancient days of Babylon." Rachel Jackson was also struck by the town's ethnic diversity. "The inhabitants all speak Spanish and French," she had written to a friend one year earlier when she and her husband were in the town. "Some speak four or five languages. Such a mixed multitude, you, nor any of us, ever had an idea of. There are fewer white people here than any other, mixed with all nations under the canopy of heaven, almost in nature's darkness." Of the town's physical dimensions and beauty she noted, "Pensacola is a perfect plain; the land nearly as white as flour, yet productive of fine peach trees, oranges in abundance, grapes, figs, pomegranates, etc., etc. . . . In the morning until ten at night we have the finest sea breeze. This is something so exhilarating, so pure, so wholesome, it enlivens the whole system." When DuVal arrived there were a number of leading men who had been there since Jackson's arrival, including Richard Keith Call, John Bronough, Henry Brackenridge, and territorial secretary George Walton. With housing scarce, DuVal boarded with Walton's family, as did Bronough.³⁴

One day after his arrival in Pensacola, DuVal wrote to both Adams and Calhoun of the conditions as he found them. To Adams he explained his surroundings but also the circumstances and challenges he faced. He noted that only five of the thirteen members of the legislative council had arrived, even though the session was to have begun ten days earlier. He found all of the governmental buildings in the military's possession and the soldiers stationed in the "heart of the City" and thus with the "opportunity to mingle in the dissipation common to all towns." Worse still, there was no money for any operations of government including the "expenses of the legislature, to furnish a house for them to meet, pay for printing the laws, or for stationary or clerks. . . . It will readily occur to you, Sir," he wrote to the secretary of state, "That nearly one year must elapse before a revenue to meet the local expense of the Government here can be collected—In the mean time without some advances from the General Government, serious inconvenience & real evil must be the consequence." DuVal asked Adams to "lay before the President this letter and give me such information & directions as he or you may deem advisable—making them so specifik that I can avoid any errors which might tend either to embarrass the Government, or myself." Ten days later the confusion still prevailed. There was still no sign of the remaining legislative council delegates, who were expected to arrive by boat from East Florida. On July 17, DuVal wrote to Adams that he feared the sloop *The Lady Washington* carrying the tardy delegates had been lost at sea, "and every soul perished." If this was the case, DuVal opined, "I have lost a brother-in-law Mr. Hynes who was also a passenger. . . . This will be a serious misfortune to our Territory." Fortunately, Hynes and the others eventually arrived, and the legislative council convened on July 22.[35]

The most pressing issue that DuVal confronted was the status of the Indians. Soon after his arrival DuVal learned that the Indians were very "uneasy" and in a "starving condition." They had lost their crops in floods, and he expected their leaders to arrive in town any day. He stated that he was not "advised of my powers & duties as superintendent of Indian Affairs" and asked for direction as to what he should tell them about what "Tract of Country it is *probable* they will occupy and in what manner and what amount they are to be furnished with rations." Calhoun offered DuVal little direction other than to say that it was expected that they would eventually be concentrated somewhere on the Apalachicola River.[36]

Indeed, Indians affairs had been in a state of flux since the transfer of flags. Jackson had met with Indians briefly, but there had been no official communication with them since his departure. In the east the situation was even less satisfactory. The first agent, Jean Penieres, had died of yellow fever in St. Augustine. Captain John Bell had served temporarily as agent but was removed, and Peter Pelham of Philadelphia served only briefly before leaving the territory due to illness. Colonel Abram Eustis filled in temporarily for Pelham but had to report to Washington that the absence of licensed Indian traders created a circumstance in which "Indians are compelled to bring their skins & other articles of trade" to St. Augustine and that "they are abundantly supplied with spiritious liquor." There was no "municipal regulation to prohibit it & even if there were the civil authorities of this City lack the *power* to enforce it." The civil authority was so weak, the colonel claimed, that he was forced to assist constables in arresting people. When Eustis wrote to Calhoun, Gad Humphreys of New York had been appointed for three months, but the former U.S. Army major would not arrive in Florida to assume his duties until December 24.[37]

Some of the answers to DuVal questions were already making their way to the Florida territory. Months earlier Secretary of War Calhoun had posted notification of Humphreys's appointment and provided the governor with copies of relevant statutes regulating his duties regarding Indian affairs. The agent was to provide DuVal with quarterly estimates of expenses of the Indian Agency to be forwarded to the secretary. The secretary would then forward funds to DuVal for distribution to the agent, the subagent, interpreters, and others who had claims against the government. The accounts must "be accompanied by a general abstract of all disbursement, within each quarter . . . detailing under distinct heads the various objects of disbursement, to wit: pay of Agent, sub agent & interpreters, presents, rations &c &c so as to leave as few as possible to be embraced under the general head of 'Contingencies.' To this abstract a statement must be annexed, shewing the names of all who have been employed in the Indian Department, by the agent or yourself, within each quarter, as Interpreters or any other capacity whatever, with the amount of wages paid them respectively. These abstracts are indispensably necessary, to enable the Department to lay before Congress the annual statement . . . as should be carefully prepared and punctually rendered." The governor would receive no additional pay for his services regarding Indian affairs, but his expenses and "suitable Compensation" would be allowed for extra work over and above his specific duties as superintendent.[38]

The condition of the Indians continued to deteriorate. As DuVal explained, the "Indians in Florida are in a wretched state." Not knowing where they would eventually live prompted them to neglect their crops. They were in such distress that "they have dug up miles of the Country in order to procure the brier root to subsist on." "The various claims of individuals to grants of Land in almost every part of Florida, Keeps the Indians in continual alarm—the settlers are crowding in their claims to the lands promiscuously, and fixing their habitations where they choose." DuVal reported that travel between the settlements was nearly impossible and recommended that the military be employed to build a road linking Pensacola with St. Augustine.[39] Though he was out of the territory Andrew Jackson continued to exert influence in Florida through the minions he left behind. Several had decided to relocate there permanently. Among those were Call, Bronough, John Overton, and James Gadsden. The General arbitrated a potential conflict between two of his lieutenants who were preparing to run against each other for the position of territorial delegate. Call, the younger man, decided to give way to Dr. Bronough, which pleased the General. Jackson wrote to Call that his friends, "among whom I include Gov. DuVal had induced [Bronough] to offer for delegate." As Jackson saw it, the main duty of the delegate would be to have "all fraudulent grants put down" and "the valid ones speedily established." The "vacant land [must be] brought into market at an early day, which will give speedily to your country's great wealth and a stable population[. U]ntill this is done, men of Capital will not emigrate to your Country and become Squatters." In addition the Indians "in the Floridas must be concentrated, or sent up to the Creek Nation."[40]

At the time DuVal arrived in Pensacola the hero's friends in Nashville and elsewhere were already plotting to have the General elected to the presidency. One step in that direction was his election to the U.S. Senate by the Tennessee legislature in 1823. At the time of his appointment DuVal knew Jackson only peripherally, perhaps through Nancy's cousin, Andrew Hynes, a Nashville merchant who served on Old Hickory's staff in his campaigns against the Creeks. DuVal appreciated Jackson's political superstardom. He understood that the General was destined for high political office—even the presidency—and DuVal carefully cultivated a cordial relationship with him, as detected in correspondence between the two. When DuVal arrived in Pensacola he found a letter from Jackson stating that "it would have given me great pleasure to have you at my house on your way to Florida" and on the new governor's next visit to Kentucky he would count on the "pleasure of seeing you. Should my opinion at any time be desirable to you, on any subject, you can command it—it will afford me pleasure to give it, or to render you any aid in my power. Permit me only to remark that upon your entering on the duties assigned you, it is only necessary to let the people know over whom you preside, that the law will be administered with energy, and impartial justice to all. This will give you ease and harmony in your Territory." This attitude of friendship naturally transferred to Jackson's cronies in Florida such as Call and Bronough, whom the General recommended specifically. Jackson concluded his missive to DuVal by declaring that he had "always endeavored to have nothing but honourable and honest men around me. I have therefore named to you a few of them who I found trustworthy, with whom any man is safe."[41]

The General's associates kept him informed of DuVal's activities, and Jackson continually solicited their impressions of him. On July 18 Jackson wrote to James Bronough that "It affords me pleasure to hear that the Govr . . . has been well received by the people, this augers well—but I know the people there, and you may look out for feuds, and party—and unless the Govr shapes his course at first, and firmly pursues an undeviating policy, he will get himself into difficulty, the council (if united) will be his efficient prop." DuVal, the General noted, must pursue an "energetic, steady course" and "convince those spirits of party, he cannot be shaken."[42]

On July 22 DuVal convened the first meeting of the legislative council at Pensacola. By that time, at DuVal's urging, Henry Brackenridge had been appointed judge of the Western District of Florida and Joseph White had been appointed land commissioner. Both men remained on hand to advise the council on the creation of the territory's first legal code, using the territorial statutes of Missouri as a guide. The delegates elected Bronough president, and DuVal made an address calling on delegates to make laws to establish courts, prepare a civil code based on the common law, and enact taxes to raise revenue.[43] As with his work in St. Augustine, DuVal was eager to demonstrate American good will toward Creoles in Pensacola, and one way to do that was to appoint talented men to political office. Writing to Secretary of State John Quincy Adams, DuVal recommended that John de la Rua and Joseph Noriega fill Brackenridge's and White's posts in the legislative council. The two were "men of information and integrity, and are looked up to by the Spanish population as their first men." These appointments would "have an excellent effect in attaching the Spanish inhabitants to our Government. I have found these people much more orderly than the Americans who are here; and I do not believe I ever have seen a more moral or better people, they can be easily governed, if treated with kindness and confidence. If the President and yourself will second me in my efforts, I think you will soon see a happy union among the People of Florida." One month later DuVal essentially reiterated that same point to President Monroe. "The Spanish inhabitants of this Territory seem much better reconciled than heretofore—they are certainly a good, quiet, and orderly people, much more so than our own populations. I hope that the Government of the United States will act towards them with the same liberality, that was extended to Louisiana."[44] The belief that Creoles could be easily be assimilated with Americans was not universal among American officials in Florida. Indeed there is little in Jackson's official correspondence to suggest that he believed it was possible. And DuVal's predecessor, William Worthington, had declared positively that "they can not amalgamate with the Americans."[45]

On September 10 DuVal wrote to President Monroe that the legislative council had nearly completed its work. But a yellow fellow epidemic, the governor explained, had forced the evacuation of Pensacola, and the legislative council was completing its business sixteen miles away. "It is with deep sorrow that I announce to you the death of my friends Doct. Bronough," the district attorney, and the navy agent. "The best and most inteligent part of our American population has already fallen victims to this distructive fever—No hope is entertained of its abatement untill frost, which will not commence untill the last of October[.]" "The distresses occasioned in Pensacola by the fever cannot be discribed, poor little children, without parents or friends are thrown on the charity of strangers we have not a cent to relieve the wretched[.] The Spanish citizens act nobley, they have done and continue to do all in their power to relieve the sick Americans many of whom are taken to houses and nursed with the utmost kindness. . . . The Spanish inhabitants of this country are the *best* even among the most quiet and orderly of our own citizens." DuVal recommended that the president appoint Richard K. Call U.S. attorney, stating that he had the best practice in the town and "has the intire confidence of Americans and Spaniards. Moreover the appointment would be most gratifying to the People of Florida to Genl Jackson and myself."[46]

The pestilence had brought civil and economic activity in Pensacola to a standstill. The land commissioners suspended their work. A proposed meeting with the Indians at St. Marks in November was also derailed, because of the yellow fever and because the new Indian agent, Gad Humphreys, had still not arrived.[47] Still,

DuVal proudly asserted to Secretary of State Adams on September 22 that the "Civil Government of the Territory is now pretty well organized." The legislative council had adjourned four days earlier. In DuVal's view, despite the obstacles, he had accomplished much. The governor took pride in the fact that the council had honored both him and Andrew Jackson by naming Florida's third and fourth counties for them. Moreover, he was glad to report to Secretary Adams that "The Spanish inhabitants are daily becoming more and more satisfied with our Government . . . throughout the Territory the utmost order and harmony prevail among the old and new inhabitants. The code of Laws enacted by the Legislative Council, I believe well calculated for the situation of the Territory. I have made it my business to conciliate as far as my duty would permit the Spanish inhabitants, and I believe I have succeeded. In the distribution of the various little offices of the Territory, I have given to the ancient inhabitants wherever I found them qualified their due proportion—I trust that this course will meet with the approbation of the President and yourself." DuVal closed his correspondence to Adams by stating that it was indispensable for him to return to Kentucky "to arrange my private affairs, before I go to St. Augustine where the Legislative Council is to meet in the spring." His year away "with the exception of the ten days last spring . . . has occasioned me some serious pecuniary losses."[48]

As DuVal prepared to leave the territory for Kentucky he may not have realized that all was not well. He likely understood that the Indian situation was a ticking time bomb. Andrew Jackson's ally Chief Blount would charge that the Americans were not living up their agreements, and Neamathla had to be dealt with. In East Florida Colonel Abram Eustis had information that Hitchiti leader Micanopy was "assembling his warriors & negroes & was determined to fight in defense of his home & his property."[49]

DuVal also was probably unaware of simmering resentments among some disenchanted elements in East Florida. About the time DuVal left the territory, an anonymous complaint reached Secretary of State Adams stating that "DuVal has become extremely unpopular in Florida. . . . His name is now never mentioned here without censure." DuVal had favored Bronough in the election for territorial delegate, and his "conduct" was "shameful in the highest degree." DuVal's decision to leave the territory was deplorable and proved that that "by obtaining the office of Governor he meant only to make a Job of it." "The people here expect the Governor to reside with his family in the Territory—to consider it his home." DuVal's departure had prevented Judge Joseph Smith from holding court because the law stipulated that he must take his oath before the governor, and as the judge "is not disposed to run after the Governor in Kentucky, consequently there can be no court until next spring."[50]

A similar communication penned to Secretary of State Adams complained that there were a number of Indians in this place "who express great dissatisfaction at the Governor's not meeting them, as he promised to do in St. Marks. Some serious consequences are feared from this neglect of the Indians in the Territory." Enclosed in the letter was an article written under the pen name "Florida" and published in the St. Augustine *Florida Herald* that further detailed the "errors and abuses" of the delegate election, charging that by his every action DuVal had supported Bronough, even declaring openly before his appointment that he favored the man. DuVal was also responsible for a defective election law that allowed the military to vote (which clearly favored Bronough). The law also allowed voting at the polling places by voice vote (a method employed in colonial Virginia and early Kentucky and favored by the upper classes).[51]

The complaint further alleged that one of DuVal's appointees in East Florida had "used his utmost influence and endeavors to induce the people" to vote for Bronough. He continually let it be known to everyone that Bronough was the "*Governor's candidate;* and that it would be highly displeasing to his Excellency if they should not support Dr. *Bronough*. He did more—he attended the poll, at the *Cowford,* and there zealously and actively electioneered for Bronough, until the news of his death reached that place, when he immediately returned home." Another DuVal appointee—the "sheriff of the new County called *Duval* . . . took a similar active part in the election of *Bronough*." He and his friends "all behaved in the most riotous and disorderly manner," and, when notified of Bronough's death, he "swore they should vote for him, *dead* or *alive.*"[52] Ironically, Bronough's death resulted in Joseph Hernandez, who polled second in the race, serving as delegate to Congress.[53]

DuVal left the territory in late October with little direction to Secretary Walton. As the acting governor explained to Secretary of War Calhoun, he lacked clear understanding as to his powers relative to Indians affairs or other matters. The next day he expressed similar concern to Secretary of State Adams, noting that "I regret extremely, that Gov. DuVal should have found it absolutely necessary to be absent from the Territory at this particular juncture. During the prevalence of the fever, domestic duties of the most imperative and irresistible character precluded me an opportunity of having scarcely any conversation with him, relative to Indian Affairs" or anything else.[54] For good or ill, the territory would be without its governor until the legislative council's meeting in the spring of the following year.

CHAPTER 4

Founder of the Florida Territory

When William P. DuVal returned to Kentucky, he found the state still reeling from the economic turmoil associated with Panic of 1819. Political fallout over the bank failures, the conflict between relief and antirelief factions, and the Old Court–New Court battle were still simmering and within months would reach near civil-war proportions. Within a year the state was rocked by political assassination when Soloman Sharp, a New Court advocate, was stabbed in the heart. The subsequent trial and execution of the assailant further inflamed the state. DuVal's relative John Pope headed the anti-Clay faction, which emerged as the Jackson party in Kentucky. The party threatened Henry Clay's ascension and had a large part in derailing his national aspirations, especially after the "Corrupt Bargain" debacle in 1825 (when Clay threw his support to John Quincy Adams and then agreed to become his secretary after the presidential contest in 1824).[1] Indeed, forces were building in Kentucky and elsewhere for Andrew Jackson's presidential candidacy when DuVal returned home, and he soon found himself caught up in the excitement.

Even though, because Florida was a territory, its inhabitants could not vote in national elections, national political battles deeply affected social and economic affairs in the Florida Territory. Nearly all political appointees owed their office to some political faction in Washington traceable directly to members of Monroe's cabinet. By 1823 the battle to succeed Monroe among William H. Crawford, John Quincy Adams, and John C. Calhoun had grown intense. The most adept at using appointments as a way to build a political machine calculated to put him in the White House was William H. Crawford. The secretary of the treasury had a vast network of political dependents scattered in various federal jobs throughout the country. Knowing that DuVal owed his appointment to

Calhoun, Crawford's lieutenants in Florida were no doubt gunning for the Kentuckian. Further complicating matters was the Andrew Jackson enigma. Old Hickory entered the Senate in 1823, and, while he was not in the administration, his impact on the appointive process was significant. Jackson's popularity was growing so rapidly that the Monroe administration could not afford to alienate the General and his friends.

Once one considers the fact that nearly every politically active migrant to Florida owed some sort of allegiance to some person or faction outside the territory, it is no wonder that political conflicts in Florida were so intense. Friction among migrants also reflected growing sectional tensions increasingly at work in the nation, especially after the inflamed political crises surrounding the Missouri Compromise. Southerners in Florida tended to distrust Northerners and vice versa. As an aspiring political appointee in what he thought was a temporary office, DuVal had to take account of what he observed in Kentucky, Florida, and Washington. Inevitably, he turned closer to Jackson. His relationship with Calhoun was secure. But the South Carolinian was aloof, and most considered him too young to actively pursue the White House. Furthermore, with Jackson men Call, Gadsden, Robert Butler, and others already in the territory, DuVal's tilt toward Jackson was not only in the cards; it was inevitable.

When DuVal returned to Bardstown in the fall of 1822, political cares probably melted away rapidly as he embraced Nancy and his large family of dependents. His financial obligations to them were obvious, and his own personal financial situation was precarious. After a warm reunion the husband and wife discussed DuVal's prospects and, no doubt, the logistics of relocating the family to the new territory. DuVal remained in Bardstown from November through January, and while in Kentucky he consulted with Secretary Calhoun on various matters, most importantly the disposition of the Indians in the Florida territory. DuVal opposed locating the Indians to any location that might cut off communications between West and East Florida. While DuVal had not yet explored the section himself, Jackson and Richard K. Call had told him that "The most valuable and fertile part of Florida is situated on the Suwanny River and running towards the old Alachua Towns, near the St. Johns River. The whole of this country from the best information I have been able to obtain is uncommonly rich, and will produce better sugar than Louisiana and I believe it is the interest of the United States, as early as possible, to have this country surveyed and brought into market. It will raise a considerable sum," he wrote to Calhoun. Jackson and Call "who saw much of it represents it to be as fertile as any part of Kentucky or Tennessee."[2]

Not long after DuVal arrived in Bardstown, Secretary of State Adams ordered him back to Florida. "Some dissatisfaction having been excited by your absence, from the Territory of Florida I have been directed by the President of the United

States to inform you of his wish that you should return to it, with all convenient dispatch." DuVal responded that it would take three or four weeks to attend to his personal affairs, and then he would "lose no time in returning to Florida." On January 13 DuVal wrote to Secretary Adams that he was leaving Bardstown for the territory. He said the dissatisfaction with him "springs only from a few men who have been disappointed—The President shall soon find that nothing like serious disquiet—really pervades East Florida. The enemies of the administration will I know use any occasion however trivial to excite the Public mind against it. I will endeavor to prevent in future any complaint, so far as I am concerned—The wish of the President for my prompt return will be promptly executed."[3]

Continuing this theme of unjust criticism of his absence from members of the territory and political factions that were already apparent in Florida, DuVal wrote to his friend Senator Samuel Southard of New Jersey. While some, he wrote, "considered it a great crime, that I should leave Florida to see me my wife and children, I feel confident you will not be among the number." DuVal explained that he had been away from them almost eighteen months except for a few days the previous spring. Also, DuVal explained that he was compelled to be in Kentucky to attend to his personal business affairs or be "ruined. [S]o I am here you see, but not before I had completely organized the government of Florida and seen everything moving on properly—except I did not choose to ride 781 miles to administer the oath of office to Judge [Joseph] Smith," he noted sarcastically. He complained that his salary was inadequate to support a chief executive in Florida. He hoped that Congress would see to increasing it. "I have not even had a servant to attend on me and yet," he explained to the senator, "all my salary was consumed and more than became due while I remained in Florida. If the common hospitalities which society demand from one in my situation (without parade or extravagance) can not be afforded, you know at once I must sink in the estimation of a people who have always been used to the habit of looking up to their governor for something more liberal than was expected from a private individual." Under the current circumstance DuVal saw no way to "remain in my present situation, unless I not only leave my family in Kentucky but also maintain them out of my private funds. So far I have done so, rather than appear fickle by resigning an office my friends took so much great pains to procure for me. I appeal to Mr. Livingston of New Orleans or any other gentleman of that Southern country if it is possible for any man in my situation with a large family to live even in the most frugal manner (as not to disgrace himself & station) on the present salary." Territorial secretary George Walton's salary was also inadequate, and a lack of travel funds forced him to remain in Pensacola. This situation had forced DuVal to order him to stay there, and thus DuVal was obliged himself to attend the next meeting of the legislative council meeting in St. Augustine and do his other work for him. "I do hope Congress will do something for our relief," DuVal wrote.[4]

While DuVal was away, Indian relations continued to fester. Secretary Walton heard continual complaints that self-appointed traders and interpreters were instigating trouble with the Indians. In the West Gadsden County grand jurors charged Stephen Richards with intriguing with Neamathla and other chiefs "and exciting them to assert and maintain their right to the lands they now occupy." In exchange for his advocacy, the accusers stated that Indians had promised Richards a six-mile tract on the Apalachicola River. Despite the rumors, Walton had little choice but to work with Richards. When the interpreter brought in ten warriors to Pensacola, the secretary paid his expenses and ordered the party to St. Marks. Indian agent Gad Humphreys would join them there.[5] In East Florida matters were much the same.

While DuVal was away from the territory, plans were already under way to build a road linking Pensacola and St. Augustine. Walton informed Calhoun that Assistant Quarter Master Daniel Burch estimated the distance between the two points at 462 miles. According to Burch a wagon road already existed from Pensacola to the Choctawhatchee, and all that was necessary was to repair a few causeways and two or three small bridges. From there the route should be cut direct to Ochesse Bluff on the Apalachicola and thence until it "intersects with the old Spanish Road (now grown up), near the Mickasukee Towns" and then to St. Marks, about twenty miles to the South. The route would then cross the St. Johns at Fort Picolata and continue on the well-traveled road to St. Augustine. In all Burch estimated that there would be 240 miles of new road to build, and the estimated cost would be just shy of $19,000. "In making this estimate I have calculated that the Road will be opened wide enough for a waggon to pass with ease & experience proves that such Roads, being shady, are most proper for a Southern climate." Provisions for the troops ought to be transported by water and deposited at various crossings of the Yellow, Choctawhatchee, Apalachicola, St. Marks, Suwannee, and St. Johns Rivers.[6]

DuVal finally arrived in Pensacola in early March. The last leg of his journey from New Orleans proved difficult when his steamer, *Fulton*, was diverted while at sea to Vera Cruz. DuVal noted that when he arrived, "factious and discontented persons were endeavoring to create dissatisfaction—I have been able to place things on proper footing. In a few days I shall proceed to St. Augustine, where I hope to put down the discontent that a few designing and disappointed men have been active in producing." In a letter to Secretary of State John Quincy Adams, DuVal attributed the bad feelings to the fact that "many persons have lately immigrated [to the territory] who are cirtainly not the best Part of our American population. These men can only hope to acquire importance by creating discontent and producing confusion, and I hope the President will make the proper allowance for me under these circumstances." As in St. Augustine, rival factions representing different states and different agendas created a volatile mix. Another problem was that rivalries among federally appointed officials, unclear mandates about their proper jurisdiction, and inadequate federal funding fueled disputes. Nowhere was this more apparent than in the enforcement and administration of the law. (At that moment Judge Henry Marie Brackenridge was in the midst of an ugly dispute with district attorney William Steele.) A few days later DuVal wrote that he was glad he came first to Pensacola "as I have at once put down the slanders and abuse which during my absence was circulated to my prejudice. It is a difficult matter to give satisfaction to such a mingled Population as inhabit this Territory but I am not without hope, that the honest and thinking part of our citizens will give me their support—more than this I do not expect."[7]

As DuVal made his way toward St. Augustine, plans were under way for major talks with the Indians. In April President Monroe appointed James Gadsden and Bernardo Sequi commissioners to work with Humphreys and DuVal to prepare Indians for talks that would result in a treaty confining them to a reservation between Charlotte Harbor and Tampa Bay. South Carolinian and Yale graduate James Gadsden had served in the U.S. Army with Jackson in the Battle of New Orleans and played a major role in his 1819 invasion of Florida. Like Humphreys's, Gadsden's career in the army came to an abrupt end when Congress ordered reduction in the armed forces. Ironically, Gadsden's career in the force was just about to take off. Monroe and Calhoun worked together to have the rising soldier nominated as adjutant general, but the Senate rejected his appointment.[8] In Charleston when appointed commissioner, Gadsden repaired immediately to St. Augustine to begin his work. As Gadsden made his way south he consulted with Jackson regarding his views on Indian affairs, and the General shared this fact, along with his own personal recommendations on the subject, with Calhoun. Included in these observations was the necessity of having troops on hand to deal with the "Renegade Creeks who have wandered" to the peninsula. "A movement of troops to Tampas Bay, previous to the *Talks* being held with them, would have a powerful influence upon their minds, and give *great effect* to the Talks of the commissioners."[9] Gadsden, DuVal, and Jackson were of one mind regarding the policy toward the Indians. Indeed, Gadsden wrote to Old Hickory, DuVal "has concurred with me on all points."[10]

Meanwhile, Gad Humphreys, who arrived in December, had had a series of talks with Indians in the St. Marks area. He reported that the Indians seemed "in general well disposed, and not inclined to be troublesome; yet there is manifest impatience felt to be informed of the Intentions of the United States towards them." Humphreys investigated the allegations against Richards and admitted that, while some were true, he did not think that another interpreter could be found. While investigating reports of illicit trade activity on the Apalachicola at "Blunt's Town," he visited the chief, who told him that Jackson had assured him and the other chiefs in Pensacola that they could remain on their lands along the Apalachicola and in old fields at Tallahassee.[11]

DuVal arrived in St. Augustine on April 28. "I find all peace and quietness here," he wrote to Secretary of State Adams. "The excitement against me was confined to a few disappointed men, who succeeded in imposing themselves on our Delegate—this will be fully proven by the events that follow hear after." Word of the disgruntlement with DuVal's leadership over the ensuing year had reached New York newspapers, and St. Augustine editor Elias B. Gould felt compelled to defend the governor. Gould questioned the motives of a person who wrote to the *New York Evening Post* to complain about DuVal and added that at home the governor is "able to sustain his own reputation, without any intervention of ours, and to give explanations wherever they are desired by anyone." Gould's own letter to the *Post* stated that "We [will] by no means have it understood that we approve of all the public acts of Governor DuVal. But we believe his intentions to be perfectly pure, and though we should differ with him in some particulars, we will not stigmatize him because he does not select us as the talisman to direct him in his public measures." Finally, Gould noted that while DuVal's "measures of policy" might not meet approval of all "our people it is not for want of integrity of character" and that DuVal held the office at "great personal sacrifice."[12]

DuVal immediately began preparing for the meeting of the legislative council scheduled to convene in early May. Another matter of business was to ascertain the precise disposition of the Indians in East Florida, and thus he turned to Horatio Dexter, offering him appointment as subagent and asking for his "assistance in the management and superintendence of the Indians." Even if DuVal realized that Calhoun and Jackson had denounced Dexter a year earlier as a man with dubious motives, DuVal understood that there was no better person to provide him with the information he needed. Humphreys was at work in the St. Marks area, and Dexter's knowledge of the peninsula was indispensable. Thus DuVal wrote to Dexter, "you will oblige me by giving me all the information of customs, habits, towns, or situation of the Seminole Indians you possess or can obtain as soon as convenient." Meanwhile DuVal informed Calhoun of his decision to employ Dexter and added that the Indians were "scattered" in such a manner that it would take more than a month to assemble them for negotiations with treaty commissioners Gadsden and Segui.[13]

While Dexter explored the Indian country, DuVal attended his second meeting of the legislative council in St. Augustine. Midway through the meeting DuVal provided Secretary of State Adams with a report of his activities. "The Council," he wrote, "occupy the only habitable room in the Governors old mansion & and it has been rendered so by Judge Smith, for the purpose of holding his Courts." He had ordered some "cheap furniture," stationery, and other materials on his own account but had no money to pay for them. He reported that the "Archives

& public records . . . were very negligently kept" and in disarray. The previous custodian had allowed persons to take papers out of the office, and when he traveled to Pensacola for the meeting of the last council, he put them in the hands of a private individual. DuVal ordered the clerks of the superior and inferior courts to take charge of the records and to make out an inventory so that frauds could be detected. DuVal asked Adams if Congress had made any appropriation for the payment of the city's expenses and the maintenance and prosecution of criminals, as the sheriff had "advanced money himself & is now in serious distress for want of it." DuVal concluded with the recommendation that Secretary Walton return to Pensacola immediately after the legislative session. "The difficulty of communications between that City and this, retards in a great measure the operations of the local Government & the sectional feeling that prevails in this territory makes it requisite that while I am in one section of the Country the Secretary should be in the other."[14] The need for a territorial capital somewhere between St. Augustine and Pensacola was obvious. The legislative council also understood this logic and provided for DuVal to appoint two commissioners to select a site for a capital midway between the two points. DuVal eventually appointed John Williams of Pensacola and Dr. William Simmons of St. Augustine. Both men set out from their prospective points that fall and eventually selected a site for the territorial capital, and DuVal announced that the next legislative council would meet there.

Appraisals of DuVal's message to the legislative council were generally favorable. The Pensacola *Floridian* called the message clear, impartial, and enlightened. "No *local* feelings are incorporated in his message; but there is evidently indicated a liberal spirit, in relation to the interests of both sections, of the territory, and a sentiment of harmony and conciliation breathed throughout every sentence." DuVal, the paper continued, "writes like the *Governor of Florida* sincerely solicitous for its future and lasting welfare, and not as the organ of sectional jealousies, and as the patron of narrow and selfish measures." Indeed, the governor had acted in every instance to "advance the prosperity and happiness of his fellow citizens and appears not disposed to mount the hobbies of demagogues in order to acquire a little temporary popularity."[15]

The article applauded the governor's efforts to locate the capital between the Suwannee and the Ochlockonee and hoped that the rivalry between East and West Florida would end. The article denounced the proposal of some in East Florida that Alabama might annex West Florida, calling it "idle and puerile in the extreme." The idea of East Florida becoming an independent state sprang from "blindness and gross misapprehension of the solid interests of the territory."[16] While the legislative council was in session, DuVal proclaimed that the election for territorial delegate for Congress would be held the first Monday in June. In the ensuing election Richard Keith Call bested incumbent Joseph Hernandez and two other candidates.[17] Finally, the legislative council concluded its work on July 5 with a resolution lauding DuVal's efforts as governor. The resolution proclaimed that the "reports [that] have gone abroad injurious to the public character of his Excellency Governor DuVal" were unfounded. The "conduct of his Excellency has met their warmest approbation," and the council expressed "their thanks to him for his uniform courteous and Conciliatory demeanor during the present Session of the Council."[18]

After the rush of events associated with the meeting of the territorial legislature, DuVal moved to catch up on correspondence he had set aside. Acknowledging a letter of support and encouragement he had received from Samuel Southard, DuVal thanked the senator for his kind words and added that his remarks, especially in light of the challenges he faced in administering the territory, "will be long remembered with pride and gratitude." As if to offer up his own evaluation of his predicament, DuVal noted that "In my station no man of experience and common sense can hope to please every body—nor will an honest man even desire it—men without principles must and will dislike him. If a public man can obtain the appropriation of his own mind and support of the honest and *thinking* part of his fellow citizens he may be considered as fortunate. I know my conduct has been vilely misrepresented at the City of Washington during the last session of Congress." According to DuVal, the territorial delegate, Joseph Hernandez, had "suffered himself to be *used* by a junto of six or eight men in this city in order to destroy my character and standing." The leader of the cabal was Alexander Hamilton Jr., who had a "mortal aversion to a *Backwoods Governor* as he stated in this place before he went to Washington last winter with a threat that he would have me dismissed." Hamilton, DuVal contended, was trying to secure the governor's chair for himself or Judge Smith. Thus he had gotten up a petition that few were willing to sign. DuVal was gratified that the scheme had failed and proudly reported that both were repudiated in the recent elections for territorial delegate largely because their scheme had been attempted and had failed. "The people ... had determined to put them both down on the ground that they had treated their governor shamefully." In Hernandez's place, Richard K. Call "is elected to Congress—a young man of sense and sterling principles." Throughout, DuVal contended, "I have taken no part in local politics but my course has been in all respects as if nothing had happened. It is to the People I look for support, they never were opposed to me, and it was a falsehood willfully stated—when this was circulated last winter in the City—I am the most popular man in this Territory and have always been so, since I entered the country. The Spanish Inhabitants are devoted to me and Hernandez now admitted that Mr. Hamilton and other Americans recently settled in Florida were the men who deceived him ... not one of the Spanish inhabitants ever said or wrote one word against me. This Genl Hernandez has publicly declared."[19]

DuVal admitted that, while the government could have found a man with "more information" and "better mind" than himself to "to fill the office I now hold," he would "yield to no man either in honesty or independence. If I act wrong it *is my own wrong*—no man ever has, or ever shall dictate to me—no faction shall claim me as their head. I will be the man of the People—their rights and interests *alone* shall influence my actions—the sectional feeling which has existed between Pensacola & St. Augustine I disregard. I have boldly opposed the claims *of both* for the seat of Government, and I have triumphed." Largely due to his leadership DuVal proudly noted that the legislative council had voted unanimously to build a "seat of government in the centre" of the territory. "This step was necessary to a fair and equal administration of the law of the Territory. I can from the seat of Government, go to any part of Florida where my presence is required in five days."[20]

And yet DuVal had had "much to do in organizing the government here. Many strong feelings of local interest and prejudice to combat . . . , the bad materials and lawless out-pourings from all the states have assembled here—and the worst of all from New York. But they are cut off at the knees, the People will place them in their proper stations as they are doing daily and by the time Congress will assemble I hope to demonstrate, to them that I have been unjustly treated." DuVal was satisfied that he had prevailed for the moment but admitted, "My feelings and a character that I prize more than my life have been cruelly stabbed." He estimated that his service had cost him more than $8,000. "I am poorly paid and worse treated, but this ever has & will be the reward of wiser and perhaps better men than myself. You must excuse me for this long and egotistical letter," DuVal wrote. "I felt I owed to my friends" to describe the "true state of things in this quarter."[21]

While DuVal had numerous political concerns, the chief challenge he now faced was Indian affairs. Horatio Dexter's "Observations on the Seminole Indians," submitted to DuVal, Gadsden, and Segui in August after his two-month journey through the Indian towns between St. Augustine and Charlotte Harbor, constitutes a truly remarkable description of the status and disposition of the Native Americans in the Florida peninsula in 1823. Dexter listed seventeen towns containing 1,395 Indians and 430 blacks. Dexter's purpose was to inform the Indians of the talks in September and to provide minute descriptions of the land, domestic habits, religious ceremonies, and principal pursuits of the Indians. He described flourishing farms and cattle-raising operations. Most alarming to DuVal and the others was likely what Indians told Dexter about the "several settlements of refugee Negroes" in the "the inner chain of Islands along the coast from Tampa to Charlotte harbour. . . who had communications with white persons who resorted to these places in armed vessels." The ships with big guns landed "packages of goods at different depots on these Islands." The Negroes at these settlements "were all completely armed with Spanish muskets, Bayonets & Cartouche boxes." Blacks cut timber and traded cattle for powder, lead, molasses, and rum. Dexter presented his report to DuVal, Gadsden, and Segui in St. Augustine on August 20, and DuVal promptly forwarded a copy to Secretary of War Calhoun, adding that slave owners continually solicited him to send a force to Charlotte Harbor to capture runaway slaves but that he had no authorization or funds to comply.[22]

While Dexter was on his journey, plans for a major meeting with all Florida Indians were being formulated. James Gadsden notified Secretary Calhoun that "expresses have been dispatched in every direction, and Indians generally have been distinctly impressed with the idea" that they must attend or have no say in the matter. Gadsden reported that there was much disagreement among the Indians as to where they wanted to relocate. Those in the peninsula were pleased with the southern section, while those in the panhandle were much opposed to moving into the peninsula. At the head of the discontented was Neamathla, and Gadsden predicted that the "enterprising and daring Savage, . . . that principal instigator of the Seminole War," would be the hardest case. Gadsden wrote to Calhoun that he favored moving the Indians south or out of the territory altogether and admitted that a reservation in the southern part of the peninsula might make Florida the "most exposed but important frontier of the Union." A military force would be necessary to prevent the Indians from "the habit of keeping up an intercourse with the Cuba Fishermen and . . . the encouragement hitherto given to absconding negroes & savage depredations committed on cattle Estates." He recommended Tampa Bay as the best place for a military post.[23]

On September 1 DuVal reported to Calhoun that the day before Humphreys had arrived with 350 chiefs and warriors from West Florida, and that the balance of those from East Florida were expected to arrive at Moultrie Creek, five miles from St. Augustine, in a day or two. He had little doubt that talks could begin as scheduled on September 5.[24] Present were DuVal, Humphreys, Gadsden, Segui, all the major chiefs in Florida, and seventy chiefs and principal men from the Indian towns. Neamathla, Blount, and Micanopy were also included in that number. Also on hand was a free black, Antonio Proctor, whom DuVal had met early on in St. Augustine and whose skills as an interpreter, he claimed years later, proved indispensable.[25] The Indians selected the Miccosukee chief Neamathla as their spokesman. The Treaty of Moultrie Creek, signed by thirty-two of the chiefs on September 18, essentially surrendered nearly twenty-four million acres for fewer than six. In exchange for the lands, a $5,000 annual annuity would be delivered for twenty years. The Indians would also receive payment for their improvements on abandoned lands and other payments. Indians were also required to return all runaway slaves and relocate to a reservation in the southern part of the peninsula between the Great Swamp of the Withlacoochee and Charlotte

James Gadsden, ca. 1820.
Courtesy of State Archives
of Florida.

Harbor. The boundaries of the reservations were drawn fifteen to twenty miles from the coast to prevent communication or trade with Cuba. Six chiefs, including Blount and Neamathla, were allowed to remain in north Florida near the Apalachicola River. To help enforce the treaty, four companies of troops established themselves on Tampa Bay. Fort Brooke was established by January 1824.[26]

Despite Dexter's comprehensive report, the commissioners lacked a full understanding of the land assigned to the Seminoles. They also anticipated (but did not know) that the land apportioned could sustain the Indians. They called for the immediate establishment of military posts on the periphery of the reservation and in the bays and harbors so that the Indians could be prevented from having any contact with foreign countries or individuals. The commissioners reported to Calhoun that, "It is scarcely necessary to state to you that a Majority of Indians now inhabiting the Territory of Florida and included as parties to the treaty just effected, are wanderers, if not Refugees from the Southern Indians—Many of them of the old Red Stick party whose feelings of hostility have only been suppressed not eradicated, and even the Native Seminoles have ever been of a most erratic disposition." They continued, "These Indians are now scattered over the whole face of Florida, but a small portion of them having any settled residence; a majority wandering about for such a precarious subsistence as the esculent roots of the woods, or the misfortunes of our Navigators on the Florida Keys may afford. To bring together these discordant and fermenting materials; to embody such a population within prescribed limits, and to conquer their erratic habits will require in some degree the exercise of authority, with the presence of a military establishment to enforce it."[27]

DuVal essentially agreed with these observations. He urged Calhoun to move rapidly to implement the treaty, and the secretary forwarded these recommendations to Monroe: DuVal wanted to "commence running the lines forthwith, and to take a military position at Tampa Bay," Calhoun told the president. "It certainly seems desirable on every account that another year should not pass away and it is believed that unless the lines should be run, without delay, it will be impossible to effect this desirable object. There is another reason for acceding to the request of the Govr. So little is known of the country, which has been fixed on for the Indians, that the commissioners have been compelled to leave the northern limits of the tract, subject to be altered hereafter, if it should appear, that there is not a sufficiency of good land, in that which has been reserved. It seems to me desirable that the line should be definitively fixed before the treaty is ratified by the Senate." President Monroe acceded to DuVal's recommendations.[28]

The Treaty of Moultrie Creek proved a disaster for the Seminoles. The land in the south could not support them, and encroachments and violations were inevitable. DuVal would find that Indian affairs would be his most vexing problem as governor. The formal agreements would oblige the government to supply the Indians with food, farm implements, and other necessities. As superintendent he would be forced to oversee a contracting system that could not help but enmesh him in controversy. And these obligations fell to him immediately after the treaty was concluded. Only days after the pact was signed DuVal wrote to authorities in Washington that corn had to be shipped to Tampa Bay from New Orleans at a cost of $.40 per bushel. Beef could be "bought on the hoof for 6 or 7 dollars the hundred weight and driven to the Indian Country."[29]

Only days before the Moultrie Creek talks began, DuVal complained to Calhoun that he deserved more compensation for his work in Indian affairs. While he agreed that his duty was to superintend and not conduct Indian affairs, the reality was that until Humphreys's arrival the previous winter he was doing just that. Pelham was ill and never made it to Florida, and the acting agent, Colonel Eustis, was confined to St. Augustine, so DuVal had carried the entire burden of Indian affairs in the west without any assistance. With the yellow fever epidemic in Pensacola, Secretary Walton was confined with his family, and DuVal had to hire his brother-in-law as a clerk, and then pay him out of his own funds. His duties in St. Augustine were also unceasing. The Indians were "scattered over the greatest part of the Territory, and since my arrival here (St. Augustine) not a day has passed in which several have not been in town, they are constantly coming and going, and almost always call on me. The Spanish invariably treated them with great respect and ceremony, as they dreaded giving them the slightest offence, and I deem it prudent not to make any change in this intercourse until after the treaty. Many of these Indians possess considerable property, and as licenses to trade had before my arrival been given to every person who applied and offered Security, various disputes have arisen between the Indians and those traders." (The disputes became so cumbersome that DuVal was eventually forced to invalidate all licenses.) Indian affairs, DuVal complained, "occupy my attentions daily, and as I feel it my duty, to have the strictest justice done in these cases, much of my time and attention is occupied in their investigation." He had been compelled to rent a large room for these purposes in St. Augustine and to hire a clerk, as noted. DuVal ended his correspondence by claiming that he presumed that territorial governors William Henry Harrison (Indiana) Ninian Edwards (Illinois), and Lewis Cass (Michigan) were in circumstances similar to his. "I am ignorant of what they received as Superintendent of Indian affairs, but I conceive myself justly entitled, to the same compensation."[30]

DuVal's complaints to Calhoun came at a difficult time for the secretary. His testing of the presidential waters had brought him into direct conflict with William H. Crawford, whose minions in Congress moved to have Calhoun's appropriations slashed. In the previous session of Congress opponents of the War Department had held hearings investigating his handling of Indian affairs.[31]

At the time DuVal wrote to Calhoun, he was contemplating resigning his office and indeed wrote to Andrew Jackson that he would have done so in Kentucky because of the "embarrassed state of my private affairs" but "for the reports from Florida vitally affecting my character. At once all other considerations were thrown aside with a determination to meet . . . suddenly the slanders and abuse that has been lavished on me and prove to my friends and my country how little my conduct had deserved the vile aspersions that a designing and unprincipled set of men had been so active in circulating." DuVal told the General that his opponents had tried to set Jackson's friends against him. Richard K. Call had seen through this and exposed the scheme, and subsequently, "I am confident that I never had a better or more noble friend than Genl Call." DuVal told Jackson that he had "enter[ed] on his duties with a determination to pursue the course that had been marked out by his predecessor," but he did not "calculate to remain long in the government of the territory. My private affairs and the pitiful salary annexed to my office will compel me to retire." He hoped that Walton would succeed him as governor and that Overton would be appointed secretary. Another reason for remaining in his post was that if he did resign, William H. Crawford, "that cold-blooded viper," would fill the post with a Jackson enemy.³²

DuVal complained that Alexander Hamilton Jr. and Joseph Smith were Crawford appointees and bound on doing him harm. DuVal acknowledged that Hamilton was the "son of our great countryman" but said he was no more "like his father than a mule is like a full blooded racer.... I know his talents would not render him valuable as a statesman and I do believe that he is mean enough to do anything that Mr. Crawford wished him. For what purpose? I answer because the fellow while he is the spirit of a hare, in forehead has the impudence of a *negro quarter dog*—he would thrust himself in all companies gathering everything that might be said against his worthy patron and dutifully make his report." Of Smith DuVal declared that the man "is a rascal." He had no "confidence in him either as a gentlemen or Judge." Finally DuVal congratulated Jackson on his presidential prospects. "I hope you will be universally throughout the states, taken up by the *People*. I am highly pleased to see my relations at the head of the meeting in Louisville Ky. I told some of your friends last March I think that they might expect . . . you are my choice as president. Next I prefer Calhoun, third Mr. Adams and last of all men on earth Mr. Crawford."³³

DuVal's letter to Jackson sets DuVal firmly in the Jackson camp. The stridency of the communication is striking and indicates the political tension among federal appointees in Florida. DuVal's reference to John Pope underlies the fact that DuVal's relative was already a principal leader among Old Hickory's operatives in Kentucky. DuVal also carried a regional prejudice against Northerners with him to Florida, and these sentiments are apparent in his correspondence. His animosity toward Hamilton and Smith are already noted; in addition, in a letter to James Barbour, a fellow Virginian, he gloried in the recent successes of James Madison's nephew Edgar Macon in his "triumph over an old and cunning Yankee lawyer" in a murder case. Macon had routed his opponent "so completely as to surprise and delight the audience. His adversary was thrown down, and actually rendered incapable of answering the arguments." As DuVal explained to Barbour, Macon's mentor, the young lawyer had "envy and cunning and meanness to contend with in several of his opponents at the bar but he will triumph over them all for he is eloquent, intelligent and his principles are purely those of old Virginia rest assured sir, that he will find me his countryman, and of course his friend."³⁴

DuVal further complained that the "yankees have been and will be my abusers." Their disappointment at not obtaining "the small places in my gift, has brought down on me all their malice and slander[.] I am now happy to inform you that that People are fast driving these men in the back ground—where I hope they will remain. New York has sent her most villainous spawn to this Territory." He intended to beat this opposition down by continually "go[ing] among the

Body of the People, and my acquaintances in East and West Florida is now general. I have made it my business to pass through the whole Territory and I intend to repeat this visit during this fall." DuVal added, "The northern men are much enraged at the influence of Virginia. Their men say in a sneering manner, 'The lord deliver poor Florida—since Virginia is the mother of us all.'"[35] Still DuVal attempted public demonstrations of civility toward all. In late October DuVal chaired a public meeting organized to establish the Bible Society in East Florida. While admitting that he had never belonged to any religious sect or denomination, DuVal noted that he "had always revered the religion of the Bible because it was the religion of the country—the religion of his fathers—but above all," he sincerely believed, "it was the religion of truth and heaven."[36]

Within months DuVal would post his letters to Jackson and to his new friend Richard K. Call to Washington. By December, Call, the territorial delegate, and Senators Jackson and John Eaton of Tennessee were attending the first session of the Eighteenth Congress and were boarding together at O' Neale's tavern. It was here that the trio first met and became captivated by the proprietor's vivacious, captivating daughter, Mrs. Margaret O'Neale Timberlake.[37]

Whether through Jackson's network or other channels, speculations on DuVal's decision to stay in Florida began to circulate. Quoting a story in his hometown newspaper, a journal in Florida noted that DuVal's intention to resign had already been conveyed to the president. The decision was based on the fact that the "perquisites of office were absolutely below the requisite means of compensating personal services and subsisting a large family in a distant and barren country, and an inhospitable climate." The information was also reprinted in other papers across the nation.[38]

Despite his disgruntlement, DuVal plowed ahead. He wrote to Secretary Adams that he planned to set out on a journey to Pensacola in a few weeks and on the way would visit the several internal counties of the territory to examine the "nature of the Country."[39] Also, on his way to Pensacola he would check on the progress of the two commissioners appointed to select a territorial capital. At the same time as DuVal's movement west, Gadsden was on his expedition to explore and survey the boundary set out by the Treaty of Moultrie Creek. In St. Augustine by November, Gadsden notified Secretary of War Calhoun that he was ready to begin his expedition on December 10. Gadsden also suggested that Calhoun send troops to Tampa Bay and that small vessels "enter occasionally the Bay of Tampa & Charlotte Harbor" so that the Indians will be dissuaded of any idea that the Americans were weak and that the British would aid them "in the event of any disturbance with the Americans." Calhoun acceded to this request.[40]

That December Governor DuVal set out from St. Augustine on his journey to Pensacola in what would be his first trip through the Upper Peninsula, visiting all known Indian towns en route. Finally reaching Pensacola after the first of the year, DuVal reported to Calhoun that he found the land between the Suwannee and Apalachicola Rivers "the most desirable and valuable region in all of the Southern Country." He would expand on this subject later, but DuVal's main focus in this communication was Indian affairs. He reported that he "could rely with some confidence, on the friendship of all the chiefs except Neamathla, he is a man of uncommon capacity, bold, violent and restless—he can not submit to a superior or endure an equal. No reliance can be placed on him. His men are the most lawless and vile of the Indians in Florida. I feel confident that they will *not remove into* the boundary given to them by the late Treaty unless there is a military force in the vicinity to *overawe them*." As an example of Neamathla's recalcitrance, DuVal noted that once troops in St. Marks had been sent to Tampa Bay, the Indians went on a rampage, threatening whites and killing their cattle. DuVal recommended that troops return to St. Marks. Newspaper accounts also reported the disturbances, ascertaining the cause as the Indians' dissatisfaction with the treaty and Captain Burch's road-building work through their lands. When DuVal complained directly to Neamathla, the chief told the governor he was unable to protect border settlers as the "blood of his young warriors was inflamed."[41]

Neamathla's ire had no doubt had been raised by the work of commissioners William Simmons and John Williams, who chose the "Old Tallahassee Fields" as the best spot for a territorial capital.[42] The chief had signed the Moultrie Creek agreement to remove to a tract west of that location, but he must have been surprised at the speed with which the treaty was implemented. Any doubts that the whites intended the location as the site for the capital would have been put to rest once he observed council buildings going up. The Moultrie Creek agreement stipulated that Neamathla would be provided with a two-square-mile tract several miles west of his present location, known as Rocky Comfort. But the chief had still not moved, and there was every indication that he intended to stay right where he was.[43]

The lands Williams and Simmons explored and reported on would eventually become the center of the rich cotton-producing lands of Middle Florida. As the historian Clifton Paisley noted, "the most attractive cotton soils of all lay east of the Ochlockonee River along the banks of four large lakes, Iamonia, Jackson, Miccosukee, and Lafayette, and between them. This country, once the center of the agricultural activities of the Apalachee, was also nearer to the principal cotton port of New York than any other farmland in Florida, for after the hills stopped eighteen or twenty miles from the Georgia line, the port of St. Marks was only as many more miles away across the flat sands."[44] Telltale evidence of a former Spanish occupation could be found whenever farmers turned the soil. Not the least of these was the ruins of the Spanish mission Fort San Luis (destroyed and abandoned in 1704), which provided a fascinating curiosity to new arrivals, including Governor DuVal.

Neamathla, ca. 1830s. Courtesy of State Archives of Florida.

Positive reports on the site began appearing in newspapers. One settler, calling himself Floridus, noted that the location was highly favorable to the purpose of trade, being within a short distance of two navigable rivers and not more than twenty-five miles from the sea. The new town of Tallahassee," Floridus predicted, will "spring up . . . like others of our Western cities, out of the woods, and will in all probability like many of them, be visited by the steam boat, before the stumps of the forest have disappeared from the streets." DuVal kept close tabs on the commissioners' work and on March 4 proclaimed that the next legislative council would meet at the new capital in May. (Ultimately it would meet in November.) DuVal proclaimed that the precise location was "about a mile southwest from the old deserted fields of Tallahassee, about a half mile south of the Ochlockonee and Tallahassee trail at a point where the Old Spanish road is intersected by a small trail running southwardly."[45]

Within weeks of DuVal's announcement, new settlers flocked to the area. One of those first on the scene was John McIver, who brought his family from Fayetteville, North Carolina. Jonathan Robinson, who as one of the first planters in the area greeted Williams and Simmons at the place, was also one of the first on the scene. Both men built many of the first structures of the village, including the first council buildings and DuVal's first homestead. (DuVal boarded with McIver when he first came to Tallahassee in the summer.)[46]

From February through April DuVal in Pensacola kept in touch with federal authorities regarding Indian affairs. By March Gadsden and his surveying party had completed their work on the southern boundary of the Indian reservation. As soon as his horses were ready, he informed Secretary of War Calhoun, he would set out for the Apalachicola to help DuVal and Humphreys in the "speedy execution of the late Treaty."[47] Apprised of his work, DuVal was anxious to placate Neamathla and suggested to Secretary of War Calhoun that the chief and his chiefs be sent to Washington. "If this chief could be attached warmly to our Government, it would cirtainly be good policy to acquire his confidence & friendship." DuVal went on to state that he was a man of "uncommon abilities and has great influence with his Nation. He is one of the most eloquent men I have ever heard." Again a month later DuVal reiterated that "Neamathla is a most uncommon man. He ought to be induced to remove with his people. This chief you will find perhaps the greatest man, you have ever seen among the Indians. He can, if he chooses to do so, control his warriors with as much ease as a Col. Could a Regiment of regular soldiers. They love and fear him. If this man can be made, as I have no doubt he can, the firm friend of our Government, no means should be spared to induce him to go with his people and to continue as the Chief of his nation." If Congress would allow him to sell his reservation and direct that the money be "laid out in cattle for him, it would awaken his gratitude to the Government and render him of essential service in commanding the nation. The chief should be seen by you; and then you can judge of the force and energy of his mind & character. Neamathla and the Chiefs who will go with him to the City have never seen the Interior of the United States, and have no precise knowledge of the strength and power of our country." Calhoun eventually authorized the Washington visit, but Neamathla, after first agreeing to go, refused the privilege.[48]

After meeting with Neamathla and Humphreys, DuVal informed Washington on April 11 that he expected many of the Indians in the vicinity of the new capital to leave Middle Florida and join the Creeks in Georgia and Alabama. It was his opinion that not more that fifteen hundred would "remove into the boundary." DuVal noted that the removal could not be accomplished until after September. To leave earlier would result in the Indians losing their crops, and rations could not be procured at the present time. DuVal asked for funds to buy rations and to carry out the removal process, noting that, while corn, salt, and flour could be bought inexpensively in New Orleans, it was cheaper to buy beef on the hoof in Florida than to purchase barrels of pork from that city. DuVal asked that funds be deposited in New Orleans for use in Florida so that from time to time he could draw on the money. "I should not like to have a large sum in my hands—for I have no place of safety—to secure it, and accident or robbery might render me responsible. I hope by the active assistance of Col. Humphreys—on whom I can confidently rely that the Treaty will be carried into effect for much less than was expected." Meanwhile, DuVal and Humphreys published proposals in newspapers throughout the territory for supplying the emigrating Indians with provisions for one year beginning in September.[49]

While in Pensacola DuVal also did his best to prepare for the legislative council's first session in the new territorial capital. By this time, DuVal's friend Samuel Southard had been appointed secretary of the navy, and he requested that the official dispatch a small vessel to transport books, records, and public furniture belonging to the Territory from Pensacola and St. Augustine to the capital site by way of St. Marks. He continued to wax eloquent on the prospects of the territory. DuVal wrote to Secretary of State Adams that he considered the land between the Suwannee and Apalachicola Rivers as, "in my opinion, the most valuable Southern Country I have ever seen," estimating the good land at greater than 1.2 million acres. "The region produces Sugar Cane and Sea Island Cotton in greater perfection than any other part of the Southern Country. The lands are uncommonly rich and finely watered. . . . I have no doubt," DuVal declared, "that this tract of Country alone will sell for more than the Florida Debt. . . . From the view which I have had of Florida I state, without fear of contradiction, that there is more good land in Florida than is to be found in Louisiana."[50]

DuVal yearned to return to his family. On February 26 he wrote to President Monroe asking permission to return to Kentucky after the next meeting of the legislative council. It had been fourteen months since he had seen his family. "My object," he wrote, "is to finally settle my private affairs in Kentucky and to remove my family to Florida." DuVal explained that he had discharged his duty "according to my best judgements and I trust I will continue to do so."[51] DuVal's request went unanswered for many months. He would not return to Bardstown until a year and a half later. The months ahead would be filled with unceasing activity, successes, failures, and frustrations. DuVal's skills and talents would be tested as he administered the territory. His immediate task was to deal with the recalcitrant chief Neamathla—and, most important, to oversee the removal of the Seminoles to within the boundary of the reservation. Also on the horizon was a presidential election that drew DuVal closer and closer into the maelstrom of national politics.

CHAPTER 5

Neamathla and a New Territorial Capitol

On May 19, 1824, as the Eighteenth Congress's first session was winding down, Senator Andrew Jackson wrote to Rachel that he was eager to return home. The tariff bill had finally passed both houses of Congress, and Jackson confided to his wife that he was now "detained only for Genl Call; I hope tomorrow to get his Bills through the Senate and leave here on Sunday morning next—I would leave here tomorrow morn[ing] but one of the Bills is to authorise the president of the u states to order; that the Florida lands shall be survayed—under which I hope to have Colo. Butler appointed survayor-Genl—and I do not wish, as I have staid so long, to leave here before I see that done, as there are but little relience here to be placed in promises." In the upcoming week Jackson's efforts paid off for Call, Butler, and the Territory of Florida. The bill to grant land for the seat of government in Florida passed both houses of Congress and became law on May 24. Also on that day the Senate confirmed Robert Butler as surveyor general of the Territory of Florida. Jackson departed Washington almost immediately thereafter, finally reaching the Hermitage on June 4.[1]

Awaiting Jackson was the expectant Rachel, but also a huge cache of letters demanded immediate attention. Among those was a letter from Governor William P. DuVal, who wrote to Jackson from his desk in Pensacola. DuVal, like Old Hickory, pined for his family in Kentucky. "It is 17 months since I parted from my family and I feel much solicitude to be with them, but as I have been put under the prison bounds. . . . I am determined under no state of things to quit the Territory unless by the President's permission—or unless I determine to resign." Of Jackson's prospects in the upcoming presidential contest DuVal wrote, "It has afforded your friends here much happiness to see the great body of the people of the Union, calling on you for further services to your country. I have long known that the people in mass were for you. If the election is given solely to the people," Governor DuVal continued, "all the cunning and intrigue that can be mustered against you will not prevent your election as President. I believe that God has determined this in favor of our country . . . in all things I pray that his will be done suddenly."[2]

Jackson's prospects in the presidential sweepstakes were indeed good. The Virginia Dynasty had run its course, and the election came down to five strong contenders. None seemed to have the popular appeal of Jackson, and the hero's supporters worked tirelessly to push their man forward. William H. Crawford, Monroe's secretary of the treasury, gained the Congressional Caucus's endorsement, but in the hands of skilled political operatives this seemed as much a political handicap as his stroke had been a physical one the previous year. Secretary of State John Quincy Adams had a large backing, especially in the Northeast. And Henry Clay, despite Jackson's popularity in the West, hoped to garner support in that section. DuVal's friend Secretary of War Calhoun also had high hopes for the White House. DuVal's fellow territorial governor Lewis Cass and his former Kentucky associate Senator Ninian Edwards of Illinois supported his candidacy. But the secretary's efforts seemed to be directed as much against his enemy William H. Crawford's interests as his own. Calhoun's hope for the presidency hinged on his Pennsylvania strategy, but when that state's legislature nominated Andrew Jackson for president and Calhoun for the second spot in March, his fate seemed sealed. Even so, the months ahead would witness much political sparing, reverberations of which trickled down to the Territory of Florida.[3]

Meanwhile, back in Pensacola, as he was preparing to set out for St. Marks, DuVal was suffering from fever. Despite his illness DuVal assured Secretary Calhoun that he would soon depart for St. Marks to take personal charge of the "necessary arrangements to carry the late Indian treaty into effect. . . . No trouble or labour on my part, shall be avoided, to accomplish the views of the Government," he promised.[4]

By the time DuVal wrote these words, Congress had created the Bureau of Indian Affairs, an agency under the direct supervision of Calhoun's War Department. The South Carolinian appointed Thomas L. McKenney to head of the bureau, and it opened for business in March 1824. A talented administrator, McKenney supervised more than one hundred employees, including superintendents, eighteen agents, twenty-two subagents, thirty-four interpreters, and twenty-one gunsmiths, clerks, and farmers. McKenney and his clerks received and answered more than eight hundred letters a year. In the upcoming years DuVal would correspond with McKenney frequently regarding all manner of subjects related to Indian affairs. But during McKenney's tenure Indian affairs in Florida were the least of the bureau's concerns. Troubles with Indians in the Old Northwest, the Cherokees in Georgia, the Choctaws in Mississippi, the Creeks in Alabama (especially after the Treaty of Indian Springs talks and the subsequent assassination of William McIntosh, who alone was the signatory)—all these consumed the War Department's time.[5]

A vexing problem concerned payment of funds involving services the governor or his agents performed, and DuVal corresponded frequently with the official regarding payment for extra duties he had to carry out. As DuVal explained, he had to oversee all the affairs of the "southern Indians" because Florida's Indian agent, Gad Humphreys, "could not attind to more than the Indians between the Apalachicola and the Suwannee. . . . I feel that, justice has not been rendered to me for, the services I have performed up to the end of the last year, and some further allowance ought to be made to me up to that time." DuVal enclosed his accounts for his personal expenses for Indian affairs, which totaled more than $1,100. His appeal was of no avail.[6]

As DuVal prepared to leave Pensacola for St. Marks, his brother John was contemplating relocating to Florida. As John DuVal explained to his father, "brother William" advised him to apply to the president for appointment as receiver of public monies in the Florida Territory. The governor had told the young lawyer and former army officer that the section where the territorial capital was to be located was one of the most promising in the Union. "The lands are so high that the country in many places can be called mountainous; the hills rising from 200 to 500 feet & the Country resounds in fine Springs of pure . . . water. The growth of the timber on the high lands in hickory, Oak, Magnolia, Dogwood. . . the climate is delightful, sugar cane and sea Island cotton will be the staples. . . . Now if you could persuade the President to make you Receiver of the public moneys in this fine country it would be worth your attention" and eventual "success." John DuVal informed his father that he had solicited his friends in Congress for a recommendation and sent a copy of the petition to his father. Among the signers of the petition were both senators and three congressmen from Kentucky, eleven congressmen from Virginia, and one from Indiana. The son also wrote to his father that "Genl Jackson waited on the President in Person and recommended me to him." Calhoun was also for him. Enclosing his brother's letter and the copy of the petition, John DuVal asked his father to forward the contents with a letter to Thomas Jefferson. "I must get you to write immediately to Mr. Jefferson, requesting him to write to the President in my behalf. Mr. Jefferson I suspect remembers me, you may say that I am the son of yours that he recommended for a commission in the US army during the War, if he would enclose the letter to the President to me directed to Middleburg, Louden county, I could deliver it to the president . . . to his [house] which is a few miles from my residence."[7]

On June 21 Governor DuVal sailed from Pensacola to St. Marks, where, as he explained to Secretary of State John Quincy Adams, he would oversee the construction of the new capital and the removal of the Indians. He asked for directions as to "what manner the appropriation to meet the expenses of this Territory must be drawn. During the last year I never drew a cent, nor will I unless specifically directed to do so."

He needed a clerk but had no funds to hire one. The previous year, he noted, he had paid several hundred dollars of his own money to a clerk, and although he sent accounts and vouchers he had not been reimbursed.[8] (Late that summer DuVal's fifteen-year-old son Burr Harrison joined him to assist his father in any way he could.) Calhoun had told DuVal that Congress had appropriated $67,700 for the purpose of implementing the Treaty of Moultrie Creek. Of that total $6,000 would go for farm tools, cattle, and hogs; $4,500 for improvements that the Indians would abandon when they moved; $2,000 for their transportation; $2,000 annually for twenty years to establish a school and hire a gunsmith; and $5,000 to run the boundary of their reservation. The secretary directed DuVal to keep all expenses within these limits and to select a suitable person to appraise the improvements made by the Indians.[9]

DuVal arrived in Tallahassee in June and immediately began overseeing construction of the council's first habitation. DuVal temporarily occupied a log cabin within the ruins of a Spanish mission, close to the council building. Years later John McIver recalled, "In the summer of 1824 Governor DuVal boarded with me in Tallahassee—the place then contained but two Houses that were occupied. One by myself and the other by Mr. W. Wyatt." The structure was the best that could be had at the time, according to another man.[10]

DuVal soon selected a site for a homestead on a quarter section of land less than a mile away from the site of the capitol that faced a beautiful cascade. DuVal claimed preemption rights of $1.25 per acre on the beautiful tract—a controversial price that his enemies charged had been obtained through unfair advantage over others. The site was indeed a majestic spot. The hill upon which DuVal's house eventually stood was crowned by majestic live oaks, and overlooked the valley through which the St. Augustine Branch curved around the town.[11] Familiar with his father's work in Richmond and his own efforts in Bardstown, DuVal assisted newly appointed Judge Augustus Woodward, who arrived in the fall, in designing the town. The scheme eventually selected called for broad avenues, a capitol square, and four other squares, named for American heroes George Washington, Anthony Wayne, Nathaniel Green, and Andrew Jackson.[12]

That summer DuVal divided his time between Tallahassee and St. Marks, overseeing shipments of supplies and soldiers. Most of DuVal's efforts were dedicated to speedily removing the Indians, but in this work he encountered considerable resistance from Neamathla, who dragged his feet in the implementation of the removal plan. Trouble was on the horizon. Not only was Neamathla uncooperative, but Humphreys and others began to report to War Department officials that the land set out for the Indians could not sustain them (a fact hotly disputed by Gadsden, who continued to defend the tract as adequate to their needs).¹³ Growing tensions accelerated once Robert Butler's surveying parties began their work in the area. In July Washington authorities ordered the new surveyor general to proceed immediately to the territorial capital and to "open his Office at that place." The seat of government would be "selected for the bases of all the surveying operations in Florida, the ranges and townships, numbered from that point." The goal was for at least twenty townships to be prepared and proclaimed for sale by the end of the next session of Congress.¹⁴

In July DuVal, Gadsden, and Humphreys continued to update Washington authorities on Indians affairs. DuVal reported that he had urged the Creeks, who had been in the area only a few years, to return to Alabama. He had ordered cattle and hogs driven to Tampa Bay by October and had ordered "Tools of husbandry to be brought from the North to be distributed at the same time." He had also paid Neamathla $500 in silver as the treaty directed. The 1,500 Indians in the area needed to be fed daily, and DuVal argued that the $65,700 appropriated by Congress was not enough to furnish 1,500 rations at 12 ½ cents each for one year. As far as practical he promised that he would "Superintend in person all the important matters in relation to Contracts, takeing care to draw them all myself." DuVal eventually selected Benjamin Chaires of St. Augustine and Micjah Crupper of Pensacola to supply rations. Crupper would supply rations at St. Marks, and Chaires would send rations to depots at Tampa Bay and Lake George on the St. Johns River. War Department officials continually frustrated DuVal's efforts to provide Indians with adequate food and other necessities, claiming that they were either too expensive or unnecessary. Calhoun insisted that 12 ½ cents per day for rations was too much and admonished DuVal to economize further. When the governor asked for more resources to carry out his objectives Calhoun responded, "I have entire confidence in your judgement and zeal to serve the public, and that you will take such measures as to conduct the concentration of the Indians in Florida, as will be most effectual and economical." Nor could DuVal expect any more troops anytime soon, "unless," as the secretary wrote, "it should become necessary to apply force to a much greater extent than I now anticipate."¹⁵

DuVal said the Indians on the Apalachicola "behave very well" and "seem Anxious to follow all my directions and are Rapidly improving in their building Fences and mode of Cultivation, I have great expectation that they will improve in Civilization, even Faster than was expected by the most Sanguine in their Calculations on this subject." The same, however, could not be said of Neamathla and his followers. Not only had the chief refused the invitation to go to Washington, but he was "assuming and insolent, he has threatened to drive out the White Setlers, I must take some decided step with this Chief—he is the only turbulent Man in the Nation—he is creating daily more and more dissatisfaction among the Indians. [H]e has avoided me since my Arrival here, although he was to meet me on the

Day appointed, which he promised and failed to do." Also alarming was the fact that Neamathla's people were "now busy clearing land and building their habitations as if they were never to remove." DuVal appealed for more troops to be sent to St. Marks and asked that they be put under his command. He promised to act with "the soundest dressscretion and Coolest and most Mature reflection. . . . But if a Single Chief should be factious or should in a Fit of rage or Drunkeness do mischief I should Certainly like to send a Detachment immediately & Arrest him—as to using any improper severity that shall not be permitted. If a Chief deserves punishment I will call the other Chiefs to try him."[16]

A showdown seemed imminent, and DuVal ordered Neamathla to meet him at St. Marks on July 25. DuVal was convinced that military force would be necessary to ensure removal. By that time Gadsden had marked the lines of the reservations for the Apalachicola chiefs Econochatomico and Blount. Neamathla's tract was also carefully designated. But as stated earlier, the chief showed no disposition to move there.[17] Writing from Charleston, Gadsden wrote to Calhoun that the governor predicted "possible hostilities near Tallahassee. I cannot believe they will proceed to extremities, though at the period of movement the discontent of a few may manifest itself in individual acts of outrage." He recommended that they be ready and punish leaders if such may occur. "[L]et the Indians be strongly impressed with the determination of our government to inflict the most exemplary punishment of all those who may attempt any outrages or manifest any indisposition to retire to the country allotted to them. Some decisive step of this character is essential in a quarter where the Indians are composed of such materials as the Savages of Florida, refugees from the 4 Southern tribes & not accustomed to any species of discipline. The sooner they are brought within the fold, the sooner will all apprehension of disturbances South be removed." To forward this end Gadsden suggested that DuVal be provided with three or four companies of troops and that they be dispatched at the governor's command "to meet any emergency" and that a military road be built "in the centre & operate toward the extremities." This would "give confidence to an enterprising class of citizens disposed to emigrate to that section of the country this fall. This double movement of military & civil will relieve Governor DuVal from much anxiety & produce all the effect we could wish."[18]

In response to the Tallahassees' and Miccosukees' threatening behavior, DuVal moved decisively to counter the threat. As DuVal explained to Calhoun, with the military not under his direct command, "I determined at once to call out the few men that reside in this quarter. They came as volunteers to the New Seat of Government well armed. In the meantime I called to the chiefs and warriors of the Apalachicola to meet me at Judge Robinsons, about 30 miles from their Towns—They all promptly attended—and were ready to act as I might order. This sudden movement so surprised the Tallahassee and Meckkcssukee Indians, that they hurried to meet me and promised to obey my Orders and respect my authority." The next day

DuVal and his interpreter confronted Neamathla and found about "300 well armed warriors. I immediately went into their square yard (which is their foram) and gave them a talk, and ordered them all to meet me on the 26th of July at St. Marks & assured them that their ruin and distruction was cirtain unless they obeyed my orders—on the day appointed about 600 Indians attended at this place and I dilivered to them a talk that made considerable impression on them, I then appointed John Hicks their head chief to lead them south to their land, I selected the oldest son of King Hijah [Tuski Hajo], as his chief councellor, these appointments the warriors confermed. These are men of sense and will execute my orders—I hope now no further difficulty will shortly occur with these people."[19]

DuVal's description of his confrontation with Neamathla would be embellished as time went on. His action certainly evidenced much bravery, but the governor's vivid storytelling ability soon gave the act legend-like proportions. Accounts of the governor's bravery began to circulate in newspapers and other sources. A few months after DuVal's confrontation with Neamathla, one newspaper wrote that once the Indians in the Tallahassee area "manifested a repugnance at leaving this country ... and some of them evinced a disposition and actually armed themselves for hostility. They were happily quelled by his Excellency the Governor, who regardless of personal danger, rode into their towns, reproached them for their perfidy, and prevented their mischief."[20]

DuVal ordered that the Indians must be in their new lands by October 1. DuVal further reported that, with Humphreys absent in Tampa, he had had been compelled to work alone to "great trouble fatigue and expense in riding over this country in order to regulate the indians, and to make contracts for the government, which are highly advantageous, and saved some thousands of Dollars. I hope that some just compensation will be allowed me, as well as for the sums I shall have to disburse." In subsequent weeks the Indians formalized Hicks (Tukosee-Mathla) as their leader, and he eventually led the Indians South.[21]

These contractual arrangements included hiring the planter John Bellamy to visit every Indian town in the vicinity, record and evaluate the improvements of Indian lands, and make a report to the governor. Bellamy had also offered to complete the road linking Pensacola and St. Augustine. For $23,000 the planter offered to finish the section from the Ochlockonee to Picolata. DuVal endorsed Bellamy's proposition and wrote to Calhoun that the planter was a man of "wealth enterprise and of strict honesty, if he makes any contract it will be fulfilled to your satisfaction. This gentleman has a number of slaves and could do the work principally with his own force I believe it would be greatly to the interest of the United States to make such a contract it would save much expense and leave the military force to be used for other projects." Bellamy had settled near the Miccosukee towns. "I know him intimately and do not hesitate to recommend him as a man who may be confidently releyed on."[22]

Samuel Southard, ca. 1820s. Courtesy of Library of Congress.

From August through October DuVal worked tirelessly to oversee removal of the Indians and to prepare for the meeting of the legislative council. The Indians were fighting among themselves, and DuVal was forced to arbitrate. They are "preparing to remove, but it is with *evident reluctance*." The governor had been ill, and this he attributed to "the exposure to the hot sun and rain in a wilderness such as this. . . . I have, for several weeks, been wholly unable to quit my cabin, and much of the time confined to my bed. . . . The want of the services of the agent, or any one to assist me, had imposed heavy duties on me, and engrossed the whole of my time." Though his son Burr accompanied him on many of his excursions in the wilderness, DuVal longed for his family. "It is now nearly two years since I have seen my family. I contemplate the ensuing winter returning to Kentucky for them," he wrote to Calhoun.[23] The fever and strain had weakened and broken him down to the point that, as he confessed to Samuel Southard, his "health and spirits have failed so much in the last nine months that I have no more life in me than a Pitcher of stale Beer." As he related to Southard, he had to pull himself together soon because the legislature would assemble the next month for its first session in the new territorial capital. After that, he would be able to see "his wife and little ones. What a sacrifice have I made to principle and duty, but the same would be done over if it was necessary." Despite these obstacles DuVal reported that "great numbers of [settlers are] now riding over and exploring this fine Country. The Indians will be removed to Tampa Bay 15th of October next. I have lived among these savages all summer, and was on the eve of battle with them."[24]

A few days later, DuVal began to regain his strength. He offered Southard a more vivid picture of the new territorial capital in the midst of the wilderness, as well as of the obstacles he faced:

> I have certainly spent the most lonely summer in this wilderness that ever passed over my head. Three poor families only live here. For the last four months, not one companion, not one intelligent person has given me an hour's conversation, with the exception of a land hunter who may now and then call on me for information relating to this country. In seventeen miles west of this place there is a flourishing settlement [Quincy] of near 60 families. My presence was absolutely required at this point to keep the Indians in order, and I apprise you it has put me to great trouble, to preserve peace. At one time I had to bring out some volunteers in order to reduce them to submission. This was done without any bloodshed—but my opinion is that the prompt manner and decisive course on my part alone prevented dreadful outrages. I had made up my mind never to quit this spot unless overpowered. I felt as if I could die sooner than it should be said I was driven from the New Seat of Government.
>
> Within the last Ten days hundreds of people from many of the states are riding over and exploring this fine country. There is no section in the Southern part of the United States to be compared with this region, between the Suwannee and Appalachicola rivers. It is rich, high, delightfully watered, and healthy—in fact here is the termination of the great Allegany chain— I have visited all the southern states—and assure you that this district of country very far exceeds any of them. Sugar cain and sea Island cotton have for two years past been cultivated on the Oclocknee & Appalachicola rivers with success—The Mississippe cannot yeald these articles in the perfection. My presence in this part of Florida has been of much service to the interests of the Territory and will rapidly advance the interests of the government. The sales of the publick lands (dispised and degraded as this country has been by cirtain politicians) will surprise the nation. For near two years have I devoted myself to my duties. Neither exposure, bad health, opposition, or the difficulties of settling a wilderness surrounded by savages, have for a moment stayed me in executing the projects which my judgement approved. This duty was required by the confidence reposed in me by the President, and the friends who recommended me for the station I fill. It was due to my own character and standing that it has been performed without regard to health, fortune, or domestic happiness—all have been sacrificed to duty and honor.

How often with bitterness and grief have my thoughts lead me to my own happy quiet fireside and how deeply have I repented of ever having abandoned my lowly, sweet, happy home. My fortune never large is shattered by the great loss in the West—Friends once affluent are reduced to poverty and thousands have fallen on me as their security—many have failed who were owing me money. The loss to me is total, and I shall have again to begin the world with a large family. These events have distressed me, but they cannot subdue my spirits. If god restores me to perfect health I will rise above such common everyday matters. I can at least command the common comforts of life—and my conscience will not render me unhappy. I know not what is going on in the world. The nearest post office to me is Hartford in Georgia 150 miles distant.[25]

DuVal reported to Secretary of State Adams that he wanted to pay the Indians as soon as possible for their improvements, call them to St. Marks, and furnish them with as many supplies as possible. "I have held out as an inducement for the Indians to go in canoes by water & thus provide for their own a certain sum of from $5 to $10 for each canoe they should make for this purpose which should be paid by me to the individuals who made them." He expected some forty or fifty canoes would be built. He urged that the Apalachicola Indians, "being stationary," ought to have their share of the annuity distributed immediately and noted that he had therefore made engagements to have them furnished with cattle & some sheep, "as many of them now spin, and several of them weave & also plough." The "houses and fields of these people," he wrote, "are equal to the best of the improvements among the white people in this Section of Florida." He estimated that there were 240 men, besides their women and children, and that that constituted roughly one-fourth of the entire Indian population.[26]

On November 2 DuVal reported to Calhoun that he hoped in a few days to "have all the Indians on their march South, who intend to go to that quarter." While DuVal had "the difficulty of reconciling the Indians to the late treaty; and restrain[ing] them from outrage had not been inconsiderable, but to purswade and threaten them into a peaceable removal from this truly delightful country required the exercise of uncommon patience, time, and prudence. I now believe confidently that they will go without force, but evidently with reluctance. I hesitate not to aver that even now, was I to leave this country not one would move; when it is recollected that the Florida Indians never were controled until the United States took possession of this country and that even since they have not the greater part of the time had either an agent or subagent with them to inform them and reduce them to order; it must be obvious that my duties have been as arduous as they are unpleasant." DuVal predicted once again that many of the Indians, including Neamathla, would rejoin the Creek nations. He urged that the

Indians be paid for their improvements as soon as possible as "they are extremely poor, more so than any Indians in all the southern country. The money distributed to them for their improvements will furnish them with blankets & such things as will render them comfortable in some degree on their march, and will give them a stronger desire to shear the annuity—I have therefore sent to New Orleans for the specie to meet this object and to provide them transportation (for they will not receive any paper money) as it is expected in eight or ten days.... I intend to pay them off by towns," the governor continued, "and will require each Chief of a town to sign a receipt, for the money paid to the Indian of his town for improvements, this is the only way that this business can be satisfactorily performed."[27]

While overseeing the removal of the Indians DuVal also did his best to prepare for the meeting of the first legislative council in the new capital. On October 23 the Pensacola *Gazette* lauded the governor's efforts and noted that he had "been laboring with an indefatigable zeal.... To the uncommon promptitude of his exertions may be attributed the early location of the seat of government, and removal of the Indians, so important to accelerating the settlement of the Interior, and his course entitles him to the gratitude and affection of the Territory." Secretary Walton and the members of the council would leave for Tallahassee in about a month. "We are informed that a large number of strangers are travelling thro' the country with a view of selecting places for settlement. On the whole we think that Tallahassee & surrounding country, have as fair a prospect of an increase of population as good society as ever was enjoyed by so young a country." Robert Butler arrived in Tallahassee on November 12 and informed authorities in Washington that within days his men would begin their surveys.[28] The legislative council convened a few days earlier without its governor. DuVal was still immersed in Indians affairs.

Since DuVal's deposing of Neamathla in favor of John Hicks, the chief had remained in the area, and the governor might well have expected that he would lead a violent rebellion against removal. But Neamathla, perhaps sensing that such an act would be futile, solemnly abdicated his leadership on November 13. A man who witnessed the ceremony at St. Marks provided an eyewitness account to the ceremony. The man described Neamathla's voice as "sonorous and I thought a tincture of melancholy appeared on his fine manly countenance." The chief was six feet two inches tall and "finely proportioned." His eyes were "coal black, and exceedingly piercing." He had an aquiline nose and a large mouth with an "expression of wit and good nature," and his physical appearance was striking. The observer regretted that there was no interpreter, but he was later given the broad outlines of his "farewell talk." Neamathla called for a spirit of "harmony and brotherly love among them in their new abode." He admonished the Indians to abstain from spiritous liquors. He called for them to place great faith and reliance on their "St Augusine Mico [Govenor Duval], who was a brave and generous man, and who would send his agent among them." Neamathla invited those assembled who wished to leave Florida to join him in his journey to live with the Creeks, "where they would be received again into the tribe from which they sprung. . . . He spoke long and ardently on this subject but without effect so he was consigned to finish his talk and bid them an eternal farewell—this he did with a single wave of the hand and returned in the same manner he came in the opening. His two attendants, however, as well as the whole remained unmoveable for the space of two or three minutes after he had retired, a particular mark of respect to their beloved chief."[29]

One day earlier John Bellamy had completed his accounts, listing payments to the Indians for their improvements. He had visited twenty-nine towns and paid out $4,693 for improvements. Just over $1,300 was paid for transportation for the approximately two thousand Indians.[30] Within days DuVal and a guard of volunteers were in St. Marks. Richard Keith Call was not an eyewitness but wrote of the scene years later that only Hicks and a few of his Indians were on hand when DuVal and the guard arrived. "No further delay was granted—the governor was unrelenting—runners were dispatched and . . . the exiles began to appear on the appointed ground—and soon all who had chosen the water passage were in attendance. It was a sad sight," Call wrote, "their poverty and dejection appealed to the hardest heart—Gov. DuVal—sympathized heartily with them—and endeavored in many general ways to reconcile them to this distressing exodus."[31]

Meanwhile DuVal directed Gad Humphreys to select a site for the Indian Agency. The location must be near the center of the Indian population, "where good land and water can be had." DuVal ordered Humphreys to make a report of the "description of the Soils, water, &c in the vicinity," as well as a "precise number of Emigrant Indians." He also outlined guidelines for the issuance of rations on the St. Johns and at Tampa Bay. DuVal ordered the annuity delivered to Humphreys at Tampa Bay, directing that $2,700 in goods and $800 in specie (for the chiefs) be distributed, and that the goods be divided among the towns according to population.[32]

Humphreys reported to DuVal that the supplies had arrived in good order and were under the care of Owen Marsh. He had borrowed a good oxen team and hired a party of "discharged soldiers, and one or two Indian Negroes to open a road to the Agency; which I hope to complete as early as the middle of February." Humphreys dispatched runners to alert Indians in the interior that he would begin distribution of the annuity on March 1. He asked DuVal to do what he could to have the boundary line extended north to include better lands for the Indians to cultivate. He also reminded the governor that the "season is at hand, when preparations should be entered into for making Crops at the Agency, wherever it may be finally located." Humphreys also warned DuVal that he foresaw many problems regarding Indian-white interaction, especially as it applied to traffic in liquor. Strict regulations for trade must be adopted. "Without this to introduce Civilization and good order among them, or to Control them in any beneficial degree, would be next to impossible. The facility for indulging in their fondness for intoxication, and its Concomitant habits of degeneracy, which a traffic with the White people residing without the Indian Boundary (many of whom feel under no moral, or legal restraint, are wholly regardless of the evils they produce) affords them an entire aversion to Industry." Humphreys had observed that Indians often sold their "Skins &c for a smaller price" to unlicensed traders for "*Rum* or other Intoxicating liquor" rather than to a "licensed trader in the Nation, who is not permitted to vend them Spirits." This circumstance was also detrimental to lawful traders because it deprived them of an "important portion of that business, which is [their] rightful due." The situation "calls loudly for some Corrective for these extensive evils, and I have pleasure in adding that knowing how much and properly, you feel in relation to the Indian affairs of the Territory, I am fully assured, you will endeavor to effect all that is required."³³

While DuVal was busy with the Indians, the legislative council met. Living conditions in the new territorial capital were primitive but tolerable. A correspondent to the Pensacola *Gazette* reported that "We are [as] well, as could be expected, for a woods-town of five months old and all the essential appointments of shelter for the head and lining for the stomach." The new settlement boasted "well-roofed houses, all with chimneys—more or less—great plenty of fuel, as old Boon required it . . . good beds and blankets plenty; some chairs and an occasional table; good flour and corn-meal, bacon, beef, pork, poultry, wild turkeys, geese and ducks, butter, potatoes both kinds, onions, apples, coffee, tea and all the variety of Bar comdits and comforts—all good and plenty."³⁴

DuVal was in St. Marks on the first day of the legislative session, and his son Burr delivered his speech to Walton, the territorial secretary, who read the governor's address on November 10. After congratulating the delegates on their first meeting in the new territorial capital, DuVal represented the site chosen by the commission as in the "centre of a beautiful and extensive body of high fertile land, finely watered and blessed with a salubrious atmosphere." The site was destined to acquire "talent, population, enterprise, and wealth" that would "render it in a few years a delightful residence." He announced that the surveyor general would arrive soon and would begin surveys of twenty townships that would be brought into the market in a short time. He urged the council to select one of the three city plans under consideration and to begin laying out the town and selling town lots so that the money could be used to build the town's first public buildings. DuVal also spoke of the road project under way linking Pensacola and St. Augustine. Congress had appropriated $23,000 to complete the 370-mile project, and the War Department had selected Captain Daniel E. Burch to direct the project. DuVal's most poignant remarks addressed the territory's relationship to the national government—the council's role in nurturing the young territory as well as the dangers of political divisions among its citizens. "The purity with which our federal government is administered, the protection, which it affords to the most remote parts of our great empire, its vigilance in watching over the various and minute interests in every quarter of the union, all conduce to prove that the national happiness, prosperity & glory of the country are the first objects of our enlightened statesmen."

DuVal warned that "divisions among ourselves and discord in our councils will render us feeble at home and contemptible abroad. . . . It is for us to unite and develop to the nation the value of Florida. Until lately no part of North America was so little known as the interior of this country. Visitors, who had taken a transient view of the extremes of East and West Florida had proclaimed it a bank of sand not worth the money paid for it." DuVal was convinced that such ignorance would soon be disproven. Louisiana, he asserted, was not as fertile as Florida. "The lands on the banks of the Apalachicola are as fertile as the banks of the Mississippi, and the climate is better adapted to the culture of sugar and sea-island cotton. The greater part of the extensive county between the Suwannee and the Apalachicola River is extremely rich and valuable, and will sustain a population of many thousands souls; while the rich lands of the Alachua, east of the Suwannee and of the Chipola west of the Apalachicola will unquestionably render Florida, at no distant period a rich and powerful state."[35]

DuVal predicted that the "bold and navigable rivers, which run through our territory will be of more value than mines of gold." The Apalachicola, Suwannee, and Ochlocknee were navigable, as were the St. Marks and Wakulla Rivers. In the West the Choctawhatchee and Escambia Rivers were "now navigated into the state of Alabama. A few years will demonstrate the value of Florida to the Unites States, and southern planters will realize in this country that wealth for which hitherto they have toiled without success."[36]

DuVal concluded by urging the legislators to promote the "happiness and interest of our country," and he reminded them that the territory's prosperity would depend on their "judgment, prudence, and independence." Finally, he looked forward to the day when, "under the direction of Divine Providence and the kindly influence of a mild and equitable system of the laws, the population of our territory may so increase as soon to enable us to take our rank among the states of the Union."[37]

While DuVal was primarily consumed with Indian affairs during the meeting of the legislative council, he did attend its final sessions. He vetoed a number of bills. He failed to sign the militia bill, for example, on the grounds that the legislation provided that the colonels of the regiments and not the governor or the companies themselves could select officers. The most thorny issue (as it would continue to be) that emerged in the session was banking legislation. The legislature passed bills to charter banks in both St. Augustine and Pensacola, but the governor vetoed both, claiming that they lacked important regulatory guidelines. There were no provisions permitting the suspension of the charters if the banks ceased specie payments or were improperly managed. The institutions were not specifically limited to dealing in gold, silver, or bills of exchange. Directors were not restrained in the amount they could borrow. Finally, too few territorial inhabitants, the governor argued, had been apprised of the legislation beforehand. Overall, DuVal expressed a natural ambivalence toward chartering banks. "In general," he stated, "I . . . consider corporate societies as unsuited to the genius and spirit of our free institutions. They tend to create petty distinctions and inflated sub-aristocracies which are ever at war with that plain manly equality so essential to the preservation of virtue and moral sentiment among the body of the people." Even so, DuVal did not preclude the possibility of ever signing a bank charter bill; however, only those measures that "strictly guarded the rights and interests of the people" and leave them as "little liable to injury" would achieve his "sanction."[38]

Several citizens expressed opposition to DuVal's vetoes of the bank measures, one claiming that the legislators themselves were better able to determine the "welfare of the Territory than any individual, who may fill the executive chair, however gifted with wisdom or adorned with learning." The governor therefore had "committed a great error; and that he has altogether misconceived the true interests of the Territory, and his objections to the establishment of these two banks, are by no means sound or convincing."[39] Another correspondent defended the governor's actions in every regard, claiming that attacks against him were done merely to "excite jealousy & angry feelings between different sections of the Territory." In the course of his arduous duties, the governor has "deprived himself of the pleasures and comforts of ordinary life; has suffered fatigue, hunger and thirst and has exposed himself to dangers, for the benefit of Florida."[40]

While observers were not universally favorable to DuVal, positive reports of his message as well as his handling of the territorial affairs were voiced throughout the territory. A correspondent to the Pensacola *Gazette* reported that DuVal's address was a "concise exposition of the character and prospects of our Territory, and we trust that under the administration of so able and energetic a chief magistrate, our prosperity will equal its anticipations, and accomplish his predictions." The governor's labors had succeeded in removing the Indians and establishing the territorial capital. Another correspondent was particularly congratulatory of the governor's efforts regarding the Indians. He had "labored beyond the knowledge of most people in their behalf."[41]

As the governor prepared his final accounts of Indian expenditures for the previous months, he could take satisfaction in a number of accomplishments. The removal of majority of most of Middle Florida's Indians had been accomplished. The territorial capital was rapidly taking shape, and the first legislative council there had ended on an upbeat note. Newcomers and expectant land purchasers were flocking to the area. After the first of the year President Monroe announced that the public lands would go on sale at the land office in Tallahassee on the third Monday in May. The territorial court of appeals held its first session under its new presiding judge, Augustus Woodward. As DuVal was preparing to depart the territory for Washington and then to join his family, one of his new acquaintances, Judge Woodward, offered his own appraisal to Secretary of State Adams of Governor DuVal's talents and accomplishments. The judge found "the public measures here have been modeled, according to my conception, with sound judgement, and with such resolution and foresight. . . . For these felicitous results our country is, principally, indebted to the talents, the activity, and the integrity of the Governor, William P. DuVal."[42]

CHAPTER 6

A "Corrupt Bargain" and New Home in Florida

In January 1825 Governor William P. DuVal set out from Tallahassee for Washington, with important papers related to his previous two years as governor of the territory. Among these papers were vouchers, bonds of the Indian suppliers Crupper and Chaires, and an Abstract of Disbursements for Indian Affairs. The important documents also included John Bellamy's schedule of payments for Indian improvements in Middle Florida. The route of DuVal's journey to Washington is unknown. He may have traveled across the peninsula along the route of John Bellamy's proposed road from Tallahassee to Picolata. At that point he could have taken a stage to St. Augustine, or he could have continued north downriver to the mouth of the St. Johns. Perhaps he boarded a sloop at St. Marks and traveled through the Florida straits, catching the Gulf Stream and then going on to the Chesapeake. More likely DuVal traveled by stage through Georgia, reaching the coast at some point, where he boarded a vessel.

When DuVal arrived in Washington, the nation was enmeshed in one of the greatest political crises in its history. In November, when Florida's legislative council was in session, citizens in the various states cast their ballot for one of four candidates for president. As the totals began to trickle in, it became clear that Andrew Jackson carried pluralities in both popular and electoral votes. John Quincy Adams ran second in both categories, followed by William H. Crawford and Henry Clay.

The mood in the capital was tense, in part because all four candidates were in Washington. Jackson was in the Senate. Adams, Calhoun, and Crawford still administered their departments in the Monroe administration, and Henry Clay was the House of Representatives' presiding officer. Calhoun, it was soon established, would become vice president in the new administration. The Constitution provided that if no candidate received a majority in the Electoral College, the election would be decided by the House of Representatives, which would choose among the top three candidates, a fact that derailed Clay's presidential hopes but ironically put him in the position of selecting the next president. When DuVal arrived in Washington in early February, the tense voting by state delegations in the House of Representatives was about to begin. The story of the deal making and intrigue, especially the supposed "Corrupt Bargain" between Adams and Clay that made the former president and the latter secretary of state, has been well told elsewhere.[1]

While he dutifully filed his reports and met with officials in the departments, DuVal no doubt got caught up in the scene. According to a source quoting the Washington *National Intelligencer,* "a great number of strangers have been attracted to the City of Washington by the interest of the then approaching crisis, and many more were expected. Lodgings had become scarce, and a 'bed was not to be had for love or money.'" Adding even more excitement to the setting was the Marquis de Lafayette's visit to Washington. The Frenchman boarded at the same inn as did Senator and Mrs. Jackson, as well as the Florida congressional delegate, Richard Keith Call, and his new bride. The couple had wed at the Hermitage the previous fall.[2] DuVal called on his friends and attended the congressional hearings. "The galleries of the House had been crowded for several days," a source reported, and "among the auditors of the debate on Monday were Gen. Lafayette, the Judges of the Supreme Court, and Gov. DuVal of Florida."[3] The official voting awarding Adams the presidency came on the afternoon of February 9. Jackson's supporters were stunned, outraged, and indignant. The poisoned political atmosphere was breathtaking. Underneath, Jackson seethed. The day after the House vote, Jackson wrote to a close associate in Tennessee, "The Election is over, and Mr. Adams prevailed on the first Ballot; Mr Clay had influence anough to barter votes of Kenty Missouri, Elinoi, Louisiana, which drew after it Ohio, These with Maryland giving way decided the vote—Thus you see here, the voice of the people of the west have been disregarded, and demogogues barter them as sheep in the shambles, for their own views, and personal agrandisement."[4] From all accounts Jackson's outward appearance was calm. He attended a reception on February 10 in honor of the president-elect and hosted by President Monroe. Eight days later he threw a party for twenty-two of his supporters.[5]

Somehow official Washington plodded along, and DuVal was among the plodders. On the day before the vote, the governor forwarded his Indian accounts to Calhoun, along with other relevant correspondence in which he provided his appraisal of the current arrangements with regard to Indian affairs. He met personally with the secretary soon thereafter. That day he would have discussed contracts, payment of interpreters, the relocation process, and especially his concerns regarding the land allotted the Seminoles under the terms of the Moultrie Creek treaty. Only a day or so after he arrived in Washington, DuVal expressed these concerns in writing to the secretary. "I feel considerable interest for these unfortunate people," he wrote to Calhoun. "From the best information I can obtain, I do believe they have not good land sufficient to support them. If the President will alter the Northern line of the Indians boundary so far as to give them the big swamp, near which the present line passes. This alteration will give intire satisfaction to the Indians and justice and humanity require they should possess it." DuVal noted that he had informed the chiefs that he had every "confidence of the justice of the Government" and that it was this "assurance that reconciled them to the treaty." DuVal's views on the matter sharply conflicted with James Gadsden's, and the South Carolinian seemed to interpret the difference as a point of honor. Even so, President Monroe eventually acceded to the request.[6]

DuVal also reported to the vice president-elect that the Apalachicola Indians were "fast improving in the arts and architecture." He requested that two official interpreters be appointed: one for the Apalachicola Indians and one for those in the lands within the Indian boundary in the southern part of the peninsula. He also requested funds to procure portraits of "distinguished warriors." He lauded the efforts of subagent Owen March and hoped that his appointment would be confirmed. Finally, DuVal recommended that Secretary Walton be issued an immediate remittance of funds to meet the contracts for rations to the Indians. The secretary acceded to these suggestions.[7]

Unfortunately, though, there was also considerable confusion over advances DuVal had paid out of his own funds for important services because public money was either unavailable or not specifically authorized. Disputes went on for years, and DuVal was forced to explain every appeal in great detail. One such dispute involved Crupper and Chaires, both suppliers of rations to the Indians. DuVal explained that he had forwarded monies to both men, "expecting to draw the amount that might be due me on a settlement of my accounts," but one of his vouchers had been "suspended untill the returns shall be made by the Agent of the issues—This subjects me to serious inconvenience, and, brings me apparently in debt to the Government, when in fact they owe me about $2000." DuVal asked for a requisition drawn on the government, but to no avail. The Chaires account became the subject of considerable controversy. There were also charges that Chaires had obtained his contract by conspiring with a man named Pindar to rig the bidding. (Pinder later charged that DuVal had wrongfully favored Chaires in the letting of the contract.) Chaires would subsequently claim that he was owed more than $31,000. Thomas McKenney, head of the Bureau of Indian Affairs, asked for an explanation from DuVal, and the governor reported that Walton had taken all the relevant documents to Washington during DuVal's absence.[8]

In the waning days of Monroe's administration, at DuVal's, Jackson's, or others' urging, the outgoing president appointed Richard Keith Call receiver of public monies in the land office in Tallahassee. There he would join Jackson loyalist Robert Butler, the surveyor general, and Kentuckian George W. Ward, who was appointed land registrar not long thereafter.[9] On March 4 DuVal joined the throng attending the inaugural ceremony, and as he attended the subsequent events of the evening, he would have grieved for Jackson, but he also would have wondered how Adams's administration would take shape. DuVal was confident that he would be reappointed (in fact, the new president had probably told him so by this time), but if he was reappointed, what form would his relations with Adams's new cabinet members take? He would have to take directions from the new secretary of state, Henry Clay, an unpleasant thought. DuVal's problems with Clay went far beyond the 1824 campaign, reaching back into the marrow of Kentucky politics. (And the recent month's events would ensure that Kentucky politics would become even more partisan.) Clay certainly understood DuVal's politics and could not be expected to do him any favors. DuVal's official business with Calhoun would cease once the South Carolinian became vice president, and the new secretary of war, James Barbour, a Virginian and a Crawford man, would now oversee the governor's Indian accounts.

DuVal joined Andrew and Rachel Jackson's processional home on March 10. The traveling party, which also included the territorial delegate, resembled an august processional. Included were stops in Baltimore and Wheeling, where the party boarded the steamboat *Gen. Naville*. The steamboat sped down the Ohio, reaching Cincinnati on March 27, in, according to one account, forty hours.[10] Everywhere he went Jackson was treated as a conquering hero cheated of his just reward. DuVal floated down the Ohio as far as Louisville and then proceeded the thirty or so miles by stage or horseback to Bardstown. Jackson arrived home in Nashville on April 13, and from there the Calls followed the Natchez Trace to the Mississippi, arriving in Pensacola on April 19.[11] Jackson's friends immediately began the campaign that would, in their view, redeem the Republic by placing their hero in the White House.[12] It was an event-filled spring and summer, and DuVal helped arrange events for the hero in Kentucky.

DuVal's homecoming must have been a warm one. He had not seen Nancy and six of his children in more than two years. DuVal's oldest son, Burr Harrison, may have remained in Tallahassee (he was identified as a speaker at the town's Fourth of July celebration).[13] DuVal's other sons, Thomas Howard (12) and John Crittenden (9), no doubt had missed their father, as had his daughters, Marcia (14), Elizabeth (8), Mary (6), and Laura Harrison (5). As DuVal reacquainted himself with his family and his surroundings, he turned to the stack of correspondence waiting for him. Included were papers dealing with pending law suits and other materials related to wrapping up his affairs in Kentucky. Among the correspondence that he answered immediately was his commission for reappointment as governor of the Florida Territory. DuVal promptly accepted his commission, writing to Secretary of State Henry Clay that "after an absence of more than two years from this state, and my family, I feel myself imperiously called upon to settle my private concerns." He asked Clay to tell the president that he would be away from his post not "one moment longer . . . than is absolutely required to make arrangements . . . for the removal of my family to Tallahassee."[14] DuVal would remain away for another six months.

DuVal returned to a state wracked by political turmoil, its chief political leader now diminished by his part in the "Corrupt Bargain" episode. In the original vote tally in 1824 that state had gone for Jackson, but as a result of Harry of the West's conniving, the argument went, Kentucky's delegation had gone for Adams. According to Merrill Peterson, the new "Jackson Party in Kentucky emerged from the Old Court–New Court Battle. Some of its leaders, like John Pope, were old political enemies of Clay, whose heart was with the Old Court faction. As Secretary of State, Clay was forced to remain aloof from Kentucky politics, and thus saw his influence and support, even among his most loyal advocates like Francis Blair and Amos Kendall, desert him in favor of the Jackson faction. Within a year, Peterson continued, "New Court radicals" had stolen the state from Clay and turned it over to Jackson.[15]

As a friend of Jackson with an ancient animosity toward Clay, DuVal accommodated himself well to this situation. DuVal did nothing to dissuade Jackson of Clay's duplicity, and, as further proof of the Kentuckian's apostasy, DuVal even confided to Jackson that during the campaign Clay had denounced Adams at Cincinnati for selling out the interests of the West in the Peace of Ghent. On that occasion, Clay had branded Adams an "apostate, as one of the most dangerous men in the union, and the last man in it that ought to be brought into the executive chair." Consequently, as Jackson wrote to DuVal, Clay's support of Adams must be viewed in an even darker light. At various parades and dinners given for Clay in Kentucky, the man must have "felt as every eye saw his corruption, and the abandonment of these republican principles which gave him the confidence of the people for the pitiful consideration for the office of the Secy of state. He must have felt his humbled situation to have kissed the hand and bowed the neck to Mr. Adams, who, as you informed me, he denounced in the presence of many of the citizens of Kentucky and in yours, as an apostate, as one of the most dangerous men in the Republic, and last man in America who ought to be brought into the Presidency. After such denunciations," Jackson continued to DuVal, "to have supported him, and received the office from him, is evidence of such humanity and want of magnanimity that every one of his constituents, must have seen, and himself most sensibly felt it. Who but such a man could have attended a dinner at Cincinnati under the public expression of disapprobation by a majority of the citizens of that place? My feelings and views of propriety say none."[16]

DuVal assisted Governor John Desha of Kentucky (his former colleague in the House of Representatives) in organizing events in the state for Jackson. In early July DuVal wrote to Old Hickory reminding him that the two had planned a visit at the springs at Harrodsburg that summer. "I hope you will find it convenient to do so and permit me to request you will write to me should you determine to visit Kentucky." Mentioning Jackson's nemesis, DuVal noted the "Clay has had several dinners given to him since his return but depend on it required the greatest efforts of his friends to get them up. I have not seen him since his return and shall not (except by accident) for to him my heart can never yield more than common politeness." DuVal assured the General that his prospects in Kentucky were bright. "I am confident," the governor wrote, "you have the people of this state with you and I believe in Lexington should you visit the springs you will have a much more splendid and warm reception at that place than was given to Mr. Clay."[17]

Some days later, Jackson confessed to a friend that he felt "great delicacy in complying with" DuVal's and Desha's invitation to visit Harrodsburg. "My political creed is neither to seek or decline office, and it might be considered a departure from this my Republican creed even to visit the springs." Yet, as he explained, given Clay's unpopularity in Kentucky because of the "corrupt combination at Washington—and when I thus view it, I think perhaps my duty is to go to the springs & if Invited to attend any dinners that I may be invited to, by a respectable assemblage but this requires deliberation." After consulting with John Eaton, John Coffee, and others, Jackson decided against accepting the invitation. Writing to DuVal on August 6, Jackson said he intended to visit the springs but was forced to take care of private business in Alabama and the West District. Still, he wrote, "Mrs Jackson and myself anticipate the pleasure of seeing you, your lady & family at the Hermitage on your way to Florida—to whom be pleased to present us. . . . Write me on receipt of this & inform me when you will be with us."[18]

Jackson remained in contact with those close to him in Florida. Robert Butler had made a "valuable purchase in Florida. . . . I have no doubt he will do well; If his family will enjoy heath in that climate, he will be able to make himself independent there." Richard Keith Call had also moved to Tallahassee and had purchased a "section of land adjoining the Town of Talisshassee, it cost him about $2,800 and I have no doubt but in ten years it will command fifty doll pr acre—I have not doubt but Call wi[ill] succeed well—he writes me & Mary writes Mrs. J that he, & she are delighted with the country." Referring to Mary's pregnancy, Jackson wrote that Mary was in "good sailing trim, good balast, & all canvass spread—she is a remarkable fine woman of great economy & industry." (In September Mary gave birth to Mary Ellinore "Ellen" Call.)[19]

Politics was nearly always the subject of Jackson's letters to associates in Florida. In a letter to Call, Jackson deplored the outcome of the recent delegate's race in which his friend James Gadsden had lost to Joseph White. Jackson had been told that White "professed friendship to him," but he doubted the fact. Jackson had exchanged words with White's father-in-law, former Kentucky governor John Adair, over the latter's role in the Battle of New Orleans.[20] Jackson said that Call might expect that the "secretary of state will wield his influence over Colo White to convert him to his views.... You may calculate him with Clay and the influence of the administration wielded to support White & prostrate his political opponents you may prepare for this, and act accordingly." With these words Jackson anticipated the shape and dimensions of Florida politics in the next decade.[21]

While in Kentucky from April through September, DuVal may have had the opportunity to visit his father in Buckingham County, Virginia. If not, he may have corresponded with him as well as with his brother John. DuVal's younger brother was yet to secure a federal appointment, and he and his father renewed their efforts with the new administration. Major DuVal's letter to Henry Clay recommending his son and congratulating the secretary of state on "your Vote in Congress in favor of election of Mr Adams as President" must have seemed as ridiculous as it would have been outrageous to DuVal's oldest son. The father informed Clay that his son desired a posting in Florida, preferably a judgeship or perhaps navy agent in Pensacola or any other position that would be worth about $1,000 a year. As he explained, "John P. DuVal before he was 21 Years Old entered the Service & before the close of the War he was promoted to a Captaincy.... I gave John a Liberal Education. His talents are above mediocrity, he is said to be a good Lawyer temperate and moral & a sincere friend to his country, he has an amiable wife and Three Children." The Major explained that he had given John good land on the Green River in Kentucky and hoped that this might "settle him with every Conveniency" but that the inability to collect debts in Kentucky made this impossible. The father had emancipated his slaves and was no longer financially able to assist his son; he appealed to the secretary to appoint him to some minor office. Major DuVal's request went unanswered, but subsequently another man who wrote in John DuVal's favor received the following terse communication from Clay: "I received, perused, and now retain Judge DuVal's letter. His wishes in behalf of his son will be considered; the fact that he has one son a governor under the general government and another holding a captain's commission (this latter now applying for another appointment), will operate somewhat against his success."[22] The facts were clear: there would be no federal appointment of John DuVal while Henry Clay was secretary of state. Assistance would have to come from the governor himself.

While DuVal was out of the territory, Secretary Walton, as acting governor, and Gad Humphreys, the Indian agent, even though they resided at great distances from each other, tried to manage things as well as they could. By the fall Humphreys had established the Indian Agency at Fort King (present-day Ocala). Close to the Silver Spring and the Oklawaha River, the location was strategically located on the northern end of the Big Swamp between the "Indian & White population of the Territory . . . thus giving it . . . the power to regulate and control the intercourse between them." The site enjoyed "good water communication with the Atlantic, by way of the Oklawaha and the St. Johns Rivers." Yet travel problems, inadequate appropriations for rations, the lack of cooperation of federal troops, and problems of communications plagued the agency. Humphreys complained that letters posted from Washington took three months to arrive in Tampa Bay because they were routed through Pensacola. He suggested that a "regular line of expresses between Tampa and St. Augustine by way of the Agency" would go a long way toward solving the problem. Humphreys suggested that "Indians, or some of their Negroes—might be induced at a moderate sum, to Transport mail between St. Augustine and the Agency; and the latter place; letters could be taken to Cantonment Brook, by a Military express." Both legs of the journey were about "eighty Miles (three easy days ride)."[23]

In the south Humphreys reported that efforts to survey the military road between Tampa and Cape Sable had bogged down because the region below Charlotte Harbor was under water. While in the area the troops had discovered fisheries in Charlotte Harbor from which the Indians had established extensive contact with Cuba. "It is a very common thing for the Indians (sometimes Chiefs) to make visits in the Vessels belonging to the Fishery to Havana, where they are welcomed by the public Authorities of the Island, and when ready to depart, are sent away loaded with presents, the injurious tendency of such a state of things is easily imagined. Through the same channel, Spirituous liquors are regularly introduced among the Indians, who do not hesitate to say, that they Can obtain it at any time, by a visit to the Fisheries." In fact, one captain saw Jumper, "one of the principal men of the Southern Indians," and the chief told him that "he was waiting for a party of his Men, who had gone to Havana, to procure him a supply of Rum. It is also well understood that Runaway Slaves are often Carried off in these vessels, sometimes as free & at others taken to Cuba and Sold." Humphreys's requests, along with other correspondence, would be taken up by Calhoun's successor, James Barbour.[24]

A number of Indian crises occurred in DuVal's absence. That summer militia commander Joseph Hernandez notified DuVal that a confrontation resulting in bloodshed between whites and Indians near a St. Augustine plantation had forced him to call out his force and alert the regular army.[25] Moreover, the uncertainty of the northern boundary of the reservation continued to be a problem. Humphreys urged Thomas McKenney to complete the "running and marking of a Northern Boundary of the Indian Territory," as white settlers "were already thronging to the Vicinity of the Indian Settlements" and taking positions near or south of it. McKenney forwarded the correspondence to DuVal, adding, that "Settlers are already appropriating land, near to, if not South of, where the line will run, which, if not checked by some visible demarkation, may involve difficulties in their removal. The line will be drawn: *The Object being to take in the Big Hammock.*"²⁶

But uncertainly arose over the precise area that was included in President Monroe's extension. As Acting Governor Walton explained to authorities in Washington, "there are two places which from a partial Similarity of names have been frequently confounded with each other; the one is called the *Big Swamp* [and it] lies North of, but near to, the Indian Northern Boundary line; the other is called the *Big Hammock* and lies near to, and West, of Indian lands." Gadsden, Walton, and Humphreys conferred on the matter in Tallahassee but failed to reach a consensus on the lands President Monroe intended.

An even greater concern was that significant numbers of Indians, claiming that the land within the reservation was too poor to sustain them, were moving back across the Suwannee. "This District of Country (formerly in the occupancy of the Indians) had been surveyed, in part sold, and is rapidly populating: and if the Indians can not be restrained within their limits, occurrences of an unpleasant nature between them and the white inhabitants must infallibly ensue." Walton urged that prompt attention be given to the matter, but, in the absence of DuVal, he was reluctant to do anything. Erroneously, he expected that DuVal would arrive in the capital at any moment. "So soon as the Governor arrives I shall make him fully acquainted with their actual situation, . . . leaving it to his experience and better judgement to decide what measures will be most proper to pursue towards them."²⁷

DuVal's continued absence became a matter of frequent comment in the journals throughout the territory. In September a Middle Floridian "regretted the "negligence of our executive officers." DuVal, the correspondent claimed, had left the territory after the meeting of the last legislative council and was not expected to return until the "setting of the next, making nearly a whole year he will have resided out of the Territory." Walton had also abandoned the executive offices in the capital to attend to "personal business" in Pensacola.²⁸ Indian affairs and all manner of other important business had been neglected.

Lands around Tallahassee were filling up quickly. Congress gave the area a promotional boost when it granted the Marquis de Lafayette a township of land adjacent to the territorial capital in gratitude for his service in the American Revolution. Publications throughout the country broadcast news of the grant as well as glowing descriptions of Middle Florida lands. In January 1826 DuVal congratulated the Frenchman on his new acquisition and urged him to locate in the area permanently.²⁹ In March of the previous year the Washington *National Intelligencer* had reported that President Monroe had proclaimed that the first sale of public lands would take place in Tallahassee that May. "The tract of country adjacent to it . . . embraces the greatest body of rich lands in Florida. These lands are well watered, interspersed with limestone, and from their position, form one of the most healthful sections of that country." Sugar and Sea Island cotton were likely to be grown there. Representative John McKee of Alabama, who was charged personally with inspecting the lands on behalf of Lafayette, reported that he had never seen land that could be cultivated to "greater advantage" than those in Middle Florida.[30]

Another paper noted that "this young capital of Florida is already attracting the attention of capitalists. Many buildings are erecting and are in a state of preparation even before the sale of lots, which will take place on the fourth day of April next. It is situated on a beautiful and commanding eminence, about eighteen miles North of St. Marks in the bosom of a fertile and picturesque country." A recent sale of town lots in the capital had netted $45,000. The article went on to describe the location that DuVal had selected for his residence. "The south side of the town is watered by innumerable springs of pure water and a clear and pleasant stream passes by the east and south sides at a distance of a few yards. . . . After passing the town . . . [the stream] falls over the rock, which beds the stream, forming a pleasant cascade & passes off to a subterraneous passage."[31]

As summer turned to fall in Kentucky, DuVal was preparing to move his family to Florida. Likely he sold his residence in Kentucky. In addition, it is not recorded whether he was able to fully resolve his pending law suits. DuVal's departure from Kentucky must have been sad for him and his family. It was in Bardstown that he had met Nancy, established a law practice, and raised children. It was from there that he had entered military service in the War of 1812 and eventually traveled to Washington to represent his district in Congress. All of these memories would have flowed back to him as he attended a public dinner in Bardstown on September 21. DuVal's friends in Bardstown and Nelson County, according to one account, "were desirous of manifesting a last testimony of consideration, esteem, and affectionate regard."[32]

DuVal's journey south with his family and their possessions was a long, tedious one. The party departed Bardstown in the first week of October and on the way south stopped at the Hermitage on October 12. Only a few days after leaving Nashville, the journey halted when one of DuVal's daughters became gravely ill.[33] When the legislative council met on November 14, Florida was still without its governor. Finally, on November 21, DuVal and his family arrived in Tallahassee at four in the afternoon to be "escorted by a number of the members of the Legislative Council, and gentlemen" into town.[34]

DuVal's first priority was probably to provide for his family, and it is likely that while he was away workmen had begun construction of his new house overlooking the cascade. With the session well under way and Acting Governor Walton having given the opening address, DuVal caught up with the affairs of the council. Chosen president of the council was Abram Bellamy, son of the previous president, planter, and road builder John Bellamy. DuVal's fellow Kentuckians

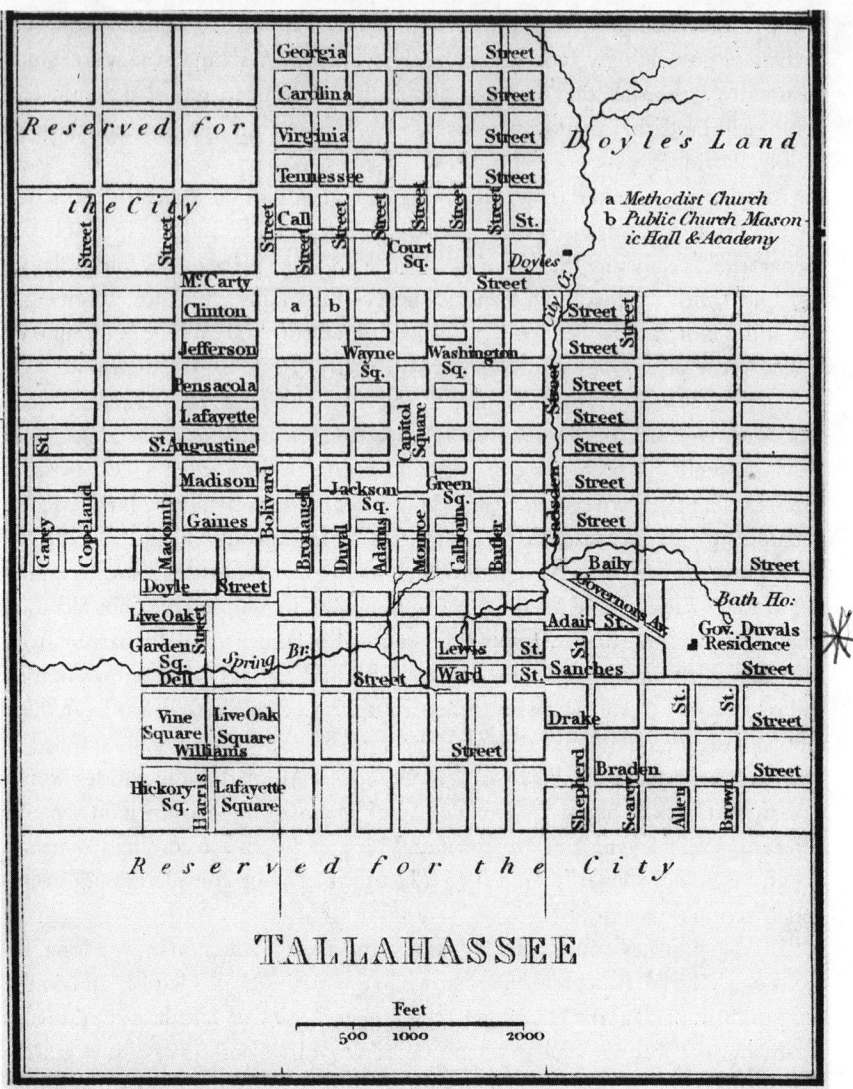

Tallahassee Plan, 1824, Showing DuVal's Homestead and Cascade. Courtesy of State Archives of Florida.

John M. Pope, Joseph B. Lancaster, and Samuel Blair were members. DuVal's first official communication came on November 25 when he addressed the council on the need to draft a new wrecking law, in lieu of the current one, which had been ruled unconstitutional by Judge Joseph Smith. Acting Governor Walton, he informed them, would proceed immediately to Key West to collect the revenue from sales at auction under the previous law. He recommended that legislation to license wreckers and regulate their operations be passed as soon as possible so as to bring in necessary revenue to the territory.[35]

Writing to Secretary of State Henry Clay on the subject, DuVal addressed the matter in more depth. He reminded the official that the "interest of the United States is deeply involved" because he was certain that more than $500,000 in property was lost on the Florida reefs per year. "The numerous Wreckers on this coast are unlicensed, and much of the property Wrecked is smuggled by them under the pretense of taking it for adjudication to different ports." As many as fifty or sixty Cuban vessels plied the waters surrounding Key West. "I believe many of them are little better than Pirates and Smugglers and are under the pretense of fishing, engaged in smuggling and Wrecking to the great injury of the country." DuVal suggested the immediate appointment of a judge to regulate wrecking activity and grant licenses. A port should be designated where all wrecked property should be taken, and only officers who have special knowledge of this coast should be appointed. "None but those best qualified and of known honesty ought to command; for the temptations are too numerous and strong in this quarter to be resisted by Ordinary Characters." There was much potential revenue for the United States at stake. Plus, "the contiguity of Cuba and other Islands to the Coast of Florida; and the numerous Keys and Inlets offer to the Smuggler the strongest temptation. In one night they can pass from the Post of Havanah and be concealed among the Keys before morning."[36]

Through the commandant of Fort Brooke DuVal also learned of continued depredations on the Gulf south of Tampa Bay. The familiar complaints that Indians were receiving liquor and other goods from Cuba were rife, but the commander also was informed that pirate ships, calling themselves Colombian vessels of war, had frequently landed on shore and robbed settlers. Also, on one occasion the commandant had intercepted a ship in Tampa Bay as its crew attempted to smuggle 150 Africans ashore.[37]

Once the lawmakers left town, DuVal was left essentially alone to conduct the affairs of the territory. Some manner of his daily activities can be gleaned from letters appealing to authorities in Washington for some assistance in his work. Clearly the strains of his office were bearing down on him on December 17, when he addressed a personal appeal to President Adams for $600 per year to hire a clerk. DuVal explained that the previous year he had employed his son Burr Harrison as a clerk, but "I lament he ever went into my office as it has materially injured his health—he has not been able to render much assistance for two weeks past." As DuVal explained, his duties had become so "oppressive that I find myself unable to perform all the writing necessary—There is no other Territory from which so many communications are required." DuVal complained that the "peculiar Situation of Florida" with its vast coastline necessitated the executive's "constant attention, to the various subjects directly under the controle of the several departments of the General Government, and these require frequently my attention. I do not know," he continued, "whither the Governors of other Territorys keep a record of their proceedings, and of their correspondence with the Several Departments of the General Government, as well as a Separate record of local business transacted in the Executive Office; Such however had ever been my practice, and its value and importance will (without detail on my part) be obvious to a Statesman—From the accumulation of business, I cannot continue the course hitherto pursued, unless some provision is made for a Clerk," he complained. "I have seriously impaired my vision by constant writing at Night, which I have been in the habit of doing even in Summer frequently until midnight. Since my return to Florida I can say truly that my business has become so pressing that for four weeks past, I have been confined to my Office to twelve at Night and frequently until two in the morning. It is impossible to stand this long, I assure you Sir, the business of the Office must be neglected unless I am permitted to employ a Clerk." Secretary of State Clay thrust DuVal's appeal aside, claiming that statutes did not permit the hiring of a clerk and that it was the duty of the secretary under the supervision of the governor to record and preserve the papers of the executive.[38]

Not surprisingly, the most pressing problem with which DuVal had to deal was Indians affairs. Many of the old problems had degenerated and had reached a critical stage. Indians were starving, and every day more were crossing the Suwannee to find better lands. Moreover, the governor had lost confidence in his Indian agent, Gad Humphreys. One month back in the territory had convinced him that, as he explained to the secretary of war, the agent had not followed his instructions, and the result was that he had "Seriously deranged my whole plan for the Government of the Indians in this quarter." DuVal stated that a force of two hundred troops was necessary at once to "bring these people to order and obedience, and I have recommended the establishment of a post on the South frontier of Allachua." Settlers there had charged that the agent had allowed Indians to "stroll about and hunt through this country in large parties," contrary to the treaty. One party of Indians had shot and killed a man and scalped him and had not been called to account in any way. At that very moment, DuVal wrote to McKenney, he was on his way to the Alachua settlements to investigate the matter.[39]

DuVal also predicted that, given the current circumstances, if the government saw fit to remove the Creeks west of the Mississippi, the Seminoles would join them voluntarily. He recommended that five Seminole chiefs "such as I know have influence be permitted to visit Washington, for I consider it important that the Secretary should converse with them and ascertain their views & disposition and the sooner the better." He suggested that the secretary write to General Edmund P. Gaines to solicit his opinion on the matter. If the general would send

Creek chiefs to Florida, DuVal would accompany them to the Indian boundary for talks. The War Department eventually authorized DuVal to offer the proposal to the Seminoles, but if his suggestion was rejected, he was to assure them that both the Big Hammock and the Big Swamp were within the boundary.[40] DuVal thought the major sticking point regarding eventual Indian removal was slaves and that every measure should be made to induce the Indians to sell their slaves. He was convinced that "it is owing to them that the Indians have not acted properly—the negroes have unbounded influence over them and are more hostile to the white people than their masters."[41]

DuVal also came under fire from anonymous sources alleging that he and the other two commissioners had pressured Indians to sign the treaty of Moultrie Creek, a charge that he disputed, claiming that all of their meetings had been public and that many people had been present every day of the talks. In the two years since the talks, the Indians themselves had never complained of any improper pressure; in addition, as DuVal claimed, "it is well known that many of our citizens (some of high standing) complained loudly at the time, and since, that the commissioners had been more liberal to the Indians, than to their Country—and I am greatly mistaken if you do not find such complaints filed in your Office." DuVal reminded McKenney that it was "at least uncommon, to arraign the veriest criminal, without specifying, the charge, and the name of the prosecutor." When the anonymous "volunteer guardian, of Indian rights" identified himself, DuVal promised to "freely state the course . . . pursued individually by me in the conduct of the Treaty without the fear of censure or the hope of applause."[42]

It was not the past but the current crisis of Indian starvation that most concerned DuVal. Benjamin Chaires joined others in offering a poor appraisal of the Indian lands: "So far as I have seen them," he wrote to DuVal," it is the poorest part of Florida, and a large portion of it is generally inundated. . . . I know of no spot of good land sufficiently large for one of the several tribes, or towns of Indians cannot possibly subsist on their present location."[43] DuVal wrote to McKenney that extending the Indian boundary would keep the Indians from starving until their crops came in. The Indians on the Apalachicola were also in desperate straits. Three times the previous year "were their Corn fields and fences Swept by the uncommon rise of the river—all these Indians live on the river, and until now had never solicited the aid of the Government for provisions. The old Chief Blunt and Tuski Harjo have just left me; they have given me a gloomy picture of distress now prevailing for want of food. Both chiefs and their warriors," DuVal reminded McKenney, "Served with Genl Jackson during the Seminole War." Further down the peninsula, Indians had again "continued to fall back on the Settlements," driving families from their homes, taking provisions, and destroying houses. DuVal urged again that a military post be established in Alachua and promised to go there personally to investigate the situation. When in Alachua DuVal promised to take proof of all the losses of cattle and other property taken and destroyed by the Indians and submit them to the War Department. All claims would be heard in a formal manner, and thus, he hoped, all "the clamour against the Indians will be silenced." Finally DuVal wrote that Acting Governor Walton had turned over to him very little cash and that he was "therefore without funds to meet many Accounts that have been presented."[44]

Responding to DuVal's and other appeals for immediate assistance of the Indians, on February 14 Secretary Barbour asked President Adams to request $50,000 from Congress. "Humanity demands that they should be kept from starving. They are there by our seeking, and their Country was exchanged as is usually the case by Treaty, doubtless with an ignorance on their part of the nature of that to which they consented to emigrate; and erroneous information on ours as to its fitness." Congress appropriated $20,000, but those funds would not become available until the summer.[45]

As DuVal prepared to set out to personally visit the Indian territories in late January, he received word from the War Department that his requests for pay for his services as acting Indian agent had been denied. Months earlier he had written to the department of his dissatisfaction at being granted a mere $750 for his extra services the year before. It was "too little and in the settlement of my accounts I have lost money by discharging my duty." This was particularly frustrating because he found himself in the same situation as the year before. As DuVal explained, he could not afford stationery, candles, fuel, or house rent on $750 per year. If not allowed proper compensation by the War Department, he continued, he must "petition Congress—to pass some law. . . . In the mean time I shall continue to take vouchers so as to cover the actual expenses of my Office—I am for two or three days together wholly ingaged in Indian Affairs, allow me to enquire if I am to receive any compensation for attending to business out of my office. My presence is necessary sometimes to prevent mischief, or broils between our citizens & the Indians—is this considered as part of my duty and if so—must I serve my country without any allowance."[46]

He complained that he had been discharging the "whole duties of Superintendent, Agent, and Sub Agent" and that his compensation had never even covered the expenses of his office. "I confess that I feel myself not fairly treated in this matter, although I have no doubt Mr. Calhoun at the time fully believed justice had been rendered to me. I do not believe it ever be the interest of our Government, to avoid paying a man well, who faithfully discharges his duty, when this is left to the discression of any Department."[47]

Territorial delegate Joseph White interceded in DuVal's favor, claiming that DuVal deserved extra compensation for serving as superintendent of Indian affairs. "I know he has encountered great difficulties and hazards in his negotiations with the Indians & I should humbly Conceive was entitled to the same Compensation as have been allowed" in other territories. "I trust you will consider the equity of his demand, & when a decission is given, cause it to be transmitted to him." Three days later, McKenney equivocated. To DuVal he wrote, "I am directed to state, in reply, that the decision in regard to your Salary, by the late Secretary, as conveyed to you in his letter of 20th April 1824, cannot be, at this time reversed—But such aid as the Secretary feels himself justified in granting to you, he will cheerfully extend." McKenney wrote that Major John Phagan would soon arrive as "sub-agent and he will report to you and follow your direction" and assist DuVal in whatever way the governor directed. He would also be allowed $100 for office rent and stationery. "You will be held accountable for all monies which you may receive on account of your Superintendency, as a matter of course—not special compensation can be allowed for either the 'risque or trouble'—This is understood to be embraced in your pay as Superintendent," the official stated. DuVal was authorized to pay Phagan $500 per year out of funds appropriated for Indian affairs.[48]

With this DuVal was forced to accept that there would be little relief for him personally or for the territory's troubled Indian affairs. He interpreted his duty as simply to plow ahead. As he set out for the Indian reservation, he must have wondered what he had gotten himself into.

CHAPTER 7

Trials, Tribulations, and "Left-Handed Justice"

In early 1826, while Governor William P. DuVal made his way to personally inspect the Indian territory, many changes were taking place in the Florida Territory. Migrants streamed into Middle Florida seeking new lands. Florida's first census, conducted four years later, recorded nearly thirty-five thousand people, with Middle Florida's population containing nearly half of the total. Well-to-do planters from Virginia, Kentucky, and the Carolinas brought their slaves and acquired the best lands for themselves, while those less fortunate were eager to rise as best they could, using their own labor to extract a living from the rich soils. Merchants, lawyers, doctors, and commercial men also migrated to Middle Florida, and often the first thing that they did once they arrived in the territorial capital was to pay their respects to the governor. To those able to survive the challenges of the new country, almost certain prosperity awaited. In 1826 Florida had ten counties: Escambia, Walton, Washington, and Jackson in West Florida; Gadsden and Leon in Middle Florida; and Alachua, St. Johns, Duval, Nassau, Monroe, and Mosquito in the Peninsula, east of the Suwannee. Migrants were most attracted to Middle Florida, and within one year growth in the district was reflected when the legislative council established Jefferson, Madison, and Hamilton Counties. Newcomers also headed to East Florida, and in that area pressure on the Seminoles was DuVal's biggest problem. Migrants to the Peninsula fanned out in haphazard fashion, settling wherever they chose. Many whites drifted in from Georgia, squatted on open lands, built a cabin, raised a crop of corn, and herded cows and pigs on the open range.

To facilitate movement and immigration to the new frontier, army personnel and others labored to create access to isolated areas. Roads were cut, surveys made, and lands soon put up for sale. Captain Daniel Burch's work crews toiled on the pathways linking Pensacola to Tallahassee and to St. Augustine. In the southern part of the territory explorations went forward. From Tampa Bay Captain Isaac Clark forged a path in a northeastern direction, linking the Indian Agency, Wanton's (Micanopy), and Black Creek on the St. Johns River. By midyear Clark reported to the quartermaster general that he had established a route that could deliver mail twice a month between Washington and the Gulf. "Communications from Washington will reach us in twenty days," he wrote from Tampa Bay, "twelve days from Washington to St. Augustine; two days from that to Wanton's, and four days from Wanton's to this place, allowing two days for delay, will make twenty days." Clark's parties also explored the region south of Tampa Bay as far as the Everglades. The interior around Talapchopco Creek (Peace River) was also explored and documented. Early in the year Bellamy and another contractor submitted bids for cutting a road from the St. Marys River south to Wanton's, using a ferry at Black Creek over the St. Johns River as a crossing point. The old "King's Road" that ran along the east coast of Florida from the St. Marys to the Tomoka River was reconditioned, and plans moved forward for cutting paths along the west bank of the St. Johns River running south to link Alachua.[1]

Meanwhile, Robert Butler's surveying teams continued their work in Middle Florida. The lands surrounding the new territorial capital were the first to be marked, but the "Chipola District" in nearby Jackson County just west of the Apalachicola River attracted settlers and speculators. From April to December 1825 official records note that Butler's teams, composed of twenty men, surveyed just over ten thousand miles of land. The times, terms, and conditions for the sale of these tracts occupied the interests of settlers, speculators, and of course officials on the scene, as well as authorities in Washington. Also of pressing concern was the thorny question of Spanish land grants (especially the Forbes Purchase in West Florida and the Arredondo tract in East Florida), and the pending claims perplexed officials and hampered the ability to grant clear titles. Officials also strove to follow up the unfinished work of surveying the boundary between Georgia and Florida. Plans also moved forward to cut a canal to link the Gulf with the Atlantic, and survey teams moved forward to explore routes.[2]

In late January 1826 DuVal boarded a sloop at St. Marks and headed toward Tampa Bay. His purpose was to visit the Indian Agency and assess for himself the true condition of the Indians. He had heard conflicting reports regarding the lands that the Indians had been allotted. Most reports judged the lands so inferior that they could not sustain the Indians. Reports also described drought-like conditions in the Peninsula. If the Indians were truly starving, DuVal was determined to report the situation and insist that a larger area be granted them. Also, the secretary of war authorized DuVal to meet with Hicks and other leaders and to sound them out regarding removal west of the Mississippi. A surveyor would be on hand to work under DuVal's direction to survey new boundary lines if the talks were unsuccessful and the Indians were to stay in Florida.[3] When DuVal arrived at the Indian Agency in February he met briefly with Hicks, stressing to the chief the need to restrain roaming Indians within the boundaries and the necessity of handing over runaway slaves who had taken up with the Indians. Hicks asked the governor to make a full reconnaissance of the lands. This DuVal agreed to do, promising that if he determined the lands to be inadequate, "I will request your Great Father to give you more."[4]

For thirteen days DuVal explored the area, and his conclusions were dismal. He reported to officials in Washington that the land leading south on the military road toward Tampa Bay was of "little value":

> The land around Okahumpki was too poor for cultivation & there is little good land in the neighborhood. Pelacklakaha is a town occupied by Indian negroes, its name signifies, <u>Scattered hammoc</u>; there is but little land fit for cultivation about it, and in the rainy season, the best of it is under water—Chicuchatty <u>Red house</u> is an Indian town on the margin of a large pond; it appears to be an ancient Settlement—and all the good lands have been exhausted by cultivation, and it is now poor unhealthy and has no water near that is fit to drink—the Big Hammoc is situated near this town. I spent some days examining it, and was greatly disappointed in its fertility, extent, and supposed advantages—The Big Hammock is much lower than the adjoining land, which is poor pine sandy hills, wholly unfit for cultivation. . . . I feel confident it has been vastly overrated. I think that a man who is a good judge of land would not give more than One dollar per acre for the best of it, above high water mark, which would be but a small [portion] of the whole Hammock. I did not travel but a short distance in going south on the military road; I left it near Okahmumpi and examined the whole country to the right of the road as far as Tampa Bay. I visited every spot where any lands were spoken of as being good, and I can say with truth that I have not seen three hundred acres of good land in my whole route after leaving the Agency. The lands on the Big and Little Withlecoucha are poor, and the land on the Hillsboro' River with the Indian Boundary, are of little value, that there is not one Indian Settlement on any of them—I did not visit Peas Creek, I had suffered so much from drinking water, alive with insects, from mosquitoes, intolerable hot weather, and my horses were so reduced by the journey, and the swarms of horse flies, that I determined to leave that point unexplored, having received Satisfactory information that there is but a small tract of good land in that quarter—I never have seen a more wretched tract of Country, than that which I entered five or six miles south of Chucuchatty –the Sand hills rise very high, and Indian trial winds over an

extensive Sand ridge for eight or nine miles; the whole of the timber for this distance as far as the eye can Survey has been killed by fire; the burnt and blackened pines, without a leaf, added to the dreary poverty of the land, presents the most miserable and gloomy prospect I ever beheld—After descending the Southern extremity of this ridge, I entered a low wet piney country, spotted with numerous ponds—I had much difficulty to pass through them, altho' the season has been uncommonly dry; had much rain fallen, I never could have reached Tampa Bay in that direction—so low was the whole country as far as the Indian boundary extends toward Tampa Bay, that after riding all day and until eleven O'Clock at night, in the hope I would find a dry spot to sleep upon, I was compelled to take up my lodging in a low wet place for the night. No Settlement ever can be made in this region, and there is no land in it worth cultivation—The best of the Indian lands are worth but little—nineteen twentieths of their whole country within the present boundary, is by far the poorest and most miserable region I ever beheld. I have therefore to advise as my duty demands, & the honor and humanity as my country requires, that the <u>Big Swamp</u> also be given to the Indians, and the northern side be fixed five miles North of the Big Swamp, and extended to the Oklawaha River east and so far west, as to include the Big Hammock—this line will take in no good land but the Big Swamp of any consequence, but by extending it into the pine barren it will keep off settlers from the Indian boundary who would otherwise crowd near the line and sell Whiskey to the Indians—the pine barren between the south end of Alachua, and the Big Swamp is poor and never can be cultivated—The distance is about twenty five miles—The Big Swamp is six miles long and is about two miles wide and is healthy, high rich land.[5]

Two days after submitting this gloomy picture to Washington, DuVal met with Hicks and the other chiefs. The talks addressed the poor lands within the boundary, the need to enlarge the reservation to include better lands, and the possibility of sending a delegation of chiefs to Washington to confer with the president and other officials on these questions. DuVal also brought up the matter of Indian encroachment on white farms, especially the killing of cattle and destruction of property. Hicks promised to investigate the matter, and he also promised to turn over any runaway slaves that he could identify but reiterated that whites had also stolen blacks from the Indians. Both agreed that there was wrongdoing on both sides. DuVal assured Hicks that, "Whatever property belonging to the Indians can be found with the white people, they shall be made to give it up; for the white and red men must be treated with the same justice." DuVal did not address the prospect of the Indians moving across the Mississippi, because, as he explained to Secretary of War James Barbour, "I felt certain it would alarm them. . . . The chiefs are disposed to do their duty but are afraid to exert their authority for fear of a part of the nation called the Mickasuky tribe, who are a very bad set of men." DuVal recommended that funds be appropriated to send a delegation of Indians to Washington, as they "have never been in the United States, and have no idea of the power or numbers of the country." DuVal urged Washington to confer on Hicks the "title of 'governor of the red men,' as he has been elected its chief by the unanimous voice of the nation." Finally, DuVal recommended that a military post be established to police the boundary. He had observed that "many white men crowd near the Indian boundary, who are worse than the Indians, and do constantly cheat them, and steal their horses and cattle." A military post near the agency would "control all such men" and have the effect of establishing "security and peace to the honest white settlers and Indians. I do hope most sincerely that you will view this subject as I have done, under all the circumstances, which has convinced me that this step is necessary."[6]

Over the next several days DuVal made an examination of ongoing work at the Indian Agency and reported what he saw. He found the smith shop well managed and in good order and noted that many of the Indians were bringing in broken tools to be mended. He reported that at least $2,500 would be necessary to complete the council house and other structures, which were absolutely necessary for the agency. DuVal suggested that the $1,000 appropriated for a school be used instead to "furnish Spinning Wheels, Looms, & that the Indians are now Soliciting," as the Indians had no interest in a school at the moment. "These people will raise Cotton immediately had they wheels to spin and Looms to weave it." It would be, he continued, "of infinite advantage to these people if a wheel wright, and a Cooper was Settled at the Agency who would take the young Indians as apprentices. The arts they are fond of Learning and in a few years, they would have workmen among themselves." DuVal also recommended that education of the Indians be confined to teaching them the "Usefull arts. We seem to forget that the wild and roving habits of the Children of the forest, can not be Changed Suddenly, it will be difficult to show for the history of any nation that its people were taught to read and write, before they learned to make their own tools for Labour or Comfortable houses for dwellings."[7]

The most vexing problem with which DuVal had to deal was the problem of slaves among the Indians. In late February Thomas McKenney had ordered Indian agent Gad Humphreys to report "immediately the number of Runaway Slaves (so far as you may be able to ascertain it) who are now within your Agency; and that you take immediate steps to restore them to their owners." Subagent Owen Marsh responded that it was impossible to "ascertain the number of runaways as they are protected by the Indians' negroes, and that many of the runaways had gone to Providence and Cuba."[8] DuVal reported that he had become "more and more Convinced that the Slaves belonging to the Indians are a Serious nusance, they have by their art and Cunning the entire Controul Over their Masters and negroes are all hostile to the white people and are Constantly Counteracting the advice and talks given to the Indians; and on Several occasions, after they have promised to the Agent in Council to attend to his advice on their return to their villages their Slaves have persuaded them to disregard it." DuVal advised that some method be employed to induce the Indians to sell their slaves and also to "clear out all free Negroes from the Nation." If this were done there would no more complaints from planters that slaves were running away and hiding out in the Indian nation. No fewer than four gentlemen had met with him personally to reclaim slaves who were "now among the Indian Negroes who are in the habit of enticing them from their masters and hiding them in the thick hammocks. I request you will grant permission to the Agent to purchase these Slaves for the use of the Agency or for his own use as he may think proper."[9]

DuVal visited the Alachua settlements to take testimony from settlers and investigate complaints against Humphreys and to investigate for himself the conditions within the area. DuVal heard continual complaints from the settlers that the Seminoles had destroyed or carried off their property, to which DuVal insisted that neither he nor Humphreys had any troops at their disposal—to which the settlers made direct appeals to the federal government.[10]

As the weeks progressed DuVal hoped to establish some legal procedure to arbitrate questions relating to runaway slaves. Judge Joseph Smith was already hearing individual cases, and in the meantime DuVal asked for specific instructions from Washington, adding that he and the agent had, in a few cases in which it appeared to them that claimants were justified, arranged for slaves to be returned to their white owners. He was unsure, however, about whether it was necessary for slaves, horses, and cattle captured by the Indians in the "late war to be given up[. A]nd and if so what indemnity is to be offered to the Indians" for property captured from "them during the war, which in value can not be less than $100,000? Am I to enquire in the right of property—in the nation claimed by the citizens of Florida, which was held by and in possession of the Indians before the delivery of Florida to the United States—and if so how far back is the examination to extend?" Also, DuVal reported that much Indian property was unethically acquired from the Indians "shortly before the surrender of Florida, by allarming the Indians by telling them that the Americans were coming immediately to take possession of the country and all their property. Indians were tricked into selling their slaves, Horses, cattle, and property for trifling sums. These slaves & other property . . . has run back to the Indian Nation. Ought this property so obtained, under these false, representations now be delivered up to such claimants?" DuVal admitted that the "difficulty and trouble that these claims produce is incalculable, [yet] I cannot consent to that sort of left handed justice which gives all that is demanded to our citizens & which withholds justice from this cheated and abused and persecuted race. . . . I assure you it is all important to secure the rights of the Indians as well as the peace of the country."[11]

Three days later DuVal reported that he would wait to survey the boundary line until he heard back from the department with regard to the report on the infertility of the Indian lands. He had promised the chiefs that he would personally supervise the task. "If I was not present," he explained, "they would be dissatisfied, and suspicious of the validity." Surveys would have to wait until the fall or early part of the winter because it was now "too late in the season to attempt it." Though the Indians had surrendered up many runaway slaves, he estimated that there were still at least twenty in the nation. "[Y]esterday [they] promised to find and deliver at the agency in eight days from this time, I believe that my presence has done much to effect this and bring the nation into order." DuVal suggested that if the president approved his recommendations it would "give to myself and the agent great influince over these People." DuVal argued that those who had previously cheated them were behind most of the settlers' claims against the Indians. DuVal reported that he had been adjudicating these claims almost daily since he arrived at the agency. "I have felt asshamed while urging the indians to surrender the property they hold, that I have not power to obtain for them their own rights and property held by our citizens." The Indians, DuVal asserted, could not get the "Justice" to which they are "intitled." In every case, on the contrary, "they surrender to our citizens. The government should have their property restored to them or pay to the Indians the value of it. To tell one of the these people that he must go to the law for his property in our courts with a white man is only adding insult to injury. I pray sir you will hear the agent on this subject who is possessed of many facts, highly deserving the attention of your department. I have taken the most unwearied pains to have justice done to all parties but I confess—the Indian under the laws of the United States have but little, shear [sic] in its advantages."[12]

As time went on, the War Department's policy on disputes arising between Indians and whites over ownership of slaves was that the courts would decide the individual cases. Subsequently McKenney directed DuVal to refer each case to the district judge: "You will address the Judge a line requesting him to decide and report the cases to you, to be forwarded to the Department for its Information." Soon Judge Joseph Smith began hearing cases involving slave disputes, and he stood firm on the premise that slave property could not be legally taken from the Indians except through the courts. Even so, seizures continued.[13]

While DuVal worked to administer Indian affairs as best he could, charges and recriminations were once again voiced against the governor, Gadsden, and other federal officials. Recognizing the suffering and the plight of the Indians, the St. Augustine *East Florida Herald* called the Moultrie Creek treaty a "perversion—a mere substitute for that of a *forced contract*. At the time this treaty was forming, it was pretty well understood that it was a matter of necessity with the

Indians and not of choice." The paper demanded that the "encroachments upon the rights of Indians ought to cease; and instead of treating them as a people whose hand is against every man, their situation is such as to call for the strongest sympathies that human nature is capable of sustaining. They have been driven from their paternal inheritance and are still pursued with relentless parsimony under the semblance of treaties, the express object of which has been the extinguishment of their title upon terms *favorable to the United States.*" The journal published letters from Lieutenant Colonel George Brooke and others speaking to the starvation of the Indians and also defended Indian agent Humphreys. "How can a single individual secure such an influence as to restrain the lawless? Is it not a wonder that 5000 Indians should be controlled so well without a protective force?" While he was no doubt angered by these representations, DuVal chose not to respond publicly to the charges. He did privately voice his frustration to Navy Secretary Samuel Southard that "some stinking rascal has given information to the war department that . . . commissioners . . . of whom I was one 'resorted to improper means to procure the Treaty.' No name is given as the authority for this long delayed and volunteer disclosure."[14]

Gadsden, on the other hand, responded publicly, stating that the treaty made was the "most favorable to the Indians regarding alike their comfort, protection and future prosperity." He asserted that DuVal's and Chaires's report was based only on "partial examination of a very limited portion of the district set apart for the Indians." He blamed current difficulties on those "lawless" elements (Miccosukees) still within the nation. "The Territory of Florida was purchased for its Military Position, to cleanse it of lawless savages who endangered and disturbed our frontiers: and to add to our means of defense and internal tranquility by diminishing the facilities to foreign invasion and to internal commotion by transatlantic excitement." These elements were "ready instruments in the hands of foreign incendiaries" and must be removed from the territory. The "Refugee Party, who merit neither the sympathy or bounty of the General Government, . . . are a band of restless savages who have infested our Southern border ever since the termination of the Creek War of 1813. Wandering Ishmalites their hands are, and will continue to be raised against every people who will assume the authority they have power to exercise." Only compulsion, not moderation, could check these people. In his public response to the *Herald*'s charges and in communications to authorities in Washington, Gadsden argued that the Moultrie Creek talks were fair. Moreover, "the lands . . . extended as recommended by the Governor to embrace the Big Swamp [would be] more than sufficient." Finally, addressing the authorities in Washington, Gadsden urged that Indians be removed west of the Mississippi as soon as possible.[15]

Traveling back to Tallahassee from Alachua by way of the Bellamy road, DuVal was able to examine the work. He was pleased at the workmanship and reported to

Washington that he had traveled 150 miles of the road and found it well executed: "considering the low and swampy situation of much of the ground over which the road passes . . . it is decidedly the best new road I have ever seen. When Mr. Bellamy shall finish the causeways by adding more earth, the road will be excellent. I do not think the stumps are too high and more labour has been bestowed on the road than I expected, knowing that the appropriation was so small for a road so lengthy."[16]

Back in Tallahassee by April 5, DuVal concluded that the settlers' complaints were largely based on the false premise that Humphreys had the authority to call out federal troops to protect them. This not being the case, DuVal was convinced that Humphreys had done all in his power and "did perform as much as any other man unbacked by a competent force could have accomplished." DuVal reported that the "whole Indian Nation is under more complete controle" than any other tribe in the United States that has so "recently come under our management. The Mickkessukee tribe I must exept from this general remark; they are and have ever been the most violent and lawless Indians in all the South. They have Set their own Chiefs at defiance, and have abandoned their limits, roving among the white inhabitants killing hogs and cattle, pillaging their plantations. There is about 200 of these Indians that can never be managed but by force. Three times they have attempted to put to death their head Chief because he has endeavored to retrain their excesses." All the chiefs in open council had denounced them and assured the governor that if the government would assist them, they would punish the outlaws and bring them into their boundary. "I have been upwards of two months in the woods, regulating and bringing the Indians to order, and have completely Succeeded except with the Mickkessukee tribe." DuVal reported that the settlers and the Indians were "exasperated at the injuries they have Sustained from this tribe and worse consequences may be expected" and that he could do nothing with them "without force." DuVal informed McKenney that Humphreys and a "deputation of Chiefs" would soon be in Washington to talk to the secretary of war. He urged authorities to send an advance party west to inspect lands west of the Mississippi. "I do sincerely hope that Mr. Barbour may be able to carry into effect his plan for colonizing the Indians and every good, and humane man must ardently desire to see the experiment fairly tested." Humphreys would be carrying his own accounts to Washington. The governor's illness made it impossible for him to examine and approve them.[17]

A few days later DuVal sent his son Burr on a mission to Washington. Writing to McKenney, DuVal explained that he wished to "introduce to you my son B. H. DuVal, he has seen very little of the world, but his principles and morals will entitled him to respect & I flatter myself in any intelligent and virtuous society. I have much pleasure in sending to you by my son a complete suit of Indian costume—which I request you will accept." DuVal promised to collect and send "more Indians curiosities" and added that there are the "remains of an old fort a few hundred yards of my house that had once been inhabited by a civilized people. We found many locks, hinges, spikes, stoneware, and composite, that were chard by fire, but in appearance, in a perfect state of preservation." DuVal reported that "growing in the midst of these ruins, under these mighty oaks, we have discovered the tabby floors of the old houses—these floors are made of shell lime & sand, and are smooth chard." He had also found large bricks that might have led up "to the Alter in a Chapel. Is it not singular that we have no account of the settlement of this part of Florida? When it is evident that this whole region between the Apalachicola and the Suwannee had once been densely populated." The "remains of the numerous roads, and ditches, is strong evidence of a great population." DuVal reported that the "lands are selling lower here than in any part of the Union." DuVal then requested McKenney to assist his son in the settlement of his "business in the offices—he is so unacquainted with the routine of business that without the aid of some friend I fear he may be long detained in the city. I hope he may be enabled to purchase me a few slaves—for I have now but two working hands—I have planted an acre and a half in sugar cane for seed, and next year I hope to have 20 acres in cane."[18]

While Burr DuVal was on his way to Washington, so were Humphreys, Hicks, and six other chiefs. (McKenney and Barbour would have been surprised and dismayed to see Humphreys and the Indians because the day before he had written DuVal not to send the delegation.) Arriving on May 9, Humphreys and the Indians met with the secretary of war, who addressed them the following day.[19] Barbour stated that the president had authorized the Indians to occupy the Big Swamp "until he had a use for it" and that he expected them to move within the limits of the survey. The secretary admonished them to plant their own crops, surrender up runaway slaves, and stay away from whiskey and from white settlements; he also stipulated that if the whites struck at them, they should not to strike back but go to the agent. Finally Barbour brought up the issue of relocation. "Your Great Father owns a great country over the Mississippi, and is willing to give you a large portion of it, whenever you may incline to go."[20]

Seven days later Hicks responded to the secretary, complaining that the president's offer to occupy the Big Swamp "until he may want to send us from it . . . does not please us." They did not want to be "put to the trouble of moving again—The hardship suffered from our first removal, gave us pain enough—We do not wish to feel it again." When they "left the good land about Tallahassee and Mickasuky which is now covered by the White Skins, we stopped at the Big Swamp because we knew we could not live further South" and because DuVal had told them that they could have the land. "We now claim the fulfillment of his promise." Hicks also declared that they would never move across the Mississippi. "We have no friends there, the people of that country are strangers to us—the

Tuko-see-Mathla.
A. K. A. John Hicks.
Courtesy of State
Archives of Florida.

Muscogees invited us to go with them, but it was only to make their party stronger—we will not involve ourselves in the troubles of the Muscogees—We are a separate people and have nothing to do with them—We came hither not to see the Muscogees but to hold a talk with our Great father on our own affairs and to claim of him more land in our own Country—Most of us were born on the land we now inhabit & that which we claim to be surrendered to us—here our naval strings were first cut & the blood from them, sunk into the earth & made the country dear to us." The Indians disputed the claims that they were hiding runaway slaves from the whites and asserted that they did not wish "to disturb our white neighbors but to live in friendship with them."[21] Satisfied as to the veracity of DuVal's statements regarding the infertility of lands within the boundary, Washington authorized the governor to extend the surveys to "embrace the Big Swamp as well as the Big Hammock."[22]

In the following days Hicks and his delegation met briefly with President Adams, had their portraits painted, and were provided with uniforms. They remained in Washington until June 4, when Humphreys put the Indians on a ship at Baltimore bound for St. Augustine. Humphreys then made his way to New York and then to Boston, where he intended to interview teachers for the Indian school at the agency. That work done, Humphreys began an extended visit with his family in Massachusetts.[23]

When the Indians returned to Florida, they soon learned that many of the old problems had grown worse.[24] Starvation led to further confrontations with whites in East Florida, and some Indians roamed west of the Suwannee. Everywhere there were signs of impending Indian outbreaks, and citizens complained to authorities in Washington that DuVal was not doing enough to protect them. In July John Rodman wrote to the secretary of war that the people of St. Augustine are "greatly excited and justly alarmed. They consider their lives and property in imminent danger." Rodman charged that it was the governor's duty to "carry the militia laws into effect." When ordered to investigate the matter, DuVal admitted that the militia was not properly organized but explained that the officers had few weapons and that it was difficult to get sufficient arms. Further explaining the difficulty of mobilizing militias, DuVal stated that the "citizens of Florida are enterprising bold men and like most of our best Citizens who have emigrated to new lands and Countrys do not bring, but come to acquire fortune. Not one in five hundred has yet had the opportunity to purchase . . . the land he has opened in the forest." DuVal had been "actively engaged during the Spring and summer in trying to excite our Citizens to form themselves into Corps," but many "are unable in a large district thinly settled to attend the muster of a Regiment." Yet, if the federal government would provide two hundred muskets and one hundred rifles, the governor would need no assistance from regular forces. DuVal went on to explain that all the disturbances were attributable to only about two hundred or so

> lawless Indians, most of whom were part of the notorious Miccosukee tribe[.] I had the honor last spring to give you this information and to assure you that Nothing short of force would control this banditti[. T]hey are the Outlaws of their own Nation and have Many of them fled from the Merited punishment which awaited at home. The great body of the Nation have in Council Condemned the Indians who have Constantly been depredating on our Settlers, but these fugitives go wandering over the Territory, dealing destruction on the Cattle and rifling the plantations. I apprehend danger is likely to arise from our own Citizens who are and have for some time been ready to redress by force of arms the wrongs and injuries they have sustained. It has required all my vigilance and influence to restrain this hostile disposition. There is no danger of the Indians in resorting to arms except in self-defense, they are entirely sensible of their feeble situation and dependence on the Government.[25]

DuVal asked that a garrison be located at the mouth of the Suwannee River and that a federal force land at St. Marks and march east and "scour all the Country between that place eastward thro' Alachua County, destroying all Indian Settlements out of their limits." DuVal communicated these sentiments to the War Department and directly to Duncan L. Clinch, commander of the garrison at Pensacola. The colonel supported DuVal's plan, and in the months ahead, the man selected to move against the unruly Indians was Captain Francis Langhorne Dade. (That officer eventually established a fort near the mouth of the Suwannee and named it for DuVal.) The governor called out militia units against the Indians, but Dade succeeded where they failed. From July 1826 to April 1827, Dade and his men moved decisively against real and perceived Indian treats in both East and West Florida. The historian Canter Brown ably recounts Dade's ruthless movements during the "Florida Crisis of 1826–1827." In this work Dade collaborated closely with Governor DuVal. Acting in response to killings in Thomas County, Georgia, and another on the Aucilla River, Dade inflicted harsh treatment on the Indians that established a deadly pattern of escalating violence between the Indians and the whites, setting the stage for the officer's own demise on December 28, 1835.[26]

Also that summer, DuVal had reason to fear for the safety of friendly Indians on the Apalachicola River. Blount and the other chiefs had been helpful to DuVal in his stormy relations with the Miccosukee tribe, and he would need their help again that summer and fall. But Blount and his people had more to fear from whites than from the Indians. DuVal ordered his subagent, John Phagan, to reside in the vicinity of the Apalachicola Indians, "owing to a sett of white men . . . whose lawless conduct has hitherto annoyed and injured them—the subagent's presence was required to protect them and their property from these men—no legal proof could be procured of their stealing the horses cattle and hogs of the Indians but I had no doubt of the fact." DuVal might have reminded officials that Indians' recourse to the courts in matters concerning whites was of no avail.[27]

Even as tensions escalated during the summer of 1826, DuVal and other settlers formed relationships with individual Seminoles who were tolerated if not accepted into white society. In later years DuVal's son John Crittenden recalled that Indians were his companions in his youth and taught him "the mysteries of 'wood craft.' I have hunted and camped with them and joined them in their sports and pastimes, and I think I can truly say that in some respects they were fully equal if not in advance of a large majority of their more civilized brethren. They were notably honest and hospitable . . . always grateful for favors shown them." As an example DuVal cited the relationship between certain Indians and the Gamble family, whose plantation twenty miles east of Tallahassee was "always open to them and never entered by them without being hospitably welcomed. The daughters of the house played the piano for them, sang comic and patriotic songs for them—gave them geegaws and ribbons, feathers and beads—while the matrons gave them physic and delicacies." The Indians, remembered DuVal, did not forget this kindness and abstained from attacking the Gamble plantation once hostilities commenced.[28]

Tiger Tail (Thlocklo Tustenuggee), a Tallahassee, whose father's village had previously occupied the site of the town, stayed in town long after others departed. As John K. Mahon has noted, Tiger Tail was "always well received because he knew how to act in white society." He was fluent in English, "kept the Sabbath, and treated his family white-style. Everyone knew him in Middle Florida because he had been a common lounger in the streets of Tallahassee." He was particularly friendly to the Gambles and the DuVals and stayed in the area until DuVal's successor, John Eaton, arrived in 1834. Tiger Tail sold fish and game and frequented the homes of the whites, including DuVal's, but sometimes he had occasion to vanish into the woods for extended periods of time.[29]

Tiger Tail may have been among the Indians that DuVal had in his house in the spring and summer of 1826. The governor complained to McKenney that "I have had my house crowded with Indians for Six months, many of them sick come to me to be taken care of—common humanity will not permit me to drive these people away when a disease is preying upon them." Droughts had ruined the Indians' crops, and they were "more destitute than ever." DuVal had provided for them out of his own funds. Otherwise, the "whole country would have been over run by them, for a starving people can not be controuled even by force." With his own "trouble and responsibility so greatly increased," he was forced to "Apply again to the Department of War, and if no Change Can be ordered by the Secretary or the President I must be content to be driven from the office I now hold. [I]t does not seem [fair] to me, that my efforts to serve my country, and their Consequent responsibility, will ruin me." Finally he asked that all responsibility for Indian affairs be given to the agent. "My duties as Governor are too much interfered with by the business of the Indian Department." McKenney ignored DuVal's personal plea for more resources. Instead, he directed the governor to see that the Indians began supporting themselves.[30]

The Indian scare of 1826–1827 reached its peak while the Florida legislative council was in session. In November a killing just over the Florida line in Thomas County, Georgia, occurred. Then, on December 12, the same day he delivered his annual message to the assembly of lawmakers, DuVal announced that six days earlier the Miccosukees had butchered the Carr family on the west bank of the Aucilla River. DuVal reported that he had ordered out militias from Jackson, Gadsden, and surrounding counties. He also ordered the Nassau and DuVal County militias to proceed to Alachua County to guard the Indian boundary. Captain Dade on the Suwannee River, he reported, "is actively engaged in arresting and disarming the Indians, many of whom are painted for war and display hostility."[31] While DuVal had no power to command federal troops, he asked that

Colonel Brooke send troops to the Suwannee to seize Seminole boats and canoes, assemble the Seminole chiefs, ascertain their temper, demand the murderers' surrender, and repel any further encroachments with force. The governor also sent an emergency appeal to Colonel Duncan L. Clinch, asking that officer to dispatch three companies into the field. This "outrage is the forerunner of some Desperate Movement of these beings of both Nations" (the Miccosukees and the Creeks). While he understood he had no authority over Clinch, he considered it "obligatory on you" to cooperate and respond to his plea. "As the Executive Officer of this Territory having Charge of the Welfare of its Citizens who belong to the great family of the Nation, I make this appeal to you claiming all and every responsibility arising out of it."[32] DuVal also reported the murders to Georgia Governor Troup, whose legislature was also in session. As one Georgia source reported, "several members belonging to the frontier counties have obtained leave of absence to return home, and it is said several troops of horse have been ordered to repair to the Florida line."[33]

In the face of the Carr family murders on the Aucilla, DuVal ordered his sub-agent, John Phagan, to lead Apalachicola warriors against the "wandering Indians" west of the Suwannee. He was soon able to report that those concerned in the Georgia killings and the Carr family murders were in custody. DuVal praised the Apalachicola Indians and Phagan. "Mr. Phagan is an excellent man and valuable officer, he divided his party and without doing any injury to the Indians he succeeded in driving them out of the Ocilla swamps." Their services, DuVal insisted, required adequate compensation. Under DuVal's direction, the captives were turned over to civil authorities for prosecution. Humphreys succeeded in having some released to him to be brought back to the agency in East Florida, but others were held in Middle Florida and, despite questions about their guilt, suffered both judicial and extrajudicial punishment.[34]

Indian affairs continued to occupy the greater portion of DuVal's time that winter and spring. On December 2, only a few days before the Aucilla attack, he ordered Owen Marsh to call the Indians to a council at the agency and deliver a prepared message of the governor. The precise contents of this message is unrecorded but it seems certain that the governor would have ordered the Indians to remain within their boundaries and demand that they surrender up all runaway slaves and also work to capture and turn over renegades wanted for depredations. After the council, Marsh reported to DuVal of the suffering state of the Indians. Game was depleted, corn would not grow in the allotted lands, and the "whole nation is suffering alike." Marsh also reported that the chiefs were "distressed" at the "disobedience of a great portion of the Mikasuky tribe who had left the reservation and seemed determined not to return. Several of the chiefs," March reported "have been traveling night and day in search of the abandoned wretches, for the purpose of persuading them to return, while their own families, have been starving at home. . . . The chiefs have been informed of the outrages committed by their people, and that they could expect no favors to be extended to them by the government until the offenders were given up."[35]

That winter and spring DuVal labored almost exclusively by himself on Indian and civil affairs. Humphreys, the Indian agent, was gone, and more than a year earlier Secretary Walton had left the capital for Key West to collect monies in his capacity as territorial treasurer. Since that time DuVal had received no word from him, and he was forced to report the situation to both President Adams and the territorial delegate, Joseph White, on January 2. "I have no personal dislike to Col. Walton and never had any personal difficulties with him and it is painful to me to make this presentation," DuVal wrote to the president, "but he ought to be removed. I shall not avoid my duty for fear of censure from any man, nor will I let my private wishes and feelings turn me aside from the interest of the territory over which I have the honor to preside." Unknown to DuVal was the fact that Walton, in Baltimore, had already submitted his resignation. It would be spring before a replacement could assist the governor.[36] Of even greater concern to DuVal, he had learned recently that he was responsible for monies that Walton had administered while DuVal was out of the territory. As he had earlier complained to Secretary Southard, "If I was the poorest fool on earth I could not believe that I am in any manner responsible for money that never came to my hands and which was transmitted to an officer who during my absence under the organizing act of this Territory possessed all the power of the governor. But such is the doctrine maintained by the Department, that I am to account for all moneys sent to the late acting governor."[37]

Even as he labored alone, DuVal continued to receive directives from Washington: he was to personally award the five Apalachicola chiefs medals "as a token of the friendship of their Great Father" in recognition of their service under Captain Dade. He was also to oversee the survey of the Indian boundary extension: "As you have been appointed to examine the Country, it was reasonable to suppose you could best fix" the boundary "so as to avoid coming in contact, as far as possible, with the settlements of the Whites. . . . Give the Indians a *sufficiency*, and avoid as far as possible embracing lands settled by Individuals." DuVal must have wondered how long it would take before any work could go forward, as the official hastened to add that no remittances could be made until "your returns are received, and settlement made on the books of the Territory. This, I entreat you not to interpret into any implication of integrity. Every confidence is felt in you on that score—but the regulations of the Department demand it."[38]

Meanwhile, General Edmund P. Gaines and Colonel Duncan Clinch set out from Pensacola by boat to Tampa Bay to make a personal investigation of the Indian situation. The officers traveled though the Indian country and frontier settlements to Tallahassee and St. Marks, returning by boat to Pensacola. Their journey of one month convinced them that there was no conspiracy among the Creeks and Seminoles. The recent outbreaks in their view were "acts of a few desperate Outlaws, three of whom it is believed have already atoned for their crimes, and efforts are making to have the others taken and brought to justice." Clinch and Gaines were confident that the troops they had stationed at strategic points would give protection and "quiet apprehensions of the Settlements on the Frontiers of Georgia and Florida."[39]

If the Crisis of 1826–1827 seemed over, DuVal's problems with the War Department seemed to get worse and worse with each passing month. If that department would not treat him fairly, he told McKenney, he would seek recourse to the attorney general, the president, or the Congress. The Chaires and Crupper situations were still in dispute. The past year's emergencies had forced the governor to put off Chaires with a promise to pay later. When Chaires complained to the government that he had not been paid for cattle purchased in 1824, McKenney responded that the government had delivered the funds for DuVal's disbursement but that the governor had seen fit to use the money for other purposes.[40] DuVal also complained to McKenney that a lack of funds adequate to operate the Indian Agency had induced subagent Marsh, the agency's blacksmith and its interpreter, to resign. "I apprehend it will be impossible under the new regulations . . . to fill the vacancies." In view of Marsh's resignation, DuVal requested that an officer at Tampa Bay be appointed until another subagent could be appointed. In the emergency DuVal had ordered Captain Burch to purchase six thousand bushels of corn in New Orleans, and it would arrive in Tampa Bay at any moment.[41]

Meanwhile, correspondence among DuVal, Humphreys, and authorities in Washington indicate that DuVal and the agent, only recently returned, had differing views of current Indian policy. Humphreys wrote to DuVal soon after he returned to his agency that he found that the "condition of the Indians of this nation is one of great suffering from hunger." There was not "at this moment . . . in the whole nation a bushel of corn, or any adequate substitute for it." Moreover, whites had used the excuse of the "recent disturbances" to take the Indians' guns, and thus they could no longer hunt. "Their appearance is sufficient to excite the commiseration of the hardest heart." Humphreys admitted the need to apprehend the culprits in the Aucilla killings but deplored the "necessity . . . of parading of military detachments through the country in warlike fashion in a time of peace." The evils of this policy, he contended, were plain for anyone to see. "Any man who reads the history of this inglorious war and its effects, will learn and see much which, as an American, a member of a nation calling itself Christian, he must blush at. . . . I find it a duty to say to you, that upon the subject of this treatment of the Indians, the chiefs exhibit great feeling. 'We cannot understand,' they say 'why unoffending men, and helpless women and children, should be made to suffer for the faults of a few turbulent spirits, whose bad deeds the nation does not justify.'"[42]

Humphreys forwarded these complaints to Washington and further decried a law passed by the recent legislative council allowing settlers to whip Indians found outside the reservation. Humphreys also said he suspected that the Carr killing was in part retaliation for such a whipping. Humphreys complained of the law to authorities in Washington, who in turn appealed to DuVal to use his influence to see that the law was not enforced. "I am directed to state," stated McKenney, "that it is hoped under the present state of excitement and the wretchedness of these people, that this act will not be enforced. It can hardly be conceived that the Indians would submit to the chastisement contemplated by the act, without seeking to be revenged. Out of this, feeble as they are, and for that very reason appealing to the sympathies of the Government and people, not of Florida only but of the U. States—they might afflict the citizens of the Territory, in the destruction of many lives, whilst the *occasion* of their excitement and revenge might make it less a matter of concern with every body." DuVal responded that to his knowledge the law "has never been executed in any instance . . . by any Citizen in the Territory" but operated mainly as a deterrent. He admitted that some of the Indians had flogged recalcitrant members of their own tribe and had even asked the white authorities to have it done, but "this was never done, but the law is well Calculated to restrain the bad Indians within their limits. They are apprised of it, and so far, without pressing its execution it has had the effect intended." DuVal also regretted that the "Agent without knowing the facts (for he has but recently returned to Florida) should have stated that the late murder near Tallahassee was occasioned by the head of the family having whipped an Indians to death." This he pronounced an "idle rumor," and he added that the "Agent has suffered his feelings to mislead his judgement and really has mistaken the facts. I hesitate not to aver, that the Citizens of Florida have evinced more good, humane, feeling, patience, and forbearing towards the Indian under severe loss and frequent insult than I ever witnessed in any frontier Country. These people have been indulged so much that they become wanton and insolent. Fed at every white man's house they called, they mistook humanity for fear, and for kindness and hospitality paid them by robbing their houses and fields and killing their Cattle. The great body of the nation has always behaved properly; but it can be expected, when the Seminole nation is formed in part of outlaws of the Surrounding tribes, that such men can be governed in any other manner than by force." Finally, DuVal indignantly rejected any suggestion that his policies lacked moral sanction. "I have never been considered as deficient in humanity—No man in my situation ever took more pains or trouble than myself to protect and Civilize those unfortunate people; but long experience had satisfied me that too much kindness is as fatal to their happiness as too much severity. There is no Consideration that could induce me to suffer the Indians to be cruelly treated—I owe it to the Character of my Government to say nothing of my own, to see them justly And Kindly treated. I hope all further difficulties are at an end—the feeling of hostility on the part of Our Citizens is fast subsiding."⁴³

As summer began, surveys of the Indian boundary to include the Big Swamp were completed. The Indians had been pushed back across the Suwannee. As Colonel Clinch explained, the "prompt and energetic measures" of Dade and his other officers "have in great measure quieted the fears & apprehensions of most of the inhabitants" near the Indian Agency. Even so, the commander insisted "in the strongest terms" that two companies should be garrisoned in the area because it was "in the immediate vicinity of the largest number of the Florida Indians, and between them and the white inhabitants."⁴⁴ The territorial delegate, Joseph White, made a personal inspection of the agency. He joined DuVal and others in the opinion that the Indians must be removed west of the Mississippi. The delegate argued that it was a mistake to give the Indians the four million acres allotted to them by the Moultrie Creek treaty. The land, he claimed was "better fixed for sugar and cotton than any in the Union" and was wasted on the Indians, who had no ability to cultivate the land. Moreover, with game exhausted, the Indians were driven to "depredations on the cattle of the whites, who by retaliation would render bloodshed," which would lead to "their utter extermination." White contrasted this situation with what was transpiring west of the Suwannee. That section was "filling with emigrants from every portion of the union—Forests falling before the axe of industry and fields of cotton blooming where they stood—I will shew you a city, in the place of a wigwam—and a press inculcating the mild principles of republicanism, where the war whoop was lately heard. And, why is this? The land claims have been adjusted, and savages expelled—it needs no comment."⁴⁵

White even resuscitated fears that in the event of invasion Indians might support the foe as they had before. "Sir, such men as Nicols and Ambrister and Arbuthnot aided by the British arms and British gold operating savage cupidity would revolutionize East Florida and massacre the whites before the people of Georgia could hear of the danger." A memorial to Congress from the legislative council perhaps summarized settlers' sentiments more cogently. "The vigilance of our Governor and the promptness of our militia have for the present checked [Indian] outrages, and in some degree quieted the fears of our citizens, but at what time, and in what place, the bent bow will let slip its arrow, the blood of our citizens, will we fear, soon proclaim." The Indians, they insisted, must be concentrated within their boundary "and talks immediately commence to send them west."⁴⁶

If the Indians had just complaints against their treatment, DuVal understood that he could not allow continued outrages by a few to go unchecked. He understood that the protection and safety of the settlements had to be his first priority. Not only was East Florida at risk, but Middle Florida was also vulnerable. Unless the region around the territorial capital was protected from Indian depredations, the territory would never reach its potential. DuVal's most important priority was to ensure safe conditions for surveying and road-building teams. If it was this very activity that triggered Indian resistance, then so be it. As DuVal understood his duty, paving the way for white settlement and establishing civil government was his primary responsibility. DuVal's own moral sense required that he treat Indians in as humane a way as he could, but they could not be allowed to stand in the way of white settlement. In the months ahead, in the face of very little assistance from Washington or from those around him, DuVal would try his best to reconcile these two competing interests. But at every turn it was Indians who lost out in the bargain.

CHAPTER 8

"I have health, activity, good spirits, and a small share of *Perserverity*"

On December 12, 1826, Governor William P. DuVal addressed the Florida legislative council on the occasion of its second meeting in Tallahassee. The governor congratulated the council for being the first body elected by the people of Florida. Thus the members had the duty to exert their "energy and wisdom" upon their legislation for the good of themselves and their posterity. Of the territory's prospects, DuVal argued, "there is no Section of the Union that combines so many advantages as Florida." Farmers were producing corn, cotton, rice, and sugar cane, and he declared that the "fisheries on our shores are decidedly the best in the South." DuVal called attention to the "confused, uncertain, and defective state of our laws." Among his recommendations were that the laws be codified and that the superior courts be vested with jurisdiction over sheriffs, collectors, and other officers whose accounts were in arrears. DuVal also urged that more superior courts be created, observing that not all counties had them and that settlers often had to travel more than seventy or eighty miles to attend court. The militia also needed attention. The governor closed with the promise to assist the body in its work in "promoting the interests of our infant country."[1]

The legislative session coincided with a much more important event, a scheduled sale of public lands. Robert Gamble of Richmond joined other expectant migrants in the capital, but postponement of the sale provided him with a good opportunity to thoroughly explore the area and to sample its social life. "I was at a Ball last night given by the Legislature of this territory," he wrote to a relative. "The company was much superior to the expectation I had formed & would have been [on a par] with any country [town] in Va, indeed [I saw] many highly respectable & well bred ladies as any place can boast of. . . . I am in the family of Governor DuVal who would not receive a refusal you know him . . . his family are very agreeable."²

The legislative council met in a village that was only two years old. From all accounts the territorial capital resembled a rough frontier outpost whose inhabitants displayed a penchant for violence. In 1827 Ralph Waldo Emerson visited St. Augustine but did not make the two-hundred-mile trek to Tallahassee. Even so, he heard many uncomplimentary descriptions of the town. He learned that Tallahassee was a "grotesque place . . . settled by public officers, land speculators & desperadoes. [It was a place of] much club law & little other." Governor DuVal, he was told, was the "button on which all things are hung." The Leon County grand jury in its fall 1827 session confirmed the picture when it lamented that a "horrible state of things has existed" in Tallahassee for some time. "The most flagrant breaches of the laws have taken place. The civil authorities have in many instances been set at defiance; and most riotous, immoral, and disorderly proceedings have taken place."³ Years later DuVal's son John Crittenden provided a description of Tallahassee when he first arrived. "When I first saw it there were perhaps fifteen or twenty families in the place, congregated around the 'Public Square'. . . the unbroken wilderness still extended in every direction. Deer, panther, and other wild animals were not infrequently killed within the 'Corporate Bounds,' one of the largest panthers I ever saw, was killed between the town and the 'Cascade.'" As DuVal's son recalled, there were only three "'blazed roads', connecting the City with the outside world—one going east to St. Augustine, one west to Pensacola, and one to St. Marks on the Gulf. No other roads traversed the country at the time, unless the numerous Indians trails could be designated as such."⁴

While DuVal's son recalled the territorial capital as an exciting place, Tallahassee presented a none-too-inviting appearance to Laura Wirt Randall of Richmond when she first arrived in the fall of 1827. "Tallahassee is a miserable looking place certainly," she wrote to her father, the sitting attorney general of the United States and man who had already invested heavily in Middle Florida cotton lands. "I expected it to be merely a village, but I thought it w'd have a more agreeable appearance." There were three taverns and a few frame houses, but "they as well as the huts composing most of the rest of the town look old from not having been painted. I see no stores—at least none that look like such—nor anything else that w'd make it look like a town." She and her husband took up temporary residence in a tavern, of which she complained, "They understand nothing of comfort or cleanliness in this tavern, whilst it is the best in the place, we continue to use our own sheets & towels. At [the] table coffee is served in a *tea—pot &* the cooking *inedible*—I scarcely can prevail on myself, hungry as I may be, to taste the burnt up & dirty food before me."⁵ And to a friend Laura Wirt Randall complained that "Tallahassee is no larger than your Maryville, and the houses there are

Legislative Council Meeting House, Tallahassee. From Francis Comte de Castelnau, *Vues et Souvenirs de l'Amérique du Nord*. Courtesy of State Archives of Florida.

palaces compared with these. The Governor, himself, lives in a log house, and many families [live] in cabins of *one room*."[6]

By 1827 the DuVal family had lived in the territorial capital for nearly one year in the house south of town, overlooking the cascade. One year earlier DuVal had written to Samuel Southard that the Florida climate had done wonders for Nancy's poor health. "Since her removal to Florida last fall, she was recovered. We have now another daughter, Miss Florida after our interval of more than six years—so a baby is a new thing with me at present. I thank God he has preserved eight of nine which he has blessed me with & I would feel yet more grateful if we could have 20 sons, and Ten daughters in addition."[7]

In 1827 William and Nancy DuVal were both forty-three years old and had a full house of children and dependents. That year the household included three sons, Burr Harrison (18), Thomas Howard (14), and John Crittenden (11), and five daughters, Marcia (16), Elizabeth (12), Mary (8), Laura (7), and tiny Florida (1), the couple's last child, born only days after the family arrived in the territory. Also in the house was Nancy's sister Mary "Polly" Hynes, who joined the family when it relocated from Kentucky to Florida.[8] The governor took great joy in his sons' diversions and often rode by their fort, making "official inspections" on his short trips through the woods while riding to and from town.⁹

Other DuVal relations came to Florida as well. In 1827 William's brother John brought his family to Tallahassee. Residing for a time in his brother's eight-room house, John DuVal eventually established a plantation two miles north of Tallahassee, where he planted sugar cane.¹⁰ After John was admitted to the bar, on October 1, the Tallahassee *Florida Advocate* announced that he would practice law in Leon and surrounding counties.¹¹ Later he would become city commissioner. The governor's cousin Samuel DuVal arrived in 1830.¹² Another nephew, DuVal's sister Lucy's son, Dr. William Price, had migrated to Tallahassee several years earlier. The DuVal home became a focal point in the community for young and old. Tiger Tail and other Indians visited the house on a regular basis, as did any number of civil and military officials. DuVal's responsibility to entertain, feed, and sometimes house visitors was substantial and must have caused financial and physical strain on the governor and Nancy.

With a house full of children, overnight guests, and officials of various kinds, the DuVal home must have been chaotic at times. The custom for all new migrants (especially those from the Old Dominion) was to call first at the governor's house. Not long after they arrived in Tallahassee, Laura Wirt Randall, the young bride of newly appointed U.S. Middle District judge Thomas Randall, called on the DuVal home before heading out to the couple's one-thousand-acre Jefferson County plantation site. She may have known that the governor had warmly endorsed her husband's appointment.¹³ She was determined to make a good first impression. But as the spoiled daughter of U.S. attorney general William Wirt and the niece of Robert and John Gamble, Laura was used to refinements unavailable anywhere in Florida, even the territorial capital. (As a child she had lived in DuVal's father's former home on Richmond's Shockhoe Hill.) Laura Randall's first impression of Florida's First Lady was unfavorable. Randall thought Mrs. DuVal a "sharp-featured, sharp-spoken lady—she does not look very amiable—tho' she rec'd me kindly."¹⁴

She was particularly unprepared for Nancy DuVal's indifferent table settings. After a visit to the DuVals' home in October 1827, Laura Randall wrote to her mother that Mrs. DuVal was a "bad house-keeper." There was "no white sugar for tea, & no coffee for their Brown Sugar, as they might have had in place if they had been as judicious house-keepers as I *intend to be*." The butter was carelessly laid about, the cakes came in cold, and the bread was like lead. Laura Randall also found Mrs. DuVal a "course woman. She opened her coarse dirty brown bosom & suckled her child before us all, without the least ceremony." To Randall the house was chaotic. The governor was in Washington, his brother's family were temporary residents, dirty children were running about, and "Miss Marcia" (who she later admitted was "quite a pretty girl") and a friend were "romping and squealing instead of entertaining us."¹⁵

John Gratton Gamble.
Courtesy of State
Archives of Florida.

Though her father and her husband were Governor DuVal's friends and associated on many levels (these included frequent visits to Randall's Jefferson County plantation, Belmont), Laura Randall's first impression of the DuVals remained unchanged. To her they were rustics in a crude frontier environment. In subsequent correspondence to her mother in Baltimore, she referred to them as the "rough, inhospitable *don't care* Duvalls." To her sister Randall admitted that the DuVals had "sons that w'd do for your Beaux—& daughters about your age—But they are very coarse sun burnt children dressed in dirty Virginia cloth frocks & not at all interesting."[16]

Elizabeth Brown, who, at eleven years old, arrived in Tallahassee from Virginia one year after the DuVal family arrived, was a frequent visitor to the household and provides one of the best descriptions of the DuVal house. "Lizzie" Brown's father, Thomas, a Richmond native, rented a house next to the DuVals. "Then there was no house nearer than Governor DuVal's which stood high up on the hill just above the spring where the Baptists . . . baptized," Lizzie Brown recalled. "Just below us was 'The Cascade,' a beautiful fall of water, a part of the Augustine Branch. The Cascade was surrounded by a beautiful grove of oaks and magnolias. It was a lovely spot and quite a resort for the young people." Of her nearest

Thomas Brown, ca. 1820s. Courtesy of State Archives of Florida.

neighbor, Governor DuVal, Brown remembered that he was "one of the most genial and amusing men I ever met. He was a true old Kentucky gentleman, and [his] house [was] the headquarters for all social meetings." Brown fondly remembered DuVal's two "grown daughters, Miss Elizabeth and Marcia, [and] Mary and Laura [who were] girls about the age of my sister Mary and I. . . . Miss Elizabeth and Miss Marcia were very beautiful and great belles in those early days" and had many suitors.[17]

As the community began to take shape, William and Nancy assumed leadership roles in social and public affairs in the new territorial capital. In April 1826 DuVal joined Judge Augustus Woodward, James Gadsden, Achille Murat, Bird Willis, Turbott Betton, and William Allison McRea in forming the Florida Institute of Agriculture, Antiquities, and Science in Tallahassee. Fourth of July celebrations were always festive occasions, and preparations for such festivities were made months in advance. That year Tallahasseans celebrated the fiftieth anniversary of the Declaration of Independence "with a degree of splendor suitable to the occasion and highly creditable to the citizens of Tallahassee and vicinity." (As DuVal led the processional from the north side of the capitol square to the meetinghouse, he had no knowledge that the Declaration's author and his father's friend Thomas Jefferson was breathing his last breath at Monticello.) Even so, the Declaration was read, orations were delivered, "Hail Columbia" was struck up, and the processional of more than 150 people went to the arbor, "where a splendid Barbecue" took place. After the meal toasts began, DuVal made a toast to "General Andrew Jackson." An unnamed participant honored DuVal with the following tribute: "The Governor of this Territory, his prudence and energy located this spot as the capital of Florida, may his anticipations be realized."[18]

As DuVal understood it, his primary responsibility as governor was to lead in the establishment of civil government for the territory. DuVal felt that his duty as governor was to ensure that the Territory of Florida reached its full potential—and for the governor that meant the establishment of a prosperous slave-based plantation economy. Thus Florida lands must be surveyed and put up for sale as soon as possible. The governor collaborated closely with Robert Butler, Richard K. Call, and George T. Ward, who served as surveyor general, collector of the public monies, and head of the land office, respectively. Richard C. Allen was also among this circle of insiders. DuVal did everything he could to promote migration and settlement in the new territory.

The Lafayette Grant had the effect of publicizing the desirability of Middle Florida lands. And DuVal's correspondence with the famous Frenchman—which found its way into print—helped spread the word about the attractiveness and availability of the land.[19] DuVal was eager to make sure that his friends, especially those who were well connected, did not miss the opportunities that were developing. For example, he wrote to Navy Secretary Samuel Southard that "this country is settling very rapidly by intelligent and wealthy people. I wish you would take the advice I gave you some time past and purchase a Section or two of good sugar lands in this region." Major Ward, he told Southard, would be in Washington soon, and he was sure the land registrar would be able to assist him in the purpose. "Should you wish me to act for you, I will do so with great satisfaction for 'Old Lang Sine.'"[20]

DuVal understood that his family's well-being depended on his taking advantage of the opportunities offered by the new lands of Middle Florida. Lamenting the fact that his lack of funds prevented him from purchasing good lands, he offered to go into partnership with Southard if the secretary, who had already expressed interest in the Lafayette tract, wanted to forward the cash. "I have made nothing by my removal to Florida," he wrote. "I am poor and my family is large. My salary is a bare support ten years hence should I retain my office I should be quite poor as now. If you determine to establish a plantation in this country I would most willingly join you and take the exclusive management—I have not the funds to procure the force requisite and must endeavor to unite with some friend that has." DuVal offered to manage the entire operation himself and perhaps resign his office to devote himself fully to "raising Sugar & Cotton. . . . I am convinced," he wrote Southard, "that more can be cirtainly made in this country by planting than in any other part of the United States and at my time of life with a large family my exertions should be turned to my private affairs."[21]

Over the past year and a half DuVal had cultivated approximately eighty acres surrounding his homestead. Reviewing his present crop as a way to demonstrate the potential to Southard, DuVal noted, "I have more than an acre in Sugar cane, as fine as ever was seen in the United States of its age. This will plant this fall 15 acres." DuVal had fifty acres of corn, seven acres of sweet potatoes, four acres of rice. His crops had been "kept in fine order, with only three men and two ploughs—fifteen acres of the land was also cleared, and fenced during last winter by the same hands. My slaves, for I have but 4 are clothed and fed well and never have received a blow; they are content, and fat, much more so than their master." Again alluding to the Lafayette township, DuVal mentioned that he "hoped to obtain a half a section for my own residence, at a fair price, for otherwise I can not purchase, for poverty is a mighty destroyer of hope. I am therefore at your service to establish a first rate plantation and if I am engaged in it, I will be ranked as a first rate planter and manager. It is not my disposition and character to lag behind in any thing I undertake—the greatest objection to forming such a partnership as I propose, is that, you must trust me largely in the business. If I do not in my old age turn rascal you will make money. If I do tell the devil to cook me after his own fashion."[22]

Offering up a more specific cause for his current financial embarrassment, DuVal explained to Southard that he had lost his fortune because of the "revolutions" that had taken place in Kentucky while he was in Florida. He had lost more than $17,000 because he had signed on as a security for friends. To meet the obligations, he had sold off one-third of his property. "I just had enough to remove my family here and am now a poor happy fellow who like many other wise men have sworn never to be security for any man again." DuVal speculated that if not for this mistake he would be worth $70,000. "I have no idea however of grieving about a loss—which my best exertions alone can repair. I have health, activity, good spirits, and small share of *Perseverity*. This, if health continues, will take me through great difficulties. If you have no intention to join me, could you please procure me a partner such as you would have yourself."[23]

Everyone, especially the governor, understood that the continuing threat from Indian attacks discouraged settlement. James Gadsden, John Bellamy, and Benjamin Chaires—who had established large plantations west of Tallahassee—encouraged DuVal to take a hard line with the Indians. DuVal understood that Florida's future rested on a secure environment for settlement. Given the challenges and the realities with which DuVal and others were faced, there was only one sure path to economic success in the Old Southwest, and that was through extracting wealth from the rich soils. The only way to achieve that was through slave labor. But the Indians were in the way. They had to be subdued and eventually removed west of the Mississippi.

Included among some of the migrants to the territorial capital who did not fit DuVal's grandiose vision of a flourishing slave-based plantation economy for Middle Florida were DuVal's friend the free black Antonio Proctor and his son George. Toney Proctor first came to Tallahassee in 1824 as a messenger, bringing important documents from East Florida on Indian affairs to the governor.[24] DuVal and William Simmons had befriended Toney and his young son George, using their influence to protect them from the uncertainties free blacks experienced in the slave South. Toney offered valuable assistance in DuVal's work with Indians affairs, but the color of his skin put him at peril in the territory. About 1826, records show that young George was apprenticed to a carpenter in St. Augustine who subsequently carried him to Tallahassee. While Toney remained in St. Augustine, the young man fell under the governor's watchful eye.[25]

Advertisements for Florida lands for sale appeared in published sources throughout the nation. For example, the Washington *Daily National Journal* advertised that Richard C. Allen and Company was "prepared with special information relative to the quality and extent of the most valuable lands, which may be offered for sale by the Government, or by individuals." The firm announced that it would "handle all business" relating to the purchase of land and any other dealings "for the benefit of early settlers in Florida."[26] More and more planters were coming to Middle Florida to inspect lands in preparation for migration to the territory. For example, in the winter of 1826, Lizzie Brown's father, Thomas Brown, a Virginia planter from the Richmond area, personally visited Tallahassee with the intention of permanently relocating. A year and a half later, Brown returned with his family and 144 slaves after traveling eight hundred miles in caravan.[27] Others, including the Eppes, Willis, Gamble, Wirt, Parkhill, Randolph, Brockenbrough, and Cabell families, also left the Old Dominion for the new Florida Territory, and DuVal often advised them on land purchases.[28] Achille Murat, a descendant of Napoleon Bonaparte and a man DuVal had met in St. Augustine, also migrated to the area. Coming also were the Branch, Bradford, and Croom families from North Carolina and the Alstons from South Carolina and Georgia.[29] DuVal already knew many of these families. Several new migrants were fortunate to enjoy federal appointments with salaries that could help tide their families over in their first few years in the territory.

Like all newcomers to new places, these migrants had past familial and political networks that they brought with them, creating factions that reproduced themselves in the new territory. DuVal was careful to keep his ties to the Virginia Dynasty strong. DuVal corresponded frequently with James Madison regarding his nephew Edgar Macon and other Virginians planning to migrate to Florida. In the fall of 1826, he wrote to the former president, promising to treat Macon "like a son." "So far as my support and limited influence could be exercised . . . for his advantage and so long as I continue in my present position he shall find me ready to render him any service in my power." DuVal told the former president that he looked forward to seeing Macon soon, as "You may have learned that the People have elected him a member of our council."³⁰

Madison thanked the governor for his solicitous attention to his relative and also asked DuVal to be on the lookout for Francis Eppes, Thomas Jefferson's grandson, who would soon visit the area. Macon attended the legislative session, and DuVal reported to Madison that the young Virginian visited his house every day. DuVal felt compelled to confide to Madison that the continued persecutions and pressure had led Macon down a path to "certain destruction." Colonel Macon had during the past winter "indulged too freely at the festive board, and altho no habit of intemperance is confirmed, to me it is obvious it will as such, if he remains in the South. I never have in any part of the Union seen so much dissipation as in the South." He urged Madison to see to it that he, Philip Barbour, and his other "friends recall him to Virginia. . . . I hope you will excuse me for writing frankly on this subject," DuVal wrote Madison, "but the deep interest and ardent desire I feel in the success and happiness of Col. Macon could only tempt me to address you on a subject so delicate. I am sure if he was apprised of the liberty I have taken with him, he would perhaps highly resent it, but I cannot consent to be silent when the happiness of his family, his success and character, may all be destroyed." Macon's stay in Tallahassee was brief. After the legislative session he bought an interest in the Tallahassee *Florida Intelligencer* (possibly in anticipation of winning a coveted printing contract under DuVal's favor). He changed the paper's name to the *Florida Advocate* but held the paper for only a few months before migrating to and dying, at the age of twenty-seven, in Key West.³¹

As early as 1826, political factions had already emerged when DuVal called out the first-ever elections to the legislative council.³² Factions in Florida grew out of from sectional, familial, and political ties but were strengthened and exacerbated by personalities and economic considerations. In St. Augustine, for example, Joseph Smith, John Rodman, and DuVal's old enemy Alexander Hamilton Jr. were Northerners and clashed with Macon and others over legal cases, particularly the procedure for adjusting Spanish land grants. Macon had even worked with Richard Keith Call to have Judge Smith removed. It will be recalled that DuVal had also clashed with the New Yorkers while in St. Augustine. The degree to which DuVal may have participated in the scheme to remove Smith is uncertain. But DuVal could have been expected to defend Macon against Smith and others, particularly when it is understood that Smith, Rodman, and Hamilton had questioned the governor's previous actions as judge and land commissioner in that quarter.³³

The most potent political force to burst on the scene to challenge DuVal and the Nucleus—the land office crowd, composed of Call, Butler, Ward, Gadsden, and other appointees who owed their positions to the political coat tails of Old Hickory—in the early years of the territory was Joseph M. White. Appointed to the first legislative council, White gained a reputation as a skilled lawyer and served as a land commissioner, before defeating James Gadsden and Joseph Hernandez in the race for territorial delegate in 1825. DuVal had known White slightly in Kentucky and had even recommended the lawyer for various federal posts. White's close affiliation with Henry Clay and John Quincy Adams, his strong appeal to voters, his legal sparring with Richard Keith Call, and the inevitable rivalry between strong personalities resulted in conflict (both verbal and physical) with Call. Even before Old Hickory's election in 1828, White was clearly identified as the leader of the anti-Jacksonians in Florida. Yet in November 1826 he was still attempting to establish a cordial relationship with Jackson. Call warned Jackson not to be misled by this deception. Had not White's own father-in-law, former Kentucky governor John Adair, and the General clashed in the past over Adair's participation in the Battle of New Orleans? White, Call reported, pretended to be Jackson's friend when he thought it beneficial to him. "I know this man perfectly, intimately, and you may depend on it a more unprincipled fellow never lived. He is plausible, and will pass well among strangers but when known will be held in contempt by all honorable and intelligent men." Call told Jackson that he looked forward to sending his wife and young daughter with the "DuVals for a visit to the Hermitage" in the spring. In the upcoming years White battled Call in the courts, in the newspapers, and in the streets.[34]

DuVal could be expected to side with Call in any controversy with White. And he did, especially once the territorial delegate might question him or fail, in DuVal's mind, to offer adequate support for his official actions. Hints of conflict arose between the governor and the delegate in November 1826 when the two exchanged words over the placement of an asylum for the deaf and dumb in Jackson County.[35] But it was DuVal's membership in the political grouping the Nucleus that ensured that White and the governor would be at odds. The Nucleus was viewed then as it is now—as a "clique" of grasping land office officials, mostly from Tennessee and Kentucky, who were intent on obtaining the best lands and political offices for themselves and their friends. Whether or not this description fit, DuVal was associated with the group, even though he tried to steer an independent course. The ascendancy of the Nucleus was ensured as long as Andrew Jackson exerted influence. Yet White's supporters effectively attacked the Nucleus as a corrupt combination of rich, politically entrenched operatives determined to favor speculators and large planters over actual settlers. Though White himself was one of Florida's largest planters and slaveholders, it was an effective strategy that would keep him in office until 1837.[36]

As had been already noted, DuVal's relationship with the Adams administration was often strained, especially his relationships with Secretary of War Barbour and, of course, with his nemesis, Secretary of State Henry Clay. Complaining of his persecution by the War Department and offering his opinions of Adams's cabinet to Navy Secretary Samuel Southard, DuVal declared, "I have had so many occasions to see, that my conduct by some of the departments never will be approved." Even so, "he was determined to bring matters to issue. . . . You know my opinion of Mr. Clay and that long before you ever were in office I have no reason to change that opinion and as to Mr. Barbour, he is just as well fitted for is station as a man [who] cannot write is fitted for secretary of state. Mr. McLean and yourself are the only good appointments that Mr. Adams has made for the departments and I told Mr. Adams so when I was last in the City. Mr. Clay is the star ascendant in the cabinet. He is providing well for all his devoted friends in the West, all of whom were the bitter enemies of Mr. Adams. . . . I now predict that Mr. Clay will either blow up the administration or blow himself up—the later is perhaps the most probable, as he is backed by the war chief. . . . I am satisfied that from the captain's course pursued against me that the object of these gentlemen is to harass me out of my office. I shall let the President act on this subject—if he acts for himself I need not fear if he does not I will of course resign. I am poor and have made great sacrifices to remove my family to Florida but I will go to the Gulph and fish for their support before I will do any thing that may be calculated to give me a mean opinion of myself." DuVal assured Southard that he was not writing to the secretary to solicit any opinion on these subjects. "Your situation forbids this and it would lessen you in my estimation were you to act otherwise so long as you are one of the cabinet. But my own views and opinions I will express without reserve. I shall and am now preparing for the worst that can happen to me and happen when it may I return to Kentucky for here I can not live without some income." Finally, on Adams and the future DuVal confided to Southard, "I like Calhoun and I am a decided friend of Genl. Jackson and I do not give up my old friends for those who may chance to hold the power. In saying this I have no personal feeling inimical to the President. I have ever found him friendly and kind to me, but I do think—as they say in the West—'He is in a bad fix,' with Mr. Clay on one side & Barbour on the other."[37]

Given DuVal's tendency to speak his mind, it was perhaps inevitable that rumors or accusations would arise about him, alleging that he was working against the administration, secretly aiding Jackson men at the expense of the administration, or, as he denied to Southard, "abusing" Adams. Such were the political dynamics of the "Futile Administration," especially for those who, like DuVal, held appointments from Monroe but who had supported Jackson in 1824 and clearly favored the General in the next election. The more he tried to convince members of Adams's administration that his personal preferences for Jackson made no difference in his administration of the Florida Territory, the deeper he seemed to fall into the trap. "What unprincipled fellow could have made such a statement" that he had abused Adams? "I hope I may discover. I never uttered such an expression disrespectful of Mr. Adams in my life," he insisted. "I have no doubt that false statements have been made in relation to my acts & conduct by base and malicious men here but I will unmask them."[38]

By that time yet another awkward situation had emerged that threatened to cause DuVal problems. In June 1826 Samuel Southard attended a party in his wife's hometown of Fredericksburg, Virginia. Present were a number of dignitaries, including former president Monroe. The conversations and the liquor flowed until someone mentioned that Andrew Jackson's victory at New Orleans entitled him the right to seek the presidency. Southard responded that it was possible that Jackson had received too much credit for singlehandedly defeating the British and reminded the gathering that Monroe was serving as secretary of state at the time and had never been given enough credit for his defense of city. The statement was interpreted as a slight against Jackson, and for the next year and a half tension escalated. Soon Jackson's friends, the newspapers, and the General himself were demanding satisfaction. DuVal no doubt knew of the situation and was not eager to mention it. The event simmered for months. Some even predicted the possibility of a duel. Even as he understood that Southard and Wirt were working arduously for Adams and against Jackson, DuVal tried to maintain his friendship with both men.[39]

As the executive of the territory DuVal had the power to shape the political leadership at the county level in the early years of the territory, and he accomplished this primarily through the appointive power. As governor DuVal had the authority to appoint nearly every county officeholder, including sheriffs, county judges, clerks of the county court, justices of the peace, coroners, surveyors, and notaries public. He also appointed officers in seven regiments of the territorial militia. In 1827, for example, DuVal appointed 149 men to positions in the county government in thirteen counties and twenty-one officers in the militia.[40] Even after most county offices became elective, in 1829, he still retained substantial appointive power. Such powers allowed DuVal to reward loyal followers and to punish those who took other positions or supported anti-Jacksonian candidates, of whom Joseph White was the primary leader. Those not favored with appointments could and would charge that DuVal was building up a cadre of loyal supporters against the people's consent. Charges that the governor was undemocratically filling the ranks of officeholders with cronies were inevitable.

As summer 1827 approached, William P. DuVal faced attacks from several quarters. Agnonides, a correspondent to a St. Augustine newspaper, proclaimed that the governor obviously wanted to be reappointed. He was planning a trip to Washington, the writer noted, saying that it ought to be the "right of the citizens to review the past in reference to him, and to see, whether it would not be right to ask the President to 'take him from us.'" The correspondent recounted DuVal's undistinguished career as judge, suggesting that his appointment came because of his "peculiar talent in making stump orations" in Kentucky.[41] Agnonides also questioned DuVal's War of 1812 service and his effectiveness as a member of Congress. More serious charges against DuVal came from Publicus, who reported that Joseph White, the territorial delegate, would prefer charges against DuVal in Washington. The correspondent charged that DuVal had given the contract to print the laws to someone in whom he had a financial interest. William Hasell Hunt, editor of the Pensacola *Gazette,* agreed with Publicus and offered to provide White with "abundant proofs" of DuVal's malfeasance. "We, with Publicus, think that it will be readily admitted that, it is the duty of the Delegate to Congress to look properly into it." DuVal, the editor continued, had appointed incompetent men and was guilty of the most "barefaced and shameful instance of favoritism and misrule." There were also "innuendoes" of mismanagement in Indian affairs, and Hunt demanded that more light be shed on that aspect of the governor's duties. Hunt was clearly frustrated by his inability to win the contract to print the territorial laws. Whether or not his charges could be substantiated, it was almost inevitable that charges of this sort would be brought against the executive. The reality was that factions existed in territorial Florida and that DuVal led the faction that was in the position to reward his friends with favors.[42]

When DuVal read these charges in Florida's two principal newspapers, he immediately attributed the attacks to his two nemeses, Joseph White and Judge Joseph Smith. Indeed, as he explained to Samuel Southard, White had gained control of the Pensacola *Gazette* and Smith the *Herald*. DuVal poured out vitriol toward the two men. Smith was perhaps the most "unprincipled man that ever held an office in the judiciary" and White, while "pretending to be friendly to me has deceived my friends—no man ever had a more specious, cunning and malicious calumny. This very man while professing to be my friend against whom I have never up to now exercised the smallest opposition, this very man was secretly engaged in base machinations against me and has organized into his party some of the most profligate and abandoned men in Florida. With the people he speaks of me highly unless when he finds a man that he can use for his purpose and I assure you that throughout all this Territory this man has had the addresses to make the people believe he was my decided friend."[43]

Meanwhile, DuVal continued to have his difficulties with the War Department over his Indian accounts. The difficulties, as he explained to Andrew Jackson, had brought him to the point of resignation. "I avail myself of the opportunity . . . to present the respects of myself and family to you and Mrs. Jackson," wrote DuVal. He would go to Washington as soon as the new territorial secretary arrived. He had been without a clerk for the past eighteen months, he complained to Jackson. Still the War Department has assailed "me as an honest man—and when I called on them to demand why such an attempt was made they have pretended that it was only done to give me an opportunity to defend myself from charges that had been made against me and not out of mere tenderness for my reputation." DuVal was unsure about whether he could convince Clay, Barbour, or Adams "that justice is denied me" but added that he would "not consent to be insulted for any office on earth while corn and meat can be had in the west on good terms. I am poor but my family lives on corn and beat it into hominy while I live, sooner than submit to the treatment I have received."[44]

DuVal's rants to Old Hickory took up the familiar theme of persecution at the hands of administration bureaucrats and sycophants who had no true appreciation of the services that dedicated public servants were rendering to their country or of the challenges they faced. It was a theme that DuVal expected would bring sympathy from Old Hickory, reminding the General that a national housecleaning would be necessary in the next election. (DuVal also may have known, through Call or Jackson's other associates, that Barbour, a Crawford man, was also attempting to accuse Jackson of defrauding the government during his days in the army.)[45] DuVal's threats to resign notwithstanding, he had little choice but to go to Washington and seek exoneration and reappointment. His family was settled in Florida, and there was little chance that the governor would move them back to Kentucky. After all, DuVal no doubt understood that change was in the offing. The next year (1828) was an election year, and DuVal had every expectation that his friend Andrew Jackson would be in the White House. DuVal enjoyed some relief when territorial secretary William McCarty assumed his official post on July 5, 1827. After spending roughly one month acquainting McCarty with his duties, DuVal left Tallahassee for Washington in early August. The arduous journey ended on October 5.[46]

CHAPTER 9

"Harassed by the persecution of their neighbors"

Governor William P. DuVal was in Washington nearly one and a half months before the first session of the Twentieth Congress opened, on December 1. Before DuVal attended any of the sessions he had important business with the administration, chiefly among which was the settlement of his Indian accounts with the War Department. DuVal might have wondered what kind of reception he would receive from Secretary of War James Barbour and Indian Affairs head Thomas McKenney. His reappointment was by no means ensured. Secretary of State Henry Clay would have been cool to his reappointment if he thought of it at all. Certainly DuVal could count on Vice President John C. Calhoun's recommendation if he sought it. DuVal could certainly count on Attorney General Wirt and Navy Secretary Southard's support, but what did John Quincy Adams have in mind?

The governor met with President Adams on October 10, but the length and the subjects of their discussions were unrecorded. Likely DuVal explained as well as he could the challenges he faced as governor of the Florida Territory, urging that the president order the War Department to reimburse him for personal expenses undertaken on behalf of supervising Indian affairs. DuVal's case was complicated. The War Department studied the governor's accounts and submitted them to President Adams for disposition. On January 17, 1828, Adams confided to his diary: the comptroller presented a volume of army laws and "some accounts of T. L. McKenney, of Governor DuVal, and of the Indian agent and stated to me the principle of his objection to their accounts. But I have no time to read the papers relating to the controversy left with me yesterday by Governor Barbour. The question requires deliberate consideration and great discretion in determining upon the principle to be hereafter pursued."[1] President Adams eventually decided the issue, but not necessarily in DuVal's favor. Yet he did see fit to reappoint the governor. Adams submitted his nomination on December 27, and the U.S. Senate confirmed him on January 9. According to Thomas Randall, who himself awaited news of his own Senate confirmation as judge for the Middle District of Florida, DuVal's "reappointment was hailed with great joy at Tallahassee."[2] Indeed, according to one account, when they learned of DuVal's reappointment, the citizens "volunteered a subscription of gun powder" for the old cannon discovered among the relics of "old for Saint Louis. We do not remember to have witnessed more unanimity and general good feeling expressed on any occasion as this."[3]

One of the most pressing personal matters that DuVal took up once Congress began its session involved the controversy regarding his homestead in Tallahassee and whether or not it included lands either reserved for the capital itself or lands embraced within the Lafayette Grant. In a statement of facts to the House Committee on Public Lands DuVal explained that his homestead did not "*adjoin* but only cornered the South East extremity of the quarter section on which Tallahassee is established." DuVal had occupied and improved his site since the summer of 1824 and thus claimed preemption status even though the surrounding area was being surveyed and sold. "But for the structure I erected at considerable expense, no other could have been obtained sufficiently large and dry, in which Public business could have been transacted, and the records and papers have been safely preserved." As DuVal explained, when he visited Washington in February 1825 he had tried unsuccessfully to get Congress to give the territory four other quarter sections of land as had been done for other territories, but the session ended before he could achieve this goal. He then called on Land Commissioner George Graham to reserve the quarter sections from sale, and the official assured him that he would forward directions to land officials in Tallahassee to that effect. When DuVal returned, he found the quarter section on which he had resided reserved from sale. "This reservation however gave the Territory no claim to the land I had settled; and under the preemption law passed by Congress to secure to actual settlers their improvements, I claimed with justice the quarter section on which I had built and resided in the year 1824." When DuVal applied to the registrar and the receiver of the Land Office in Tallahassee they refused the claim, whereupon the governor presented his petition to Judge Augustus Woodward, and, after a hearing with considerable argument on both sides, the judge ordered the officials to enter DuVal's claim. DuVal also presented the matter to a subsequent session of the legislative council, which "refused to direct further prosecution." To remove whatever controversy still existed, DuVal offered to "surrender my land & and houses to the Territory, if the Legislative Council or Congress would pay me for improvements so as to enable me to build another dwelling even as rude as the Hull I now inhabit." DuVal hoped for a final resolution of the matter, but the committee offered none. After essentially restating the basic facts as DuVal had related them, the committee report simply stated that it hoped DuVal's claim "will be arranged between the Governor and the Territory in a way satisfactory to both without any legislation on the subject." The controversy remained unresolved and would be taken up in later years by DuVal's enemies.[4]

While in Washington, DuVal made the rounds of receptions, parties, and dinners. At one such occasion, on January 8, on the anniversary of Andrew Jackson's victory at the Battle of New Orleans, a New England newspaper reported that DuVal, with Calhoun and the Speaker of the House present, provided an "excellent sample of 'wit, wisdom, and sentiment.'" Toasts to "George Washington," the "Soldiers of the Revolution," "Our Fair Country Women," "A Free Press," "the Militia," and others were given. Close to the end of the formal ceremony Governor DuVal toasted Andrew Jackson: "The 4th of July 1776 and the 8th of January 1815. The first announced our Independence, the last saw it nobly ratified." Conspicuously absent among the toasts, however, was one in favor of President Adams.[5]

Joseph White, the territorial delegate, was also in the capital during the congressional session, and the two made every effort to present a common front for the benefit for the Territory of Florida. On January 10, the governor congratulated the delegate on his efforts in the session to secure an appropriation for a lighthouse for St. Marks as well as for navigational improvements on the St. Marks and Wakulla Rivers.[6] When it came to matters regarding appropriations and the need to remove the Indians DuVal and White spoke with one voice. They worked together to urge federal officials to declare Neamathla's reserve on Rocky Comfort Creek vacated and to authorize sale of the tract. White asserted to general land office officials that when the chief abandoned the land four years ago it reverted back to the government. "Gov DuVal who is now in the City will officially report to you the facts if required. I have to request that this land be ordered into the market at the next sale & that instructions be now issued to the Registrar and Receiver to receive evidence of any preemption within the Reserve." DuVal agreed with the delegate's assertion, adding that Neamathla "has never complied with any of the provisions of this reservation, and absolutely refused to reside on it. Neamathla left Florida, in January 1825, and returned to the Creek Nation, of which he was a native and is now Chief of a Town, in that Nation."[7]

Both also agreed that the exposed territory needed more troops to protect the frontier from Indian attacks. DuVal also brought up the danger of slave revolts and rampaging pirates. On January 28 DuVal brought the attention of the secretary to the need for a permanent stationing of troops "at or near the head of the St. Marks River. When it is known that many of the slaves taken to Florida are the very worst, in the union—it must be admitted that a military post near the center of the population would not only be serviceable but highly prudent. In the event of any commotion among the slaves—a company of regular troops would become a nucleus for the militia." DuVal also called attention to the exposed condition of Key West. "This place is becoming daily more important. The revenue derived during the year from that port was $60,000. But the place was entirely destitute of defense, and the collector's office must be exposed to any pirate who may be tempted by money, which must accumulate there, from its remote situation." The War Department forwarded DuVal's suggestions to General Winfield Scott, who refused to comply with the governor's requests, citing excessive expenses and the unhealthiness of Key West.[8]

Most of DuVal's interaction with the War Department during his stay in Washington concerned Indian affairs. That winter the department heard complaints from Chief Blount (through Joseph White) that DuVal and John Phagan, the Indian agent, were cheating him. The governor and the agent had substituted worthless goods for cash in his annuities, had taken slaves from him without "tryal or hearing," had withheld from him medals, had sold him corn at exorbitant prices, and had failed to protect him from thieves. Blount said that he did not "believe that you can love the treatment that your Red Children has Received from the governor and this agent." When called to account, DuVal blamed the complaint on former interpreter Stephen Richards, whom the governor had fired. Richards's "conduct was so improper, and he was so much in the habit of violating the law—respecting the intercourse and trade with the Indians—That I felt it my duty to dismiss him from the agency. . . . Richards is known to be destitute of character and is in fact considered as a most unprincipled man by the honest citizens who know him." DuVal charged that "Phagan is greatly abused & misrepresented in this petition. He is a man of correct and humane feeling, of decided character, and tried integrity and is an excellent and faithful officer." Richards had succeeded in turning the Indians against the governor and Phagan by this "improper conduct, and deceitful influence." This was the reason the Indians had become "so refractory. This Mr. Richards has been laboring ever since Maj. Phagan settled among the Indians to destroy his character and influence with them." DuVal concluded with the observation that it "may be necessary to remove Blunt down into the nation, in the manner provided or directed by the late Treaty if he does not conform to laws provided for the regulation of trade, and the Government of the Indians." The department seemed to accept DuVal's explanation. Whatever the truth of the matter, Blount's and the other Apalachicola Indians' days in Middle Florida were numbered. Despite appeals to the War Department and even to his primary benefactor, Andrew Jackson, little was done to protect their status and property in Florida.[9]

DuVal wrote Secretary of War Barbour that if Congress would appropriate money for the Seminoles to remove elsewhere and that if Colonel McKenney could be sent to Florida in the spring, he could accomplish the objective better than any other commissioner the government might appoint. "My acquaintance with the Indians' habits, customs, and disposition, authorize me to say—that Col. McKenney is not surpassed (if he has an equal) in all that relates to these extraordinary people." The Seminoles, DuVal argued, are "poor & miserable and if not removed will in a few years become extinct. Their preservation & happiness demand the change more than the interests of Florida—though it is admitted that the growth and prosperity of the Territory depend on a considerable degree on the removal of the Indians." DuVal voiced similar appeals to War Department officials throughout the summer. If McKenney were to come to Florida, DuVal had no doubt that the official could induce the Seminoles to move. "My plan is to take one respectable Indian from each Town, not permitting the whole part to exceed twenty five—they shall be furnished each with a horse, bridle, saddle, rifle, two blankets & a Kettle and such necessaries as will be required." It might be necessary for DuVal to do the work himself, but he was ready to undertake it if "you will send me such a talk as your judgment may approve to be given to the Chiefs as from their Great Father. . . I know it will have great effect on the Indians, if they are told it is sent to them from Washington."[10]

During DuVal's several months in Washington, the governor and the secretary of war seemed to have reached a rapprochement. Whether because of their common Virginia roots, DuVal's winning ways, or their ability to find some other commonality of purpose, the governor and Secretary Barbour seemed to have reached a cordial, if not warm, working relationship. While on his way home, DuVal wrote about the situation to his friend Samuel Southard. After promising to give the navy secretary a full report on Florida matters when he returned home, DuVal stated, "I must not close this Samuel without saying to you how much I was gratified with the kind attentions of Gov. Barbour. I always believed him a man of candor and integrity—but I did not know before whether he had a good heart—so many men lose all heart when they become politicians that it is almost rare to find one in a man that has been so long in public life—But I will swear that Gov. Barbour's is as big as a tin cup and is as fresh and as sincere as it was in his days of youth. I do not only respect him and admire him, but I shall ever entertain for him the most sincere regard."[11]

DuVal remained away from Florida for nearly five months. It can be assumed that he resided for most of that time in Washington, but from to time to time he ventured out of the capital. Though the exact date for the excursion is unrecorded, a newspaper report placed the governor in company with Andrew Jackson on a campaign swing through southern Pennsylvania.[12] DuVal left the capital in early March and arrived in St. Augustine, via Augusta, Georgia, a few weeks later.[13] After making his way to Middle Florida, DuVal greeted his family, examined his crops, and caught up with his gubernatorial duties as quickly as he could. He also updated his Washington friends on land prices and purchasing possibilities in Middle Florida.[14]

Also, once he returned to town he responded favorably to Thomas Brown's invitation to attend a public dinner in his honor at Tallahassee on March 22.

After dinner, toasts were given to Washington, Jefferson, other former presidents, Andrew Jackson, and, finally, "William P. DuVal, Governor of Florida—We welcome his return to the land of his adoption, to the city of which he was the founder." Governor DuVal rose to respond. "Mr. President," he stated, while "I am opposed to the general practice of delivering set speeches at the convivial board, . . . I would be wanting in respect and gratitude to the company if I refrained from an expression of my thanks. The humble services which I have rendered to the Territory, can give me no claim to the distinguished honor of the public dinner. I owe this high mark of respect to the generosity of my fellow citizens, whose steady support and continued confidence can never be forgotten." DuVal asserted that the "steady desire to promote the interests of Florida has ever influenced me in the discharge of my Executive duties and the best and highest reward, is the gratification which springs from the approval and confidences of the people." DuVal congratulated his hearers on the growth of the population, adding that from

> personal observation of the settlement of our younger States, . . . in their original settlement, none of them in the same period could boast of so much intelligence and character as Florida. The continuance of this valuable emigration is earnestly hoped for, yet it much depends on our conduct as officers and citizens. Party spirits has in some degree already interfered with the harmony of our society—not that Florida has ever felt its effects in the same degree as many other parts of the Union, but the want of forbearance towards each other, and fostering of angry passions, will inevitably occasion that bitter and rancorous feeling which will not only destroy our peace at home and reputation abroad but also check that class of emigrants. . . . I trust my fellow citizens will unite with me in the work of conciliation and harmony.[15]

Then DuVal turned to the subject of his relationship to the territorial delegate. DuVal admitted that he and White had "not been on friendly terms, we have differed, and with some bitterness. Our intercourse while I was last in Washington the past winter went no farther than mere politeness. . . . I did closely and critically regard the conduct of that Gentleman with a disposition not friendly, yet I cannot and will not withhold from him the praise which he so justly merits for the steady and untiring discharge of his arduous duties. Yes sir," he continued, "I trust I never shall want the magnanimity to declare, no Territory ever had a more faithful, efficient & vigilant Delegate. These remarks I think due to the Delegate and myself, for the official situation in which we stand to each other, and in justice to the zeal and ability he has displayed in sustaining the best interests of the Territory." DuVal then proposed a toast to the territorial delegate: "Jos M. White, our Delegate in Congress—the zeal and ability he has manifested, to promote the interests of Florida, claim and receive our warmest praise."[16]

DuVal's speech was widely reported throughout the territory and drew varying responses. The St. Augustine *East Florida Herald* grudgingly accepted that it was right for Tallahassee to offer DuVal "some mark of respect and attachment, as our Chief Magistrate and founder of their city." It also applauded DuVal's call for an end to "party strife. We are glad his Excellency has announced his determination to 'smoke the calumet of peace.'"[17] Yet political friction in the territory would increase, and the governor and the delegate would be at the center of it.

That summer DuVal was never far away from politics (national, territorial, or domestic). Back in Bardstown, DuVal's brother-in-law Dr. Burr Harrison had aligned himself with the anti-Jackson forces. He joined other Whigs in a full-scale denunciation of Jackson's candidacy. The sentiments of Nancy's younger brother Alfred were unknown, but the younger physician's professional partnership with his older brother-in-law might have made for awkward relations with the governor's old friend.[18] Meanwhile, Nancy DuVal carefully cultivated her husband's supporters in the territory. One of these was Joseph Simeon Sanchez, a St. Augustine Creole whom her husband had appointed justice of peace. Sanchez informed DuVal that he was a candidate for the legislative council and that he hoped that he, Mrs. DuVal, and Elizabeth would be able to visit St. Augustine when the oranges were ripe. "I have no doubt it would be very agreeable to them to see our groves groaning under the immense weight of their fruit and pluck them with their own hands from the trees." Sanchez closed with the hope that DuVal would remember him "to all our friends, I say our friends because your friends are mine in the same manner that mine will always be yours."[19]

If Nancy DuVal and her daughter Elizabeth ever made their trip to St. Augustine, they likely did so without the oldest DuVal daughter, Marcia, who, in a hastily performed wedding ceremony, married her cousin Dr. William D. Price Jr. at the DuVal homestead. Lizzie Brown and her mother happened to be visiting the DuVals on April 28 when DuVal's nephew (the son of his sister Lucy) asked for Marcia (who was in the yard milking a goat). According to Brown, Marcia was a "perfect child" of about sixteen, "a very beautiful girl and full of life and fun. . . . Price brought a magistrate, and the marriage ceremony was "then and there performed and no one seemed to think it was anything but right. It was a union of May and December," Lizzie Brown recalled, as Price was a "quiet and staid man" of about thirty. By all accounts Marcia and "'cousin William' seemed to get along without any jarring though she was one of the most admired married belles in Tallahassee." The couple resided in town only a few years before moving to Aspalaga on the Apalachicola River.[20]

In early May the new Mrs. Price accompanied her father, mother, and sister Elizabeth to nearby Jefferson County for a round of visits, parties, and balls that coincided with the meeting of the spring court session at Monticello. Visiting Welaunee and Waukeenah (the Gamble plantations), Belmont (the Randall plantation), and

Lipona (Achille Murat's plantation), the DuVals enjoyed socializing with the Jefferson County planters. Laura Randall wrote her mother that she invited young Elizabeth DuVal, Charlotte Greenup, and Catherine Gamble to spend the day with her. "It was necessary too to invite their beauxs and those that remained of the party assembled the day before at Welaunee." The next day a party was given for Elizabeth and her sister Mrs. Price. According to Laura Randall, "It was neighborhood dance. . . . They danced also at Welaunee, Murat having brought his fiddler with him for the purpose." Of Murat, Randall observed, "what spirit he has. He is the life of every company & his health is much improved. He is quite fat. His wife is also devoted to dancing, company & amusement—and is as much a candidate for admiration & attentions as any unmarried Belle." The next day Charlotte Greenup and Elizabeth visited Belmont, but Marcia Price chose to sleep late and return to Tallahassee without them. Laura Randall attributed her sullen behavior to some "ridiculous notion of dignity or some equally ridiculous pique. She is a silly, spoiled child & ought to have at least one whipping every week."[21]

As the summer dragged on, DuVal was ever mindful of the national election in the fall. Looking ahead expectantly, DuVal urged Jackson to discount the claims made in a Washington paper that the governor had pronounced him unfit for the presidency. DuVal assured Old Hickory that there was "not a shadow of truth to found such a publication upon—but it is hardly necessary to tell you this. I have never supported any of the candidates before or since the last presidential election but you, such from an honest conviction, not one was as well qualified as yourself." DuVal added that:

> Mr. Adams has studied more books than yourself I never doubted but that he understands human nature as well, or has as much experience or is as practical a man or ever can be half as efficient, I do utterly disbelieve. I hope to see the scoundrels who have lived by slandering you and your friends, forever put to silence this fall . . . but let us leave politics. Our crops are very promising and will be excellent. The frost did no material injury to the sugar cane. Col. Butler is improving his plantation rapidly and General Call is well. I hope to plant 100 acres in sugar cane this fall. Mrs. Duval's health has improved very much since her residence in Florida, she desires to be remembered to Mrs. Jackson and yourself.[22]

As DuVal tended to his gubernatorial responsibilities, he and Nancy took time out to call on the Gambles and other Jefferson County planters on the Fourth of July. The mood of these visits among the men and women was always convivial, but that did not prevent discussions among the men of planting, land purchases, and any number of other serious subjects. Judge Thomas Randall informed his father-in-law, U.S. attorney general William Wirt, who was contemplating expanding his Florida holdings, that the governor had informed him of "some great

Achille Murat, ca. 1820s. Courtesy of State Archives of Florida.

scheme of purchase of lands near the Gulf in which speculation he means to embark you and Mr. [Samuel] Southard. He darkly alluded to it the other day & when things are ready I am to be called on to advise . . . to give you my judgement on the matter. It is yet however a profound secret . . . but it is public land & of course to be entered at gov't price."[23]

By that time DuVal and Southard had arranged for the purchase of the Lafayette section. Once Southard forwarded to him the cash, contract, and power of attorney, DuVal assured Southard that he would plant "as much sugar cane on our land as will I hope sell for as much money as the first installment. I will take care to make the land, yeald something handsome." As a precaution against the possibility that their first year's efforts might fall short, DuVal asked Southard whether he might wish to have some understanding with Lafayette's agent that only interest payments and not principal would be due the first year. In this, he suggested, he hoped "we may be indulged. I throw out this hint to gard myself not you against the disappointment of having the cash in due time." DuVal asked Southard if he knew of any cane stock on U.S. ships coming from China. Two weeks later DuVal wrote to his friend that he would plant as much sugar as he could on their land with his own force. "There is 100 acres now in cultivation with

William Wirt.
Courtesy of State
Archives of Florida.

convenient cabins on it. What force can you raise and send out by the first of December next? I shall plant plenty of corn, peas, and potatoes and except meat for the hands no money will be required—some hoes, ploughs, axes, and such farming utensils as are necessary—you can purchase and send by water to me. This expense will more than be balanced by the provisions I will furnish. . . . I am well apprised," DuVal added, "your riches do not weigh heavy on you, nor has fortune ever buckled a heavy pack on me, except a large portion of trouble & ill luck such that she gave me a light heart and a thin pair of breeches which suits this climate. I do not repine. My wife & children make me happy and in truth it is a high pleasure to provide for them. I think we can make money by raising sugar and sea Island cotton." DuVal noted that never since his residence in Florida had he seen crops so excellent. "Provisions this fall will sell very low and the immigrants to this country will have much better supplies than their predecessors."[24]

One week later, ever optimistic, DuVal again wrote Southard:

> I have never given you a description of land we purchased of Genl. Lafayette. It is situated between two and three miles east of Tallahassee to the left of and near the great road leading from this place to St. Augustine. Three quarters of the section are not inferior in quality to any land in the Territory. The fourth quarter is excellent oak, and hickory land, most of which is now in cultivation. There is a peach orchard now 4 years old, containing

forty or fifty fine trees. There are several good cabbins for dwellings and some out houses, for corn, etc. The land is beautifully watered by two small clear branches, formed by several excellent never failing springs. I do not know so desirable a tract of land in five miles of this place. Every person here says we have made a good bargain and consider the tract with the improvement on it now worth fifteen Dollars per acre. I consider it worth $20 per acre, if any land in the South is—I am determined to reside on it as soon as I can dispose of my present residence.

DuVal had planted apricots and nectarines and even had a number of young orange trees transplanted there. "Whatever fruits or vines you can send me will particularly be attended to. In three years if I live we shall have one of the most delightful places in the United States."[25]

DuVal also reported that Nancy's and her sister Polly's health had improved since they had left Kentucky:

> I mention these facts for the benefit of Mrs. Southard. If I was permitted to offer my opinion—it would be that Mrs. Southard and her family come out this fall and spend the winter with us. We have few inducements it is true to offer in exchange for the captivating pleasures of your grand city, but our climate alone is worth more than all she can enjoy in Washington. Such a trip would improve her health, and save her from the vilest of all slavery, that of waiting on every female biped, who visits your City for the pleasure of dashing away native grace and lovely modesty, in order to talk scandal fashionably—float about at your parties—and then abuse their entertainers. The trip will save you much expense, during the next session of Congress as without Mrs. S. you will not have . . . to give parties. I know you cannot come therefore my invitation is to Mrs. S and her family. The road from here to Washington is excellent for a carriage and I will meet Mrs. S. and family at Milledgeville in Georgia. As to the expense of the journey it will be nothing in comparison to her living next winter in the city. I do not think you ought to ridicule this proposition, as I know you will be apt to do, . . . but just submit to your better half and let her decide. I do believe if Mrs. S was to spend one winter here she would be willing to reside in Florida.[26]

DuVal then turned to the necessity of obtaining slave labor for "Southard Place." "What can negro men & boys, and girls from 25 to 16 years old be had for? In settling a new country remember that negro children too small to render any service ought not to be purchased. . . . Able and efficient lads are therefore of first importance in opening new lands," DuVal explained. " If we could purchase negroes in families provided there were not too many children on a credit of one, two, and three years, we need not apprehend about the payments unless some singular misfortune should overtake our crops. On this subject however you will determine for yourself, only I say to you if we determine on making a valuable plantation, you may calculate on my personal and devoted attention to it, so far that I will visit it generally once a day—and suffer no manager we may have to purchase any article—every expense must be submitted to me and I deem it necessary I shall make all purchases myself. I can ride to the plantation every morning before breakfast, from my residence. Economy, judgement and unceasing perseverance must combine, to insure success. I will succeed or die in trying."[27]

If such mundane references to buying and selling human beings seems cruel and shocking to modern ears, it must be understood that DuVal was a man of his times. As governor of the Florida Territory and as a politician, DuVal was convinced that slavery was essential to economic progress. Blacks were seen as an inferior race, and the rights of slaveholders must be protected. Yet, when it came to personal relationships, DuVal's attitudes did not always toe the line. His personal relationship with the Proctor family is a case in point. In January 1829 DuVal intervened on behalf of Toney's son George when the man he was apprenticed to nearly succeeded in absconding with the young boy. The Leon County Court ordered that young George be placed under the personal care of the governor until the end of his contractual term.[28]

Also that summer DuVal continued his planting operations in partnership with his brother. Without mentioning his agreement with Southard on the Lafayette section, DuVal wrote to Nancy's cousin Andrew Hynes in Nashville of his own operations. He and his brother John had fifteen hands working on an excellent tract of land. They had cleared one hundred acres, had planted twenty acres in sugar cane, and were planning ninety more in the fall. He admitted that

> the expense of maintaining the whole for one year together with a mill house &c has nearly ruined me, I have progressed thus far and now if I cannot raise the means to purchase the mill boiler and steam engine it will all go for nothing. I wish you would ride down here and view this country, come and see our plantation and let me persuade you to join us in completing the establishment. I assure you that it is better than the Mississippi country for cane. I do not mean richer or so rich, but we have land fertile enough for anything and the climate is decidedly superior to any part of the union. If I do not succeed in establishing a good sugar plantation it will be for want of funds to erect works and in that event I shall leave this country for unless I can make money in this way it would be folly for me to continue here my large family I am only getting poorer by my office. I beg you will come & see the country & then judge for yourself. There has not been a case of fever or any other serious diseases the whole year more health cannot be found on any spot.[29]

DuVal's missive to his friend betrays a sense of melancholy over missed opportunities and unfortunate decisions made over a long, disappointing life:

> My earliest and best friend—I have a thousand times wished I had remained with you, when first you located yourself in Nashville—If I had continued by you, and under your direction and management, as I ought to have done, I would have been this day a wealthy and happy man, dashing the billows of the rolling world aside with golden arms—in place of being a poor Governor in a remote corner, scuffling for a support and that too, quite precarious—with waves rolling over my head, propped on a moss pillow, with a sour, mixed, and sad, sick and lonely heart.
>
> I have never my dear Andrew felt at home in this country, and if I die here, my spirit will quit in twenty four hours—for old Kentuck—with all her faults I love her still, as my kind mother—it is true she has been treated most unnaturally by many of her children, they have reduced her to the brink of bankruptcy by infernal banks—and stop laws &c so at one time she was (even in the winter) clothed in paper—the hearty old Lady is now engaged with all her maids in making homespun & household goods I hope she will again be comfortable & independent.[30]

In September DuVal left the territorial capital and visited other Middle Florida settlements. He attended a public dinner in his honor at Marianna and a few days later traveled to the Apalachicola settlements to check on the Indians. He reported to McKenney that he found the Indians eager to visit the country west of the Mississippi. He also found them "much afflicted with the venerial disease in its worst form; many of them are very ill. I have ordered that medical assistance should be furnished them." DuVal attributed their condition to "trade . . . and intercourse with the boatman [and this would] certainly destroy them. I suppose that not less than fifty of them are now ill and Several dangerous. Humanity demands the removal of these unfortunate people as early as possible."[31] Gad Humphreys, the Indian agent, essentially reiterated the same thing to authorities after his meeting with Hicks and six other chiefs at McKensie's Pond near the agency. Humphreys said that he had discussed the idea of sending a delegation west to inspect the lands and that the Indians "understand that a removal, under suitable and fair circumstances, would tend to the benefit & happiness of the Indians themselves—distressed as I know these people are . . . and harassed by the persecution of their neighbors without and judging from the reputed character of the new country offered to them, I think it may be confidently calculated, that a visit to it, will result in a general & entire removal of the Nation." DuVal suggested that "if a party of the chiefs are invited to Washington, and I can meet them, many difficulties will be surmounted."[32]

DuVal wrote these words with every expectation that the incoming administration would deal decisively with the Indian issue. By that time he knew that

Andrew Jackson would soon be in office. He had kept careful tabs of the voting taking place from September through November by reading newspapers and through his correspondence with friends and relatives in the states. By the end of the balloting, Old Hickory had swept the South and West, while Adams carried only New England, New Jersey, and Delaware. While DuVal would have looked forward to the electoral results with every expectation of better things to come, he would have also thought of friends in the previous administration, such as William Wirt and Samuel Southard. To the latter he wrote a heartfelt letter of condolence on December 7.[33]

Altogether, it was a landslide for Jackson, and from November until the inauguration four months later, in March 1829, Jackson supporters were jubilant. But the enthusiasm was short lived once Jackson's friends learned of Rachel Jackson's death, on the afternoon of December 22. The morning before she succumbed, Jackson wrote to Richard Keith Call that in the last few days his wife had been "suddenly & violently attacked, with pains in her left shoulder & breast." Attributing her condition to the calumnies thrown on her during the election, Jackson closed with the hope that his wife would soon recover and that Call might join them in their journey to Washington. But it was not to be. The president-elect was in mourning when he set out for Washington on January 19. Yet boisterous crowds turned out to greet the hero at riverboat stops and other places until his journey ended on February 11. From that day until his inauguration, on March 4, Jackson resided at Gatsby's National Hotel, receiving well-wishers and other visitors.[34]

Things seemed to be looking up for DuVal and Jackson's other friends in Florida. As many of the General's most widely heralded exploits that led him to the pinnacle of power had been associated with Florida, certainly, his friends reasoned, Jackson would not forget them once he reached the White House. But still, nagging questions remained. Would the General's health hold out an entire term? What kind of executive would he be? Whom would he appoint to his cabinet? Would he, as his campaign had promised, sweep the federal bureaucracy clean, and, if so, would all federal appointees in Florida be replaced with his supporters? Who would be his secretary of state—and, most important for DuVal, who would direct the War Department? DuVal might also have wondered what the role of his friend John C. Calhoun (who continued in the new administration as vice president) would be. Answers to these questions would come in upcoming months, but for now DuVal could look ahead with optimism. What he and others had worked for since he had come to Florida had been achieved. Andrew Jackson was president-elect of the United States.

CHAPTER 10

Storm Clouds on the Horizon

On December 19, 1828, the Magnolia *Advertiser* announced that "Friday last, our citizens were gratified with the first visit of Governor DuVal, to our place since its establishment. His Excellency was attended by several Gentlemen from Tallahassee, on an excursion of pleasure to the mouth of the river." Though DuVal's visit to the village a few miles from Tallahassee was brief, a committee of citizens published a long statement lauding DuVal's efforts in serving the territory. "At the call of his country," the committee enthused,

> he gave up the ease and comforts of society and of an affluent fortune at home, to take up the privations and hardships in the then unexplored wilds ... at a time when all this part of our Territory was supposed to be a barren waste, inhabited only by hostile tribes of Indians. The dread of encountering these savages, and the want of enterprise among the civilized settlements of the Territory had kept them in total ignorance of the most valuable portions of it. On his appointment as Governor he determined on exploring it personally. But the undertaking was considered so wild and hazardous, that no white person could be found hardy enough to accompany him. ... Unattended by any other than a hired negro, and his own servant, he commenced his arduous attempt, and we believe for nearly two years was engaged in exploring those trackless forests, which are now becoming the most valuable portions of our country. During these two years besides the fatigues, and privations incidental to a life of constant exposure, the whole of his salary was expended in the public service. He made himself master of every bay, harbour & inlet on the coast and of all the localities of the interior, and completely developed, the resources of the country. His communications to the Government excited surprise and astonishment, and his private friends could scarcely credit his descriptions.[1]

Due to DuVal's indefatigable courage and vigor, the account continued, a "region of sterility was suddenly converted into extensive tracts of rich and fertile lands, adapted to the richest products of any country." Yet, even as he strove to improve the territory, Governor DuVal "had to contend with strong local prejudices, and combat against sectional and private interests." But Presidents Monroe and Adams stood by him, as they were "impressed by his unwearied efforts and industry." DuVal, the account continued, "surmount[ed] every obstacle, which presented itself in establishing and organizing the Territorial Government." The governor had spared "no personal or pecuniary sacrifice in forwarding his schemes for the public good. . . . The whole of the official duties and exertions of the Governor have been characterized by the most disinterested zeal, and without any of that ostentatious display. . . . We repeat therefore that no man, more richly deserves the esteem, and gratitude of our citizens." While DuVal had made some mistakes during his governorship, he did not deserve the "invidious attacks of those, who in spite of ignorance, and want of merit, have the arrogance and effrontery, to assail him with base and slanderous falsehoods."[2]

DuVal would have taken pride in the Magnolia committee's version of the governor's career. The narrative would certainly have coincided with his own views of his service to the territory since he became its governor, in 1822. Those views would find voice in Washington Irving's writings, in the governor's own storytelling then and later, and in the reminiscences of his sons in recounting the exploits of their father. A carefully cultivated "DuVal Myth" was beginning to emerge—a myth closely related to his stock in trade as a politician, lawyer, and frontier bon vivant.

But these views of the governor's sacrifices were not universally held. In fact, in his remaining years as governor DuVal faced attacks on many fronts—attacks that would eventually drive him from office. Yet as the new year dawned, William P. DuVal had every reason to be optimistic about the future. His friend Andrew Jackson would soon be in the White House, and his older friend John C. Calhoun was in the second seat with every expectation that he would one day succeed the General. Whether that would be in four or eight years, no one knew for sure, but the Jackson-Calhoun coalition seemed certain to dominate national affairs for many years to come. Perhaps, as time went on and the territory became a state, DuVal could expect that he might be selected as one of Florida's first senators or its member in Congress. Or maybe he could take a prominent role in a future Calhoun administration. For now, however, as territorial governor of Florida, he faced many old problems.

Among these problems were Indians affairs and, most important, his financial accounts related to administering the Indian Agency in Florida. His ongoing disputes with the War Department continued after Jackson's inauguration. But at that moment DuVal had every reason to expect that Jackson's new secretary of war would be easier to work with. By 1829 DuVal seemed to have fallen out with Gad Humphreys. Also, as has been previously noted, he increasingly fell out with Chief Blount, and the old Jackson ally remonstrated personally against DuVal's treatment of him. His patience strained, DuVal found his tender feelings for the Indians diminished as he was assailed by citizens and political enemies who charged him with incompetence and malfeasance in administering the Indian Agency. One thing was certain, however. Andrew Jackson's election to the presidency put perhaps America's greatest advocate of Indian removal in the White House. The General had favored the move as early as his brief time as governor of the Florida Territory. DuVal could expect that the General would push the matter forward as soon as he had completed his housecleaning of corrupt federal officials. With Old Hickory in the White House, DuVal understood that the days of the Seminoles in Florida, along with those of the other "Civilized Tribes" in the South, were numbered.

Even if his temperament had been suited to the job (which it was not), the duties of his office diverted him from the daily grind of supervising his agricultural pursuits. He was forced mostly to rely on his brother's work on their plantation. How much time he was able to devote to "Southard Place" is unclear. Nor is it certain that the slaves that he asked Southard to send out ever arrived. Even so, he did what he could in anticipation of great success, and his neighbors took notice. "The governor and his brother," Thomas Randall wrote to his father-in-law, William Wirt, "have their sugar works now commencing . . . so that we shall have the benefit of their experience."[3]

DuVal was not able to attend Andrew Jackson's inauguration on March 4, 1829, but by that time he certainly would have been apprised of Jackson's cabinet selections. It was not a distinguished group but was cobbled together through a strange array of regional and political considerations. Because he owed his victory in New York to the deft political operator Martin Van Buren, Jackson felt obliged to reward the New Yorker with the position of secretary of state. Van Buren had formerly backed Crawford's presidential aspirations, and proof of Crawford's influence in the administration can be seen in the selection of John Berrien of Georgia (who favored Indian removal) as attorney general. For the war and naval departments, Jackson chose friends: senators John Eaton and John Branch of North Carolina. (Branch's appointment was ironic. Monroe had chosen DuVal for territorial governor over Branch in 1822, and now Jackson was appointing Branch in place of DuVal's friend Samuel Southard.) In deference to Calhoun, Jackson appointed Samuel Ingham of Pennsylvania secretary of the treasury. As it stood, the cabinet seemed to balance both Calhoun's and Van Buren's interests.

Even more important than Jackson's official cabinet were the men he chose to surround himself with as political advisers after he assumed the presidency.

President Andrew Jackson. Courtesy of Library of Congress.

Known as the "kitchen cabinet," these men, several of whom lived in the White House, had been active in his campaign as personal advisers. Some were journalists. Others had served with Jackson in the military. These informal advisers came and went, but DuVal knew many of them. Principal among these advisers were newspapermen: Amos Kendall (formerly a Clay man from Kentucky), Francis Blair (former editor of the Frankfort *Argus,* whose relatives William and Samuel had served with DuVal in various appointive posts in Florida), and Duff Green (who had served with DuVal during the War of 1812). Also considered to be in this inner circle were Jackson's nephew Andrew Jackson Donelson and his wife, Emily, who assumed the role of First Lady. Major William B. Lewis was also among the select group.[4]

Even before the inauguration, DuVal may have sensed that tension between his two friends Jackson and John C. Calhoun was already beginning to be felt, and the rift could be felt in Florida. As sitting Vice President, Calhoun had supported Jackson's candidacy for the presidency as early as June 1826, with the implicit understanding that Calhoun would remain in his current position in the next administration. The next year William H. Crawford tried without success to have Calhoun dropped from the ticket. Jackson and Calhoun were not close but cordial. Both understood that they needed to accept the situation that presented itself. But before the election a number of issues emerged that threatened to increase the tension among the two. First, was the theft of a September 9, 1818, letter from Calhoun's War Department files from President James Monroe to the secretary calling into question Jackson's view of his authority to seize St. Marks and Pensacola. Sam Houston obtained a copy of the letter and forwarded it to Jackson in January 1827. Jackson eventually asked for an explanation of the matter, and on April 30 Calhoun suggested that the letter was part of a plot to discredit Calhoun and Monroe in Jackson's eyes. Circumstantial evidence related to the theft pointed to Crawford. Correspondence went on for some time, and Calhoun offered plausible explanations, but the matter festered, only to explode once Jackson became president when more revelations emerged of the true nature of Calhoun's actions vis-à-vis Jackson during the "Florida Affair."[5]

The Tariff of 1828 was an even more serious threat to the Jackson-Calhoun relationship. Jackson's precise sentiments on the tariff were unstated, but most Southerners expected that as a Southern slaveholder who derived his income from growing cotton, Jackson would oppose the tariff. Contemporary observers and historians have argued that the tariff was as much a political as an economic measure, designed as it was to attract Northern votes to the Democratic Party. As Robert Remini has written, "The tariff of 1828 deliberately sought favor from states such as New York, Pennsylvania, Missouri, Ohio, and Kentucky—which were regarded as swing states—and discriminated against New England. The South, so totally committed to Jackson, did not enter into their calculations at all."[6]

Of course, with the "Tariff of Abominations," South Carolinians and many others in the cotton-producing states were livid. Calhoun was in a bind. While he looked forward to becoming a major force in the new administration (and even the president's successor), he could only hope that the new president would use his influence to change the obnoxious legislation. From his plantation in Pendleton, South Carolina, Calhoun brooded over the problem, formulating the arguments that would eventually find voice in his "South Carolina Exposition and Protest," while at the same time expressing the hope that Jackson might intervene on the side of the South. In the same letter in which he addressed Jackson's queries regarding the Monroe letter, Calhoun observed to candidate Jackson that the tariff passed at the last session "excited much feeling in this, and other Southern atlantick States. The impression, so far as I have observed, is nearly universal, that the system acts with great severity against the staple states, and it is the real cause of their impoverishment." There was some "excess of feeling," but Calhoun cautioned against the idea that this demonstration indicated a "want of attachment to the Union. The long cherished attachment to our institutions is not easily weakened, but as strong as it is, an impression of long continued wrongs would not fail to shake it. The belief that those now in power will be displaced shortly; and that under an administration formed under your auspices, a better order of things will commence, in which, an equal distribution of the burden and benefit of government, economy, the payment of the publick debt, and finally the removal of oppressive duties, will be primarily objects of policy is what mainly consoles this quarter of the Union under existing embarrassment. That your administration may be the means of restoring harmony to this distracted country and of averting the alarming crisis before us is my sincere prayer."[7] Calhoun completed his draft of the "Exposition" in November and forwarded it in anonymous form to the South Carolina legislature, which in turn printed thousands of copies and submitted it to Congress one month later. In speculating that the "Exposition" would defuse the situation in South Carolina and also would not be offensive to Jackson, Calhoun was putting himself out on a limb. As Charles Sydnor has noted, "Calhoun was venturing to write for Jackson the platform that Jackson himself had not yet announced."[8]

The final issue that had the potential of destroying Calhoun's influence in the Jackson Administration and ultimately his chance of succession was the "Peggy Eaton Affair." No one would have predicted that such a scandal in the Jackson cabinet had the potential to bring down a vice president, but the conflict over Secretary of War John Eaton's new wife, Margaret O'Neale Timberlake Eaton, only recently widowed when she married John Eaton, on January 1, 1829, did just that. At least it could be said that, taken together with the other two issues, Calhoun's—or, more precisely, his wife, Floride's—behavior toward Peggy ensured his downfall and the elevation of Martin Van Buren in Andrew Jackson's eyes.

It will be recalled that beginning in 1823 Senators Eaton and Jackson, along with Florida territorial delegate Richard Keith Call, boarded at the O'Neale tavern in Washington. William O'Neale's daughter was the vivacious and voluptuous Mrs. Margaret O'Neale Timberlake, the wife of a naval officer who was frequently at sea. Margaret's manner was forward, open, and often flirtatious. Women hated her. Men were attracted to her, including Richard Keith Call, who, it was whispered, once tried to force himself on her. Jackson, the gallant, defended her then and after whenever tongues wagged. When Peggy's husband died, under mysterious circumstances, Eaton, also a widower, after consulting with Jackson, married Margaret three months before the inauguration. When Jackson subsequently named Eaton his secretary of war, the fallout over the acceptance of his wife in polite society poisoned relations in Jackson's cabinet. And John C. Calhoun was the primary casualty in the debacle. Floride Calhoun had led the snubbing of Peggy Eaton, and an infuriated Jackson (still embittered over Rachel's treatment) took Eaton's side. So did Martin Van Buren. If the conflict over the tariff and Calhoun's true role in the "Florida controversy" irreparably damaged the Calhoun-Jackson relationship, the "Eaton Malaria" sent it over the brink.[9]

William Pope DuVal may have understood the potential of each of these brewing crises to cause tension between Jackson and Calhoun, but he could never have fully anticipated a full break between Jackson and Calhoun. As the new administration began, DuVal expected that Calhoun would succeed the Hero, and once the old General had done his part (probably after one term), DuVal's old friend would take his rightful place as president of the United States. It was not to be. In the ensuing fallout, DuVal, as he had done earlier, was forced to choose sides in the controversy. Would Jackson's popularity force his hand in that direction? Or would Calhoun's theories of state's rights fashioned in response to the "Tariff of Abominations" attract his loyalty? Or, better yet, could he escape the choice altogether and choose not to take sides? DuVal's skills as a politician would be tested. But in 1829 DuVal was having his own problems in Florida.

Indian affairs continued to be prominent among DuVal's worries, but, as he explained to Thomas McKenney, with Jackson in the White House and John Eaton in the War Department he had every reason to expect that matters would progress much more smoothly. Evidence of a new vigorous policy toward the Indians was evident. Indeed, only nineteen days after his inauguration Jackson addressed the Creeks, urging their voluntary removal west of the Mississippi.[10] Less than a month later, Jackson's secretary of war addressed the Cherokees on the same subject. DuVal hoped that the same dispatch would be possible regarding the Seminoles. DuVal expected authorization soon for a "deputation of Chiefs of the Florida Indians to visit Washington" and conclude a "most Effectual plan for their emigration beyond the Mississippi River. I trust," he continued to McKenney, "you will bring this matter before Mr. Eaton, as I hope now to receive more Support than I have hitherto been favored with, in my repeated attempts to have the Indians removed."[11]

Soon thereafter DuVal also wrote to the new administration that change was necessary at Florida's Indian Agency. DuVal urged that John Phagan replace Gad Humphreys as Indian agent. As DuVal explained to Eaton, Humphreys had illegally purchased slaves and cattle from the Indians and had improperly created a sugar plantation at the agency. Forwarding extensive evidence that Humphreys had used his office for personal enrichment, DuVal also complained that the agent had not submitted his accounts to him as directed. Moreover, for the preceding two years, Humphreys had "counteracted the views of the Government in the removal of the Indians—I have no confidence in Col. Humphreys and as the Superintendent I must urge his removal," the governor continued. "The Government has looked to me to enforce its orders this I have in vain attempted—The agent has ever some excuse for evading them, I trust sir you will see the President on this subject and inform me of his determination."[12]

As would be expected, DuVal lost no time in advising the new administration on Florida appointments. After all, Jackson had campaigned on removing corrupt federal appointees for office, and Jackson's national housecleaning, DuVal hoped, would extend to the Florida Territory. Prominent in DuVal's mind was the hope for the final cleansing of Crawford, Adams, and Clay appointees from the ranks of federal officeholders in Florida, but in this work territorial delegate Joseph White could be expected to oppose him. Not long after Jackson's inauguration DuVal shared with the president the views of "your friends in this Territory" that the "benefits resulting from the salutary reform which you have commenced should also be extended to Florida." Among those who ought to be ousted were Humphreys; Judge Joseph Smith of the Eastern Judicial District; Adam Gordon, the U.S. marshal of the Western Judicial District; and William Allison McRea, whom Adams had appointed U.S. district attorney for the Middle Judicial District of Florida in 1827 before transferring him to the Southern Judicial District in May 1828. "No man could have been more indecently abusive of you," DuVal wrote of McRea. "Sir we look to you as the father of this Territory it is truly the child of your own creation—It was the success of your arms that first induced Spain to surrender a country she found too dangerous to maintain. When you consented to become Governor of Florida you were promised that your friends should be provided for. It was a long time ere they were noticed and then, very partially. I [hope] you remember them now and aid us in giving a character to our Territory it richly deserves." DuVal further explained that though there was "not one man in 50 throughout the Territory that does not revere you for your virtues & services, and yet nearly two thirds of all the appointments made by the Late administration, were in direct opposition to the wishes of the People, Believe me sir it is from no influence of a vindictive feelings that I call your attention to these facts—The honor, interest, and character of the Territory . . . its prosperity will in great degree depend on the changes that shall be made."[13]

Later that same afternoon, after seeing Richard Keith Call, DuVal again addressed the president, linking Jackson's reform impulses of the present to his loyal followers in the past who had relocated to Florida. "If I become in any manner troublesome to you, it will give me pain, but if any time I seem too officious, do not ascribe it to a vain desire to give myself consiquence with you." DuVal recommended that Richard C. Allen be appointed in place of the current land agent. Allen was a "sound and correct Lawyer and possesses all the industry and patience requisite for this laborious investigation." Furthermore, Allen, Jackson would recall, had served with him in New Orleans and "through your campaign in Florida." Jackson complied with DuVal's suggestions, appointing Allen and removing McRea, Gordon, and, eventually, Humphreys and Smith.[14]

One of the subjects of DuVal's conversation with Call may have been the emerging scandal in Jackson's cabinet over Peggy Eaton's acceptance in Washington society. About the time of Jackson's inauguration Call had consulted with Presbyterian minister Ezra Stiles Ely regarding the Eaton situation. These talks and others convinced Ely that Mrs. Eaton was an abandoned woman, and he urged Jackson to remove Eaton from his cabinet. In the ensuing months Jackson angrily responded to the charges against Peggy Eaton by carefully formulating a series of defenses of her character. Call addressed the president personally on the subject in late April, suggesting that Mrs. Eaton was an "unworthy associate for the Ladies of your house." Jackson was livid. The president immediately responded to Call by reminding him of Call's former indiscretions with Peggy in 1823. Moreover, he charged Call with poisoning Ely's mind against Eaton. "Gen.l you cannot regret more than I do that you assisted in giving currency to any reports about Major Eaton and his wife at the time you did." The Peggy Eaton Affair foreshadowed a break between Jackson and Call. The matter consumed Jackson's inner circle that summer and festered into the next year as Jackson invested precious energy seeking to disprove the calumny against the Eatons. Perhaps even more personally distressing to Jackson was that Emily Donelson, the wife of his nephew and personal secretary, sided with other cabinet wives against Peggy. Finally, in April 1831, Jackson accepted the resignation of his entire cabinet. The primary casualty of the affair was Calhoun, but Call's friendship with Jackson was seriously damaged. As Call's friend, DuVal was forced to consider where he stood on the issue. The president seemed desperate to convince everyone he could of Peggy's innocence. He even solicited DuVal's thoughts on the matter.[15]

On June 10, while in Washington, William McCarty, Florida's territorial secretary, resigned his post. When citizens in the Tallahassee learned of the vacancy, a number of them recommended John DuVal for the post. Instead of appointing the governor's brother, Jackson appointed James D. Westcott Jr. of New Jersey.[16] Westcott had the backing of cabinet secretaries Van Buren, Eaton, Barry, and Ingham.

A talented yet volatile young man, Westcott was rumored to have obtained his appointment because of a duel he had fought in New Jersey in defense of Jackson. Westcott's appointment was controversial, and in January 1830 both DuVal and Joseph White, the territorial delegate, personally visited the president, asking him to remove Westcott on the grounds that he was "universally odious" in Florida.[17] As time went on Westcott attained significant stature in Florida, and a kind of rivalry between DuVal and him began almost immediately.

In such transitional times DuVal might well have understood that his own situation was vulnerable. If the White faction could always be expected to oppose DuVal, darts and arrows might come from other quarters as well. In July the president received a long communication from Alexander Hamilton Jr. It will be recalled that Hamilton was a member of the East Florida faction opposed to DuVal and that included Joseph Smith and John Rodman. After congratulating Jackson on his election, Hamilton informed the president that he was among the most effective supporters of Jackson's candidacy in 1824 and in 1828 and noted that in New York there was no greater "advocate of your success." Hamilton was ready for his reward in the form of a "station of respectability." Hamilton reminded Jackson that the "Executive" of the Florida Territory had thwarted his persistent efforts in 1823 to protect the land archives from those who might fraudulently alter the documents for illicit purposes. As for DuVal, Hamilton wrote, he ought to be removed. "Gov. Duval, who was esteemed by all respectable, disinterested men there, a low, vulger, heartless fellow—To his songs, ribaldry and duplicity was he indebted for his elevation and Florida degraded by his presence." Hamilton reminded Jackson that it was his navy secretary, Branch, who should have been appointed in 1822. DuVal would be an Adams and a Clay man "if he thought it politic. . . . The vulgarity and profanity of this personage has been so disgusting, that I have frequently cautioned him against its effects on the public and he was well aware, I was always answerable to these sentiments."[18]

Hamilton's characterization of DuVal's antics and duplicitous behavior was not a universally held opinion but one that was shared by some. DuVal's singing and fondness for telling tall tales would not be acceptable in some sophisticated circles (and it would be difficult to imagine DuVal exhibiting such antics in the presence of John C. Calhoun). But they played well on the frontier. Such behavior may have been a way for DuVal to let off steam, to relax, to put his hearers at ease, or to disarm critics, but his opponents attributed it to a wish to mask devious behavior. It may have also masked a complex personality or served as an antidote to depression. At any rate, Hamilton's views of DuVal contrasted sharply with the views of others who enjoyed his company.

By the fall of 1829 Tallahassee had grown. Its one thousand inhabitants and visitors patronized three public houses of entertainment, nine stores, two groceries, an academy, two private schools, and two churches. The town also served nearly fourteen thousand farmers, planters, and slaves in Leon, Jefferson, and Gadsden Counties. One wing of the capitol had been completed, and the whole building was under contract.[19] As Tallahassee city commissioner, John DuVal administered the sale of town lots and also oversaw the letting of the contract to build the capitol, as well as its construction. When the legislative council began its sessions the governor's brother was under attack for mismanaging the funds under his supervision. Sniping at the governor himself could also be heard. One critic charged DuVal with a "premeditated determination . . . to sacrifice the great interests of Florida to promote the personal interests of a few."[20]

On October 12, when the legislative council assembled, the lawmakers heard the governor's message. The address touched on many subjects, including the unlikely possibility of statehood, the continuing conflict over the Georgia-Florida boundary, and the need to coordinate election dates and to provide for education. DuVal's address also referenced William Allison McRea's murder in Key West, which had occurred the previous May, after his removal from office. McRea and his assailant, a man named Charles E. Hawkins, had fought several duels prior to the deadly act of assassination. DuVal used the "Key West Tragedy" to argue for tougher sanctions against dueling. In 1826 laws against dueling had been weakened, and now the governor called for more stringent measures to combat the practice. One observer congratulated the governor on his "wholesome recommendation" and added that his message "breaths a kind of reconciling spirit."[21]

The most controversial issue that emerged in that legislative session involved DuVal's veto of a bill to charter the Bank of Florida and the West Florida Insurance and Banking Company. DuVal had opposed chartering similar institutions in the previous council and opposed these bills on the same grounds. In his veto message DuVal asserted, "Great care should be taken in all such acts of incorporation, to prevent the institution from getting under the control of persons who have no interest in our Territory . . . of greedy and selfish speculators—or of money brokers, and shavers, who may use it as an instrument to fleece the people—or of gradually sinking, as all monied institutions usually do . . . into the hands . . . of the monied aristocracy. Whenever . . . these contingencies occur, a Bank is one of the greatest evils that can be inflicted by Legislative enactment upon the people."[22]

The capital stock was too high. The bank's tax-exempt status was objectionable. The legislative council had no voice in the directors' election; nor would it have any effectual control over them. There was no provision to ensure that directors would reside in the territory. DuVal found the specie requirements insufficient. Banks should not be allowed to operate as insurance companies, he said. Interest rates were too high. "By those acquainted with the silent and unseen but powerful influence of the measures of banking institutions upon the community around them, the effect of the operations of a bank, with such a capital, and with such powers as are given in this charter, upon the value of property, the credit of the Territory, the whole of its monied and commercial interests, can easily be foreseen and feared." DuVal also charged that, as the legislation was written, the territorial treasurer had no authority to inspect the bank's books. The legislative council was also granted no oversight authority. It could not suspend the charter or prosecute those committing fraud. "No corporation should be so entirely without legislative control—so completely above the laws as this!"[23]

DuVal also opposed the idea that stockholders should have a proportionate voice in the bank according to the amount of stock they owned. "The doctrine that great wealth confers upon its possessor, a proportionate abundance of intellect, has not yet been established in this country. Property does not now and never should exclusively regulate any of our elections. It is sufficient evidence of the aristocratic and anti-aristocratic character of any association that such a provision should be found in its charter. The argument that the owner of many shares is more interested in a Bank, than the owner of a few applied to the facts generally existing in relation to such subjects is of no force." Finally, DuVal was unsure whether the territory had the authority to create banks. He wondered if a territorial government, being itself "an imperfect, qualified and dependent corporation, without any certain term of existence," could properly create other corporations and make them of a more "indissoluble character than itself." It thus was unclear "what effect the organization of our Territory, as a state, will have upon these charters, all of which questions are of an important character. I cannot avoid impressing upon the minds of the Council that as to all laws where there is the slightest probability of their being held binding upon the State government without the power of repeal, it is our duty to exercise doubt vigilance and care. We cannot be too cautious in guarding against evils that may fetter and cripple us in the infancy of our State Government."[24]

Within ten days after DuVal's veto the legislative council had rewritten the legislation and resubmitted it to the governor. DuVal again vetoed the legislation, recounting the failed experiments with banking in Pennsylvania, New York, Maryland, and Ohio. "The rage for Banks, which some years since, pervaded every portion of the Union, has given us so many scenes of Bankruptcy and ruin, that it was believed we had determined to avoid their dangerous influence, until the resources, population, and extended commerce of our country, might justify the experiments." "Are we never to learn the wisdom from the misfortune of others?" he asked. Though he vetoed this legislation, DuVal did assert that he would support efforts to secure a branch of the Bank of the United States in the territory. Despite DuVal's emotional appeals against the chartering of banks in the Florida Territory, the legislature passed the measure over his veto. Within a month the Bank of Florida opened its books, and it received subscriptions for its $600,000 of stock one month earlier than its proposed deadline of April. With $75,000 in specie in the vault, the Tallahassee *Floridian and Advocate* reported on February 23, the institution "will go into immediate operation, and it is supposed that the annual installments will enable it to enlarge its discounts, in proportion to the increasing commerce and agriculture of the country." For now at least, the "bills were at a premium, that is they are on a par with United States notes."[25] DuVal would eventually accommodate himself to the reality of banking in Florida. As time went on he would be a stockholder and even represent banking institutions in court.

When the legislative council adjourned, DuVal left the territory for Washington on December 8, the same day that Andrew Jackson forwarded his first address to Congress.[26] Jackson's address touched on foreign affairs, the tariff, and Indian removal. Negative comments on the Second Bank of the United States were also included. The first session of the Twenty-first Congress met until May 31, and DuVal was in Washington during the entire time.

DuVal attended the congressional sessions and met with key officials in the various executive departments. He also attended many parties and public gatherings during his six- month stay in Washington. Among those DuVal visited soon

John Quincy Adams, ca. 1830s. Courtesy of Library of Congress.

after he arrived in Washington was former president John Quincy Adams. On January 18 the ousted New Englander noted that DuVal "professed with anxiety friendly and respectful sentiments for me—I suppose with sincerity." Adams reflected that while DuVal was appointed "partly by my influence" by President Monroe and then again by himself as president, he had been a "uniform and by no means silent partisan of General Jackson; chiefly because Jackson was the enemy of Mr. Clay. DuVal is conscious of the meanness of his conduct to me," Adams recorded, "and thinks to delude me, as he perhaps deludes himself, by professions of general respect, and by assurances that he never spoke disrespectfully of me." Adams had been informed otherwise. Their conversation was a frank one. DuVal asserted that it was Clay's appointment that cost Adams the support of the western states. Adams countered (to himself and perhaps to DuVal as well) that he had appointed Clay because he considered him "the man of the Union best fitted for the place of Secretary of State."[27]

DuVal's meeting with Adams must have been awkward. But the governor was not the only Florida official to visit the former president. Territorial delegate Joseph White was also in Washington and visited Adams on both the day before and the day after DuVal's meeting. Not surprisingly, the delegate vented his anger over Jackson's removal of twelve "highly popular officers" in the Florida Territory. When the delegate confronted Old Hickory on the subject, the president, he explained to Adams, "flew into a passion; and said that he had been abused from Dan to Beersheba for his removals, and that not a single man had been removed but for oppression or defalcation." White then took the matter up with Van Buren to no avail and then complained to several senators of the bad character of many of Jackson's appointees. When Jackson summoned White to explain, the delegate "went through the list, and mentioned facts respecting almost every one of them, which showed them fitter candidates for a treadmill than for public office; to which the President listened with tolerable patience, and closed the interview by saying he would see to it." White even enlisted DuVal's help in convincing Jackson to remove Westcott, claiming that the secretary was extremely unpopular in Florida. Their meeting with the General was to no avail, the president explaining that "if the appointment had not been made, he would not now nominate him; but as it was, he did not see how he could drop him."[28]

Part of DuVal's and White's objection to Westcott and to John G. Stower of New York (who had replaced McRea as U.S. attorney) was that both appointees were Northerners. White took up the matter directly with Vice President Calhoun, asking him to lay the matter before the Senate and asking that Westcott and Stower not be confirmed. The people of Florida should not be subjected to officers from nonslaveholding states, of whom there were already six in the territory. "The Territories," the delegate insisted, "are too apt to be considered as the patrimony of the decayed, or neglected politicians of the States"—and Northern states at that. "It had not yet been proposed to fill the Government of Michigan, with cast off agitators from Georgia, or the Carolinas." The happiness of the people requires that their officers not be imported from afar but have a community of interest and feeling with the people, White argued. "It is not the purpose of my Constituents to draw invidious distinctions, but they most respectfully beg leave to question the propriety of subjecting a southern population to be governed by persons whose views and principles are so much at variance with their own. To them it seems that the danger of disturbing questions now happily at rest, is increased by appointing to office in Southern Territories, those who seldom have discretion enough to conceal opinions odious to the population." On this subject White and DuVal spoke with one voice.[29]

Controversy over appointments tended to exacerbate divisions already evident in Florida. For example, Elias Gould, the editor of the St. Augustine *Florida Herald,* also a New Jersey native, praised Westcott's handling of territorial affairs in the governor's absence, commenting that "our new Secretary . . . appears very attentive to business, greatly correcting the loose and imprudent manner which the duties of that office have heretofore been conducted" (in other words, a bit of Yankee efficiency in the governor's office was a welcome addition). DuVal strongly opposed Westcott's confirmation, but the nominee had enjoyed a near unanimous vote in the Senate. Westcott, the editor observed, executed his official duties with "independence and fearlessness."[30]

When it came to lobbying Congress or the executive for appropriations for Florida, White and DuVal could work together. White would have supported DuVal's personal appeal to Secretary of the Treasury Samuel Ingham to establish customs collections at Tampa Bay and Charlotte Harbor.[31] DuVal also consulted, almost on a daily basis, with Thomas McKenney in the War Department on Indian affairs.

But it was his financial accounts that occupied most of DuVal's time, and he expected far more sympathetic treatment from the new administration. Reviewing the dispute going back to 1824, DuVal explained to Eaton that he was entitled to far more than the $750 per year for superintending Indian affairs. DuVal declared that the territorial governor of Arkansas was paid for his work as superintendent of Indian affairs and observed that there were few Indians in Arkansas but more than five thousand in Florida. DuVal asked to be released from all responsibilities regarding Indian affairs. "It will oblige me much if this change can be made, at this, or the next Session of Congress on the same terms—this desire arises from the fact [that] in 8 years I have acted as Superintendent of Indian affairs. I have sunk $4000 having been compelled to expend $500 per annum in the discharge of my duties & expenses of my office, more than my annual compensation $9000 being the actual expenses of the office alone. The trouble and labor of my duties as Supt have always been greater than my other executive duties." "I am certain of one fact, that had I never been obliged to act as Sup't I would have saved in 8 years I have been Gov'er $500 per annum," he added. Eaton's response was not positive. "I consider this matter, as having been heretofore arranged, and hence do not feel myself at liberty to disturb the arrangement." DuVal's disputes with the War Department continued. Finally, in the summer of 1832, after Eaton had left his post, President Jackson ordered that "the accounts of Gov. DuVall for his services & expenses should be opened and reconsidered." Jackson's new secretary of war, Lewis Cass, chaffed at the order from the White House but came to what he hoped would be a final resolution of the situation.[32]

While DuVal was in Washington, political opponents in Florida accused him of improperly arranging for his brother John's appointment as Tallahassee commissioner, a position that gave him influence over the selection of contractors to build the territorial capitol. At issue were the circumstances of his appointment and his bond, and rumors were flying. Some of DuVal's supporters had suggested that Secretary James Westcott was secretly assisting DuVal's opponents in their recent charges against DuVal to the president. The secretary had all too eagerly turned over documents to DuVal's opponents to use in attacks against the governor. With his own reappointment on the line, Westcott defended himself against these accusations and clarified the situation to President Jackson's secretary, adding that these "insinuations" against him were "totally untrue." Governor DuVal himself, "I am persuaded, would not have refused them the papers himself. Prudence and propriety," the secretary wrote, "dictate to me, that I should not unnecessarily throw myself on the side of any of the several local and sectional parties or divisions, existing in Florida, and besides Gov. DuVal is amply competent to defend himself without my humble aid." Westcott also refuted the charge of DuVal's enemies that the governor "in the selection of territorial officers has improperly preferred his own relatives. I do not hesitate to say that I believe this accusation is unjust. Indeed I consider his course as far as I have witnessed it, on this point, unnecessarily scrupulous. I know of no relation of his ever appointed to office by him. None such were in office on my arrival here." Westcott went on to explain that "great pains have been taken to excite unpleasant feeling between us" and that Joseph White and William Wyatt, a Tallahassee entrepreneur, were at the bottom of the effort but that the governor's friends in the territory had "no such idea." All of this would come to nothing, and the secretary asked Donelson to assure President Jackson that the scheme would "fail in producing any abatement of the good feelings hitherto existing between us."[33] Whether DuVal ever saw this correspondence is unclear. In the upcoming months, tension between the governor and the secretary would reach a breaking point.

The Twenty-first Congress was Jackson's first while he was in the White House. The congressional sessions included the famous Webster-Hayne debate and the formal passage of the Indian Removal Act, on May 28. Outside Congress's halls, relations between Jackson and the vice president (who had arrived in Washington roughly the same time as DuVal) degenerated steadily over the "Eaton Malaria" (as Martin Van Buren called it), the tariff, and Calhoun's role in the "Florida Affair."[34]

As the Eaton Affair simmered, Jackson's confrontation with Calhoun at the Jefferson Day Dinner on April 13 brought the matter of a state's right to nullify a federal law to a head. On that festive occasion Jackson threw down the gauntlet to Calhoun when he uttered that famous toast "Our Federal Union—it must be preserved"—to which Calhoun responded, "The Union: Next to Our Liberty Most dear; may we always remember that it can only be preserved by respecting the rights of the States, and distributing equally the benefits and burdens of the Union." Nearly all official Washington attended the gathering. Toasts were carefully rehearsed and reprinted in newspapers. Though there is no specific evidence that DuVal personally attended the gathering, it is likely he was there. Among those officiating was DuVal's friend Kentucky senator Henry Bibb, who made the first lengthy speech. Bibb's address recalled Kentucky's role in the American Revolution, in the settlement of the West, and, most important, in the first sectional crisis, in 1798, in response to the Alien and Sedition Acts. Thomas Jefferson's

Kentucky Resolutions enunciated sound principles against federal legislation that threatened individual liberties; according to Bibb, a similar stand was needed in the face of the current challenge. Bibb contended that "sordid spirit of avarice, a cold calculating policy to promote the peculiar interests at the expense of the majority of the States," was at work and must be checked. Bibb's long recitation of the dangers the nation was facing even contained the words "the Union it must be preserved" (the same phrase uttered by Jackson moments later). But exactly how this would occur was uncertain. Would it be preserved by the majority overwhelming the minority, by some accommodation of the minority, or by some scheme of state nullification of federal law as Calhoun envisioned? After enunciating as best he could the Principles of '98 and their relevance to the current crisis, Bibb closed with a toast: "Our Federal Constitution—the character of limits between States and federal powers. Let us remember that the best constitutions will degenerate into tyranny if there be not a power to watch, support, and defend them against usurpation."[35]

By their selection of the first speakers at the dinner, the managers of the event seemed to have stacked the deck against Webster's view of the Union, but Jackson turned the tables on them with his direct challenge to Calhoun. The upshot of the gathering was that, despite the rhetoric and the lengthy speeches, Jackson's sentiments regarding the issues at hand were clear. He saw the choices as between good and evil; he could see no middle ground.[36] Within a month, heated private correspondence between Jackson and Calhoun over the "Florida Affair" had commenced. A final break between the two would occur by the summer, even before Duff Green published their correspondence in the Washington *Telegraph* in February 1831. By the early months of 1831 philosophical, political, and personal enmity between Jackson and Calhoun had grown so strong that official Washington held its collective breath and waited for the next shoe to drop. There seemed to be no middle position, and for DuVal and others who had hitched their wagons to and planned their futures around a peaceful coalition between the Hero and the South Carolinian, their plans began to unravel. DuVal's political skills would be put to the test. Could he straddle the fence?

The congressional session adjourned on May 31, but before DuVal left the capital, nearly one month later, a serious matter involving William Wyatt, a Tallahassee businessman who resented the Nucleus's monopoly on political appointments and favors, required DuVal's immediate attention. Wyatt had represented Leon County in the legislative council in 1826, 1827, and 1829 and aspired to greater positions of leadership in the territory, but he found himself increasingly frozen out. In 1828 he made an unsuccessful bid to build the capitol and blamed DuVal personally for not granting him the contract.[37] Only days before DuVal left Washington, Joseph White, the territorial delegate, handed President Jackson Wyatt's petition charging DuVal's administration with malfeasance and corruption.

When Jackson asked for a response from the governor, DuVal merely responded that Wyatt was a man "destitute of character and unworthy of credit or consideration." There the matter stood when DuVal left Washington.[38]

As DuVal headed south toward Tallahassee, Jackson, Eaton, Donelson, and others close to the president headed to the Hermitage for the summer. The session had been stressful, the Eaton controversy was not yet over, and Jackson needed rest. DuVal reached his destination on June 21, but while he was away from Tallahassee, Florida politics was roiling and divisions would soon be felt as local conflicts merged with factions that endorsed or did not endorse nullification. The Wyatt petition would soon be public, and DuVal's conflict with territorial delegate White would reach a breaking point.

On the home front, the prospects for DuVal's oldest son, twenty-one-year-old Burr Harrrison, were high. Parlaying his administrative experience as a secretary for his father, he was appointed customs inspector at St. Marks, and in February he was elected major in the Seventh Regiment of the Florida Militia. DuVal's oldest daughter, Marcia, and her husband, Dr. William Price, were comfortably settled at Aspalaga, where he served as unofficial physician to the Apalachicola Indians. Also through his father-in-law's influence, Price would secure appointment as inspector of the Port of Apalachicola. Burr DuVal's younger sisters and brothers were still in the DuVal household when the governor returned to Tallahassee on June 21. Elizabeth (15), Mary (11), and Laura (10) helped their mother care for four-year-old Florida. Thomas (17) and John (14) spent their time working the farm, but they also hunted and fished in the woods. The next year Nancy DuVal took her boys to Bardstown to attend St. Joseph College.

While DuVal's domestic life may have been serene, a number of problems appeared on the horizon that would threaten his hold on the Florida political scene. The challenges and controversies threatened to cost him his governorship. Indian affairs remained a problem. His financial accounts were unsettled, and he would have to oversee arrangements pursuant to the Indian Removal Act. Worse still were growing divisions among the personalities and regional sections of Florida—divisions that would come to a head in the upcoming territorial delegate race.

CHAPTER II

"I intend to examine... Your relation to the President"

On June 29, 1830, Governor William P. DuVal, only recently arrived home from Washington, attended a public dinner in his honor at Tallahassee's Planters Hotel. Presiding as president of the welcome home gathering was Robert Butler, and among the attendees were many of DuVal's closest personal and political friends. The theme for the evening was the celebration of DuVal's role as territorial founder and community builder. Among the toasts given to DuVal was the following: "He found this country a wilderness—that wilderness is now teeming with cultivated fields and populous villages—the people happy and prosperous under his administration—will no longer forget his valuable services." DuVal responded to the many accolades by refusing to accept full credit for settling the country. "There are so many here present," the governor asserted, "equally instrumental in that great work, that I cannot claim an honor as exclusive which is equally due to others. On my right and on my left I see many whom the citizens of Florida ought to regard as their benefactors. I only claim the merit of being one of the band of pioneers who, in the midst of the Red Men of the wilderness felled the primeval forest of Florida, and who now enjoy under the shade of their own vine and fig tree, the rich products of their variegated and fertile fields."[1]

A sampling of the after-dinner toasts demonstrated that the participants were well aware of the national controversies, such as the tariff conflict, the Webster-Hayne debate, and Jackson's confrontation with Calhoun during the Jefferson Day dinner. Not surprisingly, DuVal began the round by toasting Senator George Bibb of Kentucky. But DuVal's brother John threw down the gauntlet by toasting President Jackson: "Andrew Jackson—The hero who preserved the country from invasion, the statesman who preserved the Constitution from infraction." George T. Ward responded by toasting Senator Hayne of South Carolina: "While

William Pope DuVal, ca. 1830s. From the author's collection.

his voice is heard in Washington, eloquence and patriotism will not be wanting in the cause of the South." A toast to Calhoun followed, as did toasts to the two candidates in the upcoming race for territorial delegate, the incumbent Joseph White and challenger James Gadsden. According to one witness the "whole evening was passed in great harmony and cordiality of feeling." Yet these outward appearances masked deep political divisions both at the national level and within the territory. The personalities and subjects referenced in the toasts, particularly how to respond to them, consumed DuVal's energies in the upcoming months.[2]

Serious divisions within the territory were certainly as apparent to DuVal as they were to one observer who wrote about them at the time: "It has been a very difficult task to legislate for the Territory; so discordant have been the views of the people, and so diverse have been their local interests." The territory lacked consensus over important issues, and this lack of consensus had resulted in a disjointed and often conflicting code of laws. There was disarray regarding the law codes as many of the laws embraced in the first code were "repealed and re-enacted, until the whole became so changed and so complex as to render the whole uncertain or unintelligible." This uncertainty often bred contempt for the law. DuVal shared some responsibility for this situation, and his opponents were quick to point out that fact.³

DuVal would also soon come to understand that controversial issues at the national level, such as the "Eaton Malaria," the tariff question, the Nullification Crisis, and Calhoun's alienation from Andrew Jackson, were also of great concern to Florida's territorial inhabitants. DuVal also confronted growing disenchantment with the Nucleus and, by implication, with his own administration of the territory. DuVal's public break with Joseph White would grow wider and burst into open warfare during the 1831 race for territorial delegate and its confused aftermath. William Wyatt spearheaded the opposition to the governor in the territorial capital, even as he petitioned President Jackson against DuVal. Throughout the next two years Wyatt worked closely with Joseph White to expose what he insisted was DuVal's corrupt administration, with the goal of ultimately having him removed. His first public denunciation against DuVal came about the time the governor returned to the territory, through the agency of a St. Augustine newspaper.⁴ Simultaneously, Wyatt privately addressed the governor in a lengthy communication that he eventually made public months later, castigating him for telling the "President that I was a man destitute of character or consideration" and was "politically opposed to him and his administration." He charged the governor with "endeavoring to stab his reputation" by having Gadsden and others write to the president corroborating these statements. "I have also been informed," Wyatt charged, "that since you arrived home, you have denounced Col. White to be base and unprincipled, for presenting these charges." DuVal had endeavored to "impress upon the public that the Col. and myself have privately concerted a plan, with a view to put you out of office, by false accusations and clamor."⁵

The summer of 1830 was truly the season for public gatherings in Tallahassee. At the Fourth of July celebration, many of the seemingly contradictory sentiments evident at the Planters Hotel dinner for DuVal were expressed. Toasts to the Union, the tariff, internal improvements, and "women and wine—the true contentments of man" were juxtaposed with toasts to Hayne and Calhoun. Richard Keith Call toasted both Jackson and Calhoun. John P. DuVal also toasted the vice president, which brought a response from territorial secretary James Westcott, who toasted John Eaton and was himself the beneficiary of a toast, to which he responded at length, thanking his hearers for his acceptance into their circle. The proceedings concluded with a toast to the governor and to the Territory of Florida: "May his example of rectitude be an example for this Union."⁶

Another public dinner was held approximately two weeks later in the honor of territorial delegate Joseph M. White under a "large arbor tastefully arranged on the site near the Cascade attended by a large concourse of citizens from town and country." There was no evidence that DuVal attended this gathering uncomfortably close to his house, but if he had he would have heard White's speech calling for harmony among Floridians: "Let us forget and forgive all that is past.... We have higher and nobler objects in view, than the petty opinions, cabals, and intrigues of party, in which there is neither diversity of political principle, nor divisions upon contested questions of feeling. Instead of wasting our energies in generating personal feuds, or stirring up State prejudices among those who are and ought to be Floridians in character, and feeling, let us contemplate the great change in our condition when we shall pass from our infant state into that of maturity as one of the confederated members of the Union."[7]

White was in town representing Forbes and Company claimants who were suing the United States to have the huge one-and-a-half million-acre tract along the lower Apalachicola River running east to the Ochlockonee River confirmed. The disputed Forbes Purchase case went unresolved for years, eventually reaching the U.S. Supreme Court. President Jackson took a personal interest in this case; at DuVal's urging, he appointed Richard C. Allen to represent the United States. Richard Keith Call also aided the district attorney's defense against the claims to defend the United States against the claimants. Part of this task obliged Call to travel to Havana to secure documents relevant to the case. To Jackson's chagrin, not only did White represent the claimants against the United States, but his own attorney general, John Berrien, joined White's team as well. The first hearings took place in late July in the Leon County Superior Court, with White taking the first two days to plead the case of the claimants. On the other side of the courtroom was James Ringgold, U.S. attorney for the Middle District, along with Call and Allen.[8]

Soon after DuVal's return to the territory, the administration permitted Westcott to return North, and he did so, via St. Augustine. Hearing favorable reports of Westcott's administration and having himself witnessed the secretary's public speaking skills, DuVal felt obliged to write to Secretary of State Van Buren in his favor. Admitting that he and most others had opposed Westcott's appointment, he had been forced to alter his opinion. "The conduct and deportment of Mr. Westcott has gained him the confidence and respect of Jackson men in the Territory. He has discharged the duties of Governor during my absence to the satisfaction of the People, and had not only obtained my approval for his conduct and judgment, but my thanks for the correct, and able manner, he has conducted the business of the office. I have never seen any other man who is so intirely ready and accurate, in the dispatch of business. I consider it, an act of justice to Mr. Westcott to say this in his behalf, because I was opposed to his appointment."[9]

As the hot Tallahassee summer dragged on, anti-Nucleus forces mounted a campaign against the governor. Wyatt led the attack, and others followed. The current system of executive policy, they argued, was incompetent, corrupt, and calculated to reward favorites and punish enemies. If it was not already under way, the full-scale battle between DuVal and White began on September 30 when the delegate sent the governor a scathing letter accusing him of all manner of wrongdoing. White argued that the purpose of DuVal's trips to Washington was not to secure any benefits to the territory but only to convince departments of his "fabrication of large accounts against the Government." Once in the capital he "studiously and artfully" denounced Adams's administration, complaining that he had been "persecuted" because of his political opinions.[10]

White also charged DuVal with manipulating the appointive process. The delegate contended that that his own recommendations of men for office, unlike DuVal's, were not governed by political considerations. "Neither the policy of the country, nor its laws, and constitution require such a test. Honesty and capability are, or ought to be the only qualifications for public employment." DuVal, White charged, had attempted to raise his "decaying popularity at home by a demonstration of influence at Washington."[11] White charged DuVal with nefarious back-channel attacks against his opponents. DuVal did not go directly to the president with his "petty complaints and despicable insinuations." On the contrary, "it was by nocturnal visits, secret whisperings, and tortuous approaches to subordinates about the Executive Offices" that DuVal sought influence. "When I remonstrated against your interference in all the appointments of the Territory, and insisted that neither your office, nor the law creating it ever contemplated such an agency, as that which you gratuitously assumed, you in the usual swaggering style, more in the character of a Boatman than a Gentleman or Governor, with a multitude of oaths, that it would be as indecent to repeat, as it was to utter them, assured me that you would get as many of your friends into office as you could."[12]

DuVal's inappropriate interference in federal appointments was done for the purpose of manipulating elections in Florida so as to get himself reappointed, according to the territorial delegate. White charged that these machinations were done with the purpose of doing what "insignificant men have done, by attaching themselves to the train of a popular President. . . . Notwithstanding your repeated declarations written, and . . . impropriety of interfering in elections, and against the avowed opinions of this administration, for which, if consistent, they must remove you from Office—You have voluntarily taken a most decided part against me." White disputed the fact that DuVal had recommended more men for office who were favorable to Jackson than he. On the contrary, he asserted, the reverse was true.[13]

At that point White reached back nearly a decade, questioning DuVal's appointment as governor. "I intend," he charged, "to examine . . . your relation with the President, about whose success you have a sensibility nearly approaching to an agony. When did you contract your violent attachment?" White charged that

DuVal had been appointed only because of the "good feelings of President Monroe for your father, and through the influence of Mr. Adams whose devoted friend you then professed to be. . . . It was not until you saw that General Jackson very probably was to be elected, that you ventured to announce yourself in his favor, and as the prospects brightened, you became more clamorous until you supposed that if Mr. Adams failed to reappoint you that your claims as victim might entitle you to look for a foreign mission or a seat on the Supreme Bench."[14]

White charged that DuVal had done everything in his power to destroy Jackson's kind feeling toward him. White argued that the president had spoken in the "most flattering terms of me before his election. If he entertains other sentiments now, which I have no reason to believe, they have been produced by that vile system of calumny which has been so shamelessly resorted to for the purpose of driving all my friends out of office." White charged that DuVal boasted of an influence and intimacy he had never possessed and added, "It is true that when I believed General Jackson was turning out all my friends, only because they were so, under your representations, and that of others, I remonstrated as I had a right to do directly and frankly to the President himself. You howled over your grievances real or supposed in secret or blustered out (where you thought it safe to do so) your vulgar threats of personal violence . . . which you never dared to execute and which you would probably now deny. In a word I never have said as much against this administration as you have. I have never brought it into disrepute, as you and some of your party have done by boasting of influence, promising favors, and threatening punishment in its name."[15]

In various letters marked "confidential," White charged, DuVal had schemed to have numerous officeholders removed. "I have seen more of your letters marked confidential than you imagine, and I know the contents of others, which I have not seen, the recital of which would cause the blush of shame to mount into your cheeks if there is a spark of honest pride of character remaining," he continued. "Every gentleman to whom you choose to address a letter marked private does not conceive himself under any moral obligation to become the depository of your intrigues. When you were avowing to me your opposition to proscription, and at the same time writing those secret letters without notice to honorable men who were to be disgraced by removal without seeing the hand that gave the blow, I wonder did you not exhibit the cast of Countenance, which Cicero's imagination attributed to the soothsayers of Rome? With you as with them it can only be attributed to your confirmed and hardened habit of duplicity."[16]

According to White, DuVal had also acted dishonorably regarding the current disputed Forbes Purchase litigation. The duplicity reached back as far as the early 1820s, when White served as land commissioner. Despite DuVal's current attempt to make political hay out of White's and Berrien's decision to argue for the claimants against the government, White charged that DuVal had previously conspired to convince White that both might benefit by using their positions of trust for personal gain. White charged that DuVal offered to go in with White to purchase some of the Forbes tract, "alleging that I might have influence with the claimants to obtain it on good terms—I answered that I was obligated by my office to give an opinion to Congress upon the claim, and of course could not consent to decide upon my own interests, which I should have to do if I made the purchase recommended by you." Soon thereafter DuVal proclaimed to Berrien and others that the title was as good as there was in America. Then, after White secured preemption for settlers there, DuVal "not having secured a part as you desired you joined in deprecating the title and endeavored to excite vulgar prejudices against Mr. Berrien and myself for an ordinary professional duty. You never could stand a little popular excitement, and not being possessed of moral firmness, or competent capacity to examine, or to decide whether it is founded on correct principles, you always endeavor to swim with the current." Then, as soon as President Jackson's cabinet was announced, White charged, DuVal and his "Tennessee friends, began denouncing the most popular appointment he made [Berrien's appointment as attorney general], for no other reason that I could perceive but that he happened to be considered a personal friend of mine, or perhaps because he was from the State of Georgia whose Citizens you and your partisans seem solicitous to exclude from office."[17]

White's devastating critique of DuVal's administration of the territory and of his character as a man must have floored the governor. This full-scale attack from such a skilled politician, lawyer, and polemicist could only serve to convince DuVal that he was in the fight of his life. White concluded his remarks by making ten specific accusations against DuVal and hinting that White was ready to defend his accusations even on the field of honor. "Upon these and innumerable other charges I am willing to meet you in the face of the country before which you have summoned me. If however you choose to deny the jurisdiction and prefer any other resort you will find me always accessible to our invitation."[18] With the letter written as it was on September 30, DuVal might have wondered if White would use these charges as part of his reelection campaign for territorial delegate against DuVal's friend James Gadsden. And would the contents of the letter ever become public? The answer to the last question was yes.

While the contents of White's letter were known for the moment only to DuVal, Wyatt and others during the ensuing delegate's race between White and Gadsden attacked DuVal as a way of attacking Gadsden and supporting White. Approximately one month later Wyatt charged that Gadsden had run against him for the legislative council "merely to suit the speculative views of a few individuals in Tallahassee, who could not have disguised from him their shameful objects, which was a commencement of an unprecedented scheme of denunciation of me, and my friends and a misapplication of the proceeds of the reserved and donated lands, for the use of the people of Florida." Such a strategy was "reprehensible. It is well known that I have been compelled from a sense of moral as well as political duty to complain of the weak and wicked administration of Gov. DuVal, which has always been the main stay to the detestable conduct of those under the influence of Col. Gadsden. . . . Now under this state of things which cannot be denied, all will admit that the public interest call aloud, not only for the removal of Gov. DuVal but that the blighting influence of the whole party should be checked." To protect himself, DuVal and his associates were spreading false accusations against White. White had consistently opposed a "set of men and measures which I have ever considered highly injurious to the Territory, and which I am bound to suppose Colonel Gadsden is in favor of." Moreover, White had supported Jackson's policies, while "on the other hand Colonel Gadsden and some of his leading friends have opposed it, in relation to his Cabinet appointments, which must be considered one of the most injudicious measures adopted by General Jackson."[19]

From several quarters throughout the territory, attacks against DuVal and the Nucleus grew more intense in newspapers. Of the Nucleus "A Georgian" argued that "a strong party, or company, is formed at Tallahassee to guard with vigilance the surveys and sales of the public lands, and to see that no one was appointed to any office in relation to them that was suspected of complaining of an injury." The Nucleus arranged that "persons from Tennessee or those who had come into the Territory under her influence must, under all circumstances, be preferred; and finally, in order to give vigor to this *guardianship,* it was deemed important that a Delegate should be elected to this party, and that the whole Nucleus should move, with one accord, against any one who should presume to peep into their arrangements." In a thinly veiled denunciation of DuVal, the Georgian added, "It is presumable, however that there was an amendment proposed to this general plan, which was for the admission of a *Kentuckian,* because he held high office, and controlled some matters in relation to the public lands, that did not properly belong to their *department,* who although *wincing* a little in the commencement, being in harness, has nevertheless proved himself a valuable member."[20]

Whether to campaign for Gadsden, to shore up his support in the counties east of the capital, or just to get out of the town, DuVal and his family left Tallahassee for St. Augustine in early December. The traveling party would have included Nancy, along with DuVal's daughters, Elizabeth, Mary, Laura, and Florida. His sons Thomas and John may also have made the trip. While in the ancient city DuVal may have stayed with the Sanchez family; after all, Joseph Simeon Sanchez had invited Nancy and her daughters to visit on numerous occasions. Sanchez, a loyal DuVal ally, would have delighted in the governor's visit. After only a few days in St. Augustine, DuVal returned to Tallahassee via the Alachua settlements.[21] On December 24, at a dinner at Colonel Bennet Dell's at Newnansville, DuVal gave an address blasting the "hireling press, which has been employed to assail me."[22] DuVal finally arrived in Tallahassee after the opening of the legislative council.

DuVal's address to the council opened with the subject of Indian removal. "It is a subject of gratification to the people of Florida that the only cloud that checkers our sunny prospects, is fast dispersing by the wise and humane policy of the Government in permanently settling the various Indian tribes west of the Mississippi." DuVal rejoiced in the fact that the Choctaws and the Chickasaws had already signed treaties to remove and added that the remaining tribes would be soon to follow. This humanitarian policy now undertaken by the Jackson administration would save this "remnant of those numerous nations that roved free as air, over this wide continent, may yet . . . be saved from total annihilation." DuVal urged a revision of the criminal code, arguing that English common law in place before 1776 be cast aside and that in its place a clearer, less ambiguous phrasing of statutory law be employed. He recommended that the council select a distinguished jurist to "revise . . . the several codes" and "draft original bills" for the consideration of future councils.[23]

DuVal predicted that the "success of our planters will bring a flood into every section of our Territory." The quality of sugar grown in Florida was equal or superior to that of sugar grown in Louisiana. Many planters had also discovered that Sea Island cotton and Cuba tobacco would yield even greater profits. But this land, he argued, was also suitable to indigo and silk—"but this is also the country of Almond, the Olive, the Fig and Vine. The Orange, the Pine Apple and the Banana, which have hitherto been considered as appertaining almost exclusively to the Indies, have been cultivated successfully in the vicinity of Tallahassee."[24]

One of DuVal's favorite subjects was the instruction of the young, and he urged the council to "erect . . . some general system of education. Upon a subject of such paramount importance, and so intimately connected as this is, with the safety—nay the very existence of free government the liberal institutions there can surely be but one opinion." Though there was disagreement about various systems, "all must agree that knowledge and freedom are destined to be united—or the latter must sink." DuVal called for a system that would accommodate the less well-off and the well-to-do because "unless knowledge is diffused—unless it pervades through every stage and rank of society its effects however salutary are at best, but partial and inadequate." In clumsy references to Greek and Roman civilizations and to the changes wrought by the French Revolution, DuVal attributed the fall of the existing cultures to a failure to diffuse education to the masses. A few talented men could not sustain the energies of a nation. "To make the edifice secure, the foundation must be strong as the superstructure is adorned. It is the *People*—emphatically the people, that must be informed—It is for them that governments are, or should be formed; and it is *their* character, *their* knowledge, *their* patriotism, *their* moral and intellectual strength alone, that must at last in

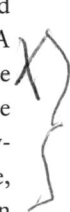

their day of trouble and commotion, sustain, invigorate, and save a nation. If they be ignorant, if they be alike unacquainted with, and regardless of their duties as citizens; of their rights as men and freemen—of what avail is it to them, that legislators plan and statesmen toil?" Referencing the current revolutionary tumult in France and in Spain's former Latin American colonies, DuVal speculated that positive changes in those lands could come only from a broadly educated populace. Returning to the situation at home, DuVal reminded the legislators that creating a workable educational system "should be a matter of engrossing public, as well as private, concern. Governments formed as ours confessedly are, on the intelligence of the people ought surely to omit no effort to keep alive that knowledge to which they owe their existence. The general government by her ample reservation of lands, avowedly for the promotion of support of schools, at some future day, as already shown how fully aware she is of the importance of education. Why should this system be delayed? Every day that is lost, is an injury to ourselves, and will be an injury to those that are to follow us." DuVal urged the legislators to immediately develop a way to solicit the general government for lands to support this great cause, predicting that "she will not deny us this last—best boon—the boon of knowledge, and consequently of virtue and of happiness."[25]

DuVal may well have been proud of his efforts at oratory. Indeed, his address gives evidence of much preparation. Yet critics charged that his address lacked sufficient specific information on the current status of efforts to remove the Seminoles. One detractor also found fault with DuVal's newfound grandiose style and eloquence. "What should have been his Excellency's inducement to abandon his usual strait-forward method and to affect . . . a style which smacks so much of Sophomorean eloquence, and is so much at variance with an ordinary tone of public and state papers, we are at a loss to imagine. We certainly want a system of general instruction, but he might have substituted a practical plan, for the Romans and Greecian lore with which we have been treated. We can overlook affection and bombast in a holy day or 4th of July oration, but they are hardly pardonable in documents which ought to relate entirely to matters of facts."[26]

In the midst of the legislative session, Wyatt unleashed his greatest salvo against DuVal when the Tallahassean published his letter to DuVal personally attacking the governor. The Pensacola *Gazette* published the letter on January 11. The Tallahassee *Floridian and Advocate* followed suit on February 10. The communication charged DuVal with lying, disingenuous behavior, inconsistency, and double dealing. In addition to the charges already touched upon previously, Wyatt cast DuVal throughout his entire career in Florida as a devious, conniving political opportunist who changed his stripes whenever it suited him. Beginning with his appointment as governor, Wyatt charged, DuVal had consistently changed course in policy and personal loyalties whenever it furthered his interests. "Your Excellency has certainly not forgotten that on your first arrival in the territory as

Governor, you told the people that you had received your appointment, through the influence of Mr. Adams, that you had not come among them to mend a broken fortune, but to correct the abuses of Gen. Jackson, whose official acts as Governor of Florida, you represented to be highly exceptionable." DuVal, Wyatt argued, had denounced Jackson's Seminole campaign, his treatment of the Spaniards, and the execution of Ambrister and Arbothnot. He professed to be an "avowed friend of Mr. Adams, after his election to the Presidency, you then chimed in with your particular friend and relative, the notorious Ninian Edwards, and denounced Mr. Crawford as being base and corrupt." Then, once it was understood that Jackson would be president, "you 'ever strong upon the strongest side,' in turn, denounced Mr. Adams, the Coalition, Mr. Clay, and all, with these vulgar epithets, so common at that day, among such Jackson men as yourself. . . . As soon as Gen. Jackson was elected, you post off to Washington, and was then loud upon the subject of removals, and wrote to some persons in Florida, that no one need expect your support, or patronage who was politically opposed to Gen. Jackson. Here, indeed, is a lesson of consistency for Tallyrand himself!" But now that Jackson's War Department had begun to scrutinize his accounts, Wyatt predicted that he would support whoever might run against the president in the next election.[27]

Wyatt further charged DuVal with unfairly trying to influence the territory's first delegate race by supporting army officer John Bronough of Pensacola. And later DuVal had even spoken of General Call's "incapacity" as a delegate and had urged that a petition be gotten up to have the governor himself go to Washington and attend to the territory's affairs. Wyatt then charged that DuVal had denounced in turn "Hernandez because he was a Spaniard, Gadsden because he was a military man even though he had left the army—all the while representing Col. White as one of the best and greatest men (save yourself) in the territory. But so soon as he was compelled as Delegate to correct some of your abuses in office, and place a check upon your executive powers, you at once became his inveterate enemy. There is no charge that a rancorous heart could make, or a vulgar tongue express, that you did not resort to against him, you told the people of Jackson county, that he was corruptly engaged in the Kentucky Asylum donation, and swore that you would cut his throat as soon as he arrived in the territory."[28]

When White came to Florida, Duval, "instead of cutting his throat . . . like a humble petitioner," "sued for peace. You sent word to the Colonel that you would meet him half way, at the little branch between your house and town, where you classically avowed you would cross the Rubicon, and from that moment swear friendship to his cause. You afterwards at a public dinner in Tallahassee, toasted Col. White as one of the purest and best men in Congress, and by a clumsy speech lauded him to the skies."

But when some of DuVal's friends protested the truce, the governor "re-cross[ed] the *Rubicon,* and swearing a new alliance to the *Nucleus.* You then swore, as a milder punishment than before that your Excellency would commit mayhem upon the body of one Joseph M. White, by cutting his ears off, as soon as he arrived in the city, which you have not done, and which it is well known you have not nerve to do, or even insinuate in his presence."[29]

Wyatt's charges against DuVal, devastating as they were, were difficult to dismiss. They also caused comment among Florida's editorial community. After printing the entire letter, the editor of the Pensacola *Gazette* observed that if "Governor DuVal is the man here represented, he is certainly unfit for the dignified and responsible station which he holds." Wyatt's charges against DuVal, "in so tangible a shape," must be answered. The editor had continually heard complaints "in most of the counties" that the governor had appointed men who "have been tools of the Tallahassee Nucleus, and use their offices for the promotion of their views. . . . We do not see how the Executive of the U.S. can continue him in office. We believe we speak the sentiments of a large majority of the people of this section of the Territory, when we say, that should Gov. DuVal not be re-appointed, it would be hailed with unfeigned pleasure."[30]

CHAPTER 12

Nullifying an Election

The question of DuVal's reappointment was a matter that occupied Florida lawmakers' time. Given White's, Wyatt's, and others' attacks against DuVal, the governor's supporters in the legislative council issued a resolution in his favor. While it denounced the move as "extra-legislative," the Tallahassee *Floridian and Advocate* reported that on January 17 Peter Gautier of Calhoun County had introduced a resolution calling for the governor's reappointment. The resolution carried by a vote of 13 to 3.[1] Petitions in support of DuVal also were forwarded to Tallahassee, prompting Abram Bellamy, the president of the legislative council, to write to President Jackson that if the "if the reappointment (at this time) of Gov. DuVal, depended on the people of Florida, he would be certain of the office." Enclosing the legislative council's resolution endorsing DuVal's reappointment, Bellamy also forwarded a petition from citizens from Alachua and Duval Counties in the support of the governor. The latter document noted that despite false "representations . . . gotten up injurious to the character and respectability of His Excellency the Governor of this Territory," the signers had full confidence in the governor and hoped the president understood that fact.[2]

Though the legislative council would muster a majority vote on his reappointment resolution, DuVal had little success in influencing legislation. He used his veto pen eight times during the session, but in every instance except one the council overrode his sanction. Among the legislation passed over DuVal's veto were bills chartering banks in St. Augustine and Apalachicola, a bill to charter a railroad linking Tallahassee with St. Marks, and several divorce bills. DuVal opposed divorce on moral grounds but in this instance stated that the courts, not the legislature, were the proper venue for such action. "Such acts are almost constantly passed on exparte statements or evidence," and courts can weigh the facts of the case, whereas legislatures can't, he argued. "I have therefore rejected the acts, leaving the parties to their remedy at law." DuVal's only sustained veto came against the legislature's attempt to repeal the antidueling law. DuVal argued that the "present law is one of the best in Our Code."³ The law would remain on the books.

As the legislative session came to a close, in early February, the upcoming delegate race between Joseph White and James Gadsden loomed on the horizon. Supporters of each candidate pled vociferously for their candidate in the newspapers, in private correspondence, and on the stump. Opponents of the governor linked his reappointment with the goal of electing Gadsden and defeating White. "They are links in the same chain," declared Cincinnatus. The White supporter complained that a new paper, the *Florida Courier,* had been gotten up to forward the cause of the Nucleus, DuVal's reappointment, and White's defeat and that that paper had been awarded the contract to print the laws, despite the *Floridian and Advocate*'s better bid. That paper's support for White had cost it the contract to print the laws; furthermore, all aspirants for office, Cincinnatus claimed, had to declare "friendship to the DuVal and Gadsden party." But matters would soon be put right once President Jackson investigated Wyatt's charges against DuVal. "Should Governor DuVal fairly refute those charges, the people will have no objection to his re-appointment; but until then, he holds his office against their will. Let his Excellency do that which every honest man should ever be proud to do. Let him publicly vindicate his reputation from charges which if unjust, will recoil upon his accusers, but if well founded render him unworthy of the station which he now holds."⁴

By the winter of 1831 DuVal's battle with White had become open, public, and vociferous. White and his allies launched a stream of personal attacks against DuVal's administration of Florida. On February 24, 1831, recounting the instances in which DuVal had lied or misled him, White charged DuVal with "inconsistency" and "duplicity." In subsequent weeks, other correspondents excoriated DuVal, Gadsden, and other Nucleus operatives. Opponents charged DuVal with favoring Gadsden in the upcoming delegate election.⁵

A common theme in the attack against the Nucleus was its decision to take Calhoun's side in the ongoing cabinet dispute. By the middle of March, Florida newspapers were reporting the imminent breakup of Jackson's cabinet, the publishing of the Jackson-Calhoun correspondence in Duff Green's *United States Telegraph,* the formation of Francis Blair's Washington *Globe,* and that paper's determination to defend Jackson in the face of Calhoun's surrogates. "Much angry political excitement will result from this controversy," one observer speculated. "What influence it will ultimately have on national politics, or the fortunes of those who are looking forward to the first office . . . is impossible to anticipate. Further developments are looked for with much interest."⁶ Relations among Jackson's cabinet members had broken down completely. No one understood this better that Martin Van Buren, and, after careful consultation with the president, the secretary of state resigned; within days Eaton and other cabinet members had

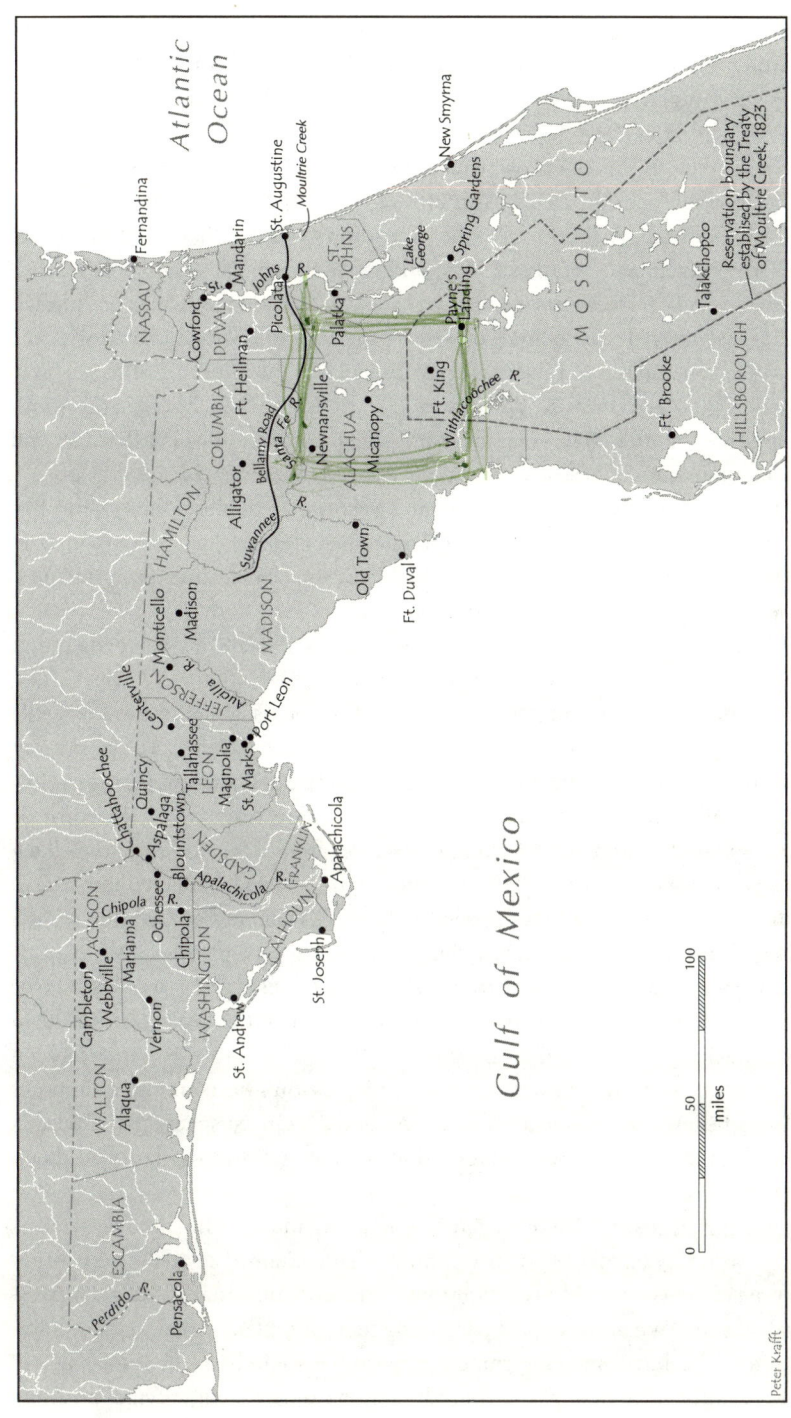

William Pope DuVal's Florida Territory, ca. 1834. Map by Peter Krafft.

also left their posts. By the end of April Jackson had appointed a new cabinet: Edward Livingston replaced Van Buren (State), Lewis Cass replaced Eaton (War), Roger Taney replaced Berrien (attorney general), Louis McLane replaced Ingham (Treasury), and Levi Woodbury replaced Branch (Navy).[7]

The conflict in Washington trickled down to Florida as Nucleus and DuVal opponents used the controversy to argue that they had been disloyal to Old Hickory. Call, Gadsden, Allen, and DuVal, according to Cato, "had successively attacked the Secretary of State, of War, and the Attorney General." They "have caused good officers to be turned out and bad ones to be put in, which has injured the administration at home & abroad & yet they are still currying favor with the administration and attempting to use its influence to the injury of others." "Will Doctor *Courier* [Dr. Edward R. Gibson]," Cato asked, "tell whether the South Carolina part of the NUCLEUS have not often expressed a wish that General Jackson might die, that the Vice President should be President? Have they not . . . predicted that they would bring General Jackson into public odium; have they not said that the Tariff was unconstitutional when General Jackson says its constitutional? If they are opposed to the administration its measures and principles, why invoke its popularity against their opponents?"[8]

When pressed about his association with the Nucleus, Gadsden denied that he was a part of a faction, whether personal or regional in nature. Such charges, he responded, were made up by "electioneering bugbears, generated in the fertile imagination of those who would alarm the people."[9] Addressing the current question of whether a state had the right to nullify a federal law, Gadsden, like DuVal, tap-danced around the question. "Our Union is based on the spirit of mutual *concession* and *compromise,* of reciprocal *burdens* and *benefits.*" Such equivocation was not acceptable to "A Voter," who asked Gadsden point blank in an adjacent column: (1) did he approve of Jackson's demand of Calhoun to "account for acts done 12 years ago, when Mr. Calhoun was his official superior or of the General's comparing him to the assassin of Caesar?"; (2) was he in favor of destroying the National Bank?; (3) was he in favor of the tariff?; (4) was he in favor of Jackson or Calhoun for president?; (5) was he in favor of removing men who opposed Jackson?; (6) was he in favor of Jackson's decision not to appoint men who believed in nullification or conventions?[10] One suspects that Gadsden was not in a hurry to answer such questions with any degree of clarity. And neither was DuVal.

That spring Joseph White was in Washington, and on March 10 he wrote a letter to Secretary of State Martin Van Buren that contained a startling revelation about the circumstances of his submitting Wyatt's petition against DuVal to President Jackson. "When the papers containing these complaints against the administration of the Territorial Government came into my hands, at the session before last, I presented them from a sense of indispensable official obligation, disclaiming all knowledge of the facts stated, and desiring not to be connected with, or responsible for anything communicated. I had no knowledge of the transactions which were made on the subject of a memorial to the President, and from a most sincere and unaffected desire, to avoid the remotest connection with it, I did not wish to make myself even acquainted with them."[11]

Instead of demanding an investigation, White charged, DuVal had "loaded the petitioner with every species of vituperation and abuse." At the secretary of state's prompting, White had presented these charges and documents to the president, upon which Jackson told him he saw "no evidence of impropriety, and as he did me the favor to exhibit to me the representations on the part of the Gov. he examined them again and formed a counter conclusion to the President. I regret to say that I cannot bring my mind to the conclusion to which the President seemed to have arrived, and with the greatest possible respect I beg leave to suggest, that if the President will take time to read the papers submitted, he will see that there has been a double charge as alleged."[12]

DuVal had charged double payments for rent of public buildings, Wyatt charged, and had favored some government contractors to supply the Indians over others in order to "fill the pockets of a favorite merchant, to whom the Governor was indebted." He was also guilty of numerous violations of the public trust. Similar charges had come from Gad Humphreys and from East Florida planter Zephania Kingsley, whom DuVal had likewise denounced. White had been told that DuVal had informed the secretary on one occasion that "'White is down!' And will be beaten '*ten* to *one*,' and that if the President would order him to Washington he would put his (White's) character before the nation in an *odious light*. This sentiment alone in my humble judgment ought to cause his dismission from office. He consults his wishes rather than his judgment in announcing the first fact, that I am down and whether I am to be beaten or not, is a question for the people to decide. How impertinent to suppose that the President would order him here to traduce me!!!"[13]

To counter the charges against DuVal, his friend Richard C. Allen wrote to Tennessee senator Hugh Lawson White, who shared with the president the letter defending DuVal and accusing delegate White and Wyatt of arranging a plan of attack against "our 'beloved Governor.'" The delegate, he charged, was the "active agent behind the curtain" of an anti-DuVal party in Florida. "This party has combined for the purpose of prejudicing the President against Gov. DuVal, and if possible to prevent his re-appointment—the Delegate is aiding and assisting as far as his popularity and official influence enables him to do." Those against DuVal, the communication declared, were "*dismissed officers* and *Northern men*." Joseph White countered that those who favored DuVal "held his commission, have benefited by his favoritism, or are his creditors and endorsers who desire to retain him to indemnity themselves from the Treasury."[14]

White defended Wyatt's character to Van Buren and represented himself as a neutral conveyor of Wyatt's petition. In fact, he explained, Wyatt was an "active political opponent who has always been heretofore against me, in local elections, and in the heat of canvass I have spoken harshly of him." Yet White said that he had never heard of any of Wyatt's acts that would be denounced as "infamous." "In his private relations he has the character of an honest man, his public conduct has been such as to secure him an election in the largest District of the Territory as long as he was a candidate, and he received more votes for Congress in the county in which he (and Gov. DuVal) lives, than Col. Gadsden and myself together. In intellectual matters and education he is superior to the Governor. His complaints cannot be disregarded upon any undefined imputation of infamy." White closed by offering up numerous memorials and a "new catalog of charges, which I pray may be placed on file," which he hoped would be sufficient to prevent the governor's reappointment. White's missive also served the purpose of a campaign document in his race against Gadsden, and on April 14 the Tallahassee *Floridian and Advocate* published the letter.[15]

DuVal answered White's and other's attacks in the Tallahassee *Florida Courier* on April 21. Gibson dedicated his entire sheet to DuVal's letter "To the Freemen of Florida" and his accompanying correspondence. Gibson also introduced the volatile issue of race and abolitionism to discredit White, with the implication that he endorsed Zephaniah Kingsley's controversial publications on relations among the races.[16]

While totally refuting the charges contained in White's letter to Van Buren, DuVal also insisted that White had published it "on the eve of the approaching election with a fond hope of producing some political effect." Up to the present, the governor stated, "I have hitherto borne patiently and [with] silence, the slanderous attacks which this man, in the name of others, and under various disguises, has caused to be circulated against me." Part of the reason DuVal had remained silent was that the complaints had been laid personally before the president, and it was to him "*alone* my defense should be properly made," but it was White's unauthorized publication of the letter for his own personal benefit that had forced DuVal to respond. The governor both refuted the charges and refused to answer them, insisting that he had answered them in the proper way more than a year earlier. "What madness there is in the delegate to attempt so miserable a deception on the people! Surely, nothing short of the despair he feels of the approaching election could have induced him to hazard so much—He hoped to escape detection until the election was over, and if the people could be *once more* cheated into his re-election, it was all he desired." White's "whole life has been a striking (I had almost said disgusting) example of cunning and deceit. From a long habit of deceit, from a sort of fixed obliquity of mind, he cannot be faithful even to his friend, Mr. Wyatt!—This friend who he pronounced 'infamous' to many gentlemen, in former days, when they were enemies."[17]

DuVal went on to deplore White's "pitiable duplicity" by citing a letter he had written to Senator Bibb stating that Wyatt's statements "could not be relied on." "Even the old maxim of 'honor among rogues,' is grossly violated, for while he used Mr. Wyatt to *steal my character* from me—keeping from himself the responsibility of the attack, he betrays his friend, and intends no doubt, if he ever *should be re-elected* by this *means* to cast him, like a loathsome weed, away; and then, indeed, if charged with treachery, with what confidence can he now appeal to the president to prove, that he once said, '*Wyatt is a trifling fellow,*' or *Wyatt cannot be relied on.*"[18]

DuVal went on to note that he had discovered correspondence between White and Wyatt in which the two men conspired to hatch a plot to have DuVal removed. The former Indian agent Gad Humphreys was also in league with them. If Humphreys was joining in the attack, DuVal warned, the former agent's own negligence while in office might come to light. "I had him removed from his office because he did not attend to his duty, and because he was not worthy in my opinion of the confidence of the Government—I should be in a lamentable condition, indeed, if the assertions of *dismissed officers* and a few other unprincipled men—the tools of the Delegate, could seriously affect my character."[19]

As far as the circumstances under which White made his charges to the president, DuVal stated that Old Hickory fully understood "my feelings" for the colonel. And "really, he [White] seems uncommonly dull not to perceive, that as the President could not in his own house with civility tell him *directly,* his opinion of his motives and conduct; he handed him my private letter, leaving him to draw the proper inference. Any man of feeling and sensibility would have understood this—but the *Colonel* considered this a favour. I venture to say that if Gen. Jackson had believed that Colonel White had acted from principle and an honest desire to perform his duty, my private letter never would have been handed to him. Gen. Jackson's known respect for honor and virtue," DuVal continued, "is such that he would not have hurt the feelings of any good man by even hinting at the contents of this private letter—if he believed them to be untrue. . . . I have been forced into this reply. My duty, my station, and my inclinations have hitherto united in withholding me from appearing before the people. You all can hear me witness that I have not sought this controversy—this *ignoble* controversy—The foul plot which has been so artfully laid to ruin my reputation, it was my duty, both as an officer and as a man, to expose—I have done so." As a final defense DuVal attached extracts of three letters from Andrew Donelson, Kentucky congressman Charles Wickliffe, and Senator George Bibb.[20]

White's response to the DuVal letter was quick and sharp. "I have seen in the *Courier* of the 21st ult. a scurrilous production over the signature of Wm P. DuVal.

The style and manner of the publication show, that it could only proceed from one who has neither the character nor feelings of a gentleman. The evident object of it was to produce some effect upon my election; the sentiments contained in it, when separated from the ribaldry are of the characteristic grossness, which must excite the disgust of all men of sense and honor." White stated that the "unworthy Governor" had forced the controversy on him because he "did not refuse a citizen of the Territory to the constitutional right of presenting a petition to the constituted authorities for a redress of grievances." Denying DuVal's accusations against White in the letter, the delegate demanded to know whether the governor had told Jackson that White was "'down and will be beaten.'"[21]

As the vitriol continued to flow in Florida, President Jackson reappointed DuVal to another term as governor on April 18, four days after White's letter to Van Buren became public. But Jackson's reappointment of DuVal was not a full-scale endorsement of the governor. Instead of the regular three-year term, Jackson's commission noted that the governor would serve until the end "of the next Session of the Senate of the United States, and no longer, unless the President of the United States for the time being should be pleased to revoke and determine his Commission." DuVal accepted this appointment, such as it was, on May 5, 1831, only days before the delegate's election and on the same day that Floridians learned of the resignation of cabinet members Van Buren, Eaton, Ingham, and Branch.[22]

If the 1831 election for territorial delegate can be viewed as a referendum of DuVal's popularity (which it shouldn't be), Florida voters would have been perceived as opposing his reappointment by voting for White. The election was extremely close, and the *Floridian and Advocate* reported that the totals in Middle Florida were slightly favorable to Gadsden but that "every artifice has been resorted to by Col. White's enemies to defeat his election. The most absurd stories were privately circulated in this and adjoining counties, which in some instances changed the vote of entire settlements. The party has played a desperate game, but it is impossible that the 'official' influence exerted too successfully here, can have extended through the territory." Results came in slowly. While Gadsden enjoyed a slight advantage in Middle Florida, White's majority in East and West Florida gave the incumbent an overall majority. But the margin was razor thin. In subsequent weeks the paper gave White's majority as 131 votes, then 77 votes, and then finally 85 votes.[23]

The counting continued, and as charges and countercharges flowed back and forth between DuVal and White, the governor wrote to the new secretary of state, Edward Livingston, requesting permission to go to Kentucky and "wind up my affairs." The governor explained that he had not been to Kentucky since 1825, when he moved his family to Florida, and the "situation of my private affairs require me to do so this summer." DuVal explained that there was nothing to prevent his leaving the territory as Secretary Westcott was fully capable of fulfilling the duties of governor. "I desire the President to be informed of my intention, with the assurance that if he should have any arrangements to execute in this Territory for the ultimate removal of the Seminole Indians or my services should be desired I would, postpone at any sacrifice my trip to the West." Jackson consented to DuVal's request on June 10, and DuVal subsequently wrote to him that he would leave for Kentucky in November and would visit Washington thereafter.[24]

Then, as Gadsden was conceding his election to White and the delegate was preparing to travel to Washington, DuVal dropped a bombshell. In a proclamation issued July 2, DuVal declared that "it appears from the returns accompanied by a transcript of the poll books, transmitted to the executive, for the several counties" that both candidates had the same number of votes. On the basis of an 1828 territorial law, DuVal ordered that another election be held on the first Monday in October and that judges and clerks of the counties appear and execute the new election. In a document prepared the day before, DuVal had carefully compiled a list of counties and precincts with vote totals, listing precincts in which poll books or transcripts from it were missing. Incredible as it may seem, even though the counted votes gave White a majority of seventy-eight votes, once DuVal deducted totals from precincts with no poll books (93 votes for Gadsden and 171 for White), the totals stood at 1,803 for Gadsden and 1,803 for White.[25]

White was indignant at DuVal's claims and that same day wrote a scathing letter to the governor, demanding that the official provide him with an accounting of the number of votes cast for White and those rejected by the governor. He also demanded official documents relating to Indian expenditures beginning in 1824. All of this should be in the "Archives of the Territory and copies of them can not be denied to any citizen—I consider them important to public practice and necessary to enable me to discharge my duties as Delegate to Congress." DuVal certainly would have understood that White's duty, as he understood it, would be to press the case in the U.S. Senate for the governor's removal. DuVal did not respond to White's appeal, and the delegate returned to the the issue five days later, demanding an official certificate of the number of votes, those that were rejected, and the grounds for the rejection. Were they, he asked, "illegal votes, or only an illegal Return of the legal votes?"[26]

White and his supporters treated DuVal's declaration with contempt. So did territorial and national newspapers. Most unbiased observers saw DuVal's stand on the election as an unvarnished attempt to punish White for his private and public denunciation of the governor. If DuVal intended a preemptive strike against White by depriving him of his ability to challenge the governor in the U.S. Congress, it failed miserably. Contending that only Congress and not the governor could challenge the legitimacy of each vote cast, White told his supporters to disregard DuVal's pronouncement and proceeded at once to Washington to assume his official duties. He was there by early August (four months before the official opening of the session).

The backlash against DuVal was not long in coming. Few took his side or were willing to support his call for a new election. Gadsden himself was silent. He had conceded to White earlier and some months after DuVal's pronouncement wrote a halfhearted letter to the governor complaining there had been "negligence" and "irregularities in the election." Newspapers universally deplored DuVal's act. The Tallahassee *Floridian and Advocate* denounced the "nullification" of the election and announced that the governor under a "flimsy pretext" was attempting to deprive the people of their choice as delegate. The Baltimore *Niles Register* observed that if half the allegations of White and his friends were true "this proceeding, on the part of Gov. DuVal. . . . [is] the most singular and unjustifiable proceedings that ever happened in America." The Washington *National Journal* presented DuVal's proclamation as a thinly veiled effort to prevent White from coming to Washington to oppose his reappointment, and the result was simply a "pretext to *nullify* a deliberate election by the people." The Richmond *Enquirer* noted that "perhaps there is no state or territory in the Union, which is so much rent in twain by political contests as Florida!"[27]

The only newspaper that took DuVal's side in the issue was predictably the Tallahassee *Florida Courier,* and that paper published his side of the controversy on July 31. Four days later, the *Floridian and Advocate* published White's long rebuttal along with letters and affidavits charging DuVal with losing poll books, containing insinuations of malfeasance, and claiming to have "evidence, as we believe, of the most damaging *foul play.*" The paper also charged that a certified list of totals from a precinct in Gadsden County was delivered to the governor and later taken from the office by the sanction of the governor "and placed under the personal control of certain distinguished members of the NUCLEUS, who are known to be personal as well as *political enemies* of Col. White; and these returns were also in the possession of *several other individuals* of the same party, under different preferences, during the same period—all of which shall be placed before the public as early as possible!" When called upon, Secretary Westcott provided a lengthy statement regarding his own part in the custody of the records. The records were in Westcott's custody before he left town about the middle of June and during that time were not:

> taken out during that time by any person, for any purpose. . . . When I went away the returns were left by me for the Governor, on my writing table in the Executive Office with other papers relating to the current business of the office. They were in a separate bundle, properly arranged, each precinct endorsed, and each county separately enveloped, and also endorsed, and the

whole placed between two file boards made for the purpose, and carefully tied. The key for the office was left with my family for the Governor, who sent for and obtained it, soon after I went away. I did not return . . . till the third of July. I immediately called on the Governor at his house and he gave me the statement of the result of the election.

Westcott insisted that he be able the next day to examine the records for himself so that he could be satisfied as to their correctness before he put his official seal on them. DuVal said he desired that Westcott do so, but then the governor told Westcott that the executive office had no "fastening to the window and no person staying in it, during the night, he felt unwilling to leave the returns there after the statement was made out." Therefore, "for greater security," the returns were taken to Richard Allen's office adjacent to the Capitol. The next day Westcott, by appointment, took them out of a locked case, made a careful examination, and found them correct.[28]

By September it seemed likely there would be no election; if one were held, it seemed unlikely that anyone would take it seriously. Local officials simply ignored DuVal's order, and most would have supported the ruling by Judge David B. Macomb of Leon County issued on July 18 and rejecting DuVal's proclamation calling the election. The governor, he charged, "acts without the pale of authority. . . . I am constrained by the paramount obligation of the U. States, and Laws of this Territory, to disregard the Proclamation and treat it as a nullity." Gadsden himself, one newspaper reported, declined to be a candidate again under the governor's proclamation. He intended not to go through with the election because, as he stated publicly, it served only to "divert the public attention from the character and qualifications of the candidate to the alleged malpractices of private personages and official agents." Thus, according to the source, "discussion . . . on the subject of the new election seems useless, as Colonel White and Col. Gadsden have both declined running under the proclamation."[29] If all this were not embarrassing enough for DuVal, one newspaper even ran a spoof article, written in the vernacular of Southwestern humor and titled "Another Steam Boat Disaster," in which the steamboat *Billy DuVal* sinks and capsizes after trying to ram the *Joe White* on "Poll River."[30] The date for the election came and went with little notice taken of it by either officials or voters. The confused situation was not helped by the fact that many in Tallahassee were ill that fall, including DuVal, Call, Butler, and their families.[31] If his health suffered, DuVal also faced the indignity of having his proclamation ignored by most of the officials and voters in the territory. Even so, as if to ratify the farcical situation, territorial secretary James Westcott proclaimed White the winner on December 5 (the same day as the official opening of the first session of the Twenty-second Congress).[32] When he received official notification of the result, White wrote to Secretary Westcott that while he did not recognize the legality of the election he was honored once again by the people's choice. Meanwhile, both to secure his election and to bolster his opposition to DuVal's reappointment, White demanded official documents from Secretary Westcott relevant to charges against the governor.[33]

The same day as the called election, DuVal wrote a long letter to President Jackson on subjects ranging from the Eaton Affair to Van Buren, Joseph White, and his upcoming investigation before the Senate. DuVal wrote to the president and others that he intended to resign as soon as he cleared his name in the Senate. As he explained to James Barbour, "I have determined to resign my office and go back to Kentucky, the want of means to cultivate a plantation and the expenses of my situation will keep me poor as long as I hold the office." His family was large, and if he were to die they would be compelled to return to Kentucky anyway. His position had cost him $10,000 more than his salary. He would settle at some point near the Ohio River, "where the steamboats come, and content myself with what I can raise from the earth." DuVal was fed up with politics. "I am sick of Public life and politicks—nor would I be willing for any situation to give up friends or ever consent to let politicks interfere with my feelings of friendship or affections."[34] Also by that time the press of other duties had caused DuVal's planting interests to fizzle. As he explained to his friend Samuel Southard, he had sold his interest in the Lafayette tract to his cousin Samuel DuVal, Richard C. Allen, and Romeo Lewis, and he suggested that Southard might wish to do the same. This was "owing to some losses and wants (in consequence) of means."[35]

Reiterating to President Jackson his pledge to retire from office once his case was heard before the Senate, DuVal stated that his resignation had become "absolutely necessary for the benefit and advancement of my family." Again he explained he had "many endeavors to remain in Florida but a large family dependent on my office as their only support cannot expect anything but poverty if I should drop off. I must as soon as I can make the necessary arrangements for a home in Kentucky and take them to a place where my death will not deprive them of a certain support."[36]

DuVal's letter to Jackson also provided his opinions of the cabinet breakup, especially Eaton's part in the fiasco. In every sense DuVal reiterated his approval of Jackson's decisions. Jackson had forwarded Eaton's exculpatory pamphlet to DuVal outlining his side of the controversy, and DuVal returned the document, commenting on it at length in a patronizing tone. Major Eaton's pamphlet, DuVal wrote, "directs to us many facts of which I was ignorant, and I presume the Public was so little informed as well as myself. The appeal bears on the face, an open and frank and convincing candor. Truth lashes out in bold relief amidst the thousand slanders that have been showered on the Public." DuVal thought Eaton more "persecuted on your account, than on his own. The reorganization of your Cabinet was required by the best interests of your country and the [proof] of real friendship and personal attachment was given by Maj. Eaton in setting the example of retiring—he saw and felt the necessity of depriving your enemies of any pretext for complaint, against you on his account while he well knew that you and not *himself* was" the target of the "set of men who were seeking to drive you from . . . the station you now occupy. The people," DuVal continued, "will not consent to this course—as they know and feel that the essential interests of our country, and this great Democratic party, can only rest in safety under your controle." DuVal went on to denounce Ingham, Berrien, and Branch. They had "never merited my approval. They should have at once resigned and taken as your friends a part of the responsibility—True friends ever seek to share responsibility and even danger. Your Secretaries are able men: Mr. Livingston, from his age, experience, and principles, and qualifications will add strength and confidence to your administration—No man can question the integrity and ability of the Secretary of the Treasury. . . . Mr. Woodbury has talents and firmness—modesty and warm heart—I am not only pleased with your selections but I rejoice at the event."[37]

DuVal reminded Jackson of a conversation they had had a year earlier when the president told DuVal that he was concerned that "there was a division in your cabinet and some changes would take place." Jackson insisted at that time that "harmony" must "prevail" but feared it might not. DuVal reminded the General that at the time the

> Secretaries knew before they accepted their offices that Maj. Eaton, a tried person of many years standing was to be associated with them and they all then appeared to be perfectly satisfied with him—and if they were not . . . , they should not have *accepted* their Departments—You then expressed fears that some combination had been formed to drive Maj. Eaton from the Cabinet and then you believed the course pursued toward his family was only one part of a plan to accomplish that object. You expressed a hope that none of the heads of Departments had entered into such a measure. But you had determined to have Harmony at any rate—You disclaimed any intention to interfere with their domestic and family arrangements, while you expressed the opinion that Mrs. Eaton was wantonly and grossly slandered—finally you closed your remarks to me nearly in these words—'I will do all in my power to restore harmony and a union among the heads of the Departments; if this cannot be effected, every man of them shall retire.' These causes were deeper (than were communicated with the Public) it now appears from Maj. Eaton's statement, and I cannot withhold my conviction and assert, so strong is truth, even if I would, without sending in my own opinion.[38]

Throughout his lengthy commentary, DuVal never once uttered Calhoun's name. Choosing to ignore the South Carolinian's role in the affair, DuVal certainly understood Jackson's warm personal feelings for Van Buren. Again, as if to soothe the feelings of the Old Man, DuVal assured Jackson that he had "gotten right" with the Little Magician.

> I confess to you that until I saw and became acquainted with Mr. Van Buren at your house—I had entertained the common opinion that he was an intriguing, cautious, cunning man—I met him under this belief that he [would] not last long—Every time I meet him, the open and bold manner in which he expresses his opinions on men and principles—astonished me, I looked at him closely and watched every sentiment that he uttered and from that time to the present I have ever declared—that so far from *secreting* his *feelings* or *sentiments*—that I have discovered him the most *bold (if not independent)* statesmen I had ever seen at Washington. I confess my opinion has utterly changed of Van Buren—and I consider him a great, good, frank and warm-hearted man nor can any *man living* have so many warm and devoted friends among the *first men* of our country—whose character was mean, selfish cunning and cautious as his was represented by his enemies—
>
> I have neither the motive or the inclination to flatter your friends—[as] my own father, I revere and admire you, my opinion of you, it was formed and decidedly when my family was with you and your sainted partner long before you were spoken of as President, I saw you at your own house, at the place of public resort and at parties among your friends. It may be vanity but I . . . know mankind—my opinion of you is my own—I trusted your character and was satisfied of its . . . purity. Major Eaton has proved to you all that the most honorable and virtuous friend ever did to any other. His appeal is a masterly defense of yourself, the style is vigorous, clear, manly, and convincing—no ambiguity, nothing concealed, or misterious—the feelings of the heart are displayed-with an ardour and warmth that I feel was answered by my own—no man feels that he had been persecuted more than myself, and not one wishes more sincerely that he may triumph over his enemies.[39]

DuVal then referenced his conflict with Joseph White by mentioning the delegate's father-in-law, who had just been elected a member of Congress from Kentucky. Anticipating the awkward confrontation with Jackson's former nemesis but newfound friend, he wrote:

> I only regret that Genl Adair's feelings will suffer from my contest with White, you know the friendly interest I have ever maintained for Genl Adair in my letters and conversations with you—this is therefore painful to me at the advanced age, to subject him at his first appearance again in public life to the scene which he must witness in the city—Col. White will not do

any man justice that he has injured so deeply as myself. I would gladly heal rather than do any act that may produce hostility among your friends—but I must not submit to imputations that affect my character.⁴⁰

I enclose to you a private letter from Worden Pope of Louisville, Kentucky to me.⁴¹ It was never designed to meet your eye or that of any person, except myself. I consider it confidential—but as he is your friend *against the world* and one too *disinterested* as you ever had in Kentucky—it may give you pleasure to see the opinions and views of a practical and strong-minded and self-taught man—Several expressions in this letter are much stronger than they would have been, to any, but to his *friend and relation*. When I reach Washington I will receive back the letter.
I am sincerely your friend,
Wm P. DuVal

The letter from Pope that DuVal enclosed provided his cousin with a candid appraisal of the elections in Kentucky and Indiana as well as their relationship to the national political scene. Pope rejoiced that the elections in those states had gone well for Old Hickory. While DuVal failed to mention Calhoun's name in his long epistle to Jackson, Pope's letter certainly did. As Pope understood things, Jackson's opponents in those states, including Clay's supporters, were "to unite all the fragments of the opposition under the banner of Calhoun, as the nucleus of the combination and to reject the nomination of the members of the new cabinet next winter in the Senate. This scheme is defeated by the Western Elections."⁴²

"Calhoun," Pope asserted, "is the real cause of the dissolution of the late cabinet. In his appeal to the people he says that we was 'neutral' between Gen. Jackson and Mr. Adams in the Election 1824—This is strange language in the mouth of one who so anxiously seeks the presidency. He was *neutral* between the two prominent candidates holding opposite *principles,* and diametrically opposed to each other in their views of national policy." Calhoun then "boldly and actively supported Gen. Jackson, in the canvass and Election of 1828. Why did he join the Jackson party? Had his own political principles and opinions, undergone a change? He does not tell us so. Did he not ascertain the course and result of popular opinion? Was it not in his aspirations for the Presidency, better to elect Gen. Jackson from the *West* for four years, and then succeed him than to elect Mr. Adams . . . from the East, and thus bring in Mr. Clay from the West for eight years. This would have been the case most certainly, had Mr. Adams been elected by the people for a second term." But Calhoun's plot to succeed Jackson had failed now that his supporters within the cabinet had been ousted.⁴³

Calhoun's miscalculations would result in his not running again. Thus Van Buren "will be right hand man and the cock of the walk." Pope then reviewed the role of the "Florida Controversy" in Calhoun's downfall, adding that Calhoun's "intrigues forced the president to write a private note of a personal nature to Mr. Calhoun. Instead of replying with frankness and candor, Calhoun publicly charged Jackson with various calumnies," appealing to "the nation for the purpose of compelling Gen. Jackson to *decline a re-election*. Van Buren & Eaton and his poor wife were made the first objects of his attack. The voluntary resignation of Van Buren and Eaton was unexpected by Calhoun and his friends removed the principal battery of attack and he required the resignations of Ingham, Branch, & Berrien. . . . Then those beautiful diamonds in his cap became enraged and fell with 'malign influence,' on the character of a woman. They have sunk their own characters for Mr. Calhoun by descending from their stations into Billingsgate abuse."[44]

The rupture between Calhoun and Jackson "made the Clay party prick up their ears like wolves—a coalition was projected between Calhoun & Clay and their friends to reject the nomination of the new cabinet and crush the present administration. If the western elections had been favorable to the opposition," Pope continued, "a combination would have been formed headed by Mr. Calhoun—in the Senate and forced Gen Jackson into retirement. From the Evils of the cabal, the Western Elections have delivered the administration and the nation. Now let Mr. Calhoun, if he dares to go on with his plan. If he shall it will make an Earthquake with the people which will shake him into Hell. Van Buren was his Mordecai in the Kings gate. Van Buren was too wise for him—in making his unexpected resignation. Mr. Calhoun will find that 'an able General' *will look behind as well as before him*. He is on the pivot. He may yet retreat and leave Ingham, Branch & Berrien to their fate, as he did [Ninian] Edwards. But if he turns over and acts in hostility against Gen. Jackson and the new Cabinet burnt Brandy will not save him. If left in the street, the Dogs would not lick his blood. Like Clay who is politically dead, he could not wait for the goose to lay her Golden Eggs. Hence I deem the result of the Western Election of the highest importance. I want Mr. Calhoun to turn his face from Mecca."[45]

As seen, the thrust of Pope's letter to his cousin was a full-scale denunciation of Calhoun, whom the Kentuckian charged with having conspired with Clay in the recent elections to destroy Jackson's administration. Pope rejoiced that the plot had failed. If DuVal did not mention the South Carolinian in his own letter, the inclusion of Pope's missive was clearly intended to convince the General that he supported the president's jettisoning Calhoun. Whether or not DuVal was sincere, Jackson accepted the intimation. On the letter's reverse, inscribed in Jackson's own hand, was the following: "Gov. Duval enclosing W. D. Pope's confidential letter. Duval on Eaton's appeal, approves it in the loudest manner. This with its enclosure to be safely preserved. A. J."[46]

DuVal acknowledged by now that Van Buren had won the war for Jackson's favor and likely was his successor. While he understood that Calhoun's hope for succession was destroyed, he also lamented the fact that partisan politics had caused him to distance himself from his friends. Commenting to his old friend Samuel Southard on the new composition of Jackson's cabinet, DuVal observed that the general had been "very much imposed upon, and I regret it. I was not in favor you know of Mr. Adams, although I ever viewed him as a good & able man. Yet somehow or other I liked Wirt, yourself, & Barbour much better than their successors—but this I must have done, from my nature, for before God, I love my friends more in adversity than in their prosperity. I never will answer for a politician if to complete the character, I must give up my friends. I would sooner rob on the highway than be such a mean speaking devil." DuVal added that if "I had the power you should fill any office in or out the Empire, so should John Crittenden of Ky." Some months later DuVal reiterated that while he had "ever been strongly and personally attached to Genl. Jackson, but I have other friends that I glory in speaking of and rejoice if I can serve." DuVal again counted Crittenden as one of that number. "I would vote for him and defend him while I have life—I have named a son after him, and a man of more virtue and talents is not in all the West." DuVal asked Southard to remember him to his wife and "your boys and tell them I can never forget them and one day hope to see them at my house in Kentucky—when they shall hunt a bear with me."47

DuVal and his family set out from Tallahassee for Kentucky by early November. Burr Harrison, whom his father had appointed Leon County justice of the peace, probably remained behind. Thomas Howard (18) and John Crittenden (15) would soon enroll at St. Josephs College in Bardstown, and their mother, Aunt Polly Hynes, and sisters resided in Bardstown as well. The family's living arrangements while there are uncertain. Perhaps they resided temporarily with Nancy's and Polly's family; more likely, DuVal may still have owned his house next to the courthouse square. Or perhaps they rented a house in town. Whether or not they intended to remain in Kentucky indefinitely is not known, but it seems likely that they did. Certainly, DuVal had shared with Nancy and his family his intention to resign his position as governor after he cleared himself in hearings before the Senate. But that was in the future. For now DuVal's immediate duty was to travel to Washington to defend himself against White's and others' accusations of wrongdoing.48 DuVal's ordeal would be one of the most trying of his life.

CHAPTER 13

"I shall return very poor to Kentucky"

When William P. DuVal arrived in Washington in the late fall of 1831 speculation was in the air with regard to Jackson's administration. Most understood that Old Hickory would seek reelection. But, given his ongoing rift with Vice President John C. Calhoun, the all-consuming question concerned who would be Old Hickory's running mate in the upcoming presidential election. The Washington *Globe* sparred with Duff Green's *United States Telegraph* over the matter: the *Globe* supported Van Buren, and the *Telegraph* backed Calhoun. When Van Buren resigned from Jackson's cabinet, the president submitted the New Yorker's name to the Senate as his nominee to serve as ambassador to Great Britain. But Van Buren's interim appointment came to an abrupt end when, on January 25, Calhoun blocked the nomination when he broke a tie in the upper chamber. Calhoun's action sent shock waves all the way across the Atlantic, and within a month Van Buren and Washington Irving, the secretary of the American legation in Britain, were on their way back to the United States.[1]

Almost immediately after Calhoun's action, if not before, speculation arose about whether Van Buren would succeed Calhoun as Jackson's running mate. In fact Green charged that the *Globe* had been gotten up not only to foist Margaret Eaton upon Washington society but also to make the New Yorker vice president. Others were mentioned for the second position, including DuVal's friend Richard M. Johnson. (In a letter to Jackson, DuVal had suggested this possibility.)[2] Unless Jackson died suddenly, Van Buren's ascendancy to the second position seemed inevitable.

Other matters of controversy debated in the halls of Congress and in the press during that session included the Second Bank of the United States, Indian removal, and tariff policy. But the most volatile issue remained nullification. Supporters of the doctrine argued that Calhoun's theory stood as heir to the theories posited in Jefferson and Madison's Kentucky and Virginia Resolutions—a natural extension of the Principles of '98. Opponents argued that this was ridiculous and that a theory such as the one Calhoun outlined was unconstitutional, unworkable, and tantamount to treason. The impending confrontation between Calhoun's South Carolina and the Jackson administration loomed large.

When considered among these pivotal issues confronting the Congress, the fate of Florida's territorial governor seems of little importance (and it was), but the controversy was inextricably entwined with national politics. DuVal and other federal appointees all over the country were feeling the pinch over the Jackson-Calhoun conflict. And the shock waves reverberated through Florida. The Tallahassee *Floridian and Advocate* may have been referring to DuVal when it opined, "The War is waxing warm in Washington—The friends of Mr. Calhoun take the lead in the opposition of Gen. Jackson—The denunciations are bitter and frequent and the political horizon indicates a STORM. . . . A word for the 'nullifiers' the friends of Mr. Calhoun in Florida—Those who used Gen. Jackson's popularity to give them office, consequence, and a coat of armour for political contests, what will they now do? They cannot serve God and Mammon; they cannot sail longer under the flag of Gen. Jackson's bitterest foe, and still use his popularity to crush their opponents—They cannot longer wear lion's skin—the deception is exposed—to the fence! To the fence must be the watchword!"[3]

Jackson submitted DuVal's nomination for another term as governor to the Senate on December 7. DuVal understood that Joseph White's and William Wyatt's charges against him would be introduced in the Senate. On December 12 Senator Ezekiel Chambers of Maryland introduced a remonstrance against DuVal's reappointment, entering into the record White's charges against DuVal for maladministration and corruption. Ten days later Louisiana senator Josiah Johnston introduced papers in DuVal's behalf, and both reports were referred to the Judiciary Committee, composed of "Van Burenite" William L. Marcy (chair), Daniel Webster, Theodore Freylinghuysen, Robert Hayne, and Felix Grundy. On January 24 Grundy entered into the official record a transcript of the Florida legislative council supporting DuVal's reappointment.[4]

DuVal understood that he would be called before the committee and worked to prepare his defense. Writing to William L. Marcy on February 9, DuVal noted that "since my arrival in the City, I have been confined by severe indisposition for which I have not yet recovered." Even so, "every moment of my time when able to labour since my arrival has been devoted to the preparation of my response to the charges which have been exhibited against me." DuVal observed that the charges against him were of a "character to require investigation of my whole conduct as Governor of Florida and Supt of Ind Affairs from the time of appointment in the year 1822 untill the present moment." This circumstance, he observed, would

The Capitol. Washington D.C. West from the City Hall. Sketched and Drawn by Childs & Inman, ca. 1832. Courtesy of Library of Congress.

"necessarily impose upon me the labor of referring to all accounts vouchers, letters &c which relate to the charges."[5] Throughout the month DuVal worked diligently to solicit and assemble affidavits, vouchers, extracts of official letters from various departments, personal testimonials, and other evidence to defend himself against Wyatt's and White's charges. The official file eventually contained more than three hundred pages. Among those who wrote in favor of the governor were early settlers of Tallahassee who could refute allegations that he had overcharged the government for services or had corruptly administered Indian affairs.[6]

DuVal's pending nomination and its acceptance or rejection by the U.S. Senate was a matter of speculation in the Washington press. On February 18 the Washington *United States Telegraph* reprinted an item from the Charleston *Post* stating that the Florida legislative council had resolved that the Senate should reject DuVal's confirmation. "A Floridian," a correspondent, vigorously disputed the report, and the paper was forced to print a retraction on February 22: "We insert the following communication [from "A Floridian"] as an act of justice to Gov. DuVal, and must offer an apology for the article to which it refers." "A Floridian" stated that he had been present at the entire session of the Florida legislative council, which met from January 2 through January 19, and that he was confident that a large majority of the delegates favored reappointment. Other rumors were in the air, including speculation that DuVal would either resign or be sacked and that James Gadsden would be appointed in his place.[7]

Meanwhile, DuVal's friend Richard Keith Call was also in Washington that winter, representing the United States against the claimants in Florida's second-largest land dispute. Once again, William Wirt's and Call's opponents in the Supreme Court were Joseph White, John Berrien, and Daniel Webster in the case *The United States, Appellant vs Arredondo et al.* At the conclusion of his trial Call wrote a lengthy testimonial in support of DuVal.[8]

On March 22 the Senate Judiciary Committee took up DuVal's case again, with the governor himself appearing before the committee. Before reading his formal response to the charges, DuVal regretted that his "indisposition" and other causes "not within my control have so long delayed its completion. Still more do I regret, that I have not time to give it a more condensed form. The labor imposed upon the committee in the investigation of the mass of matter and evidence &c involved in these charges, and the response, will be great, but I most earnestly desire, that the investigation shall be rigid and full." After his statement DuVal systematically refuted each charge against him.[9]

Other witnesses were called throughout the month, and the committee attempted to digest the massive amount of evidence for and against DuVal. Most of DuVal's supporters represented Wyatt as a disgruntled office seeker of questionable character, frustrated in his inability to win government contracts and secure federal appointments. For instance, in a letter to Andrew Jackson, a copy of which DuVal used in his defense in the Senate hearings, Isham Searcy argued that there was no "foundation" to any of Wyatt's charges against DuVal. "Mr Wyatt is a man of moderate capacity, very ambitious of popular favor, but has not intellect, talent, honesty, or courage to sustain himself. Through the force of his tavern, and his duplicity, he was elected to the Legislative Council, but has now returned to his original state of insignificance to slumber in obscurity the residue of his life. . . . I would give credit to no statement he would make about any man of standing. He is vacillating in his politics and his friendships, therefore no credit should be given to any statement of his unless supported by able authority."[10]

Robert W. Williams speculated that Wyatt's animosity against DuVal dated back to 1824, when the governor refused to allow to Wyatt to sell liquor to the Indians. The Indians at that time "were collected in large bodies in and about Tallahassee and St. Marks." Williams characterized Wyatt's charges against DuVal as "old and exploded calumnies, originated . . . in a spirit of revenge and personal hatred of Gov. DuVal—some of them I know to be false and believe them all utterly without foundation and malicious." They were the work of an "abusive slanderer" and "troublesome man." William Hall swore that he first met DuVal in June 1824 at St. Marks before the establishment of Tallahassee. "I have lived in his neighborhood and have known him ever since. I never heard that Gov. DuVal ever traded with the Indians, or sold to them whiskey, I never heard that his conduct in his treatment of the Indians by withholding their rations had produced any discontent, and as I lived in Tallahassee and had an opportunity of seeing Gov. DuVal often, I can say that his conduct was firm, liberal, and in my judgment correct. I know he endeavored to prevent the sale of whiskey to the Indians."[11] Ambrose Crane and John McIver asserted that in those early days Wyatt had continually sold liquor to the Indians to such an extent that the governor was nearly forced to jail him in the Spanish fort at St. Marks.

Moreover, Crane, David Thomas, and others disputed the claim that DuVal had paid more for corn in 1826 than was merited. They insisted that the contracts DuVal initiated with Micah Crupper and Benjamin Chaires were fair, above board, and calculated in the best interests of the Indians and the federal government. Crane witnessed ration distributions firsthand and argued that they were done to the complete satisfaction of the Indians. All of DuVal's efforts at administering Indian affairs were dedicated to conciliating the Indians and to expediting their removal. DuVal, Crane contended, had succeeded beyond any reasonable expectation and had earned the complete trust and love of the Indians. Thomas asserted that on their frequent visits to Tallahassee the Indians generally lived on DuVal's hospitality. If there were any complaints of improper treatment, they never came to his knowledge. As an example of the Indians' affection for the governor, Crane described the scene when the governor saw the Indians off from St. Marks. The Indians parted from the governor by "invoking the blessing of the good spirit—during which time the utmost silence was observed then each in his turn took his parting embrace nor did I see one of these weather beaten warriors leave him without tears in their eyes."[12]

David Thomas directly refuted charges that DuVal was "vulgar in . . . manners and odious to the people." On the contrary, Thomas insisted that DuVal's presence in Florida fostered harmony and hospitality on a scale that would be greatly missed if he were to leave the territory. "Your house is resorted to by all the genteel classes of the country. All who wish to pass a few social hours never leave your house disappointed. All, who visit go and return at their pleasure, and it is no false picture to say that your house is proverbial for its hospitality. If your family were to leave Tallahassee there would be a blank in the society of the place not easily filled up, and there are but few who would not regret it. The indignation of the community will recoil on those who are seeking to injure you in public estimation by so foul means."[13]

Richard Keith Call disputed White's claims that the governor had overcharged the federal government for rents for buildings to conduct the government. Secretary Walton, Call claimed, rented DuVal's house and continued to use it for public purposes, as it was the best structure that could be had at the time. The house was "large, well furnished, and conveniently arranged for one, situated in a newly settled community, and all the offices, and duties of the Executive Department of the Territory were kept and performed in it." On January 1, 1826, Walton moved the governmental offices to town, housing them in a frame "building consisting of two rooms, one above and the other below stairs. It was one of the most comfortable buildings in Tallahassee at the time. It was then a very difficult matter to procure a house of any disposition, and rents were exceedingly high, and have continued so until the present time." (This latter structure was actually owned by DuVal's son, Burr, who was under age at the time.) Call pronounced the charge that DuVal had "speculated on public funds" or had "sacrificed the public interest for the advancement of your own fortune" erroneous; in fact, he pronounced the charge "of little accordance with your well known disregard of pecuniary considerations, and your fidelity in office." In fact, the opposite was the case. DuVal, he asserted, had always neglected his own pecuniary interests for the good the territory. "For the last six years I have possessed as many opportunities of becoming acquainted with your transactions, public and private, as most persons, and it affords me pleasure to state, that I have never known you to commit, nor do I believe you have been capable of committing, an act in the smallest degree dishonorable. You have enjoyed that highest confidence of a large portion of your fellow citizens of the Territory, and that confidence so far as I am advised remains unshaken by the large catalog of charges preferred against you."[14]

James Gadsden argued that White's charges against DuVal were related to the recent political canvass. The governor's reappointment was in "some degree blended" with the territorial delegate election between Gadsden and White. Gadsden characterized the "Union of Wyatt & White as one of those political combinations we daily witness, in which previous repulsive materials are made to unite for an interested object." White could not carry the election, he believed, without the aid of Wyatt, and the prosecution of Governor DuVal by the latter was made the pretext for the former's uniting with a man he had previously spoken of in terms of great contempt. DuVal's "alleged mal-practices" were brought out in a newspaper "at the last hour, [and] after repeated . . . attacks, the governor found himself compelled to respond. The act was defensive on his part, and in reply to a letter written to Mr. Van Buren, and which White had caused (on April 14th) but 3 weeks before the election, to be printed in one of the papers of the Territory."[15]

As a part of his defense against White's and Wyatt's charges, DuVal included documents supporting charges against Gad Humphreys's administration of Indian affairs. James Gadsden, Phagan, and others attested to Humphreys's neglect and his improper acquisition and personal use of Indian slaves. Phagan charged that Humphreys had cheated the Indians out of their annuities and that DuVal was forced on more than one occasion to deliver the goods to them himself in Tallahassee. Gadsden agreed with Phagan's assessment and once again suggested that Wyatt's and White's charges stemmed from their political aspirations. As Gadsden explained to the Judiciary Committee, "Like all new countries populated from distant and different sections, and with a diversity of habits, opinions, interests and even prejudices, discontent and dissatisfaction has been occasionally manifested in Florida. But amid all the complaints, whether just or unjust, at different times made, and amid all the disagreements of opinion which may have been entertained or expressed, as to the wisdom or inexpediency of any of Governor DuVal's acts, I never heard until very recently his character, or motives impugned. I feel assured that 3/4ths of his fellow citizens would acquit him of even a suspicion of 'speculation or embezzlement,' or of having applied any manner the public funds to his own private use." In fact, he came to the territory "under reduced circumstances and he certainly has not improved his pecuniary affairs."[16]

The governor had prepared his defense well. DuVal's refutation of White's charges convinced the committee that the evidence was not substantial enough to deny him confirmation. In the end the choice came down basically to a question of which side to believe. Finally, on April 26 (a Thursday afternoon) the Judiciary Committee reported favorably on DuVal's nomination, but the governor was forced to wait over the weekend for the final vote. No sooner had this occurred than sparks flew in the House of Representatives between DuVal's friend Kentucky congressman Charles A. Wickliffe and White when the very next day, during debate over an appropriations bill, the territorial delegate questioned the need for a law agent for the Territory of Florida. Wickliffe hinted that White favored abolishing the office because "it was understood that he (Mr. W) was the counsel for the land claimants, whose interest this officer was employed to oppose," though he "disclaimed any personal allusion." Bristling at the implication that he was somehow speaking for his own interest, White said that "he was not now, and never had been, since the passage of the law, the counsel of any of the claimants except two, one of which was decided, and the other now pending in the supreme court." Wickliffe argued that it was the duty of law agent to "collect evidence against the claims." White responded that this is "the duty of the District Attorney, who was a man of industry, learning and ability and fully competent to protect the interests of the states," and that no other officer was necessary.[17]

Finally, on April 30, the full Senate confirmed DuVal's nomination by a vote of 32 to 10. Not surprisingly Senator Henry Clay was among the ten who voted against DuVal's reappointment.[18] When he learned of the Senate's decision to disregard his charges and reappoint the governor, William Wyatt refused to accept the result. In upcoming months Wyatt had White's rebuttal as well as his own statements contradicting DuVal defense published in anti-DuVal newspapers. The Tallahassee *Floridian and Advocate* was an eager participant in the work. "Much as we regret the agitation of any political question that has been, or is likely to be a source of personal or party violence," the editor noted, "we feel bound to afford Mr. Wyatt an opportunity to place before the public the entire proceedings connected with the effort made last winter, before the Senate, to prevent the reappointment of Governor DuVal." The journal claimed that it would have let the matter rest had not DuVal and "his friends claimed it as a triumph and indulged in the bitterest recrimination against those concerned in presenting the charges. We consider it an indispensable duty, to publish all the documents in our reach, that the public may be enabled to judge whether the governor owes his triumph to his own innocence."[19]

Closely related to the DuVal-White conflict was Andrew Jackson's decision to remove Henry M. Brackenridge, judge of the Western Judicial District. One of America's most skilled jurists and men of letters, Brackenridge had known Old Hickory since his earliest days in Florida and had been instrumental in assisting the General in his brief tenure as territorial governor. Brackenridge, who had been in office since 1822, fumed at his ouster and, in a series of blistering attacks printed in Washington papers, blamed political intrigue as the cause of his removal. (Brackenridge had ruled in favor of White and Berrien against Call in the Forbes case.) White also blasted Jackson's removal of the judge and urged the Senate to exert a check against this executive "indiscretion, imbecility, and favoritism." Up to now, he charged, "the ermine has yet preserved its purity; how long it shall remain unsullied, now depends upon the Senate." Brackenridge blamed DuVal and Call for his ouster. Indeed, most understood that Brackenridge was a casualty of the DuVal-White struggle, with Old Hickory taking DuVal's advice to remove the judge because he had sided with White.[20] Indeed, the removed judge was embittered. Not long after the Senate's confirmation of DuVal, he wrote to Wyatt from Washington, "DuVal is here acquitted or rather untried for no investigation took place, on account of the determination of the Senate not to hear *ex parte testimony*," letters, or affidavits.[21]

The six months that DuVal was out of the territory were difficult ones for James Westcott, but by most accounts he held up well under the pressure. Wyatt continually pressed the secretary to hand over documents relevant to his charges against DuVal.[22] As they had for the governor, Indian affairs occupied most of Westcott's energies. Westcott responded to Indian-settler conflicts as best he could and looked ahead to implementing Indian removal under the act of Congress. But with Joseph White's continual attacks against Indian agent John Phagan as DuVal's corrupt lieutenant, his task was not easy. While the delegate, agent, and governor were in Washington and while the Senate was deliberating DuVal's nomination, White wrote to Secretary of War Lewis Cass, blaming all the current problems of the Seminoles on Phagan's corrupt administration of their affairs. White urged the secretary to order Phagan and all his subordinates out of the territory and to appoint a new commissioner to treat with them. Cass answered White promptly, assuring White that Jackson looked forward to executing a treaty with the Seminoles as soon as the opportunity presented itself. What

Lewis Cass, ca. 1833. Courtesy of Library of Congress.

Cass did not disclose was that the man the president had already chosen for the task was James Gadsden.[23]

The winter of 1831–1832 found the Florida Indians suffering extreme hardships. Secretary Westcott wrote to Secretary of War Cass that the Indians were wandering past their boundaries and hunting on territory occupied by the whites. A number of violent confrontations were reported, and the secretary did his best to address them. In early January he ordered authorities to apprehend "a slim boy about 19 years" who had killed an Indian near the Apalachicola River. Near the middle of the month he ordered the superintendent to the Aucilla River to compel Indians to return to their boundaries. If necessary, the agent was to "call upon the nearest JOP [justice of the peace] for aid and in the case of resistance or outrage by the Indians upon the officers of the militia you will endeavor to ascertain the name of the Indians who have killed their cattle and report them to me and if you think advisable to have them whipped under the Territorial law."[24]

The condition of the five thousand or so Indians in Florida was indeed precarious. In a report to Abram Bellamy, president of the legislative council, Westcott provided an appraisal. Under the provisions of the Moultrie Creek agreement the Indians received $5,000, with about one-fifth of that total going to the Apalachicola

Indians, whom Westcott judged better off than the others. "Common Indians" received $3 or $4 per year and the chiefs, $20 to $70. Half of the Indians had guns, and some on the Apalachicola River sold game and skins to nearby villages. When the corn ran out, which it usually did by February or March, they worked for the whites. They habitually wandered outside their boundaries and when they did they created "great alarm and disquiet. If drunk they are often insolent and ungovernable. The white settlers own thousands of cattle, hogs etc. running at large in the extensive ranges over which the Indians roam, and upon their stock great depredations are committed." According to Westcott, more mayhem resulted when Indians set fire to the woods during their hunts. Though the Indians were by treaty excluded from the coastlines, fishing offered some respite to their hunger, but it also fostered contact with outside influences. Westcott had been informed that the Spanish employed some twenty or thirty Seminoles as fisherman and sailors to supply the markets of Havana and Matanzas. (DuVal had also often complained to Washington of this fact.) Westcott estimated that four hundred blacks lived among the Indians. This fact, along with the influence that these folk exerted on Seminole leaders, remained of paramount concern to Westcott, DuVal, Phagan, Gadsden, and all others charged with Indian removal.[25] But such issues mattered not to Andrew Jackson. Finally, his plan to relocate all of the Seminole people in Florida across the Mississippi—a plan he had envisioned in 1821 as territorial governor—was about to be realized.

His testimony before the Senate completed and his nomination confirmed, DuVal tarried in the Washington area for another two months. He may have attended the Democratic nominating convention in Baltimore in late May, where he would have witnessed Van Buren's nomination as Jackson's running mate. Since learning of his rejection as minister to England, the New Yorker had remained abroad, timing his return conveniently after the convention. Returning home to New York, Jackson summoned Van Buren to Washington immediately to assist him in his Bank Bill veto message, and the New Yorker arrived in the capital by July 8. A month earlier, however, Washington Irving had arrived in the capital by another route. (Irving arrived in New York City on May 21.) After turning down an invitation to attend a banquet in his honor in Philadelphia, he visited Washington in June and returned to New York by way of Philadelphia. Irving and DuVal may have renewed their acquaintance before DuVal departed for home.[26] Irving's nephew would explain years later in his uncle's edited correspondence that the writer made a "flying visit to Philadelphia in June, in the course of which he picked up his materials for Ralph Ringwood."[27] This tantalizing reference leaves many unanswered questions. Did Irving and DuVal become reacquainted briefly during the time they both were in Washington? Did DuVal follow him to Philadelphia? Did Irving have notes from previous conversations with DuVal that he had stored in Philadelphia?

DuVal finally left Washington on June 8 and arrived in Florida by the end of the month.[28] DuVal may have proceeded along the route he had recommended to James Barbour some months earlier, traveling south to Danville, Virginia, then to Salisbury and Charlotte, North Carolina, south to Macon, Georgia, then west to the eastern bank of the Flint River, and then on a road to Florida.[29] On June 26, the Tallahassee *Floridian and Advocate* reported that the DuVal had arrived in Quincy by the last northern stage.[30] Immediately upon his arrival in Tallahassee, DuVal became involved in a controversial incident involving a well-to-do man from South Carolina who had been convicted of murder in the Leon County Superior Court. David S. Rogers had been convicted on May 1 of killing a man named Farmer, and Judge Randall had sentenced him to be hanged on June 15. Secretary Westcott granted Rogers a respite until July 27 so that his relatives could visit him.[31] Immediately upon his return to Tallahassee DuVal was assailed with pleas from distraught relatives begging the governor for a pardon. Enemies of the governor charged that DuVal hid out, feigned illness, and even tried to escape out of a window in an effort evade Rogers's pleaders. Some even charged that the governor and Secretary Westcott had filled out paperwork to resign their commissions (only to retrieve them after Rogers's execution, on July 27) rather than face the condemned man's relatives. Unfortunately, the farcical story was circulated in the national press. Later the charges were thoroughly repudiated, but by that time the damage had been done.[32]

Despite the pressure of the Rogers case, that summer and fall DuVal attended dinners and balls held in this honor at Tallahassee and Apalachicola. Not surprisingly, DuVal interpreted these events and the toasts that followed as evidence that the people of the territory had supported him during his travails in Washington. Yet the opposition press, while printing accolades to the governor, editorialized that such demonstrations should not be interpreted as any sort of universal approbation of the governor's conduct. For example, the Pensacola *Gazette,* asserted, that toasts or sentiments, "VOLUNTEERED AFTER THE BOTTLE WAS WELL CIRCULATED, are no criterion, of public sentiment or even of those giving them."[33]

Throughout the fall of 1832 newspapers kept DuVal's controversy with White and Wyatt alive. The pair refused to accept the Senate's decision as an exoneration of DuVal's conduct. White betrayed no intention of giving ground. On October 17 he announced that he would seek another term as territorial delegate. (His opponent once again would be Richard Keith Call.) A week later the Tallahassee *Floridian and Advocate* published Wyatt's statements against DuVal along with all relevant correspondence in the affair. Wyatt disputed DuVal's defense, and the paper reproduced extracts of the papers DuVal had filed in his case before the Senate.[34] The combustible mix of personalities and political conflicts spilled over from the newspapers to the stump and even to the dueling ground. It will be remembered that fisticuffs among Call's and White's supporters had taken place in years past, with an affair of honor barely averted. Westcott, whom one observer described as "rough, factious, and egotistical," was slightly injured in a duel with a Thomas Baltzell near the Alabama line in September 1832. A year later, during the campaign between White and Call, Leigh Read, a recent migrant from Tennessee who supported Call, challenged Oscar White, the delegate's nephew, to a duel after the latter insulted Call during a campaign speech. At the appointed time the two exchanged shots and then closed with knives until seconds broke up the confrontation. In another encounter, Samuel DuVal, the governor's nephew, was also prosecuted under the territorial antidueling law for fighting a duel with Philip White, another relative of the delegate.[35]

Not surprisingly, White deplored Gadsden's appointment as commissioner to treat with the Indians. His recommendation of William Simmons was disregarded, and even before Gadsden arrived in Florida White charged Gadsden with botching the Moultrie Creek talks. In addition, Gadsden's and DuVal's combination of incompetence and corruption over the past ten years, White charged, had been disastrous for Indians, white settlers, and the government alike. By the time Gadsden arrived in St. Augustine in late March to begin his work, he and White had been sparring in the newspapers for weeks.[36] Nonetheless, Gadsden pushed forward relentlessly. On May 9 Gadsden hastily forged an agreement with prominent Seminole leaders on Payne's Landing, on the Oklawaha River, that called for the tribe to remove to the Arkansas Territory. The treaty stipulated that within three years the tribe would remove to a tract selected and agreed upon by a delegation of tribal leaders. The Treaty of Fort Gibson (March 28, 1833), American authorities would later contend, committed the Indians to remove to the Arkansas Territory within one year. Charges of fraud, intimidation, and corruption dogged Phagan and the other American representatives. But the key point was that by the time DuVal left office, most doubted that the Seminole leaders' signatures on the treaty represented the will of a majority, or even a sizable minority of their tribe. At that point armed resistance was probably inevitable.[37]

Even so, as soon as DuVal returned to the territory, he moved as expeditiously as he could to speed Indian removal. DuVal kept authorities in Washington abreast of Indian affairs in Florida. In August he notified Secretary of War Cass that he might need to travel to the Indian Agency to counteract the work of Humphreys and other men who were "intriguing and interfering with the Indians" in an effort to persuade them not to leave Florida. The former agent, he wrote, had a store near the boundary and consequently had influence over them. Phagan, DuVal explained, "believes it is necessary that I should visit the Agency to counteract any impressions these men have made on the minds of the Indians unfavorable to the plans and views of the Government." In October DuVal reported that

Phagan and several of the chiefs had passed through Tallahassee on their way to Arkansas Territory, staying with him several days before making their way to St. Marks and then on to New Orleans.³⁸

Separate talks with the Apalachicola Indians also commenced. On October 10 DuVal hosted talks at his house in Tallahassee that included Gadsden and himself as well as Blount and the several other Apalachicola chiefs. Blount essentially acquiesced to DuVal's and Gadsden's demands, signing an agreement the following day. But the months ahead proved difficult as misunderstandings among Blount, other Apalachicola leaders, and Gadsden hindered progress. Blount's preparations to remove to the Arkansas Territory was complicated by the fact that whites and other Indians continually harassed him. As Gadsden explained to President Jackson, "Blunt was at my house last night complaining that some Creek Indians had been treating him with outrage & that one or two white men have commenced trespassing on his reservation." It was true, Gadsden admitted, that Blount had agreed to move west, but he had been given two years to make his preparations, "which cannot be done to his satisfaction without the unmolested occupation of his land." Gadsden reported the problem to DuVal and expected him to do his best to protect Blount but confided to Jackson that the "governor might find it impossible, under the existing state of things, to extend protection." Even so, DuVal did what he could to protect Blount from further molestation. At DuVal's request, the War Department consented to the governor's appointment of his relative William S. Pope as special agent to protect Blount from marauding whites.³⁹

Meanwhile, the Senate ratified the treaty with the Apalachicola Indians and set November 1, 1833, as the date for removal. As he dealt with continuing political turmoil and conflicts over Indian removal, DuVal prepared for the meeting of the legislative council. Newspapers were already speculating about who would be Florida's next territorial governor. James Gadsden was mentioned, but so was John Eaton, Jackson's friend and the former secretary of war. Joseph White's father-in-law, General Adair, was also named as a possible successor. Even as he understood his days as governor were numbered, DuVal advised the Jackson administration on territorial appointments while deploring the fact that even by this time Jackson's enemies had not been rooted out. "In this Territory," he wrote in a private missive to Andrew Jackson's personal secretary, "it is time that our friends should not be overlooked and our enemies placed above them. I believe more than one half of all the officers in Florida are opposed to Genl. Jackson."⁴⁰

The legislative session opened on January 7, and DuVal's address to that body reflected familiar themes. He called for an end to political conflict and spoke of the need to create an educational system for the young. DuVal also spoke to the controversial issue of banking and reminded the solons that formerly he had used his veto pen to oppose the institutions that were currently in operation, largely because they acted primarily to the benefit of merchants rather than planters. The Bank of West Florida in Pensacola, the Bank of Florida in Tallahassee, and the Bank of Magnolia, chartered in 1829 and 1830 over his veto, were not fulfilling what he thought were the primary responsibility of banks—to provide capital to planters. In DuVal's view the present institutions had brought "little or no additional capital among us." But DuVal signaled to the legislators that he was willing to consider new charters in light of current capital needs for the territory. "If an institution could be established on suitable terms, and under such ample security, as to induce the investment of *foreign capital* in it, this prominent objection would not exist. But to meet my approval it must be in fact, as well as in name, truly the *Planters Bank*."[41]

Casting a shadow over the council was the impending conflict between South Carolina and the Jackson administration. Florida papers carried stories of the Nullification ticket prevailing in South Carolina by a large majority, Governor Hayne's calling of a special session of the legislature to consider nullifying the federal tariff, and Jackson's proclamation to the people of South Carolina.[42] When DuVal addressed the legislative council, South Carolina was making preparations to resist federal authority. These were "most distressing" occurrences to every "true patriot," he noted. "It was a maxim of an ancient and renowned government most similar to our own, 'never to despair of Republic.' We will not forebode evil; we will hope and believe that both parties, by forbearance, and that spirit of concession should be employed, will avert the terrible catastrophe of disunion. That such may be the result and the cause of the desire of every good citizen—and may God grant a speedy termination to this unhappy contest."[43]

Attending the legislative sessions and visiting Tallahassee for the first time was the newly appointed judge Robert Raymond Reid of the Eastern Judicial District. A thoughtful, introspective man with a passion for philosophy and poetry, Reid formed an opinion of Tallahassee that was not flattering. He found a "noisy, senseless crowd; a legislative council with little wisdom, and a fashionable circle with little taste." Reid's first impressions of DuVal were also negative. Their personalities clashed. DuVal, the Georgian recorded in his diary, was a fine storyteller but, "if I mistake not, a weak man and wants dignity." The governor, Reid recorded, was "shallow, blasphemous, and course." Even so, Reid made attempts at cordiality, and on January 31 he saluted the governor on the street and "asked him what the Legislative Councils were about," to which DuVal responded, "Making banks."[44]

Indeed, by 1833 the momentum to expand and extend Florida's banking system was almost irresistible. Throughout his twelve years as executive of the territory DuVal had continually vetoed bank legislation, but he likely understood that further resistance was impossible. Judge Reid opposed banks. As he confided to his diary, "There is a passion for bank making existing at present in the Territory, which must prove injurious to the general interests. Banks must be founded on capital and the superstructure." Any other "basis," the judge noted to himself, "is erroneous. Such schemes are fit only for the brains of speculators who care not who loses so *they* make a lusty hit, but they do not become wise Legislators. In this free country, Banks . . . favor monopoly, make aristocracy, and create slaves."[45] DuVal would have agreed with Reid, but inevitably he deferred to the will of the legislative council. After vetoing the original bill to charter the Union Bank of Florida, he eventually reconciled himself with an altered version. Sentiment in favor of expanding Florida's banking institutions was overwhelming, and DuVal did what he could to accommodate his views to the eventuality of the legislation's passage. DuVal signed the bill into law on February 13. DuVal may have realized that his decision to sign the legislation might cost him politically in the future. But, probably thinking most of the immediate political necessity and even inevitability of the measure, he did what he could to ensure that the legislation was the best that could be obtained at the time. Whether or not he fully understood it at the time, DuVal signed a bill into law that made the Territory of Florida liable for up to $2 million in "faith bonds." It was an act that would come back to haunt him in years to come.[46]

If DuVal acquiesced in creating territorial banks, he was a loyal supporter of Andrew Jackson in his war against the Second Bank of the United States. DuVal shared the sentiment of his fellow westerners that the Bank was hostage to Eastern financial interests. As he wrote to Congressman James K. Polk while the Bank War was raging in Congress, "I have been with you heart and judgment throughout the protracted discussion on the Bank question and the deposits and rejoice sincerely on the very able defense and argument you delivered on this subject." DuVal desired a seat in Congress himself so as to join the struggle. He deplored "the politicians of the day, who have changed their principles at least as often as their coats as so many devils hirelings, who for pay will fight for any banner. I feel the danger which so daringly threatens the happiness and liberty of our country and if there was not another man in this nation who would do it humble as I am I would never cease to denounce this monopoly of curses—*the Bank*." The present crisis, he wrote, reminded him of the first Bank crisis preceding the War of 1812. "I remember the crys, speeches, and public meetings, when the old Bank was put down. The present are facsimiles of the occurrences of 1811." Still, DuVal was confident that the people would sustain the president because of the "purity of the agricultural community and I thank god they constitute 19:20ths of the nation." In good Jeffersonian tradition DuVal deplored the merchant class and the inhabitants of cities. "As to the merchants—when was it ever known that patriotism with them interfered with *trade*. I look at the large cities as corrupt and the smaller ones as apeing the larger." DuVal concluded his missive with his prediction that the scheme of the Bank interests to "force a recharter, is, and ought to be sufficient warning to honest men of all parties, to unite in putting it down." In an obvious reference to Jackson, DuVal asserted, "This Hidra has I trust met with a Hercules that will yet strangle the Monster."[47]

Not long after the legislative session DuVal once again left the territory for Kentucky, leaving Westcott to oversee Indian removal and other pending matters. In his absence whites' pressure on the Apalachicola Indians continued to mount. In early May special agent William Pope reported to DuVal that "ruffians" named Oaks and Ralls had broken down the door of Blount's house, assaulted the family with "sticks and clubs," robbed the house of most of its valuables, and made off with between $700 and $800 in cash. With the governor out of the territory, Pope reported the incident to Westcott and U.S. Attorney J. K. Campbell. Warrants were issued—all to no avail. Westcott made a personal visit to Blount's homestead to investigate the matter. Over the next several months Westcott and Blount finalized plans to remove the Apalachicola Indians, and the date was set for July 20.[48] Also while DuVal was out of the territory, John Phagan's financial records came under close scrutiny. Though DuVal steadfastly supported him against White's charges, by August 1833 Jackson had sacked the agent and appointed in his place Georgia military leader and politician Wiley Thompson, who arrived in the territory that November.[49]

Also while DuVal was out of the territory, his friend Richard Keith Call suffered yet another political setback at the hands of anti-Jacksonian Joseph White, who once again bested Jackson's protégé. Call's narrow defeat ensured White's continued influence and signaled a weakening of the power of Jackson's forces in the territory. White's mastery of Call was not limited to politics. A close student of the delegate's career has noted that in fourteen cases argued before the U.S. Supreme Court from 1832 through 1835, White bested Call every time.[50] The president himself was livid and chose to believe that Call's electoral defeat was attributable to "treachery in your ranks, and Nullifiers in your Territory." Jackson interpreted Call's defeat as a personal slap at the administration. He wrote to the defeated Call, "[H]ow has this happened? I wish you to explain to me—there are so many rumors. . . . I am anxious to be correctly informed." Old Hickory even suspected that James Gadsden might be the culprit. "Is it possible that G is a Nullifier? And his political friends voted against you—or did not vote at all."[51]

Meanwhile, books were opened on April 10 for subscription of stock of the Union Bank of Florida. Overseeing the process were John G. Gamble, William Nuttall, Ben Chaires, and William Bailey. Investors could buy stock not only in the capital city but also in Pensacola, St. Augustine, Jacksonville, and Key West. In DuVal's absence Westcott was called upon to appoint directors, but on July 8 he shared his reservations about the validity of the legislation itself: "I doubt the existence of any official obligation upon me, to do the various acts prescribed to be done by the Governor and the Secretary. I have also strong apprehensions that if this bank goes into operation under this charter, it will be found pregnant with the most mischievous and disastrous results to the credit and prosperity of the Territory and its citizens." Even so, he eventually appointed the directors, who immediately began soliciting mortgages in exchange for bonds.[52]

In Kentucky DuVal divided his time between Louisville and Bardstown, where his family resided. Nancy's youngest brother, Alfred Hynes, was practicing medicine with Burr Harrison, her sister Elizabeth's husband. It is unclear where her oldest son and the namesake of her distinguished brother-in-law was at the time, but the DuVal's next oldest son, Thomas, then nineteen years of age, was enrolled at nearby St. Joseph College. Nancy's cousin William Hynes had moved back into town and was operating a store on the southeast corner of the public square. Hynes's antislavery views along with previous legal conflicts over Nancy's father and uncle's estate may have strained relations among the in-laws. Together with like-minded citizens in the community William formed the Nelson County Colonization Society, which styled itself an auxiliary to the American Colonization Society.[53]

Conscious of the fact that he would soon be out of office and perhaps out of Florida, DuVal renewed political contacts while investigating opportunities in the Bluegrass State. As he made his rounds, DuVal felt obligated to offer President Jackson his appraisal of the political scene in Kentucky. Writing from Harrodsburg Springs, DuVal confided to Old Hickory that the congressional race for that district was too close to call, but he was glad to report that "my kinsman Patrick H. Pope is elected by a few votes over Mr. Crittenden. This I consider a just triumph over the powerful influence of the bank in Louisville." Despite all manner of devious operations by the "Clay Party," the Jackson forces, DuVal was delighted to report, had prevailed. He also mentioned that he looked forward to seeing Jackson's former postmaster general, William T. Barry, in Louisville in a few days. Curiously, as if to assuage the president's ego, DuVal congratulated Jackson on his recent triumph against the Bank and offered a kind of retrospective analysis. "I never could see why the representative principle that pervades our general and state governments should not be introduced into a great National Bank. Let the Gen. Government take a certain portion of the stock—that each state in the rate of its representation in Congress take stock—and the one third of the Capital be taken by individuals—Let each state legislature elect one or more directors as their legislators might authorize annually and it seems to me the three distinct interests would act as guards on each other—and thus preserve a correct and healthy action throughout the Union." Such a system, he was convinced, would "firmly bind the Union together. I would sooner have state banks" than the current Bank of the United States, because the latter was "little more under the control of the United States than the Bank of England. I pray to God sincerely that no man may ever be elected as President of the United States who should again sign such a charter as the one which created this Private Bank." DuVal closed his missive by informing Jackson that thus far he and his family had escaped the cholera and that he would return to Florida with them as soon as weather permitted.[54]

On September 4 DuVal accompanied William Barry and John Pope, a relative and the territorial governor of Arkansas, to a public dinner in Louisville. A local newspaper noted that DuVal was the featured speaker on the occasion.[55] Also while he was in Kentucky, the tragedy of the dueling ground once again struck William P. DuVal's family. Only a year or so earlier his daughter Elizabeth had married John K. Campbell, a young lawyer from South Carolina who had migrated to Tallahassee. Campbell's skills as a lawyer were evident to everyone, and DuVal succeeded in having Andrew Jackson appoint Campbell U.S. attorney for the Middle District of Florida. The couple's future seemed bright until, unknown to Elizabeth, Campbell was struck down in a duel with a merchant from St. Marks on August 28. Family members brought the widowed Elizabeth to Bardstown to be with her parents. She married Bardstown merchant Samuel Beall in November.[56]

By early November, leaving his daughter Elizabeth behind with her new husband, DuVal began making his way back to Florida. When he arrived he found numerous communications waiting for him from the War Department, ordering him to execute the removal of the Apalachicola Indians. Once in Tallahassee DuVal consulted with Westcott and ordered Wiley Thompson (who had already arrived) to proceed at once to Fort King to take charge of the Indian Agency and order Indians from Blount's and other Apalachicola towns to emigrate with their chiefs. DuVal thereupon informed authorities in Washington that he hoped the evidence collected against Blount's robbers would be sufficient to have the chief reimbursed by Congress. Another pressing matter involved the return of Blount's son and other Indian boys who were in Kentucky at the Choctaw Academy. (Blount refused to leave until the boys returned to Florida.) Once at Fort King Thompson reported to authorities in Washington and to DuVal that he found conditions around the agency deplorable. The Indians were starving, and, worse still, corrupt traders were making "disgraceful profits" by trading whiskey for stolen cattle. "The convenience of pond water, tempts them to make two barrels of whiskey out of one. They are thus reaping a golden harvest, which will be blasted by the removal of the Indians. Hence, their efforts to exert Indian hostility to emigration."[57]

As the new year dawned DuVal prepared for what he certainly understood would be his last address to the legislative council as Florida governor. DuVal's message urged that the legislators enact tougher criminal sanctions to suppress "licentiousness and vice" and the growing illegal trade between "certain white men" and slaves. Contrasting the British with the American peoples, DuVal noted that the British depended on commerce and its workshops while "nineteenth twentieths of our population are engaged in agriculture" and suggested that this was as it should be. "With us, Commerce must be the maid, not the mistress of Agriculture; and Manufactures must yield to and depend on both." Americans and Floridians must look to science to assist agriculture. DuVal predicted that the Union Bank of Florida would assist planters, as would the new road already under construction that would link Tallahassee with the St. Johns and Withlacoochee Rivers. Improvements to Pensacola Bay and to the Apalachicola and St. Marks Rivers, as well as DuVal's grandiose proposal of building a series of canals linking the Atlantic with the Gulf, would foster an agriculture boom in Florida. The "whole line of communication between the Mississippi and Atlantic," he said, "if taken up the Suwannee River" through the Okefenokee and St. Marys River out to the Atlantic, would cost shippers less than half of what it cost to send goods through the Florida Straits. Finally, removal of the Seminoles, which he predicted would be completed within three years, would be the final ingredient necessary to usher in a period of unequaled prosperity for the settlers of Florida. With the departure of the Seminoles, a "fine country better adapted than the larger portion of Florida for the cultivation of sugar cane and sea island cotton, will be opened to the enterprising emigrant of capital and industry. . . . With care and economy [he] may, in a few years, be rewarded most amply for his expenditures and privations." The removal would benefit both races and would allow the Indians to "receive all the benefits and advantages, which our humane government will kindly extend for their permanent residence, instruction and government. [The removal,] while it secures their happiness, [will also] reflect honor on the national character." Their new home in the West was "better adapted, in every respect to advance their civilization and more improvement, than their present residence, surrounded as they are by our white population."58

During and after the legislative session DuVal worked closely with Wiley Thompson in making arrangements for removal of the Seminoles. On March 9 Thompson reported to DuVal that Blount and other Apalachicola Indians were, despite a delay in their receipt of funds promised them, ready to emigrate and that he would set out the next day for Apalachicola Bay for the purpose of embarking with the Indians immediately. But upon arrival he discovered that many of the Indians had not arrived. He thus found it necessary to visit bands remaining on the Apalachicola and Chattahoochee Rivers to take testimony of more Indian claims and round up, if possible, some Indians belonging to Blount's Band, who were lurking about these upper towns. Thompson complained that he was not able to get a steamboat and thus "paddled myself down in a canoe from Ochessee to this place (upwards of one hundred miles) where I arrived today. I trust I shall be able to embark the Indians for New Orleans, by the day after tomorrow."59

City of Washington from Beyond the Navy Yard. ca. 1834. Courtesy of Library of Congress.

By late winter DuVal was preparing to wrap up his affairs in Florida. His last official act as governor, on April 16, was to sign and deliver to the Union Bank the first installment of "faith bonds" in the amount of $360,000.⁶⁰ The following September Union Bank president John Gamble traveled to New York and sold off the bonds. Days after this official act DuVal was on his way to Washington. DuVal's twelve-year stint as governor of the Territory of Florida had come to an end. It may not have actually been so, however, because President Jackson had actually renominated the governor on March 19, only to withdraw his name from the Senate six days later. DuVal's status is further confused by the fact that the governor actually had one more year to serve, having received his commission for three years on April 30, 1832.⁶¹ Did DuVal ask that his name be withdrawn? Had others encouraged the president not to renominate DuVal?

Rumors of DuVal's intention to resign were everywhere. The governor had discussed the matter with President Jackson, and some believed that DuVal had assured members of the Senate investigating committee that if he was exonerated of charges and reconfirmed for another term, he would resign. Joseph White, re-elected territorial delegate over Richard Keith Call the previous year, was convinced of this. Calling for DuVal's removal some weeks before the president nominated John Eaton to serve as governor, White argued that "since that time he [DuVal] has made the office a sinecure—He was for seven or eight months before December last actually been living in Kentucky—His secretary acting as governor & there are now claims . . . before Congress for clerk hire, because the Secretary was the Governor & there was no Secretary." DuVal, the delegate, warned was planning another extended absence in Kentucky and was fully expecting to have the taxpayers foot the bill.⁶²

Interestingly, not long after it was announced that Eaton would succeed DuVal, territorial secretary James Westcott predicted to Andrew Jackson Donelson that Eaton's appointment would be popular in the territory: "Governor DuVal's friends go warmly for him and most of the planters are pleased."⁶³ Even though his tenure as territorial secretary was soon to end, Westcott's political situation continued to brighten. He would soon be favored with an appointment as U.S. district attorney for the Middle District.

Whatever the circumstances, DuVal left Florida, leaving his duties as governor behind. DuVal's plans were to settle in Kentucky permanently. As he revealed to his friend Senator Samuel Southard, "I shall return very poor to Kentucky and will resume the practice of law. It will be my only means of support but I love my old state and its people and I hope to die among them." Also to his old friend a sanguine DuVal lamented the passing of their dear "pure, good, and great" friend William Wirt. DuVal hoped to be see Southard again, "but if it should not be my fortune ever to meet again in this world yet never will I cease to cherish the kindest and most lasting regard for you. If we meet in another world (I hope in bliss)

I will meet you (with the blessing of the great father of the universe) in a congregation of millions and take you by the hand, with honest and warm affection."[64]

Before traveling to Kentucky, however, DuVal and his friend Achille Murat made what must have been a pleasant sojourn to West Point, New York. Appointed by the secretary of war, DuVal and Murat and sixteen others attended the annual examination of the cadets at the military academy on June 17.[65] Along the way DuVal and Murat may have enjoyed a brief repast with Washington Irving. Murat and his wife, Catherine, had entertained the New Yorker at their house in London in 1831. Though the writer would not acquire Sunnyside, his home at Tarrytown, until the next year, he was in the area, and, although specific evidence of a meeting is not recorded, the two may have sought him out.[66]

As DuVal made his way to New York and then to Kentucky, statements on DuVal's twelve-year stint as governor of the Florida territory began to appear. Reviews were mixed. Benjamin Wright of the Pensacola *Gazette* gave a fair appraisal. DuVal, he noted, had left many friends and some bitter enemies. Wright viewed DuVal's unpopularity in some circles as the inevitable plight of all territorial governors. "History of all new countries shews," he said, "that no Territorial Governor can be popular with the people. Citizens of this 'free country' quite naturally refuse to submit to the authority of rulers not of their own choosing." Early on, DuVal's enemies had charged that he "wanted *dignity*. . . . Certain it is, that Governor DUVAL never walked with a golden or even an ivory-headed cane. If he took snuff at all, (which we do not recollect,) it was not done in a manner to give him a place among the *distingue* of fashionable life." DuVal, Wright asserted, treated all men alike. "Though a Governor, he lived and acted like an ordinary man and a gentleman. But he wanted dignity! And who says so? They who, had his conduct been in accordance with their pretended *beau ideal*, would have denounced him for a solemn fop—a vain and pompous official coxcomb." DuVal had dedicated his "time and his talents to the prosperity of the country, while his salary was consumed in a somewhat profuse hospitality, which his grateful guests, oftentimes repaid by detailing new evidences of this *want of dignity*. May he long live in the enjoyment of that exuberance of social feeling, which while it delighted his friends, subjected him to this monstrous imputation" of wanting dignity. "We have to say in conclusion, that we hope, we may have no cause to regret his absence."[67]

By August, his trip to New York concluded, DuVal was back in Kentucky. A card was published in various newspapers in Florida, Virginia, Kentucky, and other Southern states: "Wm P. DuVal, having removed from Florida, will open his law office in Louisville, Kentucky, and resume the practice of Law."[68]

CHAPTER 14

"Do all you can for Texas"

In the summer of 1834, when William Pope DuVal arrived in Louisville, the town contained approximately eighteen thousand people. The town at the falls of the Ohio had, since its founding by George Rogers Clarke during the American Revolution, served as an important river town. But with the advent of steamboat travel Louisville became the leading commercial center for the region and the largest town on the Ohio below Cincinnati. Approximately forty-five miles north of Bardstown, Louisville offered convenient steamboat transit east toward Frankfort and Cincinnati. The town also offered easy access to ports in the other direction. According to the Louisville *Public Advertiser,* during the month of October DuVal could have boarded any one of fourteen different steamboats bound for New Orleans via the Mississippi River.[1] In October 1834 Nancy DuVal's cousin Andrew Hynes, now a prominent merchant and civic leader in Nashville, along with others was promoting the idea of linking that city with Louisville by rail.[2]

Under the leadership of civic leader James Guthrie, the town was about to experience a great building boom. A huge waterworks project was on the drawing board. Also, to further the goal of luring the state capital to the town, city fathers undertook a series of construction projects they hoped might someday house the state government. The Bank of Louisville (a successor to the city's branch of the Bank of the United States) offered easy credit for this and other ventures, including a new medical university established a few years later. The town also boasted a city theater and famous hotels: the Galt House and the larger Louisville Hotel, as well as the nationally known Oakland Racecourse. In 1837 the "Falls City" became the first town in the West to illuminate its streets with gas lighting.[3]

If the fifty-year-old former governor of Florida had left the cares of Indian affairs, partisan politics, and banking controversies behind, his most pressing concern was figuring out how to make a living in a state that he had not lived in

Louisville, Kentucky, Street Scene, ca. 1834. From Samuel Thomas, *Views of Louisville Since 1766.* 1971.

permanently since 1820. He certainly had many contacts and past acquaintances to draw on, but supporting his large family was not made any easier by the fact that much had changed in Kentucky since he had left so many years before. DuVal planned to handle land claims, especially for those claimants in Virginia who sought clear titles. Whether or not DuVal kept an office in Louisville is unclear, but newspaper accounts note that he had decided to live in Bardstown. Nancy DuVal was already in Kentucky when her husband arrived. Burr, age 23, was in the area. John, age 18, was attending St. Joseph College in Bardstown.[4] Thomas had already graduated from that institution and was reading law in the area. DuVal's daughters Mary (13), Laura (12), and Florida (8) were also in the household. The DuVals' older daughter Marcia and her husband, Dr. William Price, also joined the family on a visit from Apalachicola that fall. The proximity of their family no doubt helped console the Prices after the loss of their six-year-old son, who had died the previous March. DuVal's recently widowed and remarried daughter, Elizabeth Beale, also was nearby with her new husband.[5] DuVal's brother John had left his sugar plantation north of Tallahassee, but his plans for earning a living in Kentucky were unclear.[6]

In early September citizens in Bardstown gave DuVal a public dinner, as one newspaper account stated, "as a token of their respect for his public services and private worth. We notice as a circumstance highly creditable to the citizens of Bardstown that all parties united in tendering Gov. Duval this testimonial of respect."[7] The guests at the lavish dinner included DuVal's oldest son, Burr, his son-in-law Dr. William Price, his brother John, and many of his old friends from Bardstown. The festivities began with a toast to *"His Excellency William P. Du-Val*—A friend to the poor, companion of the brave, a citizen in peace, and a soldier in war. Long may he live to enjoy the unfeigned respect due to him by the citizens of Bardstown and Nelson County." DuVal gave a long address recalling his many fond memories of his life in the town. He also used the occasion to speak of his trials and tribulations in Florida, "growing out of the distracting and conflicting opinions of a new community." DuVal chose his words carefully, addressing the audience with an almost certain understanding that his controversial Florida past would be a subject yet discussed in Kentucky, Florida, and elsewhere. DuVal explained that his most serious challenges in his role as the territory's first governor arose from the difficulty of organizing "a new government depending for its action on a mingling population coming from every quarter of our country. . . . Yet under all these disadvantages, aggravated by local causes and local politics, sometimes violent and seldom dispassionate," he asserted, "I [am] under many lasting obligations to the people of Florida for their liberal and uniform support. . . . With all my defects of judgment and all the errors of my administration, together with occasional detraction and abuse to magnify these errors and exasperate the ardent and unreflecting against me, it will ever remain to me, a lasting consolation that I retired from the Government of Florida, with the esteem and confidence of the greater portion of her citizens." DuVal admitted that his political "connection with the people of Florida, have terminated, and there is little probability of its renewal"; however, he declared, "I have never known in any new country a better, bolder or more generous race of men. I shall long remember their fine traits of character and manly virtues. Their few defects are already forgotten." DuVal hastened to add that he had left many "dear and valued" friends whose "disinterested conduct I can never forget—friends whose intelligence and virtues reflect honor on our race and who are destined to shine on a greater theatre than the limits of their own territory. Wherever I may live—humble and powerless as I am—should the interests or the rights of Florida be assailed, one voice, feeble and unavailing as it may prove, shall be raised in defense of her rights and in defiance to her enemies."[8]

DuVal concluded with a reference to Bardstown. "I look upon this spot [Bardstown] with fond and lively emotion. Silent and rural as it is, compared to the great and busy world amidst the rolling of whose cars and sounding commerce, the modest name of Bardstown is unheard.... Let the great world then, overlook our little village—we will defy them to overlook or forget the statesmen, orators and jurists, she has given to the nation."[9]

As he made the rounds reintroducing himself to his Kentucky friends and associates, DuVal could not help being drawn into state politics. As a token of respect, Democrats in the Kentucky legislature tapped him to represent the seventh congressional district at the national nominating convention in Baltimore. Richard M. Johnson, Martin Van Buren, and Hugh Lawson White were contenders for the nomination, but the body asserted that its delegates would act in concert "cheerfully and zealously by the decision of the grand national convention." DuVal's relative Worden Pope was also selected delegate.[10]

That spring DuVal attended to his practice and readied himself for the Baltimore convention. As he wrote to Andrew Jackson from Louisville on May 17, "I am a hard student in my profession, and in all most daily attendance on the courts." But as he explained to Old Hickory, a sudden medical setback prevented his attendance. Having "prepared to attend the convention at Baltimore—my trunk ready to go on board of a steam boat," he "was taken most violently ill with bilious fever." He had been "confined" to his "bed until yesterday." DuVal reported that though he was "up and moving about my room," it was decided after consultation with other Democratic leaders to send another man to Baltimore. DuVal assured Old Hickory that the whole Kentucky delegation favored Van Buren as his successor. DuVal predicted that Richard M. Johnson would be nominated for vice president and that Van Buren would carry the whole West. DuVal offered his unequivocal support to Van Buren, whom he had "ever found frank" and "candid" and to whom "we owe more than any other man in the

John Eaton at the time he became territorial governor of Florida, in 1834. Courtesy of State Archives of Florida.

country for the bold and manly support he has given your administration." DuVal also provided Old Hickory with an update on Florida affairs as reported to him from friends there. Those he had heard from in Tallahassee spoke in the "highest and warmest terms of Gov. Eaton & and nothing has afforded me more sincere gratification than the uniform support that all my friends have given to his administration."[11]

John and Peggy Eaton had arrived in Tallahassee in late December. On December 13 a large gathering gave an official welcome to the new governor. Among the toasts given in salute of the new governor was a toast in honor of the former executive: "Wm P. DuVal—Our highly esteemed ex-Governor—We know the man, and knowing him, admire him."[12] Only weeks later, the territorial legislative council also recognized DuVal's service to the territory. The council resolved that the governor's "long faithful [service], his integrity of purpose and his devotion to the interest and welfare of the Territory" merited the "kind feelings of its members, with the hope that he may return and spend the evening of his days in the land so long benefited by his faithful service and embellished hospitality."[13]

Herbert J. Doherty has argued that John Eaton's appointment in place of DuVal in 1834 all but ended the Nucleus's influence in the territory. Eaton was of

Tallahassee Street Scene. From Francis Comte de Castelnau, *Vues et Souvenirs de l'Amérique du Nord*. Courtesy of State Archives of Florida.

course Richard Keith Call's enemy, and some, including Achille Murat, interpreted the former secretary of war's appointment as a victory for Joseph M. White. Call's cousin George K. Walker succeeded James Westcott as territorial secretary, and he exerted strong leadership when the governor was out of the territory, which he often was.[14] While it could be expected that Walker's appointment redounded to the benefit of Call, such was not the case. Indeed, as DuVal himself had explained to Andrew Donelson a year earlier in a "private" letter, Walker was actually Call's enemy and ought to be removed. He had spoken out against the president as well.[15] If Call's political fortunes seemed to be on the wane, such was not the case for his economic situation. His law practice grew, his planting interests prospered, and his selection as president of the Tallahassee Railroad Company portended great wealth and influence. Capitalized at $100,000, the company proposed to build a railroad from Tallahassee to St. Marks. Not long after Eaton arrived in the territory, construction began.[16]

John Eaton's tenure in Florida was uneventful and temporary, and most in the territory rightly considered Eaton's appointment one of the many sorry outcomes of the Jackson cabinet debacle. Even so, Peggy Eaton remembered her time in Florida fondly.[17] One might expect that Eaton's tenure as war secretary might have prepared him well for dealing with the building Seminole threat, but there is little evidence that he took much interest in the issue. The situation on that front continued to degenerate while DuVal was in Kentucky. In April 1835 Colonel Duncan Clinch wrote to authorities in Washington that he was convinced that the Indians had "not the least intention of fulfilling their treaty obligations, unless compelled to do so by a stronger force than *mere words.*" Again writing from Fort King in October, Clinch pleaded for more troops to protect his isolated outpost and the surrounding settlements; "otherwise many lives & much property may be lost."[18]

Another negative legacy that DuVal bequeathed to Eaton was the divided sectional and political nature of the territory. On one of his frequent trips to his daughter's plantation, Blackwood, near Tallahassee, Judge Robert Raymond Reid noted the divided nature of the territory. On February 27, he wrote in his diary, "There is an Eastern, and Western, and Middle Party, a Call Party, a White Party, a Nuttall, a Gadsden—the whole community from the point of the Peninsula to the St. Mary's and Pensacola split up into bits. This should not be so," the judge observed, adding that "the parties should divide on principle. No body can tell when we shall get into the Union but 'tis to be regretted that there are not separate Governments for East and West Florida."[19]

Precisely what property DuVal had left in Florida is unclear. Records show he took out a $3,500 mortgage on his 160 acres and slaves and received thirty-five shares of stock in the Union Bank of Florida.[20] As previously noted, he had sold off whatever interest he held with Southard in the Lafayette tract. Still, the uncertainty of that situation was a matter of concern for Southard, and he inquired about the disposition of the land to George T. Ward, the public land registrar, who in turn told him that as best as he could tell, the land had reverted to the original owners once DuVal left for Kentucky. Ward added that Lafayette's agent had told him that as far as he knew "no written contract for the land" existed."[21]

That fall DuVal, his sons Burr Harrison and John Crittenden, and other Kentuckians became keenly aware of events brewing on America's western frontier. Since the 1820s Americans, especially Southerners, had been migrating to Texas seeking fertile cotton lands along the Brazos River. (This migration occurred simultaneously with the opening up of the Florida Territory in the 1820s.) The Republic of Mexico had fostered this influx by the creation of its Empresario System, a scheme to populate its northern province with Americans who agreed to acquire large grants under closely regulated conditions. By the 1830s approximately thirty thousand Americans had migrated either legally or illegally to Mexico's northern province. By 1835 conflicts and disputes between Mexico and the Americans had led to a virtual breakdown of comity between the two distant regions. By the middle of the year, armed resistance and eventual independence appeared inevitable. DuVal had many friends and associates who were in Texas or who had a financial stake in the region. A few years earlier, for example, Achille

Murat and a consortium of investors from Tallahassee had formed a company to invest in Texas lands.[22] After a series of political setbacks DuVal's friend Sam Houston had decided to cast his lot with Texas and had been there off and on since 1832. When fighting broke out in the San Antonio area in October 1835, calls went out all over the United States for assistance. It took no leap whatsoever for patriotic Americans to equate the Texas cause with the American cause of 1776. Towns throughout the United States, especially in the South, held meetings, raised money, and sent troops in support of the cause.[23]

In Bardstown, Kentucky, William P. DuVal and his sons Burr and John were drawn to the cause. The crusade offered adventure, and Burr and John were among the first Kentuckians to answer the call. The proud father wrote to Sam Houston that he had "sent you *two* of my *three* sons—my eldest B. H. [you] saw at Washington City, [John Crittenden] my youngest son about 20 years old—to your generous feelings I recommend[. They] have not one bad habit that I would change." DuVal had the "utmost confidence . . . in their integrity and courage—If I could have borrowed $10,000 I would have done so without delay—and I could have joined you at the head of a noble regiment." Instead DuVal noted that he was forced to travel to Florida on business, and both there and upon his return to Kentucky he would do his utmost to "have troops sent from that quarter." Equating the Texas cause with the American Revolution, he stated that he was surprised that Texas had not yet formally declared its independence but noted that, "The United States was engaged in active war for more than a year before our declaration of Independence. I have no hesitation knowing that Texas should pursue this course as soon as circumstances will admit."[24]

While DuVal was on a steamboat heading for Florida, Burr and John DuVal were on their way to Texas. At the head of approximately twenty-five Kentuckians, Captain Burr DuVal arrived at Quintana, at the mouth of the Brazos River, on December 28.[25] The "Kentucky Mustangs" eventually joined a force under the overall command of James Fannin and for the next two and a half months prepared for a confrontation with the Mexicans, while also keeping abreast of events at the Texas Consultation, which served as Revolutionary Texas's provisional government. On January 18 Burr wrote to his brother Thomas that he expected that independence would be declared by March. "Tomorrow," he wrote, "we are ordered to embark for Copano—from thence to we will proceed by land to San Patrick [San Patricio], which is the place of general rendezvous for the army from which point, as soon as the forces have assembled, we will make a descent on Matamoros. So you see, it is as I anticipated; Mexico and not Texas is to be the invaded country. Should we proceed in taking Matamoros (of which no one seems to have a doubt) I think there is reason to believe that another and I hope more successful attack will be made on Tampico. The town of Matamoros is situated near the mouth of the Rio del Norte," Burr continued. "It contains about 7000 inhabitants, and is a place of considerable wealth and commercial advantages. The possession of it will be of no small consideration with Texas. Since my arrival here I have been so busily engaged that I have not been able to see anything of the country, but from all accounts, some parts of it must be the most desirable in the world. I am told that the country about San Antonio, cannot be surpassed for beauty and health."[26]

On the same day Burr and John DuVal arrived in Quintana, what General Duncan Clinch and other Florida officials feared most occurred. On December 28 Seminoles attacked and decimated Major Francis L. Dade's command as it headed north from Fort Brooke to reinforce the isolated outpost at Fort King. (The rotting corpses of the one hundred men lay on the battlefield where they fell until they were discovered and buried by a force some one and a half months later.) That same afternoon the Seminole chief Osceola murdered Indian agent Wiley Thompson as he walked outside the Fort King stockade. In what were clearly coordinated attacks, Seminole bands ravaged isolated farms and plantations throughout the peninsula. Three days after Dade's Battle, General Richard K. Call and his militia forces and General Clinch's regulars fought the Seminoles on both sides of the Withlacoochee River. Call's militia forces, trapped on one side of the river, could not be adequately deployed. The regulars bore most of the fighting, and recriminations would follow.[27]

William P. DuVal arrived in Tallahassee only weeks after the Florida Territory erupted into warfare. The mood was somber and unsettled. Even so, local leaders invited the former governor to a public dinner in commemoration of "the grateful recollection of the many valuable services rendered to this Territory." DuVal promptly accepted, thanking them for the "flattering testimony of regard, from a community, with whom I resided so many years." At the appointed time a dinner was given at the City Hotel. Governor Eaton presided, assisted by General Call and Colonel Robert Gamble, in a large "hall crowded to overflowing—Good feeling and good cheer were the order of the day." After the dinner the cloth was removed and toasts were offered to "the States of this Union, The President, both Houses of Congress, Florida," and of course, "Our Distinguished Guest." Also recognized was the memory of Major Dade, and a toast was raised to Burr H. DuVal, "a noble son of a noble father."[28] A similar gathering found DuVal in Marianna on April 1. An account recorded that the "honored guest was in fine spirits" and sang a couple of songs in commemoration of the event.[29]

By this time Middle Florida residents had learned that DuVal intended to return permanently to Florida. A local newspaper announced the fact, and in an accompanying column a card listed DuVal as forming a partnership to practice law with Richard C. Allen. The firm would have offices in Tallahassee and St. Joseph and practice in the superior courts of Leon, Jefferson, Gadsden, Jackson, and Franklin Counties as well as in the territorial court of appeals.[30]

For the next two months DuVal worked in Middle Florida as best he could to launch his law practice. Meanwhile, President Jackson had appointed Richard K. Call to replace Eaton as territorial governor, and the new executive took the oath of office three days later. By that time the war had descended into chaos. Not long afterward, DuVal wrote to General Clinch offering to raise a thousand men in Kentucky and entrust them to Clinch. "I have confidence in your judgment and knowledge of the Indian character, and if you cannot fight them with success no other officer can. The campaign will not open until Autumn. I shall return to Kentucky and will organize a mounted force which will be offered to the President of the United States . . . and I . . . will be perfectly content to be under your command & General Calls—indeed I desire no other to command me."[31] DuVal forwarded a circular letter from Governor Call to authorities in Kentucky, and soon a call for volunteers to serve in Florida was publicized.[32]

By May the conflict between generals Winfield Scott and Edmund Pendleton Gaines over the leadership of the regular forces could not be resolved. Both commanders refused to collaborate with Governor Call. This debacle left settlements and isolated pioneers in Middle and East Florida exposed to Indian attacks, and the spring was extremely bloody. Scott's campaign in April failed, and the commander called off the offensive for the summer. Not surprisingly, this hiatus brought intense condemnation throughout the territory. Newspapers denounced the general for abandoning Florida. Tallahassee citizens burned Scott in effigy. The leadership conflict and the exposed condition of the frontier were reported in newspapers throughout the nation. One Georgia newspaper reported, for example, that "Osceola, the famous Seminole Chief, proclaims that he will hold his green corn dance in the public square, opposite the Tallahassee City Hotel." "[E]very building in Black Creek and Newnansville has been destroyed by the Indians," the report continued. "The posts of Fort King, Fort Drane, and the settlement of Micanopy and Newnansville will have to be abandoned, because it will be impossible to maintain them."[33]

Governor Call scrambled as best he could to raise militia forces and appealed continually to Washington for assistance. After numerous unanswered appeals, Call penned a desperate letter to President Jackson's personal secretary. "I have been writing to the secretary of war relative to the exposed and defenseless condition of the territory, ever since I came in to office, but can get no answer from him. I have to beg sir you will bring this subject to the attention of the President, and urge the adoption of some measure for our relief. I have received no letter from Genl. Scott who has left the field to the enemy." Call feared that the Seminoles might "link and strengthen with the Creeks" and that in that case "Florida will be between two fires."[34]

While most of the devastation centered in East Florida, Middle Florida was not immune to the violence. In the midst of the crisis Governor Call called on

Louis M. Goldsborough to form an expedition to march against the Seminoles. Goldsborough had significant military experience as a naval officer and was at that time managing his father-in-law's plantations. Goldsborough had married William Wirt's daughter Elizabeth in 1831 and had migrated to Middle Florida soon thereafter, joining Elizabeth's sister Laura Randall and other Wirt relations. One day after Call wrote to Donelson, Goldsborough, writing from Wirtland Plantation, recounted to his wife the expedition he had led on the Wacissa and Aucilla Rivers against marauding Indians in retaliation for recent attacks committed against their rural community. Goldborough speculated that the group was a "small straggling party, no doubt some of Tiger Tail's concern." The marauders had attacked "killed and scalped Judge [Thomas] Randall's negro Tom. Next they way-laid your uncle John's [Gamble] Plantation, but committed no mischief. . . . Next they shot Mr. William Gorman, a most excellent and worthy citizen, in two places, in his thigh and neck. . . . Next they burned to the ground the dwelling and smokehouse of Captain Murray's plantation. Next they visited several abandoned houses lying on the road leading from Belmont to Magnolia, robbed them all of what they wanted . . . broke crockery and last they murdered and scalped a boy." Goldsborough wrote to his wife that Governor Call had asked him to participate in an expedition to relieve a blockhouse on the Withlacoochee River but that he had declined because it was an *"aquatic expedition."* Governor Call had already given command to Leigh Read, and he "could not take it from him without hurting his feelings; and as far as my serving" in such an expedition "under him or any one else in the territory, it was out of the question." Goldsborough concluded his missive with an appraisal of Winfield Scott's unpopularity. His conduct, he explained, "only emboldens the savages." "Great excitement prevails against him. I certainly believe that if he were to attempt to pass through Middle Florida, he would be shot down by some of the more desperate of its population."[35]

While DuVal tried as best he could to launch his law practice, he must have thought often of his sons in Texas. By April DuVal may have learned of the formal declaration of Texas independence on March 2 or the fall of the Alamo on March 6. Loved ones in Florida and Kentucky must have despaired of the whereabouts and condition of the Kentucky volunteers. On March 9 Captain Burr H. DuVal wrote to his father from Goliad, explaining that he had given the letter to a man going north but did not think he would get out as "we are surrounded by Mexican troops." As far as he knew, the Alamo was still holding out even though its inhabitants had been "fighting desperately there for 10 or 15 days against 4 or 5 thousand Mexicans. Santa Anna is there himself and has there and in this vicinity at least six thousand troops." The Mexican dictator had invaded unexpectedly. Burr speculated that by the time his father received his letter San Antonio would have fallen. "I cannot believe it possible so small a band could maintain it against such fearful odds—D. Crockett is one of the number in the fort," he wrote.[36]

Burr DuVal wrote to his father that Fannin was unpopular and that his men wanted to put the young man himself at the head of the army but that he had resisted. "I have seen enough to desire no office for the present in Texas higher than the one I hold—I have fifty men in my company who love me and who cannot be surpassed for boldness and chivalry—with such a band I will gain the laurels I may wear or die without any—I am situated at present with my company in a strong stone house immediately across the street and opposite one of the Bastions of the fort—from the bastion I have built a bridge to the top of the house on which is placed a brass six Pounder, the best and most commanding situation we have—before I am driven from it hundreds must perish."[37]

DuVal went on to explain to his father that Texas was a "decidedly richer country than I expected to find, and must be more healthy than any other southern country." It is "high and dry tho' generally level and the rivers, at least this, the San Antonio descends with the velocity of a mountain stream." DuVal thought Florida's climate better, but Texas's soil was more fertile. DuVal had no doubt that with independence declared the Americans would "whip the Mexicans—For young men who wish to acquire distinction and fortune now is the time—Tell all who are friendly to the cause of Texas to lend a helping hand and that quickly. The little band of volunteers now in the field must breast the storm and keep a powerful army in check until relief is at hand or all is lost—We want provisions, arms, & men. I have never seen such men as this army is composed of—no man ever thinks of retreat, or surrender, they must be exterminated or whipped—Nothing can depress their ardour—we are frequently for days without any thing but Bull beef to eat, and after working hard all day you could at night hear the boys crowing, gobbling, barking, bellowing, laughing, and singing you would think them the happiest and best fed men in the world. Do all you can for Texas—Your affectionate Son, B. H. Duval." In a postscript he added, "If there should be anything in my letter that could benefit Texas make it public."[38]

It is not known when DuVal received his son Burr's March 9 letter. Whether the missive reached him in Florida or Kentucky is also unknown. The ultimate fate of Fannin's army remained uncertain. Rumors of its capture, surrender, and massacre began to trickle in. On May 11 the Bardstown *Herald* reported a rumor that Colonel Fannin and his men had been massacred after entering into articles of capitulation, but the paper doubted the veracity of the claim. "The thing is incredible." But the account proved accurate. Finally, on June 1 the journal reported the gory details: 350 men in eight companies, including the "Kentucky Mustangs," had been surrounded. After several day's fighting they decided to surrender on March 20 and were marched to Goliad. The terms stipulated that they would be treated as prisoners of war according to the rules of civilized nations, paroled immediately, and sent home. Yet, after seven days of brutal treatment, they were marched out of town in four columns and shot. Only a few of the men were able to escape the firing by running into the river.[39] One of those was John Crittenden DuVal. When the shooting started DuVal jumped into the river, wandering for several days until he reached Brazoria. From there he was able to make his way back to New Orleans and then to Bardstown. The thrilling narrative of his miraculous escape would soon find its way into the newspapers.[40]

The full details of the catastrophe remained unknown outside Texas for months after the incident. Even the Houston *Telegraph and Texas Register* was unable to verify the identities of all the victims of this "unprovoked, cold-blooded, and unnecessary murder committed on those illustrious champions of Texas liberty" until November 11, 1836. Precisely when William P. DuVal learned of his sons' fate is unknown, but when he left Florida in early June for Kentucky he thought that both his sons had perished at Goliad. As he explained to Governor Call, shortly after arriving in Bardstown in late June, he said had not heard of his son John's "extraordinary escape . . . until I was [within] 45 miles of this place." DuVal enclosed a paper describing his son's escape. DuVal explained to his friend that since his return home John had become "diffident, that he has kept himself actually secreted . . . to avoid the notice and attention, which were crowded on him—he can not be persuaded to speak of his own actions. But he says there never were 400 men together so brave and determined as those under Fanning." John declared that "not a man, was down hearted and all fought with coolness and judgments. Poor Burr was butchered but John says he was the favorite of the corps. *His* was the only rifle that could carry a bullet a great distance with certainty of execution." DuVal reported that his wife, Nancy, was "wasted to a shadow" at the loss of her son. "If John had not returned home," he confided, "there is little doubt she would by this time have been in her grave." For his part John had grown weary of recounting the episode, but, as DuVal explained, John's brother Thomas had reminded him that people were "anxious to hear all about his escape." For his part, John DuVal, whether still grieving at the loss of his brother or perhaps uncomfortable that he had survived while his brother had perished, resisted his newfound celebrity status. He told his brother Thomas that people had "made too much of a common affair, that he felt ashamed for them."[41]

DuVal then switched to the topic of the Florida War. He informed Call that he had written to President Jackson, begging to be allowed to raise a mounted corps of 1,200 men under Call and Clinch. He was convinced that Call and Clinch alone could "bring the war to a close in six weeks, from the time you enter the enemy's country." DuVal also informed Call that he was delighted that Leigh Read had rescued the besieged blockhouse on the Withlacoochee and that, despite Scott's wanton and malicious calumnies against the officer, Read was just the man to head a new regiment of troops mustered into the regular army. "[T]his I have proclaimed at Milledgeville and at my town & village and every house from that place to this. A braver man than Reed cannot be found."[42]

When DuVal arrived in Kentucky, he found a state that had caught fire for Texan independence. Word had reached the state of Sam Houston's victory over Santa Anna at San Jacinto. Dramatic demonstrations in support of the cause erupted everywhere; one such demonstration was chaired by DuVal's brother John and his brother-in-law Dr. Burr Harrison on May 9 in Bardstown. The gathering resolved that Texas should be independent and that an agent should be appointed in each Kentucky county to solicit donations for the Texas cause.[43] On May 23, the editor of the Louisville *Daily Journal* declared, "We never before witnessed such a scene of general rejoicing, as was exhibited in this city, on Friday night, on account of the downfall of Santa Anna and the Texian revolution. . . . Thousands of lights were gleaming in every direction: the whole city was beautifully and gorgeously illuminated; moving bonfires of surpassing brilliancy were drawn through the streets; blazing rockets were seen streaming in all directions through the air; cannon and small arms were roaring amid the loud shouts of the multitude; and every street exhibited a dense mass of men, women, and children rejoicing in the general jubilee. How deeply and fervently the hearts of a republican people can sympathize in the triumphs of Liberty."[44] Even with the victory at San Jacinto and the capture of Santa Anna on April 21, most Kentuckians were convinced that the war was not over and that more troops would be needed.

On June 30 DuVal wrote to General George Chambers that, although he had been in Bardstown only a few days, he was "determined to devote my life to the cause of Texas, and to avenge the murder of my son Capt. DuVal and his brave companions who were butchered at Goliad."[45] DuVal offered to assist in raising men and supplies, and Texas authorities in Kentucky appointed DuVal adjutant general, Army of the Reserve. Jointly with General Chambers he issued a broadside entitled *Magnanimous and Chivalrous Sons of the West* on July 15. Writing glowingly of the Texas cause, DuVal declared that Texas had again been "invaded by a "ruthless and sanguinary foe, and she renews her call to the brave and the free . . . to participate in the glory of sustaining the principles of civil and religious liberty, against tyranny and fanaticism."[46]

DuVal reminded his hearers that while Santa Anna had been defeated and captured, "the war has not been terminated by his fall. He was but the creature and instrument of a party; that party still lives; and the object of those who compose it is to sweep from the nation every vestige of civil liberty, and to establish upon the ruins of the Federal Constitution, an absolute military and ecclesiastical despotism." It was "liberty that the party fear—it is the contagious and all pervading influence of North American liberty that they seek to counteract and destroy; and extermination is the means by which they propose to effect it. The cause of Texas," DuVal continued, "is not an isolated one peculiar to herself; it is the cause of human liberty; it is the cause of all mankind."[47]

That summer DuVal divided his time between Bardstown and Louisville. Soon papers throughout the nation took notice of DuVal's activities. The Charleston *Southern Patriot* on August 2 reported, for example, that "Governor DuVal, whose Son among others was murdered at Goliad, has determined to avenge him by raising *two thousand troops* in Kentucky, and, with them, joining the Texas forces by the first of October." DuVal felt it his duty to inspire the troops. He circulated around the entire area that summer. On July 2 DuVal and his brother John joined Andrew Hynes, Dr. Burr Harrison, and four other Bardstown leaders who passed six resolutions in support of the Texas cause after John explained the nature and object of the meeting and offered six "resolutions to which Gov. DuVal delivered an address explanatory of the objects and inducements, which have made it necessary to adopt the above resolutions." After the resolutions were adopted unanimously, DuVal "tendered his thanks to the meeting, and pledged himself to lend his all in the cause of bleeding liberty."[48]

Similar occasions followed throughout the month. On July 13, at a meeting in Elizabethtown, he spoke at a recruiting meeting. According to one source, "Gov. Duval made an able and eloquent speech, which is said to have produced a powerful effect." Approximately one week later DuVal "addressed the people of Hardinsburg on the subject of Texas. His speech," according to a witness, was "very eloquent... produced a thrilling effect." Another man added feelingly that when DuVal "spoke of the destruction of our citizens at the Alamo, the contracted brow, the clenched hand, and the glistening eye, told of sympathy of our people. When he spoke of the treacherous and cowardly butchery of Fannin's corps, of the death of his noble son Burr, and of the escape, the privations, and sufferings of his other son John," the man continued, "the deep indignation of the people could scarce be restrained within bounds. It broke out in audible murmurs, and many a heart bent high with the determination to avenge their murder." When DuVal announced his determination to raise a force for Texas and "advance the cause of Independence," the declaration was "received with a wild hurrah of approbation."[49]

Meanwhile, back in Florida, Governor Call prepared for renewed operations against the Seminoles. But Call's recruiting efforts for the East Florida campaign had been less than inspiring: "I am deeply mortified," he wrote President Jackson, "to give you the results of my recruiting efforts. It is ever more dishonorable to the territory than my worst apprehensions could have anticipated." Only one regiment had shown any "particular, manly feeling." He predicted that only one-third of them would be ready to march with the Tennessee volunteers when they arrived. Even during this time of crisis, partisan politics had raised its ugly head. James Westcott, Call complained to Jackson, was obstructing his efforts.[50] The Tennessee troops arrived nearly a week after Call wrote to Jackson. William Campbell, an officer in the corps, was impressed with Tallahassee. According to

Campbell, the town that DuVal had founded fourteen years earlier was "well laid out in squares, the streets being broad & running at right angles. There are a good many very excellent houses," Campbell explained to his wife, "and from every appearance I think it ought to be healthy for this climate, but for this far South I am well satisfied there is no such thing as health."[51]

Campbell had good reason for concern about the hostile climate and terrain that he was entering. In the months preceding the time the volunteers set out for East Florida, Micanopy and surrounding forts in the middle peninsula had been abandoned and troops and settlers had fallen back to Fort Heileman on Black Creek to wait for reinforcements and provisions to be brought in by steamboat. On September 27 a correspondent from that post explained, "Indians hover about, deliver their fire and fly off, without the possibility of getting at them. They have trails through their immense hammocks, with which they are familiar and in this way they harass us with impunity. . . . A new campaign is about to open, but no one, can anticipate the result. . . . Gen. Call has advanced as far as the Suwannee with the brigade of Tennesseans, and the militia of West Florida, making 1,900 men." General Thomas Jesup, who had replaced Scott, was "advancing from Tampa Bay with about 800 regulars and 600 Indians, while Major [Benjamin] Pierce, the commanding officer at this Fort, will advance soon, with about 200 regulars and form a junction with Gen. C at Camp King."[52]

As Call and his men made their way across the Suwannee River, William P. DuVal and his family boarded a steamboat in Louisville and headed to Florida. He would have wondered what lay in store for him as he decided for the second time in his life to settle in the Florida Territory. Perhaps he hoped to revive his planting efforts. But the lands in the Lafayette tract that he and Samuel Southard had hoped to cultivate had reverted to their original owners. Rich outside interests or migrants representing them had appropriated most of the best lands still available in Middle Florida. In addition, DuVal had no cash to buy land and slaves. But he did have contacts. He would somehow have to wrest a living out of the law.

CHAPTER 15

Canals, Banks, and a Constitutional Convention

As William P. DuVal set out from Louisville down the Ohio and Mississippi Rivers to Florida in November 1836, the United States set about selecting its ninth president. The choice was between Jackson's handpicked successor, Martin Van Buren, and three Whig candidates chosen to run in different sections of the country: Daniel Webster in New England, William Henry Harrison in the West, and Hugh Lawson White in the South. The Whig strategy to throw the election into the House of Representatives failed when Van Buren won a comfortable margin of nearly seventy electoral votes over the combined totals of the three Whig candidates. Jackson's firm support for the New Yorker plus the candidate's own political skills in creating the Democratic machine had clearly made the difference. Yet a cursory glance at the electoral map indicated that the South supported Van Buren, and its continued support would be crucial. The Van Buren-Johnson ticket secured the electoral votes of Alabama, Arkansas, Louisiana, Mississippi, Missouri, North Carolina, and Virginia. Taking these states along with Michigan, Illinois, Pennsylvania, and New York allowed Van Buren to claim that his was truly a national victory. As most understood, sustaining this coalition would be difficult without the star power of Old Hickory. Running second to Van Buren was William Henry Harrison, who ran strong in the Midwest, and only months after the election his supporters were already plotting a strategy for the 1840 election. As it turned out, the Whigs would focus their attention on the South. They understood that the Little Magician was most vulnerable there.

These thoughts may have also coursed through William P. DuVal's brain as he and his family headed south toward the Florida Territory. DuVal stopped first in Pensacola before arriving at St. Joseph. DuVal's daughter Marcia and her husband, Dr. William D. Price, the town's port collector (a position that DuVal had himself secured for him), were on hand to greet the new arrivals. Peter Gautier, local booster and proprietor of the St. Joseph *Times,* hailed DuVal's return. Writing glowingly of the former governor, Gautier enthused, "The services rendered by Gov. DuVal to this territory while in its infancy are now generally acknowledged by many who assailed his motives, and his administration of our laws, while filling the executive chair. He was induced to visit the western country last winter on account of the distressed situation of his family, growing out of incidents of the Texian War, and had made arrangements for the raising of a large corps of volunteers destined to act against the Mexicans." DuVal had also labored long to assist Florida as he offered President Jackson 1,200 Kentuckians for the Florida war. But, as Gautier explained, the president had turned them down in the belief that the Tennessee volunteers along with their Florida and U.S. army counterparts would be sufficient to bring the war to a "speedy conclusion." The newspaper declared that "Governor DuVal merits and will receive wherever he goes, the kind greetings of his numerous friends."[1]

DuVal's visit to St. Joseph was no haphazard affair. The former governor and his law partner, Richard C. Allen, understood the town's potential as a commercial center. Sheltered by Cape San Blas, the location had a good harbor. But without roads, canals, or a railroad linking the town to the Apalachicola River, St. Joseph's potential could never be realized. Major transportation facilities required federal support, and DuVal had the contacts and the skills to push these projects forward.

The DuVals returned to a territorial capital flush with cotton profits. Citizens appeared oblivious to the war raging in East Florida. Nor did they appreciate the national economic picture. A visitor from Pensacola visiting Tallahassee at the time speculated that there was "perhaps no community taken as a body more prosperous than this. The lands are . . . peculiarly adapted to the culture of Cotton and capable of being made to endure almost forever."[2] True, cotton prices were high. But the commentator failed to understand that much of the apparent prosperity was due to the easy credit policies of John Gamble's Union Bank of Florida, which lavished loans and mortgages on its stockholders with little regard to their ability to repay these obligations. Yet some wiser heads understood that the bubble could not last forever. A reckoning was on the horizon.

The DuVals reacquainted themselves with their friends and former associates. John Crittenden may have accompanied the family to Florida. Twenty-three-year-old Thomas Howard returned to Florida and assisted his father's legal practice. Within a short time he was serving as clerk of the Leon County Superior Court and the territorial court of appeals.[3] Thomas DuVal eventually married his cousin Laura Peyton DuVal, his Uncle John's daughter. Nancy DuVal and her daughters Mary (17), Laura (16), and Florida (10) also reunited with friends. Among these were their former neighbors Thomas and Elizabeth Brown, whom they had known since 1828 when the Browns had migrated to the area from Virginia. By 1836 Thomas Brown was one of the leading businessmen in Tallahassee. He had erected the City Hotel, owned a brickyard, and built and operated the Marion Race Course, on the south of town. Sixteen-year-old Laura DuVal and her friend "Lizzy" Brown were no doubt happy at the return of the DuVals. That year Laura accompanied the Browns on an excursion to Cuba. Also along on the trip was Arthur M. Randolph, the son of Thomas Eston Randolph and a student at the University of Pennsylvania Medical School. A romantic relationship between the two developed.[4] A rival of Randolph for Laura's affections would soon arrive in Tallahassee in the person of Captain Samuel Peter Heintzelman, stationed in the territorial capital as a member of the U.S. Quartermaster Corp. As paymaster Heintzelman came to know and associate with many of the town's political and economic leaders. He and his fellow officers participated in the vibrant social scene in town and on outlying plantations, frequently escorting Laura DuVal, Elizabeth Brown, and their friends to balls, parties, and other social gatherings. DuVal's home, as it had been when he was governor, continued as a focal point for these affairs.

John DuVal also returned to Tallahassee with his family about the same time. Like his brother, DuVal planned to resume his law practice. DuVal hoped that handling settlers' claims for property lost in the war against the Seminoles might prove lucrative. In February a card in the Tallahassee *Floridian* announced that DuVal had become associated with another attorney from the U.S. Department of the Treasury. They would "prosecute all claims for Negroes and other property destroyed or taken off by the Indians and for horses &c killed in service or taken for the army." He could be found in the "office lately occupied by [Richard K]. Call and [George] Walker."[5] John DuVal also eventually secured a contract to write a compilation of the territorial laws.

Meanwhile, Richard Keith Call's campaign against the Seminoles had gone badly. After Jackson appointed Call to head all military operations in Florida, bad luck and Call's own shortcomings soon intervened. Things went from bad to worse. His wife died before he could depart. Call's health faltered, as did his recruiting efforts. The Tennessee volunteers arrived late. Once his offensive was finally put into effect, it proved too complicated to execute, and, after a short movement toward the Withlacoochee River (the stream that essentially shielded the Seminoles from his army), Call decided to fall back on his supply bases at Fort Drane and Black Creek. Though the governor-general considered this episode a minor setback, the Jackson administration became impatient. President Jackson was so angered by his protégé's lack of success against a foe he had mastered twenty years earlier that he sacked him from command on November 4. Military operations in Florida reverted to General Thomas Jesup. At first mortified and then indignant, Call sent off a series of blistering attacks to the War Department, charging that the president had acted on incomplete information and mere rumor and innuendo. Call's correspondence and extensive editorial comment made their way into print in the next several months.[6] Not since the Eaton affair had Call and Jackson had such cross words, but the breach reopened, never fully closed. As he often did, Call took the slight personally. The affair and its aftermath also soured Call's relationship with the Van Buren administration even before it started. His relations with the administration went from bad to worse, eventually resulting in his removal in 1839. Soon thereafter Call and other likeminded men formed a nascent Whig movement in Florida.[7]

Most Middle Floridians rallied around their governor, and DuVal led in defending his friend. On December 15 he organized a public meeting in Tallahassee for the purpose of planning a suitable reception for Call's return to the capital. Called to chair the gathering, DuVal made an impassioned speech in support of Call. DuVal proclaimed that no one could have achieved more than Call against such "an alert and daring foe." This was especially true given the many "difficulties which were to be encountered, and the many chances by which the best laid plans might be disconcerted in a vast country without roads or the means of communication." Indeed, "more had been done than we had a right to expect, and much more than had been accomplished with superior means by his predecessor." Governor Call, DuVal continued, "is entitled to our gratitude for affording in the late brilliant engagement an opportunity to our citizen soldiers of silencing forever the calumnies against them, which have been propagated through ignorance, wantonness or malice." The gathering received DuVal's remarks "with the warmest testimonials of approbation." Plans for a public dinner in Call's honor progressed, and the assembly unanimously appointed DuVal to deliver an address to Call "on his arrival, expressive of the sentiments entertained towards him by the citizens of Tallahassee."[8]

But it turned out that DuVal would miss Call's grand homecoming. DuVal had pressing matters in Washington to attend to and left before the first of the year. Taking DuVal's place as head of the official welcoming party was John Branch. The North Carolinian was certainly an appropriate choice. Branch had known Call since the early 1820s, when they served in Congress together. They both had warned Old Hickory of the perils of Peggy Eaton, and Branch had lost his cabinet post in the debacle. Soon thereafter, at Call's urging, the North Carolinian had settled in the Tallahassee area in 1832, bringing his wife, two daughters. and two sons, Joseph and O'Brien.[9] It is difficult to know whether DuVal's absence from the territory when Call returned was planned or just coincidental. Did he not want to share the limelight with Branch? Did the North Carolinian still harbor a grudge against DuVal for having been appointed governor of the territorial in 1822 instead of him? Whatever the case, there is no mention of Branch taking part in the earlier gathering DuVal had presided over.

Once he had provided for his family, William P. DuVal set out for Washington. Arriving in the capital city not long after the first of the year, DuVal invited his friend Senator Samuel Southard to a dinner at Brown's Hotel on January 7.[10] DuVal was in Washington as Jackson's remaining days in the White House wound down. One of the principal purposes of DuVal's visit to the capital was to lobby for legislation to fund transportation facilities linking St. Joseph Bay with the Apalachicola River and points north. In this work DuVal received support from an unexpected source—Joseph M. White. In January 1837 White was serving his few remaining days as Florida's territorial delegate. That month White wrote to his old enemy that he understood that DuVal felt "an interest in the improvements of that part of Florida, contiguous to St. Joseph's Bay." White assured DuVal that he would "present any memorial which you may choose to offer in their behalf; I will submit to any committee of Congress your views in a less formal manner, if you prefer to communicate them." White also explained that that he was willing "to propose and support an act of Congress, giving the right to the St. Joseph Company to make a rail road" to any point along the Apalachicola River.[11]

It is difficult to define DuVal's precise relationship to these transportation proposals, but it can be assumed that his role was substantial and might have brought him substantial legal fees. Whatever the result for DuVal, Congress authorized the creation of companies to create links between St. Joseph Bay and the Apalachicola and Chipola Rivers. One such company was the Lake Wimico and St. Joseph Canal and Railroad Company, founded by DuVal's law partner, Richard C. Allen. By March 1837 the company had surveyed its twenty-nine-mile route from St. Joseph to the Apalachicola river and had placed the construction of the road under contract. Company authorities estimated that the cost of the road exclusive of necessary buildings, stations, engines, cars, and tools would approach $450,000. Within a year, Allen would request gifts of federal land in alternating sections to support the enterprise, arguing that this road "forms the first link in the great line which is to extend from the Atlantic Ocean, across the peninsula of Florida, to the Gulf of Mexico." As justification for this largess Allen's petition stated that the "Bay of St. Joseph, from its position on the coast, the depth of water into it, the entire security of the harbor, and perfect salubrity of the climate, all combine to render it of the highest importance in a national point of view, and sooner or later must receive the attention entitled to it."[12]

At that time a rivalry between St. Joseph and Apalachicola, the town at the mouth of the river, was at fever pitch. At stake was the possibility of securing the lion's share of commerce on the Apalachicola and on the Chattahoochee River systems, providing Gulf access to some of the richest planting regions of Alabama and Georgia. By the 1830s vigorous steamboat traffic facilitated commerce with and regular travel to such upriver towns as Bainbridge, Irwinton (Eufala), and Columbus.[13]

Captain Samuel Heintzelman, for one, thought St. Joseph far superior to Apalachicola. Arriving in the latter town on December 27, 1836, on a steamboat with a load of supplies from Columbus, he found the wharves so covered with cotton that he could not unload his cargo. He explored Apalachicola and recorded in his diary that "it is not very extensive & very few good houses, all built in deep sand." The next day he unloaded more supplies in St. Joseph and found that town much more to his liking. "St. Joseph is a beautiful situation & some fine buildings. A locomotive carried us to the Depot, on the Bay, eight miles in less than an hour," yet he conceded "it was not the best in the world." At the depot were two "fine warehouses." From there Heintzelman "passed through the bayou, a beautiful piece of water, but narrow, a distance of eight miles to Lake Wimico," then traveled another four miles until he finally reached the Apalachicola River, and then went on to Columbus.[14]

DuVal also had other business in the nation's capital; he worked to secure federal appointments for his brother John as Florida's territorial secretary and also sought a position for his cousin Samuel DuVal as marshal for the Middle District of Florida. Indeed, John DuVal very much desired the appointment; as he explained to Congressman John Campbell, he had decided to relocate permanently to Florida as he had "made some speculation in sugar lands on the Gulphe." Recommendations on DuVal's behalf to president-elect Martin Van Buren came from a majority of the members of the legislative council and three of Florida's four territorial judicial district judges. The judges presented John P. DuVal as a "lawyer of very respectable talents, of most exemplary worth, and high standing." He had a "deep interest in the prosperity of this territory." William P. DuVal himself wrote Andrew Jackson Jr. on behalf of his brother, noting that George Walker was about to resign as secretary and wanted John P. DuVal to be appointed. Though Van Buren might appoint DuVal after his inauguration, DuVal noted three days before Van Buren's inauguration that "It would have been much more gratifying to my brother and myself to receive the nomination from Genl Jackson as we have ever been his sincere friends and admirers." DuVal added that he would come to the White House at 4 o'clock that day and "take a family dinner with you when you may have it in your power to inform me of the determination of the President. I feel much interest in my brother as you may naturally suppose—I have no other brother, and yet I feel the greatest diffidence and delicacy in urging his appointment *only because he is my near relative.*" Of his cousin Samuel DuVal, the former governor explained that the current marshal was dying and that for some time Samuel DuVal had been his "principal deputy," and was actually conducting his duties. Samuel DuVal also received recommendations from the same three district judges and James Westcott.[15] DuVal felt it his duty if not his privilege to offer the new president advice on Florida appointments, and he did so often.[16]

DuVal's cousin and his brother eventually received their appointments, but John DuVal's tenure as secretary of the Territory of Florida eventually caused his brother pain and strained his relationship with Governor Richard Keith Call. If anything, the circumstances of DuVal's appointment are among the most convoluted imaginable and point up the difficulties of travel and the uncertainties of the mail during the period. As he wrote to authorities in Washington, Call was convinced that John DuVal had solicited the office in bad faith, promising to stay in the territory until he was notified of his appointment. Instead, as Call explained, immediately after he had secured their recommendations, DuVal set out with his family on a trip to the North.[17] DuVal was in Philadelphia when he learned of his appointment on May 15. Writing to Secretary of State John Forsyth from that place on June 6, DuVal intoned, "I see by the *Globe* that I have been appointed Secy. of Florida, which I accept." DuVal explained that he had left Florida for Bardstown with his family before he learned of his appointment with the intention of wrapping up his affairs in Kentucky. He hoped to be allowed to stay in Kentucky until the fall so that he could "devote the summer to the compilation of the laws of Florida, and secondly that I may have an opportunity to arrange my private affairs previous to my return to Florida . . . having however accepted the appt. of Sec. of Florida, I feel it my duty to comply promptly with the wishes of the President, and shall wait at Bardstown Ky for instructions." John Forsyth ordered DuVal immediately back to Florida. DuVal complained of illness but was warned that if he did not return immediately he would forfeit his appointment. As of September 10 DuVal had still not arrived, "nor has any intelligence been received here of his having set out for Tallahassee," an exasperated Call complained. "I have not the least expectation of seeing him here before October. He possibly may have commenced his journey at the time mentioned, but he will complete it at his leisure." DuVal finally arrived in Tallahassee on October 15, whereupon he wrote to Forsyth: "I am gratified to find since my arrival here that the public service has suffered no detriment by my absence, and as I expected there are no duties of my office requiring my immediate attention. My health has been restored, and it will afford me pleasure to discharge any official duties which may be required."[18]

One can only imagine Call's reception of DuVal when the secretary arrived in the capital. The relationship degenerated even further as time went on. No sooner had DuVal arrived in Tallahassee than he began to complain that his annual salary of $1,500 was inadequate to support his family. Writing to territorial delegate Charles Downing, DuVal asserted that it cost $2,300 per year to board his family at a private boarding house, and at Brown's it would be double that sum. Admitting that his duties were light when the governor was in town, DuVal reminded the delegate that he would be "forced to play Govr whenever his Excellency may think proper to leave the territory." DuVal asserted that he should receive at least

John P. DuVal. From the author's collection.

as much money as would feed him and his family. "You know something about the *expenses* of *Tallahassee*," he reminded Downing.[19]

William P. DuVal was in Washington during Jackson's last days in the White House, and he would have likely been among the estimated twenty thousand spectators who attended Van Buren's inaugural ceremonies. March 4 was a bright, sunny day. The large crowd turned out as much to wish Andrew Jackson a fond farewell as to hear Van Buren's inaugural remarks. After Roger B. Taney swore in the new president, Van Buren gave his long inaugural address, which included most of the usual optimistic pronouncements of an incoming administration. Van Buren's hearers were most interested in the new president's references to slavery. Would the new president reference the Gag Rule that had just passed in the House of Representatives, the abolitionist movement, or the possibility of the annexation of Texas—all issues relevant to the "institution of domestic slavery"? Van Buren noted that "our forefathers were deeply impressed with the delicacy of this subject, and they treated it with a forbearance so evidently wise in spite of every sinister foreboding [that] it never until the present period disturbed the tranquility of our common country." Van Buren urged his fellow citizens to follow this well-trodden path laid down by the forefathers. Moreover, he proclaimed that he would oppose any attempt by Congress to ban slavery either in the District of Columbia or in the states where it already existed.[20]

Van Buren's inaugural address made no specific references to the economic situation confronting the nation. While its dire effects were slow to take effect in the Florida Territory, Van Buren's administration soon foundered on the economic rocks of the Panic of 1837. Brought on by the economic instability surrounding Jackson's killing of the Second Bank of the United States, the Panic of 1837 was the worst financial crisis in American history up to that time. With federal deposits removed from the Second Bank, federal revenues were deposited in state "pet" banks, which recklessly loaned money for dubious internal-improvement projects. Individuals also benefited from these practices. Credit was overextended, and the economic downturn was already evident before Jackson left office. Near the end of his term, the lame-duck president issued the Specie Circular, banning the acceptance of discounted bank notes for federal land purchases. Senator Thomas Hart Benton argued in his memoirs that Jackson's decisive order "saved the public lands from being converted into broken bank paper," but the damage to the economy had already been done. Among the financial institutions involved in the boom and bust associated with the financial crisis were those chartered by Florida's legislative council, especially Gamble's Union Bank of Florida, whose bank notes DuVal had signed in his final days in office.[21]

The nation's economic picture turned gloomy in the days following Van Buren's inauguration. It was clear by the time DuVal left Washington in the fall that the country was experiencing serious problems. The "pet banking" system was collapsing, and Van Buren called Congress into special session to address the crisis on September 4. In an address to that body, Van Buren called on Congress to enact legislation and included in his proposals plans for an "independent treasury," a measure dedicated to divorcing the government entirely from banks.[22]

In Florida the lending practices of the Union Bank of Florida should have caused concern, but, with cotton prices rising so fast, few worried at the time. That institution loaned planters money on the basis of questionable valuations of slaves and land. According to one historian, "loans to planters often involved fraudulent or unsubstantiated security." It often occurred that planters temporarily transferred slaves from one plantation to another, and "specie requirements were sometimes fulfilled when the stockholders borrowed the proper amount of specie to commence operations and satisfy the law, then returned it after the bank's opening." Further, in order for the banks to raise sufficient capital to support these demands, the legislative council, largely because of the political influence of banking advocates, issued "faith bonds" based on the full faith and credit of the territory. Gamble's bonds sold rapidly, both in the United States and abroad.²³

By 1837 in the Florida Territory there came to be a political coalescing of an antibank movement in Middle Florida. The leader of this political movement was James Westcott. From 1834 to 1836 Westcott had served as U.S. district attorney for Middle Florida, but in 1837 he was using his political skills to organize a party opposed to the interests of the Union Bank of Florida. Westcott's political organizing methods were similar to Van Buren's. Indeed, before coming to Florida in 1829, the thirty-five-year-old lawyer had studied and been associated with the Little Magician's party-building efforts in New Jersey. Westcott, it seemed, was intent on building and controlling an antibank Democratic organization in Florida that was loyal to Van Buren. In this work Westcott ran up against the planter-based Nucleus, most of whose members were the primarily supporters, stockholders, and beneficiaries of the Union Bank. Of course, the Nucleus had also been the primary recipient of Democratic patronage, and Westcott's new political movement threatened that monopoly. Arthur Thompson has noted that the Nucleus would eventually "become the hard core of the Florida Whigs and paradoxically the old 'Jackson men' would bitterly oppose the rise of the newer political and economic tendencies embodied in the 'Jacksonian Democrats.'" The radical, antibank, anticorporation Democrats would come to be known as "Loco-Focos" among their enemies. As the territory's economy worsened, Westcott's movement gained more adherents. The Union Bank proved an effective scapegoat.²⁴

DuVal must have perceived and anticipated this new political movement. He would have been wary of Westcott, even as he tried to stay on good terms with the new administration. Shortly after his return home to Tallahassee DuVal wrote to President Van Buren congratulating the president on his recent message, noting that it was the "most able document of the kind I ever read. It accords so entirely with my views and with the great principles by which our nation should be governed that for the first time in many years, I regret that I am not in Congress to give the administration my humble support. No president," DuVal assured Van Buren, "ever assumed his station surrounded by such formidable enemies and backed as they are against you. . . . I honestly believe that the people will sustain you, and that the extravagant and reckless opposition to your administration will react on your opponents with recuperative power. I have not seen any project of a single opposition member of either house of Congress that would relieve the embarrassing state of our commercial affairs. . . . The thinking men throughout the nation who love their country more than their parties will sustain you in the firm and correct and patriotic course you are pursuing." DuVal had seen no papers "opposed to your administration *since your message*. . . . I think that *cuckoo song* is forever ended."²⁵

In March 1838 the DuVals celebrated the wedding of another daughter when nineteen-year-old Mary married twenty-six-year-old Dr. James S. Robinson. Robinson and his widowed mother had migrated to Middle Florida from North Carolina with the Bradford and Branch families; he and his mother had resided with the Branch family since his father's death, in 1812. In 1832 Robinson entered Medical School at the University of Pennsylvania. Returning to Tallahassee to practice in 1834, Robinson took up residence with his mother. Robinson took an active part in community affairs. He served as clerk for the legislative council and was elected an officer in the Citizen Guards. After the wedding ceremony the bride's family hosted a grand party at their house. One guest reported to relatives in North Carolina that the festivities were "on the real old fashion—much dancing, plenty to eat, and plenty to Drink." The couple decided to settle in St. Joseph.[26]

Even as he kept abreast of political affairs, DuVal concentrated on his law cases. As noted in court records and newspapers, DuVal and Richard C. Allen handled many cases in the Middle Florida courts and the territorial court of appeals. DuVal and Allen rode circuit and practiced with and against other leading attorneys in Florida such as DuVal's brother John, Thomas Baltzell, and James Westcott. Thomas DuVal often joined his father in these cases.[27] Thomas Hagner, a young lawyer from Maryland and Judge Thomas Randall's nephew, wrote to his father that he had met DuVal and his son while on his way to Quincy. The young man noted that he saw much of DuVal in and out of court and on one occasion had dined with the DuVals at their residence in Tallahassee. At the conclusion of the meal DuVal had asked Hagner to join his practice, but, after considering the offer and discussing it with his uncle, the young man declined.[28]

DuVal understood at the time that his law partner, Richard C. Allen, was about to be appointed to federal office. In 1838 Congress created the Apalachicola Judicial District, which encompassed superior courts in Washington, Jackson, Calhoun, and Franklin Counties, and President Martin Van Buren appointed Allen as its new judge.[29] Casting about for a new law partner, DuVal decided on the twenty-six-year-old William H. Brockenbrough. From a well-to-do Richmond family and a man with obvious talent, Brockenbrough had migrated first to East Florida, where he practiced law with Charles Downing in St. Augustine. At the time he met DuVal, Brockenbrough was representing Mosquito County in the 1838 session of the legislative council. The advertisement announcing the new partnership noted that DuVal would reside in Tallahassee and Brockenbrough in Apalachicola. Both would attend the court of appeals and other courts in Middle Florida, as well as Jackson and Calhoun Counties on the west bank of the Apalachicola River. An adjoining column noted that Thomas DuVal would practice in the same office as his father in the first floor of the Union Bank building. Among DuVal and Brockenbrough's clients were the Union Bank of Florida and the Lake

Wimico and St. Joseph Canal and Railroad Company. DuVal's son-in-law William Price was an agent of the Union Bank in St. Joseph.[30]

The nature of DuVal's clients reflected his support for Florida's banks and railroad companies. Though he was never a major investor or stockholder in the Union Bank, his personal friendship with the bank's directors and the realities of making a living as an attorney meant that he was forced to alter his earlier view of banks. Perhaps he rationalized that banks at the territorial or state level were necessary institutions. Thus he could oppose a national bank and not a state bank under the belief that such institutions would be under the control of local interests. Moreover, DuVal's personal familiarity and association with Robert Gamble, John and Samuel Parkhill, Richard Keith Call, Thomas Brown, George T. Ward, and other bank supporters and functionaries made the decision to represent the bank an easy one.

Also at that time DuVal and Brockenbrough became involved in one of the area's most celebrated law cases. It concerned the estate of a wealthy planter, Hardy Croom, who was lost at sea when the steamboat *Home*, traveling off Cape Hatteras, went down. DuVal, Brockenbrough, and DuVal's old nemesis Joseph White filed a bill of complaint in behalf of Croom's North Carolina heirs in the Leon County courthouse on January 24, 1839. Thomas Baltzell and James D. Westcott represented Bryan Croom and the Tallahassee heirs. The case went on for years and was eventually resolved in the Florida Supreme Court in 1857.[31]

Even as he continued his law practice, DuVal found time to enjoy his family's and friends' company—and increasingly these pleasant get-togethers took place in the emerging coastal village of St. Joseph. In the summer of 1838 the intimate circle of the DuVals and the Prices at the seaside community on the Gulf included the Gambles, the Parkhills, the Randolphs, and the Goldsboroughs. While his family remained there most of the summer, DuVal visited in June and August. Mary Gamble wrote to her cousin Catherine Wirt of the many lazy, enjoyable days with the DuVals and the Prices. Mary Gamble thought of the DuVals as "more like relatives than mere friends often are." Though she boarded at the Mansion House, she was with them so often that friends often asked her whether she paid board at the hotel or at the DuVals' home. As she explained, she spent the "greatest portion of my time there. As soon as I eat my simple breakfast of Bakers bread, crumpled into a glass of milk & I pack up my work basket & protected against the rays of the sun which even at that early hour are powerful, put [on] a large sun bonnet, mask, & parasol, I go to Dr. Prices & never return until the 9 O'clock bell rings. At 11 O'clock we all go to the bathing house and luxuriate for 15 minutes in the most delicious bath I ever enjoyed." The facility had a "great many conveniences—A very long wharf . . . and a space 45 feet square is enclosed for a bathing room. Over this is built three or four rooms for dressing in and one is fitted up for the purpose of keeping refreshments of various kinds.

Around the whole is a pleasant balcony which affords an agreeable resort about sunset." On August 30, Mary Gamble noted that Governor DuVal had been with them for several days but was on the "eve of his departure" for Tallahassee.[32]

Events continued to move forward in positive fashion for St. Joseph. The 1838 session of the legislative council created Calhoun County, and the town on the Gulf became its new county seat. Moreover, settlers in St. Joseph were not content to wait for rails to provide access to the interior. The previous year a road linking the town with Marianna and other settlements in the planting districts of the upper panhandle was already under construction. According to one account, "The entire route is not yet marked but we presume the road will pass St. Andrews Bay . . . thence by the settlements on the Econfina to Marianna."[33]

St. Joseph boosters also scored a success when the legislative council voted to have St. Joseph host the state constitutional convention and set December 1, 1838, as the date of its first meeting. By April, campaigns for delegates were under way. William P. DuVal and Richard C. Allen were elected to represent Calhoun County. DuVal also was successful in his bid to represent the Middle District in the Florida Senate.[34] Taking note of DuVal's candidacy for the Florida Senate and his volatile temper was Benjamin Wright of the Pensacola *Gazette*. "There is scarcely an individual familiar with the early history of Florida who was not rejoiced at the return to the Territory of the distinguished individual whose name heads this paragraph." DuVal was a little more "'thin skinned,' than he was at twenty. . . . As Governor of Florida, no man could move him to anger. His hospitable doors were thrown open to all alike, and not a few of those who fed upon his bounty, went away and abused him; but he regarded not their abuse and without, perhaps, having the Christian's reason for it, he returned good for evil, and when they came again, he entertained them as he had done before. In this way he conquered all his enemies except those who were the enemies also of all merit and virtue." DuVal was now, Wright continued, "a candidate for office, and we regret to see that he is harshly treated by one of the presses in his county, and hardly sustained, if sustained at all, by the other—We do not undertake to decide the merits of the controversy into which he has been precipitated, but we do undertake to say (and in this we mean no particular disrespect to others) that he is worth cords of such people as are trying to pull him down. We have spoken of his infirmities. They all lean to virtue's side, and if we are not mistaken, the people of Middle Florida will so decide by their votes." Finally, Wright concluded, it was only right that a man who had "sacrificed the best part of his life for the Territory" be entitled to seek now "some humble station at the hands of the people of this District."[35]

John DuVal also sought to represent Leon County at the convention (the fact of his serving as territorial secretary notwithstanding) but failed.[36] Not surprisingly, given its rough start, John DuVal's service as Florida's territorial secretary remained controversial. His disagreements and angry confrontations with Governor Call were a continual subject of conversation in Tallahassee. The breach between the two officials was even a subject of editorial comment. In August and September "Enquirer" and "W" traded insults with DuVal in the columns of the *Floridian*. The conflict began when "Enquirer" complained that the secretary was too often absent from Tallahassee and that since he had been in the territory he had sought to create discord and excite opposition against the governor to "gratify a pitiful personal malevolence." DuVal responded by denouncing "Enquirer," after which another correspondent, "W," weighed in against DuVal, charging that he should never have been appointed, given the fact he had been appointed brigadier general of the Army of the Republic of Texas. DuVal's title, "W" asserted, came not from any real service in the field but only from his recruitment of Kentucky volunteers for a war against Mexico, "a power then at peace with the United States. This is considered by the laws of the United States as a high misdemeanor" and subjects the person to severe penalties. "If true Gen. D. ought not to have been appointed to his present responsible situation—and we presume that the President and Senate were ignorant of the fact." Supposedly also, according "W," DuVal "it is said is subject to the orders of the President of the Texas, and is bound to assume command of his brigade whenever required." Since when, the man asked, "should [we] select *distinguished* officers of foreign armies to fill our civil appointments?"[37]

While Governor Call was away in Washington and these recriminations played themselves out on the streets and in the newspapers, Florida prepared to hold its state constitutional convention. In May 1837 voters voiced their preferences for or against statehood, and the results reflected substantial regional divisions in the territory. The total vote was 2,214 for "State" and 1,274 for "No State." Of the four districts, Middle Florida overwhelmingly supported statehood, while voters in West Florida also supported the measure. In East Florida voters opposed statehood by more than a two-to-one margin.[38] East Florida's opposition to statehood was based primarily on its suffering condition during the Second Seminole War, the cost of state government, and the likelihood that the section would be dominated by more populous and financially powerful Middle Florida. Many in East Florida also called for separation from West and Middle Florida. "Division" was the natural outcome of the antistatehood sentiment in East Florida.[39] This issue proved intractable and was emblematic of the sectional divisions within the territory. Throughout the year citizens in East Florida held public meetings and petitioned Congress in opposition to statehood, calling for division of the territory.[40] The St. Augustine *Florida Herald* took up the cause with enthusiasm.[41] No doubt DuVal read and perhaps was even sympathetic to these sentiments in East Florida. While mulling these issues as he prepared to serve, DuVal joined the other elected delegates who began arriving in St. Joseph by late November.

The St. Joseph convention met without interruption (except for Sundays) from December 3 until January 11, 1839. Before the work began in earnest, DuVal took advantage of the opportunity to visit friends in the area. Nancy, their daughter Laura, and her friend Elizabeth Brown accompanied him on his rounds. Among those the DuVal family visited was Louis Goldsborough. William Wirt's son-in-law was angling to succeed Richard C. Allen as president of the St. Joseph and Lake Wimlico Company, and he was attending a stockholders' meeting in the town. On December 13 Goldsborough offered his observations on the convention and its participants to his wife in Baltimore, writing that St. Joseph presented a "dreary aspect and judging from all I see, I think its business has declined since I last visited it. . . . My heart quails at the idea of living here. . . . The convention here," he continued, "I regret to say is, in the majority for Agrarianism, Loco-Focoism, Fanny Wrightism, &c, &c. A desperate effort is making to tear the Union Bank to pieces, with [James] Westcott at the Head of the party—poor dirty, insignificant creature! . . . All the truly respectable men are Conservatives, yet strange to say the Blackguards in the majority; and as to their ultimate measures, no man can devine. . . . A weaker set of men I have never known assembled before to carry out so solemn a purpose as that of framing a Constitution."[42]

According to Goldsborough, of all the men at the convention DuVal clearly occupied first place. "The Convention gets on very slowly and very badly" on account of the poor abilities of its members. "There is in reality not a solitary man of more than any ability in the whole Convention. Gov. DuVal, to my mind is decidedly, the first man among them, and indeed, he is generally thought to be so by everyone else. He has made already, two or three very handsome speeches, containing sound and solid arguments, such as have been felt by all present and such too, as have provided the greatest effect." Goldsborough wrote to his wife that the day before he had spent a pleasant day with young Elizabeth Brown and Laura DuVal, eventually accompanying them to the railroad depot and then to the steamboat that was to convey them to Chattahoochee and back to Tallahassee. "Mrs. DuVal," he wrote proudly, "entrusted them to my charge."[43]

As Goldsborough indicated, the most controversial issue at the convention was territorial banking. By the time the delegates met, John Gamble's bank as well as other Florida banking institutions were under attack, and the Convention became a battleground for the banks' supporters and opponents. But the first order of business was to select a president, and DuVal's name was immediately put into nomination by Sam Parkhill of Leon County, whose brother John just happened to be cashier of the Union Bank. Others quickly moved to endorse Parkhill's nomination of the former governor. As the correspondent to the *Floridian* reported, Parkhill "alluded to the past service of the nominated in various official stations in Florida. As Judge, as Governor for upwards of twelve years, and as a citizen, his course has been such as to commend him the grateful feelings of every Floridian. He was one of the earliest emigrated to Florida, and had encountered as many privations as any other citizen." Thomas Brown of Leon County added his endorsement. "The oldest and the youngest citizen of Florida, when they heard his name, called to mind his eminent services and moral worth." It was only proper, Brown added, that this position of honor "should be conferred upon one of the oldest residents and public servants of Florida; who had done his duty faithfully, who was well known to the people, and in whom they had the fullest confidence. The station was a sort of Past Master's degree given for long, well tried, and honest service." Alfred Woodward of Jackson County agreed. "The wreath of honor now proposed to be placed around his [DuVal's] brow by the assembled delegates of the people had been well-earned. He was well known to be an ardent advocate of organizing our Territory into a sovereign and independent State at the earliest period."[44]

Parkhill "trusted that [DuVal] would be elected without opposition," but it was not to be. Leon County's Gen. Leigh Read, son-in-law of John Branch, and a rising star in the anti-bank faction of the Democratic Party, nominated Judge Robert Reid. In a flamboyant speech Westcott supported Reid, asserting that no man "had a claim or pre-emption right, for any services, however eminent, to any station." A spirited debate followed. As an anti-bank Democrat, confidant of Van Buren's Secretary of State, John Forsyth, the St. Augustine resident seemed the perfect candidate for Middle Florida anti-bank statehood advocates. Dorothy Dodd has speculated that Reid's candidacy as President emerged out of a deal struck between anti-bank delegates from Middle Florida and the East Florida delegation, who they feared might break up the convention unless Reid was named the leader. At any rate, the whole Eastern delegation, combined with delegates from Madison and Hamilton counties; John M. Partridge and Abram Bellamy of Jefferson county; James Westcott, Leigh Read, and Leslie Thompson, of Leon; Cosam Emir Bartlett of Franklin, and William Marvin of Monroe voted for Reid. The final tally was 27 for Reid and 26 for DuVal.[45]

Westcott's speech favoring Reid for the leadership was political; it also betrayed personal animus against DuVal. The former governor most certainly was piqued when James S. Robinson, DuVal's son-in-law, was nominated as secretary of the convention, only to have Westcott nominate another man, who was subsequently elected. According to one observer, "considerable feeling appeared to exist between some of the delegates from your county (Leon), who divided in vote for President between Governor DuVal and Judge Reid, but nothing unpleasant occurred. I think the complexion of the Convention is what is called Loco Foco. The Bank question is the all engrossing topic of conversation now." James Westcott, the commentator wrote, chaired the banking committee. The main question was whether the "State will assume the Territorial faith pledged for the Union and Pensacola Banks."[46]

Samuel Parkhill and his brother John were born in Ireland and came to Tallahassee via Richmond, Virginia, in 1828. Both became successful in planting and banking. Courtesy of State Archives of Florida.

Fundamental disagreement over whether the territory was ready to come into the Union almost derailed the convention before it even got started. Some delegates used the imperfect census returns as a way to question the convention's legitimacy. Others proposed a resolution calling for a vote to test whether there was a majority favoring state government. Jackson County's Samuel Bellamy asserted that "it was too late to debate the duties of this Convention, and the policy and right of our admission into the Union." The task of the delegates, he insisted, was simply to create a state constitution, nothing else.⁴⁷

At that point DuVal joined the debate. He asserted that he had come to the "Convention with straight forward purposes; he came here to do his humble part in aiding Florida to take that stand in the Confederacy to which she is of right entitled." The population question was irrelevant to the task at hand. It was time, he said, to present "our claim for admission in the halls of Congress." DuVal challenged those who agreed with him to raise their hands. "It is time for the advocates of a State Government to know who are the friends of Florida," he stated. DuVal admitted that his call for the resolution was a test and did not hesitate to avow it.⁴⁸

Richard Long of Jackson County suggested that for East Florida delegates not to favor state government was tantamount to perjury. But DuVal dissented vehemently from this insinuation. Intending to "cast no imputations upon gentlemen who differed from him, least of all did he insinuate perjury against any honorable member of that body. What sir, are we to be told, that because the people had elected Delegates to the Convention, that therefore the persons so elected were bound to vote for and advocate a State form of government or be taunted with the charge of perjury? I say no such thing and repel the insinuation as groundless and illiberal. Gentlemen here are sent to speak for the parts, as well as the whole of this Territory, and if the constituents of any member on this floor believe it impolitic and ruinous for Florida at this time to seek admission into the Union, he for one, would never censure that member for faithfully representing their wishes. It is a new and strange doctrine sir that every man here is bound to advocate a State Government because he has sworn to do his duty as a member of this Convention."⁴⁹

DuVal reminded other delegates that each delegate could eventually vote for or against the finished version of the document as his conscience directed. "Mr. Chairman, on a subject of so much importance as the organization of a new state, a diversity of opinion as to the mode, time and policy of the measure must be expected. If the gentlemen from the East—representing their constituents are not ready for the application; If the East borne to the dust by long continued calamity, and suffering under the privations of a barbarous war are not prepared for the change—are we, honorable Delegates to be taxed with perjury because they may utter the language of their constituents? When was the free voice of the

American people ever restrained by a construction so arbitrary. Sir, upon this subject all opinion must be heard—all views fairly considered. If Middle and West Florida are in favor of the measure and East Florida from her particular condition opposed to it—let her be heard. I for one am not disposed to trample upon the rights to stifle her voice, and say to her Delegates you must go in for a State right or wrong, because you have sworn to do your duty as member of this Convention—That duty may require them to oppose it." DuVal then asserted that all that the resolution was intended to do was to determine whether a majority of the convention was in favor of state government and, if there was in fact a majority in favor of statehood, "let us say so and go on to form a Constitution for the new State." "If there is a majority opposed to the measure, let us know it—or it is unnecessary to consume the time and money of the people if no good is to result from our deliberations." DuVal's call for a vote on resolutions failed, and the matter was dropped. At that point the delegates began the work of writing a state constitution.[50]

On Monday, December 10, President Reid startled the convention by proclaiming that the one-vote majority he had secured was tainted by the fact that the delegate from Hillsborough County who had voted for him by proxy had not actually been elected to the convention. He immediately tendered his resignation. "The chair, gentlemen, is vacant," he announced. After it was declared that a new election would be necessary, DuVal promptly nominated Reid and Reid was elected unanimously.[51]

The opponents of banking scored a victory when Reid appointed James Westcott chair of the banking committee. Reid appointed DuVal chair of the committee on the executive department. Sparks between Westcott and DuVal flew after DuVal submitted his committee's report, calling for candidates for the governor to reside in Florida at least five years before becoming eligible for election as Florida executive. Westcott moved to amend the third section of the report to require three years' residency instead of five, noting that when the chairman was first appointed governor he had no residence in the territory. "And yet, sir, I must do him the justice to say, he was thought to be at least well acquainted with the interests of this Territory, and fully competent to foster and protect the same."[52]

Westcott's remarks brought a swift rejoinder from DuVal. It was clear DuVal interpreted Westcott's remarks as both a personal attack and an attempt to take over the work of the convention. The tension in the gallery was palpable. DuVal said that whether the "member from Leon intended his remarks for wit or as a compliment to him he would leave to the opinion of the house. If intended as a compliment, he must decline its acceptance." DuVal explained that it had taken more than three if not six years' residence in the territory before he was able to acquire even a "general knowledge of the wants of the scattered population of the country. Its resources for years were but little known, and yet he had done as

Canals, Banks, and a Constitutional Convention || 259

Robert Raymond Reid, a native of Georgia, served as judge of the Eastern Judicial District of Florida from 1832 to 1840. In 1838 he bested DuVal for chair of Florida's constitutional convention. In 1840 Martin Van Buren appointed him territorial governor. Courtesy of State Archives of Florida.

much in exploring the country and hunting out its settlements and resources, and providing for its citizens, as most officers in his situation." DuVal asserted that he was willing to "risque losing all the talent that the member from Leon supposes will certainly emigrate to this land if you only change this feature of your constitution, and make three instead of five years the term of residence. For one, I do not court such selfish and ambitious aspirants, if the only desire to remove to Florida rests on the hope of speedily becoming its Governor." At that point, DuVal addressed Westcott: "The member from Leon is too conscious of his own high powers of mind—confident, from experience, of his complete ability to play the part of Governor with wisdom, integrity, and unusual dignity, he estimates others by his own uncommon qualities and powers." By this point DuVal's contempt Westcott was palpable. All would admit, DuVal sneered, that the member "deserves thanks for his universal action and unlimited efforts to conduct the entire business of this body, and give to the country a constitution worthy of its acceptance—a constitution containing a clear and bright epitome of the high principles, purity and wisdom of the distinguished legislator from Leon. No member of this house admires more than myself, a genius so rare—a wisdom as profound, and a devotion and love of country, so sincere as is constantly manifested by that generous and candid member. He has so far, conducted the business of this house; follow him with submission and reverence and wonder, on most subjects, and if, on so small a matter as this, he should find himself in a minority he will have ample reward in ultimately reviving the despairing hopes of the friends of the State Government, and securing to his admiring countrymen, by the efforts of his uncommon mind, a constitution which will insure their lasting happiness and independence. Such generosity," DuVal continued, "not to say model deportment of the distinguished member from Leon call for our thanks and gratitude. Where, let me ask, was ever such a indefatigable activity, such willing sacrifice, of watching and labor enticed on this part of a single individual, to relieve his fellow laborers for the trouble of thinking and acting for themselves. . . . We should congratulate the people of Florida that among the happy selections they have made on this great and interesting occasion, they have served in their service at least one, whose mind is so clear, virtuous, and comprehensive, as to grasp at once the machinery of government, even to its smallest details; a mind so adorned, so improved by learning experience, so imbued with refined and delicate modesty, yet so beautifully balanced by principles of such rare moral and political excellence, that make him to know what the pillar of fire was to the Israelites of old, a burning light to lead thorough the night of ignorance, to the temple of virtue, wisdom, and liberty."[53]

The battle between DuVal and Westcott was only beginning. On December 21 Duval and Westcott sparred on banking resolutions.[54] At issue was whether the charters of the Union Bank and the other financial institutions in operation at the time (and their financial obligations) would be carried forward or could be repudiated by the future state. As Dorothy Dodd explains, DuVal and banking advocates insisted that there was no "question either of the validity of charters and bonds or of the essential soundness of the financial theory on which they rested. Anti-bank men, such as Westcott, [Leslie] Thompson, [William] Marvin, [David] Levy, and Abram Bellamy, contended either that charters were illegal in the first place or that, even if the bonds were valid, a primary convention of the people had the right to repudiate them."[55]

DuVal vehemently opposed such a course, arguing that the honor of the territory and its future was at stake. The issue was not one of mere "local interests . . . but general principles . . . of preserving the inviolability of contracts" as opposed to "breaking the solemn pledge of the state and its people." Canals, railroads, and banks operated under the clear mandate of the legislature under terms fully agreed to by both parties. "If, after money was loaned and improvements made, the Legislature could step in, under pleas of supremacy of the law, and destroy all the privileges it had granted there would be an end of all public improvements. It would be a death-blow to corporations. Nobody would put faith in, or lend money, upon such a hazardous condition. The House should deliberate coolly, and weigh well the consequences of its decision. If the influence of corporations was shown to be injurious, limit their power and definitely fix their privileges." DuVal asserted that he had done much in his career to "advance the internal improvement of the country," and he "could vote for nothing that would imply an intention of bad faith, or infringe upon the character of the State. For the good of the State he would give corporations power to improve the country and protect both their privileges and the privileges of the people under the shield of the Constitution."[56]

DuVal said he "would have it the law of the land that the obligation of contracts could not be impaired by the proposed clogs; it might be understood that the Legislature might impair these obligations.... We know not when or for what occasion the faith of the State might be required, but it might be when they had neither money nor credit to enable them to defend their wives and children or their hearths. They might in making application for assistance, be looked upon as a money making race, ever ready to break engagements honorably entered into—as a people, without honor, and more than Carthagenian perfidy."[57]

Duval offered the example of the War of 1812 when the United States' credit helped stave off defeat. "She triumphed, and triumphed nobly but could she have raised the means, had her credit been a matter of speculation or if perfidy had been anticipated? When we want credit or means, what would be our character with such a condition in our constitution as that proposed by the member of Leon? In event of a foreign war, Florida would be the theatre of naval operations, and the scene of a deadly and terrible conflict, with a servile population, more formidable in our midst, than a legitimate contest with a most powerful nation." If such circumstances were to occur and Florida were to need credit, "what could we effect with a blighted name, with a time serving and tarnished reputation? The example of the U.S. was worthy of consideration. To insist upon clogs and qualifications would destroy all chance of our becoming a State. Let the House, therefore, leave local details for the present, and meet the question of the inviolability of contracts, face to face."[58]

In the end the antibank advocates prevailed. Article XIII of the Florida Constitution, "Banks and other Corporations," contained numerous provisions restricting banking. Bank officers were prohibited from holding state office. Banks could not deal in real estate and manufacturing and were subject to regular legislative investigations. Stockholders of banks, in case of forfeiture of a bank's charter, were individually liable for payment of all debts in proportion to the stock they owned. Most important, the state was prohibited from pledging its faith for any bank liability. If the antibanking forces had not succeeded in voiding the territory's obligations to the current institutions, the door seemed open on that score.[59]

Westcott, Reid, and another up-and-coming politician from East Florida, David Levy, emerged from the convention in a strong position. Westcott's strident stands against banking and his imperious statements had earned him the warm enmity and contempt of his political opponents. Louis Goldsborough proclaimed him the "veriest Loco Foco I ever knew." Westcott "holds himself to be a Magnus Apollo of the whole and therefore speaks and does more than all the rest together. What a terrible state of society where such a creature—where denounced on all hands as unworthy of trust—should be permitted to occupy such a position. He is, however, vividly more knave than fool, and it is to this fact alone that I ascribe his ascendancy over the rest."[60]

While DuVal and the banking interests were not entirely defeated, clearly the political tide and the economy were going against them. But the battle would be joined in another forum. Even before the St. Joseph convention closed officially, Florida's legislative council convened, on January 8, and DuVal was in Tallahassee for the opening session. (Having left St. Joseph, DuVal voted in favor of the final version of the constitution by proxy but was not present to affix his name to the document.) When the Florida Senate met, the first order of business was to select a president and a secretary. As a correspondent to the Pensacola *Gazette* reported, the body selected DuVal to serve as president and his son-in-law James S. Robinson to serve as secretary. But DuVal declined the honor. Whether DuVal thought he could better push the policies he believed in as a member and not as leader is unclear. But what was clear to everyone was that the question of banking would dominate the deliberations of the Florida Senate as it had at the constitutional convention. "Great excitement prevails here in regard to the Union Bank," the correspondent noted. "It has warm friends as you may suppose, but it has many bitter enemies too. It has worked much seeming good, but the proverb that 'all is not gold that glitters' is especially applicable to the state of apparent prosperity which reigns around me."[61]

CHAPTER 16

Faith Bonds, Division, Depression, and a Plague

By the time of the opening session of the legislative council in early January 1839, Florida's political landscape had changed. Energized by their successes in the St. Joseph statehood convention, the antibank Democrats swept into the 1839 Florida legislative council with great momentum. They had prevailed in the recent elections and were determined to rein in the banks. With the antibank forces on the attack and the probank forces on the defensive, DuVal and his friends were under the gun. With Middle Florida's economic situation continuing to deteriorate, the antibank Democratic Party was able to blame the crisis on a corrupt banking system and the well-connected political operators who had aided and abetted it.

Other uncertainties regarding statehood confronted the legislators. When and under what conditions would Florida submit its constitution to Congress? Settlers debated the issue at courthouses, taverns, and country stores, while plans to hold a referendum were being considered. And when would the referendum take place? Even more divisive was the question of whether the territory would be divided. Some proponents advocated dividing the territory at the Suwannee River, making Middle and West Florida a state, thus allowing East Florida to become a state on its own at some later date. West Florida's future was also in doubt because in that region there was only tepid support for statehood. Some advocated dividing the territory at the Apalachicola River and annexing Florida's western portion to Alabama. Thus, even though the St. Joseph convention had produced a state constitution, there was still much uncertainty as to what mode or manner a new state would take. Timing was also uncertain. Sectional tensions at the national level augured against admission anytime soon. And for the next six years "division" continued as a popular proposal for East

Floridians, but Middle Florida statehood advocates did all in their power to beat the measure back. And they were not above using any and all methods to discredit their opponents.

DuVal found himself in an awkward position. A probank Whig senator representing Middle Florida, DuVal supported division. Indeed, in the opening days of the legislative session, while he did not sign a petition to Congress circulated by ten East Florida delegates of the legislative council calling for division, DuVal introduced a similar resolution in the Florida Senate calling for dividing the territory. (The measure did not come to a vote.)[1] DuVal's motives for introducing the measure in favor of the East Florida delegates can only be speculated upon. Was he in communication with friends in Washington who supported the proposal? Perhaps he was plotting some measure or enterprise that required support from the East. For the moment at least, conflicts over banking policy overshadowed statehood or division.

At the national level, the economy had enjoyed a temporary boost in 1838 when federal surpluses were distributed to the states. Late that year banks resumed specie payments. But this miniboom soon came to an abrupt end in 1839 when bumper crops of cotton sent prices through the floor. Those states that had borrowed to build roads, canals, railroads, and other internal improvements could not meet their obligations, and the resulting defaults furthered the downward spiral. Default followed default. Investors, especially foreign ones, were driven away. Trade that required credit nearly came to a standstill.[2]

The economic downturn was particularly devastating for Florida's economy because of the newly created and unstable banking system, the challenges of the Indian War, and the already perilous territorial economy. The degenerating situation proved a disaster for planters and for lawyers dependent on legal fees. Also, those associated with the establishment and support of banking paid the price at the polls. While a detailed examination of DuVal's personal finances and business is impossible, it is clear that DuVal had cast his lot with Florida's banking interests. He would come to represent the Union Bank in court, and more and more he would be linked economically and socially to men like John Gamble, John and Samuel Parkhill, George T. Ward, and Thomas Brown.

DuVal's new position would subject him to criticism. For example, "A Voter of Gadsden" questioned why DuVal and others had opposed banking previously and then supported the banking institutions at the St. Joseph convention. Voters with long memories, especially those opposed to banks, increasingly charged DuVal with inconsistency.[3] By 1839 DuVal was clearly aligned with former Jacksonians like Call, who favored maintaining the banks and protecting the territory's obligations under their original charters. Formerly known as the Nucleus (the Jackson-sponsored political force that had once controlled the land office and many of the most lucrative federal political appointments), the political group

Martin Van Buren, ca. 1840. Library of Congress.

morphed into a nascent Whig party in Florida. On the other side were the antibank Democrats, sometimes referred to as Loco-Focos by their opponents. Also influencing these shifting coalitions was the growing disenchantment with the Van Buren administration among former Jacksonians who transferred their loyalty to the national Whig Party in 1840. Probank Whigs also counted territorial delegate Charles Downing as an ally. While DuVal was careful not to openly desert Van Buren's standard, he was clearly moving in the other direction. On the other hand, Governor Call was less oblique.[4]

The political fallout against the probanking factions was severe. In the campaign for seats on the legislative council, candidates representing James Westcott's newly organized Democratic Party called for repudiation of "faith bonds." Intertwined inextricably with banking policy was the question of statehood. Not only were the timing of Florida's possible statehood and the circumstances under which it might take place at issue; even more perplexing was the question of whether the territory should be divided. East Floridians advocated division of the territory, with Middle Florida becoming a state and East Florida being constituted as a separate territory. They argued that the sections had developed differently. Middle Florida had developed more rapidly and had outstripped the East and the West in population, and it therefore had greater influence in the legislative council. Middle Florida's thriving cotton economy had brought to Middle Florida such power in the territorial government that East and West Florida understood that the section would dominate political affairs in the new state, as it had done in the territorial period. In addition, the Indian War had wiped out East Florida plantations, devastated the section's economy, and curtailed emigration. As a result, the section relied heavily on federal largess, which many predicted would cease once Florida became a state. A state government, opponents argued, would result in an overwhelming tax burden for modest farmers and cattle herders. East Florida's deep-seated distrust of its more powerful neighbor went back at least as far as DuVal's second term as governor.

As a general rule Middle Floridians favored statehood and banks while East Floridians opposed both. But of course there were many exceptions to these general rules, the most obvious of which was that Florida's two leading advocates of statehood were David Levy and Robert Raymond Reid, both of East Florida. While both supported statehood, so did DuVal's enemy James Westcott, of Middle Florida, who also led the charge against the banks as leader of the Middle Florida Democrats. In yet another inconsistency, Charles Downing of East Florida, the territorial delegate, opposed division, even as he dutifully submitted a petition gotten up in East Florida in favor of division. Downing saw the measure as an abolitionist scheme to add another free state to the Union.[5] In the upcoming months, harsh words and recriminations on the floor of the legislative council and in the newspapers led to violence in the streets and bloodshed on the field of honor.

Near the end of the legislative session, DuVal took a brief respite from his labors in the Florida Senate along with some friends. At a public dinner in Tallahassee to honor Downing on his recent return from Washington, DuVal joined his son John Crittenden and his friends Governor Call, Judge Richard C. Allen, Thomas Brown, Green Chaires, and Samuel Sibley. Among the many toasts was the final one to DuVal: "[T]he long tried and enthusiastic friend of Florida . . . In song or in sentiment or politics, he is our Apollo—Territory or State will be sure to award him his deserts. To the above," an observer reported, "Governor DuVal made a suitable reply."[6]

Also enjoying the social scene of Tallahassee that spring was Captain Samuel Heintzelman and his fellow officers. The previous months they had taken a survey of the various military posts between Tallahassee and the Suwannee, but by January 27 he was back in Tallahassee. That evening he spent a delightful evening with Elizabeth Brown and Laura DuVal at the homes of both the DuVals and the Browns. The next night he attended a party at the Browns' home and danced until after midnight. Heintzelman also attended parties in the country. On February 15 he and about a dozen "uniformed officers" attended a costume party at Judge Randall's Belmont plantation. The place was so crowded that, as he recorded in his diary, "I could not find a seat. Dr. Robinson and I sat at the counter table in the drawing room & took our dinner." Soon guitar playing and dancing commenced and did not end until 3:00 A.M. March 31 found Heintzelman at DuVal's house, where Charles Downing, the territorial delegate, and Mrs. Downing and others were being entertained. He stayed until after midnight listening to Downing talk about Washington and the "old claims of the public officers. He exaggerates some," Heintzelman noted, "but I have no doubt, but we will settle our accounts with much less difficulty than I had first apprehended." Several days later, he and a small party "serenaded old Gov. DuVal." Heintzelman and his fellow officers continued to party and to visit with Laura DuVal, Elizabeth Brown, and other ladies throughout that spring and summer. The captain and a few of his associates rented U.S. Marshal Samuel DuVal's house for the summer while he and his family were away in Virginia.[7] Also that summer Arthur Randolph returned to Tallahassee, having recently graduated with his medical degree. He and Laura DuVal increasingly found themselves alone together, separated from the other partygoers. "That will be a match," Heintzelman predicted.[8]

One can only imagine the strain such constant entertaining and partying must have put on Nancy DuVal and her husband. Ellen Wirt Vass, a friend from Jefferson County, certainly sensed the burden when she visited the DuVals after a day of shopping in town. When she arrived, she found Lizzie Brown hard at work on embroidering and other visitors lounging about. She promised her mother that she was "going to make herself *scarcer* at that house, for I see plainly enough that they are very tired of entertaining company."[9]

The major topic of conversation at gatherings all over Middle Florida was the Van Buren administration's handling of the Second Seminole War. One issue that united Floridians of every political stripe was the determination to remove the Seminoles. Thus all Floridians denounced General Alexander Macomb's late treaty with the Seminole Indians, which seemingly allowed them to remain in the territory. At a public meeting at the Leon County Court House, DuVal joined Thomas Brown and others in interpreting the pact as a dangerous capitulation. DuVal offered resolutions denouncing "all elements" of the treaty. On the motion of DuVal's old enemy William Wyatt, the word "unanimous" was inserted to the resolutions. In an "animated and eloquent speech" DuVal conjured up apocalyptic visions in which Seminoles and emancipated slaves from the West Indies joined forces with a foreign power (Britain or Spain), bringing "utter ruin" to Florida and adjoining states. For DuVal and those of his generation who had lived through the bloody scenes of the War of 1812, Native Americans who lived at the extremities of the nation's borders were always the potential allies of America's greatest foe, Great Britain. DuVal joined most Southerners in thinking that Britain's decision in favor of abolition and its perceived hostility to American slavery posed the most dangerous threat to American expansion and even its existence as a nation. "The danger," DuVal warned, "will become greater than we now undertake to anticipate."[10]

DuVal and Nancy spent a considerable part of the summer on the coast, visiting St. Marks, the new village of Port Leon, Apalachicola, and St. Joseph, where their daughter Marcia lived with her husband, Dr. William Price. Another DuVal daughter, Mary, and her husband, Dr. James Robinson, also lived in St. Joseph. DuVal and Nancy, the Robinsons, the Prices, and other family members enjoyed their respite from the heat (both thermal and political) in Tallahassee. On an excursion to Port Leon on the Fourth of July Captain Heintzelman found DuVal out fishing when he arrived. "He soon came in with a number of fish & and a sawfish about 12 feet long. It is the first I have seen & to me a great curiosity. We sat down to a very abundant dinner at 2 P.M. with a very motley crowd. There were a number of gentlemen from Tallahassee. . . . We had a number of toasts, more songs & several speeches. That of the Govs in reply to a toast in the honor of Andrew Jackson was very good."[11] Later in the month Heintzelman visited Apalachicola and St. Joseph, where he enjoyed fishing, boating, and excursions to Dog Island with the DuVals, Robinsons, and Prices.[12]

But all was not rest and relaxation for DuVal that summer. While DuVal divided his time between St. Joseph and Apalachicola, local merchants complained to him of their dissatisfaction with the Union Bank. The rapidly degenerating economic picture that summer induced bank officials to slow their exchanges to merchants south of Tallahassee. DuVal wrote from St. Joseph, explaining the situation to John Parkhill. "The merchants here complain loudly of the partiality of the Union Bank. They say none of your exchange ever gets to them—that they hold certificates of deposits on the Bank and when they get to Tallahassee it is all gone. They talk of calling a meeting and withdrawing their deposits and pledging themselves not to receive a Dollar of you." DuVal urged Parkhill to come to St. Joseph himself and address these complaints. "There are many vague, foolish, and even absurd reports about your Bank that discounts are made to certain merchants in Tallahassee and refused to Merchants in other towns." DuVal suggested that Parkhill examine his agency in St. Joseph. "It seems to me that the Bank ought either to place a certain capital here, to meet the wants of the business here or withdraw this Agency[. A]s things are and have been for some time—this *dead* Agency, had only done harm—by doing nothing."[13]

Also that summer Governor Call and DuVal's brother John continued to battle each other both privately and publicly. DuVal would later reveal to a Florida House committee investigating banks that the governor and his clerks were often in the habit of using the official territorial seal to endorse Union Bank bonds.

DuVal was appalled at this unauthorized use, for it was only he who had the authority to use the seal. But for now Call complained to Secretary of State John Forsyth that the territorial secretary "considers himself independent of the authority of the Governor, and at liberty to leave the Territory, for any length of time he may think proper." Call's directives notwithstanding, John DuVal, with his family, had left his post to spend the summer in Virginia. Call also denied DuVal's accusations that he had continually spoken out against the Van Buren administration.[14]

A year and a half earlier, on January 23, 1838, John DuVal had chaired a gathering composed mainly of antibank men in Tallahassee, complaining that no adequate measure had been taken to inform General Thomas Jesup of the Indian threats to Middle Florida. Not surprisingly, Call interpreted this meeting, in which resolutions were drawn, as an attack against his leadership. William P. DuVal, embarrassed at his brother's insinuation, called another meeting the next week that adopted a resolution arguing that "we view with regret and pain that any misconception should have arisen from the said resolution." Furthermore, it was the "opinion of this meeting, that our chief magistrate has done all that he had the power or means of effecting, in providing for and giving protection, not only to our frontiers in Middle Florida, but in West Florida." Floridians' confidence in their governor, the resolution continued, was "undiminished"; they had every confidence in the "virtue, capacity, energy, and ability of Gov. Call to protect and guard our frontiers" and believed that "he has done, and . . . will do, all that his limited means . . . can accomplish."[15]

Responding to Call's complaints against John DuVal, Secretary of State Forsyth ordered the territorial secretary to return at once to his post or face removal. Whether DuVal returned to Tallahassee for this reason or for his own purposes is unknown, but when he tried to enter the capital Call ordered him away. DuVal drew his pistol; in response, as Call wrote to President Van Buren, "I proceeded to disarm him without the least unnecessary violence."[16]

Tiring of these contretemps and taking advice both from his secretary of war and from Democratic stalwarts inside Florida, especially James Westcott and David Levy, Van Buren removed both Call as governor and John DuVal as territorial secretary, appointing Robert Raymond Reid and Joseph McCants in their stead. An old friend of John Forsyth and staunch defender of the administration, Reid was a natural choice for Van Buren. Reid was also an antibank Democrat who opposed division and favored statehood. Predictably, Call lashed out against the administration. The break with Van Buren was complete, and he would salve his wounds by working tirelessly for William Henry Harrison's election in 1840.[17]

With the antibank Reid in the governor's chair, the legislative council packed with antibank delegates, and the economy in a tailspin, most observers understood that there was trouble on the horizon for banking interests and their supporters. As

Richard Keith Call, ca. 1840. Courtesy of State Archives of Florida.

Reid made his way from St. Augustine to Tallahassee, harsh words in the newspapers, on the stump, and between political factions led to violence. During the recent campaign for legislative council seats probanking Whigs had suffered a humiliating setback at the polls. As retribution, a clique of Whig leaders in Middle Florida had lured Leigh Read, a young, up-and-coming politician, into a duel with one of their stalwarts, Augustus Alston. (Read had traded insults with his opponent in the recent campaign.) Read had counted Richard Keith Call as a mentor, but personal and political differences had ended their friendship. Read had also joined in the attack against banks at the St. Joseph convention, placing Robert Raymond Reid's name in nomination for president of the convention. A rising star in the Democratic ranks, Read had made a name for himself in the war against the Seminoles, had married John Branch's daughter Eliza Branch, and, most recently, had taken a leading role in John DuVal's "anti-Call" meeting the preceding January.[18]

In an effort to remove Read from the picture, as noted, a clique of Whigs decided to call out Read. Several men challenged Read but were refused. Finally, after being branded a coward, Read challenged the man he was convinced was behind the plot. Much to the surprise of many observers, Read killed Alston, and the event touched off a cycle of violence that consumed the territorial capital for the next year and a half. Though the duel was judged a fair fight, Alston's well-connected friends and family swore vengeance against Read and would not let the matter rest.[19] Less than a month later, on January 4, 1840, Willis Alston, the slain man's brother, shot and stabbed Read nearly to death at a Democratic gathering at Tallahassee's City Hotel.[20] (Only three days earlier, at a similar gathering at the same venue, Read and Westcott had jointly proclaimed division the scheme of "Spanish land claimants, Bankites, and Abolitionists.")[21]

DuVal must have been repelled at the violence. He certainly took no personal part in the mayhem, and he and his law partner, William Brockenbrough, were out of town for much of November and December. While attending the Calhoun County Superior Court they brought suit in favor of their clients, the Lake Wimico & St. Joseph Canal and Railroad Company.[22] But politics, economic relationships, lifelong friendships, and familial connections certainly made DuVal no unbiased observer.

Unfortunately, just when they needed it most, Governor Reid and other civil authorities could not call on strong law enforcement officials to keep the peace, for, as Florida's territorial delegate Charles Downing explained to President Van Buren, U.S. Marshal Samuel DuVal was "now dying of the Consumption." DuVal's cousin had been seriously ill for more than a year. His trip to Virginia for his health had done him no good. He eventually succumbed to his disease on March 3 while traveling from Tallahassee to Pensacola.[23] In the absence of strong civil law enforcement, Governor Reid, who had arrived in Tallahassee only one day before Alston's near-fatal assault on Read at the City Hotel, asked for but was refused the assistance of federal troops to apprehend Alston and enforce the peace. Still Alston eluded capture. He eventually slipped out of town and returned to Texas, assisted by a loan from Captain Heintzelman.[24]

Such was the scene on January 6 when DuVal and his son-in-law Dr. James Robinson (who would serve as secretary of the Senate) attended the first day of the legislative session. The session began with the majority party nominating its wounded hero as its leader. The provocative move served only to stir the pot. The antibank Democrats certainly had momentum on their side. And they were strengthened by the fact that President Van Buren had recently "called attention to the Bank Charters of Florida, and to the necessity of their supervision by Congress." The executive also called for an end to the issuance of "faith bonds." One commentator hoped that the matter would be taken up in Washington. This would "abate the cause of excitement here" as battles over "'plighted faith,' 'vested rights,' 'obligation of contracts,' 'Territorial honor,'" and the power of the legislature to "issue such bonds will now be fought in Washington, and not here."[25] If the commentator hoped that Washington would relieve the territory of the combustible mix of politics, banking, and violence, he would be disappointed.

On January 12 an obviously shaken Governor Robert Raymond Reid addressed the legislative council. In his first formal address since assuming office, Reid admonished the legislators to address antidueling laws with "a care commensurate with the known evasions upon this subject." Dueling, he asserted, had no place in a civilized society. In closing Reid referred specifically to the incident of the previous week. "The outrage recently committed upon the whole community and upon the person of the gentleman who was subsequently honored by the House of Representatives, in his appointment to the chair of that body, cannot be too much deplored; as also, the fact that the offender has not been arrested, and brought to answer to the laws for their signal violations." Reid declared that the "public indignation as well as the law" must be relied upon to "bring the community back to the paths of peace and good order."[26]

As DuVal heard these words he would have recalled many bloody scenes of family and friends on the field of honor. Though he was Reid's opponent and perhaps even still smarted over the Georgian's besting of him at the St. Joseph convention, DuVal needed no persuading on the subject of dueling. A lifelong opponent of dueling, he set about to answer the governor's call for a new antidueling law. Two days later, while serving on the judiciary committee, DuVal introduced an antidueling bill on the Senate floor, the final version of which went down to defeat as a kind of "overkill" piece of legislation. The bill proposed to disfranchise anyone involved in a duel. If anyone was killed in the duel, all survivors were to be hanged. Their heirs would be compelled to pay the debts of survivors as well as, if applicable, a pension to surviving widows. One Democratically aligned newspaper called the Senate version of the bill "the most ridiculous tissue of crudities and fudgeries ever sanctioned by a grave legislative body." Perhaps as a veiled insult to DuVal, the journal labeled the failed measure "a specimen of legislative quackery as could be compounded by ignorance and silliness, or manufactured by folly."[27]

Midway through the legislative session, DuVal solidified yet another link to probanking interests when his daughter Laura married Dr. Arthur Moray Randolph. The DuVals, Randolphs, and other friends celebrated the nuptials on January 16, midway through the legislative session. Arthur Randolph's role in the Read-Alston duel is unrecorded, but his brother John, six years older, also a doctor and Alston's friend, had provoked the affair, only to bring back the dead man's corpse to his plantation after the fight. At the time of the duel the brothers were practicing together. Both brothers were the sons of Thomas Eston Randolph, a cousin of Thomas Jefferson. At the time of their father's death, in 1842, Arthur acquired an interest in his father's eight-hundred-acre San Luis plantation, encompassing the old San Luis mission. Thus Laura became the mistress of a large plantation, with many slaves.[28]

Predictably, the Florida House of Representatives moved with dispatch to rein in Florida's banking system. Though probank supporters held a slight majority in the Senate, they could do little to obstruct the Democrats. A House report asserted that there was no basis for chartering banks with "exclusive privileges and that pledges of the faith and credit of the people of Florida were null and void." While the Union Bank increasingly came under scrutiny, the House also called for Reid to appoint a commission to examine the books of the Southern Life and Insurance Company in St. Augustine, the Bank of Pensacola, and branches of another institution in Apalachicola and St. Joseph. (Interestingly, DuVal himself had called for the repeal of the Bank of Pensacola's charter.)[29]

While the bank question was the principal matter of controversy during the legislative session, the Territorial Senate Committee also considered the question of division. Predictably, the measure failed. Senator Isaiah Hart of Jacksonville issued the minority report advocating the division of the territory at the Suwannee River. Such a move, the senator reasoned, would eventually create two southern states with two senators each. Both territories would be capable of attracting much larger populations. "Their present union appears to be unnatural, and their geographical position will present a state of most awkward shape, whilst a controversy and conflict of interests growing out of it, will forever destroy that harmony so essential to the prosperity of a political body." There the matter stood at the session's close. But supporters of division soon learned that they had a powerful ally in the U.S. Senate—John C. Calhoun.[30]

After about a month and a half of convalescence at his father-in-law's plantation, Leigh Read was able to attend the few remaining days of the legislative session. On March 3, the Democratic caucus named him its chairman. Read then traveled to St. Augustine to inspect the books of the St. Augustine Life and Trust Company. Returning not long thereafter to Middle Florida, Read assumed command of a 1,500-man militia unit called into service by Governor Reid. Then, on May 22 President Van Buren appointed Read U.S. marshal for the Middle District of Florida. The Whigs were appalled. DuVal for one was convinced that the selection was a blatant political maneuver by the Van Buren administration calculated to gain the support of John Branch in the hope that he would use his influence to see that North Carolina would support the New Yorker in the upcoming presidential contest. DuVal wrote to authorities in Washington questioning Read's ability to serve impartially in a time of great political instability. Read, DuVal claimed, was a "man of violent passions and prejudices" and, worse, was a "professed Duelisto who had been engaged in some the most savage contests that ever occurred in any country." Moreover, Read's appointment, DuVal contended, "united . . . civil power & the military . . . in the same individual"—something that should never be done "except in the case of the president and governors of states & Territories."[31]

For the next year Read neglected his duties as marshal as he was engaged in the field against the Seminoles. While he was away, Tallahassee simmered throughout the spring, summer, and fall of 1840. Also that spring Van Buren raised more eyebrows when he declined to reappoint DuVal's friend John Randall as judge of the Middle District of Florida and in his place appointed Alfred Balch of Tennessee, an Andrew Jackson loyalist. Balch reported to the president upon his arrival in Tallahassee on April 3 that Call, DuVal, and other of Randall's friends "felt some displeasure" toward him. Balch added that the "condition of affairs in this territory is deplorable. The leading men are divided into bitter parties and violence is the order of the day. Heretofore the Banking influence has been predominant, but now the most determined resistance is made to it and in fact it is tottering to its foundation as well it may since the paper of the Union Bank here is 25 per cent below Virginia paper and Virginia paper is 8 per cent below specie."[32]

Meanwhile, violent rhetoric became ever more combustible. On the day after Balch wrote to President Van Buren, the Tallahassee *Floridian* charged that the "faith-bond Bankocracy" was scheming to elevate "the granny Abolitionist, Harrison to the Presidency and the fanatical and incendiary gang was . . . seeking the destruction of the interests and rights of the South." Thus the Democratic press began to take up the argument that somehow Whigs, defenders of the banks, and supporters of division, were in league with Abolitionists. Such accusations would be akin to charging political opponents with being communists in the 1950s or supporters of Islamic terrorists in the post-9/11 world.

And William P. DuVal was also in on the plot. The *Floridian*'s account continued with a report that Senator John Pope, DuVal's relation, again representing Kentucky in the U.S. Senate, had introduced a bill to divide the territory. If such a measure were to pass, the "germ of an Abolitionist State in East Florida" in less than five years would be the result. "[I]t will be a receptacle for runaway slaves from the contiguous States, more dangerous than the Seminole nation has been. Hordes of immigrants from the North, gathered up by colonizing emissaries and agents, are waiting but for the Indians to give place to make settlements, and not a few of these emigrants will be infected with the Abolition monomania. Many will be from Europe." The peninsula was "literally shingled with Spanish grants, confirmed and unconfirmed, genuine and forged, honest and fraudulent." Much of the land, the article asserted, would "eventually fall into the hands of wealthy speculators from New York" who would be the means by which "emigrants of this sort" would come to Florida.[33]

The truth of the matter was that DuVal, along with a large segment of the population of East Florida, was trying to slow down the process of statehood. DuVal and others in East Florida, with counseling from John C. Calhoun and other Southern leaders, advocated severing East Florida from West and Middle Florida. Settlers in East Florida, they argued, were not ready for the financial obligations of statehood; when they were ready, the argument went, East Florida could come in as another slave state.

While the political sparring in the press continued, DuVal attended to his law practice. By that time he had dissolved his partnership with William Brockenbrough, as Van Buren had appointed Brockenbrough U.S. attorney for the Apalachicola District. In November 1839 an announcement noted that DuVal would practice as part of the firm of W. P. and T. H. DuVal.[34] Either father or son could be found in Tallahassee at their office under the Union Bank of Florida.

The DuVals had a number of important cases pending in the several superior courts of the Middle District that spring term, but one of the most sensational took place in the Apalachicola District. It involved the Passmore brothers, accused of brutally murdering a man named Raffenburg in Ochessee, Calhoun County. The Passmores were rich and powerful and could afford the best legal counsel in the territory. DuVal and Thomas Baltzell defended William Passmore and George Hawkins defended Thomas Passmore in the St. Joseph trial. Prosecuting the case before DuVal's other former partner, Judge Richard C. Allen, was William Brockenbrough. According to one account, the district attorney so skillfully laid out the case against the Passmores in such a "bold, startling" manner, that there was little doubt of the brothers' guilt. "The counsel for the prisoners aware of the desperate nature of the case, employed every artifice that legal learning and eloquence in a bad case could bring to their rescue. But it was to no avail, the crime of murder, damning murder, was too clearly made out." Judge Allen's "calm clear charge . . . summed up the evidence and applied the law, left the guilty parties no hope save what sorrow and repentance might bring beyond the grave." The brothers were sentenced to hang on May 15 but eventually escaped from the Calhoun County jail while their case was under appeal.[35]

By far the most important case DuVal was involved in that summer was the suit brought against him by the United States. In *The United States vs William P. DuVal* the federal government argued that DuVal was more than $2,000 in default from accounts dating back to his time as superintendent of Indian affairs. DuVal counterclaimed that the government owed him for daily expenses incurred while he was serving in the post. The War Department, he also asserted, had wrongly rejected more $8,000 worth of vouchers he had submitted. The dispute had gone on for more than twelve years. The two-day trial in the Leon County Superior Court included a "full and patient examination by the Court and jury of the great mass of written and oral testimony." At the conclusion of the trial the jury awarded the former governor $18,200. As a witness to the trial recorded, "after years of procrastination after the defendant was reduced to poverty," justice was finally done. If interest had been added, DuVal might have been entitled to more than $30,000, but Judge Balch declared that interest ought not to be levied against the United States.[36]

DuVal must have exulted at this vindication of his official acts and of his financial claims against the government. Peter Gautier of the St. Joseph *Times* editorialized, "the friends of this gentleman will rejoice with us, that at length there has been a fair adjudication of the matters between" him and the federal government. "Gov. DuVal as Superintendent of Indian Affairs necessarily incurred heavy expenses, and it was preposterous and unjust that the burden should be thrown upon him as an individual. The Government was the party for whom these expenditures were made, and they ought to have been done long since—what the jury have now said they should do—Justice then would have been done to an honest man and worthy efficient officer, and the Government would have escaped the odium of withholding justice from one who deserved it."[37] Though the court ruled in DuVal's favor, it would take a congressional appropriation before he could collect the funds. On December 30, 1841, Senator James Morehead of Kentucky began the process, which would take many years to complete, when he presented DuVal's petition for payment before the Senate Committee on Claims.[38] DuVal continued in very difficult economic circumstances.

An important part of DuVal's and his son Thomas's law practice involved the prosecution of claims of Florida citizens who had lost property during the Seminoles wars. DuVal's knowledge of and familiarity with these issues provided him with the necessary skills to present these claims before Congress. As an advertisement for his services outlined, DuVal would prosecute their claims "before Congress, or any other tribunal that may be created by law" for the purpose. Those who desired this service could "call on Thomas H. DuVal, Esq. at Tallahassee, who will prepare the requisite powers of attorney, containing terms upon which the business will be undertaken by me." This work would sometimes require travel to Washington. Eventually, a Board of Army Officers was established in Tallahassee to adjudicate claims. Its first sessions would meet roughly a year later. Subsequent sessions were also held in other locations through the territory, necessitating DuVal's travel to Suwannee Springs, Newnansville, Black Creek, and St. Augustine.

On Sunday, May 17, after church, Samuel Heintzelman called at the DuVals' home and found DuVal, Richard Keith Call, and George Walker ready to sit down to dinner. After the meal, the men saw DuVal off on the stage to Washington. By July 27 Heintzelman found him returned and "full of news from Washington."[39] During DuVal's absence, violent confrontations between Democrats and Whigs had continued in Tallahassee, and Willis Alston's return to Tallahassee from Texas swearing to avenge his brother's death only added to the disorder. Within a week after Heintzelman greeted DuVal on his return from Washington, the territorial capital exploded in violence.

The trouble began on August 3 when an angry delegation of Whigs surrounded the office of the *Floridian*, threatening to tear it down unless Samuel Sibley, the editor, disclosed the names of persons who had authored resolutions that had appeared in the paper and that linked bank advocates with the abolitionist movement. Sibley stalled them until several men appeared to take credit for authoring the resolutions. Within hours angry groups of Whigs and Democrats faced each other in the streets. Taking a prominent role in the mayhem was Willis Alston. He and other Whigs assaulted several bank opponents, including William Francis, a merchant; Walker Anderson of the House Judiciary Committee, which had reported against the banks; and another antibank man whose surname was Brown.[40]

Governor Reid called out the nearby federal troops to restore order. The next day a militia force from Quincy arrived in town. But this only made matters worse. (The fact that the force's leaders were General Leigh Read and Major E. E. Blackburn, a prominent Democrat and candidate for the Florida Senate, served only to further antagonize the Whigs.) DuVal led a delegation of citizens to Reid's office to protest the move but was rebuffed. On August 5 he and several others lodged a written complaint directly with Governor Reid. Five days after that, DuVal chaired a "Committee of the Citizens of Tallahassee," which drafted a formal appeal against Reid's actions to President Van Buren. Among the eight signatures on the document were those of Thomas Brown and DuVal's old enemy William Wyatt. The petition called for Reid's removal, claiming that he had wrongfully suspended civil law. The petition likened Reid's behavior to the arbitrary "conduct of the British Governors in the incipient stages of the Revolution." The document cast Reid's actions as the "grossest outrage upon the personal and civil rights of our citizens, ever perpetrated by an Executive officer since the foundation of the republic." Reid, the petition continued, had acted in a partisan manner and could not tolerate any group or faction opposed to his party.[41] Charles Downing, the territorial delegate, also joined in the attack against Reid. Penning an angry letter to President Van Buren, he accused the chief executive of appointing people solely on the basis of party loyalty to his administration and charged him with thus excluding Florida's best citizens. "You had placed an unwelcome ruler over an unwilling people—one totally unfit for the duties that are now his—either of war or of peace."[42]

As various political slants on the behavior of participants in the outbreaks began to appear in Florida and throughout the country (the "Tallahassee Troubles" had even attracted national attention), DuVal's role in the affair came under scrutiny. E. E. Blackburn complained that DuVal should have been the last person to accuse Reid of abusing power by suspending the law. "I allude to his celebrated order for holding a new election in 1831, which was treated by the people with sovereign contempt as they will his vain-glorious effort to make Whig capital out of the recent occurrences at Tallahassee."[43] But perhaps the most devastating attacks against DuVal came from "W," who published his open letter "To William P. DuVal." Instead of playing the role of elder statesmen and calming things down, DuVal, "W" charged, had tried to manipulate the situation to achieve political advantage. Also as evidence of DuVal's inconsistency, "W" exposed the irony of DuVal working with his old enemy William Wyatt. As governor "your complaints against this individual were loud and repeated. You stated he had given you more trouble than all the men in the Territory together. He is understood to have preferred charges against you; and yet we find you, now no longer Executive united with this same man in the honorable employment of assailing your successor."[44] Few who read "W"'s attacks against DuVal would have doubted that the author of these words was James Westcott.

Certainly a contributor to the violence were the upcoming political contests that would take place in the fall. The presidential sweepstakes pitting Van Buren and William Henry Harrison also kept the pot boiling. That summer Richard Keith Call did not participate in the Tallahassee upheavals; he was campaigning in New Jersey with Daniel Webster in support of William Henry Harrison, a circumstance that must have made Andrew Jackson boil over. Later Call was reported to have made a "powerful speech" in Harrison's favor in New York City.[45] In Florida both rival parties had nominated a slate of candidates for the upcoming elections. The Tallahassee *Floridian* noted that the "Conservative Bank Ticket" included DuVal (attorney for the Union Bank); in addition, all the other Whig nominees for the Florida Senate were large stockholders or directors of the institution. Those on the Democratic slate, which included Blackburn and four other men, pledged to use their "best exertions so far as their power as legislators may extend, to bring the Banks of the Territory to a sound and healthy condition."[46]

Only days before the balloting in Middle Florida the St. Joseph *Times* on October 5 ran on its front page "The Early Experiences of Ralph Ringwood," with the following observation on the second page: "We extract from the *Knickerbocker* on our first page the quaint graphic and original narrative of Ralph Ringwood and commend it to the perusal of our Florida friends, many of whom have heard these tales orally from Ralph himself. The speaker or narrator is a candidate for the Florida Senate for the Middle District [and has] talked politics and poetry (as the case might be) with almost every man, woman, and child in Middle Florida." The "Experiences" recounted DuVal's setting out from his boyhood home in Richmond for the Kentucky frontier, his growing to manhood in that state and hunting on the Green River, and, finally, his courtship of Nancy.[47] Reprints also appeared in other papers in Florida and in other parts of the nation.[48] While Washington Irving's authorship of the stories was not immediately revealed, DuVal would have immediately known that fact. It is impossible to know when DuVal first saw Irving's stories or what would he have thought of them. Would he have been angered by Irving's publishing his tall tales? Would they have embarrassed him? Would he have used them to political advantage? Would the stories be used against him by his opponents? Time would tell.

Washington Irving, ca. 1840. Courtesy of Library of Congress.

In the elections a few weeks later the entire Whig ticket prevailed. DuVal received more votes the any other senatorial or house candidate in Leon County. He also received the most votes in Jefferson and Madison Counties. The only county in which he did not obtain more votes than other senate hopefuls was Gadsden, where Charles DuPont bested him by two votes. Of course, DuVal and his friends also rejoiced in Harrison's victory over Van Buren. Especially pleasing to them was the certainty that the general would sack Reid. But that eventuality would have to wait.

Captain Heintzelman arrived in Tallahassee on October 17 after a month away and paid a visit to the DuVals. He was sorry to find "Gov. DuVall a little unwell." Alston was still in town, and rumors swirled that Leigh Read had hired an assassin to kill him. "I find Gen. Read has pretty well d—d himself by a letter he wrote to get a man to assassinate Alston. . . . They say he is afraid to show himself. . . . A fine man he to command in the U. States service. . . . The vols ought to compel him to resign. . . . Read's race is nearly run."[49] Heintzelman continued to enjoy DuVal's hospitality that fall and winter. Dining with DuVal and Nancy on December 7, the captain visited the new DuVal house under construction on elevated hills approximately a half-mile from his previous home site. The new residence was a "fine house on a beautiful situation. The house is still unfinished & the grounds unimproved." From there the party "adjourned to Gov. Call's & took tea & spent the evening." As a New Year's gift the captain bought DuVal a snuff box.[50]

The new legislative session opened on January 8. The senators selected DuVal their president, and once again Dr. Robinson was elected secretary.[51] On the House side, Peter Gautier, the editor of the St. Joseph *Times*, bested Thomas Brown for speaker. The major issues confronting the solons were the same as in the previous session. Conflicts over banking and division dominated the debates. In his opening message Governor Reid argued that any talk of division should be postponed until after Florida became a state. He warned that "Speculators [were] greedily expecting a termination" of the Second Seminole War. Abolitionists were ready to pounce, and "Blacks from the British West India Islands, are, I am credibly informed, holding intercourse with the Mainland." Division at this time would only assist their nefarious schemes, the governor warned.[52]

DuVal busied himself with the passage of legislation for the territory. He introduced bills to suppress riots, public brawls, and breaches of the peace, reported out a bill to charter a railroad, and joined other legislators in a Memorial to Congress "against any course calculated to suffer the Indians to remain in the Territory." DuVal also joined his fellow Whigs in lobbying the incoming administration of William Henry Harrison. DuVal and his friends called for Richard Keith Call's reinstatement as governor and Leigh Read's sacking as U.S. marshal. Writing to a Harrison operative, DuVal asserted that "we have had the most worthless and inefficient men appointed to office in our territory, and I trust that the president elect will let all such retire."[53]

By the end of the session antibank forces in the legislative council had passed a resolution favoring repudiation. Even more distasteful to the banks was the issuance of an unfavorable report on the condition of the Union Bank. William Brockenbrough had authored the report, and DuVal also likely participated in its writing. One Democratic newspaper reminded its readers that both men had served as counsel to the bank. It poked fun at their "*ingratitude* to all those favors in one shape or another." Negative public opinion as well as a thoughtful reconsideration of the facts no doubt caused this change. Retribution against DuVal was swift. On April 3 he announced to the public that, "the Union Bank of Florida having transferred its business to other gentlemen of the bar," he and his son "can now be employed to defend those who have been sued by the bank." Of course, that also meant that DuVal was now free to sue the bank as well. Within a year and a half the legislative council had suspended the charters of the banks and repudiated the "faith bonds." The action brought suit after suit in the courts. DuVal would have all the legal work he could handle. The only problem was that with the economic collapse no one had any money to pay legal fees.[54]

As the legislative session came to a close, DuVal attended to his law cases and occasionally took time out from his practice to enjoy the delights of springtime in the capital. One of the favorite locations for doing so was the site of Fort San Luis on the grounds of the Randolph plantation. On March 30, DuVal, Nancy, and a party of about twenty others, including Richard Keith Call and Mrs. Murat, had a picnic on the grounds. According to Captain Heintzelman, who escorted Elizabeth Brown to the affair, "everything passed all delightfully. We had cards, back-gammon, singing & guitar & dancing." A few days later DuVal left Tallahassee for St. Joseph to attend court but returned with Judge Allen and Thomas Baltzell on board the *Commerce* via Port Leon on April 19. Three days later DuVal threw a large party at his house.[55] For DuVal and his friends, Reid's sacking and Call's reinstatement as governor were certainly cause for celebration. Leigh Read was also removed from his post as U.S. marshal. As he had in terminating Reid's tenure, President Harrison followed the recommendation of DuVal and others and selected Minor Walker for the post.

But the relative calm that seemed to be returning to Tallahassee was shattered when Willis Alston shot down Leigh Read on April 26. The killing occurred in cold-blooded fashion in the streets of Tallahassee, and Read expired at his brother-in-law's law office. That afternoon, Heintzelman recorded in his diary, "There is great excitement in town. Willis gave himself up & is in the charge of a guard. This is the result I have long anticipated. I hope it will quiet the community." Though the captain despised Read, he felt "very sorry for him. His course has been such as he can only blame himself for his violent end." Read's father-in-law, John Branch, Heintzelman continued, "became perfectly crazy & accused some of the most respectable citizens with being accomplices to Read's death. He accused Gov. Call" and others of having a hand in the assassination, but the distraught man apologized after he calmed down. "Alston gave himself up to the civil authority & is now in jail. He intends to stand trial. The affair excited the town very much but now all appears to have become quiet. I am in hopes now the town will remain so."[56]

But such was not to be the case. The murder threw the entire community into an uproar. As it had in the summer of 1840, pandemonium reigned once again, especially after Alston and his friends connived to have him released on bail. As the new U.S. marshal, Minor Walker, explained to Secretary of State Daniel Webster, "It is impossible for you to imagine the excitement which prevails in this place & vicinity. Altho Judge Allen refused to admit Alston to bail, nevertheless two of the Justices of the Peace in this county did bail him out of Jail." Governor Call issued a proclamation for Alston's arrest once it was learned that the commissions of the justices of the peace had expired. By that time it was too late. Alston had already fled to Texas.[57]

It seemed to many that DuVal was fed up with the Florida political scene. He confirmed the fact when he announced his resignation from the Florida Senate. In a lengthy speech to the "Electors of the Middle District of Florida," DuVal expressed his regret at his decision but cited the defeat of bills he had proposed against dueling. He attributed an "intemperate zeal of party" as the cause of these defeats. "Surrendering into your hands the power you confided in me is induced by imperious necessity. For three years I have endeavored to serve you, my professional interests have greatly suffered." His service in the Senate in the winter months had prevented him from arguing cases in the court of appeals. Even though custom and tradition might have sanctioned his doing so, his own sense of propriety had dissuaded him from the act. He also noted that his obligation to prosecute military claims in Washington during the next winter on behalf of his clients necessitated his retirement from legislative service.[58]

DuVal concluded his remarks by speaking of a subject on which most of his hearers disagreed with him. Making the case for renewed thoughtful consideration of division, DuVal asked, "Shall we force the East into state government? Would it be just and wise to drag so large and respectable a portion of our fellow citizens into the Union, when all of us know that, under present circumstances, it will be impossible for them to sustain that portion of expense that will certainly be necessary, and for which they must provide?" Then he asked again rhetorically, "If Middle Florida had been overrun by the savage foe—our plantations ruined—houses and crops and stock destroyed—our citizens many of them wanting bread, driven for protection into a few forts, what would we have said had East Florida been exempt from these misfortunes, and was now urging our admission as a sovereign state?" DuVal asserted that East Florida would eventually become a slave state, observing that "the North West Territories are not only extensive, but are rapidly increasing in population. It seems just and proper that Wisconsin and Iowa should be balanced with East and West Florida, to preserve that unity of interest so well designed to protect the Middle, South, and South-Western States, from the dangerous encroachments on our domestic institutions, which have and yet continue to agitate the Union. As patriots, desiring the perpetuity of our confederation, we should be willing to make some sacrifice on the altar of our country to secure our general interests and happiness." DuVal closed with the assertion that he did not oppose statehood but advocated only that Congress include a provision that East Florida be allowed to become a separate state "when she is ready and in a situation to accept the privilege."[59]

DuVal's retirement, his advocacy for postponing statehood, and his call for separating East Florida from the rest of Florida received considerable comment. The Tallahassee *Sentinel* regretted DuVal's retirement but predicted that at some future day "the people will show that they have not forgotten his past service." DuVal had always served his country "wherever and whenever she asked him, without regard to his private interests; and though we regret that he could not serve out the term for which he was elected, we know his reasons are conclusive for resigning." As for his views on the admission of Florida into the Union, the journal noted, "We have been from the very start in favor of state government." Yet, as DuVal had reminded everyone, "a change has come over the prospects of the country. The war is unclosed—the treasury is empty—currency bad—people in debt. Under these circumstances, we are in favor of delay. Delay until our circumstances are more prosperous, and then, in harmony with the East, let us go in as a whole, with the understanding that two states may hereafter be formed if all desire it, and other states consent to it."[60]

On May 31 DuVal wrote his old friend Senator Samuel Southard in Washington that he had "flattered myself [to see you] at least as early as you will [receive] this letter but the illness of Mrs. DuVal has detained me here and I fear it will for a few days yet." DuVal deplored the recent division among the Whigs, which had led to the election of a "Loco Foco delegate, and he is a *foreign Jew*." Of David Levy, DuVal wrote, "I do not believe he was ever naturalized and I trust that the committee on elections of the House will inquire into this matter." DuVal told Southard that he had "quit public life" and for a long time had taken "but little interest in public affairs. . . . So when you see me have no apprehensions that I am seeking office."[61] In June DuVal dissolved his law partnership with his son Thomas. An announcement noted that Thomas would form a partnership with Benjamin Allen. Allen would remain in Tallahassee while Thomas DuVal would be in St. Joseph.[62] Meanwhile, Thomas's father was preparing to pack himself off to Washington to pursue their clients' claims. Leaving Nancy and his daughters behind, he had little idea that he would never see his wife alive again. Her health already weakened when she left Tallahassee to be with her daughters in St. Joseph, Nancy DuVal died of yellow fever on July 14.

CHAPTER 17

"Tyler Too," Washington Intrigue, and St. Augustine

It is impossible to determine how William P. DuVal learned of his wife's death. Newspapers available in Washington contained information about the St. Joseph yellow fever epidemic, and most of these accounts contained news of Nancy DuVal's passing. Her obituary also circulated widely and was reprinted in various papers across the eastern seaboard. Nancy died only a few days after arriving in St. Joseph to stay with her daughters. According to one account, when the dreadful news reached Tallahassee, it "wrapped this whole community in mourning. Where Mrs. DuVal has been long known, she was beloved by all, and her loss will be wept by all; for she was truly the mother of our society at Tallahassee." Nancy DuVal's many contributions to the territorial capital's earliest days were recounted as she presided over "Governor DuVal's house," which was in those days "in measure *head quarters*." It was "ever open to the needy; his hospitalities to all, and thus from the position of Mrs. D a state of society grew up around her, receiving a tone and impulse from her example, which will long characterize it above all other newly settled countries." The account could only speculate as to the condition of her absent husband. "But what consolation can we offer the husband of ... thirty six years" who contemplated "her as his chief good, whose existence was interwoven with every fiber of his heart, and who was not permitted, in the last hour, to watch over her dying pillow, and catch her parting words?" Sickness in St. Joseph, Tallahassee, and elsewhere in Middle Florida continued, claiming the lives of hundreds of settlers, including DuVal's former law partner Judge Richard C. Allen, Samuel Parkhill, and former governor Robert Raymond Reid, who died at his daughter's plantation in Leon County.[1]

Despite Nancy's death, DuVal remained in Washington. He would have shared his grief with his friend George T. Ward, who had lost his sister and his mother

John Tyler, ca. 1840.
Courtesy of Library
of Congress.

in the St. Joseph epidemic. Governor Call was also in the capital that summer, as were Captain Samuel Heintzelman, Thomas Baltzell, Thomas Randall, Peter Hagner, and numerous other Floridians. Arriving in the capital city after the opening of the special session on May 31, DuVal and his friends witnessed firsthand the confused transition from the Van Buren to the Harrison-Tyler administration. Further complicating matters was the president's death after only one month in office. The aged military hero was the first president to die in office, and there was no consensus about John Tyler's role. Would he be president in his own right? Or would he operate as "vice president and acting president," essentially ceding to Congress any and all executive functions? When he arrived in Washington in mid-April, Tyler left little doubt as to what policy he would pursue—he would be president. By the time DuVal arrived in Washington the battle between the new president and the Whig leader Senator Henry Clay was already in full swing. Tyler, a states'-rights Virginian and an opponent of Andrew Jackson, had been put on the ticket primarily to attract Southern votes. He had little sympathy for the Whig agenda, especially Clay's rechartering of the National Bank. Clay, already bitter from being left off the ticket in the 1840 election, was bent on dominating the new president. This drama began playing itself out even before the opening of the special legislative session on May 31.[2]

DuVal attended to his business and pressed his clients' and his own claims against the government. Despite the judicial verdict in his favor, DuVal had yet to be paid for his expenses while governor. A congressional appropriation of the funds was necessary, and legislators had other priorities. DuVal was on friendly terms with Tyler and paid a visit to the new president on September 15. The two discussed Florida appointments and perhaps even a position for DuVal himself. He also counted Secretary of the Navy Abel Upshur of Virginia (whom he had known for more than thirty years) among his friends in the new administration. His old Bardstown crony Charles Wickliffe served the president as postmaster general. On September 7 DuVal dined with Captain Heintzelman. Earlier that day Heintzelman had heard John Quincy Adams and other House members debate David Levy's right to his seat in the House of Representatives. Later that evening the territorial delegate paid his respects to the captain and DuVal. By that time DuVal had reconsidered his former opinion: "Gov. DuVal says there is no doubt he [Levy] is entitled to his seat," Heintzelman recorded in his diary. Later that evening DuVal introduced Heintzelman to a number of other legislators, including Congressman James Buchanan, who represented the captain's district in Pennsylvania.[3]

DuVal left Washington after the conclusion of the special session in late September. By that time Tyler and Henry Clay had broken completely after the president's veto of Clay's bank bill and other Whig legislation. Arriving in Tallahassee close to the first of October, DuVal reunited with his sons Thomas Howard and John Crittenden and his daughters, Marcia Price, Mary Robinson, Laura Randolph, and fifteen-year-old Florida DuVal. All would have shared with their father memories of Nancy's final moments. It must have been a tearful reunion. By that time President Tyler had appointed Thomas DuVal territorial secretary and James and Mary Robinson had relocated to Tallahassee. Dr. Robinson formed a partnership with a medical school friend named Pope, a distant relative of DuVal's family in Virginia. The two physicians bought a drug store in the town, and prosperity beckoned.[4]

Also home to greet DuVal was his brother John. Thomas DuVal's appointment to John's old post as territorial secretary must have proved awkward for his uncle and father-in-law John DuVal. (Thomas DuVal after all had only recently married his cousin Laura Peyton DuVal.) After his sacking as territorial secretary John DuVal continued his law practice in Tallahassee. Brooding over his fall from grace, he resumed his bitter enmity with Richard Keith Call. Shortly before the inauguration he wrote Vice-President elect Tyler a long letter explaining how Van Buren had unjustly removed him at the urging of a "low fellow here by the name of Westcott." John DuVal sought another appointment, writing similar letters to Kentucky senators John Crittenden and John Pope. One source speculated that the "quondam ex-Secretary, *ie devant* Texas General" might be appointed judge of the Middle District and that Governor Call, as if to "conciliate a man with whom, two years ago he had a bout of fisty cuffs," might have even recommended him for the post. But nothing materialized. DuVal continued his sparing with Call in the press over past disagreements, especially the manner in which official seals were affixed to faith bonds. Their animus toward one another became a matter of ridicule. John DuVal continued a bitter, angry man.[5]

On his return to Middle Florida William P. DuVal, a widower at the age of fifty-two, contemplated his future. His law practice provided only a meager income, especially given the economic hard times. Relief came in the form of tidings from Washington when President Tyler appointed him to yet another federal post, law agent. An office created by Congress in 1828, the law agent was responsible for representing the United States in land claims cases dating back to the beginning of the American acquisition of Florida. During the Jackson administration Richard Keith Call and William Wirt had handled such claims against the United States. In their work, they had mostly failed—bested by Joseph White, John Berrien, and Daniel Webster in numerous battles in the Supreme Court.[6]

By 1841 most of these cases had been settled, but a substantial number still remained unsettled. DuVal's background on the bench and bar, his familiarity with land cases, and his experience as governor made him a promising candidate for the post. The majority of the cases were based in the East Florida counties of St. Johns, Nassau, Duval, Alachua, Columbia, Hillsborough, and Mosquito. DuVal's appointment required that he travel to East Florida, where claims had arisen. Some critics saw the office as an unnecessary expense. One critic likened the "useless law agent" to the "Grand Falconer of England," who at one time might have performed necessary duties but was no longer needed. The needless post, the critic charged, was merely a way for a new administration to reward "hungry partisan office seekers."[7]

Before he could assume his duties DuVal had to wrap up his clients' affairs in Middle Florida, and he was eager to do so. Soon after he returned to Florida, DuVal wrote to Charles Wickliffe from Tallahassee that he had approximately $100,000 in suits to be collected in the Apalachicola District. He and other members of the bar desired a competent U.S. marshal to collect the money and pay it over to them. Not only was the area suffering from an incompetent marshal, but sickness, even with the cooler weather, was still prevalent. "There has been buried here the last season up to this time 400—out of a population of about 1600, it is now more healthy but hot, a few cases of yellow fever are occurring." Though DuVal's son John

William P. DuVal, ca. 1840. From the author's collection.

Crittenden was well, his daughters Florida DuVal and Mary Robinson were sick, as were two of his servants. Indeed, the "whole country is truly a land of mourning—I do not know what will become of us all," he lamented.[8]

A year before Nancy DuVal's death, a visitor to Middle Florida offered a lengthy description of DuVal. Governor DuVal, the man wrote, "wears a much more youthful appearance" than his age might suggest. He had little gray hair, no whiskers, and was about 5' 7", and was just about as portly as a well fed Alderman. His appearance, whether sitting, standing or walking—whether waking, or sleeping, eating or sleeping or drinking, indicates the cheerful, contented, happy man. And such most truly and literally he is; as thousands can attest, who have visited Tallahassee during the last twelve years." He still practiced law "with the zeal and activity of man just admitted to the bar." His greatest skill was not in the "intricacies and depths of the law," but "few are his superiors in persuasive eloquence before a jury." Because of his "urbane manners, his social disposition, and his well-known hospitality, he is the most popular man in the country." His reading was "miscellaneous and somewhat extensive—his acquaintance with human

Born in Connecticut in 1790, Thomas Douglas came to Florida from Indiana in 1826, after his appointment as U.S. district attorney for the Eastern District of Florida. In that capacity he worked closely with DuVal defending land claims against the United States. Courtesy of State Archives of Florida.

nature practical, apt, and indeed profound. . . . As a Statesman he is practical and shrewd—as a debater ready and strong."[9]

But it was as a social companion, the observer noted, that DuVal was "perhaps better, and more universally known and beloved. He is an inexhaustible fund of anecdote full of pith and humor, gathered during the early part of his life." These stories, the writer noted, were in circulation through the writings of Washington Irving in recent editions of the *Knickerbocker Magazine*. The governor "most pleasantly deals these out to his friends at his own fireside. . . . It is then that his kind countenance wears all its sunny hues. His mouth, indicative of comic humor and ready wit, speaks from the very heart . . . and in his eye swims the liquid light that gushes and sparkles up from a generous soul."[10]

But DuVal's loss of Nancy, the further deterioration of his economic situation, concern over his family's future, and, finally, his new duties as law agent robbed his face of most of its "sunny hues." Still, near the first of the year DuVal headed to East Florida to begin work on the Florida land cases. There he would work closely with U.S. District Attorney Thomas Douglas. While on his way east he learned of his father's passing. William DuVal died quietly at his residence in Buckingham County, Virginia, at the age of ninety-four.[11] When DuVal had last seen his father is unrecorded. Nor is it known whether he visited his father's grave when he traveled to Virginia that spring.

After preparing appeals on behalf of the United States in five cases emerging from the Eastern District Court, DuVal headed to Washington in February 1842 to plead these cases in the Supreme Court. DuVal failed to have the verdicts overturned in all but one of the cases. He also had received no compensation for his work. "I have received no allowance or compensation whatever since I was appointed," DuVal wrote to a functionary in the Tyler administration. "If the enclosed account from services is allowed—my future compensation—may commence from this date, as the President may direct—with the understanding that if I am requested to attend the Supreme Court—that a reasonable allowance may be granted for expenses." DuVal also added that to perform his duties, he must "reside in St. Augustine the greater part of the year, where most of the claims will be tried and that office rent, stationary &c should be allowed me." For his services he claimed a fee of $1,300 and $6 for every twenty miles traveled between Tallahassee and Washington. President Tyler granted DuVal's request for his fee and expenses and ordered his deputy in the Department of the Treasury to set DuVal's salary at $2,000 per annum to commence March 1. Even so, Tyler observed that the "permanent expenses of the law agency are at present too great—considering the number of cases now pending there can be no necessity for a principal and assistant agent. Let the assistant agency cease." Tyler also reduced the extra compensation of the district attorney from $1,500 to $1,000.[12]

Congress was also in a cost-cutting mood. In April territorial delegate David Levy informed DuVal that Congress wanted to hear directly from the law agent as to "the necessity of retaining the appropriation for his services," and DuVal dutifully testified before the House Ways and Means Committee. His formal statement reviewed the history of the office and reminded the legislators that its continuance was still critical. DuVal then reviewed his recent cases before the Supreme Court. He explained that he had rescued from private claimants in behalf of the United States lands taking in the Cantonment Brooke, the falls of the Hillsborough, and the most important points on the shores of Tampa Bay in East Florida. The land was vital for naval and defensive purposes, and he estimated its worth in the millions. He added that there were twelve cases yet to be adjudicated and three other huge suits about to be entered that encompassed millions of acres in the peninsula. The value and importance of these lands to the United States, he argued, had induced the president to appoint him. As DuVal explained, his duties were to attend any court where suit against the United States was brought. He was obliged to take evidence everywhere throughout Florida, superintend all the testimony taken by the claimants, collect and record evidence, and argue cases on behalf of the United States. While the district attorney answered all petitions or bills, drew up pleadings, took the necessary steps in the suits, and placed them on the trial docket, he had to remain in his district and could "not attend elseware." DuVal reminded the committee that because the president had discontinued the assistant counsel position, he would be forced to take up even more of the duties.[13]

Meanwhile, back in Florida, the territory's once-prosperous cotton economy had all but collapsed. As newly appointed Judge Samuel Douglas reported to Secretary of State Daniel Webster, "the situation in this territory (especially the Middle District) is most distressing. It is now shingled over with Judgments: this county (Leon) is indebted to the amount of three millions. This arises from the extravagant habits of the people—Some years ago when cotton was high, and the facilities for procuring money from Banks great, almost all mortgaged their property in whole or in part; the money was procured and spent in luxury & extravagance & and thus entirely lost. Now banks themselves are ruened, and there can be no relief from that quarter, it seems to me their situation is almost hopeless." Douglas reported that since arriving in late November of the previous year he had been engaged in court from ten in the morning until ten at night. He had already disposed of two thousand cases and estimated that he would not finish until June.[14]

The economic desperation had created civil unrest. Recognizing an oft-noted characteristic of political affairs in Middle Florida, Douglas noted the people there had no "sittled political creed it is all faction. . . . When I first reached here I found much difficulty in conducting the business of court. From the delay in executing the Laws, society had become disorganized, and the best citizens were unable to withstand the threats of violence made by the offenders." The previous week Douglas had presided in the agonizing trial of Michael Ledwith, prosecuted as Willis Alston's accomplice in Leigh Read's murder. (The fact that Ledwith was William Wyatt's son-in-law made things even more politically volatile.) With Alston's flight to Texas, Read's friends, including his powerful father-in-law, John Branch, wanted Ledwith hanged. When Douglas sentenced Ledwith to death, Wyatt charged the judge with malfeasance and called for his impeachment. The grand jury defended the judge's behavior as beyond reproach and considered a true bill of indictment for libel against Wyatt. Then, only a week before Ledwith was to hang, Governor Call pardoned him, which brought forth a scathing attack from John Branch accusing the governor of pardoning Ledwith to prevent his implicating others close to the governor.[15]

Branch took his complaints to Washington, where he personally complained to President Tyler of Call's action. Acknowledging a letter that Call had written to DuVal a week earlier, DuVal wrote to Call that Branch had visited the president the previous day and had "made every effort to rouse the prejudices . . . against you." DuVal and Wickliffe followed the next day, and they had some further conversations with the president on the Ledwith case. "The President," wrote DuVal, "thought it would have been hasty to have your pardon arrested.... Mr. Wickliffe boldly contended you have acted properly and told the President he could himself have done no less."[16]

More important, DuVal began his letter to Call by bringing up the painful subject of his brother's continued feud with him and the awkward irony that his son Thomas was working in the same position that John DuVal had vacated. "My son will ever I trust prove his affection to me by his devotion to his duties and regard for you. I felt it my duty as his father to explain to him the cause of difference between my brother and yourself, and told him with truth that his uncle was wrong and that you have just cause of complaint for his conduct towards you. No man has lamented with more sincerity than I have, this difference but conscious of all the circumstances under which you have acted, a love of justice, truth, and friendship, has placed me among your defenders. I know you better than most of your friends and every passing year, has added to my esteem, and friendship for you."[17]

Florida's impending admission to the Union was also a subject of discussion in Washington, and DuVal offered his own appraisal. "I believe," he wrote, "that it is the decided interest of the People of Florida to come into the union with as little delay as possible." Florida was likely to prosper as a state. "The pressure of the times is an objection with many against our becoming a state, but I am not sure it may not in the end be beneficial to Florida. The salary and the expenses of government will be measured out with more economy, than would be done in a state of general prosperity. I am for a state Government as early as practicable, but I am well convinced that will not occur until Iowa seeks admission also. This she will certainly do at the next session of congress." DuVal then provided his thoughts on Levy. Of the delegate DuVal noted, "I felt it due to you to urge upon him the respect, and punctuality, due from the delegate, to the Executive—and he has promised to attend to this. I do not know what his correspondents may infuse into his mind against you, or who they are, but I have repeatedly warned him against the insidious and cunning acts & opinions of Westcott."[18]

DuVal then turned to his own situation. "It is true that Congress in their zeal for retrenchment has abolished, after the present year, the office of Land Agent but I am compelled to go to St. Augustine, when I leave this." Finally, DuVal complained to Call of his frustration with Congress over his unpaid claims against the federal government. "My own claims seem to deter the committee. There are so many papers that as yet I can not get them even to read them. The consolidation of Congress is not favorable to justice . . . the violent party feeling—all tend to delay, or deny justice to the creditors of the nation. The moment I can get some knowledge as when, & how, the committee will act, and report, on my claim, I shall leave here, and if this can not be known in a few days I will withdraw all papers & quit."[19]

DuVal tarried several more months in the Washington area. He visited Baltimore often and may have even taken the opportunity to visit Richmond. At his Capitol Hill boarding house DuVal dined with members of the Virginia delegation—the so-called Virginia Cabal. Henry Wise, Edmund Hubard, Thomas Gilmer, and R. M. T. Hunter were among that number, and they had much influence with Tyler. John Mason, a U.S. district judge, also kept company with this group and DuVal. The historian Craig Simpson has identified this group as "unofficial counselors with easy access" to Tyler. These "designing men" intended to reclaim the "Old Dominion's fading glory" by a rejuvenation of the Virginia Principles of 1798, formulated by James Madison and emphasizing state sovereignty. These were principles with which DuVal agreed wholeheartedly, and with which he naturally affiliated.[20]

Washingtonians, congressmen, and out-of-town visitors were particularly fond of the Marine Band concerts on the south portico of the White House that President Tyler hosted on summer evenings. One such occasion, on June 25, found DuVal and Captain Samuel Heintzelman paying their respects to the president on his portico.[21] As they had the year before, DuVal and Heintzelman saw one another continually. On July 12 the captain called on DuVal at his Capitol Hill boarding house and found him "at tea" with John C. Calhoun, Thomas Gilmer, and several other congressmen. Though the captain was welcomed wholeheartedly and introduced politely, the gathering ended abruptly because DuVal and the other gentlemen excused themselves to keep an appointment to see the president.[22]

DuVal finally left Washington in late July. Arriving in Charleston on August 1 on board the steam packet *Gov. Dudley* from Wilmington, DuVal eventually made his way south in another vessel to St. Augustine.[23] DuVal found a community of perhaps 1,800 to 2,000 souls, composed of fishermen, merchants, Minorcans, and, despite the winding down of the Second Seminole War, many soldiers. The most remarkable landmark in the town was the Castillo de San Marcos, renamed Fort Marion by the Americans. According to Captain Heintzelman the troops had added buildings onto the ramparts for quarters. One of the most popular pastimes on summer evenings was to stroll along the one-mile sea wall. Indeed, the "Ancient City" presented an attractive appearance. George Fairbanks, who clerked in Judge Isaac Bronson's court, wrote to his brother soon after arriving from New York that the town was "very compactly built, indeed it resembles Montreal more than any place I have ever seen." It had "the same narrow streets and stone houses—which are built of the coquina stone which is composed of

St. Augustine, Plaza ca. 1840s, painting by George Harvey. Trinity Parish Episcopal Church is on the right. Catholic Parish Church is on the left. Courtesy of National Archives.

shells." Fairbanks described his office in the Government House fronting the public square as very "pleasant and cheerful. . . . I am sitting with doors open and as comfortable as in our Summer months."[24]

Known for its parties and masquerades, St. Augustine had its share of eccentrics, probably the most notorious of whom was the brilliant but erratic Joseph Smith, still practicing law at the age of seventy-six. DuVal's old enemy was still known for his late-night binges. A year earlier Captain Heintzelman and many of his fellow officers had stayed up one night until long after midnight singing. As they were about to turn in, "Judge Smith came in & was as wild as any." Taking off his wig and exposing his bald head, he joined in the raucous celebration. "He is an extraordinary man for his age," Heintzelman observed, but it was "a great pity—he takes a drop too much."[25]

When William P. DuVal wrote to his friend Governor Call soon after he arrived in St. Augustine in early September, he was in no mood for celebration. He found little to cheer him. By that time he had probably learned that his son-in-law Dr. James Robinson had died, and he would have understood the further financial burdens this situation would entail. Unlike Fairbanks, DuVal found little in the community in St. Augustine that pleased him. "This community," he wrote to Call, is "split up into miserable little factions, so much so that among the little society here, that slender, & and cold formal intercourse is held." DuVal said that he had "lived like a hermit" since his arrival there. "I attend to my own business and seek companionship with none," as he had little in common with anyone. He took no interest in local affairs, choosing instead to lose himself in his work. In his broodings, DuVal, as never before, was tempted to see the worst in others. "I am no doubt as much changed as the world perhaps even more," he wrote, "but I declare to you the more I see of mankind the less, & less, I respect them. I now speak of the politicians, the demagogues, the little hair trigger intriguers, the flys that blow on the political carcass.... The great mass of the people are honest, and wish prosperity to our country, and if not misled by designing and selfish & unprincipled men they would seldom err in their actions or conduct. This it is feared, however, must continue to be the case, until education and knowledge is more universally defused among the People."[26]

Worse still, as he explained to Call, everything that had previously animated his existence seemed gone. Every day, as he explained to his old friend, he felt more and more "disposed to quit this Territory. The hour of gloom & melancholy often deeply shadow my mind & thoughts—When I look to Tallahassee and think of the days of life & joy that that once shed their happy influence around me, it is only by the contrast with the present that gives a darker view of my condition." DuVal's inner self called him to "*go home, return to your former haunts & seek friendship and affection where you once found it.* Alas, for what, to find the voices I used to love silent & the faces that gave it light are gone; to see in my chamber; in its ornaments & shrubbery that flourish and round & grace my house, at every turn, some memorial of the dead, while each well known object is a new source of grief; it may be a mingled feeling of the pure good and death, all combined with every scenes and object. The fairy spell is broken; and the sick sunshine of the heart is changed, its cold and starless night." As DuVal lamented to his old friend, he was no "longer interested in the affairs of men; [yet] with a few sterling hearts, I shall ever feel a deep and lasting affection, and if the poor and unavailing prays of so insignificant a being as I am, could weigh a feather, to increase their happiness, it would serve to gild the last glimmering of my life.... If I live I shall be in Tallahassee early in November as soon as the court is over."[27]

DuVal expressed similar sentiments to his friend Congressman Edmund Hubard, who represented his late father's district in Virginia. He was particularly bitter about not having his claims paid after waiting for the Senate committee for more than five months. "All my papers were lost (not one of which they had read)," he complained. He had waited an extra six weeks in Washington hoping to have his case heard, but the session concluded without "hearing one word on the subject." DuVal told Hubard he had neither the "inclination or the means to attend again to urge my claim, upon the Congress—I can not *beg* for that justice which under the constitution of my country is guaranteed to every White citizen—If such disregard is manifested by the dominant party in Congress to the solumn obligation they have refused to sustain the constitution—no effort of mine will avail—I thank the author of all good that he has blessed one with a spirit too proud to cater to men no better than myself, or to fawn and creep, in humble swooning to obtain what of *right* I demand. . . . I never will . . . forgive the manner I have been treated by the committee of the Senate—but we will let this pass with things that have vanished before the flood."[28]

DuVal concluded his letter to the congressman with information on his son-in-law's death. Dr. Robinson, he wrote, "ranked high for a young man in his profession, and was entering a busy life with the brightest prospects. He died in very humble circumstances and during the absence of his wife & family—my daughter and her little girl, and the Doct's mother were all very ill at Tallahassee a year since, and had not recovered their health in May last when I urged him to send them to Kentucky." They had all recovered, but the news of Robinson's death would be a "severe shock to my poor daughter, and his excellent mother. I must remove from this doomed land, as I shall see perhaps the last of my children carried to the grave." DuVal understood that his widowed daughter, child, and mother-in-law would come under his protection, but "this, so far as any trouble may fall on me I view as nothing. But declining in life, and poor as I am with only my profession to maintain them, which must fail with either sickness, or death, it renders me sad and unhappy." DuVal was contemplating moving them all to Kentucky and asked Hubard whether he had any good land in that state to sell him on credit of one, two, or three years. His son John was in Kentucky and could inspect it, assess its "quality and advantages, for health, pure water, and its convenience to Steam boat navigation." He spoke of leaving Florida in the spring with his sons and sons-in-law for Kentucky or Texas, where John Crittenden had been granted seven thousand acres. "I have no friends here," he explained. "Twenty years ago I had—but they are all dead or removed away—I am a stranger to the society here if any exists—worth knowing—I read write and think, too much I fear for my own peace—but in a few years it will be all the same to me, and it is some consolation even to know this."[29]

Despite his despondency DuVal set himself to work on the law cases pending in the Eastern Judicial District. He worked closely with Thomas Douglas. A veteran lawyer with a good reputation, Douglas had come to St. Augustine in 1826 upon his appointment by President John Quincy Adams as U.S. district attorney for the Eastern Judicial District of Florida. Few men possessed more knowledge of and experience with the intricacies of Spanish land grants. As well as preparing defenses against private claims, DuVal felt it his duty to advise federal officials on any number of issues he felt needed attention. He warned his friend Navy Secretary Upshur that much valuable live oak and other ship timber along the coast was at risk. "Parties are forming in the North," he wrote, "under the pretense of settling in this country & under the armed occupation law to take out permits for lands in order, to cut and ship off the live oak, and other valuable ship timber, and then abandon the lands." The area west of the Suwannee to the Gulf was practically uninhabited and had some of the best stands of live oak and red cedar in Florida. DuVal predicted that unless the federal government took some action the "best will be taken off before next March. . . . This information is of interest to the government and I feel it a duty to make you this communication," he wrote to Upshur.[30]

DuVal and Douglas worked arduously in the fall session of the St. Johns County Superior Court. Their goal was to wrap up the litigation as best they could, but, as Douglas explained to Charles Penrose in the Department of the Treasury seven days after the session ended on December 3, none of the cases was decided. This being the case, none of his and DuVal's duties would be lessened. "On the Contrary they will be materially increased during the ensuing year by a reference back from the Supreme Court of Seventeen Cases; Seven of them for dismission . . . so that the claims yet to be acted upon by the Court amount to between 700,000 & 800,000 acres. . . . As the lands in East Florida are about to be generally surveyed by the United States, it is exceedingly important, not only to the Claimants, *but to the Government* that *all* these vexed questions of boundary should be speedily & correctly settled." Thus, Douglas reasoned, his and DuVal's duties "instead of being at all diminished will be (as stated before) *very materially increased* during the coming year." He therefore asked the administration to reconsider its decision to discontinue the agency.[31]

DuVal also shared his views on the situation. Writing from Jacksonville, DuVal explained that he and Douglas had made every exertion to bring up the cases for trial and warmly contested the right of the parties after so much delay to continue the causes. But their objections were overruled because the court interpreted the affidavits as cause for continuance. "I regret this postponement," DuVal declared, "as I have devoted my time for several months in preparing myself to argue those cases which it is probable I shall never do, as my Agency in behalf of the United States will terminate with the present year." Like Douglas, DuVal made every effort to explain what the United States had at stake. He also shared the many complexities, intricacies, and obstacles standing in the way of a correct adjudication of the claims. DuVal insisted that the Spanish surveys did not conform to the grants and in many cases were at a great distance from them. Therefore the court would be obliged to order new surveys. "Many of the grants are so vague, and uncertain," he continued, that "it will be impossible to locate them." Many of the surveys undertaken under "Spanish rule in East Florida were manufactured in the chimney corner, nor did they ever go on the land to mark a corner or a line." A trusted agent of the United States, DuVal asserted, must oversee the work on the ground "and direct the . . . survey delineated on the plat, as he may deem proper, so that the court may be enabled to decree justly between the parties. . . . From my examination of many of the grants, & comparing them with surveys it is evident that the grantees have sought out the best lands without regard to the calls of the grants. If these surveys are admitted as valid, the parties of course may cull the finest lands in the Territory, without reference to their location according to their grants." Finally, DuVal observed, "If the law of the last session of congress repealing all the powers granted to the law Agent & district Attorney should remain unchanged it does not require much foresight to perceive that the interest of the United States in the soil of Florida will be sacrificed."[32]

Douglas and DuVal successfully won over Penrose on the need to continue the agency. After studying their reports, the officer wrote a long letter to President Tyler urging him to reauthorize the funding. Given the "minute knowledge which Gov. DuVal has of the Territory, and of the history of the outstanding claims, I feel it my duty to suggest whether the reestablishment of the office of Law Agent for these claims is not required by the true interests of the United States."[33] President Tyler authorized Penrose to forward DuVal's report to the chairman of the Committee on Public Lands in the House and requested that it authorize an appropriation for the law agency. The committee supported the authorization unanimously, but the session ended before a bill could be voted on. Penrose wrote to DuVal in March asking that DuVal continue his work without pay in the hope that the next Congress would compensate him. Penrose explained that he and the territorial delegate, Levy, pledged themselves to do what they could to urge Congress to pay him. Still, Penrose wrote, "I have no authority in the premises and can hold out no promise of Compensation—All that I can Say is that I deem your Services of great importance to the Government—And that I believe Congress will at the next Session provide a reasonable Compensation for those Services. In this opinion your Delegate as he will inform you Concurs—If in view of these Circumstances and upon this reliance for Compensation you can serve consistently with a proper regard for your private interests, continue your attention to these Cases I shall be greatly gratified. Please advise me of your determination in the matter at your earliest Convenience."[34]

Whether out of a sense of duty or because he had no other prospects at the moment, DuVal acquiesced. Writing from Tallahassee, DuVal declared, "I am well aware that you have no authority in the premises, but as my services are deemed important, I will take the risk of depending on the future action of Congress, who no doubt will do whatever is right and just from the interest of the United States. . . . Should Congress think proper to appropriate any thing for my services, they will no doubt take into consideration the delay, and expense I incur previous to their action." DuVal noted that once it became known that his work for the government had been terminated, numerous persons had approached him to argue their claims. "This I have declined doing for several reasons, but principally on account of my having acted for the United States heretofore, and in their service obtained a knowledge of the claims, which might be used to their injury. Obtaining all the information on one side as their Agent, I would prefer to continue in their Service—I cannot view it as compatible with the honor and dignity of my profession voluntarily to change sides in cases I have once managed, however liberal may be the offers to do so." DuVal wrote that he would travel immediately to St. Augustine and be ready for the June session of court.[35]

As DuVal continued his work on the land claims, efforts were under way to see that the $18,250 that the Middle District Court had awarded him would be paid. This time DuVal's friends in the legislative council took up the initiative in his behalf. As territorial secretary, Thomas DuVal performed his official duty, forwarding certified copies of resolutions passed by both houses and signed by Governor Call to Levy asking that his father be reimbursed for his services and advances laid out during the twelve years of his superintendence of Indian affairs in Florida. Levy and the chairmen of the House and Senate Committees on Claims received the resolution, which recognized "sacrifices made and losses sustained by" DuVal and expressed an "anxious desire that justice should be done him in the premises and his claim be no longer delayed."[36]

While this appeal made its way to Washington, DuVal labored arduously in St. Augustine while still keeping track of the recent midterm elections. In May he wrote to his friend Edmund Hubard congratulating him on his reelection to Congress. Much to DuVal's delight, Henry Wise was reelected, but unfortunately his friend R. M. T. Hunter lost at the polls. Even so, DuVal predicted that Hunter would return to Congress. Indeed, DuVal believed that Hunter "at no distant day" would eventually be a "great and shining light to all our nation." DuVal asked about his friend Gilmer and wondered aloud whether John Mason would again enter politics. DuVal then turned to the political situation in Florida. He recalled that in 1840 he had campaigned hard for the Whigs "(for which I hope God and my country will forgive me) and . . . by a large majority [they had] carried the Whig ticket." This year DuVal proudly declared that he had rectified the situation. Exulting in the Democratic triumph in Florida, DuVal proclaimed, "I have rode over much of this territory previous to the election and done all that was in my power to set up our people right, and now they will remain steady and firm." Levy, he reported, was "much gratified at the result."[37]

DuVal explained to Hubard that he had returned to his duties in East Florida with no guarantees that his services would be paid for but with every expectation that "Congress will do what may be right on the subject." If it did not, "it will not lessen the belief that my services were of benefit to the country." DuVal also updated the congressman on his efforts to have his other claims addressed by

Congress. The committee had lost the original paperwork submitted, including the depositions. With most of the witnesses dead, DuVal predicted that Levy would do all in his power to obtain justice for him but that if his claims were "ever paid it will come to my heirs—long after my death."[38]

Despite such fatalistic speculations DuVal plowed forward in his work. By that time he had decided to relocate permanently to St. Augustine. Indeed, with the Second Seminole War winding down, East Florida offered a fine prospect for prosperity. The Armed Occupation Act was luring settlers. Immigrants were arriving in Jacksonville and using the St. Johns to reach various locations on the river. Conversely, Middle Florida's economy had not yet recovered from bank failures, and the distractions of the yellow fever epidemic had all but sealed the fate of once-prosperous St. Joseph. As if to put an exclamation point on this gloomy picture, Florida's capital literally went up in smoke in late May. The blaze consumed the entire business district, including John DuVal's law office.[39] Indeed, with Nancy, Dr. Robinson, and many of his friends dead or gone and so many painful memories of the people and places he once knew, DuVal found that there was little left in Middle Florida to entice him to remain there. Abandoning his unfinished and unpaid-for house in Tallahassee, DuVal set out for St. Augustine.

Whether or not DuVal purchased or rented a house in St. Augustine is uncertain. Newspapers frequently mention DuVal's comings and goings in St. Augustine and note that he stayed at the Florida House when in town.[40] Writing to his friend George Burt, a St. Augustine merchant who was spending the summer in Vermont, DuVal noted that he would soon have his household furniture shipped from Port Leon to St. Augustine. DuVal complained of the summer heat and playfully juxtaposed his own situation against Burt's cool, delightful surroundings. "Several mornings I have waked at the first dawn of day feeling like a fat . . . duck stirring in his own gravy," he wrote. "I have more than once wished to be near a mountain spring gushing, like ice water, clear & refreshing over some mossy rock, glittering and humming its lively song through wooded glen giving life & beauty, and fragrance to flowers and shrubs but wake from this far off delight and find by contrast our bay boiling nearly red hot, the tide down, and the sun swarming over the sandy beach, like a mighty army of bumblebees." DuVal requested that Burt send down a lamp with wicks and tubes suitable for night reading and writing and two "can bottomed lounges—no sides to them, but turned up at each end only and ten pounds of superior *green tea*."[41]

DuVal and Thomas Douglas kept Washington updated on their progress on defending against the claims. Again, the hearings in the June session of the St. Johns Superior Court failed to reach a verdict. Three cases involving the heirs of Arredondo and covering more than 350,000 acres were continued. Reports forwarded to Washington listed seventeen cases yet to be disposed of. DuVal and Douglas found many of the same difficulties that Richard K. Call had experienced, especially the inability to obtain access to important documents in Havana. DuVal explained that the plaintiffs had prepared their pleadings on the basis of copies of documents that they had seen in Havana. The originals remained in Havana, and DuVal was convinced that the copies were forgeries. He explained that he was certain that roughly a decade ago, Call, despite being assisted by Spanish officials, had been unable to find these very same documents. DuVal and Douglas urged officials in Washington to have the U.S. consul in Havana investigate the matter. The stakes were substantial. As DuVal explained, several of the tracts included lands on the northern side of the Manatee River, "a bold & navigable river . . . which flows into Tampa Bay." Lands bounded by this grant were as "firtile as any land in Florida," and these, together with lands on the other side of the peninsula, would sell for not less than ten dollars an acre. "[B]etter sugar lands, or for the culture of tropical fruits & plants, is not to be found in our limits."[42]

In his work in the East Florida courts DuVal developed cordial relationships with Thomas Douglas, Judge Isaac Bronson, and his clerk, George Fairbanks. DuVal thought Bronson was "one of the best judges in the United States." Bronson, according to DuVal, was "more devoted to the duties of his station than any other judge I have ever known and his services greatly exceed his salary."[43]

Even as he labored on his court cases, DuVal kept in touch with friends in Washington and with national political affairs. Apprising his friend Virginia Congressman Henry Wise of Florida affairs, DuVal also spoke to national issues. "I can do but little to rouse up the people for the annexation of Texas, [the] Revenue Tariff, Oregan, and the admission of two states by dividing Florida . . . we are too poor to enter into the Union. If our territory was divided as it should be we can soon be in a condition to enter . . . at least East Florida would in a short time have the required population. It is settling up very fast." If both Floridas were admitted to the Union in time for the next election, DuVal predicted that Calhoun would be their first choice for president, with Tyler second. "If Mr. Calhoun is juggled by Van Buren, Mr. Tyler would carry the two states of Florida, should they be admitted, and they must be, if the two north western territories are brought into the Union. I would ride through every part of Florida, to aid in defeating Mr. Van Buren, if he is nominated by the convention. I would labour zealously for Mr. Tyler, or any man spoken of for the Presidency who has the best prospects to defeat the red-fox, even Cass—who I consider a poor apology for President, and am half inclined to believe—bad as I think of Clay—I would vote for him before that impudent, spoiled hound dog Van Buren."[44]

DuVal knew at that time that his friends Congressmen Henry Wise, Thomas Gilmer, Abel Upshur (who had replaced Webster as secretary of state), and Duff Green were secretly pushing to have Calhoun replace Tyler in the 1844 presidential sweepstakes. DuVal's friend R. M. T. Hunter, though temporarily out of office, was also assisting Calhoun by encouraging Postmaster General Charles

Wickliffe to use patronage to forward the South Carolinian's cause. At the time Calhoun was enjoying his "retirement" at his Fort Hill estate in the South Carolina piedmont. Tyler's scheme of annexing Texas was also enmeshed in the intrigue. Duff Green began to spread the rumor that Great Britain intended to annex Texas by offering interest-free loans to the Republic for the purpose of emancipating slaves. Britain's goal, he charged, was not only to block American expansion but also to foment discord between North and South with the hope of fostering secession and thus the destruction of the United States. As the historian Norma Lois Peterson has written, "Upshur, Green, Gilmer, Wise, and others of the so-called Tyler circle were resolved to add Texas to the Union by whatever means necessary, and they wanted the next president to be John C. Calhoun, who had resigned from the Senate in the Spring of 1843 to prepare for the campaign. To achieve their ends they played 'fast and loose' with Tyler, who naively was unaware of what was happening. Secretly, his 'trusted and confidential advisers' were keeping Calhoun informed of everything that was going on in the Tyler administration."[45]

Throughout the remainder of the year Tyler instructed Secretary of State Abel Upshur to continue back-channel discussions with Texas officials regarding annexation. The offer to pay Texas's bonded debt at par sweetened the deal. Secret talks with Britain over Oregon also moved forward. Tyler was soon ready to submit an annexation treaty to the Senate. Then, on February 28, tragedy struck during a lavish celebration on board the new U.S. gunboat *Princeton*. On board for the excursion were several hundred partygoers, including President Tyler, Upshur, and Thomas Gilmer (the president's new secretary of the navy). Numerous congressmen, military officers, and diplomats, along with their wives, were also on the craft. After a morning's ride up and down the Potomac, one last ceremonial firing of the gun was called for. This time the huge gun's breech burst, sending iron fragments flying like shrapnel skyward and in all directions. Pandemonium ensued, and when the smoke cleared Upshur, Gilmer, and five others lay dead.[46] As the wounded were slowly offloaded from the *Princeton* and official Washington mourned the dead, many speculated on the future. What would become of the Texas treaty? Who would succeed Upshur at the State Department? Southerners both in and out of the Tyler administration were convinced that that man had to be John C. Calhoun. Indeed, DuVal's friend Henry Wise declared that Calhoun was "the one man left who was necessary above all others to the South in settling and obtaining the annexation of Texas."[47] And so it was done. Tyler submitted Calhoun's name to the Senate, and the South Carolinian was confirmed unanimously. Also, DuVal's friend John Mason succeeded Gilmer as navy secretary.

When DuVal heard of the *Princeton* tragedy, he would have grieved at the news of Upshur's and Gilmer's death, but he would have rejoiced at his old mentor's selection as secretary of state. He would also have thought of what it might mean for him. Even better, with Calhoun a likely candidate to succeed Tyler, DuVal's political prospects brightened. What would the next few years bring? Would Florida indeed be admitted to the Union soon? If so, would Florida come in as DuVal and his friends in East Florida hoped—as two states? If so, DuVal perhaps would be considered Florida's elder statesman—and be selected by East Florida's state legislature as one of its first senators; election as its member of the House of Representatives might also be in the offing. Time would tell.

CHAPTER 18

State of Texas—State of Florida

By the time John C. Calhoun arrived in Washington on March 29, 1844, to take up his duties as secretary of state, the broad outlines of an annexation treaty between the Republic of Texas and the United States had already been formulated. One of Calhoun's first actions after familiarizing himself as much as he could with the status of the Texas negotiations was to put Britain on notice that he interpreted its meddling in Texas affairs as a threat to the United States. Britain was the leader of the world abolition movement, and its designs on Texas were calculated to block the cotton South's expansion. Moreover, as Calhoun understood it, Britain's intervention in Texas was its current method of sowing discord between the North and the South. In a lengthy communication to the British minister Richard Pakenham, Calhoun charged that Britain's scheme of abolishing slavery in Texas aimed to destroy the American economy for its own benefit. Given this hostile intent, the United States had no choice but to annex Texas. But Calhoun's communication did not stop there. He also went on to characterize slavery as a "positive good" and essential to America's domestic and economic security as well as its future as an independent nation. The "Pakenham Letter" was subsequently leaked to the press and inspired much comment. Predictably, a backlash erupted among antislavery forces in the United States. Despite Tyler's efforts to cast the annexation of Texas as a "national" and not a "sectional" priority, most chose to understand it otherwise.[1]

On April 22 Calhoun submitted the annexation treaty along with accompanying documents to the Senate for ratification. Almost immediately Northern politicians and the press voiced strong opposition. Most outspoken were Senator Benjamin Tappen of Ohio (who was suspected of leaking the Pakenham Letter to the press), and House members Joshua Giddings and John Quincy Adams. At that moment Van Buren was biding his time, anticipating another run at the White House. After careful consideration, he came out against the treaty. Henry Clay, the Whig nominee for president, also opposed the treaty. Then, on May 29, in Baltimore, the Democrats rejected Van Buren and nominated James K. Polk, a strong supporter of annexation, for president. Just as the campaign between Polk and Clay was heating up, the Senate rejected Texas annexation by a vote of 16–35 on June 8.[2]

Among those who saw the annexation of Texas as essential to America's economic and domestic security was William P. DuVal. His correspondence with friends and associates in Florida, Washington, and other parts of the Union trumpeted Calhoun's contention that Southern rights and the integrity of the Union itself rested on the acquisition of Texas. Before the crucial vote on the treaty and only weeks before the Democratic convention, DuVal wrote continually to the South Carolinian on annexation, as he did on other matters he felt important. On May 20, writing from St. Augustine, DuVal addressed Calhoun as "one of your long tried and unwavering friends." DuVal congratulated Calhoun on his letter to Pakenham and added that it would "sustain your high character and proves that a few patriots are yet to be found among our statesmen." Clay and Van Buren are "fit companions, either would sink half the States to become President of the nation."[3]

As old War Hawks, DuVal and Calhoun viewed the current conflict between the United States and Britain similarly. Britain was using the false philanthropy of abolitionism as a way to thwart American expansion and prosperity. As it had in 1812 and again with its machinations in Florida in the subsequent decade, Britain was plotting to choke off American advancement. It was also using slavery as a way to stir discord among sections of the country. Britain's imperial designs had to be confronted immediately. Oregon and Texas must be occupied, DuVal asserted. They would be the best "safety-valves, to prevent the explosion of the Union. Oregon will make three free states—and Texas as many, the latter having the most fertile soil—thus keeping up the proper balance between the States. If we are so madly wicked, as to exclude Texas, and thus throw her into the arms of England, she will soon bring us to witness our consummate folly." DuVal then offered up a vision of the apocalypse: Britain's emissaries "will combine [with] the Indians tribes, on our western borders, against us—and Missouri, Arkansas, and Louisiana, will be covered with the blood of our people. What man of common mind can doubt this? In this event, will not the slaves of those States unite with the savages in spreading death and conflagration to the banks of the father of waters? Yet controlling Texas she will flood the great valley of the Mississippi with goods—through the red river, & other channels. What then becomes of our revenue? What then will be the fate of our petted manufactures? As a nation we are older in folly than any other in existence, and younger in wisdom, than the least enlightened of the sister republics."[4]

All those who opposed the annexation of Texas were either dupes or conspirators of the evil British Empire. DuVal particularly condemned Francis Blair, editor of the Washington *Globe,* for his opposition to Calhoun's statesman-like stance. Of Blair DuVal wrote to Calhoun that he was "only shewing his cloven foot which he has cunningly put 'into' a *boot* since he became a *Jackson man.* The nation will do you justice, such a corrupt creature as Blair, cannot tarnish your fame. He is like a child, crying to pull down a star." DuVal warned that a "combination of the leaders of both great parties is now formed to destroy the administration—and the *prosperity of our country.* I yet believe that the Texas treaty and the action of the Senate on it, will result in as signal a revolution in public opinion as occurred in 1800. The voice of the people is now rising, and those who have given up their country's banner for the British flag, will have little, honor by the exchange. The light of wisdom is shining on your path and it will lead you, Mr. John Tyler and the nation to Glory. I well know the steady firmness of the President, his purity and love of country. I know too the energetic power of your mind & principles—the iron nerve that braces your determination, never to yield under the most trying circumstances, those principles to secure the union & prosperity of your country. You are engaged in a mighty struggle which must soon result either in triumph over British influence, and the honor of the union—or the treacherous & mortifying disgrace to the nation. The people are coming to the resque & and like a mighty wave, will wash the decks of our national ship clear, of the virmin that now defiles her."[5]

Meanwhile, DuVal served as Calhoun's best source of information on all matters involving Florida. He offered his thoughts, prejudices, and personal observations to the secretary of state. He embroiled himself in a dispute between Governor Call and District Attorney Charles Sibley in which the latter had prosecuted the governor for unlawfully blocking the St. Mark River after a hurricane had blown down the railroad trestle. Sibley held Call, as president of the railroad company, personally liable for blocking the river. Call countered that Sibley was using his office to benefit himself. DuVal took Call's side in the matter. DuVal favored Call's reappointment as governor but accepted the fact that Tyler did not like him and thus urged Calhoun to use his influence to have James Gadsden appointed. Also spoken of for the post was William Brockenbrough, DuVal's former law partner—a man DuVal had grown to despise. "He was my partner in the practice of law for somewhat more than a year. I found him the most selfish and avaricious man I ever knew. He will hate a man who confers signal favour on him and you could as soon, obtain the gratitude of a cat, as his—cold, cautious & selfish, he is incapable of friendship or noble feeling. I am somewhat of a judge of men," he wrote Calhoun, "and depend on it I am not mistaken in this man's temper feeling & character."[6]

While DuVal offered his opinions to Calhoun and others on territorial and national affairs, he also strove with East Florida leaders to sever the district from the territory. Thus, on March 27, 1844, DuVal joined Thomas Douglas, B. A. Putnam, James M. Gould, William Simmons, George Fairbanks, William A. Forward, and other leaders at a public meeting at the St. Johns County Court House in calling for the division of the territory. Florida, the gathering resolved, should be admitted to the Union as two states. Several months earlier, Florida's legislative council had adopted such a resolution. In a "forcible and eloquent" address DuVal "presented the great advantages that will result from a division of the Territory, both from a general and local point of view." Resolutions cited the rapid advance in population in the upper Mississippi River valley and the likelihood that Iowa and Wisconsin would soon be ready for admission. The speakers also recounted the long-standing differences between the interests of those living east of the Suwannee and those living west of it as a cause for division. The past twenty-five years had shown an "irreconcilable dissimilarity in the circumstances and pursuits of the people" in the east of the territory and those of people in the west such that there was no "real community of feeling and interest to make such a connection desirable or expedient." The gathering concluded with the order that 250 copies of the proceedings of the meeting be distributed to newspapers and sent to the president, to the speaker of the House, to the president of the Senate, and to Florida's delegate to Congress.[7]

By August 1844 Tyler had selected John Branch as Florida's territorial governor in place of Call. It was clear long before that Call had favored the Whigs over the Democrats, and the former governor made no secret of his support for Clay over Polk in the upcoming presidential election.[8] The month before, DuVal had joined other Democrats assembled in Palatka to nominate candidates. Elected president of the body, DuVal was determined to arouse his fellow Democrats to the danger Great Britain posed to the United States.[9] And Texas was the vehicle through which Britain conspired to block and eventually enslave America. DuVal's remarks to the delegates have not survived, but his fiery oratory likely resembled the overheated rhetoric of his letter written to Calhoun on the Fourth of July. In that missive DuVal attributed the Senate's recent rejection of the treaty to the work of "unprincipled leaders" who were the "minions of England. . . . Nothing short of war with England, will put down the native traitors of this nation—trade, commerce, and speculation, have corrupted our cities—they have extended their baneful influence deep & wide, thro' the land." Only another war with Britain would stop "her interference in American affairs," which "ought and should be arrested at all hazard." Britain's influence was rapidly advancing in Congress and "increasingly throughout the Union. . . . We have the option to become vassals of Great Britain, or we can rally the people and overthrow her influence, and expose our secret enemies, and traitors to the odium of public opinion."¹⁰

In words reminiscent of statesmen in the late nineteenth and early twentieth centuries, DuVal asserted that war would cleanse the United States of its evils. "War at all times is an evil," he explained, "but it is a necessary one for us. The cankers of a long war are often felt, even after years of succeeding peace. The cankers of a long peace are more dangerous, because they strike at the vital principle on which freedom, and patriotism is based. The scars & bruises of war, are on the surface," he continued, "the plotting intrigues, and silent workings of unprincipled men, in days of peace, when the public mind, is slumbering in security." These "are the moments, when the unwatched enemies, the demons of our land, fasten on the wings of liberty, producing inward decay—never manifested, until disease & corruption had struck deep into the heart of the constitution. War is necessary to unite and save our country, no sacrifice is too great to accomplish this end."¹¹

Not long after the Palatka convention's conclusion, DuVal prepared to travel to Washington. Throughout the entire month of June DuVal and Thomas Douglas had labored mightily in defending the United States against one of its biggest claimants of land. In three separate cases, the heirs of the Arredondo tract had sued to confirm claims for lands totaling nearly 360,000 acres in East Florida. The largest of the three suits, involving 256,000 acres, was pressed by Moses Elias Levy, the territorial delegate's father. For the moment at least DuVal and Douglas had succeeded in fending off the suits. DuVal proudly asserted that the claimants were unable to prove evidence of title and had decided not to pursue the cases at that time. "I have no fear," he wrote to the Department of the Treasury, "that the complainants can ever succeed in establishing their tittle to lands claimed by the Heirs of the Arredondos. These three large claims, [will give the United States] now, disposed of, some of the finest lands in the Territory. And if surveyed & brought into market, will command a fair price." In his report DuVal listed seven other cases: one confirmed, one under advisement, and five continued.¹²

Thomas Douglas also wrote to Washington to remind treasury officials that the rigors of the one-month trial had required "much labour and responsibility" on his and DuVal's part. Douglas reminded the official that Congress had failed to appropriate funds to pay their expenses for defending the claims and asked for clarification as to where the matter stood. The official forwarded Douglas's claims to the secretary of the treasury and added that "the services of Gov. DuVal were deemed of great importance to the U. States; and that the Solicitor entertained a Strong Confidence that Congress would make a Special appropriation to Compensate Him." Yet at the moment no compensation had been made. When DuVal boarded a vessel in St. Augustine for Washington, he had every expectation that he would be paid. John Tyler had just appointed his old friend George Bibb secretary of the treasury.¹³

As DuVal made his way north, the conflict between Governor Call and District Attorney Charles S. Sibley reached a conclusion as Call's term as governor came to an end. Indeed, DuVal's son Thomas (still serving as territorial secretary) was presiding as "acting governor" in the place of John Branch (who was in Washington) when Calhoun concluded that Call's charges against Sibley were groundless. The affair is interesting because it demonstrated the factions that had developed in Florida politics. Nearly alone in his support of Call was DuVal. On the other side of the ledger, writing to Calhoun in support of Sibley was DuVal's son Thomas and, not unexpectedly, DuVal's brother John P. DuVal. Also defending Sibley were James D. Westcott, Thomas Baltzell, Joseph Branch, Charles DuPont, William Brockenbrough, David Levy, and Judge Samuel Douglas.[14]

While DuVal sailed north he may have thought of Nancy, his sons Thomas and John Crittenden, and his daughters—especially his responsibilities toward them. DuVal's widowed daughter Mary Robinson; her mother-in-law, Maria Robinson; and probably eighteen-year-old Florida DuVal still lived in Tallahassee. They would soon join him in St. Augustine. About that time, DuVal's well-to-do son-in-law Dr. Arthur Moray Randolph contracted tuberculosis but recovered enough to pursue surveying. DuVal helped Randolph secure a federal appointment in East Florida, and he and Laura moved to St. Augustine in March 1844.[15] After the Department of the Treasury discontinued the port collectors' post in St. Joseph, Marcia DuVal Price relocated with her husband, Dr. William Price, to Galveston, Texas. John Crittenden was already in Texas, and his brother Thomas was also making plans to move there. Several months earlier DuVal himself had confided to Calhoun that he intended to migrate to Texas—that is, until the annexation treaty was defeated. DuVal had written that he "would have been gratified to have gone there as Charge d'Affaires, but I never asked for the office, as that sort of solicitation is repulsive to my pride & principles." Even so, DuVal added that his personal acquaintance with Texas citizens and "the services of two gallant sons in defense of her cause—one of whom was murdered by Santa Anna in cold blood—my popular manners, and the facility of becoming acquainted with men, give me decided advantage over most men."[16] For now, however, relocation would have to wait.

While in Washington DuVal pursued his own personal claims, renewed political acquaintances, and represented a number of clients, among whom was his old friend John Lee Williams from Picolata.[17] Congress was not in session, but DuVal could have visited Tyler, Calhoun, Bibb, and other members of the executive branch. John Branch was also in Washington, and DuVal may have congratulated him on his appointment as governor. One familiar face he did not see was his old friend Samuel Southard. The former New Jersey senator and navy secretary had died in 1842 and was buried in the Congressional Cemetery.[18] By that fall the campaigning between Clay and Polk had reached a fever pitch. Whether

DuVal campaigned actively for Polk is unknown, but he no doubt spoke for the Tennessean and the annexation of Texas every opportunity he got.

As DuVal returned to St. Augustine, most white male Americans who lived in states and not territories cast their votes for either James K. Polk or Henry Clay. When the counting was concluded, Polk had squeaked by with a narrow victory. Clay's equivocating on Texas, most assumed, had cost him the election. Also costing Clay was the candidacy of John Birney, a former slaveholder from Alabama who was running on the ticket of the Liberty Party, a party openly favoring abolitionism. Birney's votes in New York and Michigan probably contributed to Clay's loss. DuVal could take grim satisfaction that his old nemesis had been defeated a third time for the presidency, but the fact that Polk might have owed his election to abolitionists and newly enfranchised foreign voters would have given him pause.[19]

DuVal stepped off the boat in St. Augustine on November 12 and immediately began assessing his domestic and political circumstances.[20] Living close to his daughter Laura Randolph and his widowed daughter, Mary, and her mother-in-law, Maria Robinson, DuVal pursued his law practice but also kept abreast of political doings in East Florida. Although the Democrats had clearly prevailed at the national level with Polk's election, everyone understood that balloting in Florida was likely to commence subsequent to Florida's admission to the Union—and that admission was likely to occur in the next legislative session. DuVal began making the rounds at various Democratic functions in East Florida. He knew that Levy's star was rising and acquiesced in the fact. On December 3 he attended a barbecue for Levy in St. Augustine. According to one account of the proceedings, DuVal "made a very complimentary speech in his peculiar style" in favor of Levy's "untiring industry and attention to business" in the previous legislative session, and another participant offered a toast to "Gov. DuVal our old friend. We love him for his generous heart and noble bearing."[21]

As predicted, events moved rapidly toward both the admission of Florida into the Union and the annexation of Texas. By that time the prospect of Florida entering the Union as two states was still alive, but it was fading fast. The House Committee on the Territories even reported out a bill calling for admission of the two territories, but DuVal and his friends were disappointed when the final version of the bill passed both houses of Congress without the division. The annexation of Texas also proceeded with dispatch. Interpreting Polk's election as a mandate for the annexation of Texas, Tyler's supporters in Congress arranged to have Texas annexed by a joint resolution of Congress. On March 3 Tyler sent the resolutions to Texas, the same day he signed the Florida and Iowa admissions bill. Fifteen days later Governor Branch called for elections for members of the state legislature and other officials to be held on May 26.[22]

With Branch's proclamation Democrats and Whigs moved mightily to achieve victory at the polls and thus take control of the new state. That April DuVal did his part. As he explained to his friend Senator Robert J. Walker of Mississippi (who had just resigned to become Polk's secretary of the treasury), he had "just returned from a trip of eight days in the country where I have been organizing our friends." DuVal had addressed voters in Duval County and in the subsequent days would speak to others at courts in Levy, Marion, Benton, Alachua, and Columbia Counties. He was confident of a Democratic victory and confided to Walker the scheme of electing Levy to the House and then selecting him as senator once the Democrats took the General Assembly. Levy, he said, would do "good & efficient service . . . in support for our virtuous and patriotic administration." DuVal's talents for inspiring rhetoric were brought to their full effect on several occasions that month. On April 5, for example, DuVal addressed a Democratic gathering at Garey's Ferry after a militia muster. After the day's events, soldiers and other voters were brought into a room prepared for political speechifying. According to "A DEMOCRAT," a correspondent to a St. Augustine newspaper, DuVal addressed the gathering in his "usual eloquent, happy style, and in a very plain, full, and satisfactory manner." DuVal explained the party's principles "to the entire satisfaction of every Democrat present, and to the confusion of our political opponents. While he was speaking so great was the attention that prevailed, you might almost have heard a pin fall: But when he brought this . . . meeting to a close, the applause was indeed deafening. May he long live to honor and be honored by his country men," the observer concluded.[23]

Despite his work for the party, DuVal coyly sat out the April Democratic convention in Madison. Did he expect at the last minute to be drafted for a run for the House? Or might he be considered for the Senate? With Levy clearly a certainty for one of the Senate seats, the choice for the other one seemed to be between DuVal and James Westcott. DuVal had his supporters. In a lengthy biographical sketch of DuVal, "An Old Planter" made a strong case for DuVal's selection as one of Florida's two senators in the columns of the Tallahassee *Star*. "Shall we, the freemen of Florida, neglect and abandon this old and faithful servant? God forbid this sin of ingratitude! Let us manifest to the Government and our Country, our unshaken confidence in his talents, integrity, and patriotic devotion to Florida, by bestowing upon him the highest office in the gift of a Free and Sovereign State—that of Senator in the Congress of the United States." Thus the Democratic papers in Tallahassee, the *Floridian* (for Westcott) and the *Star* (for DuVal), battled over this issue. The Tallahassee *Star* accused Westcott of "political juggling in Madison" and further charged that the *Floridian* had succumbed to his personal ambition and control of the Democratic Party.[24]

For the moment at least, DuVal could only watch from the sidelines as Westcott took control of the Madison convention. As one commentator put it, "a better scheme for perpetuating the Westcott dynasty could never have been devised" for carrying out "the projects of the Tallahassee Locofoco unit." Westcott's men, the observer noted, were "keen as hungry wolves" and would "howl down opposition."[25]

As David Levy had played the crucial role in Florida's admission to the Union, he also ensured that the new state of Florida would fall into the Democratic column. Levy carefully worked both in Congress and in East Florida, where he knew that latent opposition to statehood without division lingered. After the Whigs prevailed on Call to run for governor of the new state, Levy worked tirelessly to ensure the election of a Democrat for the first office. Most important, Levy desired a Democratic majority in the state legislature because he knew that was his ticket to the U.S. Senate.[26] The Whigs were clearly outgunned, and they knew it. One newspaper even resurrected DuVal's antistatehood remarks back in 1841 to try to convince voters that the election of Call as governor and of a Whig general assembly was the only way to block Levy's path to the Senate. They circulated DuVal's 1841 address to the Florida Senate as a broadside titled "Expenses of State Government," but the ploy failed, and the scheme must have embarrassed DuVal.[27]

In the subsequent balloting William D. Moseley prevailed as governor and Democrats took both houses of the state legislature. When the General Assembly first met in June, four Democrats—Walker Anderson, Branch, Levy, and James D. Westcott—aspired to the two Senate seats. DuVal's name still circulated as a possible selection. On June 13 the Tallahassee *Star* identified DuVal, Anderson, William Brockenbrough, and Westcott as the likely candidates. (Levy, who had won the race for the House, was not mentioned.)

DuVal provided John C. Calhoun with an appraisal of the recent elections in which he proudly asserted the "signal overthrow of the Whig party in Florida. I took the field and hope I rendered . . . aid in securing the democratic victory. . . . My friend Mr. Levy will be one of our senators to congress where I hope you will once more take your stand in defense of southern rights and principles." DuVal explained that he could have joined Levy in the Senate if "I had sought the station in the manner & way too often resorted to by politicians. I cannot electioneer for myself, although, I am, not backward in the service of men whose conduct and principles are in accordance with the democratic doctrines of 1798. I am a candidate for no office, and in my public speeches said so to the people, and am now convinced, my disinterested support had influence with the voters." As for himself, DuVal told Calhoun that, despite his friends' urgings, he would not go to Tallahassee while the legislature was sitting. "If that body believes that any other gentleman of our party will be more serviceable to our State—they should elect him. I will under no circumstances blow my own trumpet, and shall be content to act in the service of our cause, with all the energy and limited influence I can possess. I am so much gratified at the success of our principles in this State and conscious that Florida will never desert you or your doctrines, that personally I care little for myself."[28]

The day after he wrote these words, probably with no sense of irony, DuVal joined St. Augustine mayor E. B. Gould, Judge Isaac Bronson, George Fairbanks, Thomas Douglas, Joseph Hernandez, Joseph Sanchez, and other community leaders at a meeting memorializing the death of Andrew Jackson.[29] As he participated in this solemn ceremony, would DuVal have thought of his first days as territorial governor succeeding Old Hickory and of those warm visits to the Hermitage? Would his memory have flowed back to the election of 1824, his campaigning for Jackson in Kentucky, and then his witnessing his counting out in the House of Representatives? Would he have pondered Jackson's triumphal election in 1828 and his subsequent falling out with his friend Calhoun? Would he have bitterly recalled Van Buren's influence with the old General and his eventual elevation to the White House? For the moment at least DuVal could take satisfaction in the fact that it appeared that Van Buren's influence in the Democratic Party was diminished, if not at an end. For DuVal, commemoration of Jackson's career did not necessitate opening any old wounds. Yet, as he understood it, Calhoun was the statesman of the age—the man whom all Southerners expected to protect their interests. At the moment Calhoun was in retirement at Fort Hill. But the South Carolina legislature would soon return him to the U.S. Senate.

If DuVal refused to go to Tallahassee, Westcott already lived there. According to his enemies—among whom DuVal counted himself—Westcott took up residence in the halls of the General Assembly. According to one observer, "It is amusing to watch Mr. Westcott's maneuvers in the field of politics and observe, notwithstanding a great show of disinterestedness, how skillfully he turns every thing to his advantage." Westcott, the observer continued, has an "eye to the Senate . . . as well as an eye to the interest of his party." He fought for Levy, for his party; "he cares nothing for the spoils, but like a gallant now leaves them for the mercenaries who follow in his wake. But now the victory is won, the scene is changed and Mr. Westcott's disinterestedness gone; he can no longer resist the temptation of preferment, and the things which he once affected to despise he now covets." Levy, according to another witness, was but "one of the puppets in his hands and one of the creatures of his power."[30]

Writing from Palatka, DuVal confided to John C. Calhoun that "disgusting scenes have occurred at our seat of Government." Westcott, "the most unprincipled man in Florida," had secretly organized a faction to defeat Mr. Levy's election to the Senate. Failing in this, he had "the cunning" to prevail on Levy's backers to support him. Such a ploy was a "disgrace to the Senate of the United States." Westcott "came out last winter as soon as he saw Mr. Van Buren's letter against the annexation of Texas. He was sent to the state by Van Buren and he will carry out his wishes." Once he found that Floridians opposed Van Buren and favored Texas annexation and Calhoun, he changed his tune. He then induced "certain men who are utterly without principle, but cunning rascals like himself, to offer for the legislature in many of the counties pledged to go for him against Mr. Levy." The scheme succeeded, as Levy's supporters were forced to vote for Westcott also or have their own man go down to defeat. "This bribery and corruption succeeded in making" him a senator.[31]

Westcott's next move, DuVal explained to Calhoun, was to have "his gang nominate Brockenbrough who is no more your friend than Westcott. They will exert themselves to entrap, and break down Mr. Levy." Westcott and Brockenbrough (if elected) would join the Northern Democrats; Levy would be for the South. DuVal warned Calhoun that if he returned to the Senate he should not trust them and should be "guarded in what you utter before them. Westcott will endeavor to worm himself into your confidence and betray you. This is his usual game, and the more he avers he is your friend then rest assured he intends to play the spy & hippocrite. I have heard this man by the half hour describe the various tricks and deceptions he has practiced and boast of the artful lies—that he has propagated in order to accomplish his objects. When told in public company of some infamous act he has committed and denounced as a rogue & rascal I have heard him say to his accuser, 'That is nothing new, if you will go to the business part of our town you can find fifty men who will prove your charge.'" DuVal once again reminded Calhoun that he was not a candidate for the Senate even though many of his friends had urged him to throw his hat into the ring. He thought his entry in the race might harm Levy's chances. Such "disgraceful proceedings stain our character. I will either go to Texas this fall or settle in Tallahassee to kill off rascals."[32]

In a lengthy postscript to his letter to Calhoun, DuVal noted that "if I determine to settle in Tallahassee, I will organize the best and ablest of the Democratic Party that will sustain southern interests. And if I live at another congressional election, a man, worthy of the confidence of your friends will represent us in congress. I will as certainly down Westcott and his junto as I live." DuVal doubted Levy's capacity to protect himself from Westcott's intrigues. Westcott's minions were already "setting the people against him—by saying he played them false by pretending he would serve them, as their representative when he knew he would not as he would go into the Senate and then hold another election—and I tell you this slang is having its effect. You shall hear from me," he promised Calhoun, "as soon as I decide where I shall locate myself. The temptation is on me, strongly, to remain at Tallahassee & If I do you shall in time, know the course I shall pursue."[33]

There was no question that Westcott understood DuVal's animus against him. It was also no secret that DuVal opposed his old law partner's candidacy. Westcott was not silent on both counts. In a startling letter to Levy about that time, Westcott complained to Levy that:

> Gov. DuVal is doing his best to excite Eastern sectional feeling against Brockenbrough and to get up another candidate. Read the article signed

'Franklin' in the St. Augustine *Herald*—it has his ear mark.... His course in politics national and local show him to be one of the most depraved political harlots that ever disgraced any party. He was in 1816 a U.S. Bank man ... as Governor he vetoed all the Territorial Bank charters till 1833 when he approved the Union Bank ... the most abominable of them all ... he ... lauded it as the very paragon of bank charters ... he went for John Q. Adams in 1824, 5, 6, 7, & 8 then for Gen. Jackson ... he tried to satisfy Jackson, Van Buren & Calhoun all three of them ... that he was his ... devoted friend. In 1840 he denounced Van Buren and returning to Florida ... sold himself to the Union Bank for money & ran as one of its candidates for the Territorial Senate and stumped ... this district for Harrison ... the old prostitute raised money from ... candidates for office in 1841 to go to Washington and secure their appointments, which he has never repaid ... so too the Union Bank paid him for attending to her interests.³⁴

Westcott's diatribe against DuVal's various political stands failed to take into account his long political career, during which he had been forced to alter his stances in light of changing circumstances. Yet most of DuVal's political principles had remained constant: (1) his devotion to the Principles of '98; (2) his belief that slavery was the social and economic foundation of the South, which had to be protected at all costs, and, finally; (3) his belief that Britain still presented the greatest threat to U.S. security. Thus, by 1845 DuVal was clearly among the ranks of extreme states'-rights Southerners.

The Whigs nominated the Virginian Edward C. Cabell of Jefferson County for Florida's lone House seat. (Cabell had run and lost to Levy in the original election.) One source predicted that the Democrats would "pitch upon" Cabell's "shoulders ... that 'horrid critter,' the Union Bank, and he must be a strong nag, who can carry all that and make a fast race."³⁵ Despite DuVal's prediction of an easy victory for Brockenbrough, the race was very close. In fact, the final count gave Cabell a narrow victory, and he joined Westcott and Levy as Florida's first delegation to the U.S. Congress. As DuVal himself reported to a friend on November 25, "Brockenbrough yet pretends and perhaps may really think he is elected to Congress but up to this time, the returns are against him, and Cabell has received from the Governor his Certificate of Election and has gone to Washington. Mr. B. I am told has given him notice he will contest for the seat." Brockenbrough did indeed contest the election, traveling personally to Washington to make his case. In the week-long debates in the House of Representatives, both men presented their cases. Brockenbrough eventually prevailed on January 24, 1846.³⁶

As he kept up with the political happenings in Tallahassee, DuVal also attended to his law practice. By that time he and Thomas Douglas had decided, despite possible charges of a conflict of interest, to do legal work for Moses Levy in his never-ending quest to have his land claims confirmed. They certainly had the knowledge necessary to undertake the task. When Douglas took sick, DuVal took on the lion's share of the work. In a subsequent dispute over DuVal's payment the senator's father claimed that "governor DuVal charged too much and estimated his services too highly." A formal contract for DuVal's services was never drawn up. When Levy refused to pay him, DuVal sued. Douglas testified in DuVal's behalf, claiming that, while DuVal spent many days and nights working on the case, he was not in a position to know the precise value of his services. Douglas observed that DuVal's work on the case had nearly broken his health. DuVal, he declared, looked "more fatigued, harassed, and care worn, more so than I ever saw him on any other occasions." Douglas argued that DuVal was deserving of payment, but it is unlikely that he ever saw a cent for his labor, as Levy had no money to pay him. Levy's legal battles continued until 1849, when the courts finally confirmed his claims. Meanwhile, it is likely that Levy considered DuVal one among the many "Insatiable Lawyers" he often complained about.[37]

Despite his labors in the law, politics was never far from DuVal's thoughts or his actions. As he did with Calhoun, DuVal wrote numerous missives to the new administration offering advice on appointments and other issues. President Polk acknowledged this advice in a letter to DuVal in which he apologized for not being able to answer DuVal's "several letters. . . . The truth is my time is so constantly occupied," Polk wrote DuVal, "that I have been compelled to neglect almost entirely my correspondence with my friends. . . . I hope My Dear Sir that you will continue to write to me concerning all matters which you may think important and especially those relating to the interest of the new state of Florida."[38] As he had confided to Calhoun, DuVal considered a move from St. Augustine to Tallahassee or Texas. DuVal's son Thomas, with his position as territorial secretary coming to an end, decided to move to Austin, Texas. By November DuVal had returned to Tallahassee to reestablish his law practice, and he was there as Thomas and his family, DuVal's widowed daughter, Mary, and his nineteen-year-old daughter Florida were all "impatiently waiting to sail to Texas. They hope now they will soon be off in a few days," he wrote to his friend George Fairbanks.[39]

DuVal also explained that he had "determined to stand fast at this point to do battle for the honest democracy." DuVal found the Middle Florida Democrats even more divided than those in East Florida. They were disgusted with the Westcott faction. The new senator was about to leave for Washington, but, according to DuVal, "he is a miserable man for locating myself here. He has tried every expedient to get me to speak to him, sent message after message, and just a day or two since on the event of his departure for Washington wrote me a note, full of professions and desire to serve me. I took no notice of his messages . . . so he went off with great reluctance at leaving me here as the legislature was in session."

Westcott had even conspired to get DuVal out of the way by offering him the judgeship of South Florida. "Depend upon it," DuVal declared, "I will physic the Tallahassee clique, before I have done with them, . . . and I am fast doing so, and with visible effect—If I live one year longer, the result will astonish the bipeds & tails of the democratic party for they will find that they are going back fast to their true place—*the rump*. The true democratic party will cut asunder from the faction that have disgraced our State." The most "meritorious and prominent men of our party from the West and the Middle Florida . . . are anxious to unite with the reform we contemplate." DuVal delighted in the fact that, for the moment at least, Brockenbrough seemed to have lost the election. Thomas Douglas was also "much delighted that Mr. B is not elected to Congress . . . as predicted when last in the East. Tell Judge Bronson never to trust any man, with carrot colored hair and black whiskers—he who owns such has two faces but no heart or principles and as for a soul, I tell you, the souls of ten thousand such men can be put into a seed of Tobacco—and then will be left rooms to rent."[40]

DuVal's living arrangements in Tallahassee are uncertain, but he may have occupied the large unfinished house he had abandoned in 1841 when he relocated to St. Augustine. The structure, as well as the twenty acres it stood on, was mired in dispute, as even by that time DuVal had still not secured clear title to the land. In fact, in 1840 he had sold the unfinished house to his son-in-law Dr. James Robinson and his mother for $250 contingent on his being able to transfer clear title to the land and property to them. DuVal made a bond to Robinson to that effect and got the money. It seems Robinson, Mary, and her mother-in-law, Maria Robinson, moved into the property and invested heavily in completing the house. After Robinson died, DuVal's widowed daughter and her mother-in-law left the house vacant and joined him in St. Augustine. DuVal was never able to transfer clear title, so in April 1845 he settled the obligation to Mrs. Robinson by transferring to Mrs. Robinson all the household and kitchen furniture in his house and his law office in St. Augustine except for his personal possessions and law library. Included in the more than one-hundred-item inventory were mahogany tables, wardrobes, washstands, silver goblets and crystal wine glasses, thirty maple chairs, and four maple bedsteads. Also among the items was one purple tea set of 75 pieces and a 180-piece Canton dining set.[41] Whether Mrs. Robinson auctioned off the items or brought some of the items back to Middle Florida is unknown. Mrs. Robinson did actually return to Middle Florida with DuVal and her daughter-in-law but chose to remain there rather than migrate to Texas with DuVal's son and daughters.

In January DuVal provided his friend Fairbanks with an update on the General Assembly. He began by discussing the distribution of the judgeships but soon turned to "dissatisfaction prevailing in Middle & West Florida with the Democratic Party." Levy's application to the "Legislature to change his name to *Eulie*

David Levy Yulee was a lawyer, planter, territorial delegate to Congress, and one of Florida's first U.S. senators. Courtesy of State Archives of Florida.

has given offense to many of his warmest friends—the devotion of several influential men who have hitherto . . . named their sons David Levy are seriously offended and mortified. . . . I do not see any good reason why Mr. Levy should not assume his family cognomen—but trifles light as air will sometime produce strong results—one fact is certain, Mr. Eulie, has so identified himself with Mr. Westcott, that the same fate will attend both, when the lark joins with the crow or flocks with the thieving black bird he is apt to be shot for one."[42]

Numerous rumors circulated as to why Levy sought to add Yulee to his name. Did he fear that the Senate might challenge his citizenship as the House had done? If so, some speculated that it was to distance himself from his father and perhaps even to prove that he was not his son, thus making it immaterial whether Moses E. Levy had come to Florida after the change of flags. According to one source, "This will go a long way to establish the Hon. Mr. Yulee's claim to citizenship."[43] But he had not dropped the Levy name. He merely added Yulee. Another critic lambasted Levy's resolutions to acquire Cuba. "This is his first session in the Senate." The precipitate act "complicates our foreign relations, already sufficiently entangled by the rumor that the Government is in negotiation to purchase the Californias. . . . These resolutions are not only impolitic—they are foolish." Perhaps, the critic noted, this was a mere attempt to "change the subject" from charges that he was an alien.[44] But it would soon be reported that Yulee's efforts were turned to more productive results as his efforts to woo Nannie Wickliffe, the daughter of DuVal's longtime friend Charles Wickliffe resulted in matrimony. The New Orleans *Tropic* reported that the ceremony had taken place on April 7 at Wickland, Nelson County, Kentucky. "Mr. Yulee," the newspaper jested, "having failed to annex this country to Cuba, has shown his honesty of purpose by going from Washington to *Have-annie*."[45]

By the first of the year John C. Calhoun was back in his old Senate seat, and DuVal congratulated him on the fact. DuVal predicted that the Oregon dispute with Great Britain would soon be settled. He also noted that a new newspaper, the *Southern Journal,* had been founded in Tallahassee and that it was "speaking the doctrines that should govern the action of the South." Proudly displayed on its masthead were principles sacred to Calhoun: "Free Trade, Low Duties, Separation from Banks, Retrenchment, Economy, and Strict Construction of the Constitution."[46] DuVal complained that the Whigs in Florida were gaining because of the divisions within the Democratic Party. DuVal told Calhoun that should there be another House election he would be a candidate, but he warned the South Carolinian not to breathe a word of this as Westcott would soon learn of it. DuVal confided to Calhoun that Yulee's popularity had slipped and that if he were to run again for Congress he would not poll half the vote he had earned the year before. He attributed this fact to Yulee's connection to Westcott. Both, he predicted, would go down together.[47]

Offering up an explanation of Florida's unique political landscape, DuVal opined that it was the policy of "our friends here to treat the great portion of the Whigs kindly, for many of them are as sound as democrats of the 1798 school as can be found in any state. You must understand," he continued, "a Florida democrat is one who has mixed himself up with all the local questions that were agitated under our territorial government. The broad and great principles of the democracy, had little to do with the true Florida democracy—hence many of our best men are branded as Whigs, either because they were in favor of our sustaining [banks] and some local system or corporation at the time. Our object should be to unite all sound men of either party, to *proscribe none* who wish to unite in the Southern policy. These views will govern me, because they are just and prudent. I never fear responsibility where I know I am right."[48]

Westcott, DuVal predicted, would support Calhoun in the Senate because he knew that was what Floridians wanted. "But don't trust the man, for a moment, however he may appear to act with you. I tell you I know the man, and if ever you should be induced to confide in him, remember what I now say—he will betray you whenever it may suit his views. Such has been his course through life." DuVal also predicted that John Branch and all his friends in Middle Florida would join their cause, as would Governor Moseley. He was "heart and hand with us—and it is gratifying to me to say, you have no truer, or warmer friend in Florida." DuVal also offered to have "our *Southern Journal* publish any papers or document" that Calhoun might send. "I will see that every thing you deem proper to give for publication shall be printed for the people of Florida. You would not like perhaps to be considered as the directing course of the journal, and it is for this reason I request that I may act." The *Floridian*, DuVal noted, merely served as Westcott's organ, "speaks *his doctrines* not for the party, but for himself. Our object is to compel that paper to follow our lead and it will be compelled to do so or it will sink if it does not pursue the right track. We will make no war on it, but treat it with respect, for my policy as before stated is to conciliate and strengthen our Southern phalanx. Let all join our cohort and march in order, and the victory will be ours."[49]

DuVal closed his missive to Calhoun with the statement that he would rather be in the next House than the Senate. "The only representative in the popular branch, if a sound practical man, can have more influence, and effect more for the Southern democracy, than both of our senators." If elected, he would seek only one term. "I am too poor to remain in Congress." DuVal assured Calhoun that, whatever "you may communicate to me in confidence, no other shall see or know—such communications may sometimes be necessary to guide the course of your friends—and if so, will be used so, as not to commit you, for any view or opinion thus given."[50] Thus William P. DuVal pledged himself to be John C. Calhoun's special confidant in Florida. He hoped that he and his associates could wrest control of the Democratic Party in Florida away from Westcott and his followers and forge it into a unified front to protect Southern interests both in the state and in the nation. Like Calhoun, DuVal sought to build a party based on strong Southern principles. The names "Democrat" and "Whig" meant little to him. But would his political operations merely serve to weaken the Democrats and make them vulnerable to Whig efforts to regain control of the state? As DuVal pondered these questions, he also pondered his future. Would that future lie in the law or in politics? And would it take place in Florida, Texas, or elsewhere?

CHAPTER 19

"I will not be the cause of disunion in our ranks"

On April 21, 1846, the Tallahassee *Southern Journal* contained a law notice that Thomas H. DuVal, Attorney and Counselor at Law, would practice law in Austin, Texas, having permanently settled there. DuVal would specialize in land sales, examination of titles, procurement of patents, and the transaction of all business usually appertaining to a General Land Agency. As references DuVal offered the names of two men who had preceded him in the well-worn path from Florida to Texas: A. S. Thruston, a Kentuckian who had lived in Tallahassee in its first decade, and James Webb, a Virginian who had settled in Middle Florida before becoming the first judge of the Southern District of Florida. Webb had migrated to the state in 1838, holding many important offices in the Republic of Texas, including secretary of state and attorney general.

In October of the previous year, Texas voters had approved annexation to the United States by a massive margin. The U.S. Congress accepted the Texas Constitution, and President Polk signed the annexation act two days before the end of the year. Elections for state officers went forward, and in a dramatic ceremony held on February 19, the opening day of the state legislature, the Texas Republic flag was lowered and the American flag took its place. As if to emphasize the point of transition, Sam Houston caught the Texas flag as it descended. Shortly thereafter, Houston would take his seat in the U.S. Senate.[1]

Thomas DuVal and his wife, Laura, and his widowed sister, Mary, and his youngest sister, Florida, may have witnessed this spectacle as they arrived in Texas about the first of the year. Also in the party that day would have been Thomas and Laura's two children Florence (5) and Burr (3), along with Aunt Polly Hynes. It is also possible that Thomas's brother John Crittenden may also have been in Austin that day, and he may have even greeted his brother's family when they arrived in Galveston. One of the few survivors of the Battle of Goliad, John Crittenden, as his father explained to John C. Calhoun, had been on the western frontier attached to the Texas Rangers for about a year and a half.²

The new state capital offered promise for lawyers, and it was likely to become a thriving commercial village. Formerly known as Waterloo, the site on the Colorado River had been chosen by the leaders of the Republic as the capital in 1839. When Thomas DuVal and his family arrived in 1845, the town had approximately a thousand inhabitants, and there was every expectation that it would grow rapidly. The selection of the site was controversial at the time. While it was almost at the center of the claimed territory, it still was quite isolated, as it lay far beyond the settled sections of the country in the east. It also was close to the Comanche Indians. While Thomas DuVal put out his legal shingle with James Webb and others, he was fortunate to obtain a steady income by working with Webb as reporter for the Supreme Court of Texas, a post he continued once Texas became a state.³

After seeing his family off at St. Marks, William P. DuVal returned to Tallahassee and pondered his future. Would he be able to revive his law practice in the Florida capital? Would he be able to influence political affairs in the new state? And would he be an active participant in the process, or would he be content to stand on the sidelines? With his connections to President Polk and Senator John C. Calhoun, DuVal would certainly play an important role in linking Florida with politics at the national level. But DuVal's precise role was uncertain. For the moment at least he was content to serve as Calhoun's eyes and ears (and his mouthpiece) in Florida.

But it was soon learned that Governor Moseley had a special mission for DuVal. Near the first of the year the governor appointed DuVal and John Branch commissioners to settle the boundary controversy between Georgia and Florida. The Florida-Georgia boundary had been disputed since colonial times. The first serious American attempt to clarify the border occurred after the Pinckney Treaty (1795), when Congress appointed surveyor Andrew Ellicott to locate the St. Mary's River's source and then run a line west to the junction of the Chattahoochee and Flint Rivers. The task of running the boundary line seemed simple enough, but hostile Indians prevented Ellicott's survey parties from completing their work, and disputes over the precise source of the St. Mary's River (as depicted by "Ellicott's Mound") caused confusion. Not unexpectedly, Florida authorities were convinced the true source of the St. Mary's was many miles north of Ellicott's Mound. DuVal and Branch met with Georgia commissioners first at St. Mary's, Georgia, and for nearly two weeks in Bainbridge, Georgia, and then again in Tallahassee in March without resolving the conflict. From there the matter was handed over to the Florida legislature, which expressed frustration at the lack of progress. A select committee complained that the continued uncertainty over the boundary "renders the disputed territory an asylum for the most dangerous criminals. Order, peace, and justice, are sacrificed by a continuance of this controversy." The committee report might have added that for years duelists had taken advantage of the uncertain boundary to avoid prosecution. Finally, the General Assembly resolved to sue the State of Georgia in the U.S. Supreme Court and authorized Governor Moseley to secure an attorney and pay him out of revenue in the treasury. The dispute went unsettled for years.[4]

As DuVal prepared to meet the Georgia commissioners, he wrote to Calhoun about Florida and national affairs. DuVal congratulated Calhoun on the "sound policy you have so ably maintained on the Oregon question." It would prevail "unless all common sense and patriotism are thrown away." DuVal offered once again to distribute and publish in the *Southern Journal* Calhoun's full views on Oregon and all other questions. "I know all the men of standing in the counties and would take an interest, in spreading your opinions."[5] The Polk administration only grudgingly came around to Calhoun's view that the dispute with Britain over Oregon's boundary did not merit going to war. Calhoun's strong stand against "54–40 or Fight" threatened to isolate him from his president and also from the majority of Democrats in Congress, but it was a risk he was willing to take. His purpose was to play a moderating role, as if to demonstrate his statesmanlike qualities. Such a course would further his credentials as a conciliator and thus keep alive his faint hopes for a final run at the White House. But to Calhoun what was most important was protecting Southern slaveholding interests, and Oregon had nothing to do with that. Splitting the difference with Britain at the forty-ninth parallel would settle the annoying dispute and would allow the country to focus on the most dangerous question, the disputed boundary between the new state of Texas and Mexico. Calhoun did not want war with Mexico, either. But he considered war with that country the greater likelihood, and if such were to occur the United States must have peaceful relations with Great Britain.

DuVal agreed with this policy, noting that Calhoun's strategy for settling the Oregon issue was the appropriate one. "I consider it undignified and intirely too boasting and insulting to England. The wordy, Chinese, tumbling, and vaulting in the advance of war is too ridiculous for a thinking people—we want no gasconading speeches to back our courage. . . . The Senate of the United States is surely the last place that such inflammatory speakers should receive countenance or support." Calhoun worked feverishly and successfully in the Senate to beat back the Hannegan resolutions, which proclaimed that "all the country west of the Rockies and lying between 42 and 54–40 was a part of the territory of the United States; that the government possessed no power to alienate the soil or transfer the allegiance of the United States citizens; and that to give up a portion of Oregon would be to abandon the 'honor, character, and the best interests of the American people.'" Senator Edward Hannegan of Indiana represented the extreme position, and Calhoun was successful in defeating it, arguing that it was within the constitutional power of the president with the advice and consent of the Senate to determine a boundary by treaty. After debate had gone on for weeks Calhoun took the floor on March 16 and made one of the greatest speeches of his career. By the end of the day Calhoun had successfully defended the position that finding a way to renew negotiations with Great Britain was the proper course. Events had indeed moved in a positive direction. Britain had repealed its Corn Laws, and the likelihood of renewed opportunities for free trade favored the reopening of negotiations.[6]

DuVal praised Calhoun's stand. Having read his speech several times, he "found it out of the compass of my language to express my opinion of the wide and statesmanlike views you have delivered to the nation. Throughout this state but one opinion prevails on the wisdom of the far-seeing judgment. You have displayed on this important and dangerous question, so well calculated by intemperate politicians to involve, the peace if not the ruin of our institutions." Both Democrats and Whigs in Florida "unite in commending your profound reasoning on this vital question, in acknowledging no man in our national Legislature has so clearly and so ably, discussed the effect and consequences that would result for a violent and partisan action, demanding 'all of Oregon.'" The *Tallahassee Southern Journal* published Calhoun's address on March 31, adding, "This speech will make Mr. Calhoun President of the United States." DuVal predicted that Calhoun's speech was "destined to have powerful effect on Parliament, and throughout Great Britain. The Statesmen of that nation will accord to you a station preeminent among the highest of the age."[7]

DuVal reiterated to Calhoun that he desired a seat in Congress as a way to help forward Calhoun's presidential aspirations. "I care nothing for a seat in Congress on my own account, for under no contingency would I consent to remain longer than one congress. It is alone my object to sustain our great Southern principles in the coming contest for another President." DuVal even encouraged Calhoun to urge Yulee and Westcott to "write to those they confide in to unite in support of my election. No man in this State could do more, if as much, in Congress as myself." DuVal even offered his son Thomas's support in the cause to make Calhoun the next president. Since his arrival in Austin, Thomas DuVal had taken up the editorship of the Austin *New Era*, owned by James Webb, for whom DuVal sought Calhoun's support for a federal judgeship. DuVal sent to Calhoun Thomas's letter explaining the circumstances of his editorship of the paper. "I have consented to edit this paper," the son wrote to the father, "with the understanding that I would write nothing of a partisan character, so far as relates to politics here. . . . Being a stranger in the country, with nothing to depend upon for a living, but my profession, and the good will of the people, I don't choose to make enemies of one half, and embroil myself in difficulties, by taking sides for this, or that man. I may hereafter do so, but it would be of no service to me just now." Still, Thomas DuVal knew that Calhoun was popular in Texas. He concluded his note to his father, perhaps with the wish that his words would reach Washington: "Whatever I may write therefore of a political cast, shall be in praise of *Democracy* in general and *Mr. Calhoun in Particular*." "This," DuVal wrote to Calhoun, "is the language and feelings of myself and my sons and must ever be such."[8]

For the moment at least, Calhoun seemed to be the master of Polk, the Senate, and the Democratic Party. Within months the Senate ratified a treaty with Britain largely along the guidelines he had suggested. Yet his stand in opposition to the war with Mexico played a large role in dashing whatever hopes he had for the White House. Spurned in his attempt to purchase California from Mexico, Polk ordered troops under Zachary Taylor's command to the northern bank of the Rio Grande. Calhoun predicted to himself that the provocative move would result in bloodshed. He was correct in that assumption; on May 10 the predicted clash between U.S. and Mexican troops on "American Territory" occurred. The next day Polk delivered his war message to Congress. In his opposition to war, Calhoun bucked his president, his party, and the vast majority of Southerners. His reasons for opposition were numerous. Not only might a long, protracted guerrilla war result, but also war would unsettle relations among the sections of the United States. "Mexico is to us the forbidden fruit; the penalty of eating it [is] to subject our institutions to political death," he declared.[9] Ironically, Calhoun joined Polk's few Whig critics in the House by opposing Polk's war. Calhoun did not vote against war, but he was one of only two senators who "abstained." The effect was the same.

Calhoun's premonitions about the results of ingesting the tainted fruit proved correct. Even so, for the moment most Southerners welcomed the war as an opportunity to spread their civilization west. But the dangers of doing so were brought home to all in August 1846 when an obscure New York congressman offered an amendment to an appropriations bill that declared that no territory won in war with Mexico would be open to the spread of slavery. A firestorm over the so-called Wilmot Proviso broke out immediately. The measure passed narrowly in the House on a sectional vote but failed of passage in the Senate. Even so, the principle embodied within the Wilmot Proviso (that is, to halt the spread of slavery in the territories) would haunt the republic until the Civil War.

Back in Florida, DuVal's hopes to run for Congress in 1846 foundered, as did Calhoun's presidential aspirations. Yet DuVal did what he could to rally Floridians to their responsibilities in the war with Mexico, even as he railed angrily against the Wilmot Proviso. In early May DuVal "made a highly patriotic and eloquent address" to the Sixth Regiment of Florida volunteers assembled in front of the Leon County courthouse. Also on hand to see the men off to Pensacola were hundreds of other Tallahasseans.[10] DuVal also advised Governor Moseley on Florida's defenses. As astonishing as it may sound to modern ears, DuVal, when requested, provided his opinions on Florida's coastal defenses in anticipation of an attack by

Mexican naval forces. "I know from my personal observation," he wrote Moseley, "much of our sea coast and all the important points that require military protection, except Key West and Cedar Keys—against Mexican cruisers, we are fully competent" to repel any invasion without outside assistance. Yet cannon and other arms would have to be provided to the volunteers. DuVal then went on to lay out how many troops would be necessary to repel an invasion and where they should be stationed. Included in his summary were not only locations on the Gulf but also Jacksonville, St. Augustine, and points along the St. Johns River. DuVal added that, given the "exposed condition of this state, having a seacoast of thirteen hundred miles to defend renders it the duty of the U. States, to arm our militia for its protection. The folly of limiting this state the weakest and most exposed of all in the Union to an insignificant armament of no effective service is too obvious for comment. . . . The refusal to arm the militia of a country, this thinly settled, and so unprovided for defense, would be as reasonable and as wise, as to count and fix the flints in their muskets while the foe was charging our army."[11]

John DuVal, like his brother, resided in Tallahassee. He chaired a Democratic meeting in Tallahassee on June 20, at which the business of the moment was to appoint delegates to attend the state convention at Suwannee Springs in July. John DuVal joined twenty other delegates at the meeting. William P. DuVal was conspicuously not among the men involved in all these doings or among those attending the convention. For the moment at least, his political ambition to return to the U.S. Congress after more than thirty years seemed dead. It took eight ballots for the Democrats to nominate a candidate for the House. The delegates chose Franklin County's William Kain for Florida's congressional seat, bypassing Brockenbrough, the incumbent; Chandler C. Yonge; and Isaac Bronson. The convention went on to pronounce its adherence to principles of strict construction of the Constitution and opposition to the protective tariff and a national bank. "Congress's power to create either of these institutions," the convention declared, "was neither given nor implied by the Constitution." Finally, the body recognized Senator John C. Calhoun as the "great advocate of strict construction and a devotion to the principles of justice and equal rights which commands our admiration. For his nativity he is claimed by the South; but his talents, his political integrity, and private worth, are the property of the whole Union." And those "multitudes in this State and who entertain . . . preference for him for the next Presidency, will, we are convinced, come forward with the hearty, whole-souled enthusiasm, to ensure the election of William A. Kain."[12]

Though they differed on many issues, John DuVal joined his brother in the belief that the nation was clearly divided into two sections. That fall he addressed the readers of the Tallahassee *Southern Journal,* arguing that the proceedings of the previous Congress "prove that the nation is now divided into two great sectional parties: the manufacturers of the North—whigs and democrats; who have united to fatten on the Planters of the South—whigs and democrats." In good demagogic fashion DuVal reminded his readers that "you are tenants to the manufacturers of the North: every third bale of cotton is the rent you pay to the Lords of the loom and the spindle. The Democrats of the South are defending themselves and their property against this unjust opposition." DuVal called on all Florida Whigs to "stand by us, shoulder to shoulder in this our common cause."[13]

For all their bluster the Democrats faltered as Kain lost to the Whig candidate, Edward Cabell. This time Cabell served his entire term without challenge. John DuVal also lost his bid for election to the Florida House.[14] Even if he stumped for other Democrats, William P. DuVal attended primarily to his law practice. If called again, though, he would be ready.

Midway through the campaign, DuVal found himself in a sensational criminal trial in Quincy involving a gang accused of murder, slave stealing, and mail robbery. The prosecution was so complicated that Judge Thomas Baltzell appointed DuVal to assist Thomas Hair, the Middle Circuit solicitor, in the case, and their efforts netted four convictions. A grateful Gadsden County grand jury spoke for many in the area when it thanked DuVal for his service in the trial. The body regarded DuVal as "almost the father of the county" and offered him its "warmest approbation."[15]

For the next year and a half DuVal bided his time in Tallahassee, practicing law and following the progress of the Mexican War. By June or July 1846 John Crittenden had probably joined other Texas volunteers in the fighting against Mexico along the Rio Grande. His former commander of the Texas Rangers, Jack Hays, had joined Zachary Taylor's army in its assault on northern Mexico. Though documentation is sparse, it is likely that John Crittenden was among the Texas soldiers who fought at Monterrey in September 1846 and at Buena Vista in February 1847.[16]

Elsewhere on the Texas front, Thomas, still in Austin with his family, continued his law practice and his work for the Texas State Supreme Court. As for Thomas's siblings, Marcia Price's husband had died in Galveston, and she resided alone there with her son Bill. Soon after William Price's passing she wrote her brother Thomas, "I am as near living dead with the blues as any mortal can be & think I should die outright if you were not coming down." Her prospects soon brightened, however. Marcia would eventually marry Judge George Washington Paschal and move to Austin. DuVal's youngest daughter, Florida, would also find a companion, eventually marrying a man named Enoch Everett, who took her to New Orleans. Mary Robinson lived in Austin with Thomas's family but eventually married a Galveston developer named Samuel Hopkins. Eventually settling in Fort Worth, the Hopkinses had three boys and two girls. Back in Florida, DuVal's fatherly responsibilities were about to grow, as his daughter Elizabeth Beall, widowed for the second time, brought her children from Kentucky and joined her father in Tallahassee.[17]

Meanwhile, as controversies surrounding the fallout from the Wilmot Proviso coursed through the American political bloodstream, DuVal found himself called upon to give local voice to national events. At the very beginning of 1848 DuVal joined other Tallahassee Democrats in denouncing those Southern congressmen who had voted for Robert C. Winthrop of Massachusetts, a "Wilmot Proviso man," for speaker of the House. The attack was obviously targeted at Florida's Whig congressman, Edward Cabell. DuVal, who followed his friend George Fairbanks on the rostrum, "made one of his happiest efforts." DuVal joined the others in resolutions in support of Mr. Polk's War, while denouncing the Wilmot Proviso and any other measure to "hinder, impede, or delay the Government of the United States from prosecuting the war with Mexico." Finally, the gathering resolved that in forming a political association with the North, Southern men should connect themselves with like-minded men who opposed the Wilmot Proviso. Such men were likely to be found only in the Democratic Party since nearly all the leaders in the "other party" were in favor of this "unconstitutional and mischievous principle."[18]

Thus even though it was a northern Democrat who introduced the Wilmot Proviso in the House of Representatives, the Democrats denounced the Whigs as "un-Southern" or dangerous to Southern interests because the Whig Party represented itself as a national party. For example, a critic of Cabell could score points against him by quoting statements in which Cabell noted that the "Whig Party embraces in its comprehensive views, *the whole country* and is *not influenced by a selfish or sectional policy.*"[19] Sparring between the Democrats and Whigs continued as the year progressed, especially as both parties began to organize their state conventions in the spring. In February one observer warned that "there was no time to spare." All loyal Democrats should "at once go to work to select their delegates. County meetings should be had in all the counties and all the democrats should attend. . . . The Democracy must be aroused. The spirit which animates and stirs them on all great occasions, and in all scenes of trial, must be thoroughly wakened." Meetings in Tallahassee, St. Augustine, Madison, Marianna, Quincy, Monticello, Apalachicola, and other communities moved forward in preparation for the March 26 convention.[20]

DuVal was conspicuously absent from these meetings because he knew that he was the likely nominee for Florida's lone U.S. House seat. He had been in contact with a number of his Democratic friends who supported him. In a letter to George Fairbanks DuVal noted that he was delighted that Jefferson County planter William Bailey had announced for governor and that "he would lay his opponent out. I find the democracy seem well pleased that he has announced himself as a candidate and that I approve of his course as it is certain no other democrat would oppose him of our party." After going through the likely electors from the western, middle, and eastern parts of the state, DuVal spoke of his own chances in the upcoming election for Congress. But if "it should so happen that any serious division should take place in the convention my name shall be promptly withdrawn. I will not be the cause of disunion in our ranks," DuVal asserted. Even so, DuVal was able to report that his friends Walker Anderson, C. C. Yonge, and George Baltzell had told him that "public opinion in the west & middle is manifestly in my favor. His old friend, Benjamin Wright, though a Whig, had written to him that he would "support me against any candidate." But above all DuVal stressed unity for the Democrats. "I wish the convention to act so as to maintain the unity of our party—and throw me off if it will give strength to our cause."[21]

As DuVal speculated on his chances in the upcoming political sweepstakes, an important debate was taking place in the U.S. Senate in which Florida senator David Yulee was one of the primary participants. For four days beginning on February 14 New York senator Daniel Dickinson and Yulee, following John C. Calhoun's lead, debated the principle that came to be known as "popular sovereignty." In an effort to tamp down difficulties arising over the acquisition of territory from Mexico, Northern Democrats had proposed that the question of whether slavery should be banned or allowed to spread be left to territorial inhabitants. Senator Dickinson had carefully articulated this position earlier in December and proposed resolutions supporting the concept. Calhoun rose in opposition, offering his own resolutions, and a month-long debate over not only the future of the territories but also Polk's war policy against Mexico began. (Polk had adopted Dickinson's approach to the territorial questions and also was contemplating a complete conquest of Mexico.)[22]

Finally, by February, when Dickinson again offered his resolutions, Yulee took the floor in opposition. As one witness to the debates reported, Yulee responded that the "consequences of such a doctrine would be equally fatal to the rights of the South, as the doctrine contained in the Wilmot proviso itself. The latter would give the power of the federal government to infringe upon the Constitutional rights of the South; the former proposition would give it to the territorial government." Yulee countered with other resolutions stating that territories were the common property of the Union and that "sovereignty over the same vests in the people of the several States comprising the Union." Yulee also argued that the federal government has no delegated authority. Nor does the "territorial community have any inherent right, to exercise any legislative power within the said territories, by which the equal rights of all the citizens of the United States to acquire and enjoy any part of the common property may be impaired or embarrassed."[23] Yulee's assertion that the "Popular" or "Squatter Sovereignty" Doctrine was a basic violation of Southern rights protected in the Constitution essentially restated John C. Calhoun's position that neither Congress nor territorial inhabitants had the right to exclude slavery. If territorial inhabitants possessed the right to exclude slave property within their limits and territories were the joint possessions of all Americans, then the rights of Southerners as protected in the Constitution would be violated. The upshot was that neither Congress nor territorial inhabitants had the right to exclude slavery. Finally, in the end, nothing was settled, as the arrival of the Treaty of Guadalupe Hidalgo from Mexico had the effect of shutting off debate, as the senators would be consumed with studying its provisions. A decision on slavery in the territories would have to wait.

Yulee's speeches resonated with Florida Democrats, especially as they prepared for their state convention in Madison in March. Even before the convention met, Democrats questioned whether they should send a delegation to the national convention in Baltimore. What if the convention should try to nominate a "Wilmot Proviso man"? All the more reason, according to one observer, that Florida should attend, as "her Southern sisters are standing shoulder to shoulder, battling with the enemies of the Constitution for our rights." If Florida failed to appear in this hour of need, it might be charged "with treachery, a culpable disregard for the rights and honor of the South." No, the man asserted, "Florida may yet stand in line with her Democratic sisters in this matter."[24]

At the Democratic convention in Madison, things fell into place for DuVal. The final vote saw DuVal besting Dennett Mays by a vote of 74–18. Immediately, after the vote was taken, the runner-up rose and stated that the "selection of the 'old Governor' met with his hearty approval." He assured the convention that Governor DuVal would be "a hard colt to beat." DuVal formally accepted the nomination two weeks later after arriving home from the Jefferson County Court to find the letter notifying him of his nomination. By return mail DuVal noted that twenty-seven years had passed since he became a resident of Florida; he added that the "distinguished honor and continued confidence, manifested by my fellow citizens, through their Delegates to the State Convention, is the highest reward that can be offered to an old public servant." DuVal closed with this statement: "My past conduct as a public man is the best guarantee I can offer for my future action should it be the will of the public to place me in Congress." The Whig press later excoriated the statement as the "richest joke of the season."[25] In selecting DuVal the delegates must have understood that his long political past might haunt him in the upcoming campaign. Even so, they decided that DuVal's campaign skills would enable him to overcome charges of political opportunism. Moreover, DuVal, the majority reckoned, through his long service to Florida, had earned the right to represent the state in Congress.[26]

In ten well-crafted resolutions Florida Democrats denounced the Wilmot Proviso and any attempt to bar slavery from the territories by Congress, by territorial inhabitants, or in any other manner whatever. Perhaps the most striking of these resolutions was the avowal that while they adhered to the principles of the

Democratic Party, they believed that there were "interests vital to the South, which we hold to be above all party ties or considerations." Thus they ordered their eleven delegates to the national convention to oppose any presidential candidate who would support barring slavery from the territories either by congressional action or by a decision of the territorial inhabitants. Thus, the Florida convention adopted the hardline position of Calhoun and Yulee. One observer noted, "The greatest unanimity and enthusiasm prevailed and one sentiment seems to animate the Convention. . . . There can be little doubt, even with our opponents, as to the fact that Florida is a democratic State, and we only have to give a 'long pull, a strong pull, and pull together,' to sweep this State like a tornado. With such a ticket as BAILEY and DUVAL . . . we enter upon the canvass with old-fashioned, patriotic zeal and ardor." While the convention stressed unity and the correctness of the delegates' positions, it also threw darts at the Whigs. For example, one commentator declared that Whig policies in effect provided "aid and comfort" to the abolitionists.[27]

For their part the Whigs held no central convention but nominated their candidates first in county meetings and then separately in three divisional conventions. Although the process seemed confusing, in fact all the meetings coalesced around the incumbent Cabell for the House and Thomas Brown for governor. When push came to shove, as Herbert Doherty has noted, Florida Whigs differed little from their Democratic counterparts in their support for slaveholders' property rights as protected in the Constitution. The main differences were over the degree to which these rights needed to be pushed. "The Whigs were more disposed to compromise on the extension of slavery to the territories." Yet even before 1850, he wrote, there was a free-soil element among the Northern Whigs which troubled Southerners."[28] Through the columns of the Marianna *Whig*, the Tallahassee *Sentinel*, and other like-minded journals, the Whigs argued that their moderate and conservative principles were safest for the state and the nation.

The Democrats expected DuVal to be a hard campaigner, and they were not disappointed. Within a few weeks after his nomination DuVal had made speeches in Monticello, at the Leon County courthouse, and in Quincy, countering the charges that at sixty-four he was too old to run. According to one observer who heard his speech in Tallahassee, DuVal still had a "full share of the young fire still remaining. He spoke with warmth and energy, such as the importance of the crisis demands, exposing the crooked ways of the Whig politicians." DuVal, the observer continued, laid "bare the spirit of faction" among the Whigs and contrasted in a "very happy manner" their conduct and policies with those of the Democratic Party. "If not 'too old' he has at least lived long enough to see a thing or two . . . and is willing to speak fully and freely. All he wants is a tolerable showing, and, with that, he will ask the princes of whigdom for no further favors." DuVal, the commentator argued, had effectively fended off the attacks about his past votes in Congress and his support for Harrison against Van Buren in 1840. DuVal declared that he opposed Van Buren's handling of the Seminole War and his "notions on the subject of slavery."[29]

DuVal's principal message then and throughout the rest of his campaign was the threat to the South inherent in the Wilmot Proviso. This was also, he asserted, to be the great question for the South in the coming contest for the presidency. Without mentioning Cabell's vote for Winthrop for House speaker, DuVal asserted that Wilmot Proviso men must be repudiated and rejected by every Southern man. Without question DuVal's Whig opponents knew they faced a formidable adversary on the stump. One Whig commentator, satirically commenting on DuVal's skills on the stump, derisively noted that "we can almost give Cabell up for a 'gone coon.' What with the Governor's old Kentucky electioneering tricks of *swapping tobacco, kissing Polly and chucking Sally under the chin, talking horse and cotton* to the farmer, singing 'John Anderson my Jo John' to the old ladies, reciting 'Tam O'Shanter,' and rehearsing 'Ralph Ringwood' to the gals, Cabell will shure be beat all hollow!"[30]

"Wakulla," a DuVal supporter, admitted that, while his man would have some opposition, "it will be that of pigmies against a giant. No old citizen of Florida, who remembers William P. DuVal when Governor of the then Territory," the commentator continued, would deny him support now. None who "recollects the free and open hospitality, with which he was ever welcomed at the executive mansion; none who recollect the sacrifices of wealth and comfort made by that individual, in developing the resources and promoting the future success of the youthful territory placed under his care; none such, I am sure, will refuse their suffrage to so old, so faithful, and well tried a public servant, and one too, grown gray in their service, and that without the usual attendant of wealth to compensate him for his sacrifices and services."[31]

Nearly two months after the Madison gathering, on May 22 the national Democrats assembled in Baltimore. The national Democratic Party was in disarray. Polk would not run again, and there were numerous candidates for the nomination and few front-runners. The "Hunker" and the "Barnburner" factions among New York Democrats symbolized the divisions within the Democratic Party. The Barnburners looked kindly upon the Wilmot Proviso, supporting a ban on slave expansion, while the Hunkers opposed any discussion of the issue to the degree that it might annoy their Southern friends. Thus Hunkers were represented as callous party operatives bent on squelching controversial discussions that might harm their goal of attaining national office.[32]

If the New York Democrats represented an extreme situation, that same ambivalence between Northern and Southern delegates was pervasive. In such a situation the convention sought to find a candidate acceptable to all. The convention chose Senator Lewis Cass of Michigan, a man who sided with Senator Daniel

Dickinson and others who believed that the decision to extend slavery in the territories should rest with their inhabitants. As a presidential hopeful, Cass was slow to speak about the issue in detail, but he eventually came around to support the principle. The Democratic platform carefully dodged any mention of popular sovereignty, but most observers understood that Cass was in sympathy with the doctrine. Cass, according to his biographer, "succeeded in his quest for the nomination because, as a western nationalist, he bridged the expanding gap between northern and southern Democrats."[33]

When word reached Florida of Cass's nomination, DuVal was campaigning in East Florida. What DuVal thought of Cass's nomination is not recorded, but as events unfolded he must have opposed the choice. He certainly knew Cass well. Both had fought the British in the Old Northwest. Like DuVal, Cass had served as the governor of a territory (Michigan), in Cass's case for eighteen years. DuVal would have remembered Cass as the man he sparred with over his accounts when Cass served as Jackson's secretary of war. Since that time Cass had served in diplomatic posts and in the U.S. Senate. DuVal knew Cass as a moderate, reliable, but boring and less-than-inspirational politician. DuVal must have realized immediately that Cass's nomination would be trouble for him because of his perceived support for popular sovereignty. Indeed, he was correct. Cass's nomination divided the Florida Democrats. While some might take comfort in Cass's opposition to the Wilmot Proviso, others, perhaps a majority of Florida Democrats, were still displeased that he acquiesced in the popular sovereignty principle. When the State Executive Committee decided to support the national convention, the committee chairman resigned, only to be replaced by DuVal's brother. A Jacksonville newspaper voiced disgust, suggesting a fracture between East and Middle Florida Democrats.[34]

Both contemporary observers and those who came after often noted the irony that it was a Democratic war that produced two Whig candidates for president in 1848 and 1852. Zachary Taylor and Winfield Scott both emerged as heroes from the war, and it was to heroic generals that the Whig Party often turned as presidential candidates. Of the two, Taylor was the least political and thus the one the Whigs desired most. Also, as a slaveholder, the argument went, Taylor would be acceptable to Southerners. It will be recalled that during the War of 1812, Taylor, a lifelong soldier, had fought in the same region of the Old Northwest as DuVal. In Florida he had served with distinction and was one of the few regular army officers who saw his career undiminished by service there, emerging as the "Hero of Okeechobee." Whigs hoped that Taylor's aloofness from political conflicts would serve them well in these volatile times. Like DuVal, Taylor had links to Kentucky, and it was DuVal's friend John Crittenden who served as his primary political adviser in the election of 1848. As Taylor's running mate the Whigs nominated Millard Fillmore of New York.[35]

DuVal and Florida Democrats had difficulty convincing the voters and themselves that Cass, a Northerner who had come out for popular sovereignty, was a better choice than Taylor, a slaveholder and a plainspoken military man who had circulated among them during the war against the Seminoles. Unfortunately for DuVal, his long career in which he had been forced to take many seemingly contradictory positions in light of changing circumstances allowed the Whigs to effectively cast him as a political chameleon. Most devastating for DuVal were his various stands on banking. Whigs dug up his old voting record in Congress, charging that he was a "BANK FEDERALIST, having cast three distinctive votes in favor of A UNITED STATES BANK." Worse still, DuVal faced charges that he was the "FATHER OF THE UNION BANK, that upon his head rests the responsibility of all the oppression saddled upon the people by that corrupt institution." DuVal, the Whigs charged, had signed his name to "THREE HUNDRED AND SIXTY THOUSAND DOLLARS worth of Faith Bonds."[36]

DuVal's abandonment of Van Buren in favor of Harrison in 1840 and his support for Polk in 1844 were brought up as reasons why DuVal could not be trusted. According to one critic, in nominating DuVal the Democrats had adopted a "heathen Deity as their patron saint"—"a Janus" with "two faces."[37] DuVal's flamboyant persona, his storytelling antics, his personification in Washington Irving's "Ralph Ringwood Tales," and his adeptness as a public speaker were used against him. Such behavior, they argued, was proof of DuVal's shiftiness and unreliability.[38]

Despite the attacks, DuVal pressed on. At Alligator he addressed the people at the Columbia County courthouse, which was "crowded to suffocation." The speech was reported as "highly applauded and gave general satisfaction."[39] On July 1, at a meeting of Alachua and Marion County Democrats in Wakahoota, DuVal made a "most eloquent and forcible address touching upon the various political questions of the day, and enforcing with great ability the doctrines of the Democratic Party."[40] Democratic meetings throughout the state formally issued resolutions endorsing DuVal. Franklin County and Pensacola Democrats endorsed DuVal, as did those in Columbia County, proclaiming that DuVal, the "Son of the Old Dominion, the Hunter of Kentucky, is the man of our choice to represent us in the next Congress."[41]

In July and August both DuVal and Cabell made the rounds in East Florida. DuVal preceded Cabell in St. Augustine, speaking to a very large and enthusiastic meeting of Democrats at the courthouse.[42] "VERITAS," a participant at the gathering, noted that "During the whole time he was on the stand not a sound was to be heard; all listened with profound attention, until he arrived at the end of some touching and eloquent passage, when the room resounded with approbation. The old gentleman favored us with what was pronounced by all who heard him, a truly eloquent, able, statesmanlike speech. There was no trick—nothing to trap the unsuspecting—nothing but such as should at all times characterize the actions

Edward Carrington Cabell, ca. 1848. Born in Richmond in 1816, Cabell migrated to Jefferson County, Florida, in 1837, became a planter, and eventually became Florida's most successful Whig politician. Courtesy of State Archives of Florida.

of one who seeks popular favor. He did not deal in self adulation," the observer continued. "Nor did he descend to the scurrilous abuse of his opponents."[43]

As far as the content of the speech, VERITAS reported that "he discoursed freely and at length of the time when he came to Florida, informed us of the condition of the country, the hardships he underwent, and finally the triumph of civilization in the then unknown country. He spoke of the Tariff of '42—exhibited how it protected the wealthy few to the oppression of the industrious class composed of agriculturists, mechanic, seamen, etc." He denounced the "the visionary schemes of internal improvement, engendered by the distribution of proceeds of the public money of the several states, which was well calculated to consolidate the government in the hands of the few, thereby totally destroying State sovereignty and make the created greater than the creator." DuVal then went on to repudiate the National Bank, rhetorically asking his audience: "May I be permitted to ask whether the Whigs will not endeavor to re-enact a Bank Charter, should they have a majority in Congress, with the Automaton as President?" DuVal also "lashed" Martin Van Buren's "course of conduct" and "in the manner peculiar to himself—illustrated Martin's course occasionally, with anecdotes very opportunely introduced." DuVal concluded his address to rounds of applause. Three "hearty cheers were given," and the "crowd dispersed with animated countenances and spirits, rendered buoyant from the certainty of success."[44]

The path to victory did not get any easier for the Democrats when in August Barnburners, Conscience Whigs, abolitionists, and a whole host of other antislavery forces assembled in Buffalo, New York, and formed the Free Soil Party. The Free Soilers nominated Martin Van Buren as their standard-bearer. As predicted, the party siphoned off more voters from the Democrats than from the Whigs. Thus, in the nation as in Florida, the Whigs represented Taylor and the Whigs as the only true national party. In Florida Van Buren's candidacy mattered little to DuVal. In fact, it may have even helped him, as it may have served to defuse Whig charges that DuVal, like many Southern Democrats, had abandoned the New Yorker for Harrison in 1840.

Van Buren's candidacy was largely irrelevant to Floridians, but not so the standard-bearers representing the two major parties. Both parties tried their best to represent their candidates' position on slavery as in accord with the views of Florida voters. Florida Democrats claimed that Cass opposed the Wilmot Proviso but unfortunately were forced to admit that he seemed to accept the assertion that territorial legislatures had the right to determine the fate of slavery in their territories. Supporters took heart in the fact that Cass denied Congress's right to restrict slavery. One newspaper even quoted Cass's statement that "Congress has no more right to take from a man his slave than his wife. . . . We should think this language at least strong enough to dispel every doubt," the commentator asserted.[45] But doubters there were, and the Whigs homed in on Cass's nativity. At a speech in Jacksonville Cabell himself ridiculed Democratic attempts to identify Cass with Southern interests, reminding his hearers that Taylor owned a plantation on the Mississippi River while Cass lived on Lake Michigan. Cass, Cabell argued, secretly supported the Wilmot Proviso. Another critic charged that Cass was an "enemy in disguise, with the smiling looks he would lure to him the people of the South, that unexpectedly . . . he may stab them in the vitals."[46]

Other than portraying Taylor as a political neophyte—a charge that probably was no detriment at all—the Democrats could say little against him. Yet Fillmore, who coddled "abolitionists," was dangerous to Southern interests. He had failed to denounce Joshua Giddings when the latter had said that "Murder and treason by slaves was JUSTIFED" during the *Creole* affair in 1840. Fillmore, they charged, was among those Whig politicians of the North who had "latched on to the 'abolition of slavery' as a 'means of acquiring place and power at the sacrifice of our happy Union." Fillmore, Democrats warned, was a dangerous gamble should Taylor not survive.[47]

DuVal and Cabell both finished their campaigns in Middle Florida. Addressing the Democratic Club of Tallahassee, DuVal provided his hearers with accounts of his enthusiastic reception in East Florida and predicted victory for the

Democrats.⁴⁸ The canvass concluded with two huge events in Quincy and Marianna in which both parties participated. On September 14 and 15 an estimated 1,200 voters turned out in Quincy to hear speakers from both parties speechify before enthusiastic crowds. According to one account the "combat grew more interesting" on the second day as Richard Keith Call, Jesse Finley, and George T. Ward spoke for the Whigs and Augustus Maxwell, John Milton, and the gubernatorial candidate William Bailey spoke for the Democrats. Glee clubs from Leon, Jackson, and Gadsden Counties serenaded the attendees, and a "rich, ample, and sumptuous" barbecue enlivened the occasion.⁴⁹

The campaign concluded in Marianna with what was supposed to be a bipartisan affair but instead resembled a Whig victory celebration. The day began with Whig delegations from various parts of the county marching into town playing music and with banners flying. Each processional marched around the square giving cheers for Cabell, Brown, Taylor, and Fillmore. Cabell himself took the rostrum, speaking of his legislative accomplishments. John Milton then took his stand for Democrats, "in vindication of Mr. Polk's war, and Mr. Cass's anti-Southern position upon the subject of slavery extension." A Whig commentator speculated that "not one was convinced of Mr. Cass's soundness even to his own party." In an enthusiastic rejoinder, Cabell "destroyed the flimsy tissue woven by his antagonist, gave a triumphant vindication of the Whigs, and Whig candidates," presenting "reasons and arguments showing so plainly and conclusively that Gen. Taylor was the *man for the South* and for these times of crisis."⁵⁰

DuVal must have understood by this time that the Whigs had the momentum—such was the obvious conclusion—but he may have held out hope that his long service to the people of Florida would put him over the top. If these were his sentiments, he would be disappointed. Whigs prevailed everywhere. It was a blowout. Surveying the carnage, the Tallahassee *Floridian* admitted on October 7, "Our state elections, so far as heard from, have resulted disastrously for the democrats—The Legislature, Governor, and Congressman all lost: at least present probabilities leave but little hope of any different result. So be it. We have struggled hard for a victory but as our opponents have snatched it from us; we must abide the loss as best we may." The final totals saw Cabell besting DuVal by a vote of 4,382–3,802. Cabell ran ahead of DuVal in every county in West and Middle Florida except Washington, Franklin, and Jefferson Counties. DuVal bested his opponent in East and South Florida, but his margins were not significant enough to overcome Cabell's majorities in West and Middle Florida.⁵¹

One month later, after the presidential totals came in, the results were the same. The *Floridian*'s editors, Samuel Sibley and Charles Dyke, admitted again on November 11 that "we are soundly thrashed, and we cheerfully 'acknowledge the corn.' Our opponents have out-footed us in the race, though we gave them as good a pull for it as we were able, under all the circumstances. All we have now

Thomas Brown, DuVal's old friend and neighbor, was elected governor of Florida on the Whig ticket in 1848. Courtesy of State Archives of Florida.

to do is gather up our armor, like Wellington's Guards at Waterloo, 'up and at them, again.'"

When all was said and done, the Whig attacks and his opponent's youth (Cabell at thirty-two was half DuVal's age) doomed DuVal's candidacy. "Rough and Ready"'s status as a slaveholder and war hero and the lack of enthusiasm for Lewis Cass also played a part in DuVal's defeat. In fact, rightly or wrongly, DuVal chose the latter as the primary cause that had doomed his candidacy. Instead of blaming himself for dividing Middle Florida's Democrats over the past three years, DuVal chose to blame Cass for his defeat. In the first sentence of a four-page letter to John Crittenden congratulating his old Kentucky friend on the Whig victory, DuVal stated, "The popularity of Gen. Taylor defeated my election to Congress." Until the Whigs put Fillmore on the ticket he was for Taylor, as were nearly all the Democrats in Florida. DuVal acknowledged that Taylor's "manly character and his patriotism, . . . his honesty and his virtues and his intimate acquaintance with the actions and policy of the government for the last forty years" may carry the nation though. "He is no trading politician—If he has a pure & able cabinet our country will continue to prosper and I sincerely hope

& trust he will select you for Secretary of State." No "Whig in the Union has so much confidence of the Democracy as yourself. All believe in your patriotism & integrity." DuVal took some solace in the fact that Van Buren, "a traitor to all parties," did not receive any electoral votes.[52]

After offering his opinions on the perilous nature of the Union, DuVal closed by providing Crittenden with an appraisal of his personal situation. "Many causes have intervened to prevent my writing to you and a few other esteemed and valued friends. My pecuniary situation has weighed upon me heavily. I have lost all I possessed in this country and am struggling for my daily bread. I am so depressed in my circumstances that now I neither own a house to shelter me & my daughter Mrs. Beall & her children, nor do I own a servant." He had for the past three years been without the "usual comforts of life. The practice of law is almost worthless. The business in this country is so much decreased in our courts that not a member of the bar can do more than live in a frugal manner. I am often in want of a dollar to go to the market—clients in the desperate state of business can not pay." DuVal also understood that the likelihood of future political office seemed remote. "I have never been an applicant for office . . . and never expect to beg for office. I am well convinced that he who will not solicit patronage and court office, will not have it thrust upon him. I for one will starve rather than curry after political favors."[53]

William P. DuVal had hit rock bottom. At sixty-four years of age and with a widowed daughter and her children to care for, he had no money, few friends, and no prospects. In his mind the people of Florida had repudiated him. How could he recover his self-respect after such a heartbreaking loss? What would DuVal do now? Where would he turn? Everything tended to point westward. DuVal would to go to Texas. But how? And when?

CHAPTER 20

Gone to Texas—
Gone to Washington

As the full measure of DuVal's defeat began to sink in, his family in Texas reacted with a mixture of compassion, despair, and indignation. When he learned the news Thomas DuVal expressed his regret and urged his father to migrate to Texas. DuVal's response to his son was that it was "useless to fret or complain. Florida is the only country whose people never *forgive the man who renders them great service*. I am satisfied with the results of the election, and shall remain. My quiet & happiness does not depend on the fickle popularity of the passing hour—popular applause springs like a mushroom in a night from mere fungus—it comes often without merit, and perishes without cause or crime."[1]

What most concerned DuVal at the moment was his family; especially on his mind was the fate of Elizabeth and her children. No one in Leon County was able to make a living practicing law. "The pecuniary distress is great in this state," he wrote to Thomas. "Cotton sells so low that our planters instead of making anything are in debt. No man ventures to incur any liabilities that owns property and the business in my profession is yet declining so as to render it a starving pursuit." All DuVal's fellow members of the bar were seeking judgeships. "They can not live by the present practice." DuVal confessed that several times the previous winter he had gone without eating. "I look steady at the result and nothing but the balding head of poverty presents itself before me."[2]

DuVal told his son he would have joined him in Texas had Elizabeth and her children not been with him. He could not raise funds sufficient even to transport them to New Orleans. "I can no more move to Texas than I could swim over the Pacific. Here I am fastened by poverty and in my present condition am doomed to die here. . . . I go to no man's house here," he continued despairingly. "I live like a hermit. My thoughts and cares & distress are preying on my vitals—I am in a perpetual fever, so that night after night I can not sleep. I have no enjoyment. Life is a mountain pressing me down and God grant it would pass me under the earth."[3]

DuVal then reminded Thomas that he and his brother John had discussed the prospect of establishing a ranch south of Austin near San Antonio. "If I come with your sister, houses or cabins must be ready. I can do nothing else. I can live by hunting and fishing—I want to get away from scenes here that distress and destroy my mind." But for the moment at least there were no funds to accomplish anything. DuVal's brother was also in desperate straits. "Your Uncle John is much embarrassed with old debts from Virginia and he can do nothing for you or myself." Finally, DuVal suggested that Marcia Price might raise money to meet her sister Elizabeth and her children in New Orleans and then return with them to Galveston. If such were possible, DuVal "would follow as soon as I could arrange my little matters here."[4]

For the moment at least, DuVal was stuck in Tallahassee. Though beaten down by financial and physical burdens, he followed national events as best he could through newspapers and whatever other sources of information he could obtain. In the waning days of the Thirtieth Congress several territorial bills were being presented. Senator Stephen Douglas of Illinois, chairman of the committee on territories, was conferring with President Polk on a bill to create one huge territory consisting of California and New Mexico. The massive size of this territory mitigated against having it encompass one territory, and eventually two bills would be offered: one for the New Mexico Territory without mention of slavery and another bill admitting California as a state, thus bypassing the territorial stage altogether. Also, word leaked out of Washington that another committee was drafting a bill to abolish the slave trade in the District of Columbia.

In response to these dangerous omens John C. Calhoun organized Whig and Democratic congressional leaders to issue a bipartisan address to the Southern people on the subject of the impending danger. The final address emerging from these discussions was largely the work of Calhoun himself. It denounced the Wilmot Proviso as part of a conspiracy of the North to steal Southern property despite constitutional protections. Once this encirclement was completed, emancipation would be forced upon the South, and the result would be utter ruin as free blacks and profligate whites would, in their unholy alliance with opportunist politicians from both North and South, plunder the region.[5] It was indeed an apocalyptic vision that DuVal in his miserable mental state could envision perfectly. On February 13 DuVal rose from his sickbed to write to Calhoun that he had read his report to the Southern members of Congress. "It is all it should be," DuVal stated, "clear, forcible and temperate."

John C. Calhoun, ca. 1850. Courtesy of Library of Congress.

It is such a report as will stand the scrutiny of the wisest heads of the nation.... The time is past for conciliation, this has long been the mistaken policy of the South. For one I am ready to meet the worse that can now occur. My native State Virginia has stood forward, nobly under her lead the South will rally in spite of the traitors that has stolen into her confidence and now like scorpions are stinging her bosom. Virginia has an immense store of arms and she will distribute them to sustain the South. When the time shall come (and I fear it is near) I will return to my native state, and leave nothing undone to procure 1200 stand of arms for a corps that I will raise & command in this State and hold ready to march to any point where their services may be required.

If slaves must wrongfully be taken from us, we will try and settle them in the north, we will give them freedom and let them conquer our enemies, and give them their cities and country that they win by their arms. The coloured race will have much to encourage them in this attempted freedom, a country they can call their own, wealth and honor the result.

> Able leaders, discipline and arms will carry that destruction & ruin to our enemies that they are preparing for us. The fancied security of the north may be shattered by a volcano—over which they little dream they are preparing for themselves. I rejoice to see so many of the Southern members uniting on your report, and if further action is determined on by our Southern friends, I am ready to act with them at all hazard.... Let me hear of your health, and let me also have your opinion of the *hope or prospect* of any compromise of the all engrossing question of slavery. I trust providence will preserve your health and enable you to bring to a favorable issue to the agitating and dangerous controversy that so seriously threatens the perpetuity of our union.[6]

Finally, DuVal expressed his hope to Calhoun that there were still yet some Northern politicians who would respect Southern rights. He rejoiced that Cass had returned to the Senate, where he would have the opportunity to demonstrate that his "professions are as sincere as I believe them to be. I sacrificed my election to congress, to sustain him, from the conviction he stood firmly by the constitutional rights of the South. Could I have sustained General Taylor, no man in this State, could have defeated my election. I have never sacrificed principle for office. I go for my country & her honor & rights and prefer death on principles and honor [rather than] office without them."[7] DuVal eventually came to believe, if he did not believe it already, that Calhoun's vision of creating a pure Southern states'-rights party—a party that would stand for the protection of slaveholders' rights in the territories and throughout the nation—was the only hope of preserving the Union.

DuVal was certain that the future of the Union rested on the rights of slaveholders to take their property into the territories. Thus he despaired of the future of the Union. As he wrote to John Crittenden,

> The great questions that have agitated, and so long divided the people of the Union (with the exception of *one*) have never for a moment caused any obvious fears in my mind as to the safety of the Union. The question of slavery (as it exists under our constitution) and the insidious attempts as well as declarations of the abolitionists and not the all absorbing question of the Wilmot Proviso threaten the disunion of the states. The Tariff, Bank, &c are mere subjects of policy and within the constitutional powers of Congress. We may honestly differ about measures of mere expediency without any fear of effecting the Union. The slave question is the rock which will certainly dash the Constitution, into fragments, unless the wisdom of our statesmen can provide against so great a calamity.[8]

DuVal also wrote as part of his missive to Crittenden his thoughts on the future of the West. He thought it strange that Polk's treaty with Mexico did not include in it provisions for free blacks to migrate to Mexico. After all, he asserted, "nine-tenths of that nation are of the coloured race, the mongrels of Indians, Spaniards, and Negroes. I believe Mexico would have willingly received the free blacks of this country. They would have accessed their physical power and I believe added to their *mental improvement.*" Because we "held the Mexican Empire in our hand we should have enforced such a provision to relieve our country from the eminent danger of disunion," he asserted. This should be immediately "accomplished by treaty with Mexico. . . . Such a provision will work as a safety valve & prevent an explosion of our Confederacy. The Valley of the Ohio and Mississippi would be the broad road for the Negroes to travel to Mexico—provisions would be cheap and the honest fannaticks of the North, seeing the broad road thus freely open to the negroes, they would be satisfied that in time, the slave states would become free states—and they would know that this policy could not be carried into effect immediately, but that it would so result eventually. This hobby would at once be swept away from the unprincipled demagogues who now urgently excite the certain destruction of the Union."⁹

The only other way to save the Union, DuVal asserted, was to "let New Mexico be set apart, specifically for the free negros, and every person throughout the Union who may liberate their slaves, should be compelled to send them to New Mexico." The United States must not allow foreign access to the region and then could at some future time as "Congress should think proper permit New Mexico to become a separate & distinct government—it could be so declared—*but not as a state of this union.* This plan would relieve us of the danger of dissolution & no man who loves this country would hesitate to give up this portion of our territory obtained from Mexico to save our glorious Union." DuVal suggested that his plan was the only sure way to "to secure the peace and stability of our country." DuVal concluded by suggesting that "if Gen'l Taylor & his cabinet can settle the question of slavery in this or any other manner to the satisfaction of the parties—it will be the greatest service and the most essential, blessing that can be considered or bestowed on our country. God grant it may be accomplished."¹⁰

Thus did DuVal offer up his advice to the man everyone understood was the odds-on favorite to become the president-elect's secretary of state. But Crittenden refused Taylor's invitation to join his cabinet, deciding instead to fulfill his election promise of serving as Kentucky's governor. Yet he would still exert a profound influence on Taylor's administration.¹¹

In the spring of 1849 DuVal's physical and mental state was precarious. Like other lawyers in Middle Florida, he was in desperate straits. His goal was still to move to Texas. But he was ill, he had no money, and he admitted to his son Thomas that he could not leave Elizabeth and her children in Tallahassee "without a dollar to support them. I never was so tied down, as now, in the most grinding servitude—it is a painful struggle to obtain the most common daily support for my little family & often after all my efforts want meat & bread. My health & spirits are sinking under it—and care will soon perform its last office for me. So far from treading with regret at such a termination, it is my greatest consolation, disgusted and tired of life, I have no object in desiring its continuance." DuVal noted that the "Bar throughout this state are idle & dispairing." Having just attended the courts in Madison and Hamilton Counties, he had made only $8.00, not even enough to pay expenses, and these were among the highest receipts among members of the bar. Many of his fellow lawyers were heading to California.[12]

Thomas had offered his father the opportunity to sell Texas lands in Florida. But DuVal told his son it would be impossible to sell them in Tallahassee because the "best lands near this place can be had for a trifle." DuVal told Thomas that he had had heard from his brother John Crittenden that he was heading to Austin but that he was uncertain where he would eventually reside. DuVal was reluctant to go to Texas until they had decided on some fixed location. "I can not think at my time of life of floating about uncertain as to where I shall reside."[13]

By December DuVal had finally raised sufficient funds to transport himself and Elizabeth and her children to Texas. Once it became known that DuVal was planning the move, friends and well-wishers began inviting the old man to farewell events. In late December a party of his friends traveled to St. Marks to see their friend off. Days earlier an assembly of the bar offered DuVal a personal tribute. "We have ever found you able and skillful," they asserted. "Virtue and Justice have always found in you a powerful advocate—but to oppressions and wrong, an indignant and seething opponent. We have seen the weak, the widow, the orphan look to you with perfect confidence for protection, and we have witnessed the haughty oppressor tremble beneath your rebuke. In your intercourse with us you have even been kind and courteous, never availing yourself of your superior learning and experience to take advantage. . . . These virtues, and many others which we have not space to enumerate, have endeared you to us all, and there is not a lawyer in Florida who will not shed a tear of regret at your departure."[14]

Another similar tribute announced that this "true patriot, and noble and generous hearted man, has left the State with whose interest, history, and fame Floridians of every description are so connected. . . . Gov. DuVal leaves behind him in every part of Florida, a multitude of hearts that are inexpressibly sad at his departure. Their warmest wishes will follow him for his prosperity, happiness, and lengthened days in his new home. He needs no introduction there. His name and his fame have gone before him. There is no part of this immense nation from Canada to Mexico, from Maine to California, where that name would be a strange sound. That Texas, whose most devoted friend he has ever been, in whose defense his chivalrous son poured out his blood will give him a hearty and generous welcome, we have no doubt."[15]

From St. Marks DuVal, Elizabeth, and her children reached New Orleans and then finally boarded the steamer *Palmetto* on December 19 bound for Galveston. The two-day journey must have been an unpleasant one. On board were ninety-six people, of whom sixty-eight were slaves. Twenty-one horses and nineteen sheep were also on board. Once in Galveston DuVal wished first of all to make the four-day journey to Austin. A stage to the capital was available every Monday and Wednesday, with taverns available along the two-hundred-mile-route.[16]

DuVal adjusted to his new surroundings in the Texas capital. He likely found a friend in Governor Peter Hansborough Bell, a native of Virginia. Meanwhile, events in Washington were moving toward resolution of the vexing territorial controversy springing from the acquisition of California and other western lands. President Zachary Taylor angered Southerners in his insistence that California be admitted as a state on the basis of the will of its own people. As Henry Clay, Daniel Webster, and other elder statesmen labored with Stephen Douglas to cobble together a compromise, John C. Calhoun, aged, sick, and dying, made one last effort to secure for the South a permanent protection of its institutions despite its minority status in the Union. Calhoun's demands went unfulfilled, as the final version of the compromise contained no such provision. DuVal followed these events closely through the newspapers.[17] He also read of Calhoun's final speech in the Senate, read for him on March 4 by Senator James M. Mason of Virginia. Calhoun died on the last day of the month. An obstinate President Taylor would follow him to the grave in July. With the president and the South Carolinian gone, Clay, Webster, and Douglas consummated the compromise. The final agreement reached in September admitted California as a free state and created the New Mexico and Utah Territories without mention of slavery (the result being, much to DuVal's disgust, that they were organized under the principle of popular sovereignty). The slave trade but not slavery was abolished in the District of Columbia. The only item the South received in the bargain was a new federal fugitive slave statute. Time would tell whether this law would be enforced in the North, for there were already assertions by Senator William H. Seward of New York and others that they would resist the law's enforcement.[18]

One of the thorniest issues the senators grappled with (but one that received little comment given the gravity of the other measures) was the controversy over the Texas boundary with New Mexico. Of course, this question was of paramount concern to Texas. When the United States annexed Texas, the treaty was vague regarding the precise western and northern boundaries. Most Texans assumed that the boundary reached west to the Santa Fe settlement, but the matter did not come to a head until after the Mexican War, when U.S. troops occupied the town. In March 1848 the Texas legislature created Santa Fe County and sent out administrators to implement Texas laws by creating a state court. But opposition from settlers and the U.S. Army brought an end to the attempt to incorporate the area into the state of Texas. President Taylor's actions clearly demonstrated that he opposed Texas's claims, as he encouraged the Santa Fe residents to write their own constitution and apply for statehood. As the proposed state would certainly enter the Union as a free state, Texas leaders were doubly outraged at the prospect. On the final day of 1849, responding to an appeal from Governor Bell, the Texas legislature redefined the Santa Fe County boundaries and created several other counties, and the governor dispatched Robert S. Neighbors to bring the new counties into Texas's jurisdiction. Neighbors's efforts failed just as the U.S. Senate was considering its compromise measures. Governor Bell and his fellow Texas were indignant. In August he proclaimed that Texas must defend its rightful claims "at all hazards and to the last extremity."[19]

Temperament and inclination naturally drew DuVal into political discussions in the state capital. And when called upon, he eagerly provided his views on the issues under discussion. Two months earlier in June, 1850, in a long address at a public meeting DuVal had spoken in response to a series of resolutions passed by a public meeting in Austin with regard to the boundary issue. He denounced the Taylor administration's action as a violation of Texas's "rights and sovereignty." By encouraging "a convention of her rebellious citizens in Santa Fe County to organize an independent government within her defined and acknowledged territory," he charged, the administration had violated the Constitution. In the same speech DuVal also faulted the U.S. army for not doing enough to protect the Texans from the Comanches.[20]

After Clay's omnibus bill failed in the Senate, DuVal rejoiced in the fact and wrote to Senator R. M. T. Hunter of Virginia, enclosing Governor Bell's address and adding that the "people of this state are calmly determined to take possession of the Santa Fe country. There is no noise or violent excitement about this subject. When a people know they are rightfully protecting their own dignity and honor and have determined to do it at every hazard it is pretty certain that they will effect their own object. The first hostile gun that is fired in this contest dissolves the union." DuVal predicted that "every southern State will stand by Texas. Hers is the common cause of the South. . . . Our Governor's message speaks as the voice of this state and you can rely upon it that his views will be carried out by the Legislature." DuVal wrote to his fellow Virginian that their native state "will have to head the Southern Confederacy. She has arms for herself and two [other] Southern States, and the union if broken, we will save the North all further trouble with California and New Mexico, for we will take them to our exclusive use."[21]

DuVal remained a strident advocate for Texas's right to its western boundaries, and, assuming the role of an elder statesman—and a fiery one—he spoke out continually of the threats of submission.[22] But he was dismayed when the final compromise included an amicable resolution to the boundary dispute. Senator

Sam Houston led the Texas congressional delegation in the acceptance of the Texas Boundary Bill, which fixed the western boundary of Texas at its present limits in exchange for ten million dollars' worth of bonds to satisfy the debts incurred by the state as a republic. At first DuVal joined other extremists in denouncing the "Texas Bribery Bill," but he soon accepted the inevitability of the compromise.[23] DuVal was naturally drawn into politics and could not resist, when called upon, to publicly express his views. Thus, on one occasion, at a Democratic meeting at the Travis County courthouse in Austin, the gathering called DuVal to the chair. While the assembly "cheerfully acquiesced in the compromise measures adopted at the late session of Congress . . . at the same time we warn our brethren of the Northern states, that a faithful and prompt enforcement of the fugitive slave law, can alone make that settlement of a vexed question binding upon us of the South," DuVal asserted. He then, according to an account of the gathering, "delivered a very eloquent and forcible speech on the politics of the day."[24]

Even as his inner demons haunted him, DuVal still had the capacity to draw people near. Some years later, one old Austin resident recalled DuVal as a "genial, entertaining old fellow" who "possessed an inexhaustible store of anecdotes gathered from the varied experiences of a long life. His appearance in public was signal for all lovers of good stories to assemble around him." DuVal often referred to his time as governor of Florida as a kind of purgatory, noting that "if he went to hell when he died and the authorities who presided over that institution did not give him credit for those years, he should always think they did him injustice." His "situation" there, he asserted, so "nearly resembled that ascribed to the infernal regimes as any he could imagine." As ever before, young people were attracted to DuVal. One child who heard his tales was Burr Grayson DuVal, who remembered his grandfather's stories many years later, recalling that his most vivid childhood memories were "connected to the old man and his fascinating stories."[25]

But DuVal's primary concern at the moment was with the mundane questions of making a living. Soon after his arrival in Austin, DuVal joined his son Thomas's law practice. Their work saw no diminishment once Governor Bell appointed Thomas DuVal Texas's secretary of state. One of their primary fields of practice was pressing claims of Texas citizens for property taken from them by the Comanche Indians. An advertisement for their services noted that DuVal would personally pursue the claims in Washington.[26] While DuVal worked to establish himself in Texas, he kept in touch with issues back in Florida. John DuVal wrote him that he should have held out a little longer in Florida. The area's economic prospects had brightened. Business was on the increase, and cotton prices were rising. Florida's political climate had also changed. "I am satisfied from all I hear that the people are mortified at your removal from Florida and I have no doubt if you had only made a visit to Texas holding your citizenship in this State you would certainly have been returned to the Senate in place of Levy." The

Washington—Capitol (East View), ca. 1848. Courtesy of Library of Congress.

senator was "now the most unpopular man in East Florida." Yulee's stand against the compromise had "ruined him with the Whigs and Democrats" and all opposed him except for Florida's small "South Carolina faction." DuVal urged his brother to return to Florida and offered to assist him in reestablishing his law practice. "You as well as myself are getting old. Come back amongst your old friends and live in peace the balance of your days."[27]

But DuVal looked not to Tallahassee but to Washington. Not long after witnessing his widowed daughter Marcia Price's marriage to George W. Paschal on March 25, 1852, DuVal set off for the nation's capital.[28] The town had grown in the seven or so years since he had visited, but it had not reached its potential. It lacked the quality of a settled town. According to one description of the place, the capital was "a combination of town and pasture. . . . Even after half a century it still looked unfinished. Pennsylvania Avenue was the principal commercial street, lined on both sides with buildings from the Capitol to the White House. Beyond it Washington was a town of monotonous red brick row houses, usually mounted on raised, or 'English,' basements, with high stairs leading to the front doors. Here and there a row boasted a fine house, wider than its neighbors. . . . Many of the lots were vacant, and some of the stately circles barren, occupied by only two or three houses and seas of grass. . . . Some streets were paved with stones; others were gravel or dirt. The Mall was a prodigious grassy field. Cows and sheep grazed there, making bare dirt paths that ran string-like from one side to the other. To a farmer's eye it seemed a vast waste. At the East end the Capitol stood taller than any building around, but even so, it was not sufficiently imposing for its size."[29]

DuVal arrived in Washington during the waning days of the Thirty-second Congress. Settling into Mrs. Peyton's boarding house on P Street, DuVal surveyed the scene. Many of his former associates such as Mason and Hunter of Virginia were still in the Senate, as were Cass and Sam Houston, who was being mentioned as a presidential candidate. Clay, though ailing (he would die in June), was still there. DuVal found Florida senators Yulee and Westcott replaced by Jackson Morton and Stephen R. Mallory. Cabell was still in the House, but that session would be his last. DuVal found a friend in Peter H. Bell, who had resigned as Texas governor to enter the House. DuVal's brother John and his wife, Anne, were also living in a boarding house on Capitol Hill.[30]

While he took on work for many clients, including Sam Houston, DuVal's primary duties involved securing compensation for property taken from Texans by the Comanche Indians since the annexation.[31] DuVal argued before the appropriate congressional committee and set forth the rationale for payment of the claims, carefully laying out the previous case law in relation to states and territories with other tribes, including the Creeks and Seminoles. His pamphlet *The Argument of Wm. P. DuVal on the Claims of Citizens for Compensation for the Property Taken from Them by the Comanche Indians, since the Annexation of that State by the United States* (1852) circulated widely. One commentator noted that DuVal's publication was "better calculated than any thing we have seen to put the case in its true light."[32]

DuVal argued that compensation was just and that if it was denied settlers might take matters into their own hands. If their women and property were plundered, settlers' own "rifles will clear and square the account with these Comanches." Moreover, as the pioneers were in the vanguard of settlement, the U.S. government owed these hardy pioneers protection. "Who has thought for the frontier," DuVal asked rhetorically, "for the bold and daring pioneer? These seem to be forgotten. Yes, these brave and fearless men, who have in so many instances, and under so many privations, won from the fierce warriors the wilderness and the waste, and created an empire, now occupied by many prosperous and happy millions of people daily adding strength and wealth to the nation. They are neglected and forgotten." DuVal contrasted the settlers' plight with the federal money showered on the railroads, owned by wealthy stockholders. It was the settlers who made railroad building possible by their "daring and gallantry."[33]

DuVal's efforts on the part of claimants taxed his health. At sixty-eight years of age, he found his energy limited. While working on his treatise, DuVal suffered a collapse that resembled a stroke. DuVal's sister-in-law Anne DuVal described the episode to her daughter in Austin: "Your Uncle William . . . was looking very well until a few days since when he was taken with paralysis. We knew nothing about it until he came up on Sunday evening and told us about it. He looked very badly—it only affected his tongue, which makes him articulate very badly & his spirits were a good deal affected."[34] Like others of his age, DuVal fell victim to a whole battery of torturous treatments such as "cupping" and "blistering" that were intended to increase blood flow. As he wrote to his son Thomas, he protested the treatments, but still they were performed. "I was barbecued accordingly," he complained.[35]

Though his infirmities prevented him from pursuing the active life he had once enjoyed, DuVal constantly kept abreast of national affairs. Proof that he still exerted influence in his old age came in a letter to his old friend Thomas Brown only days after Franklin Pierce's inauguration in March 1853. In a shaky hand that betrayed his physical frailty, DuVal proudly informed the governor that he had secured port collection positions for his old Florida friends, Hugh Archer and George Hawkins. His primary purpose in writing to Brown was to secure a judgeship for his friend Benjamin Wright, and the Florida governor had authority to do that before an election was mandated. "I need not tell you his virtues, modesty, and true manly principles. His legal acquirements and long practice & experience in our courts render his appointment highly expedient & proper. Judge Wright [was in Florida] from the *beginning of our Territorial Government* and no man is more respectable and esteemed."[36]

DuVal hoped to return to Texas, but his condition steadily worsened, and he fell in his boarding house not long after his seventieth birthday. As they had previously, physicians diagnosed DuVal's condition as apoplexy and once again prescribed a series of treatments, all to no avail. He died on March 18, 1854. Peter Bell was at his side. In a lengthy letter to Thomas DuVal, Bell noted that DuVal's passing was "easy and tranquil as ever fell to the lot of a human being struggling with the dread Messenger." Bell assured Thomas that his father had retained "his mental faculties to a wonderful degree to the last moment, often calling your name & other members of his family." He was playful to the last; Bell noted that when asked if he needed anything, DuVal "would always evade a direct reply, and make some jocular remark about his situation." Bell assured Thomas DuVal that his father had died in peace. "In looking upon the corpse this morning I was struck with its natural appearance indicating clearly that he died without the usual agony of pain and with great composure of mind." Another friend on the scene who had known DuVal from his days in Florida assured Thomas that his father had enjoyed the constant attention of a "numerous circle of devoted friends, who surrounded his dying bed & ministered to his every wish & want. It should be a consoling reflection to you to be assured that he received all the care & attention which affection & the most devoted friendship could render. He could not have been more kindly & affectionately attended, had he died in the bosom of his family."[37] The day after his death DuVal was laid to rest in the Congressional Cemetery, within sight of his friend Samuel Southard's headstone.

News of DuVal's death spread rapidly. The Austin *Texas State Gazette* reported DuVal's passing, noting that "Governor DuVal was a member of the Congress of 1812, and leaves only one associate in that patriotic assembly now alive—Gen. Lewis Cass. The deceased filled with honor to himself and the benefit of his country, many important offices under the Federal Government; he was a man of strictest integrity," the report continued, "and usually fascinating in the social relations of life."[38]

DuVal's death was also noted in Boston, Baltimore, and other major cities.[39] The Washington *National Intelligencer* noted that it was unfortunate that DuVal had died far from home. But it assured its readers that he was "not among strangers," "for in this City and in Congress he had friends, whose kindness and attentions during his illness soothed his sufferings and tranquilized him in his dying moments." DuVal bore his illness with "uncomplaining fortitude and encountered death with calmness and resignation." DuVal, "whilst distinguished in public life," the account continued, "was much esteemed and beloved for his virtue and estimable qualities in private. He was a man of cheerful, equitable temper, kind, sociable, sincere and in all the accidents and exigencies of life reliable and true, and those who best knew him are those who will most deplore his loss."[40]

Naturally newspapers in Florida recognized DuVal's passing. The Pensacola *Gazette* on March 25 noted that "thus has gone one of the fastest and most faithful friends of our young state. In all his sufferings he maintained the same lofty spirit and the same self-sacrificing disposition which distinguished his public and private life in Florida. Peace to his ashes." A memorial from the Tallahassee bar appeared in the Tallahassee *Floridian and Journal* on April 1, 1854. Perhaps DuVal's greatest memorial appeared in the Washington *National Intelligencer* more than a month after his death. In a lengthy biographical account drawn largely from DuVal's own stories as depicted in Washington Irving's writings, the piece recounted his life in Virginia and Kentucky and on the Florida frontier. "Few men who have led such a varied life have left behind so pure and spotless a name. His public services, and the integrity and ability with which he acquitted himself, in his public trusts, are widely known. His dauntless courage, too, has been proven on various trying occasions. But it is among his [intimates] that his loss will be more especially lamented, among those who delighted in his simple, unaffected goodness, his genial humor, his devoted and unwavering friendship, in the kind and generous qualities of his heart, and the manly independence of his spirit." William P. DuVal, the commentator asserted, was "a type of the genuine American character."[41]

Epilogue

In 1925 Senator Duncan Upshaw Fletcher of Florida observed before a gathering of the Florida Historical Society that Governor William Pope DuVal's grave in Washington's Congressional Cemetery lacked proper recognition for a man so important to his state and to the nation's early development. DuVal's monument was "rough and darkened with age and elements," and the "only inscription was simply his name, William P. DuVal. . . . It is now in order," the senator asserted, "to give some attention to the monument and add the date of birth and death and the words, 'First Governor of the Territory of Florida, 1822–1834.'"[1] And so today the large obelisk that marks DuVal's resting place in the nation's capital reflects this brief description.

Since the governor was laid to rest, the nation, as he predicted, had sundered over the question of the expansion of slavery in the territories. As it had for other families of the time, the conflict strained relations in DuVal's family. DuVal's son Thomas, a federal judge at the time of the Civil War's outbreak, opposed secession but experienced the pain of a son fighting for the Confederacy. Sitting out the war in Austin and New Orleans, Thomas DuVal ultimately traveled to Washington, where he consulted with the Lincoln administration over the reconstruction of Texas. After the war DuVal continued as a federal judge until his death in 1880. He died a Republican.[2]

DuVal's other son, John Crittenden, though no ardent secessionist, drifted in and out of Confederate service and drifted about his entire life. He never married and often appeared as a welcome guest at his family's houses. He eventually returned to Texas, where he wrote prolifically about his adventures on the Southwestern frontier. After dying, in 1897, at his sister Mary's house in Fort Worth, John Crittenden DuVal would be widely hailed as the "First Texas Man of Letters."[3]

William P. DuVal's descendants went on to make substantial contributions to their nation. One of these was DuVal West. As Senator Fletcher made his address to his hearers in Florida, DuVal's grandson, already having served President Woodrow Wilson as a diplomat in Mexico, was a sitting federal judge.

Today thousands of revelers trudge down DuVal Street in Key West. But few know for whom the street is named. Streets in Tallahassee, Jacksonville, St. Augustine, and Lake City, Florida; Lexington, Kentucky; Austin, San Antonio, Fort Worth, and Galveston, Texas; and Richmond, Virginia, also bear DuVal's name—as do counties in Florida and Texas. How to sum up DuVal's legacy? He was in every way a man of his time, influenced and affected by the places and times in which he lived. Coming of age on the Kentucky frontier as a War Hawk politician, DuVal inherited from his surroundings and his father a lifelong antipathy to Great Britain. A firm believer in expansion, DuVal shared the sentiments of his fellow Westerners that until Great Britain was ousted from its borders, the United States would never reach its potential. DuVal believed, as did Andrew Jackson, John C. Calhoun, and others, that the British were constantly plotting to undermine American expansion by enlisting and inciting Indians and enslaved Africans against Americans where they were most vulnerable—on the frontier, the periphery of settlement. Through their manufacturing and banking prowess, the British were also not above bribing American manufacturing and banking interests and the politicians who did their bidding. DuVal was certain that British duplicity was America's number one national security problem.

DuVal chose to fight these enemies and, later, Northern abolitionist interests through the Democratic Party. Coming of age in Jefferson and Madison's Democratic-Republican Party, DuVal was weaned on the Principles of '98—a doctrine of limited federal power with a deference to states' rights. DuVal deviated briefly from these principles, once while in Congress when he voted to charter the Second Bank of the United States (a measure President Madison himself favored) and later, in 1840, when he supported William Henry Harrison in place of the Democratic Martin Van Buren. DuVal's abandonment of Van Buren in support of Harrison, like that of most Southerners who had followed Old Hickory, was largely personal. Though he worked closely with John Tyler (in fact, he could almost be considered an "insider" in his administration), he returned to the Democratic Party almost immediately once his fellow Virginian left office. DuVal paid a heavy price for his temporary desertion of the Democratic Party.

DuVal grew to manhood in an agrarian age and had difficulty adjusting politically—and even psychologically—to a market economy. While he joined his mentor Old Hickory in his opposition to the National Bank, the trend of events in the Territory of Florida and elsewhere forced him to the conclusion that banks were inevitable. In DuVal's last year as governor (1834), after vetoing bank measure after bank measure, he finally signed into law a bill chartering the Union

Bank of Florida. When he returned to Florida a few years later after a brief time in Kentucky, DuVal even represented the institution in court. Thus, when the bank crashed and burned, DuVal handed a bludgeon to his opponents with which they could hammer him. It was about that time (1840) when Washington Irving first published his stories about DuVal. DuVal's son John Crittenden remembered some years later that, although his father was a "great admirer of Irving and they were warm personal friends, I do not believe he ever fully forgave him for putting these things in print. It seems that Irving had skillfully 'drawn him out' on convivial occasions, without the least suspicion on the Governor's part for the express purpose of 'taking notes.'" John Crittenden DuVal remembered that, while his father relished more than anything recounting his "personal experiences for the amusement of his friends and acquaintants, he had no desire at all to see them figuring in print." But, according to the son, DuVal eventually "came to the conclusion that authors considered themselves a privileged set, and had an acknowledged right to make use professionally of any material that might aid in catering to the public."[4]

As the "hungry forties" began to bite, DuVal, a widower and alone in his misery, fell increasingly under the spell of John C. Calhoun and others who called for a unified Southern front against the British, abolitionists, and any others who sought to block the South's access to the territories. The politics of the time catered to DuVal's worst instincts and embittered the man, who had always been able to mask his demons with his storytelling and singing.

But perhaps it is DuVal's talents as an orator, tall-tale teller, and man of the frontier, not his career as a lawyer or politician, for which he should be remembered. One year after DuVal's death, Washington Irving published *Woolfort's Roost: And Other Papers, Now First Collected* (1855), a work bringing together the writer's earlier sketches from his notebooks that had appeared in *Knickerbocker Magazine*. "The Seminoles," The Conspiracy of Neamathla," "The Origin of the White, the Red, and the Black Man: A Seminole Tradition," and of course, "The Early Experiences of Ralph Ringwood" were among the essays included in the collection. To a nation eager for a respite from the complicated and conflicted age of the 1850s, the book harked back to a simpler time before sectional politics cast a dark shadow over the future of the Union. Fortunately, DuVal did not live to experience his worst nightmare—the breaking up of the Union—and the ultimate defeat of the South he loved so much. Whether as a politician, teller of tall tales, or frontier bon vivant, William P. DuVal was without question certainly "a type of the genuine American character."

Notes

Abbreviations in Notes

Calhoun Papers Wilson, ed., *The Papers of John C. Calhoun*
Jackson Papers Feller, et al., *Papers of Andrew Jackson*
       LC Library of Congress
      NA National Archives
   PKYL P. Y. Yonge Library of Florida History, University of Florida
      PU Firestone Library, Princeton University
      TP Carter, ed., *Territorial Papers of the United States*

Preface

1. Mahon, *History of the Second Seminole War,* 61.
2. Little, *Ben Hardin,* 171, 193–94.
3. "Reminiscences of Governor Duval by the Late Judge S. J. Perry," Jacksonville *Florida Times Union,* February 10, 1910.
4. Horatio Waldo, "Florida Sketches," Apalachicola *Florida Journal,* March 17, 1841.
5. Irving, "Early Experience of Ralph Ringwood"; Irving, "The Seminoles"; Irving, "Conspiracy of Neamathla"; Irving, "Account of Duval's Visits to the Chief who Opposed Treaty of 1823."
6. Johnston, *The Heart that Would Not Hold,* 87–89, 123.
7. *The Lion of the West* first appeared at the Park Theatre, New York, on April 25, 1831. In March 1833 the play debuted in England under the title *A Kentuckian's Trip to New York* in 1815 at the Theatre Royal, Covent Garden. After playing in theaters in Edinburgh and Dublin, the Nimrod Wildfire character played to enthusiastic audiences in New York and other U.S. spectators for more than twenty years. Tidwell, ed., *The Lion of the West,* 8–9. Whether or not DuVal was actually the inspiration for Paulding's Nimrod Wildfire character is a matter of dispute. Some scholars claim the Nimrod Wildfire character was modeled after Davy Crockett. The plausible Crockett connection to the Nimrod Wildfire character is explored in Seelye, "A Well-Wrought Crockett," 23. Richard Boyd Hauck contends that Crockett was likely the source but admits that he "was not the sole

inspiration for Wildfire." Hauck, "Making It All Up," 103–11; Derr, *The Frontiersman,* 189–91. Also on Paulding see Herold, *James Kirke Paulding;* Arpad, "Jarvis, Paulding, and Col. Nimrod Wildfire," 92–106; Aderman, ed., *The Letters of James Kirke Paulding,* xvi–xxiv, 112–13.

CHAPTER 1: **Scion of the Old Dominion**

1. Ocala *Argus,* June 8, 1848.

2. Washington Irving's "Ralph Ringwood Tales" first appeared in 1840 as "The Early Experiences of Ralph Ringwood, by Geoffrey Crayon, Gent" in the *Knickerbocker or New-York Monthly Magazine.* Based on Irving's conversations with William P. DuVal in the 1810s, the stories told of DuVal's coming of age on the Kentucky frontier. Neither DuVal nor Irving made any attempt to hide Ringwood's true identity. Indeed, as Irving himself stated in a note, "Ralph Ringwood though a fictitious name, is a real personage: the worthy original is now living and flourishing in humble station. I have given some anecdotes of his early and eccentric career in . . . the very words in which he related them." See Snyder, "William Pope DuVal," 204–7; Knauss, "William Pope DuVal," 97; Swift, *Civilizers,* 6–7, 15–17. Irving's stories were widely circulated and soon became available to Floridians via newspaper reprints. The positive political spin for DuVal, a candidate for office in 1840, was not lost on the reader. For example, on October 5, 1840, the St. Joseph *Times* reprinted the stories and added, "We extract from the *Knickerbocker Magazine* on our first page the quaint graphic and original narrative of Ralph Ringwood and commend it to the perusal of our Florida friends, many of whom have heard these tales orally from *Ralph* himself. This spirited auto-biographist, is now a candidate for the Senate from Middle Florida, has drank the good old *Vernacular,* talked politics, religion, love and poetry (as the case might be) with almost every man, woman and child in Middle Florida. The fun, the frolic and the indomitable enterprise of his youth, is as sparkling and fresh yet, as when he first set out for the Buffalo or tracked the wild deer to its covert." See also "Extract from the Crayon Papers, The Seminoles," St. Joseph *Times,* November 7, 1840; Quincy *Sentinel,* October 16, 23, 1840; Tallahassee *Star of Florida,* December 29, 1840. In 1855, one year after DuVal's death, Irving published *Woolfort's Roost and other Papers.* Ralph Ringwood is specifically identified as Governor William Pope Duval of Florida in the first edition of the published book on p. 249n.

3. "Ralph Ringwood, or a Scene in the Late Democratic State Convention," Pensacola *Gazette,* May 13, 1848; Marianna *Florida Whig,* May 24, 1848.

4. According to the family historian, Margaret Gwin, "the Mount Comfort Plantation rested in the area that would later become known as the Chesnut Hill and Highland Park Addition." See Buchanan, *Duvals of Kentucky,* vii, 3–10. Most of the foregoing information on Duval's ancestors comes from the previous source and from Grabowski, *The DuVal Family,* 187–93; Swift, *Civilizers,* 1–5.

5. Van Schreeven, *Revolutionary Virginia,* 1: 98, 141, 221, 235; Jackson, *The Diaries of George Washington,* 3: 316.

6. Stokesbury, *A Short History of the American Revolution,* 247–48; Simkins, *Virginia,* 256–60; Rubin, *Virginia,* 60–63.

7. John Pope served in the Kentucky legislature and was a U.S. senator from 1807 until 1812. John's brothers William and Benjamin also came to Kentucky. His brother Benjamin

brought his son Worden to Louisville, Kentucky, in 1779. Later Worden moved to Elizabethtown, where he practiced law. Haycraft, *Haycraft's History of Elizabethtown, Kentucky*, 174, 180–82.

8. Anne DuVal died on October 3, 1792. Richmond *Gazette and General Advertiser*, October 10, 1792.

9. Mordecai, *Richmond in Days Gone By*, 105–6; Scott, *Old Richmond Neighborhoods*, 145.

10. To Be Rented, Richmond *Enquirer*, April 4, 1805.

11. Richmond *Enquirer*, August 20, 1805.

12. DuVal reminded Clay of their association in a letter. "Our old friend Chancellor Wythe & myself discovered in you when Young a Capacity that would make you an Ornament to your Country—I had your Grand Father Hudson & your Father as my friends, whose Virtues endeared them to me & my Esteem & affection naturally extended to the Son of your Father." William DuVal to Henry Clay, June 14, 1821, in Hopkins, ed., *Clay Papers*, 3: 89–91. See also on the legal scene in Richmond in those years Remini, *Henry Clay*, 9–14; Heidler and Heidler, *Henry Clay*, 19–25.

13. "DuVal Addition" Plats, Wilkinson, Adams, and Harvie, trustees of Courts, to William DuVal. Deed dated July 4, 1791, recorded in Henrico Co. Court, August 1, 1791, Robinson Papers, Virginia Historical Society.

14. William Duval to Thomas Jefferson, April 12, 1792, Thomas Jefferson Papers, LC.

15. For the settlement of Kentucky after the Revolution see Harrison and Klotter, *A New History of Kentucky*, 48–80; Friend, ed., *The Buzzel about Kentuck*; Friend, *Along the Maysville Road*, 9–58; Friend, *Kentucke's Frontiers*; Chinn, *Kentucky*; Rubin, *Virginia*, 65–66; Abernethy, *Three Virginia Frontiers*, 63–96; Rohrbough, *The Trans-Appalachian Frontier*, 9–46.

16. Jillson, *The Kentucky Land Grants*, 7–9, 45, 169.

17. Jillson, *Old Kentucky Entries and Deeds*, 411, 487.

18. Christopher Waldrep, "Opportunity of the Frontier: South of the Green," in Friend, ed., *The Buzzel about Kentuck*, 157–58.

19. Abernethy, *Three Virginia Frontiers*, 68.

20. Remini, *Henry Clay*, 14. Also on the confused nature of land titles and their litigation in Kentucky see Harrison and Klotter, *New History of Kentucky*, 52–55; Rohrbough, *The Trans-Appalachian Frontier*, 38–39; Tachau, *Federal Courts in the Early Republic, Kentucky*, 167–90.

21. Kincaid, *The Wilderness Road*, 11; Chinn, *Kentucky*, 365–75.

22. George Washington to Alexander Spotswood, July 31, 1799, in Fitzpatrick, ed., *The Writings of George Washington*, 37: 320–21.

23. Christopher Greenup (who represented Kentucky in Congress, 1792–1797, and became its governor in 1804) had acquired some of his brother-in-law Major DuVal's land warrants and had offered them for sale as early as 1788. See Lexington *Kentucky Gazette*, November 1, 1788, May 9, 1798; Jillson, *The Kentucky Land Grants*, 7–9, 45, 169; Jillson, *Old Kentucky Entries and Deeds*, 411.

24. Snyder, "William Pope DuVal," 204–7.

25. Agreement between John Cowan and Samuel P. DuVal, January 19, 1799, in *John Cowan vs William Duvall, heir-at-large of Samuel P. DuVal, deceased*, 1805, Chancery

Cases, Nelson County, Kentucky, copies in Frank Snyder Collection, box 28, f. 1, University of South Florida Library.

26. Agreement between William P. DuVal and Samuel P. DuVal, May 23, 1800 in *John Cowan vs William Duvall, heir-at-large of Samuel P. DuVal, deceased*, 1805, Chancery Cases, Nelson County, Kentucky, copies in Frank Snyder Collection, box 28, f. 1, University of South Florida Library.

27. Statement of William P. DuVal, November 10, 1805, in *John Cowan vs William DuVal*, 1805, Nelson County Court, copies in Frank Snyder Collection, box 31, f. 4, University of South Florida Library.

28. Ibid.; Nelson County, Performance Bond Book, 1792–1803, 152, in *Nelson County Pioneer* 10 (Fall 1986), 30.

29. In 1823, in an answer to a complaint filed against DuVal and his father, William P. DuVal responded that before he died, his brother Samuel had sold their property and "applied it to his own use"—property "for which he had never received a cent." Affidavit of William P. DuVal filed in St. Augustine, Florida, August 14, 1823, in *Robert Todd vs Samuel P. DuVal*, Nelson County Court, copies in Frank Snyder Collection, box 28, f. 1, University of South Florida Library.

30. Buchanan, *DuVals of Kentucky*, 90; Washington Irving's "Adventures of Ralph Ringwood," tells the story and DuVal's granddaughter Betty Paschal O'Connor repeats the tale in *My Beloved South*, 17–20; Snyder, "Nancy Hynes DuVal," 19–22.

31. Power of attorney recorded in Nelson County, Kentucky, on April 18, 1803. Nelson County, Kentucky, Deed Book 8, 1–2. Notes in Frank Snyder Collection, box 25, f. 2, University of South Florida Library. See also *Nelson County Pioneer* 14 (Winter 1990), 57.

32. Little, *Ben Hardin and His Times*, 27.

33. Ibid., 26.

34. Order Book, 1804–1808, Nelson County Court, 27.

35. William P. DuVal to Samuel Greenup, December 4, 1807, Christopher Greenup Papers, Kentucky State Archives.

36. William P. DuVal and Nancy Hynes were married on October 3, 1804. Antoniak, *Kentucky Marriage Records*, 626–29; Ellsberry, *Marriage Records of Nelson County*, 9; Nelson County, Executors Bonds, 1804–1813, 8, 9, in *Nelson County Pioneer* 11 (Spring 1988), 81.

37. McChord, *The McChords of Kentucky*, 22–28; McClure, *Two Centuries in Elizabethtown*, 168; Hynes, *Our Heritage*, 15–18; Chinn, *Kentucky*, 439. Hynes's will provided that his five slaves would be set free once they reached the age of twenty-five. Will of Andrew Hynes, September 5, 1800, Will Book A, 415–21, Nelson County Court, Bardstown, Kentucky, copy in Frank Snyder Collection, box 25, f. 6, University of South Florida Library.

38. Elizabeth Hynes's will provided that her children would each receive an equal share of her property, and on November 11, 1804, Dr. Burr Harrison and Thomas Hynes supervised the sale of all of Elizabeth Hynes's personal effects and household furniture. Will of Elizabeth Hynes, (1803), Nelson County, Will Book A, 728 in *Nelson County Pioneer* 5 (Spring 1982), 73; Bardstown *Western American*, November 2, 1804.

39. In 1806 Nancy's cousins William and Andrew formed a mercantile firm called Andrew Hynes & Company. But Andrew soon left Bardstown for greener pastures. In 1809,

at the age of twenty-four, he relocated to Nashville, Tennessee, where he opened a store and became prosperous. "Articles of Agreement between William and Andrew Hynes," February 18, 1806, in *Nelson County Pioneer* 8 (Winter 1984), 64; Harrison Taylor to William R. Hynes, February 20, 1805, Andrew Hynes Papers, 1804–1870, Tennessee State Archives, Nashville, Tennessee; McChord, *The McChords of Kentucky,* 22–28; McClure, *Two Centuries of Elizabethtown,* 168; Hynes, *Our Heritage,* 15–18; Goodstein, *Nashville,* 34–35, 50; *Jackson Papers,* 3: 73n.

40. In 1812 Dr. Burr Harrison and William P. DuVal filed a complaint against William Hynes on the part of "Burr Harrison and Elizabeth and his wife, William P. DuVal and Nancy his wife, Thomas Hynes, Polly Hynes, of lawful age and Abner Hynes and Alfred Hynes under the age of 21." Harrison and DuVal brought suit against William Hynes claiming that he had mismanaged the business and thus had damaged the claims of the others. The complaint charged that Hynes had used at least $20,000 that he had "had in his hands ten or twelve years, and has employed that same very advantageously in trade as a merchant yet refuses to settle . . . the estate of . . . Andrew and Elizabeth with Interest." The complaint also charged that William had allowed numerous accounts receivable dating back years before Andrew Hynes's death to go uncollected and that these funds were thus lost by "removals and insolvencies of such persons, by the statute of limitations owing solely to the inattention and neglect of the defendant." The case was not settled until 1823. *Heirs of Andrew Hynes vs. William R. Hynes, Executor, 1812,* in Nelson County (Kentucky) Court, copies in Frank Snyder Collection, box 25, f. 6, University of South Florida Library.

41. Bardstown *Western American,* June 22, 1804.

42. Little, *Ben Hardin and His Times,* 27; Spaulding, *Biography of a Kentucky Town,* 42; Parks, *Felix Grundy,* 19; Heller, *Democracy's Lawyer,* 36–37.

43. Quoted in Little, *Ben Hardin and His Times,* 29.

44. Abernethy, *Three Virginia Frontiers,* 69–70; See also Harrison and Klotter, *New History of Kentucky,* 55–57; Parks, *Felix Grundy,* 7–18.

45. Remini, *Henry Clay,* 29. The 1792 state constitution protected rights of slaveholders but provided that people could bring slaves into the state only for their own use, and migrants were required to sign an oath to that effect. Eventually restraints were loosened. For Kentucky's early political development as well as the question of slavery in Kentucky see Harrison and Klotter, *New History of Kentucky,* 61–80; Peterson, *The Great Triumvirate,* 10–17; Coward, *Kentucky in the New Republic,* 62–68, 136–39; Baylor, *John Pope Kentuckian,* 18–26, 59–81; Heller, *Democracy's Lawyer,* 27–30.

46. Remini, *Henry Clay,* 35–40; Parks, *Felix Grundy,* 19–31; Abernethy, *Three Virginia Frontiers,* 88–96; Peterson, *The Triumvirate,* 14; Heller, *Democracy's Lawyer,* 60–75.

47. Clift, *The Corn Stalk Militia,* iv, xviii, 171.

48. "Minutes of Bardstown Trustees, 1789–1827," printed in Bardstown *Kentucky Standard,* December 17, 27, 1936.

49. Lexington *Kentucky Gazette,* September 20, 1808; Buchanan, *DuVals of Kentucky,* 15.

50. Bill of Indictment, *Commonwealth of Kentucky vs Negro Isaac,* 1811, copies in Frank Snyder Collection, University of South Florida Library.

51. Niven, *Martin Van Buren,* 119–20.

52. Boles, *A Guide to William Wirt Papers, 1784–1864*, 1–6; Jabour, *Marriage in the Early Republic*, 63, n10.

53. William Pope and his brother John Pope, a student at Washington College, divided the land between themselves when their brother Nathaniel died. Nelson County, Deed Book 6, 624; Jillson, *Old Kentucky Entries and Deeds*, 411; John P. DuVal, "Lands for Sale in the State of Kentucky," Richmond *Enquirer*, April 23, 1811; Alexandria *Herald*, February 5, 1817.

54. William DuVal to Thomas Jefferson, June 4, 1806, Jefferson Papers, LC.

55. See William Duval to Thomas Jefferson, June 8, 14, 19, 29, November 21, 1806, and Thomas Jefferson to William DuVal, June 14, 19, 22, July 17, 1806, Jefferson Papers, LC. Scholars have thoroughly investigated the Wythe poisoning, especially as it relates to race and miscegenation in early national Virginia. See Boyd, "The Murder of John Wythe"; Malone, *Jefferson The President*, 135–40. Fawn Brodie was the first to analyze it in the context of Thomas Jefferson's own racial thinking, especially as it may have affected his ongoing relationship with his own slave, Sally Hemings. See Brodie, *Thomas Jefferson*, 522–26. One recent work disputes the likelihood of a sexual relationship between Wythe and Broadnax. See Chadwick, *I Am Murdered*.

56. On July 10, 1807, it was recorded that Major DuVal would emancipate Claiborne, age 19, and his wife, Kitty Thomas, age 17. They were to be freed July 1, 1811, but both were to serve DuVal's son William P. DuVal until that time. Also it was recorded that five more slaves were to be emancipated, but "they [were] to serve son William P. DuVal.... Molly Thomas now 16, when she is 25, Violet, daughter of Violet in Virginia, now 16, when she is 21, James, a mulatto, to serve 2 1/2 more years, America, daughter of Grace to serve three years, and she is now 18, and Scipio to be freed on August 25, 1810." Nelson County, Deed Book 6: 655, 656, in *Nelson County Pioneer* 9 (Spring 1986), 85; William DuVal to Henry Clay, June 14, 1821, in Hopkins, ed., *Clay Papers*, 3: 89–91.

57. Richmond *Virginia Argus*, February 10, 1807; Richmond *Gazette and General Advertiser*, February 11, 1807.

58. Lots in DuVal Addition advertised for sale in Richmond *Enquirer*, January 11, 1806. See also "DuVal Addition" plats and "Plan of Lots Purchased by G. Pickett and Robert Pollard of Wm DuVal, March 28, 1808." DuVal also sold to Samuel Greenhow four other lots in the DuVal addition on June 8, 1809, Robinson Papers, Virginia Historical Society.

59. William DuVal to Supporters, September 24, 1808, Thomas Jefferson Papers, LC.

60. Guild, *DuVal: Past and Present Owners of Mt. Comfort Plantation*, 5–6, 32–34.

61. Johnson, "Aaron Burr," 1–32; Heidler and Heidler, *Henry Clay*, 54–64.

62. *Richmond Virginia Argus*, March 27, 31; April 3, 1807.

63. Parmet and Hecht, *Aaron Burr*, 288. Also on the Burr trial in Richmond see ibid., 295–305; Malone, *Jefferson the President*, 310–46; Little, *History of Richmond*, 108–17; Burstein, *The Original Knickerbocker*, 56–61; Williams, *The Life of Washington Irving*, 1: 93–98.

64. Irving quoted in Burstein, *The Original Knickerbocker*, 58.

65. Washington Irving to James Paulding, June 22, 1807, in Irving, ed., *Life and Letters of Washington Irving*, 1: 94–96; Aderman et al., eds., *Letters of Washington Irving*, 1: 240.

66. Collins, *History of Kentucky*, 1: 26.

67. Third Census of the United States, 1810, Nelson County, Kentucky; Nelson County Tax Rolls (1811), 7, Nelson County Public Library.
68. Frankfort *Palladium*, December 11, 1811.
69. Little, *Ben Hardin and His Times*, 162.
70. Haycraft, *Haycraft's History of Elizabethtown, Kentucky*, 185–86.
71. Little, *Ben Hardin and His Times*, 193–94.
72. Ibid., 34.
73. Haycraft, *Haycraft's History of Elizabethtown, Kentucky*, 185–86.
74. Ibid., 36, 193–94.

CHAPTER 2: **Soldier and War Hawk Politician**

1. Lexington *Kentucky Gazette*, August 4, 18, 1812; Lexington *Reporter*, August 15, 1812.

2. Remini, *Henry Clay*, 75–93; Wiltse, *John C. Calhoun: Nationalist*, 53–66; Coit, *Calhoun*, 70–81; Bartlett, *John C. Calhoun*, 69–76; Hickey, *The War of 1812*, 24–26. Pope was burned in effigy, as a Federalist. Pope's biographer contends that though he voted against the declaration and supported other Federalist measures, Pope was a committed Democratic-Republican. See Baylor, *John Pope Kentuckian*, 82–93, 102–22. See also Lexington *Kentucky Gazette*, October 27, 1812; Hammack, *Kentucky and the Second American Revolution*, 9–14.

3. Horsman, "Battle of Tippecanoe," in Heidler and Heidler, eds., *Encyclopedia of the War of 1812*, 514–15.

4. Message of Governor Charles Scott, Frankfort *Palladium*, December 11, 1811.

5. Lexington *Kentucky Gazette*, May 5, 12, 1812. See also "To the Freeborn Sons of Kentucky," Bardstown *Repository* quoted in Frankfort *Palladium*, June 10, 1812; Governor Charles Scott, "To the Free Men of Kentucky," Frankfort *Palladium*, May 6, 1812.

6. Hammack, *Kentucky and the Second American Revolution*, 14.

7. Ibid., 20–21, 28.

8. Lexington *Kentucky Gazette*, August 4, 18, 1812.

9. Lexington *Kentucky Gazette*, August 18, 1812.

10. Adjutant General's Office, General Orders, July 27, 1812, in Lexington *Kentucky Gazette*, August 18, 1812; Fay, *War of 1812 Veterans in Texas*, 93–94.

11. Parsons et al., *The United States Congressional Districts*, 152–55; *Biographical Directory of the American Congress*, 1140.

12. Shelby quoted in Hammack, *Kentucky and the Second American Revolution*, 35–37; Harrison and Klotter, *A New History of Kentucky*, 90–93; Hickey, *The War of 1812*, 80–86.

13. Shelby quoted in Hammock, *Kentucky and the Second American Revolution*, 44.

14. Haycraft, *Haycraft's History of Elizabethtown*, 110–11; McMurtry, *Elizabethtown, Kentucky, 1779–1879*; Kirwin, *John J. Crittenden*, 18; Belko, *The Invincible Duff Green*, 19–24; Green, *Facts & Suggestions*, 7.

15. Lexington *Kentucky Register*, September 22, October 6, 13, 1812.

16. Samuel Hopkins to Governor Shelby, September 29, 1812, in *Niles Register*, November 14, 1812.

17. Hammack, *Kentucky and the Second American Revolution*, 43; Bauer, *Zachary Taylor*, 14–17.

18. Bauer, *Zachary Taylor,* 14–17.

19. In 1990 the historian Frank Snyder discovered an undated manuscript story entitled "Relief of Fort Harrison," as told to Washington Irving by William P. DuVal in Washington Irving Autographs at the Henry E. Huntington Library, San Marino, California. Snyder and his wife, Helen, transcribed the seven pages of Irving's handwritten "Notes of Conversation with William P. DuVal, the Original of Ralph Ringwood." Copies of the original and transcriptions are in the Frank Snyder Collection, box 30, f. 7 (transcript), and box 47 (original), University of South Florida Library.

20. Bauer, *Zachary Taylor,* 17; Irving, "Notes of Conversation with William P. Duval," 4–5.

21. In his report Hopkins thanked the "officers commanding brigades, many of the field officers, captains." General Hopkins to Governor Shelby, October 26, 1812, in Lexington *Kentucky Gazette,* November 10, 1812. See also William Russell to the Secretary of War, October 1812, TP, 16: 268–69; Green, *Facts and Suggestions,* 13–16.

22. Samuel Hopkins to Governor Isaac Shelby, November 27, 1812, in Esarey, ed., *Messages and Letters of William Henry Harrison,* 2: 231–34.

23. Irving, "Notes of Conversation with William P. DuVal," 5.

24. La Plante quoted in Quisenbury, *Kentucky in the War of 1812,* 30. Also on the Hopkins expedition see *Niles Weekly Register,* October 31, November 14, 21, December 26, 1812; "Extract of a Letter from a Gentleman in Bairdstown dated October 26, 1812," in Lexington *Kentucky Gazette,* November 24, 1812; Hammack, *Kentucky and the Second American Revolution,* 44–48; Gilpin, *The War of 1812 in the Old Northwest,* 47–50; Brackenridge, *History of the Late War,* 63; Mahon, *War of 1812,* 68–70; Belko, *Duff Green,* 19–24; Bauer, *Zachary Taylor,* 17–19; McAfee, *History of the Late War,* 157–62; Ferguson, *Illinois in the War of 1812,* 87–93.

25. Irving, "Notes of Conversation with William P. DuVal," 6; James Paucha to Andrew Hynes, February 1, 1813, Andrew Hynes Papers, Tennessee State Archives; A. Hite to Governor Isaac Shelby, October 31, 1812, Isaac Shelby Papers, box 4, f. 12, Kentucky State Archives.

26. Lexington *Kentucky Gazette,* January 12, February 16, 1813.

27. Irving, "Notes of Conversation with William P. DuVal," 6.

28. Roy Swift discovered that Thomas Howard DuVal's gravestone in an Austin, Texas, cemetery notes that he was born in Buckingham County, Virginia. Thus, the extended visit of the family in early 1813 at Major DuVal's is plausible. See Swift, *Civilizers,* 18–19.

29. Heidler and Heidler, eds., *Encyclopedia of the War of 1812,* 343–44, 195; Hickey, *War of 1812,* 85–86, 126–58.

30. Remini, *Andrew Jackson and the Course of American Empire,* 171–77; Goodstein, *Nashville, 1780–1860,* 34–35; *Jackson Papers,* 3: 73.

31. Abernethy, *The South in the New Nation,* 405, 410–13, 415–16; Hammack, *Kentucky and the Second American Revolution,* 87; Parks, *Felix Grundy,* 82–86.

32. Young, *The Washington Community,* 66, 24, 90; Green, *Washington: Village and Capital,* 1–201.

33. Young, *The Washington Community,* 89–92, 98–104.

34. Goldman and Young, *The United States Congressional Directories: 1789–1840,* 59, 61–62.

35. Remini, *Henry Clay*, 101–2.
36. *Debates and Proceedings of the Congress of the United States*, 13th Congr., 1st sess., 372–76.
37. Ibid.
38. *Debates and Proceedings of the Congress of the United States*, 13th Congr., 1st sess., 500. For the reaction in Kentucky see Hammack, *Kentucky and the Second American Revolution*, 87; Abernethy, *The South in the New Nation*, 412–13, 415–16, 418–19. Calhoun reversed his course and sided with the administration in the second session. Bartlett, *John C. Calhoun*, 79; Hickey, *The War of 1812*, 167–73.
39. McKee et al., *Reflections on the Law of 1813, for Laying an Embargo*, 1.
40. Ibid., 10–14; Hammack, *Kentucky and the Second American Revolution*, 87.
41. Heidler and Heldler, eds., *Encyclopedia of the War of 1812*, 354–55, 508–10; Millett and Maslowski, *For the Common Defense*, 107, 111–12; Hickey, *War of 1812*, 147–51, 137–39.
42. Johnston, *The Heart That Would Not Hold*, 87–89, 123; Williams, *The Life of Washington Irving*, 1: 133–34; Aderman, *The Letters of James Kirke Paulding*, xvi–xxiii.
43. For the attack on Washington see Green, *Washington: Village and Capital*, 60–65; Millett and Maslowski, *For the Common Defense*, 110; Remini, *The House*, 97–99; Drake quoted in Heidler and Heidler, eds., *Encyclopedia of the War of 1812*, 544–45.
44. Lexington *Kentucky Gazette*, August 22, 1814.
45. Goldman and Young, eds., *The United States Congressional Directories: 1789–1840*, 61–62.
46. Green, *Washington: Village and Capital*, 64.
47. Quoted in Green, *Washington: Village and Capital*, 65. For other descriptions of the scene see Hurd, *Washington Cavalcade*, 50–59.
48. William P. DuVal to Governor Isaac Shelby, November 1, 1814, Isaac Shelby Papers, Kentucky State Archives.
49. Andrew Jackson to Andrew Hynes, September 26, 1814, *Jackson Papers*, 3: 147.
50. Remini, *The House*, 101.
51. *Debates and Proceedings of the Congress of the United States*, 13th Congr., 3rd sess., 496–98, 1026, 1028–31; Petersburg (Va.) *Daily Courier*, November 11, 1814; Bartlett, *John C. Calhoun*, 80–81; Coit, *Calhoun*, 95–96; Hickey, *War of 1812*, 249–51.
52. Secretary Pope to Delegate Stephenson, October 20, 1814, in TP, 17: 35–36; Richard M. Johnson to James Madison, November 22, 1814, in "Letters of Col. Richard M. Johnson," 327–28.
53. *Debates and Proceedings of the Congress of the United States*, 13th Congr., 3rd sess., 530–33.
54. Ibid., 800–808; "Mr. DuVall's Speech," Lexington *Western Monitor*, January 6, 1815.
55. Ibid.
56. J. H. Hawkins to Isaac Shelby, January 17, 1815, Isaac Shelby Papers, box 1, f. 4, Kentucky State Archives; Peterson, *The Great Triumvirate*, 43–44.
57. Green, *Washington: Village and Capital*, 65–66.
58. William P. DuVal to James Monroe, September 13, 1815, TP, 17: 216.
59. Blakey, "Rendezvous with Republicanism," 233–50.

60. Harrison and Klotter, *New History of Kentucky*, 96–97; Collins, *History of Kentucky*, 1: 28–29; Remini, *Henry Clay*, 198–99.

61. On the boom-and-bust conditions in the West that culminated in the Panic of 1819 see Rothbard, *The Panic of 1819*, 98–110; Sydnor, *The Development of Southern Sectionalism*, 104–19; Remini, *Andrew Jackson and the Course of American Freedom*, 39–47; Kirwan, *John C. Crittenden*, 46–65; Parks, *Felix Grundy*, 103–112; Meyer, *Colonel Richard M. Johnson*, 225–32.

62. The leaders of the Relief Party were John Adair, William T. Barry, George Bibb, Amos Kendall, and Joseph Desha; the antirelief group included Robert Wickliffe, Ben Hardin, John Pope, and John J. Marshall. Remini, *Henry Clay*, 198–99; Harrison and Klotter, *New History of Kentucky*, 109–12; Baylor, *John Pope Kentuckian*, 149–67.

63. Bardstown *Repository*, August 3, 1814.

64. *Felix Grundy vs William P. Duval*, 1819, copy in Frank Snyder Collection, box 25, f. 2, University of South Florida Library.

65. Fourth Census of the United States, Population Schedule, 1820, Nelson County, Kentucky, 49.

66. William P. DuVal to John Quincy Adams, October 7, 1819, in Tallahassee *Floridian and Journal*, April 21, 1831.

67. There is disagreement among historians regarding Jackson's authorization to seize Florida. The "smoking gun" letter from Monroe to Congressman John Rhea, which Jackson asserted gave him official authorization, has never been found. Daniel Feller, in a recent reappraisal of the incident uncovering new evidence, speculates that letter may have actually existed. See his "The Seminole Controversy Revisited." David S. and Jeanne T. Heidler make the case that it never existed. Robert Remini insists that there is ample correspondence from administration officials to conclude that Jackson had the backing of the administration. The best treatment of the First Seminole War is Heidler and Heidler, *Old Hickory's War*. See also their *Andrew Jackson and the Quest for American Empire*, 119–20; Remini, *Andrew Jackson and His Indian Wars*, 134–42; Remini, *Andrew Jackson and the Course of American Empire*, 341–77; Remini, *Henry Clay*, 162–68; Wiltse, *John C. Calhoun, Nationalist*, 155–63; Burstein, *The Passions of Andrew Jackson*, 129–33; Missall and Missall, *The Seminole Wars*, 32–51.

68. John C. Calhoun to William P. DuVal, October 22, 1820, *Calhoun Papers*, 5: 406–7.

69. Ninian Edwards to John Quincy Adams, February 21, 1821, Letters of Recommendation during the Administration of James Monroe, 1817–1825, NA, RG 59, Letters of the Department of State M 439, Reel 6.

70. John C. Calhoun to John Quincy Adams, February 17, 1821, and William P. DuVal to John C. Calhoun, January 27, 1821, and Commission of William P. DuVal as Judge of East Florida, May 18, 1821, TP, 22: 3–4, 42–43.

71. Robert Butler to John Quincy Adams, July 11, 1821, and Robert Butler to the Secretary of War, July 12, 1821, TP, 22: 112–13, 115.

CHAPTER 3: **Judge and Governor**

1. Andrew Jackson to the President, August 4, 1821, TP, 22: 160–61; Doherty, "Andrew Jackson's Cronies," 3–29. For a good summary of Jackson's three-month sojourn in Florida see Remini, *Andrew Jackson and the Course of Empire*, 401–24; Burstein, *The Passions of Andrew Jackson*, 147–49; Doherty, *Richard Keith Call*, 16–23.

2. Secretary of War to Commissioner and Governor Jackson, March 31, 1821; Secretary of War to Jean Penieres, March 31, 1821, TP, 22: 25–28.

3. Covington, *The Seminoles of Florida*, 50. On the number and disposition of Native Americans in Florida at the time of the transfer see ibid., 34–51; Mahon, *History of the Second Seminole War*, 30–33; Brown, *Florida's Peace River Frontier*, 3–16; Hoffman, *Florida's Frontiers*, 286; McReynolds, *The Seminoles*, 95–98.

4. Wright, *Creeks and Seminoles*, 220–21.

5. For the long heritage of Florida as a refuge for runaway slaves and the Spanish policy re: slavery in Florida see Landers, *Black Society in Spanish Florida*; Landers, ed., *Colonial Plantations and Economy in Florida*, 121–35; Weisman, "The Plantation System of the Florida," 136–49; Schafer, "'A Class of People Neither Freemen Nor Slaves,'" 587–92; Cusick, *The Other War of 1812*; Brown, *Florida's Peace River Frontier*, 7–9; Rivers, *Slavery in Florida*, 4–8; Rivers, *Rebels and Runaways*; Porter, *Black Seminoles*, 3–26.

6. Wright, *Creeks and Seminoles*, 73–99.

7. James Forbes to John Quincy Adams, July 14, 1821, TP, 22: 119; John R. Bell to the Secretary of War, July 17, 1821, Secretary of War to John R. Bell, August 4, 1821, TP, 22: 125–27, 164–65. See also Brown, *Florida's Peace River Frontier*, 17–22.

8. Andrew Jackson to John Quincy Adams, April 2, 1821, *Jackson Papers*, 5: 24; Commissioner and Governor Jackson to the Secretary of War, May 26, 1821, TP, 22: 58.

9. Andrew Jackson to John C. Calhoun, September 17, 1821, Governor Jackson to Acting Governor Worthington, September 18, 1821, John C. Calhoun to Andrew Jackson, November 16, 1821, TP, 22: 205–9, 209–10, 278–79. On Wanton and Dexter see Monaco, *Moses Levy*, 100–102; Frank Marotti Jr., "Edward W. Wanton," 456–77; Boyd, "Horatio S. Dexter," 65–95; Mahon, *History of the Second Seminole War*, 33–34.

10. "Extract of a Talk held by Gen. Jackson with Three Chiefs of the Florida Indians at Pensacola, September 18, 1821 in St Augustine," *East Florida Herald*, March 8, 1823; Governor Jackson to the Secretary of War, September 20, 1821, TP, 22: 210–13; Andrew Jackson to William Worthington, October 1, 1821, *Jackson Papers*, 5: 108–9.

11. Governor Jackson to the President, November 14, 1821, President to Governor Jackson, December 31, 1821, TP, 22: 276, 316.

12. Robert Butler to the Secretary of State, May 21, June 6, 1821, TP, 22: 48–49, 60–61.

13. Acting Governor Worthington to Governor Jackson, October 6, 1821, Acting Governor Worthington to the Secretary of State, November 12, 1821, Horatio S. Dexter and Edward M. Wanton to Abraham Eustis, October 5, 1821, in Abraham Eustis to the Secretary of War, October 8, 1821, Temporary Organization of St. Augustine, July 16, 1821, TP, 22: 238–41, 272, 243–44, 120–21.

14. William P. DuVal to the Secretary of State, November 29, 1821, TP, 22: 284–85.

15. William P. DuVal to the Secretary of State, December 10, 1821, TP, 22: 299–300.

16. William P. DuVal to the Secretary of State, November 29, 1821, TP, 22: 284–85.

17. Martin, "The Public Domain in Territorial Florida, 174–75; Martin, *Florida during Territorial Days*, 6–7, 69–76. From 1830 to 1834, in fourteen decisions, the U.S. Supreme Court confirmed Florida claims, including the Arredondo, Levy, Fleming, and Hernandez claims. Gates, *History of Public Land Law Development*, 87–90, 104.

18. Robert Butler to the Secretary of State, June 6, 1821, TP, 22: 60–61.

19. This, along with British influence among the Indians, enraged Andrew Jackson.

Even after he left the territory, he continued to rage against the situation and to insist that Spanish officials had colluded with other Spaniards and corrupt Americans to fraudulently alter records so that they might legitimize fraudulent claims to land. Also, to Jackson the Spaniards' handling of the archives suggested foul play at every turn. "The attempt to carry away a number of those documents from St. Augustine and Pensacola in a clandestine manner was considered, as a flagrant violation of the Treaty, and I began to entertain the opinion, that a systematic combination had been formed amongst the Officers of Spain to deprive the honest citizens of the country all the evidences of their right to property, secured to them by the provisions of the cession." Andrew Jackson to the Secretary of State, January 22, 1822, TP, 22: 338–39.

20. Judge William P. DuVal Charge to the Grand Jury of East Florida District Court, December 5, 1821, in St. Augustine *Florida Gazette*, December 10, 1821.

21. Governor DuVal to Richard M. Johnson, November 26, 1822, TP, 22: 566–67.

22. TP, 22: 4 n3.

23. Recommending DuVal for governor were Senators Ninian Edwards (Ill.) Jessee Thomas (Ill.), James Pleasants (Va.), Benjamin Ruggles (Ohio), Waller Taylor (Ind.) James Noble (Ind.), and Caesar Rodney (Del.), as well as other congressmen from Pennsylvania, Massachusetts, and Maryland. Also recommending DuVal were congressmen Joseph Kent (Md.), John Scott (Mo.), George Holcolmb (N.J.), Edward Jackson (Va.), Rapheal Neal (Md.), Daniel Cook (Ill.), Thomas J. Rogers (Pa.), Samuel Allen (Mass.), and Arkansas Territorial Delegate James W. Bates. Recommendation of Judge DuVal as Governor, March 3, 1822, TP, 22: 372–73.

24. Francis Johnson to James Monroe, April 54, 1822, Letters of Recommendation during the Administration of James Monroe, NA, RG 59, M439, Reel 6.

25. Recommendation of Judge DuVal as Governor, March 3, 1822, TP, 22: 371.

26. Commission of William P. DuVal as Governor, April 17, 1822, TP, 22: 469.

27. H. G. Burton to John Branch, April 16, 1822, Branch Family Papers, box 1, f. 1, Southern History Collection, University of North Carolina.

28. Secretary of State John Quincy Adams recorded in his diary that "Branch was pressed upon Monroe as a test for Crawford's influence over appointments in the administration." Adams, ed., *Memoirs of John Quincy Adams*, April 19, 1822, 6: 494. Once it became clear that Monroe would nominate Branch for judge and not for governor, Senator Nathaniel Macon of North Carolina asked Monroe to withdraw the nomination, which he refused to do. According to Adams, "Macon . . . takes it in high dudgeon that his friend Branch was not nominated as Governor. The President also read to me the draft of his answer declining to revoke the nomination and assigning his reasons for nominating Mr. DuVal, which were very sufficient." Adams, ed., *Memoirs of John Quincy Adams*, April 16, 1822, 6: 491.

29. Memorial to Congress by the Inhabitants of East Florida, January 28, 1822, An Act Establishing the Territory of Florida, March 30, 1822, TP, 22: 348–50, vii–viii, 389.

30. DuVal recommended William Gibson (S.C.), Greenbury Gaither (Md.), Edmund Law (D.C.), Zephaniah Kingsley (Fla.), Peter Mitchell (Ga.), Joseph Hernandez (Fla.), Dr. William Simmons (S.C.), and Bernardo Sequi (Fla.). Judge DuVal to the President, April 16, 1822, and Commission of Members of the Legislative Council, May 4, 1822, TP, 22: 406–7, 422–23. See also Joseph M. White to the President, April 15, 1822, TP, 22: 406.

DuVal had claimed in 1819 that White was "a young gentleman of high reputation and his standing at the bar of Frankfort, in this State, among the eminent lawyers of our Country, (for a young man) is deservedly high. He hopes, by his merit and qualifications of the office to obtain the appointment of United States Attorney in one of these new states [Alabama or Mississippi]. I do believe that Mr. White is every way qualified for such an office, and would discharge the duties with credit to himself and honour to the Country." William P. DuVal to John Quincy Adams, October 7, 1819, in Tallahassee *Floridian and Journal,* April 21, 1831.

31. William DuVal to Henry Clay, June 14, 1821, in Hopkins, ed., *Clay Papers,* 3: 89–91.
32. Snyder, "Nancy Hynes DuVal," 25.
33. Pensacola *Democrat,* June 22, 1822; Alexandria *Herald,* July 29, 1822.
34. Pensacola *Floridian* quoted in Davis, "Pensacola Newspapers, 1821–1900," 421; Rachel Jackson to Elizabeth Kingsley, July 23, 1821, *Jackson Papers,* 5:79–81; Governor DuVal to the President, September 10, 1822, TP, 22: 531–32.
35. Governor DuVal to the Secretary of State, June 21, 30, July 17, 1822, TP, 22: 470–71, 478–79, 489–90.
36. William P. DuVal to the Secretary of War, June 21, 1822, Secretary of War to Governor DuVal, July 17, 1822, TP, 22: 471–72, 488.
37. Commission of Gad Humphreys as Indian Agent, May 8, 1822, Secretary of War to Peter Pelham, June 24, 1822, Abraham Eustis to the Secretary of War, July 23, 1822, Acting Governor to the Secretary of War, January 9, 1823, TP, 22: 429–30, 474, 495, 597–98.
38. Secretary of War to Governor DuVal, June 11, 1822, TP, 22: 452–55.
39. Governor DuVal to the Secretary of War, July 18, 1822, TP, 22: 491–92.
40. Andrew Jackson to Richard Keith Call, May 20, 1822, *Jackson Papers,* 5: 183–87, 197.
41. Andrew Jackson to William P. DuVal, June 1, 1822, Andrew Jackson Papers, Reel 9, Scholarly Resources edition.
42. Andrew Jackson to James Craine Bronough, July 18, 1822, *Jackson Papers,* 5: 202–03.
43. Commission of Henry M. Brackenridge, June 5, 1822, TP, 22: 451, 490n; Denham, "A Rogue's Paradise," 6–7.
44. William P. DuVal to the Secretary of State, July 17, 1822, Governor DuVal to the President, August 17, 1822, TP, 22: 489–90, 505–6.
45. Acting Governor Worthington (East Florida) to the Secretary of State, December 11, 1821, TP, 22: 301–2.
46. Governor DuVal to the President, September 10, 1822, TP, 22: 531–32.
47. Secretary of War to Gad Humphreys, September 18, 1822; Governor DuVal to the Secretary of War, September 22, 1822, Nathaniel Ware and Samuel Overton to the Secretary of State, TP, 22: 532–34, 552–53; John C. Calhoun to Colonel Abram Eustis, October 23, 1822, *Calhoun Papers,* 7: 314; *Niles Register,* October 19, 1822.
48. Governor DuVal to the Secretary of State, September 22, 1822, TP, 22: 534–36.
49. Colonel Abraham Eustis to Governor Duval, October 16, 1822, in Abraham Eustis to the Secretary of War, October 17, 1822, TP, 22: 549.
50. A Resident Inhabitant of East Florida to the Secretary of State, October 14, 1822, TP, 22: 539.

51. Florida, "The Election," St. Augustine *East Florida Herald,* October 1822, in Anonymous to the Secretary of State, October 15, 1822, TP, 22: 542–46.

52. Ibid.

53. Hernandez attended Congress from January 3 to March 3, 1823. TP, 22: 528n. Also on the election controversy see Knauss, "William Pope DuVal," 104–7.

54. Acting Governor Walton to the Secretary of War, November 4, 1822, Acting Governor Walton to the the Secretary of State, November 5, 1822, TP, 22: 554, 556–63.

CHAPTER 4: **Founder of the Florida Territory**

1. Baylor, *John Pope Kentuckian,* 157–60. For Kentucky politics and the Beauchamp murder trial see ibid., 101–22, 149–67, 176–276, 309–12; Remini, *Henry Clay,* 198–99, 206–7; Peterson, *The Great Triumvirate,* 149–51.

2. William P. DuVal to John C. Calhoun, November 27, 1822, *Calhoun Papers,* 7: 355.

3. Secretary of State to Governor DuVal, November 22, 1822, Governor DuVal to the Secretary of State, December 17, 1822, January 13, 1823, TP, 22: 563, 583, 599.

4. William P. DuVal to Samuel Southard, December 13, 1822, Samuel Southard Papers, box 9, f. 6, PU.

5. Thomas Wright to Acting Governor Walton, December 7, 1822, in Acting Governor Walton to the Secretary of War, December 8, 1822, Acting Governor to the Secretary of War, January 9, 1823, TP, 22: 578, 597–98; Gadsden County, Presentment of the Grand Jury, April Term, 1824, in Pensacola *Gazette,* May 15, 1824.

6. Acting Governor Walton to the Secretary of War, January 31, 1823, and Acting Governor Walton to Daniel E. Burch, January 30, 1823, TP, 22: 606–9.

7. Governor DuVal to the Secretary of State, March 16, 22, 1823, TP, 22: 649, 652; William P. DuVal to Samuel Southard, March 4, 1824, Samuel Southard Papers, box 14, f. 11, PU.

8. *Calhoun Papers,* 7: xiv, xvii, xxxix–xl.

9. Secretary of War to James Gadsden and Bernardo Segui, April 7, 1823, TP, 22: 659–60; John C. Calhoun to William P. DuVal, April 14, 1823, John C. Calhoun to Bernardo Segui, May 29, 1823, *Calhoun Papers,* 8: 19–20, 79; TP, 22: 42n; Andrew Jackson to the Secretary of War, July 14, 1823, TP, 22: 719–20.

10. James Gadsden to Andrew Jackson, July 30, 1823, *Jackson Papers,* 5: 285.

11. Gad Humphreys to Secretary Walton, April 19, 1823, in Secretary Walton to the Secretary of War, April 26, 1823, TP, 22: 670–73.

12. Governor DuVal to the Secretary of State, May 1, 1823, TP, 22: 675; A Friend to Merit, St. Augustine *East Florida Herald,* June 28, September 27, 1823.

13. Governor DuVal to Horatio Dexter, May 10, 1823, TP, 22: 681; William P. DuVal to John C. Calhoun, May 13, 1823, *Calhoun Papers,* 8: 78–79.

14. Governor DuVal to the Secretary of State, May 26, 1823, TP, 22: 687–88.

15. Pensacola *Floridian,* July 5, 1823.

16. Ibid.

17. Notice of Election for Delegate to Congress, May 31, 1823, TP, 22: 693. Call received all but six of the votes cast in West Florida. St. Augustine *East Florida Herald,* September 27, 1823. See also Doherty, *Richard Keith Call,* 27–28.

18. Resolution by the Legislative Council, July 5, 1823, TP, 22: 715.

19. William P. DuVal to Samuel Southard, July 13, 1823, Samuel Southard Papers, box 11, f. 12, PU. DuVal's trouble with Hamilton continued. Some months later DuVal wrote Southard again. "I am getting on in my Government better than I had any right to expect. Mr. Hamilton tries to injure me by scribbling against me. I take no notice of him. The cause of offence on my part is that I *would not oblige him so far,* as to become an *unprincipled villain to suit his purpose in the late election of our delegate to Congress.* [He] wanted me the day before the election to open Polls in several new places, where he said he had many friends and to out several judges who had been appointed to hold the election on the ground that he had ascertained *they would vote for him.* I bursted on him like a bomb—and was very near kicking him out of my office. [S]ince that time I do not let him approach me and was it not for the respect I feel as a man for Mr. Monroe, and knowing the fellow has married Mr. Monroe's niece (undignified) as it might be, I would have put my mark on him with some emphasis. This man is perfectly odious to the people here and his society is actually shunned by all the men of standing in this city. He is a noisy, intermeddling, intriguing, shuffling, trifling, *remote circumstance,* in the affairs of the country." William P. DuVal to Samuel Southard, October 14, 1823, Samuel Southard Papers, box 11, f. 12, PU.

20. William P. DuVal to Samuel Southard, July 13, 1823, Samuel Southard Papers, box 11, f. 12, PU.

21. Ibid.

22. Boyd, ed., "Horatio S. Dexter and Events Leading to the Treaty of Moulrie Creek with the Seminole Indians," 81–95; Governor DuVal to John C. Calhoun, September 23, 1823, and Petition to the President by the Inhabitants of the Territory, October 4, 1823, vol. 22, TP, 744–45, 762.

23. James Gadsden to the Secretary of War, June 11, 1823, TP, 22: 694–96; John C. Calhoun to James Gadsden, June 30, 1823, *Calhoun Papers,* 8: 140.

24. William P. DuVal to John C. Calhoun, September 1, 1823, *Calhoun Papers,* 8: 251.

25. In 1848, in support of Proctor's application for compensation for his services, DuVal swore that Proctor was a man "truth and integrity. The Indians were scattered over Florida and Proctor was often required to summon the chiefs to meet me on business. . . . Proctor was of great service in controlling the Indians and rendered me, and the country, most essential benefits from his usefulness with the Indians and his prudence and good sense—no man could have possessed their confidence in a higher degree . . . his services were invaluable to the United states—in the management of the Florida Indians at a period when no other person could have preserved the peace of the country." DuVal quoted in Parker, "The Proctors–Antonio, George, and John," 20–21. Warner, *Free Men in the Age of Servitude,* 22–23; Smith, *Slavery and Plantation Growth in Antebellum Florida,* 114.

26. On the Treaty of Moultrie Creek see Mahon, *History of the Second Seminole War,* 42–50; Wright, *Creeks and Seminoles,* 232–37; Covington, *The Seminoles of Florida,* 52–54; McReynolds, The Seminoles, 88–101; Brown, *Florida's Peace River Frontier,* 29–33; Brown, *Tampa before the Civil War,* 3–17; Hoffman, *Florida's Frontiers,* 287–88.

27. The Indian Commissioners to the Secretary of War, September 26, 1823, TP, 22: 747–51.

28. William P. DuVal to John C. Calhoun, October 4, 1823, John C. Calhoun to James Monroe, November 3, 1823, *Calhoun Papers,* 8: 299, 333.

29. Governor DuVal to the Secretary of War, September 26, 1823, TP, 22: 746–47.

30. Secretary of War to Governor DuVal, May 27, 1823, and Governor DuVal to the Secretary of War, September 2, 1823, and Secretary of War to Governor DuVal, October 25, 1823, TP, 22: 689–91, 732–34, 774–75.

31. Wiltse, *John C. Calhoun, Nationalist*, 249–63; Bartlett, *John C. Calhoun*, 110–20; Remini, *Andrew Jackson and the Course of American Freedom, 1822–1832*, 12–38.

32. William P. DuVal to Andrew Jackson, August 26, 1823, Jackson Papers, Reel 32, LC.

33. Ibid.

34. William P. DuVal to James Barbour, August 12, 1823, in *Gulf States Historical Magazine* 1 (March 1903): 367–68.

35. Ibid.

36. St. Augustine *East Florida Herald*, November 1, 1823; Salisbury (N.C.) *Western Carolinian*, December 19, 1823.

37. Doherty, *Richard Keith Call*, 28–33. See also Remini, *Andrew Jackson and the Course of American Freedom, 1822–1832*, 53–73; Marszalek, *The Petticoat Affair*, 22–24.

38. Bardstown *Repository* quoted in St. Augustine *East Florida Herald*, September 6, 1823; "Florida Affairs," Bardtown *Repository*, September 27, October 11, 1823. See also Boston *Daily Advertiser*, October 7, 1823; Boston *Columbian Centinel*, October 8, 1823; Norfolk *City Advertiser*, October 10, 1823.

39. Governor DuVal to the Secretary of State, September 29, 1823, TP, 22: 751.

40. James Gadsden to John C. Calhoun, November 29, December 1, 1823, *Calhoun Papers*, 8: 383, 388, John C. Calhoun to James Gadsden, December 23, 1823, *Calhoun Papers*, 8: 420.

41. Governor DuVal to the Secretary of War, January 12, 1824, TP, 22: 823; Pensacola *Gazette*, February 2, 1824; Mobile *Register* quoted in New London *Connecticut Gazette*, January 28, 1824.

42. Simmons, *Notices of East Floridas*, xxviii–xxx.

43. Pensacola *Gazette*, May 29, June 5, 1824.

44. Paisley, *The Red Hills of Florida*, 69.

45. Floridus to the Editor, St. Augustine *East Florida Herald*, January 10, 1824; Proclamation of Governor DuVal, March 4, 1824, TP, 22: 854–55; St. Augustine *East Florida Herald*, April 3, 1824; Pensacola *Gazette*, March 13, 1824.

46. Affidavit of John McIver, January 31, 1831, Executive Proceedings of the Senate, 22nd Congress, Papers Re. Nominations: Governor William Pope DuVal, File Number Sen. 22B-A3, f. 1, Records of the United States Senate, RG 46, NA.

47. James Gadsden to John C. Calhoun, February 20, March 16, 1824, *Calhoun Papers*, 8: 549, 582–83; St. Augustine *East Florida Herald*, March 20, 1824.

48. Governor DuVal to the Secretary of War, March 19, 1824, TP, 22: 904; William P. DuVal to John C. Calhoun, April 11, 1824, *Calhoun Papers*, 9: 27–28; John C. Calhoun to William P. DuVal, April 8, 1824, *Calhoun Papers*, 9:21; Pensacola *Gazette*, July 24, 1824.

49. Governor DuVal to the Secretary of War, April 11, 1824, TP, 22: 922–23. The proposal called for three thousand rations per day to consist of one and a quarter pounds of beef, one quart of corn or an equivalent in flour and four quarts of salt to every hundred rations. St. Augustine *East Florida Herald*, May 29, 1824; Pensacola *Gazette*, May 1, 1824.

50. Governor DuVal to the Secretary of the Navy, February 27, 1824, Governor DuVal to the Secretary of State, March 25, February 13, 1824, TP, 22: 853–54, 907, 847–48.
51. Governor DuVal to the President, February 26, 1824, TP, 22: 852–53.

CHAPTER 5: **Neamathla and a New Territorial Capitol**

1. Andrew Jackson to Rachel Jackson, May 19, 1824, *Jackson Papers*, 5: 410, 411 n1, 413 n1.
2. William P. DuVal to Andrew Jackson, May 23, 1824, PKYL.
3. On the race for the presidency see Remini, *Andrew Jackson and the Course of American Freedom*, 63–66; Remini, *Henry Clay*, 235–41; Wiltse, *John C. Calhoun, Nationalist*, 276–84; Bartlett, *John C. Calhoun*, 110–20; Klunder, *Lewis Cass*, 48–49; Peterson, *The Great Triumvirate*, 116–24.
4. Governor DuVal to the Secretary of War, June 3, 1824, TP, 22: 964.
5. *Calhoun Papers*, 9: xxiii–xxiv; Viola, *Thomas L. McKenney*, 95–98; Belko, "John C. Calhoun and the Creation of the Bureau of Indian Affairs," 193–97.
6. Governor DuVal to the Secretary of War, March 26, 1824, and Secretary of War to Governor DuVal, April 20, 1824, TP, 22: 908, 925.
7. John P. DuVal to William DuVal, June 10, 1824, Thomas Jefferson Papers, LC. DuVal also solicited his friend Samuel Southard in John's behalf. "I know his worth—he is a man of business and strict principles. [H]e is however my brother, I would stake my life as security for his qualifications and integrity if you can aid me in getting him this appointment. [I]will put him to death if ever he travels one inch out of the line of his duty. I dislike asking for any thing in the gift of the government for near a relation, but trust you will excuse the feeling of an only brother." William P. DuVal to Samuel Southard, September 3, 1824, Samuel Southard Papers, box 14, f. 11, PU.
8. Governor DuVal to the Secretary of State, June 21, 1824, TP, 22: 979; *Pensacola Gazette*, June 26, 1824.
9. John C. Calhoun to William P. DuVal, June 2, 1824, *Calhoun Papers*, 9: 133.
10. Affidavit of John McIver, January 31, 1831, Executive Proceedings of the Senate, 22nd Congr., Papers Re. Nominations: Governor William Pope DuVal, File Number Sen. 22B-A3, f. 1, Records of the United States Senate, RG 46, NA.
11. Archeologists have identified the mission as Purification de la Tama, built in 1675 roughly two miles south of San Luis Mission. Boyd, "Enumeration of Florida Spanish Missions in 1675," 184–85. See also early descriptions of the site in Williams, *A View of West Florida*, 34.
12. Paisley, *The Red Hills*, 74–77. Also on the founding of the capital see Shores, "The Laying Out of Tallahassee," 41–47; Dodd, "Old Tallahassee," 63–71; Davis, "Tallahassee through Territorial Days," 48–50; Baptist, *Creating an Old South*, 13–15; "Notes of Clifton Paisley," box 1223, f. 4, and box 1226, Red Hills of Florida Collection, Manning Strozier Library, Florida State University.
13. Lieutenant Jeremiah Yancy to John C. Calhoun, June 30, 1824, *Calhoun Papers*, 9: 191. After exploring the tract in June, Gadsden wrote to Calhoun that "combining the three objects of agriculture, stock & hunting will therefore, within the limits allotted, furnish more than an abundant supply of the subsistence of life for a greater Indians population than the one contemplated." James Gadsden to John C. Calhoun, June 15,

1824, TP, 22: 968. Gad Humphreys disagreed with Gadsden's assessment. He wrote to DuVal, "I can only say that the land throughout where I visited is wretchedly bad, and in my opinion cannot long sustain the Indians should any considerable number come from the West." Humphreys noted that Micanopy and Jumper insisted that the Indian boundary be moved north. Gad Humphreys to Governor DuVal, June 1, 1824, TP, 23: 76–77.

14. George Graham to Robert Butler, July 9, 1824, and George Graham to Governor DuVal, July 10., 1824, TP, 23: 6–9, 11.

15. Governor DuVal to the Secretary of War, July 12, 1824, TP, 23: 14–17; William P. DuVal to John C. Calhoun, July 22, 1824, *Calhoun Papers,* 9: 239; Secretary of War to Governor DuVal, August 17, 1824, TP, 23: 43–45.

16. Governor DuVal to the Secretary of War, July 12, 1824, TP, 23: 14–17.

17. William P. DuVal to John C. Calhoun, July 22, 1824, *Calhoun Papers,* 9: 239; James Gadsden to John C. Calhoun, June 15, 1824, TP, 22: 968.

18. James Gadsden to John C. Calhoun, July 24, 1824, *Calhoun Papers,* 9: 242.

19. Governor DuVal to the Secretary of War, July 29, 1824, TP, 23: 22–24.

20. Tallahassee *Florida Intelligencer* quoted in Pensacola *Gazette,* April 23, 1825. Writing in later years, Richard Keith Call reiterated the standard account of the event by stating that DuVal, "angered" by Neamathla "beyond endurance, and recognizing that he was the cause of the disobedience to the Executive Order— Governor DuVal charged him with disaffection and treachery and in the presence of his people—then seized him by the throat and shaking him bodily, thrust him out of the assembly—and John Hicks an Indian of the Suwannee District was proclaimed the Chief of the Nation." "Journal of Richard Keith Call," 154–55, Florida Historical Society Library. By the time Call wrote these words, Washington Irving's "Conspiracy of Neamathla" (1840), had been well circulated and had become the accepted account.

21. In a subsequent election for head chief of the Seminoles held at the Indian agency at Fort King, Hicks bested Micanopy. By August 1826 Hicks was formally inaugurated. Mahon, *History of the Second Seminole War,* 52–63; Covington, *The Seminoles of Florida,* 55–56.

22. Governor DuVal to the Secretary of War, September 1, 1824, TP, 23: 62–64.

23. William P. DuVal to John C. Calhoun, August 31, 1824, *Calhoun Papers,* 9: 296–97; TP, 23: 45n.

24. William P. DuVal to Samuel Southard, September 3, 1824, Samuel Southard Papers, box 14, f. 11, PU.

25. William P. DuVal to Samuel Southard, September 11, 1824, Samuel Southard Papers, box 14, f. 11, PU.

26. Governor DuVal to the Secretary of State, October 2, 1824, TP, 23: 78–80; Governor DuVal to the Secretary of War, October 26, 1824, TP, 23: 88–91.

27. Governor DuVal to the Secretary of War, October 26, 1824, TP, 23: 88–91.

28. Robert Butler to George Graham, November 15, 1824, TP, 23: 110–11.

29. "Sketches of Florida" in Scotio (Ohio) *Gazette* quoted in Easton, Maryland, *Republican Star,* May 10, 1825.

30. Statement of John Bellamy for Services as Indian Commissioner, November 12, 1824, TP, 23: 101–5.

31. "Journal of Richard Keith Call," Florida Historical Society Library, 341. For an account of the trek south see Pensacola *Gazette,* December 11, 1824.

32. John C. Calhoun to Gad Humphreys, November 26, 1824, *Calhoun Papers,* 9: 403; Governor DuVal to Gad Humphreys, November 27, 1824, TP, 23: 115–16.
33. Gad Humpherys to Governor DuVal, January 20, 1825, TP, 23: 163–64.
34. Pensacola *Gazette,* December 11, 1824.
35. Message of Governor William P. DuVal, November 10, 1824, in St. Augustine *East Florida Herald,* November 27, 1824; Pensacola *Gazette,* December 11, 1824.
36. Ibid.
37. Ibid.
38. St. Augustine *East Florida Herald,* January 25, 1825; Pensacola *Floridian* quoted in St. Augustine *East Florida Herald,* April 9, 1825.
39. Decus, "The Governor's Veto," St. Augustine *East Florida Herald,* February 8, March 1, 1825.
40. A Late Resident at Tallahassee, March 11, 1825, in Pensacola *Gazette,* March 19, 1825.
41. Pensacola *Gazette,* December 11, 1824.
42. Proclamation of Public Land Sales, January 26, 1824, Judge Woodward to the Secretary of State, January 3, 7, 1825, TP, 23: 167, 151–52, 153.

CHAPTER 6: A "Corrupt Bargain," and New Home in Florida

1. Remini, *Andrew Jackson and the Course of America Freedom,* 92–99; *Jackson Papers,* 6:13–50; Remini, *Henry Clay,* 253–72; Burstein, *The Passions of Andrew Jackson,* 154–58; Peterson, *Great Triumvirate,* 116–31; Heidler and Heidler, *Henry Clay,* 176–85.
2. Pensacola *Gazette,* August 14, October 9, 1824.
3. Washington *National Intelligencer* quoted in Salem (Mass.) *Essex Register,* February 14, 1825; New Haven *Connecticut Herald,* February 15, 1825; Milledgeville *Georgia Journal,* February 22, 1825.
4. Andrew Jackson to John Overton, February 10, 1825, *Jackson Papers,* 6: 28.
5. Remini, *Andrew Jackson and the Course of America Freedom,* 96–97.
6. William P. DuVal to John C. Calhoun, February 8, 11, 1825, John C. Calhoun to William P. DuVal, February 12, 1825, Statement of President James Monroe, February 24, 1825, Thomas McKenney to William P. DuVal, February 25, 1825, *Calhoun Papers,* 23: 549, 553, 557, 593–94, 595; Thomas McKenney to George Graham, February 25, 1825, TP, 23: 192–93.
7. William P. DuVal to the Secretary of War, February 11, 1825, TP, 23: 177; Thomas L. McKenney, February 21, 1825, *Calhoun Papers,* 9: 577.
8. Governor DuVal to the Secretary of War, February 27, 29, 1825, TP, 23: 193–94, 177n; "Correspondence Relative to Provisioning the Indians during 1825, which was done under Contract with Benjamin Chaires," *American State Papers: Indian Affairs,* 2: 630–40. When called to account, DuVal claimed "as far as I had any agency in making the contract, no man was favored; and I hazard nothing when I say that the Government, by my attention in making the contract has saved many thousand dollars in the rations; nor could the Government at any time since or now under the same circumstances obtain a contract so favorable." William P. DuVal to Thomas L. McKenney, January 24, 1826, House Doc. #17, 19th Congr., 2nd sess., 8–10; McReynolds, *The Seminoles,* 110–11.
9. George Graham to Richard K. Call, February 28, 1825, George Graham to George W. Ward, May 28, 1825, vol. 23, TP, 197, 253.

10. St. Augustine *East Florida Herald,* April 30, 1825.

11. Pensacola *Gazette,* April 23, 1825.

12. Remini, *Andrew Jackson and the Course of American Freedom,* 103–4; *Jackson Papers,* 6: xxx–xxxi, 96 n2.

13. At the Fourth of July celebration Burr proposed the follow toast: "Bolivar, the Washington of the South." Pensacola *Gazette,* September 17, 1825.

14. Governor DuVal to the Secretary of State, April 24, 1825, TP, 23: 242–43.

15. Peterson, *Great Triumvirate,* 150–51; Remini, *Henry Clay,* 281.

16. Andrew Jackson to Henry Lee, October 7, 1825, *Jackson Papers,* 6: 103–5. The subject is also referred to in John Henry Eaton to John Overton, February 7, 1825, *Jackson Papers,* 6: 27; Andrew Jackson to William P. DuVal, July 25, 1825, *Jackson Papers,* 6: 95–96.

17. William P. DuVal to Andrew Jackson, July 5, 1825, Jackson Papers, Reel 33, LC.

18. Andrew Jackson to John Coffee, July 23, 1825, *Jackson Papers,* 6: 92–93, 97; Andrew Jackson to William P. DuVal, August 6, 1825, Olin Library, Rollins College.

19. Andrew Jackson to John Coffee, July 9, 1825, *Jackson Papers,* 6: 91–92.

20. John Adair to Andrew Jackson, March 20, 1815, Andrew Jackson to John Adair, April 2, 1815, John Adair to Shelby, April 10, 1815, in Bardstown *Repository,* May 18, 1815.

21. Andrew Jackson to Richard Keith Call, June 24, 1825, *Jackson Papers,* 6: 84–85.

22. William DuVal to Henry Clay, August 10, 1825, in Hopkins, ed., *Clay Papers,* 4: 572–73; Henry Clay to Francis Brooke, September 2, 1825, in Colton, ed., *Private Correspondence of Henry Clay,* 127.

23. Gad Humphreys to Thomas McKenney, February 22, September 20, 1825, TP, 23: 253, 323–24.

24. Gad Humphreys to the Secretary of War, March 2, TP, 23: 202–3.

25. Joseph M. Hernandez to Governor DuVal, July 10, 1825 in Joseph M. Hernandez to the Secretary of War, August 9, 1825, TP, 23: 291–96; Sprague, *The Florida War,* 28–34.

26. Gad Humphreys to Thomas McKenney, August 20, 1825, Thomas McKenney to Governor DuVal, September 15, 1825, TP, 23: 310, 318.

27. Acting Governor Walton to Thomas McKenney, October 6, 18, 21, 1825, TP, 23: 335–37, 343–44, 345–46.

28. A Middle Floridian, Pensacola *Gazette,* September 3, 1825.

29. William P. Duval to the Marquis de Lafayette, January 10, 1826, in *Gulf States Historical Magazine* 1 (November 1902): 200.

30. Washington *National Intelligencer* quoted in Pensacola *Gazette,* March 19, 1825; John McKee to George Graham, April 21, 1825, TP, 23: 238.

31. "Tallahassee," St. Augustine *East Florida Herald,* April 2, 1825; Pensacola *Gazette,* April 23, 1825.

32. Bardstown *Western Herald,* September 21, 1825; Pensacola *Gazette,* November 5, 1825; St. Augustine *East Florida Herald,* December 6, 1825.

33. Nashville *Whig* quoted in Pensacola *Gazette,* November 19, 1825.

34. St. Augustine *East Florida Herald,* November 29, 1825; Pensacola *Gazette,* December 10, 1825; Richmond *Enquirer,* January 5, 1826.

35. Pensacola *Gazette,* December 24, 1825, January 21, 1825.

36. Governor DuVal to the Secretary of State, November 29, 1825, TP, 23: 363–65.

37. George M. Brooke to Quartermaster General (Jesup), November 30, 1825, TP, 23: 365–66.

38. Governor DuVal to the President, January 16, 1825, in Governor DuVal to the Secretary of State, December 17, 1825, and Secretary of State to Governor DuVal, January 9, 1826, TP, 23: 388–89, 408.

39. Governor DuVal to the Secretary of War, December 12, 1825, Memorial to Congress by the Citizens of Alachua County, n.d., 1825, in Thomas McKenney to Governor DuVal, January 4, 1826, TP, 23: 385, 405–6; Governor DuVal to Thomas L. McKenney, March 20, 1826, in Thomas McKenney to Governor DuVal, January 4, 1826, TP, 23: 482.

40. Governor DuVal to the Secretary of War, December 12, 1825, January 12, 1826, TP, 23: 385, 413–14; Thomas McKenney to Governor DuVal, December 27, 1825, TP, 23: 396.

41. Governor DuVal to Thomas McKenney, January 12, 1826, TP, 23: 413–14.

42. Governor DuVal to Thomas McKenney, January 22, 1826, TP, 23: 421.

43. Benjamin Chaires to William P. DuVal, January 13, 1826, in St. Augustine *East Florida Herald*, May 9, 1826; Pensacola *Gazette*, May 27, 1826.

44. Governor DuVal to Thomas McKenney, January 23, 1826, TP, 23: 423–24.

45. Secretary of War to the President, February 14, 1826, TP, 23: 443–44.

46. Governor DuVal to Thomas McKenney, December 13, 1825, TP, 23: 386–87.

47. Ibid.

48. Delegate White to the Secretary of War, January 8, 1826, Thomas McKenney to Governor DuVal, January 11, 1826, TP, 23: 407–8, 412–13.

CHAPTER 7: **Trials, Tribulations, and "Left-Handed Justice"**

1. Isaac Clark to Quartermaster General, September 29, 1825, Daniel Burch to the Quartermaster General, October 3, 1825, February 10, March 26, 1826, Quartermaster General to Daniel Burch, April 5, 1826, Daniel Burch, the Quartermaster General, May 18, 1826, TP, 23: 328–29, 332–33, 439–43, 492–93, 502–3, 551–54.

2. Robert Butler to George Graham, March 24, 1826, Abstract of Payments made to Deputy Surveyors by the Surveyor General, May, 5, 1826, George Graham to Richard K. Call, April 14, 1826, John Scott to George Graham, April 10, 1826, George Graham to John Scott, April 10, 1826, George Graham to Robert Butler, April 24, 1826, Memorial to Congress by Robert Mitchel and Others, January 16, 1826, The Chief Engineer to Simon Bernard, March 15, 1826, Simon Bernard to Paul H. Perrault, March 18, 1826, TP, 23: 487–89, 533–34, 517, 518, 519, 416–20, 522–23, 470–71, 476–82.

3. Thomas McKenney to Joshua Coffee, February 6, 1826, TP, 23: 436.

4. Copy of a Talk Delivered to the Indians of the Seminole Nation, by his Excellency Wm. P. DuVal, Governor of Florida, and Superintendent of Indian Affairs in the Same, February 1826, in U.S. House of Representatives, *Information . . . Relating to the Present Location of the Florida Indians*, Document No. 17, 19th Congr., 2nd sess. (1826), 16–19.

5. Governor DuVal to Thomas McKenney, February 22, 1826, TP, 23: 445–48; James Barbour to the Honorable Speaker of the House of Representatives (enclosures 1, 2, and 3), April 17, 1826, in Pensacola *Gazette*, May 27, 1826.

6. Reply of Colonel Hicks, Head Chief of the Seminole Nation, to His Excellency William P. DuVal, Governor of Florida, February 24, 25, 1826, *American State Papers:*

Indian Affairs, 2: 691; William P. DuVal to James Barbour, March 2, 1826, *American State Papers: Indian Affairs,* 2: 689.

7. Governor DuVal to Thomas L. McKenney, March 2, 1826, TP, 23: 453–54.
8. Thomas L. McKenney to Gad Humphreys, February 28, 1826, TP, 23: 451.
9. Governor DuVal to Thomas L. McKenney, March 2, 1826, TP, 23: 454.
10. Memorial to the President by the Inhabitants of St. Johns County, March 6, 1826, TP, 23: 462.
11. Governor DuVal to Thomas L. McKenney, March 17, 1826, TP, 23: 472–73.
12. Governor to Thomas L. McKenney, March 20, 1826, TP, 23: 482–84.
13. Thomas L. McKenney to Governor DuVal, May 5, 1828, TP, 24: 8; Joseph White to Gad Humphreys, May 10, 1828, in Sprague, *The Florida War,* 53–54.
14. St. Augustine *East Florida Herald,* March 28, 1826; William P. DuVal to Samuel Southard, January 23, 1826, Samuel Southard Papers, box 21, f. 14, PU.
15. James Gadsden to the *Herald,* April 26, 1826, in St. Augustine *East Florida Herald,* May 16, 1826; James Gadsden to the Secretary of War, March 25, May 17, 1826, the Secretary of War to James Gadsden, May 2, 1826, TP, 23: 489–90, 527–28, 545–47; James Gadsden to the Secretary of War, June 5, 1826, TP, 23: 581–82.
16. Governor DuVal to Daniel E. Burch, May 29, 1826, in Daniel E. Burch to the Quartermaster General, May 29, 1826, TP, 23: 567–72. See also Daniel E. Burch to the Quartermaster General, June 3, 1826, TP, 23: 573–81.
17. Governor DuVal to Thomas L. McKenney, April 5, 7, 1826, TP, 23: 500–501, 504–5.
18. William P. DuVal to Thomas McKenney, April 15, 1826, Letters Received, Office of Indian Affairs, RG 75, NA, copy in Frank Snyder Collection, box 28, f. 20, University of South Florida Library.
19. Tuckkasee Mothla (Hicks), Micanopy, Holata Mico, Tulcee Mathla, Fokee Lustee Hajo, Nea Mathla, and Itcho Tustenuggy made the trip. St. Augustine: *East Florida Herald,* April 4, May 23, June 13, 1826.
20. James Barbour to Delegation of Florida Indians, May 10, 1826, in Thomas L. McKenney to Gad Humphreys, May 11, 1826, TP, 23: 539–41.
21. Talk by the Delegation of Florida Indians, May 17, 1826, TP, 23: 548–51; Pensacola *Gazette,* August 4, 1826.
22. Thomas L. McKenney to Governor DuVal, May 22, 1826, TP, 23: 557.
23. Thomas L. McKenney to Gad Humphreys, May 11, 1826, TP, 23: 538–39 n45; Pensacola *Gazette,* August 4, 1826; Gad Humphreys to William P. DuVal, June 4, 1826, in Executive Proceedings of the Senate, 22nd Congr., Papers Re. Nominations: Governor William Pope DuVal, File Number Sen 22B-A3, f. 1, Records of the United States Senate, RG 46, NA.
24. St. Augustine *East Florida Herald,* July 4, 1826.
25. John Rodman to the Secretary of War, July 11, 1826, Secretary of War to Governor DuVal, August 6, 1826, Governor DuVal to Thomas L. McKenney, August 29, 1826, TP, 23: 603–6, 627, 635–37.
26. Governor DuVal to the Secretary of War, August 10, 1826, Duncan L. Clinch to Adjutant General, October 18, 1826, TP, 23: 628–29, 651–53; Brown, "The Florida Crisis of 1826–1827," 419–42.

27. Governor DuVal to Thomas McKenney, November 9, 1826, TP, 23: 661–62.

28. DuVal, "Sketch of Gov. William DuVal," Call Papers, Florida Historical Society Library, typescript copy in Frank Snyder Collection, box 9, f. 11, p. 7, University of South Florida Library.

29. Mahon, *History of the Second Seminole War*, 281; Sprague, *The Florida War*, 99, 502–3; McReynolds, *The Seminoles*, 136; Ellen Call Long, *Florida Breezes*, 60–61, 111.

30. Governor DuVal to Thomas L. McKenney, July 27, 1826, TP, 23: 624–25; Thomas L. McKenney to Governor DuVal, November 6, 1826, TP, 23: 656–57; Governor DuVal to Thomas L. McKenney, November 30, 1826, TP, 23: 671–73

31. Pensacola *Gazette,* December 1, 1826; William P. DuVal to the President of the Legislative Council, December 12, 1826, in Pensacola *Gazette,* December 28, 1826, *Niles Register,* January 13, 1827.

32. Governor DuVal to Duncan L. Clinch, December 7, 1826, in Governor DuVal to the Secretary of War, December 8, 1826, TP, 23: 684–86.

33. Savannah *Georgian,* December 25, 1826.

34. Governor DuVal to Thomas L. McKenney, January 9, 29, 1827, TP, 23: 721–22, 744–45; William P. DuVal to George Troup, January 6, 1827, RG 151, Ser. 2153, Territorial and Early Statehood Records, box 6, f. 26. See also Brown, "The Florida Crisis of 1826–1827," 437.

35. Owen Marsh to William P. DuVal, January 1, 1827, RG 54, Territorial Papers of the Senate, M200, NA, frame 165–69.

36. William P. DuVal to President John Q. Adams, January 2, 1827, and William P. DuVal to Joseph White, January 2, 1827, Papers Relating to the Florida Territorial Council, Museum of History/Miami; Secretary Walton to the Secretary of State, December 14, 1826, TP, 23: 688–89.

37. William P. DuVal to Samuel Southard, November 14, 1826, Samuel Southard Papers, box 21, f. 14, PU.

38. Thomas L McKenney to Governor DuVal, December 7, 1826, TP, 23: 682–84.

39. Duncan L. Clinch to the Commanding General, February 13, 1827, TP, 23: 757–59.

40. Governor DuVal to Thomas McKenney, February 27, 1827, Thomas McKenney to Governor DuVal, March 20, 1827, Governor DuVal to Thomas McKenney, April 17, 1827, Thomas McKenney to Benjamin Chaires, April 26, 1827, TP, 23: 771–72, 794–95, 818–19, 825–26.

41. Gad Humphreys to Governor DuVal, March 11, 1827, in Governor DuVal to Thomas McKenney, March 20, 1827, TP, 23: 796–97.

42. Gad Humphreys to William P. DuVal, March 6, 1827, in Sprague, *The Florida War,* 37–38.

43. Thomas L. McKenney to Governor DuVal, March 22, 1827, Governor DuVal to Thomas L. McKenney, April 17, 1827, TP, 23: 800–801, 816–18.

44. Joshua A. Coffee to Thomas L. McKenney, June 13, 1827, Duncan L. Clinch to the Adjutant General, July 8, 1827, TP, 23: 860–64, 856–57.

45. Delegate White to the Secretary of War, June 15, July [?], 1827, TP, 23: 864–67.

46. Delegate White to the Secretary of War, July [?], 1827, Memorial to Congress by the Legislative Council, July, 1827, TP, 23: 898–901, 896–97.

CHAPTER 8: "I have health, activity, good spirits, and a small share of *Perserverity*"

1. Governor William P. DuVal, Message to the Legislative Council, in Pensacola *Gazette*, December 28, 1826.
2. Robert Gamble to James Breckenridge, January 19, 1827, Breckenridge Papers, Virginia Historical Society.
3. Gilman and Ferguson, *Journals of Ralph Waldo Emerson*, 3: 115; Pensacola *Gazette*, November 2, 1827.
4. DuVal, "Sketch of Gov. William DuVal," Call Papers, Florida Historical Society Library, typescript copy in Frank Snyder Collection, box 9, f. 11, 3, University of South Florida Library.
5. Laura Wirt Randall to William Wirt, September 30, 1827, Reel 9, Wirt Papers, Maryland Historical Society.
6. "Letters from Laura H. Wirt to Louisa Elizabeth Carrington, 1819–1831" (typescript), 252b, Laura Wirt Randall Papers, Virginia Historical Society.
7. William P. DuVal to Samuel Southard, August 8, 1826, Samuel Southard Papers, box 21, f. 14, PU.
8. Snyder, "Nancy Hynes DuVal," 26–27.
9. Dobie, *John C. DuVal*, 15–16.
10. Tallahassee *Floridian,* November 25, 1828, reprinted in Baltimore *Patriot,* December 23, 1828.
11. Tallahassee *Florida Advocate,* September 29, December 15, 1827; Leon County, Minutes of the Superior Court, 1824–1833, Book 1, 36.
12. Samuel DuVal farmed and served as deputy marshal of Middle Florida under Thomas Eston Randolph. In 1837 he was appointed marshal of the Middle District of Florida. See Thomas E. Randolph to the Secretary of State, August 18, 1837, TP, 25: 412.
13. When he learned that Judge Augustus Woodward was "dying" due to "hard drinking," DuVal urged Samuel Southard to do all in his power to have William Wirt's son-in-law Thomas Randall appointed. His appointment would give "general satisfaction, and a man more competent will not be appointed. He has formed an acquaintance with almost every gentleman of standing in this district and is highly esteemed." William P. DuVal to Samuel Southard, June 12, 1827, Samuel Southard Papers, box 26, f. 2, PU.
14. Laura Wirt Randall to Elizabeth Wirt, September 30, 1827, Reel 9, Wirt Papers, Maryland Historical Society.
15. Laura Wirt Randall to Elizabeth Wirt, October 13, December 16, 1827, Reels 9 and 10, Wirt Papers, Maryland Historical Society; Jabour, *Marriage in the Early Republic,* 63 n10.
16. Laura Wirt Randall to Elizabeth Wirt, January 8, 1828, Laura Wirt Randall to Sister, December 24, 1827, Reel 10, Wirt Papers, Maryland Historical Society.
17. Groene, "Lizzie Brown's Tallahassee," 157–58.
18. Tallahassee *Florida Intelligencer,* April 14, May 5, July 22, 1826.
19. See for example Lafayette to William P. DuVal, February 27, 28, 1827, and David B. Macomb to Lafayette, July 16, 1827, in Milledgeville *Southern Recorder,* October 1, 1827.
20. William P. DuVal to Samuel Southard, January 23, 1826, Samuel Southard Papers, box 21, f. 14, PU.

21. William P. DuVal to Samuel Southard, June 12, 1826, Samuel Southard Papers, box 21, f. 14, PU.
22. Ibid.
23. Ibid.
24. Abstract of Disbursements for Indian Affairs by Wm. P. DuVal, Governor of Florida, December 1824, TP, 23: 142.
25. Warner, *Free Men in the Age of Servitude*, 22–23; Parker, "The Proctors—Antonio, George, and John," 20–21.
26. A Tennessean with ties to Andrew Jackson, Richard C. Allen offered Governor DuVal, Richard K. Call, James Gadsden, Benjamin Chaires, and Jonathon Robinson as references. Washington *Daily National Journal*, September 15, 1826.
27. Groene, "Lizzie Brown's Tallahassee," 155.
28. Thomas Randall to William Wirt, April 17, May 22, 29, 1827, Wirt Papers, Reel 9, Thomas Randall to William Wirt, December 5, 1827, Reel 10, Wirt Papers, Maryland Historical Society
29. Baptist, *Creating an Old South*, 16–119; Paisley, *The Red Hills of Florida*, 57–94; Smith, *Slavery and Plantation Growth in Antebellum Florida*, 9–27; Shofner, *History of Jefferson County Florida*, 21–34.
30. William P. DuVal to James Madison, November 14, 1826, Madison Papers, Reel 21, LC.
31. James Madison to William P. DuVal, January 11, April 18, 1827, William P. DuVal to James Madison, February 11, 1827, Reel 21, Madison Papers, LC; Knauss, *Territorial Florida Journalism*, 24; Key West *Register and Commercial Advertiser*, April 23, 1829; Washington *Daily National Intelligencer*, December 17, 1829.
32. DuVal proclaimed that elections would take place on the first Monday of October 1826. Proclamation Re Election by Governor DuVal, July 23, 1826, TP, 23: 619–23; Pensacola *Gazette*, August 25, 1826.
33. Doherty, *Richard K. Call*, 36–37, 46–47; Manley et al., *The Supreme Court of Florida*, 27–29.
34. Richard K. Call to Andrew Jackson, November 8, 1826, *Jackson Papers*, 6: 233; Tallahassee *Florida Intelligencer*, October 27, 1826, December 3, 1826; Pensacola *Gazette*, December 21, 1826, April 13, 1827. On the White-Call conflict see Baptist, *Creating an Old South*, 88–89; Doherty, *Richard Keith Call*, 36–37, 42–43, 46–48; Dibble, *Joseph Mills White*, 1–47.
35. Pensacola *Gazette*, November 23, 1826.
36. Counted among members of the Nucleus were Call, Ward, Butler, Richard C. Allen, George K. Walker, Robert W. Williams, Isham D. Searcy, Romeo Lewis, and William B. Nuttal. In East Florida Joseph Sanchez and Charles Downing were also associated with the group. On the Nucleus see Baptist, *Creating an Old South*, 92–94; Thompson, *Jacksonian Democracy on the Florida Frontier*, 3–4; Doherty, *Richard Keith Call*, 41–42, 46–51, 70–83; Doherty, "Andrew Jackson's Cronies"; Manley et al., *The Supreme Court of Florida*, 29.
37. William P. DuVal to Samuel Southard, July 28, 1826, Samuel Southard Papers, box 21, f. 14, PU.
38. William P. DuVal to Samuel Southard, June 12, 1827, Samuel Southard Papers, box 26, f. 2, PU.

39. Birkner, "The General, the Secretary," 243–53; Remini, *Andrew Jackson and the Course of American Freedom*, 121–22.
40. List of Territorial Appointments, February 1827, TP, 23: 778–81.
41. St. Augustine *East Florida Herald* quoted in Pensacola *Gazette*, July 13, 1827.
42. Pensacola *Gazette*, October 9, 1827.
43. William P. DuVal to Samuel Southard, June 12, 1827, Samuel Southard Papers, box 26, f. 2, PU.
44. William P. DuVal to Andrew Jackson, June 12, 1827, Papers of Andrew Jackson, Reel 34, LC.
45. This subject is covered in Remini, Andrew Jackson and the Course of American Freedom, 126–27.
46. TP, 23: 784; Tallahassee *Florida Advocate* quoted in Pensacola *Gazette*, August 17, 1827; Augusta *Chronicle and Georgia Advertiser*, August 29, 1827; Charleston *City Gazette and Commercial Daily Advertiser*, October 12, 1827.

CHAPTER 9: "Harassed by the persecution of their neighbors"

1. Adams, ed., *Memoirs of John Quincy Adams*, 7: 341, 407.
2. Commission of Governor DuVal, January 9, 1828, TP, 24: 3; Thomas Randall to William Wirt, February 13, 1828, Reel 10, Wirt Papers, Maryland Historical Society.
3. Milledgeville *Georgia Journal*, February 25, 1828.
4. Governor DuVal to Jacob C. Isacks, January 6, 1828, Report on the House Committee on Public Lands, January 11, 1828, TP, 23: 992–95, 999. On October 14, 1826, a "mandamus" was issued commanding Ward and Call, Registrar and Receiver of the Western Land District of Florida, to let DuVal enter Northwest corner of section six, township one, range one, South & East. Leon County, Minutes of the Superior Court, 1824–1833, Book 1, 26; *William P. DuVal vs Richard Keith Call and George T. Ward*, 1826, and William P. DuVal to the President of the Legislative Council, January 1, 1826, Office of the Secretary of State, RG 151, ser. 2153, box 5, f. 42, Florida State Archives.
5. Keene *New Hampshire Sentinel*, January 25, 1828; Bennington *Vermont Gazette*, January 29, 1828.
6. Governor DuVal to Delegate White, January 10, 1828, TP, 23: 996–98.
7. Delegate White to George Graham, December 25, 1827, Governor DuVal to Thomas L. McKenney, May 30, 1828, TP, 23: 959, 24: 16.
8. William P. DuVal to James Barbour, January 28, 1828, New York Historical Society; Winfield Scott to Adjutant General, April 5, 1828, TP, 23: 1059–61.
9. Chief Blount (through interpreter Stephen Richards) to Colonel Joseph White, December 10, 1827, in DuVal Papers, PKYL, typescript copy in Frank Snyder Collection, box 9, f. 10, University of South Florida Library; John Blunt and Cathron to the Secretary of War, October 27, 1827, Letters Received, U.S. Bureau of Indian Affairs, RG 75, NA; John Blount to Andrew Jackson, October 28, 1827, *Jackson Papers*, 6: 595; Governor DuVal to Thomas L. McKenney, January 10, 1828, TP, 23: 995–96.
10. Governor DuVal to the Secretary of War, January 28, July 17, 1828, Governor DuVal to Thomas L. McKenney, July 17, 1828, TP, 23: 1013–14, 24: 40–41.
11. William P. DuVal to Samuel Southard, March 10, 1828, Samuel Southard Papers, box 29, f. 12, PU.

12. That spring Jackson, DuVal, and others passed through Uniontown and Brownsville, Pennsylvania. Cooperstown (N.Y.) *Watch-Tower,* November 3, 1828.

13. Joseph White to William P. DuVal, March 16, 1828, Correspondence of the Territorial Governors, 1825–1836, RG 101, ser. 177, box 1, f. 4, Florida State Archives; William P. DuVal to Samuel Southard, March 10, 1828, Samuel Southard Papers, box 29, f. 12, PU.

14. DuVal told Samuel Southard the lands are "rising in value, daily.... The land that we propose to get of General LaFayette" he estimated was worth $30 per acre, and DuVal hoped to be able to obtain it for $1.25 per acre. William P. DuVal to Samuel Southard, April 15, 1828, Samuel Southard Papers, box 29, f. 12, PU.

15. Tallahassee *Florida Advocate* quoted in Pensacola *Gazette,* May 16, 1828.

16. Ibid.

17. St. Augustine *East Florida Herald* quoted in Pensacola *Gazette,* May 16, 1828.

18. To Harrison the question of the election was between Adams and "liberty" and Jackson and "despotism." See Burr Harrison et al., "To the Citizens of Nelson," and Burr Harrison, "Kentuckians!," Bardstown *Western Herald,* October 18, 1828, December 17, 1828.

19. Joseph Simeon Sanchez to William P. DuVal, June 27, 1828, Correspondence of the Territorial Governors, 1825–1836, RG 101, ser. 177, box 1, f. 4, Florida State Archives.

20. Groene, "Lizzie Brown's Tallahassee," 159; Hammond, *The Medical Profession,* 509–11; Leon County Marriages, Application #27, Record Book X, 4. In a far different account of the wedding ceremony, Laura Wirt Randall wrote to her parents that, although she was not able to accept the governor's invitation to the wedding, she had heard that the match was "opposed to the wishes & almost the commands of her parents & family." The ceremony had only a "few witnesses and was a very melancholy affair. I have heard Mrs. D ... left the room as soon as it was over." Laura Wirt Randall to Elizabeth Wirt, February 2, 1828 , Wirt Papers, Reel 10, Maryland Historical Society.

21. Laura Wirt Randall to Elizabeth Wirt, May 25, 1828, Wirt Papers, Reel 10, Maryland Historical Society.

22. William Pope DuVal to Andrew Jackson, June 23, 1828, Jackson Papers, Reel 35, LC.

23. Laura Wirt Randall to Mother, July 4, 1828, Thomas Randall to William Wirt, July 11, 1828, Reel 11, Wirt Papers. Southard as well as Wirt would eventually be involved in litigation involving the Forbes purchase. Benjamin D. Wright to George Graham, November 17, 1830, TP, 24: 454.

24. William P. DuVal to Samuel Southard, July 1, 17, 1828, Samuel Southard Papers, box 29, f. 12, PU.

25. Ibid.

26. William P. DuVal to Samuel Southard, July 25, 1828, Samuel Southard Papers, box 29, f. 12, PU.

27. Ibid.

28. Parker, "The Proctors," 21; Warner, *Free Men in the Age of Servitude,* 23–24.

29. William P. Duval to Andrew Hynes, September 18, 1828, typescript in St. Augustine Historical Society.

30. Ibid.

31. Pensacola *Florida Argus* quoted in Pensacola *Gazette,* September 30, 1828; Governor DuVal to Thomas L. McKenney, October 12, 1828, TP, 24: 83.

32. Gad Humphreys to Thomas L. McKenney, October 20, 1828, Governor DuVal to Thomas L. McKenney, January 28, 1829, TP, 24: 92–93, 147–48.

33. William P. DuVal to Samuel Southard, December 7, 1828, Samuel Southard Papers, box 29, f. 12, PU.

34. Andrew Jackson to Richard Keith Call, December 22, 1828, *Jackson Papers*, 6: 546–47; Remini, *Andrew Jackson and the Course of American Freedom*, 145–48; Burstein, *The Passions of Andrew Jackson*, 162–72.

CHAPTER 10: **Storm Clouds on the Horizon**

1. Magnolia *Advertiser*, December 19, 1828.
2. Ibid.
3. Thomas Randall to William Wirt, August 22, 1829, August 22, 1829, Reel 12, Wirt Papers, Maryland Historical Society.
4. On the formation of the official cabinet and the "kitchen cabinet" see Remini, *Andrew Jackson and the Course of American Freedom*, 159–68, 181–82; Van Deusen, *The Jacksonian Era*, 31–34; Wiltse, *John C. Calhoun, Nullifier*, 19–25; Bartlett, *John C. Calhoun*, 136–38, 160–63.
5. Samuel Houston to Andrew Jackson, January 13, 1827, *Jackson Papers*, 6: 261–63, 263 n1; John Henry Eaton to Andrew Jackson, March 4, 1828, *Jackson Papers*, 6: 428; John C. Calhoun to Andrew Jackson, April 30, 1828, *Jackson Papers*, 6: 450; Andrew Jackson to John Caldwell Calhoun, May 25, 1828, and John Caldwell Calhoun to Andrew Jackson, July 10, 1828, *Jackson Papers*, 6: 461, 480; Wiltse, *John C. Calhoun, Nationalist*, 363–64.
6. Remini, *Andrew Jackson and the Course of American Freedom*, 137. Also on the formulation of the tariff and Calhoun's reaction to it see Remini, *Henry Clay*, 329–30; Bartlett, *John C. Calhoun*, 144–46; Wiltse, *John C. Calhoun, Nullifier*, 65–74; Sydnor, *The Development of Southern Sectionalism*, 186–91; Van Deusen, *The Jacksonian Era*, 39–40.
7. John Caldwell Calhoun to Andrew Jackson, July 10, 1828, *Jackson Papers*, 6: 481.
8. Sydnor, *The Development of Southern Sectionalism*, 191.
9. The principle work on the Eaton affair is Marszalek, *The Petticoat Affair*. See also Remini, *Andrew Jackson and the Course of American Freedom*, 203–16; Van Deusen, *The Jacksonian Era*, 37–38; Bartlett, *John C. Calhoun*, 163–65; Satterfield, *Andrew Jackson Donelson*, 21–23, 27–36, 41. An excellent summary of the break between Jackson and Calhoun is contained in Peterson, *The Great Triumvirate*, 183–94; Sydnor, *The Development of Southern Sectionalism*, 187–202; Remini, *Andrew Jackson and the Course of American Freedom*, 217–47; Wiltse, *John C. Calhoun, Nullifier*, 1–97.
10. Andrew Jackson to the Creek Indians, March 23, 1829, *Jackson Papers*, 7: 112–13.
11. Governor DuVal to Thomas L. McKenney, April 20, 1829, TP, 24: 195.
12. Governor DuVal to the Secretary of War, May 4, June 9, 1829, Governor DuVal to Thomas L. McKenney, June 23, 1829, TP, 24: 209–10, 230–34, 240. Jackson eventually removed Humphreys and appointed Phagan in his place. Thomas L. McKenney to Governor DuVal, March 18, 1830, TP, 24: 381.
13. Governor DuVal to the President, April 21, 1829, TP, 24: 197–98; William Pope DuVal to Andrew Jackson, April 21, 1829, *Jackson Papers*, 7: 169–70. See also TP, 23: 734–35, 24: 11–12.
14. Governor DuVal to the President, April 21, 1829, TP, 24: 198, 219, 220.

15. Richard K. Call to Andrew Jackson, April 28, 1829, Andrew Jackson to Richard K. Call, May 18, July 5, 1829, *Jackson Papers,* 7: 187–88, 226–28, 325–28. See also Marszalek, *The Petticoat Affair,* 23, 77–78; Doherty, *Richard Keith Call,* 31–33, 53–55; Satterfield, *Andrew Jackson Donelson,* 21–23, 27–36, 41.

16. John DuVal desperately sought the post, explaining to the Richmond postmaster that Henry Clay, who "has ever been opposed to all my kin and Clan, induced the President to appoint Mr. McCarty" when George Walton resigned the post. John P. DuVal to James Preston, June 6, 1829, Preston Papers, Virginia Historical Society; Recommendation of John P. DuVal as Secretary, June 5, 1829, Secretary McCarty to the President, June 10, James D. Westcott Jr. to the President, June 12, 1829, Commission of James D. Westcott, June 15, 1829, TP, 24: 227, 235, 238–39.

17. Adams, ed., *Memoirs of John Quincy Adams,* 8: 176–77.

18. Alexander Hamilton to Andrew Jackson, July 4, 1829, *Jackson Papers,* 7: 323–25.

19. Tallahassee *Floridian and Advocate,* September 8, 1829, December 7, 1830.

20. Tallahassee *Floridian and Advocate,* October 2, 1829.

21. TP, 24: 194 n41; St. Augustine *Florida Herald,* October 28, 1829. The address was also reprinted in Tallhassee *Floridian and Advocate,* October 1, 1829; Pensacola *Gazette,* October 27, 1829.

22. William P. DuVal to the President of the Legislative Council, November 13, 1829, in Tallahassee *Floridian and Advocate,* December 15, 1829.

23. Ibid.

24. Ibid.

25. William P. DuVal to the President of the Legislative Council, November 23, 1829, in Tallahassee *Floridian and Advocate,* December 22, 1829. See also Tallahassee *Floridian and Advocate,* January 5, 26, February 23, March 30, 1829.

26. Tallahassee *Floridian and Advocate,* December 15, 1829.

27. Adams, ed., *Memoirs of John Quincy Adams,* 8: 176–77. The former president and his wife were staying at their son's residence during the holiday season. Washington *Daily National Intelligencer,* January 5, 1830.

28. Adams, ed., *Memoirs of John Quincy Adams,* 8: 176–77. Two days earlier, on January 16, White had told Adams that Jackson's Florida appointments were "all bad and extremely odious to the people of the territory. White was retailing to me the characters with which he gave of them," Adams recorded in his diary, "one after the other, to the General; and if he had extracted the quintessence of all the penitentiaries of the Union to represent the virtues of the Government of Florida, he could not have done worse." Adams, ed., *Memoirs of John Quincy Adams,* 172.

29. Delegate White to the Vice President, January 26, 1830, TP, 24: 333–37; *Calhoun Papers,* 11: 105.

30. St. Augustine *Florida Herald,* May 12, 1830.

31. William P. DuVal to S. D. Ingham, January 22, 1830, U.S. Department of the Treasury, Correspondence of the Secretary of the Treasury with Collectors of Customs, 1789–1833, RG 56, M-178, Reel 38, NA.

32. Governor DuVal to the Secretary of War, May 6, 1830, and the Secretary of War to Governor DuVal, May 7, 1830, TP, 24:406–9; Secretary of War to William B. Lewis, June 25, 1832, TP, 24: 718–19.

33. James Westcott to Andrew Jackson Donelson, May 18, 1830, Andrew Jackson Donelson Papers, LC, Reel 2.

34. Remini, *Andrew Jackson and the Course of American Freedom*, 300–309; Bartlett, *John C. Calhoun*, 163–74; Peterson, *The Great Triumvirate*, 186–88; Remini, *The House*, 117–20.

35. Washington *Daily National Intelligencer*, April 20, 1830.

36. One observer noted that the addresses were "carefully prepared, were of a strong anti-tariff and rather of an anti-federal complexion." Washington *Daily National Intelligencer*, April 19, 1830.

37. William Wyatt to William P. DuVal, April 22, 1828, Records of the Secretary of State, RG 151, Ser. 2153, Territorial and Early Statehood Records, box 1, f. 42, Florida State Archives.

38. William Wyatt to Joseph White, June 20, 1830, in Pensacola *Gazette*, January 11, 1831; Tallahassee *Floridian and Advocate*, February 10, 1831; Joseph White to William Wyatt, July 15, 1830, in Tallahassee *Floridian and Advocate*, February 10, 1831.

CHAPTER 11: "I intend to examine . . . Your relation to the President"

1. Tallahassee *Floridian and Advocate*, July 6, 1830.
2. Ibid.
3. St. Augustine *East Florida Herald* quoted in Key West *Register and Commercial Advertiser*, April 23, 1829.
4. William Wyatt to Editor of the St. Augustine *Florida Herald*, June 16, 1830; St. Augustine *Florida Herald*, July 21, 1830.
5. William Wyatt to William P. DuVal, n.d., in Pensacola *Gazette*, January 11, 1831; Tallahassee *Floridian and Advocate*, February 10, 1831.
6. Tallahassee *Floridian and Advocate*, July 13, 1830.
7. Tallahassee *Floridian and Advocate*, July 27, 1830.
8. Tallahassee *Floridian and Advocate*, July 27, 1830. On the Forbes Purchase and litigation see Doherty, *Richard Keith Call*, 57–68; Coker and Watson, *Indian Traders of the Southeastern Spanish Borderland*, 350–62; Manley et al., *The Supreme Court of Florida and its Predecessor Courts*, 50–51; Knetsch, *Faces on the Frontier*, 137–39; Rogers, *Outposts on the Gulf*, 5–7, 11, 45–47.
9. St. Augustine *Florida Herald*, August 12, 1830; Governor DuVal to the Secretary of State, July 30, 1830, TP, 24: 435.
10. "This short-sighted artifice," declared White, "succeeded to some extent in some of the Departments, whilst in others it was despised and rejected as I am sure it must have been by the President. Neither your boast of influence in producing the late political revolution as it is called, nor the numerous stories you told, while acting the Sycophant before the friends of the Executive, availed you of the several thousand dollars of your accounts, with an administration over whom you claim at home a predominant influence—When I saw you bewailing your pennyless condition and cursing the Secretary of War in terms of characteristic grossness, I hardly supposed you would so soon have returned, and claimed the merit of obtaining appropriations which cost me the most diligent attending , and which you know are to be attributed exclusively to my individual exertions. Nor did I suppose that you had the audacity enough to recover so soon from the disappointment in the rejection of your accounts to use to my injury the popularity of the administration you had abused—You knew

so little of what was going on at Washington unconnected with your own intrigues, that I remember you repeatedly inquired of me what I had before Congress, and complimented my extraordinary zeal, as you have repeatedly done in clumsy letters addressed to me, and upon one occasion in a speech at Tallahassee for which the Nucleus gave you a crown of thorns until you respoke it all in commendation of another. The new edition restored you to credit perhaps in more respects than one." Joseph White to William P. DuVal, September 30, 1830, in Tallahassee *Floridian and Advocate,* May 26, 1831.

11. Ibid.
12. Ibid.
13. Ibid.
14. Ibid.
15. Ibid.
16. Ibid.
17. Ibid.
18. Ibid.
19. William Wyatt to the Editor, n.d., in Tallahassee *Floridian and Advocate,* October 26, 1830. One week later Wyatt again drew the connection between support or lack of support for the governor's administration, arguing that "the reappointment of Governor DuVal and the universal complaints of his public acts, are in my opinion closely connected to the next delegate's election, for it is a matter of great importance to the people of Florida, to know the sentiments of the candidates upon this subject as it is well known that there is a large majority of them opposed both to his re-appointment and administration, and would not vote for any one if they know it, that would support either." Tallahassee *Floridian and Advocate,* November 2, 1830.

20. Georgian to the Editor, n.d., in Tallahassee *Floridian and Advocate,* December 21, 1830. For similar charges against the Nucleus see Orlando to the Pensacola *Gazette,* November 30, 1830.

21. The St. Augustine *Florida Herald* reported on December 30, 1830, that "During his short stay in this City, [DuVal] was treated with the respect and attention, that was due his rank, by all parties."

22. Tallahassee *Floridian and Advocate,* February 17, 1831.
23. Address and comments in Tallahassee *Floridian and Advocate,* January 6, 1831.
24. Ibid.
25. Ibid.
26. Ibid.
27. Pensacola *Gazette,* January 11, 1831; Tallahassee *Florida Advocate,* February 10, 1831.
28. Ibid.
29. Ibid.
30. Pensacola *Gazette,* January 11, 1831.

CHAPTER 12: **Nullifying an Election**

1. Tallahassee *Floridian and Advocate,* January 20, 27, 1831.
2. Abram Bellamy to the President, January 5, 1831, TP, 24: 476–79; Abraham Bellamy to Andrew Jackson, January 19, 1831, *Jackson Papers,* Scholarly Resources edition, Reel 17.

3. William P. DuVal to the President of the Legislative Council, February 2, 1831, in Tallahassee *Floridian and Advocate,* March 3, 1831; Baltimore *Niles Register,* March 26, 1831.

4. Cincinnatus to the People in Florida, in Tallahassee *Floridian and Advocate,* March 10, 1831. Dr. Edward R. Gibson published the Tallahassee *Florida Courier* beginning in December 1830. Few issues of the paper have survived, and it went out of existence in March 1832. When the paper folded, Gibson went to Washington, where he worked for Duff Green at the Washington *United States Telegraph* before returning to Tallahassee in 1840. Knauss, *Territorial Florida Journalism,* 25–26.

5. Tallahassee *Floridian and Advocate,* February 24, 1831. Philo Jefferson claimed that in Gadsden DuVal had finally found someone who will "vindicate his administration." The "forced and unnatural union of Col. Gadsden and Gov. DuVal is a bad omen." Tallahassee *Floridian and Advocate,* March 24, 1831. A Georgian also spoke of the DuVal-Gadsden alliance. Ibid. One of the people predicted that Leon County Sheriff Romeo Lewis, a DuVal appointee, would attempt to sway votes for Gadsden in Leon County. Tallahassee *Floridian and Advocate,* April 21, 1831.

6. "Gen. Jackson and Mr. Calhoun," Tallahassee *Floridian and Advocate,* March 17, 1831. For the creation of the Washington *Globe* as the administration's newspaper and the alienation of Duff Green from the administration see Remini, *Andrew Jackson and the Course of American Freedom,* 292–99; Wiltse, *John C. Calhoun, Nullifier,* 94–97; Niven, *Martin Van Buren,* 262–66.

7. The only cabinet officer to retain his post was DuVal's friend Postmaster General William Barry. On the cabinet resignations and subsequent fallout see Remini, *Andrew Jackson and the Course of American Freedom,* 311–30; Wiltse, *John C. Calhoun, Nullifier,* 103–6; Niven, *Martin Van Buren,* 267–71; Van Deusen, *The Jacksonian Era,* 45–46; Marszalek, *The Petticoat Affair,* 157–79.

8. Tallahassee *Floridian and Advocate,* March 17, 1831.

9. James Gadsden, Address to the Voters in Jefferson County, March 14, 1831, in Tallahassee *Floridian and Advocate,* April 7, 1831.

10. "A Voter," in Tallahassee *Floridian and Advocate,* April 7, 1831.

11. Delegate White to the Secretary of State, March 10, 1831, TP, 24: 508–13.

12. Ibid.

13. Ibid. See also Gad Humphreys to Joseph M. White, March 2, 1831, in Tallahassee *Floridian and Advocate,* June 2, 1831; William C. Allen to William P. DuVal, March 5, 1832, Executive Proceedings of the Senate, 22nd Congr., Papers Re. Nominations: Governor William Pope DuVal, File Number Sen 22B-A3, f. 1, Records of the United States Senate, RG 46, NA.

14. Extract of letter from Richard C. Allen to Hugh Lawson White, February 3, 1831, in Andrew Jackson Donelson to Richard C. Allen, May 28, 1831, *Floridian and Advocate,* newspaper clipping in Andrew *Jackson Papers,* Scholarly Resources edition, Reel 17.

15. Delegate White to the Secretary of State, March 10, 1831, TP, 24: 508–13.

16. In an accompanying column Gibson attempted to discredit White by linking him with Zephaniah Kingsley's controversial pamphlet, which many Floridians denounced as incendiary and abolitionist in nature. Of Kingsley and White Gibson wrote, "Mr. Kingsley the other favorite of the Col. is a rich man and a classical scholar. Mr. Van Buren probably cares very little about Mr. K's riches. He might think a little more of him on account of this

classical scholarship. To satisfy him upon that point, we should like to know if the Col. sent on to the Department of state a certain pamphlet published by Mr. K advocating the breeding of Mulattos. There seems to be something ominous in this union of the Col. with Mr. K and with the Webster Party of Massachusetts. They have repealed the law in Massachusetts which prohibits the marriage of blacks and whites. And the Col. is praising Mr. Kingsley for his classical attainments. Mr Kingsley's hopes must be reviving and we shall perhaps see a new edition of the '*amalgamation* pamphlet,' revised and corrected by our late Delegate." In a flagrant attempt to link White to an inflammatory idea that was obnoxious to all white Floridians, Gibson asked, "Does the Col mean to become the advocate of certain doctrines advanced by Mr. Kingsley in a celebrated pamphlet two years ago? As the Col. favors *no party* and has no '*particular creed,*' it may be that he may extend his impartiality so far as to favour no *peculiar colour.*" Tallahassee *Florida Courier,* April 21, 1831.

17. William P. DuVal, "To the Freemen of Florida," in Tallahassee *Florida Courier,* April 21, 1831.

18. Ibid.

19. Ibid.

20. On March 8, two days before White wrote the letter to Van Buren, Donelson wrote to DuVal that White "has withdrawn his objectives to you, and that after a thorough examination of your accounts and the evidence which you have submitted in refutation of the charges presented by Wyatt that your whole conduct stands unimpeached in the eyes of the government—so that a renewal of your commission will be not merely a proof of the President's regard for you, but a highly complementary evidence of your official merit. P. S. I have read the forgoing to the President. He requests me to add, that White has withdrawn the charges for *the present*—and unless he finds when he reaches Florida, *reason* to think that they can be sustained, he will let the subject alone." Andrew J. Donelson to William P. DuVal, March 8, 1831, Tallahassee *Florida Courier,* April 21, 1831. DuVal's friend Congressman Charles Wickliffe confided to DuVal that the president had said that White had told him that Wyatt was a "trifling fellow and not deserving consideration but that as the Delegate he could not refuse to hand the charges in." After inquiring with the State and Treasury Departments, the president told him that he found them "groundless." C. A. Wickliffe to William P. DuVal, March 21, 1831, Tallahassee *Florida Courier,* April 21, 1831.

21. Joseph White to the Public in Pensacola *Gazette and Chronicle* quoting Tallahassee *Floridian and Advocate,* May 19, 1831.

22. Commission of Governor DuVal, April 18, 1831, TP, 24: 525. Washington *National Intelligencer* quoted in Tallahassee *Floridian and Advocate,* May 5, 1831.

23. Tallahassee *Floridian and Advocate,* May 5, 12, 19, June 2, 1831. The final total was given as 1,988 for White and 1,903 for Gadsden.

24. Governor DuVal to the Secretary of State, May 26, 1831, TP, 24: 528.

25. On the basis of the failure to turn in poll books or transcripts within the specified two-month period, DuVal rejected returns in precincts in Mosquito, St. Johns, Duval, Alachua, Hamilton, Gadsden, Jackson, Washington, and Walton Counties. William P. DuVal, Election Returns for Delegate to Congress, July 1, 1831, TP, 24: 535–38; William P. DuVal, "Proclamation to the Judges and Clerks of the Several Counties in the Territory," July 2, 1831, in Baltimore *Niles Register,* August 20, 1831.

26. Joseph M. White to William P. DuVal, July 2, 7, 1831, Territorial Governors Correspondence, RG 101, Ser. 177, box 1, f. 4, Florida State Archives.

27. TP, 24: 539; Tallahassee *Floridian and Advocate,* July 7, 28, August 4, 1831; Baltimore *Niles Register,* July 30, 1831, 396; Richmond *Enquirer* and Washington *National Journal* quoted in Tallahassee *Floridian and Advocate,* August 24, 1831.

28. See James D. Westcott to Charles E. Sherman, August 3, 1831, in Tallahassee *Florida Courier,* August, 10, 1831. The Pensacola *Gazette* ridiculed Westcott's statement. See paper quoted in Tallahassee *Floridian and Advocate,* September 7, 1831; Pensacola *Gazette,* August 20, 27, 1831. For other accounts of the dispute see Savannah *Georgian,* July 30, 1831.

29. Tallahassee *Floridian and Advocate,* August 10, September 7, 1831.

30. Tallahassee *Floridian and Advocate,* August 17, 1831.

31. William P. DuVal to Andrew Jackson, October 4, 1831, *Andrew Jackson Papers,* Reel 40, LC.

32. Proclamation of James D. Westcott, December 5, 1831, in Tallahassee *Floridian and Advocate,* December 27, 1831. The Baltimore *Niles Register* reported on November 19, 1831, that on the day appointed for the election "some places of voting were neither attended by the judges of the election nor the people. At others, however, they were partially attended, and the votes appear to have been nearly unanimous for Col. White." Other national papers kept the matter alive. See Washington *Daily National Journal,* October 14, 25, November 26, 1831; Washington *Daily National Intelligencer,* January 2, 1831. Also on the election and its confused aftermath see Baptist, *Creating an Old South,* 101; Doherty, *Richard Keith Call,* 70–74; Shofner, *History of Jefferson County,* 32–33; Dibble, *Joseph Mills White,* 61. Clifton Paisley calls DuVal's decision to intervene in the election his "worst decision" as governor. See Paisley, *The Red Hills of Florida,* 92.

33. Joseph M. White to James Westcott, December 16, October 22, 1831, Territorial Governors Correspondence, William P. DuVal, RG 101, Ser. 177, box 1, Florida State Archives.

34. William P. DuVal to James Barbour, August 28, 1831, Barbour Papers, Alderman Library, University of Virginia.

35. William P. DuVal to Samuel Southard, May 7, 1831, Samuel Southard Papers, box 1, LC. Four months later DuVal wrote to Southard that "My own private fortune has been seriously diminished since my removal to Florida. I have made many sacrifices for the interest of this country and have been rewarded as you have by abuse, and slander. I do not mean to imply that Genl Jackson has ever treated me unkindly. I have ever found him a warm and decided friend. I disdain to complain and will stand only on my own merit and my own principles." William P. DuVal to Samuel Southard, August 11, 1831, Samuel Southard Papers, box 38, f. 7, PU.

36. William P. DuVal to Andrew Jackson, October 4, 1831, Andrew Jackson Papers, Reel 40, LC; James D. Westcott to P. W. Bower, September 27, 1831, Correspondence of the Secretary of State, RG 150, ser. 24, box 1, 76, Florida State Archives;.

37. William P. DuVal to Andrew Jackson, October 4, 1831, *Andrew Jackson Papers,* Reel 40, LC.

38. Ibid.

39. Ibid.

40. Ibid. One newspaper reported that Jackson's "courting of Adair's favor" would be unsuccessful because "we trust [Adair] has not yet forgotten the vile treatment of his son-in-law, Mr. White the delegate from Florida, both by that weak instrument Gov. DuVal, and by the national executive. He will not be deficient in civility, but we mistake the man, if he can be flattered out of his firmness and consistency." New York *Evening Journal* quoted in Easton, Maryland, *Republican Star,* January 3, 1832; Baltimore *Patriot,* December 13, 1831.

41. Worden Pope to William P. Duval, August 19, 1831, in William P. DuVal to Andrew Jackson, October 4, 1831, Andrew Jackson Papers, Reel 40. LC.

42. Ibid.

43. Ibid.

44. Ibid.

45. Ibid.

46. Ibid.

47. William P. DuVal to Samuel Southard, May 7, 1831, Samuel Southard Papers, box 1, LC; same to same, August 11, 1831, Samuel Southard Papers, box 38, f. 7, PU.

48. "A Sketch of John C. DuVal's Life," 6–7, in Ruth West Emerson Collection, San Antonio, Texas; Appointments to Office by the Governor, February 12, 1832, TP, 24: 660.

CHAPTER 13: "I shall return very poor to Kentucky"

1. Henry Clay and Daniel Webster led the charge against Van Buren in the Senate. Senator William L. Marcy of New York led the Van Buren defenders. Critics charged that Calhoun had conspired with Clay and Webster to block the nomination, even suggesting that they persuaded Kentucky senator George Bibb to absent himself on the day of the vote, thus opening the way for Calhoun to break the tie. On Calhoun's role in Van Buren's rejection in the Senate and its political ramifications see Remini, *Andrew Jackson and the Course of American Freedom,* 347–50; Remini, *Henry Clay;* Niven, *Martin Van Buren,* 295–99; Wiltse, *John C. Calhoun,* 126–31; Bartlett, *John C. Calhoun,* 184–85. Washington Irving had served in the American legation in Great Britain since 1830 and was with Van Buren on the day he learned of his rejection. Nevin, *Martin Van Buren,* 289, 293, 295–96; Burstein, *The Original Knickerbocker,* 228–30.

2. "I have always loved R. m. Johnson, brave, virtuous, and honorable, he was never known to flinch from either danger or truth—I have always said no man from Kentucky ever rendered such important services—He is slandered and abused, because of his virtues and warmth." William P. DuVal to Andrew Jackson, October 4, 1831, Andrew Jackson Papers, Reel 40, LC; Washington *United States Telegraph,* January 28, 1832.

3. Tallahassee *Floridian and Advocate,* February 28, 1832.

4. *Journal of the Senate of the United States of America,* Executive Proceedings of the Senate, 22nd Congr., 1st sess. (1831), 493, 497, 499, 507; Tallahassee *Floridian and Advocate,* January 3, 1832; Washington *National Intelligencer,* December 7, 1831.

5. Governor DuVal to William L. Marcy, February 9, 1832, TP, 24: 652; TP, 24: 694 n92.

6. Among those writing statements in support of DuVal were Isham Searcy, Ambrose Crane, James Gadsden, Abram Bellamy, Jonathon Robinson, William Hall, Robert W. Williams, David Thomas, Richard Keith Call, Benjamin Chaires, John McIver, and John

Phagan. Executive Proceedings of the Senate, 22nd Congr., Papers Re. Nominations: Governor William Pope DuVal, File Number Sen. 22B-A3, f. 1, Records of the United States Senate, RG 46, NA.

7. In actuality the will of the legislative council regarding DuVal reappointment is not that clear. On January 5 John Love, a delegate from Gadsden County, introduced a resolution calling for the Senate to reject DuVal's nomination, which brought about another resolution abrogating the last legislative council's resolution endorsing DuVal's nomination on the grounds that such a resolution did not "come within the province of the duties of the council." It was subsequently agreed by a vote of 12–3 that both resolutions and amendments would be postponed. *Journal of the Florida Legislative Council* (1832), 18; Tallahassee *Floridian and Advocate,* January 10, 17, 1832; St. Augustine *Florida Herald,* February 1, 16, 1832. On March 20, 1832, the Tallahassee *Floridian and Advocate* disputed "A Floridian"'s construction of the resolution as an "expression of DuVal's favor— The truth is, the council was not disposed to interfere in the matter, when it was known charges had been made against him to the Senate and would be investigated before that body." For the rumors see Charleston *Mercury* quoted in Richmond *Enquirer,* March 3, 1832; Tallahassee *Floridian and Advocate,* May 29, 1832; Peter Alba to the President, January 15, 1832, TP, 24, 629–31.

8. The trial took place on March 3, 5, 6, and 8. Washington *United States Telegraph,* March 8, 1832; Washington *Daily National Intelligencer,* March 1, 14, 1832.

9. Washington *Daily National Intelligencer,* May 1, 1832; *Journal of the Senate of the United States of America,* Executive Proceedings of the Senate, 22nd Congr., 1st sess. (1831), 510, 511. Response of William P. DuVal to the Charges and Specifications Exhibited Against Him by Joseph White, Gad Humphreys, and William Wyatt, Before the Senate of the United States, March 22, 1832, in Executive Proceedings of the Senate, 22nd Congr., Papers Re. Nominations: Governor William Pope DuVal, File Number Sen 22B-A3, f. 2, Records of the United States Senate, RG 46, NA (Hereinafter Response of William P. DuVal to the Charges).

10. Isham Searcy to Andrew Jackson, May 30, 1830, Response of William P. DuVal to the Charges, in Executive Proceedings of the Senate, 22nd Congr., Papers Re. Nominations: Governor William Pope DuVal, File Number Sen 22B-A3, f. 2, Records of the United States Senate, RG 46, NA.

11. Robert W. Williams to Andrew Jackson, April 26, 1830, Response of William P. DuVal to the Charges, in Executive Proceedings of the Senate, 22nd Congr., Papers Re. Nominations: Governor William Pope DuVal, File Number Sen 22B-A3, f. 2, Records of the United States Senate, RG 46, NA.

12. Ambrose Crane to William P. DuVal, n.d., Affidavit of John McIver, January 31, 1831, David Thomas to William P. DuVal, February 29, 1832, Affidavit of William Hall, October 18, 1830, Response of William P. DuVal to the Charges, in Executive Proceedings of the Senate, 22nd Congr., Papers Re. Nominations: Governor William Pope DuVal, File Number Sen 22B-A3, f. 2, Records of the United States Senate, RG 46, NA.

13. David Thomas to William P. DuVal, February 29, 1832, Response of William P. DuVal to the Charges, in Executive Proceedings of the Senate, 22nd Congr., Papers Re. Nominations: Governor William Pope DuVal, File Number Sen 22B-A3, f. 2, Records of the United States Senate, RG 46, NA.

14. Richard K. Call to William P. DuVal, March 12, 1832, Response of William P. DuVal to the Charges, in Executive Proceedings of the Senate, 22nd Congr., Papers Re. Nominations: Governor William Pope DuVal, File Number Sen 22B-A3, f. 2, Records of the United States Senate, RG 46, NA.

15. Affidavit of James Gadsden, n.d., Response of William P. DuVal to the Charges, in Executive Proceedings of the Senate, 22nd Congr., Papers Re. Nominations: Governor William Pope DuVal, File Number Sen 22B-A3, f. 2, Records of the United States Senate, RG 46, NA.

16. Affidavit of John Phagan, February 13, 1832 and Affidavit of James Gadsden, n.d., Response of William P. DuVal to the Charges, in Executive Proceedings of the Senate, 22nd Congr., Papers Re. Nominations: Governor William Pope DuVal, File Number Sen 22B-A3, f. 2, Records of the United States Senate, RG 46, NA.

17. Adding up the costs of litigation—$1,500 to assistant counsel in two cases ($3,000 and $500), plus $2,000 to William Wirt in the second case, plus the law agent's salary and perquisites for several years—White concluded, "It is very evident that if there was not some 'reform and retrenchment' in this branch of public service, the sums paid for the adjudication in future cases would be more that the land was worth." Washington *United States Telegraph*, May 4, 1832.

18. *Journal of the Senate of the United States of America*, Executive Proceedings of the Senate, 22nd Congr., 1st sess. (Printed by Duff Green, 1831), 510–11. For the daily action on DuVal's nomination from December 13, 1831, to April 30, 1832, see *Executive Journals of the United States Senate, 1789–1866* (1831), 185, 186, 189, 203, 204, 243, 245, 246, 251.

19. Tallahassee *Floridian and Advocate*, September 18, 1832. Documents continued to appear in that newspaper on September 25, 1832, January 5, 1833.

20. Joseph White to the Senate of the United States, February 21, 1832, in St. Augustine *Florida Herald*, June 14, 1832. Washington *United States Telegraph*, April 17, 1832; May 9, 1832. See also Washington *Daily National Intelligencer*, March 19, 1832; Henry Brackenridge to Joseph M. White, May 14, 1832, and Joseph M. White to Henry M. Brackenridge, May 16, 1832, in Washington *National Union* quoted in Tallahassee *Floridian and Advocate*, June 12, 1832; Henry M. Brackenridge to the Citizens of the Western District of Florida, in Tallahassee *Floridian and Advocate*, August 7, 1832; Bardstown *Herald*, May 19, 1832; Hall, *The Politics of Justice*,16–17; Manley et al., *The Supreme Court of Florida*, 37.

21. Joseph M. White to William Wyatt, May 14, 1832, Henry M. Brackenridge to William Wyatt, May 26, 1832, in Tallahassee *Floridian and Advocate*, October 23, 1832.

22. James Westcott to William Wyatt, November 14, 1831, in Tallahassee *Floridian*, October 23, 1832.

23. Charging Phagan with corruption and demanding an investigation of his affairs, White declared, "I solemnly believe that the history of no nation or Country can furnish a parallel of the fraud, oppression and inhumanity to which the Florida Indians have been subjected—A part of them are now endeavoring to hire an interpreter to come at their own expense & the lay their complaints before the President—These miserable people are now reduced to utmost extremities for the necessarys of life, indeed they have been in penury & wretchedness for years & many have perished from starvation—this is brought

upon them by combinations to decoy them into intoxication, the more effectually to cheat and defraud them out of their property & to paralyze their efforts to make a support so the new appropriations may be asked only to be wasted." Joseph White to the Secretary of War, January 23, 1832, Secretary of War to the Delegate White, January 25, 1832, TP, 24: 637, 641. For Phagan's answers to White's charges see John Phagan to the Secretary of War, February 7, 1832, TP, 24: 651–52.

24. James D. Westcott to Superintendent of Indian Affairs in Florida, January 17, 19, 1832, Isaac Brown to James D. Westcott, January 3, 1832, James D. Westcott to Lewis Cass, January 17, 1832, Correspondence of the Secretary of State, RG 15, Ser. 24, 99–101, Florida State Archives.

25. James D. Westcott to Abram Bellamy, President of the Legislative Council, February 2, 1832, Letters Received, Bureau of Indian Affairs, RG 75, NA. In 1831 DuVal estimated that the illicit trade between Florida and Cuba involving the Indians exceeded $100,000 annually. Indians and Spanish salted and dried fish at several villages along the coast. DuVal complained that English and Spanish delivered liquor from Cuba and even transported chiefs on business trips to Cuba. William P. DuVal to the Secretary of State, October 7, 1831, TP, 24: 557–63.

26. Tallahassee *Floridian and Advocate,* July 10, 1832; Remini, *Andrew Jackson and Course of American Freedom,* 355–58; Niven, *Martin Van Buren,* 301; Baltimore *Gazette and Daily Advertiser,* June 14, 1832; James Kirke Paulding to M. C. Paterson, May 28, 1832, in Aderman, ed., *The Letters of James Kirke Paulding,* 121–22; Washington Irving to Gentlemen, June 9, 1832, in Irving, ed., *Life and Letters of Washington Irving,* 3: 24–24; Burstein, *The Original Knickerbocker,* 248–56.

27. Irving, ed., *Life and Letters of Washington Irving,* 2: 265.

28. On June 12, 1832, the Washington *Daily National Intelligencer* reported that "Governor Duvall left this city on Friday last for Baltimore on his way to Florida."

29. William P. DuVal to James Barbour, August 28, 1831, Barbour Papers, Alderman Library, University of Virginia.

30. Tallahassee *Floridian and Advocate,* June 26, 1832; St. Augustine *Florida Herald,* June 28, 1832.

31. Tallahassee *Floridian,* May 1, 8, 15, June 19, July 12, 1832.

32. "The Case of Rogers Before the Executive of this Territory," Tallahassee *Floridian,* August 14, 1832. Various national newspapers reprinted the story. St. Augustine *Florida Herald,* September 1, 1832; Baltimore *Niles Register,* October 6, 1832; Hartford *Connecticut Mirror,* September 22, 1832; Boston *Daily Courier,* September 20, 1832.

33. Pensacola *Gazette* quoted in Tallahassee *Floridian and Advocate,* October 9, 1832. For the ball held in Apalachicola in DuVal's honor see Tallahassee *Floridian and Advocate,* October 30, 1832.

34. Tallahassee *Floridian and Advocate,* October 23, 1832.

35. Robert Raymond Reid Diary, February 18, 1833; Tallahassee *Floridian and Advocate,* October 30, 1832; Leon County, Minutes of the Superior Court, Book 1, 546, 561; Denham, "Dueling in Territorial Middle Florida," 36–45.

36. Secretary of War to James Gadsden, February 23, 1832, TP, 24: 662; Joseph White to William Wilson, February 14, 1832, in Tallahassee *Floridian and Advocate,* March 6,

1832, James Gadsden to William Wilson, March 21, 1832, in Tallahassee *Floridian and Advocate*, April 3, 1832; St. Augustine *Florida Herald*, March 15, 1832.

37. On the Treaties of Paynes Landing and Fort Gibson see McReynolds, *The Seminoles*, 122–31; Mahon, *History of the Second Seminole War*, 69–86; Sprague, *The Florida War*, 72–83; Covington, *The Seminoles of Florida*, 63–66; Wright, *Creeks and Seminoles*, 243–44; Missall and Missall, *The Seminold Wars*, 82–89; Hoffman, *Florida's Frontiers*, 304–5; Klunder, *Lewis Cass*, 85.

38. William P. DuVal to the Secretary of War, May 30, August 21, 1832, TP, 24: 711, 725–26.

39. Governor DuVal to the Secretary of War, August 21,1832, James Gadsden to the Secretary of War, September 19, November 30, 1832, Governor DuVal to the Acting Secretary of War, October, 11, 1832, Secretary of War to James Gadsden, December 19, 1832, James Gadsden to Elbert Herring, March 30, 1833, TP, 24: 725–26, 734, 740, 752–54, 765–66, 824–25; James Gadsden to Andrew Jackson, February 12, 1833, Jackson Papers, Reel 40, LC; Elbert Herring to Governor DuVal, March 16, 1833, Secretary of War to Governor DuVal, April 12, 1833, Acting Governor Westcott to the Secretary of War, April 27, 1833, TP, 24: 822–23, 829, 834–35.

40. William P. DuVal to Andrew Jackson Donelson, January 26, 1833, Andrew Jackson Donelson Papers, Reel 3, LC.

41. Tallahassee *Floridian*, December 1, 15, 1832; Message of William P. DuVal, in Pensacola *Gazette*, January 25, 1833.

42. Locally the Tallahassee *Floridian* proclaimed on October 30, 1832, "The efficacy of the *peaceful remedy* of nullification will soon be tested. It is a fearful experiment and we only hope that it may not result in consolidation or a dissolution of our happy government." The paper also reprinted Jackson's proclamation vis-à-vis the nullification in South Carolina on December 29, 1832. See also on the issue St. Augustine *Florida Herald*, October 25, November 29, December 6, 27, 1832.

43. Message of William P. DuVal, in Pensacola *Gazette*, January 25, 1833. For coverage of events in South Carolina in Florida newspapers see Tallahassee *Floridian*, October 30, December 29, 1832; St. Augustine *Florida Herald*, October 25, November 29, December 6, 27, 1832.

44. Diary of Robert Raymond Reid, January 31, February 18, 1833, State Library of Florida.

45. Ibid.

46. DuVal admitted that the "time has arrived when the great planting interest of Florida calls for such an institution." The bill as he understood it "guaranteed the Territory against any possible loss arising from the responsibility assumed." William P. DuVal to the President of the Legislative Council, February 8, 1833, Tallahassee *Floridian*, February 16, 23, 1833. The bill creating the Commercial Bank of Apalachicola also passed that session. Baltimore *Niles Register*, April 6, 1833, 83. On DuVal's stand on banking see Cash, *History of the Democratic Party in Florida*, 11–13; Thompson, *Jacksonian Democracy on the Florida Frontier*, 4–7; Abbey, "The Union Bank of Tallahassee," 207–31; Brevard, *History of Florida*, 202–4, 212. The best treatment of the economic, social, and political ramifications of the Union Bank of Florida's creation is Baptist, *Creating an Old South*, 112–19.

47. William P. DuVal to James K. Polk, March 26, 1834, in Weaver et al., eds., *Correspondence of James K. Polk*, 2: 376–77.

48. William S. Pope to Governor DuVal, May 10, 1833, Acting Governor Westcott to the Secretary of War, May 18, 1833, TP, 24: 846, 847. Blount's possessions were never recovered. Reporting on the matter some time later, Westcott reported that he had no doubt that Blount had lost the "money and goods he alleges. Every possible effort was adopted to bring the perpetrators of this outrage to punishment and they were apprehended but escaped from the custody of the officer." One man confessed, but another shot dead a pursuer and fled to Alabama and then to Texas. Acting Governor Westcott to Elbert Herring, September 1, 1833, TP, 24: 878.

49. James B. Thornton to the Secretary of War, August 29, 1833, Daniel Kurtz to John Phagan, August 30, 1833, TP, 24: 873, 876; St. Augustine *Florida Herald,* October 31, 1833.

50. Dibble, *Joseph Mills White,* 173–81.

51. Andrew Jackson to Richard K. Call, July 14, 1833, *Jackson Papers*, Scholarly Resources edition, Reel 23.

52. James D. Westcott to Commissioners of the Union Bank, July 8, 1833, in House Report on Banks, March 2, 1840, in Tallahassee *Florida,* April 4, 1840. Westcott selected the following directors: John Gamble, William Nuttall, G. H. Chaires, J. K. Campbell, Thomas Preston, Isham Searcy, L. A. Thompson, C. H. DuPont, J. McBride, J. L. Doggett, and Jonathon Robinson. House Committee on Banks Report on Union Bank of Florida, February 25, 1840, in Tallahassee *Floridian,* March 7, 1840.

53. Bardstown *Herald,* December 17, 1828, February 2, 1831. See also Bardstown *Herald,* "Colonization," January 21, March 3, May 12, 19, 1832.

54. William P. DuVal to Andrew Jackson, August 17, 1833, *Jackson Papers,* Scholarly Resources edition, Reel 23.

55. Pensacola *Gazette,* October 2, 1833; Richmond *Enquirer,* September 17, 1833.

56. Charleston *Southern Patriot,* September 9, 1833; Charleston *Courier* quoted in Richmond *Enquirer,* September 17, 1833; Richard K. Call to the President, August 28, 1833, TP, 24: 872; Groene, "Lizzie Brown's Tallahassee," 169; Marriage Bond, October 1, 1833, Nelson County (Kentucky), Kentucky State Archives.

57. Elbert Herring to Governor DuVal, October 31, 1833, Acting Governor Westcott to the Secretary of War, November 13, 1833, TP, 24: 898–99, 912–15; William P. DuVal to Wiley Thompson, November 23, 29, 1833, Letters Received, Bureau of Indian Affairs, RG 75, NA; Wiley Thompson to the Secretary of War, December 2, 1833, Elbert Herring to Governor DuVal, December 13, 1833, TP, 24: 916–18, 925–26; Wiley Thompson to William P. DuVal, House Document, No. 271, 24th Congr., 1st sess. (Washington, 1838), 7–11.

58. Message of His Excellency William P. DuVal, Governor of the Territory of Florida, January 7, 1834, in St. Augustine *Florida Herald,* January 30, 1834.

59. Wiley Thompson to William P. DuVal, March 9, 20, 1834, Letters Received, Bureau of Indian Affairs, RG 75, NA.

60. Brevard, *History of Florida,* 212; Abbey, "Union Bank of Tallahassee," 212.

61. *Journal of the Executive Proceedings of the United States of America, 1829–1837,* 376, 378. Most commentators at the time, even Jackson, assumed that DuVal's term had expired, but documents clearly show otherwise. See Commission of Governor DuVal,

April 30, 1832, TP, 24: 694, and Commission of John Eaton as Governor, April 24, 1834, TP, 25: 3; Richmond *Enquirer,* April 8, 1834, quoted the Winchester *Virginian*'s report that Jackson had nominated Eaton, in "room of Gov. DuVal, that gentleman having signified a wish not to be re-nominated." The St. Augustine *Florida Herald,* April 17, 1834, noted that DuVal's "term of Office expires in the present month." See also Washington *National Intelligencer* quoted in *Niles Register,* April 26, 1834.

62. Delegate White to the Secretary of War, March 21, 1834, TP, 24: 992–93.

63. James D. Westcott to Andrew Jackson Donelson, May 1, 1834, Andrew Jackson Donelson Papers, Reel 3, LC.

64. William P. DuVal to Samuel Southard, April 20, 1834, Samuel Southard Papers, box 45, f. 11, PU.

65. Richmond *Enquirer,* June 3, 1834; Nashville *Banner and Daily Advertiser,* June 16, 1834; Baltimore *Patriot,* May 26, 1834; Report of the Board of Visitors to the Military Academy, West Point, New York, June 17, 1834, Baltimore *Patriot,* July 17, 1834.

66. Burstein, *The Original Knickerbocker,* 276–80; Hanna, *A Prince in Their Midst,* 168–69.

67. Pensacola *Gazette,* June 28, 1834.

68. Pensacola *Gazette,* August 16, 1834; Richmond *Enquirer,* July 15, 1834.

CHAPTER 14: "Do all you can for Texas"

1. On October 1, 8, 14, 15, and 30, 1834 the Louisville *Public Advertiser* advertised the steamboats *Polander, Bunker Hill, Kentuckian, Navaring, Arkansas, Orleans, Ohioan, Revenue, Champion, Planter, Compromise, Chief Justice Marshall, Dover,* and *Powhatan*—all bound for New Orleans.

2. E. T. Bainbridge to Andrew Hynes, October 9, 1834, and Andrew Hynes to E. T. Bainbridge, October 25, 1834, in Nashville *Republican* quoted in Louisville *Public Advertiser,* November 8, 1834.

3. Yater, *Two Hundred Years at the Falls of the Ohio,* 48–59; Louisville *Public Advertiser,* November 11, 1834. Also on Louisville see Share, *Cities in the Commonwealth,* 33, 55; Wade, *The Urban Frontier,* 64–66, 188–91, 197–200.

4. Bardstown *Herald,* February 1, 8, 1834.

5. William P. DuVal to James K. Polk, March 26, 1834, in Weaver et al., eds., *Correspondence of James K. Polk,* 2: 376–77; William P. DuVal to Samuel Beale, August 27, 1834, Norborne Beale Papers, Filson Club Historical Society.

6. On January 18, 1834, the Tallahassee *Floridian* advertised that DuVal would sell at auction at his plantation sugar cane, mules, hogs, farming utensils, roller gins, and other items.

7. Louisville *Public Advertiser,* September 21, 1834.

8. "Governor Duval," St. Augustine *Florida Herald,* October 30, 1834; Tallahassee *Floridian* October 18, 1834.

9. Ibid.

10. Frankfort *Argus* quoted in Louisville *Public Advertiser,* February 26, 1835.

11. William P. DuVal to Andrew Jackson, May 17, 1835, Andrew Jackson Papers, Reel 46, LC

12. "Dinner to Gov. Eaton," Pensacola *Gazette,* January 3, 1835; St. Augustine *Florida Herald,* January 10, 1835.

13. *Journal of the Legislative Council* (1835), 49; Jacksonville *Courier,* February 12, 1835.

14. Doherty, *Richard Keith Call*, 82–83.

15. William P. DuVal to Andrew Jackson Donelson, January 26, 1833, Andrew Jackson Donelson Papers, Reel 3, LC.

16. "Tallahassee Railroad Company Organized," Tallahassee *Floridian* quoted in St. Augustine *Florida Herald,* July 10, 1834; "Bill to Authorize a Railroad Upon the Public Lands for Tallahassee to St. Marks in Florida," Pensacola *Gazette,* January 31, 1835.

17. "They were beautiful years to me," Peggy Eaton recalled fondly. "My neighbors were pleasant. I had no ugly passages in my history, and I was away from my husband's political persecutors. . . . We had two happy years in Florida. To me it was the land of flowers as Washington had been the land of briars." Eaton, *The Autobiography of Margaret Eaton,* 170, 174. Also on Eaton's tenure as governor of Florida see Marszalek, *The Petticoat Affair,* 208–13.

18. Duncan L. Clinch to the Adjutant General, April 24, 1835, October 8, 1835, TP, 25: 129–31, 182–84.

19. February 27, 1835, Diary of Robert Raymond Reid, State Library of Florida.

20. DuVal was among approximately 110 other stockholders in the Union Bank of Florida. John G. Gamble to the Secretary of the Treasury, February 21, 1835, TP, 25: 109–12. DuVal's obligation was recorded on April 1, 1835, Leon County, Deed Book D, 508–9.

21. George T. Ward to Samuel Southard, April 28, 1835, Samuel Southard Papers, box 1, LC.

22. Denham, "The Peerless Wind Cloud," 3–14.

23. Campbell, *Gone to Texas,* 128–47; Fehrenbach, *Lone Star,* 174–215.

24. William P. DuVal to Sam Houston, December 6, 1835, in Jenkins, ed., *The Papers of the Texas Revolution,* 3: 99.

25. In December 1835 Robert Wilmot Scott of Frankfort, Kentucky, recorded in his journal that he had met "Governor DuVal late of Florida, a gentleman of urbane manners kind heart & extensive information" while on a steamboat on the Mississippi River. Clark, ed., *Footloose in Jacksonian America,* 100–101; B. H. DuVal to P. W. Grayson, December 30, 1835, in Binkley, ed., *Official Correspondence of the Texan Revolution,* 1: 257.

26. "A Memorial of Volunteers at Refugio to the Convention, [Feb. ?, 1836]," in Binkley, ed., *Official Correspondence,* 1: 429–30; Burr DuVal to Thomas DuVal, January 18, 1836, in Bardstown *Herald,* February 29, 1836. Also on the Kentucky Volunteers in Texas see Thomas, "Kentuckians in Texas," 237–54; Corner, "John Crittenden Duval," 47–67; Winston, "Kentuckians and the Independence of Texas," 27–62.

27. On the outbreak of the Second Seminole War see Mahon, *History of the Second Seminole War,* 99–113; Missall and Missall, *The Seminole Wars,* 92–103; Sprague, *The Florida War,* 88–114; Doherty, *Richard Keith Call,* 96–98.

28. Tallahassee *Floridian,* January 30, February 6, 13, 1836; Pensacola *Gazette,* February 13, 1836; Bardstown *Herald,* February 19, 1836.

29. Apalachicola *Gazette,* April 13, 1836.

30. Tallahassee *Floridian,* January 30, 1836.

31. William P. DuVal to Duncan L. Clinch, April 28, 1836, Duncan Lamont Clinch Papers, PKYL.

32. Bardstown *Herald*, June 9, 1836.

33. Georgia newspaper quoted in the Louisville *Journal*, June 14, 1836.

34. Richard Keith Call to Andrew Jackson Donelson, May 16, 1836, Andrew Jackson Donelson Papers, Reel 4, LC. Also on this phase of the Second Seminole War see Doherty, *Richard Keith Call*, 96–100; Mahon, *History of the Second Seminole War*, 114–73; Missall and Missall, *The Seminole Wars*, 106–22.

35. Louis M. Goldsborough to Elizabeth Goldsborough, May 20, 1836, Louis M. Goldsborough Papers, Vol. 3, LC.

36. Burr H. Duval to William P. Duval, March 9, 1836, Duval Papers, Eugene C. Barker Texas History Center, University of Texas.

37. Ibid.

38. Ibid.

39. On April 27, 1836, the Bardstown *Herald* despaired of hearing of Burr DuVal's regiment. The journal wondered whether or not it had left the besieged outpost at Goliad and joined the main Texian army on the Colorado. "We are confident of ONE thing only—and that is that Capt. Duval and his company, no matter what situation they may have been placed in, *have done their duty*, both as soldiers and Kentuckians." Also on the Goliad Massacre see the Bardstown *Herald*, May 4, 11, June 1, 1836; Louisville *Daily Journal*, June 11, 1836; Campbell, *Gone to Texas*, 150–52; Roell, *Remember Goliad!*

40. See John C. DuVal's "Awful and Thrilling Narrative," in Bardstown *Herald*, June 15, 1836; "Statement of John C. Duval," Louisville *Daily Journal*, June 9, 1836; "Narrative of C. B. Shain of Louisville: A Volunteer in the Cause of Texas," Louisville *Daily Journal*, June 30, 1836; Dobie, *John C. Duval*, 101–5.

41. William P. Duval to Richard K. Call, June 27, 1836, New York Historical Society.

42. Ibid.

43. Bardstown *Herald*, May 12, 1836.

44. Louisville *Daily Journal*, May 23, 1836.

45. William P. DuVal to George Chambers, June 30, 1836, in Louisville *Daily Journal*, July 6, 1836. Commenting on the contents of DuVal's letter, the editor of the journal noted that "Gov. D is resolved to give himself to the cause of Texas. He evinces a spirit that no damages or difficulties can intimidate or subdue. The Kentuckians are called on for their aid. The field of honorable fame is before them, and they may reap its glorious harvest. If such men as DuVal and Chambers with a Brigade of Kentuckians march to Texas, we doubt whether they will rest satisfied with the achievement of the independence of that country. We believe that they will follow up their conquests until the single star, the emblem of their adopted country, shall blaze and burn like a meteor over the minarets of the city of Montezuma."

46. Chambers and DuVal, *Magnanimous and Chivalrous Sons of the West*, July 15, 1836, in Louisville *Daily Journal*, July 18, 1836.

47. Ibid.

48. Louisville *Daily Journal*, July 9, 1836.

49. Louisville *Daily Journal*, July 15, 28. See also A to the Editors, Louisville *Daily Journal*, August 1, 1836.

50. R. K. Call to Andrew Jackson, July 9, 1836, Andrew Jackson Papers, Reel 48, LC.

51. William Campbell to Fanny Campbell, September 14, 1836, Campbell Family Papers, Duke University.

52. "Latest from Florida," Correspondence of the Fredericksburg *Arena* quoted in Louisville *Daily Journal*, October 21, 1836.

CHAPTER 15: **Canals, Banks, and a Constitutional Convention**

1. St. Joseph *Times* quoted in St. Augustine *Herald*, December 8, 1836.
2. Pensacola *Gazette*, January 28, 1837.
3. Tallahassee *Floridian*, January 27, February 3, 1838.
4. Lewis, "Thomas Brown," 93; Hammond, *The Medical Profession in 19th Century Florida*, 514–15.
5. John P. DuVal and Francis Dickens, "Florida Claims," Tallahassee *Floridian*, February 18, 1837.
6. Doherty, *Richard Keith Call*, 98–106. In his fourteen-page response to the War Department Call asserted that he would "surrender most cheerfully" the command to Jesup but added, "I must be permitted to say that I regarded your letter as the most extraordinary document I have ever read." After discussing his entire campaign Call noted that crossing the Withlacoochee "river with the means I possessed, and within the time in which our supplies required it to be done, was a rational impossibility, and could not have been accomplished by General Jackson himself." Acting Secretary of War to Governor Call, November 4, 1836, TP, 25: 339–41; Acting Secretary of War to Thomas Jesup, November 4, 1836, TP, 25: 341–43; Governor Call to the Acting Secretary of War, December 2, 1836, TP, 25: 344–59.
7. See Doherty, *Richard Keith Call*, 114–45; Doherty, *The Whigs of Florida*.
8. St. Augustine *Herald*, December 29, 1836.
9. Tallahassee *Floridian*, December 31, 1836; Doherty, *Richard Keith Call*, 30, 56, 86; Baptist, *Creating an Old South*, 24, 29; Baptist, "The Migration of Planters to Antebellum Florida," 527–54.
10. William P. DuVal to Samuel Southard, January 7, 1837, Samuel Southard Papers, box 57, f. 14, PU.
11. Delegate White to William P. DuVal, January 3, 1837, TP, 25: 360–61.
12. Petition to Congress by the Lake Wimico and St. Joseph Canal and Railroad Company, January 2, 1838, TP, 25: 452–53.
13. On the rivalry between Apalachicola and St. Joseph see Rogers, *Outposts on the Gulf*, 10–15; Knauss, "St. Joseph," 178–95; Willoughby, *Fair to Middlin'*, 12.
14. Journal of Samuel Peter Heintzelman (1836), December 27–31, 1836, 175–76, Papers of Samuel Peter Heintzelman, LC.
15. John P. DuVal to John Campbell, April 29, 1837, Robert Butler to Martin Van Buren, January 31, 1837, Undersigned members of the Legislative Council, to Martin Van Buren, February 11, 1837, Thomas Randall, James Webb, and John Cameron to Martin Van Buren, February 24, 1837, William P. DuVal to Andrew Jackson, Jr, February 28, 1837, in "John P. DuVal," Letters of Application and Recommendation during the Administrations of Martin Van Buren, William Henry Harrison, and John Tyler, 1837, RG 59, M687, Reel 9, NA; William P. DuVal to John Forsyth, March 1, 1837, James Westcott to Martin

Van Buren, February 16, 1837, Thomas Randall, James Webb, and John Cameron, to the Secretary of State, January 23, 1837, in "Samuel DuVal," Letters of Application and Recommendation during the Administrations of Martin Van Buren, William Henry Harrison, and John Tyler, 1837, RG 59, M687, Reel 9, NA.

16. William P. DuVal to Martin Van Buren, August 25, 1837, *Martin Van Buren Papers*, Series 1, Chadwyck-Healy edition, Reel 24.

17. "It now appears," Call wrote to the secretary of state, "that Mr. DuVal was making arrangements to leave Florida, and on the 15th of May the very day on which he expected to be appointed Secretary he took his departure. Being informed of his intention, Mr. Walker called on him to redeem his pledge but he coolly replied that it was impossible and left the Territory, no doubt to avoid meeting his appointment here, and to enable him to spend the summer and enjoy his salary abroad. . . . The present embarrassed and unsettled condition of the country is such as to require every officer to be at his post, and I have again to request that Mr. DuVal may not be permitted to evade the duty and responsibility of his office." Commission of John P. DuVal as Secretary, May 17, 1837, TP, 25: 391; Governor Call to the Secretary of State, June 3, 1837, TP, 25: 392–94; Secretary of State to Governor Call, June 16, 1837, TP, 25: 399, 400n.

18. Governor Call to the Secretary of State, September 10, 1837, TP, 25: 419; Secretary DuVal to the Secretary of State, June 6, 1837, TP, 25: 397–98. As further explanation of his tardiness in reaching Tallahassee, DuVal explained, "My Commission as Secretary of Florida was not received by me until a day or two since, in consequence of the absence of my brother Gov. DuVal by whom it was taken from the office with his papers. This circumstance will account for my silence. I accept the commission. The place of my nativity is Richmond Virginia." Secretary DuVal to the Secretary of State, October 15, 21, 1837, TP, 25: 428, 430.

19. Secretary DuVal to Delegate Downing, December 20, 1837, TP, 25: 445–46.

20. James D. Richardson, ed., *A Compilation of the Messages and Papers of the Presidents*, 4: 1534–35. Also on Van Buren's inauguration see Cole, *Martin Van Buren*, 298–90; Niven, *Martin Van Buren*, 410–11.

21. Benton, *Thirty Year's View*, 2: 14. On the Specie Circular see Schweikart, *Banking in the American South*, 60–62, 170–74; Niven, *Martin Van Buren*, 412–24, 428–29; Curtis, *The Fox at Bay*, 64–85; Cole, *Martin Van Buren*, 285–312; McGrane, *The Panic of 1837*, 61–69.

22. Richardson, *Messages and Papers of the President*, 4: 1541–63. See also Remini, *Daniel Webster*, 470–71; Remini, *Andrew Jackson and the Course of American Democracy*, 427–31; Curtis, *The Fox at Bay*, 87–109.

23. Schweikart, *Banking in the American South*, 59, 170–74, 197–98; Abbey, "The Union Bank of Tallahassee," 207–31; Dovell, *History of Banking in Florida*, 26–29. A particularly negative view of the Union Bank, especially its attempt to control Florida politics for the purpose of enriching its stockholders, is found in Baptist, *Creating an Old South*, 113–19.

24. Thompson, *Jacksonian Democracy on the Florida Frontier*, 1–8, quotation on p. 7. Ed Baptist represents the struggle as one primarily between "planters" (rich) and "countrymen" (poor); he also recognizes family groupings as a primary aspect of the factions. Baptist, *Creating an Old South*, 161–63.

25. William P. DuVal to Martin Van Buren, October 12, 1837, "Richard C. Allen," Letters of Application and Recommendation during the Administration of Martin Van Buren, William Henry Harrison, and John Tyler, 1837–1845, NA, RG 59, M687, Reel 1.

26. Tallahassee *Floridian*, March 24, May 19, 1838; Joseph Branch to Lawrence Branch, March ?, 1838, Mrs. Lawrence Branch Papers, North Carolina Archives; Hammond, *The Medical Profession in 19th Century Florida*, 536–38.

27. For DuVal and Allen's law cases see Tallahassee *Floridian*, February 24, 1838; Tallahassee *Florida Watchman*, April 21, 1838.

28. Thomas Hagner to Peter Hagner, November 13, 1838, Hagner Papers, Southern History Collection, University of North Carolina.

29. DuVal had recommended his friend for the judgeship. Writing personally to Van Buren, DuVal asserted, "this gentleman's reputation for legal learning is well known throughout the territory and no man now residing in this country would be more acceptable to the people." William P. DuVal to Martin Van Buren, March 3, 1838, "Richard C. Allen," Letters of Application and Recommendation during the Administration of Martin Van Buren, William Henry Harrison, and John Tyler, 1837–1845, NA, RG 59, M687, Reel 1.

30. Phelps, *The People of Lawmaking*, 12; Tallahassee *Floridian*, December 1, 1838; St. Augustine *Florida Herald*, May 19, 1838; Apalachicola *Courier*, April 24, May 8, 1839. For DuVal and Brockenbrough's law cases see St. Joseph *Times*, February 2, 23, June 15, October 8, November 13, 1839; Apalachicola *Courier*, October 15, 1839; St. Joseph *Times*, August 1, 1838.

31. Rogers and Clark, *The Croom Family and Goodwood Plantation*, 79–80, 81, 163–85.

32. Mary Gamble to Catherine Wirt, June 29, August 30, 1838, Wirt Papers, Reel 18, Maryland Historical Society.

33. St. Joseph *Times* quoted in Pensacola *Gazette*, August 19, 1837.

34. Tallahassee *Floridian*, February 3, August 11, October 6, 20, 1838.

35. "Gov. Duval," Pensacola *Gazette*, September 22, 1838.

36. Tallahassee *Floridian*, April 17, 1838.

37. Tallahassee *Floridian*, August 11, 18, 25, September 15, 1838.

38. See totals in Proclamation of Governor Call and Returns of the 1837 Election, July 27, 1837, in Dodd, *Florida Becomes a State*, 109–12.

39. St. Augustine *Florida Herald*, April 12, 1837. One commentator noted that many Floridians seek "to remain a SEPARATE AND DISTINCT TERRITORY. EAST FLORIDA is content to remain a while longer in leading strings not to Middle and West Florida, but of the General Government." St. Augustine *Florida Herald*, February 17, 1838.

40. See Memorial to Congress of Inhabitants of St. Augustine, February 5, 1838, in Dodd, *Florida Becomes a State*, 122–26. For statehood and "division" question in Florida see also Baptist, *Creating an Old South*, 159–61; Martin, *Florida during the Territorial Days*, 258–77.

41. See St. Augustine *Florida Herald*, June 2, 16, 30, September 1, 1838.

42. Louis M. Goldsborough to Elizabeth Goldsborough, December 9, 21, 1838, Louis M. Goldsborough Papers, Vol. 4, LC.

43. Ibid.

44. Tallahassee *Floridian*, December 15, 1838.
45. Ibid.; Dodd, *Florida Becomes a State*, 48. Also on the St. Joseph Convention see Hoskins, "The St. Joseph Convention," 33–43, 97–100, 242–50; Porter, "The Reception of the St. Joseph Constitution."
46. *Journal of the Proceedings of a Convention of Delegates to Form a Constitution for the People of Florida Held at St. Joseph, December 1838* (St. Joseph: Times, 1839), in Dodd, *Florida Becomes a State*, 137; Tallahassee *Floridian*, December 6, 1838.
47. Tallahassee *Floridian*, December 15, 1838.
48. Ibid.
49. Ibid.
50. Ibid. See also St. Joseph *Times* quoted in *Tallahassee Floridian*, December 22, 1838. See also Dodd, *Florida Becomes a State*, 47–51, 146, 150.
51. *Journal of the Proceedings*, in Dodd, *Florida Becomes a State*, 149–50.
52. Ibid.
53. Debates in the Constitutional Convention, December 17, 1838, from St. Joseph *Times* printed in Tallahassee *Floridian*, January 12, 1839.
54. Ibid.
55. Dodd, *Florida Becomes a State*, 56–57, 447 n47. Some years later accusations were made that the "Faith Bond Bank faction became more and more violent denunciatory and abusive" at the convention. Probank men from East Florida were aided and abetted "by the Union Bank Junto headed by their attorney Ex. Governor DuVal. . . . While the Convention was in session, the Bank minority held on Sunday a caucus, to decide whether they should not break up the Convention, unless the Democrats yielded their opposition to the recognition of the Faith Bond Banks. . . . Ex Gov. DuVal was one of the prime getters up of this meeting, which might justly be called a blood cousin to the Hartford Convention." St. Augustine *Florida Herald and Southern Democrat*, September 12, 1840. See also Martin, *Florida during the Territorial Days*, 157.
56. Debates in the Constitutional Convention in Tallahassee *Floridian*, January 5, 1839.
57. Ibid.
58. Ibid.
59. "A Constitution, or Form of Government, for the People of Florida," in Dodd, *Florida Becomes a State*, 322–24; Schweikart, *Banking in the American South*, 174; Baptist, *Creating an Old South*, 160–61; Dovell, *History of Banking in Florida*, 37–40.
60. Louis M. Goldsborough to Elizabeth Goldsborough, December 20, 1838, Louis M. Goldsborough Papers, Vol. 4, LC.
61. Tallahassee *Floridian*, January 12, 1839; Pensacola *Gazette*, January 19, 1839.

CHAPTER 16: Faith Bonds, Division, Depression, and a Plague

1. Dodd, *Florida Becomes a State*, 67.
2. Garraty, *The American Nation*, 276.
3. "A Voter of Gadsden" to the Editor of the Tallahassee *Floridian*, April 27, 1839.
4. For coverage of these complicated political dynamics see Thompson, *Jacksonian Democracy on the Florida Frontier*, 23–36; Baptist, *Creating an Old South*, 159–74; Brown, *Ossian Bingley Hart*, 38–40; Doherty, *Richard Keith Call*, 106–12, Doherty, *The Whigs of Florida*, 8–9.

5. Downing quoted in Dodd, *Florida Becomes a State*, 41.

6. Tallahassee *Floridian*, April 6, 1839.

7. Journal of Samuel Peter Heintzelman (1838), January 11–April 6, 1838, 25, 28, 70, 74, Papers of Samuel Peter Heintzelman, LC.

8. Journal of Samuel Peter Heintzelman (1838), June 22, 1838, 117, Papers of Samuel Peter Heintzelman, LC.

9. Ellen Wirt Vass to Catherine G. Wirt, June 23, 1839, Wirt Papers, Reel 18, Maryland Historical Society.

10. Apalachicola *Gazette*, June 15, 1839; Tallahassee *Floridian*, June 8, 1839. For Macomb's Treaty and the reaction to it see Mahon, *History of the Second Seminole War*, 256–58; Missall and Missall, *The Seminole Wars*, 163–65.

11. Journal of Samuel Peter Heintzelman (1839), July 4, 1839, 123, Papers of Samuel Peter Heintzelman, LC.

12. Journal of Samuel Peter Heintzelman (1839), July 13–14, July 28–30, September 10, 1839, 130, 137–39, 170, Papers of Samuel Peter Heintzelman, LC.

13. William P. DuVal to John Parkhill, July 23, 1838, John Parkhill Papers, f. 1838–1839, box 1, John Parkhill Papers, Southern History Collection, University of North Carolina. For the degenerating situation of the Union Bank in the summer of 1839 see Abbey, "The Union Bank of Florida," 217.

14. Thompson, *Jacksonian Democracy on the Florida Frontier*, 30–31; Governor Call to the Secretary of State, June 1839, TP, 25: 616–18.

15. Resolutions by Citizens of Tallahassee, January 23, 1838, TP, 25: 457–58; Resolutions by Citizens of Tallahassee, January 29, 1838, TP, 25: 464–65; Tallahassee *Floridian*, February 3, 1838. William P. DuVal was first to sign the petition. Among the forty-one other signers were John Parkhill, Samuel Parkhill, George K. Walker, Samuel S. Sibley, David S. Walker, Robert W. Williams, John G. Gamble, H. W. Braden, Francis Eppes, and Thomas Eston Randolph.

16. Acting Secretary of State to Secretary DuVal, August 21, 1839, TP, 25: 621; Call quoted in Doherty, *Richard Keith Call*, 115.

17. Mahon, *History of the Second Seminole War*, 264–65; Doherty, *Richard Keith Call*, 115–17.

18. Tallahassee *Floridian*, January 29, 1838.

19. On the Read-Alston duel see Denham, "The Read-Alston Duel," 427–46; Baptist, *Creating an Old South*, 169–172; Tallahassee *Floridian*, December 21, 1839.

20. On Willis Alston's attack of Read see St. Augustine *News*, January 24, 1840; Tallahassee *Floridian*, January 11, 1840; St. Joseph *Times*, January 22, 1840; St. Augustine *Florida Herald and Southern Democrat*, January 30, 1840.

21. Tallahassee *Floridian*, January 4, 1840.

22. St. Joseph *Times*, November 13, 1839.

23. Delegate Downing to the President, December 29, 1839, TP, 26: 16–17; Tallahassee *Floridian*, March 14, 1840; St. Augustine *News*, April 3, 1840.

24. Heintzelman was no friend of militia officer Leigh Read. Commenting frequently in his diary about the conflict brewing between Read and his Whig opponents in November through December, he found Read mostly at fault in the matter. He also admired Alston's father, Robert, who was ill. Read, he predicted, would not fight. On November

1, after visiting DuVal's residence, he confided to his diary, "Gen. Reed had fallen into the hands of men who will not be trifled with. He must fight or be disgraced." A month and a half later, on December 17, he was visiting Robert Gamble's plantation when he learned that Read had killed Alston in the duel. "Old Col. Alston and his family are almost heart broken," he wrote. Journal of Samuel Peter Heintzelman (1839), November 1, December 17, 1839, 218, and Journal of Samuel Peter Heintzelman (1840), January 17, 1840, 13.

25. Tallahassee *Floridian*, January 11, 1840.
26. Robert Raymond Reid, "Message to the Legislative Council," January 12, 1840, *Florida House Journal* (1840), 16.
27. Tallahassee *Floridian*, January 15, 25, February 1, 22, 1840.
28. Hammond, *The Medical Profession in 19th Century Florida*, 513–18; Baptist, *Creating an Old South*, 171; Paisley, *The Red Hills of Florida, 1528–1865*, 88, 169–70.
29. Thompson, *Jacksonian Democracy on the Florida Frontier*, 28; Tallahassee *Floridian*, February 22, 1840.
30. Minority Report of the Territorial Senate Committee, 1840, TP, 26: 76–80; St. Joseph *Times*, February 12, 1840; Jacksonville *East Florida Advocate*, April 21, 1840.
31. William P. DuVal to B. Penrose, February 19, 1841, TP, 26: 272–73.
32. Alfred Balch to the President, April 3, 1840, TP, 26: 128–29.
33. Tallahassee *Floridian*, April 4, 1840.
34. Tallahassee *Star*, May 21, 1840; Tallahassee *Floridian*, January 4, 1840; St. Joseph *Times*, March 4, 1840; Apalachicola *The Florida Journal*, December 23, 1840; Apalachicola *Courier*, November 12, 1839; Quincy *Sentinel*, December 26, 1839.
35. St. Joseph *Times*, April 21, 1840, January 23, 1841; Quincy *Sentinel*, January 1, 1841; Tallahassee *Floridian*, December 26, 1840.
36. Extract of a Letter to the Editor, May 4, 1840, St. Joseph *Times*, May 5, 1840.
37. Ibid., May 12, 1840.
38. *U.S. Senate Journal* (1841), 59–60.
39. Journal of Samuel Peter Heintzelman (1840), May 17, July 27, 1840, 105, 166.
40. "Troubles in Tallahassee," Quincy *Sentinel*, August 7, 1840; Tallahassee *Floridian*, September 19, 1840; St. Augustine *Florida Herald and Southern Democrat*, September 18, 1840. See also Thompson, *Jacksonian Democracy on the Florida Frontier*, 68–70.
41. Tallahassee *Floridian*, August 15, 1840; Pensacola *Gazette*, August 22, 1840; Petition to the President by the Citizens of Tallahassee, August 10, 1840, and Committee of Tallahassee Citizens to Governor Reid, August 5, 1840, TP, 26: 186–93.
42. Charles Downing to the President, August 28, 1840, TP, 26: 206–8.
43. Baltimore *Niles Register*, August 29, September 5, 1840; Tallahassee *Floridian*, August 22, 1840.
44. Tallahassee *Floridian*, August 15, 1840.
45. Apalachicola *Commercial Advertiser*, August 29, 1840.
46. Tallahassee *Floridian*, September 5, 1840. See also St. Joseph *Times*, September 4, 1840; Quincy *Sentinel*, October 9, 1840.
47. "The Early Experiences of Ralph Ringwood, Notes Drawn from his Conversations by Geoffrey Crayon, Gent." was serialized and first appeared in *Knickerbocker* or *New-York Monthly Magazine* 16 (August 1840): 152–65, (September 1840): 258–66.

48. The Tallahassee *Star of Florida* reprinted "The Seminoles" on December 29, 1840. So did the Easton, Maryland, *Gazette,* November 7, 1840. The Baltimore *Sun* on October 14, 1840, carried the "Conspiracy of Neamathla," as did the Quincy *Sentinel,* November 6, 1840. See also Hartford (Conn.) *Daily Courant,* December 3, 1840; Salisbury (N.C.) *Western Carolinian,* December 11, 1840.

49. Journal of Samuel Peter Heintzelman (1840), October 16, 17, 18, 1840, 244, 246–50. For Read's conspiracy against Alston see also Apalachicola *Commercial Advertiser,* October 3, 1840.

50. Journal of Samuel Peter Heintzelman (1840) and (1841), December 7, 1840, 313, January 2, 1841, January 24, 1841, 3.

51. Tallahassee *Floridian,* January 9, March 20, 1841; Pensacola *Gazette,* January 16, 1841; Quincy *Sentinel,* January 15, 1841.

52. Quincy *Sentinel,* January 22, 1841.

53. Ibid., February 5, 1841; Recommendation of Richard K. Call for Appointment as Governor, January 25, 1841, Recommendation of Minor Walker as United States Marshal, February 2, 1841, William P. DuVal to B. Penrose, February 19, 1841, TP, 26: 245–46, 252–54, 272–73. Call sought reappointment. "I was turned out most unjustly by Van Buren," he wrote to Congressman Henry Wise of Virginia. "It would be somewhat gratifying to my feelings to be restored to office." Richard Keith Call to Henry Wise, February 15, 1841, "Richard Keith Call," Letters of Application and Recommendation during the Administration of Martin Van Buren, William Henry Harrison, and John Tyler, 1837–1845, NA, M687, Reel 4.

54. Tallahassee *Floridian,* April 3, 8, 1841. See also Thompson, *Jacksonian Democracy on the Florida Frontier,* 29–31; Dovell, *History of Banking in Florida,* 18–20; Schweikart, *Banking in the American South,* 171–74; Abbey, "The Union Bank of Tallahassee," 224–28.

55. Journal of Samuel Peter Heintzelman (1841), March 30, April 19, April 22, 1841, 105, 124.

56. Journal of Samuel Peter Heintzelman (1841), April 26, 29, 1841, 134, 136–37.

57. John Camp to the Secretary of State, June 7, 1841, TP, 26: 327–29; Tallahassee *Floridian,* June 12, 19, 1841; Proclamation of R. K. Call, June 16, 1841, in Tallahassee *Floridian,* July 24, 1841.

58. William P. DuVal Speech to the Electors of the Middle District of Florida in Tallahassee *Sentinel,* May 21, 1841, and St. Augustine *News,* June 11, 1841.

59. Ibid.

60. Tallahassee *Sentinel,* May 21, 1841.

61. William P. DuVal to Samuel Southard, May 31, 1841, Samuel Southard Papers, box 74, f. 1, PU.

62. Tallahassee *Floridian,* June 12, 1841; Tallahassee *Star,* August 11, 1841.

CHAPTER 17: "Tyler Too," Washington Intrigue, and St. Augustine

1. St. Joseph *Times* quoted in Tallahassee *Star,* August 18, 1841. See also Pensacola *Gazette,* August 7, 28, 1841; Tallahassee *Sentinel,* July 30, 1841; Tallahassee *Floridian,* July 10, August 28, 1841; Paisley, *The Red Hills of Florida,* 105. On the yellow fever epidemic see Baptist, *Creating an Old South,* 187–88; Miller, "Tallahassee and the 1841 Yellow Fever Epidemic."

2. Peterson, *The Presidencies of William Henry Harrison and John Tyler*, 57–75; Morgan, *A Whig Embattled*, 7–45; Chitwood, *John Tyler*, 202–36; Seager, *And Tyler Too*, 147–63; Remini, *Henry Clay*, 578–99; Peterson, *The Great Triumvirate*, 301–18; Simpson, *A Good Southerner*, 50–57.

3. Journal of Samuel Peter Heintzelman (1841), September 7, 15, 1841, Reel 3, 289, 291, 305–6, Papers of Samuel Peter Heintzelman, LC.

4. Commission of Thomas H. DuVal as Secretary, September 13, 1841, TP, 26: 371. Earlier Thomas DuVal had written to the president-elect, William Henry Harrison, requesting appointment as U.S. consul to Matanzas in Cuba. "I pretend to have no claims upon your friendship other than being the son of your old friend Wm. P. DuVal and what may be given to me by the unanimous recommendation of our Territorial Legislature and Judges of the Court of Appeals. . . . As an excuse for myself, I can only say that nothing but my having been foolish enough to get married, whilst so poor, could have induced me to trouble you with such a request." Thomas H. DuVal to William Henry Harrison, February 28, 1841, "Thomas DuVal," Letters of Application and Recommendation during the Administration of Martin Van Buren, William Henry Harrison, and John Tyler, 1837–1845, RG 59, NA, M687, Reel 9; Hammond, *The Medical Profession in 19th Century Florida*, 502–3, 537.

5. John DuVal to John Tyler, February 14, 1841, and John DuVal to H. Breckenridge, February 22, 1841, "John DuVal," Letters of Application and Recommendation during the Administration of Martin Van Buren, William Henry Harrison, and John Tyler, 1837–1845, RG 59, NA, M687, Reel 9. For the rumor and ridicule see Tallahassee *Floridian*, October 9, 1841, April 2, 1842; Tallahassee *Star*, March 31, 1842. Two years later John DuVal was still writing that "Van Buren done me injustice," and he was still seeking a judicial appointment. See John DuVal to the Secretary of State (Abel Upshur), January 7, 1844, TP, 26: 825–27.

6. For the disputed land claims and how they were adjudicated in Florida see Martin, *Florida during Territorial Days*, 69–82; Gates, *History of Public Land Law Development*, 89–90; Doherty, *Richard Keith Call*, 57–69.

7. Commission of William P. DuVal as Law Agent, November 4, 1841, TP, 26: 390; St. Augustine *Florida Herald and Southern Democrat*, November 26, 1841.

8. William P. DuVal to Charles A. Wickliffe, November 13, 1841, TP, 26: 398.

9. Horatio Waldo, "Florida Sketches," in Apalachicola *Florida Journal*, March 17, 1841.

10. Ibid.

11. Richmond *Whig and Public Advertiser*, April 22, 1842.

12. William P. DuVal to Charles Penrose and Account of William P. DuVal, February 24, 1842, The President to Charles B. Penrose, March 16, 1842, TP, 26: 449–52, 459.

13. William P. DuVal to Millard Fillmore [Chair, House Ways and Means Committee], April 13, 1842, TP, 26: 463–64.

14. Judge Samuel Douglas to Daniel Webster, February 12, 1842, TP, 26: 435. Also on the economic collapse in Middle Florida see Baptist, *Creating an Old South*, 181–86.

15. Ibid. See also Leon County Grand Jury Presentment, November 26, 1842, Letters of Application and Recommendation during the Administration of Martin Van Buren, William Henry Harrison, and John Tyler, 1837–1845, RG 59 NA, M687, Reel 9; John Branch to Richard K. Call, March 25, 1842 in Tallahassee *Floridian*, April 2, 1842.

16. William P. DuVal to Richard Keith Call, May 21, 1842, Call Papers, box 27, f.1, Florida State Archives.

17. Ibid.

18. Ibid.

19. Ibid.

20. Simpson, *A Good Southerner,* 53–54.

21. Journal of Samuel Peter Heintzelman (1841), June 25, 1841, 170, Papers of Samuel Peter Heintzelman, LC; Seale, *The President's House,* 1: 238.

22. Journal of Samuel Peter Heintzelman (1841), July 12, 1841, 182–83.

23. Charleston *Southern Patriot,* August 1, 1842.

24. Journal of Samuel Peter Heintzelman (1841), July 12, 1841, 229; George Fairbanks to Samuel Fairbanks, November 5, 1842, Fairbanks Papers, box 69, f. 4, PKYL, UF.

25. Journal of Samuel Peter Heintzelman (1841), November 20, 1841, 387.

26. William P. DuVal to Richard K. Call, September 5, 1842, PKYL.

27. Ibid.

28. William P. Duval to Edmund W. Hubard, September 16, 1842, Hubard Papers, Southern History Collection, University of North Carolina.

29. Ibid.

30. William P. DuVal to the Secretary of the Navy, October 15, 1842, TP, 26: 558–59. DuVal continued to advise Upshur on similar matters. See, for example, his letter of December 10, 1842, in TP, 26: 581–83.

31. Thomas Douglas to Charles B. Penrose, December 10, 1842, TP, 26: 580–81.

32. William P. DuVal to Charles B. Penrose, December 12, 1842, TP, 26: 583–84.

33. Charles B. Penrose to the President, January 14, 1843, TP, 26: 599.

34. William P. Duval to Charles Penrose, April 20, 1843, TP, 26: 647–48.

35. Ibid.

36. Secretary DuVal to Delegate Levy, February 9, 1843, TP, 26: 616–17.

37. William P. DuVal to Edmund Hubard, May 27, 1843, Hubard Papers, Southern History Collection, University of North Carolina.

38. Ibid.

39. Tallahassee *Star,* June 4, 1843; Apalachicola *Watchman of the Gulf,* August 12, 1843.

40. St. Augustine *Florida Herald and Southern Democrat,* January 1, March 12, 1844.

41. William P. DuVal to George Burt, July 31, 1843, Burt Papers, box 1, f. 7, St. Augustine Historical Society.

42. Thomas Douglas to Charles B. Penrose, July 10, 1843, William P. DuVal to Charles Penrose, July 7, 1843, William P. DuVal and Thomas Douglas to Robert Campbell, September 29, 1843, in William P. DuVal to Charles B. Penrose, September 29, 1843, Thomas Douglas to Charles B. Penrose, February 17, 1844, TP, 26: 681–83, 678–81, 752–56, 864.

43. William P. DuVal to A. P. Upshur, January 22, 1844, "Isaac Bronson," Letters of Application and Recommendation during the Administration of Martin Van Buren, William Henry Harrison, and John Tyler, 1837–1845, RG 59 NA M687, Reel 3.

44. William P. DuVal to Henry Wise, December 27, 1843, Miscellaneous Manuscripts, #218, PKYL, UF.

45. Peterson, *The Presidencies of Harrison and Tyler,* 185–87. For Tyler's goals of annexation of Texas, his cabinet intrigues, and Calhoun's presidential aspirations during

this period see ibid., 165–210; Peterson, *The Triumvirate*, 334–49; Wiltse, *John C. Calhoun*, volume 3, 89–160; Chitwood, *John Tyler,* 342–350; Morgan, *A Whig Embattled,* 128–38; Bartlett, *John C. Calhoun,* 286–310; Coit, *John C. Calhoun,* 350–64; Campbell, *Gone to Texas,* 182–84; Niven, *John C. Calhoun,* 248–73; Seager, *And Tyler Too,* 209–27.

46. On the accident see Peterson, *The Presidencies of Harrison and Tyler,* 201–3; Chitwood, *John Tyler,* 397–98; Coit, *John C. Calhoun,* 360.

47. Wise quoted in Peterson, *The Presidencies of Harrison and Tyler,* 203; Chitwood, *John Tyler,* 284–89. For the politics and circumstances of Calhoun's appointment see Simpson, *A Good Southerner,* 57–58; Nevin, *John C. Calhoun,* 272–74; Witse, *John C. Calhoun, Sectionalist,* 161–63; Seager, *And Tyler Too,* 204–7.

CHAPTER 18: State of Texas—State of Florida

1. John C. Calhoun to Richard Pakenham, April 18, 1844, *Calhoun Papers,* 18: 273–78. Also Calhoun and annexation controversy see Silbey, *Storm over Texas*; Peterson, *The Presidencies of William Henry Harrison and John Tyler,* 203–59; Wiltse, *John C. Calhoun, Sectionalist,* 161–86, 199–216; Chitwood, *John Tyler,* 350–66; Seager, *And Tyler Too,* 209–30; Niven, *John C. Calhoun,* 264–82; Bartlett, *John C. Calhoun,* 310–24; Coit, *John C. Calhoun,* 364–81; Campbell, *Gone to Texas,* 184–86; Morgan, *A Whig Embattled,* 137–46.

2. Wiltse, *Calhoun, Sectionalist,* 165–83; Silbey, *Storm over Texas,* 43–64; Seager, *And Tyler Too,* 228–30.

3. William P. DuVal to John C. Calhoun, May 20, 1844, *Calhoun Papers,* 18: 561–63.

4. William P. DuVal to John C. Calhoun, May 1844, *Calhoun Papers,* 18: 689.

5. William P. DuVal to John C. Calhoun, May 24, 1844, *Calhoun Papers,* 18: 599–600.

6. Richard K. Call to John C. Calhoun, May 22, 1844, TP, 26: 905–7; William P. DuVal to John C. Calhoun, May 20, 1844, in *Calhoun Papers,* 18: 561–63.

7. Division of the Territory of Florida, March 27, 1844, Territorial Papers of the United States Senate, 1789–1873, RG 46, NA, M200, Reel 11. See also Resolution of the Governor and Legislative Council, March 16, 1844, in Dodd, *Florida Becomes a State,* 405–7.

8. Doherty, *Richard Keith Call,* 132–34.

9. St. Augustine *Florida Herald and Southern Democrat,* July 16, 1844.

10. William P. DuVal to John C. Calhoun, July 4, 1844, *Calhoun Papers,* 19: 269–70.

11. Ibid.

12. William P. DuVal to Charles Penrose, June 28, 1844, TP, 26: 925–27.

13. Thomas Douglas to Charles B. Penrose, July 12, 1844, Charles B. Penrose to George M. Bibb, August 15, 1844, TP, 26: 929, 945.

14. Richard K. Call to John C. Calhoun, August 16, 1844, Thomas P. DuVal to John C. Calhoun, July 29, 1844, Samuel Douglas to John C. Calhoun, September 8, 1844, John C. Calhoun to Charles S. Sibley, September 27, 1844, *Calhoun Papers,* 19: 596–97, 463, 719, 873.

15. For Randolph's surveying activities in the Tampa Bay and the St. Augustine area see Knetsch, *Faces on the Frontier,* 7, 65, 95–96, 113, 132, 135–36. He eventually returned to Tallahassee in the early 1850s. See Hammond, *The Medical Profession in 19th Century Florida,* 515; Paisley, *The Red Hills of Florida,* 169–70.

16. William P. DuVal to John C. Calhoun, July 4, 1844, *Calhoun Papers*, 19: 269–70.

17. John Lee Williams to George Burt, August 1, 1844, Burt Papers, St. Augustine Historical Society.

18. *Biographical Directory of the American Congress*, 1730–31.

19. On the election of 1844 see Peterson, *The Great Triumvirate*, 349–66; Remini, *Henry Clay*, 642–67.

20. William P. DuVal to Thomas Baltzell, December 30, 1844, St. Augustine Historical Society; St. Augustine *Herald*, November 12, 1844.

21. St. Augustine *Herald*, December 3, 1844.

22. Campbell, *Gone to Texas*, 185–86; Dodd, *Florida Becomes a State*, 85–86, 426–30.

23. William P. DuVal to Robert J. Walker, April 9, 1845, New-York Historical Society; A DEMOCRAT to the St. Augustine *Florida Herald and Southern Democrat*, May 6, 1845.

24. St. Augustine *News*, April 26, 1845; An Old Planter to the Editor, Tallahassee *Star*, April 25, 1845.

25. Apalachicola *Commercial Advertiser*, April 12, 1845.

26. Doherty, *Richard Keith Call*, 132–34; idem, *The Whigs of Florida*, 14–17; Thompson, *Jacksonian Democracy of the Florida Frontier*, 78–81.

27. St. Augustine *News*, April 5, 1845; "Expenses of State Government Handbill," Sanchez Papers, box 2, f. 2, St. Augustine Historical Society.

28. William P. DuVal to John C. Calhoun, June 23, 1845, *Calhoun Papers*, 21: 600–601.

29. St. Augustine *News*, June 28, 1845.

30. Pensacola *Gazette*, June 28, July 26, 1845.

31. William P. DuVal to John C. Calhoun, September 9, 1845, *Calhoun Papers*, 22: 136–38.

32. Ibid.

33. Ibid.

34. James D. Westcott to David Levy, August 28, 1845, PKYL.

35. Pensacola *Gazette*, August, 2, 1845.

36. William P. DuVal to George Fairbanks, November 25, 1845, Fairbanks Papers, box 374, Manning Strozier Library, Florida State University; Tallahassee *Southern Journal*, February 10, 1846; *Biographical Directory of the American Congress*, 143.

37. Affidavit of Thomas Douglas, September 28, 1846, before Oscar Hart, Clerk of the Duval County Circuit Court, in *William P. DuVal vs Moses E. Levy*, 1846, Circuit Court Papers, box 106, f. 12, St. Johns County Circuit Court, St. Augustine. Levy quoted in Monaco, *Moses Levy of Florida*, 162, 165.

38. James K. Polk to William P. DuVal, September 17, 1845, in Weaver et al., eds., *Correspondence of James K. Polk*, 10: 488.

39. Thomas H. DuVal to the Secretary of the Treasury, September 18, 1845, TP, 26: 1084; St. Augustine *Florida Herald and Southern Democrat*, March 17, 1846; William P. DuVal to George Fairbanks, November 25, 1845, Fairbanks Papers, box 374, Manning Strozier Library, Florida State University.

40. William P. DuVal to George Fairbanks, November 25, 1845, Fairbanks Papers, box 374, Manning Strozier Library, Florida State University.

41. William P. DuVal to Mrs. Maria Robinson, Sale of Personal Property, April 18, 1845, Miscellaneous Records, St. Johns County Court.

42. William P. DuVal to George Fairbanks, January 6, 1846, Fairbanks Papers, box 674, Manning Strozier Library, Florida State University.

43. Pensacola *Gazette,* January 24, 1845.

44. Charleston *Evening News,* New Orleans *Picayune,* New Orleans *Tropic,* and Charleston *Mercury* quoted in *Pensacola Gazette,* January 17, 1846.

45. *Tropic* quoted in Pensacola *Gazette,* April 25, 1846. See also Tallahassee *Floridian,* April 25, 1846; St. Augustine *Florida Herald and Southern Democrat,* April 28, 1846.

46. On the first day of the newspaper's publication, the editors declared that we "believe in the correctness and truth of those leading principles, generally known as the *States Rights Doctrines* of the Southern Democrats in contradictions to the Whig or Federal Doctrines, taught by some of the Northern politicians." "To the Public," Tallahassee *Southern Journal,* January 13, 1846.

47. William P. DuVal to John C. Calhoun, January 15, 1846, *Calhoun Papers,* 22: 447–50.

48. Ibid.

49. Ibid.

50. Ibid.

CHAPTER 19: "I will not be the cause of disunion in our ranks"

1. Campbell, *Gone to Texas,* 186; Barkley, *History of Travis County and Austin,* 65–66; William P. DuVal to George Fairbanks, January 6, 1846, Fairbanks Papers, box 374, Manning Strozier Library, Florida State University.

2. DuVal asked for Calhoun's help in securing for his son a captaincy in one of the new rifle regiments proposed to be raised. "That my son is deserving of this commission, his bravery, and sufferings in the cause of Texas proves. Few men are better fitted for the command of a company. . . . It would gratify me much. I am too poor to place my son in business. He is in truth a military man and if he has the opportunity (and should live) he will make himself a name, worthy of his family & country." William P. DuVal to John C. Calhoun, March 7, 1846, *Calhoun Papers,* 22: 673–75. DuVal also wrote directly to President Polk on his son's behalf. See Weaver et al., eds., *Correspondence of James K. Polk,* 10: 488; Swift, *Civilizers,* 75–77; Galveston *Weekly News,* May 5, December 12, 1848.

3. Campbell, *Gone to Texas,* 172; Fehrenbach, *Lone Star,* 259; Swift, *Civilizers,* 76.

4. Knetsch, *Faces on the Frontier,* 131–36; W. D. Moseley to George H. Crawford, January 3, 1846, Branch Papers, Southern History Collection, University of North Carolina; Tallahassee *Floridian,* January 10, March 28, 1846; St. Augustine *Florida Herald and Southern Democrat,* April 14, 1846, February 2, 1847.

5. William P. DuVal to John C. Calhoun, March 7, 1846, *Calhoun Papers,* 22: 673–75.

6. Wiltse, *John C. Calhoun: Sectionalist,* 252–53. Also for Calhoun and the Oregon question see ibid., 260–61; Peterson, *The Great Triumvirate,* 417–20; Niven, *John C. Calhoun,* 296–301; Bartlett, *John C. Calhoun,* 330–34.

7. William P. DuVal to John C. Calhoun, March 31, 1846, *Calhoun Papers,* 22: 788–90.

8. Ibid.

9. Calhoun quoted in Peterson, *The Great Triumvirate,* 423. For Calhoun's position on the War with Mexico see Wiltse, *John C. Calhoun, Sectionalist,* 273–89; Bartlett, *John C. Calhoun,* 335–49; Niven, *John C. Calhoun,* 301–13.

10. Tallahassee *Floridian*, May 23, 30, June 6, 1846; Tallahassee *Southern Journal* quoted in Charleston *Southern Patriot*, June 1, 1846.

11. William P. DuVal to William D. Moseley, June 14, 1846, RG 151, Office of the Secretary of State, Ser. 2153, Territorial and Early Statehood Records, box 4, f. 16, Florida State Archives.

12. Tallahassee *Floridian*, June 20, July 18, 1846; St. Augustine *Florida Herald and Southern Democrat*, June 7, July 21, August 11, 18, 1846.

13. John P. DuVal, "To the People of Leon," Tallahassee *Southern Journal*, September 22, 1846.

14. Tallahassee *Floridian*, October 24, 1846.

15. Tallahassee *Southern Journal*, September 22, 29, 1846; Gadsden County Grand Jury Presentment, September 29, 1846, in Tallahassee *Floridian*, October 10, 1846; Denham, *A Rogue's Paradise*, 188–90.

16. Campbell, *Gone to Texas*, 188–89; Swift, *Civilizers*, 79.

17. Marcia Price to Thomas DuVal, October 7, 1848, DuVal Family Papers, Possession of Samuel Maclin, San Antonio, Texas; Swift, *Civilizers*, 80–82, 87–88.

18. Tallahassee *Floridian*, January 5, 1848. Also for attacks on Cabell in the vote for speaker see Tallahassee *Floridian*, January 29, 1848; St. Augustine *Florida Herald and Southern Democrat*, February 3, 24, 1848.

19. "Q" to the Editor of the Savannah *Georgian* quoted in St. Augustine *Florida Herald and Southern Democrat*, February 24, 1848.

20. Tallahassee *Floridian*, February 5, 1848. For other Democratic meetings see Tallahassee *Floridian*, February 12, March 4, 11, 1848; St. Augustine *Florida Herald and Southern Democrat*, February 24, March 2, 1848.

21. William P. DuVal to George R. Fairbanks, February 10, 1848, Fairbanks Papers, Manning Strozier Library, Florida State University.

22. Wiltse, *John C. Calhoun, Sectionalist*, 325–29; Nevins, *Ordeal of the Union*, 16–19, 29–30.

23. Correspondent to the *Herald*, February 19, 1848, in St. Augustine *Florida Herald and Southern Democrat*, March 7, 1848. Yulee's speeches printed in St. Augustine *Florida Herald and Southern Democrat*, March 14, 21, 28, 1848.

24. S. B., a Correspondent to the *Floridian*, in Tallahassee *Floridian*, February 26, 1848.

25. William P. DuVal to J. A. Baughey, J. S. Broome, C. T. Jenkins, April 10, 1848, in Tallahassee *Floridian*, April 22, 1848; Marianna *Florida Whig*, May 3, 1848.

26. Tallahassee *Floridian*, March 25, 1848; A LOOKER ON to Editor, March 22, 1848, St. Augustine *Florida Herald and Southern Democrat*, March 28, 1848.

27. A LOOKER ON to Editor, March 22, 1848, St. Augustine *Florida Herald and Southern Democrat*, March 28, 1848. Also on the 1848 campaign in Florida see Doherty, *The Whigs of Florida*, 25–29.

28. Doherty, *The Whigs of Florida*, 22–23.

29. Tallahassee *Floridian*, April 8, 1848.

30. Apalachicola *Commercial Advertiser*, April 6, 1848; Marianna *Florida Whig*, April 12, 1848.

31. Tallahassee *Floridian*, April 15, 1848; St. Augustine *Florida Herald and Southern Democrat*, May 6, 1848.

32. On the Barnburner-Hunker conflict in New York see Klunder, *Lewis Cass*, 183–94; Niven, *Martin Van Buren*, 542–65.

33. Klunder, *Lewis Cass*, 187. Cass had publicly stated his position to a man named Nicholson in Tennessee in December 1847. During the campaign Cass refused to forthrightly address questions regarding his position on the territories. He merely invoked the so-called Nicholson Letter, which was obscure enough to shield Cass from charges that he was an outright supporter of the controversial principle. See Klunder, *Lewis Cass*,166–71, 175–88; Nevins, *Ordeal of the Union*, 30–32.

34. Doherty, *The Whigs of Florida*, 27–28; Tallahassee *Floridian*, June 10, 1848; St. Augustine *Florida Herald and Southern Democrat*, June 28, 1848. Also on the ambiguity and ambivalence of Cass's position vis-à-vis the Madison Convention's mandates for Florida delegates to the Baltimore Convention see Apalachicola *Star of the West*, August 16, 1848.

35. Bauer, *Zachary Taylor*, 143, 215–38.

36. Marianna *Florida Whig*, August 19, September 9, 23, 1848. See also Pensacola *Gazette*, August 28, September 30, 1848.

37. Marianna *Florida Whig*, April 12, 1848.

38. For the attacks on DuVal see Marianna *Florida Whig*, April 5, May 3, 24, 1848; "Great Political Sweepstake," Ocala *Argus*, June 8. 1848; Pensacola *Gazette*, May 13, 1848; Apalachicola *Commercial Advertiser*, September 6, 16, 1848.

39. Tallahassee *Floridian*, May 27, 1848.

40. St. Augustine *Florida Herald and Southern Democrat*, July 20, 1848.

41. Pensacola *Democrat*, August 16, 1848.

42. St. Augustine *Florida Herald and Southern Democrat*, August 9, 24, 1848

43. VERITAS to the *Floridian*, August 14, 1848, in Tallahassee *Floridian*, August 19, 1848.

44. Ibid.

45. Apalachicola *Star of the West*, August 16, 1848.

46. Marianna *Florida Whig*, September 9, August 19, 1848.

47. Tallahassee *Floridian*, July 15, 22, 29, 1848; Pensacola *Democrat*, August 24, 1848.

48. Tallahassee *Floridian*, September 2, 1848.

49. Marianna *Florida Whig*, September 23, 1848.

50. Marianna *Florida Whig*, September 20, 1848.

51. Election totals in Marianna *Florida Whig*, December 2, 1848; Tallahassee *Floridian*, November 25, 1848.

52. William P. DuVal to John Crittenden, November 26, 1848, John Jordan Crittenden Papers, LC, Reel, 6.

53. Ibid.

CHAPTER 20: **Gone to Texas—Gone to Washington**

1. William P. DuVal to Thomas H. DuVal, January 18, 1849, DuVal Family Papers, Ruth West Emerson Papers, Antonio, Texas.

2. Ibid.

3. Ibid.

4. Ibid.

5. Niven, *John C. Calhoun*, 324–26; Wiltse, *John C. Calhoun, Sectionalist*, 374–88; Peterson, *The Great Triumvirate*, 447–48; Nevins, *Ordeal of the Union*, 247–52.

6. William P. Duval to John C. Calhoun, February 13, 1849, *Calhoun Papers*, 26: 289–90.

7. Ibid.

8. William P. DuVal to John J. Crittenden, November 26, 1848, John Jordan Crittenden Papers, Reel 6, LC.

9. Ibid.

10. Ibid.

11. Bauer, *Zachary Taylor*, 249–52.

12. William P. DuVal to Thomas DuVal, March 22, 1849, DuVal Family Papers, Ruth West Emerson Papers, Antonio, Texas.

13. Ibid.

14. Tallahassee *Sentinel* quoted in Tallahassee *Floridian and Journal*, December 15, 1849.

15. Tallahassee *Floridian* quoted in Austin *Texas State Gazette*, January 12, 1850.

16. Galveston *Weekly News*, December 24, 1849.

17. Austin *Texas State Gazette*, April 6, May 4, 25, June 1, 1850.

18. Wiltse, *John C. Calhoun: Sectionalist*, 452–75; Nevins, *Ordeal of the Union*, 253–345; Peterson, *The Great Triumvirate*, 449–76; Niven, *John C. Calhoun*, 339–43.

19. Campbell, *Gone to Texas*, 234–35. Bell quoted in ibid., 235. See also Pool, *A Historical Atlas of Texas*, 82–85; Nevins, *Ordeal of the Union*, 327–30.

20. "Public Meeting" and "Remarks of Gov. Duval, On the Report of Resolutions adopted by a Meeting of the Citizens of Travis County, on the 11th of June, 1850, in Reference to the Rights of Texas in New Mexico," Austin *Texas State Gazette*, June 15, 1850.

21. William P. DuVal to R. M. T. Hunter, August 13, 1850, in Ambler, ed., *Correspondence of R. M. T. Hunter*, 2: 115.

22. DuVal, his son Thomas, and James Webb hosted a dinner for an U.S. Army major who had been court-martialed for assisting neighbors. See Austin *Texas State Gazette*, September 21, 1850.

23. Campbell, *Gone to Texas*, 235–36; Fehrenbach, *Lone Star*, 276–78; Nevins, *Ordeal of the Union*, 341; Pool, *Historical Atlas of Texas*, 83.

24. Austin *Texas State Gazette*, November 1, 1851.

25. Burr Grayson DuVal to Ella Moss, June 1, 1879, in Swift, *Civilizer*, ix–x.

26. Austin *Texas State Gazette*, November 30, 1850; Austin *Southwestern American*, June 11, 1851; Galveston *Weekly News*, February 11, 1851.

27. Smithwick, *The Evolution of a State*, 265; John P. DuVal to William P. DuVal, July 3, 1850, DuVal Family Papers, Possession of Sam Maclin, San Antonio, Texas.

28. Austin *Texas State Gazette*, April 3, 1852. Paschal would leave Galveston and reside permanently in Austin. See Galveston *Weekly News*, July 20, 1852; Austin *Southwestern American*, May 5, 1852.

29. Seale, *The President's House*, 1: 272.

30. Anne DuVal to Anne Steel (daughter), June 30, 1852, DuVal Family Papers, Ruth West Emerson Papers, Antonio, Texas.

31. Sam Houston to Washington D. Miller, June 30, September 13, 1853, in Barker and Williams, eds., *Writings of Sam Houston*, 5: 450, 457.

32. Austin *Texas State Gazette,* July 17, 1852.

33. DuVal, *Argument of William P. DuVal.*

34. Anne DuVal to Anne Steel (daughter), June 30, 1852, DuVal Family Papers, Ruth West Emerson Papers, Antonio, Texas.

35. William P. DuVal to Thomas H. DuVal, March 13, 1852, in Bass, "A Sketch of John C. DuVal's Life," 11, in DuVal Family Papers, Ruth West Emerson Papers, Antonio, Texas.

36. William P. DuVal to Thomas Brown, March 19, 1853, Territorial and Statehood Records, RG 151, ser. 2153, box 5, f. 3, Florida State Archives.

37. Peter Bell to Thomas DuVal, March 19, 1854 and R. T. Burchett to Thomas DuVal, March 19, 1854, DuVal Family Papers, Ruth West Emerson Papers, Antonio, Texas. Also for DuVal's last days in Washington see Swift, *Civilizers,* 89–93.

38. Austin *Texas State Gazette,* April 4, 1854.

39. Baltimore *Sun,* March 21, 1854; Boston *Daily Atlas,* March 22, 1854.

40. Washington *National Intelligencer,* March 24, 1854.

41. "Account of the Late Governor William P. DuVal," Washington *National Intelligencer* quoted in Seguin (Texas) *Texan Mercury,* May 20, 1854. See also Booneville (N.Y.) *Ledger,* June 10, 1854; Hartford (Conn.), *Daily Courant,* April 19, 1854.

EPILOGUE

1. Fletcher, "Address before the Florida Historical Society," 26.

2. Swift, *Civilizers,* 112–49; Marten, *Texas Divided,* 65–71, 81–82; Thomas DuVal Diary, Eugene C. Barker Texas History Center, University of Texas.

3. Dobie, *John C. DuVal.* Among John Crittenden DuVal's works are *The Adventures of Bigfoot Wallace* (1870) and *Early Times in Texas or the Adventures of Jack Dobell* (1892). See also Swift, *Civilizers,* 274–87.

4. DuVal, "Sketch of Gov. Wm DuVal," Call Papers, Florida Historical Society Library.

Bibliography

PRIMARY SOURCES

Archival Sources

University of Texas Archives, Eugene C. Barker Texas History Center, Austin, Texas
Hugh H. DuVal Papers
John C. DuVal Papers
Thomas Howard DuVal Papers
Thomas Howard DuVal Diary

Maryland Historical Society, Baltimore, Maryland
William Wirt Papers

Nelson County Public Library, Bardstown, Kentucky
Genealogy Collection
Tax Rolls
Nelson County Pioneer

Wilson Library, University of North Carolina, Chapel Hill, North Carolina
John M. Berrien
Branch Family Papers
Duff Green Papers
Hagner Papers
Hubard Papers
John Parkhill Papers

Alderman Library, University of Virginia, Charlottesville, Virginia
Barbour Family Papers
Breckenridge-Watts Papers

Correspondence of the Breckenridge, Gamble, and Watt Families
Correspondence of the Ambler and Barbour Family Papers
Thomas Jefferson Papers

Florida Historical Society Library, Cocoa, Florida
Richard Keith Call Journal
Richard Keith Call Papers

Perkins Library, Duke University, Durham, North Carolina
Campbell Family Papers
John Henry Eaton Papers

Kentucky State Archives, Frankfort, Kentucky
Governor James Garrard Papers (1796–1804)
Governor Christopher Greenup Papers (1804–1808)
Governor Charles Scott Papers (1808–1812)
Governor Isaac Shelby Papers (1812–1816)
Governor Gabriel Slaughter Papers (1816–1820)
Governor John Adair Papers (1820–1824)
Governor Joseph Desha Papers (1824–1828)
Nelson County, Ky., Tax Rolls 1811, 1812, 1816, 1817, 1820, 1821, 1835

Library of the Kentucky Historical Society, Frankfort, Kentucky
Felix Grundy Papers

P. K. Yonge Library, University of Florida, Gainesville, Florida
Richard Keith Call Papers
Duncan Lamont Clinch Papers
William P. DuVal Papers
Fairbanks Papers
Phillip Yonge Papers
David Levy Yulee Papers

Filson Club Historical Society Library, Louisville, Kentucky
Norborne-Beale Papers
Sanders Family Papers

Museum of History/Miami, Miami, Florida
Papers Relating to the Florida Territorial Council

Tennessee State Archives, Nashville, Tennessee
Hynes Family Papers

New-York Historical Society, New York, New York
Miscellaneous Manuscripts
Walker Papers

New York Public Library, New York, New York
Barbour Papers

Olin Library, Rollins College, Winter Park, Florida
Andrew Jackson Letter

Pace Library, University of West Florida, Pensacola, Florida
Henry Marie Brackenridge Papers

Princeton University, Princeton, New Jersey
Samuel Southard Papers

North Carolina State Archives, Raleigh, North Carolina
Branch Papers

Virginia Historical Society, Richmond, Virginia
Beverly Family Papers
Thomas Brown Letters
Abraham Cabell Papers
Cabell Family Papers
William DuVal Papers
Mason Papers
Massie Family Papers
Preston Papers
Laura Wirt Randall Letters
Robinson Papers
Thomas Family Papers

Ruth West Emerson Collection, Private Possession Samuel E. Maclin, San Antonio, Texas
DuVal Family Papers
Donald Grant Bass, "A Sketch of John C. DuVal's Life"

St. Augustine Historical Society, St. Augustine, Florida
Sanchez Papers
Burt Papers

Manning Strozier Library, Florida State University, Tallahassee, Florida
Fairbanks Collection
Memoir of Frances Elizabeth Brown Douglass, May 1894
Red Hills of Florida Collection

State Library of Florida, Dorothy Dodd Room, R. A. Gray Building, Tallahassee, Florida.
Diary of Robert Raymond Reid, 1833, 1835

University of South Florida, Tampa, Florida
Frank Snyder Collection

Library of Congress, Washington, D.C.
Crittenden Papers
Andrew Jackson Donelson Papers
John Eaton Papers
Duff Green Papers
Margaret O'Neale Eaton Papers
Louis M. Goldsborough Papers
Samuel Peter Heintzelman Diaries and Papers
Andrew Jackson Papers
Thomas Jefferson Papers
James Madison Papers
James Monroe Papers
Samuel L. Southard Papers
William Wirt Papers
Martin Van Buren Papers

National Archives
RG 46 Records of the United States Senate
    Executive Proceedings, Twenty-second Congress, Papers Re: Nominations: Governor William Pope DuVal, File Number Sen 22B-A3
    Territorial Papers of the United States Senate, 1789–1873, M200, Reels 9–11
RG 59, Records of the Department of State
    Letters of Application and Recommendation during the Administration of James Monroe, 1817–1825, M439
    Letters of Application and Recommendation during the Administration of John Quincy Adams, 1825–1829, M531
    Letters of Application and Recommendation during the Administration of Andrew Jackson, 1829–1837, M639
    Letters of Application and Recommendation during the Administration of Martin Van Buren, William Henry Harrison, and John Tyler, 1837–1845, M687
RG 75 Records of the Bureau of Indian Affairs
    Letters Sent, 1816–1830
    Letters Received, 1816–1824
Records of the Office of the Secretary of War Relating to Indian Affairs
    Letters Sent, 1815–1824
    Letters Received, 1816–1823
    Records of the Bureau of Indian Affairs
    Registers of Letters Received
    Letters Received, 1826–1842, Apalachicola
    Letters Received by the Office of Indian Affairs, Seminole Agency Emigration, 1827–1859, M234, Roll 806
    Letters Sent, 1824–1844

Florida State Archives, R. A. Gray Building, Tallahassee, Florida
RG 101, Correspondence of the Governors
    Ser. 32, Letter Books, 1836–1909, vols. 1–7
    Ser. 177, Correspondence of the Territorial Governors, 1825–1845
    Ser. 755, Correspondence of Thomas Brown, 1849–1853
RG 151, Office of the Secretary State
    Ser. 1325, Correspondence of the Secretary of State, 1831–1917
    Ser. 2153, Territorial and Early Statehood Records

County Court Records
Escambia County Court House, Pensacola, Florida
    Superior Court Minutes, 1822–1833, Book 1
Jefferson County Court House, Monticello, Florida
    Superior Court Minutes, 1828–1841, Book 1
Leon County Courthouse, Tallahassee, Florida
    Superior Court Minutes, 1824–1833, Book 1
    Superior Court Minutes, 1841–1843, Book 3
    Superior and Circuit Court Minutes, 1843–1847, Book 4
    Circuit Court Minutes, 1847–1855, Book 5
St. Augustine County Historical Society
    St. Johns County, County Court Minutes, 1827–1845
St. Johns County Court House, St. Augustine, Florida
    Minutes of the Superior Court, 1846–1860, Book A
    Circuit Court Papers, 1845–1861
University of South Florida
    Nelson County, Ky., Court, Nelson County Case Files, 1800–1834, in Frank Snyder Collection

Newspapers
Alexandria (Va.) *Herald,* 1817, 1822
Apalachicola *Apalachicolian,* 1840–1841
Apalachicola *Commercial Advertiser,* 1840–1851
Apalachicola *Courier,* 1839–1840
Apalachicola *Florida Journal,* 1840–1844
Apalachicola *Gazette,* 1836–1840
Apalachicola *Star of the West,* 1848
Apalachicola *Watchman of the Gulf,* 1843
Augusta *Chronicle and Georgia Advertiser,* 1827
Austin *Southwestern American,* 1849–1853
Austin *Tri-Weekly State Gazette,* 1852–1853
Austin *Tri-Weekly State Times,* 1853–1854
Baltimore *Gazette and Daily National Advertiser,* 1832–1834
Baltimore *Niles Register,* 1812, 1827, 1831–1832
Baltimore *Patriot,* 1831

Baltimore *Sun*, 1840, 1854
Bardstown (Ky.) *Candid Review*, 1807, 1808, 1810
Bardstown (Ky.) *Repository*, 1814–1816
Bardstown (Ky.) *Western American*, 1803–1805
Bardstown (Ky.) *Western Herald*, 1825, 1826, 1828, 1831–1834, 1836, 1854
Bennington *Vermont Gazette*, 1828
Booneville (N.Y.) *Ledger*, 1854
Boston *Daily Advertiser*, 1823
Boston *Daily Atlas*, 1854
Boston *Daily Courier*, 1832
Boston *Columbian Centinel*, 1823
Charleston *City Gazette and Commercial and Daily Advertiser*, 1827
Charleston *Patriot*, 1833, 1846
Danville (Ky.) *Danville Mirror*, 1804, 1806–1807
Danville (Ky.) *People's Friend*, 1819
Easton (Md.) *Republican Star*, 1825, 1831, 1840
Frankfort *Kentucky American Republic*, 1810–1813
Frankfort *Kentucky Journal*, 1805
Frankfort *Kentucky Journal*, 1803–1813
Galveston *Civilian and Gazette*, 1853–1854
Galveston *Journal*, 1850–1855
Galveston *Weekly News*, 1844–1854
Georgetown *Kentucky Telegraph*, 1811–1813
Hartford *Daily Courant*, 1840, 1854
Hartford *Connecticut Mirror*, 1832
Jacksonville *Courier*, 1835–1837
Jacksonville *East Florida Advocate*, 1839–1840
Jacksonville *Florida News*, 1846–1857
Jacksonville *Florida Republican*, 1848–1856
Jacksonville *Florida Times-Union*, 1901
Jacksonville *Tropical Plant*, 1844
Keene *New Hampshire Sentinel*, 1828
Key West *Enquirer*, 1831–1836
Key West *Gazette*, 1831–1832, 1845
Key West *Register and Commercial Advertiser*, 1829
Key West *South Floridian*, 1838–1839
Lexington *Gazette*, 1810–1819
Lexington *Kentucky Register*, 1812
Lexington *Reporter*, 1812
Lexington *Western Monitor*, 1814
Louisville *Kentucky Western Courier*, 1813–1816
Louisville *Daily Journal*, 1836
Louisville *Public Advertiser*, 1832–1835
Magnolia *Advertiser*, 1828–1830
Marianna *Florida Whig*, 1847–1852

Milledgville *Georgia Journal*, 1825
Nashville *Banner and Daily Advertiser*, 1834
Newport (R.I.) *Gazette*, 1846–1848
New Haven *Connecticut Herald*, 1825
New London *Connecticut Gazette*, 1823
New York *Evening Journal*, 1831
Norfolk *City Advertiser*, 1823
Ocala *Argus*, 1848
Ocala *Conservator*, 1851–1852
Ocala *Florida Mirror*, 1853
Ocala *Southern Sun*, 1854
Palatka *Whig Banner*, 1846–1847
Pensacola *Florida Argus*, 1848
Pensacola *Florida Democrat*, 1846–1851
Pensacola *Floridian*, 1821–1824
Pensacola *Gazette*, 1821–1854
Pensacola *Neutral*, 1848
Quincy *Sentinel*, 1839–1841
Quincy *Times*, 1848
Salisbury (N.C.) *Western Carolinian*, 1823, 1840
Sequin (Tex.), *The Texan Mercury*, 1854
Richmond *Enquirer*, 1804–1838
Richmond *Virginia Argus*, 1807
Richmond *Virginia Gazette and General Advertiser*, 1784, 1785, 1791, 1792, 1793, 1795, 1799, 1805, 1807
Richmond *Whig and Public Advertiser*, 1842
St. Augustine *Ancient City*, 1850–1856
St. Augustine *Florida Herald*, 1829–1837
St. Augustine *Florida Herald and Southern Democrat*, 1838–1846
St. Augustine *Florida Gazette*, 1821
St. Augustine *News*, 1838–1847
St. Joseph *Times*, 1838–1841
Salem (Mass.) *Essex Register*, 1825
Savannah *Georgian*, 1819–1831
Tallahassee *Florida Advocate*, 1827–1829
Tallahassee *Florida Courier*, 1831
Tallahassee *Florida Intelligencer*, 1826
Tallahassee *Florida Sentinel*, 1841–1854
Tallahassee *Florida Watchman*, 1837–1838
Tallahassee *Floridian*, 1836–1840
Tallahassee *Floridian and Advocate*, 1829–1831
Tallahassee *Floridian and Journal*, 1846–1854
Tallahassee *Tallahassee Southern Journal*, 1846–1849
Tallahassee *Star Florida*, 1839–1845
Washington, D.C., *Daily National Intelligencer*, 1829–1832

Washington, D.C., *Daily National Journal*, 1831
Washington, D.C., *United States Telegraph*, 1829–1832

Printed Primary Sources

Adams, Charles, ed. *Memoirs of John Quincy Adams Comprising Portions of His Diary from 1795–1848.* 12 vols. Philadelphia: J. B. Lippincott, 1874–1877.
Aderman, Ralph M., ed. *The Letters of James Kirke Paulding.* Madison: University of Wisconsin Press, 1962.
Aderman, Ralph M., Herbert L. Kleinfield, and Jenifer S. Banks. *Washington Irving Letters.* Vol. 1: 1802–1823. Boston: Twayne, 1978.
Ambler, Charles Henry, ed. *Correspondence of Robert M. T. Hunter, 1826–1876.* 2 vols. Annual Report of the American Historical Association for the Year 1916.
American State Papers: Indian Affairs. 2 vols. Washington, D.C., 1832–1834.
American State Papers: Miscellaneous. 2 vols. Washington, D.C., 1834.
Antoniak, Eleanor. *Kentucky Marriage Records from the Register of the Kentucky Historical Society.* Baltimore: Genealogical Publishing Co., 1983.
Barker, Eugene C., ed. *The Austin Papers.* 3 vols. Washington, D.C.: U.S. Government Printing Office, 1919–1926.
Barker, Eugene, and Amelia Williams, eds. *The Writings of Sam Houston, 1813–1863.* 8 vols. Austin: University of Texas Press, 1938–1943.
Bassett, John Spencer, ed. *Correspondence of Andrew Jackson.* 7 vols. Carnegie Institution of Washington Publication. Papers of the Department of Historical Research, no. 371. Washington, D.C.: Carnegie Institution, 1926–1935.
Benton, Thomas Hart. *A Thirty Year's View, or A History of the Working of the American Government for Thirty Years, from 1820–1850.* 2 vols. New York: Appleton and Co., 1856.
Binkley, John Spencer, ed. *Official Correspondence of the Texan Revolution, 1835–1836.* 2 vols. New York: D. Appleton and Co., 1936.
Biographical Directory of the American Congress, 1774–1971. Washington, D.C.: U.S. Government Printing Office, 1971.
Brackenridge, Henry M. *History of the Late War Between the United States and Great Britain.* Philadelphia: James Key Tun and Brother, 1846.
Carter, Clarence, ed. *Territorial Papers of the United States.* 26 vols. Washington, D.C.: U.S. Government Printing Office, 1934–1962.
Castelnau, Francis de. "Compte de Castelnau in Middle Florida, 1837–1838. Notes Concerning Two Itineraries from Charleston to Tallahassee." Translated by Arthur Seymour. *Florida Historical Quarterly* 26 (April 1948): 300–24.
———. "Essay on Middle Florida, 1837–1838." Translated by Arthur Seymour. *Florida Historical Quarterly* 26 (January 1948): 199–255.
Chambers, T. Jefferson, and William P. Duval. *Magnanimous and Chivalrous Sons of the West: Texas is Again Invaded by a Ruthless and Sanguinary Foe, and She Renews Her Call to the Brave and the Free.* Louisville, Ky., July 15, 1836.
Coleman, Ann Mary Butler. *The Life of John J. Crittenden with Selections from His Correspondence and Speeches.* 2 vols. Philadelphia: J. B. Lippincott, 1871.

Colton, Calvin, ed. *The Papers of Henry Clay.* 6 vols. New York: A. S. Barnes and Burr, 1855.
———. *The Private* Correspondence *of Henry Clay.* New York: A. S. Barnes, 1856.
Crockett, David. *A Narrative of the Life of David Crockett.* Philadelphia: E. L. Carey and A. Hart, 1834.
Cullum, George W. *Biographical Register of the Officers of the United States Military Academy, West Point.* 2 vols. New York: D. Van Nostrand, 1868.
Dexter, Horatio S. "To His Excellency William P. Duval, Governor and Superintendent of Indians Affairs of the Territory of Florida." In *Devane's Early Florida History,* edited by Park DeVane. Vol. 2. Sebring: Sebring Historical Society,1979.
DuVal, John C. *Adventures of Big-Foot Wallace, The Texas Ranger and Hunter.* Macon, Ga.: J. W. Burke and Co., 1871.
———. *Compilation of the Public Acts of the Legislative Council of the Territory of Florida Passed Prior to 1840.* Tallahassee: S. S. Sibley, 1839.
———. *Early Times in Texas.* Austin: H. P. N. Gammel and Co., 1892.
———. *The Story of an Escape from the Massacre at Goliad: Extract from 'Early Times in Texas.'* Houston: Union National Bank, 1936.
DuVal, William P. "Origin of White, Red, and Black Men: A Seminole Tradition." *Knickerbocker Magazine* (October 1840), 1. Reprinted in Cincinnati *Advertiser and Journal,* November 18, 1840.
Duval, William Pope. *Argument of Wm. P. Duval on Claim of Citizens of Texas for Compensation for the Property Taken from Them by the Comanche Indians, since the Annexation the United States.* Washington, D.C.: Goggins and Sanders, 1852.
Eaton, Margaret. *Autobiography of Margaret Eaton.* New York: Charles Scribner's Sons, 1932.
Esarey, Logan, ed. *Messages and Letters of William Henry Harrison, 1812–1816.* 2 vols. Indianapolis: Indiana Historical Collections, 1922. Reprint, New York: Arno Press, 1975.
Executive Journals of the United States Senate, 1789–1866.
Feller, Daniel, et al. *The Papers of Andrew Jackson.* 8 vols. Knoxville: University of Tennessee Press, 1980–2010.
Fitzpatrick, John. C. *Writings of George Washington from Original Manuscript Sources, 1745–1799.* Washington: Government Printing Office, 1934–1940.
Florida General Assembly Acts and Resolutions. 1845–1861.
Florida Territorial Legislative Council Acts. 1822–1845.
Giddings, Joshua R. *The Exiles of Florida: or the Crimes Committed by Our Government against the Maroons, Who Fled from South Carolina and other Slave States, Seeking Protection Under Spanish Laws.* Columbus, Ohio: Follet, Foster, and Co., 1858.
Gilman, William H., and Alfred R. Ferguson, eds. *The Journals and Miscellaneous Notebooks of Ralph Waldo Emerson.* Vol. 3: 1826–1832. Cambridge, Mass.: Belknap Press of Harvard University Press, 1963.
Green, Duff. *Facts & Suggestions; Biographical, Historical, Financial, and Political Addressed to the People of the United States.* New York: C. S. Wescott and Co., 1866.
Heitman, Francis B. *Historical Register and Dictionary of the United States Army.* 2 vols. 1903. Facsimile reprint, Urbana: University of Illinois Press, 1965.

Hopkins, James F., ed. *Papers of Henry Clay*. 11 vols. Lexington: University of Kentucky Press, 1959–1992.
Irving, Pierre M. *Life and Letters of Washington Irving*. 4 vols. New York: Putnam and Sons, 1883.
Irving, Washington. "Account of Duval's Visits to the Chief who Opposed Treaty of 1823." *New Yorker* 10 (October 10–17, 1840): 55–56, 71.
———. "The Conspiracy of Neamathla." *Knickerbocker Magazine* 16 (October 1840): 343–47.
———. "The Early Experiences of Ralph Ringwood, Noted Down from his Conversations by Geoffrey Crayon, Gent." *Knickerbocker Magazine* 16 (August 1840): 152–65; (September 1840): 258–66.
———. "Origin of the White, Red, and Black Men." *Knickerbocker Magazine* 16 (October 1840): 341–42.
———. "The Seminoles." *Knickerbocker Magazine* 16 (October 1840): 339–41.
———. *Woolfert's Roost: And Other Papers, Now First Collected*. New York: G. P. Putnam, 1855.
Jackson, Donald, ed. *The Diaries of George Washington, 1771–75, 1780–81*. Vol. 3. Charlottesville: University of Virginia Press, 1978.
Jenkins, John H., ed. *The Papers of the Texas Revolution, 1835–1836*. 9 vols. Austin: Presidial Press, 1973.
Kingsley, Zephaniah. *A Treatise on the Patriarchal or Co-operative System of Society as it Exists in Some Governments: and Colonies in America, and in the United States, Under the Name of Slavery, with its Necessity and Advantages*. 1829.
Little, Lucius P. *Ben Hardin: His Times and Contemporaries with Selections from His Speeches*. Louisville: Courier-Journal, 1887.
Long, Ellen Call. *Florida Breezes, or Florida New and Old*. 1883. Reprint, Gainesville: University of Florida Press, 1962.
Martin Van Buren Papers, Series 1, Chadwyck-Healy Edition. Microfilm.
McAfee, Robert B. *History of the Late War in the Western Country Comprising a Full Account of all the Transactions in that Quarter, from the Commencement of Hostilities at Tippecanoe, to the Termination of the Contest at New Orleans on the Return of Peace*. Lexington, Ky.: Worsley and Smith, 1816.
McKee, Samuel Y., William P. Duvall, and Thomas Montgomery. *Reflections on the Law of 1813, for Laying an Embargo on all Ships and Vessels in the Ports and the Harbors of the United States*. 1814.
Mordecai, Samuel. *Virginia, Especially Richmond in By Gone Days with a Glance at the Past Being Reminiscences and Last Work of an Old Citizen*. Richmond: West and Johnson, 1860.
Moser, Harold, Sharon Macpherson, John H. Reinbold, and Daniel Feller, eds. *The Papers of Andrew Jackson*. Wilmington, Del.: Scholarly Resources, 1987. Microfilm, 39 reels.
———. *The Papers of Andrew Jackson: Guide and Index to the Microfilm Edition*. Wilmington, Del.: Scholarly Resources, 1987.
Murat, Achille. *America and the Americans*. New York: W. H. Graham, 1849.
———. "Florida: A Sketch of Its Civil and Natural History, with Reviews of Books about the Region." *American Quarterly Review* 2 (September 1827): 214–37.

———. *The United States of North America.* London: Effingam Wilson, 1833.
"Roster of State and County Officers Commissioned by the Governor of Florida, 1845–1868." February. Jacksonville: Florida Historical Records Survey, 1941.
Simmons, William Hayne. *Notices of East Florida: With an Account of the Seminole Nation of Indians By a Recent Traveler in the Province.* Introduction by George Buker. 1822. Floridiana facsimile and reprint, Gainesville: University of Florida Press, 1973.
Sprague, John T. *The Florida War: The Origin, Progress, and Conclusion of the Florida War.* 1848. Reprint, Tampa: University of Tampa Press, 2000.
Thompson, Leslie A. *A Manual or Digest of the Statute Law of the State of Florida, of a General and Public Character, in Force at the End of the Second Session of the General Assembly of the State, on the Sixth Day of January, 1847.* Boston: Charles C. Little and James Brown, 1848.
U.S. House of Representatives. *Information . . . Relating to the Present Location of the Florida Indians, their Country, Its Soil, and Water, Etc.* Document No. 161, 19th Cong., 1st sess. Washington, D.C.: Gales and Seaton, 1826.
———. *Law Agent in Florida.* Report No. 190, 27th Cong., 3rd sess., February 28, 1843.
———. *Letter from the Secretary of War . . . In Relation to the Condition of the Indians in Florida.* Document No. 82, 19th Cong., 2nd sess. Washington, D.C.: Gales and Seaton, 1827.
———. *Letter from the Secretary of War, Transmitting the Information Required by a Resolution of the House of Representatives of the 16th of May Last in Relation to the Florida Indians.* Document No. 17, 19th Cong., 2nd sess. Washington, D.C.: Gales and Seaton, 1826.
———. *Message from the President of the United States Transmitting Information in Relation to the Present Suffering Condition of the Indians of Florida.* Executive Document No. 111, 19th Cong., 1st sess. Washington, D.C.: Gales and Seaton, 1826.
———. *Report of the Committee of Claims (Senate) in the Case of Duval and Carnes.* Report No. 74, 21st Cong., 2nd sess., February 9, 1831.
———. *Treaty with the Florida Indians. . . . Instructions Given to the Commissioner for Negotiating with the Florida Indians, &c. &c.* Document No. 74, 19th Cong., 1st sess. Washington, D.C.: Gales and Seaton, 1826.
U.S. Senate. *Message from the President of the United States transmitting A Report from the Secretary of War on the Claim of Econchatta Nico.* 25th Cong., 2nd sess., April 23, 1838.
Weaver, Herbert, Paul Bergeron, and Wayne Cutler, eds. *Correspondence of James K. Polk.* 10 vols. Nashville: Vanderbilt University Press, 1969–2004.
West, Elizabeth Howard. *Calendar of the Papers of Martin Van Buren.* Washington, D.C.: Library of Congress, 1910.
West, Lucy Fisher, ed. *The Papers of Martin Van Buren: Guide and Index to General Correspondence and Miscellaneous Documents.* Chadwyck-Healey, 1989.
"William P. DuVal to James Barbour, August 12, 1823." In *Gulf States Historical Magazine* 1 (March 1903): 367–68.
"William P. Duval to the Marquis de Lafayette, January 10, 1826." *Gulf States Historical Magazine* 1 (November 1902): 200.
Williams, John Lee. *The Territory of Florida or Sketches of the Topography, Civil and Natural History, of the Country, the Climate, and the Indian Tribes, from the First*

Discovery to the Present Time, with a Map, Views, &c. 1837. Facsimile reprint with Introduction by Herbert J. Doherty, Gainesville: University of Florida Press, 1962.

———. "Journal of John Lee Williams, Commissioner to Locate the Seat of Government of the Territory of Florida." *Florida Historical Quarterly* 1 (April–July 1908): 37–44, 18–30.

———. *A View of West Florida, Embracing its Geography Topographical &c With An Appendix, Treating its Antiquities , Land Titles, and Canals, and Containing a Map, Exhibiting a Chart of the Coast, a Plan of Pensacola, and the Entrance of the Harbor.* Philadelphia: H. S. Tanner, 1827.

Wilson, Clyde N., et al., eds. *Papers of John C. Calhoun.* 28 vols. Columbia: University of South Carolina Press, 1959–2003.

Secondary Sources

Theses and Dissertations

Crandall, Robert C. "Academy Education in Antebellum Florida, 1821–1860." Ph.D. dissertation, Florida State University, 1987.

Denham, James M. "Dueling in Territorial Middle Florida." Master's thesis, Florida State University, 1983.

———. "A Rogues' Paradise: Crime and Punishment in Antebellum Florida, 1821–1861." Ph.D. dissertation, Florida State University, 1988.

Thompson, Arthur W. "David Yulee: A Study of Nineteenth-Century American Thought and Enterprise." Ph.D. dissertation, Columbia University, 1954.

Books

Abernethy, Thomas Perkins. *The South in the New Nation, 1789–1819.* Baton Rouge: Louisiana State University Press, 1961.

———. *Three Virginia Frontiers.* Baton Rouge: Louisiana State University Press, 1940.

Anderson, John Q. *John C. DuVal: First Texas Man of Letters.* Austin: Steck-Vaughn, 1967.

Baptist, Edward E. *Creating an Old South: Middle Florida's Plantation Frontier before the Civil War.* Chapel Hill: University of North Carolina Press, 2002.

Barkley, Mary Starr. *History of Travis County and Austin, 1839–1889.* Waco: Texian Press, 1963.

Bartlett, Irving H. *John C. Calhoun: A Biography.* New York: Norton, 1983.

Bassett, John S. *The Life of Andrew Jackson.* Garden City: Doubleday, Page, 1911.

Bauer, K. Jack. *Zachary Taylor: Soldier, Planter, Statesman of the Old Southwest.* Baton Rouge: Louisiana State University Press, 1985.

Baylor, Orval W. *John Pope Kentuckian, His Life and Times, 1770–1845: A Saga of Kentucky Politics from 1792–1850.* Cynthiana, Ky.: The Hobson Press, 1943.

Belko, W. Stephen. *The Invincible Duff Green: Whig of the West.* Columbia: University of Missouri Press, 2006.

Birkner, Michael. *Samuel Southard: Jeffersonian Whig.* Rutherford, N.J.: Farleigh Dickinson University Press, 1984.

Boles, John B. *A Guide to the Microfilm Edition of the William Wirt Papers, 1784–1864.* Baltimore: Maryland Historical Society, 1971.

Brands, H. W. *Andrew Jackson: His Life and Times.* New York: Doubleday, 2005.

———. *Lone Star Nation: How a Ragged Army of Volunteers Won the Battle for Texas Independence—and Changed America.* New York: Doubleday, 2004.

Brevard, Caroline Mays. *A History of Florida from the Treaty of 1763 to Our Own Times.* 2 vols. Deland: Florida State Historical Society, 1924–1925.

Brown, Canter, Jr. *Florida's Peace River Frontier.* Orlando: University of Central Florida Press, 1991.

———. *Ossian Bingley Hart: Florida's Loyalist Reconstruction Governor.* Baton Rouge: Louisiana State University Press, 1997.

———. *Tampa before the Civil War.* Tampa: University of Tampa Press, 1999.

Buchanan, Margaret Gwin. *DuVals of Kentucky from Virginia, 1794–1935: Descendants and Allied Families.* Lynchburg, Va.: J. P. Bell Co., n.d.

Burstein, Andrew. *The Passions of Andrew Jackson.* New York: Random House, 2003.

———. *The Original Knickerbocker: The Life of Washington Irving.* New York: Basic Books, 2007.

Campbell, Randolph B. *Gone to Texas: A History of the Lone Star State.* New York: Oxford University Press, 2003.

———. *Sam Houston and the America Southwest.* New York: HarperCollins, 1993.

Cash, William T. *History of the Democratic Party in Florida.* Tallahassee: Florida Democratic Historical Foundation, 1936.

Chadwick, Bruce. *I Am Murdered: George Wythe, Thomas Jefferson, and the Killing That Shocked a New Nation.* Hoboken: Wiley, 2009.

Chinn, George Morgan. *Kentucky: Settlement and Statehood, 1750–1800.* Frankfort: Kentucky Historical Society, 1975.

Chitwood, Oliver Perry. *John Tyler: Champion of the Old South.* 1939. Reprint, Newtown, Conn.: American Political Biography Press, 1990.

Clark, Thomas D. *Footloose in Jacksonian America: Robert W. Scott and His Agrarian World.* Lexington: University of Kentucky Press, 1989.

Clift, G. Glenn. *The Corn Stalk Militia.* Frankfort: Kentucky Historical Society, 1957.

———. *Second Census of the Kentucky, 1800.* Baltimore: Genealogical Co., 1966.

Coit, Margaret. *John C. Calhoun: An American Biography.* Boston: Houghton Mifflin, 1950.

Coker, William S., and Thomas D. Watson. *Indian Traders of the Southeastern Spanish Borderlands: Panton, Leslie & Company and John Forbes and Company, 1783–1847.* Pensacola: University of West Florida Press, 1986.

Cole, Donald B. *Martin Van Buren and the American Political System.* Princeton: Princeton University Press, 1984.

Collins, Richard H. *History of Kentucky.* 2 vols. Covington, Ky.: Collins and Co., 1878, 1882.

Cooper, William. *Liberty and Slavery: Southern Politics to 1860.* New York: Knopf, 1983.

Covington, James W. *The Seminoles of Florida.* Gainesville: University Press of Florida, 1993.

Coward, Joan Wells. *Kentucky in the New Republic: The Process of Constitution Making.* Lexington: University of Kentucky Press, 1979.

Curtis, James C. *The Fox at Bay: Martin Van Buren and the Presidency, 1837–1841.* Lexington: University of Kentucky Press, 1970.

Cusick, James G. *The Other War of 1812: The Patriot War and the American Invasion of Spanish East Florida.* Gainesville: University of Florida Press, 2003.

Denham, James M. *A Rogues' Paradise: Crime and Punishment in Antebellum Florida, 1821–1861.* Tuscaloosa: University of Alabama Press, 1997.

Denham, James M., and Canter Brown Jr. *Cracker Times and Pioneer Lives: The Florida Reminiscences of George Gillett Keen and Sarah Pamela Williams.* Columbia: University of South Carolina Press, 2000.

Denham, James M., and Keith Hunecutt. *Echoes from a Distant Frontier: The Brown Sisters Correspondence from Antebellum Florida.* Columbia: University of South Carolina Press, 2004.

Diamond, Robert A., ed. *Congressional Quarterly's Guide to U.S. Elections.* Washington, D.C.: Congressional Quarterly, 1975.

Dibble, Ernest F. *Joseph Mills White: Anti-Jackson Floridian.* Cocoa: Florida Historical Society, 2003.

Dobie, J. Frank. *John C. DuVal: First Texas Man of Letters.* Dallas: Southern Methodist University Press, 1939.

Dodd, Dorothy. *Florida Becomes a State.* Tallahassee: Florida Centennial Commission, 1945.

Doherty, Herbert J., Jr. *Richard Keith Call: Southern Unionist.* Gainesville: University of Florida Press, 1961.

———. *The Whigs of Florida.* Gainesville: University of Florida Press, 1959.

Dovell, J. E. *History of Banking in Florida, 1828–1954.* Orlando: Florida Bankers Association, 1955.

Derr, Mark. *The Frontiersman: The Real Life and Many Legends of Davy Crockett.* New York: William Morrow, 1993.

Ellsberry, Elizabeth Prather, compiler. *Marriage Records of Nelson County, Kentucky, 1785–1815.* Chillicothe, Missouri: Elizabeth Prather Ellsberry, 1965.

Fay, Mary Smith. *War of 1812 Veterans in Texas.* New Orleans: Polyanthos, 1979.

Fehrenbach, T. R. *Lone Star: A History of Texas and Texans.* New York: Collier Books 1968.

Ferguson, Gillum. *Illinois in the War of 1812.* Urbana: University of Illinois Press, 2012.

Fernald, Edwin A., and Elizabeth D. Purdum, eds. *The Atlas of Florida.* Gainesville: University Press of Florida, 1992.

Freehling, William W. *Prelude to Civil War: The Nullification Controversy in South Carolina.* New York: Harper and Row, 1966.

———. *The Road to Disunion: Secessionists at Bay, 1776–1854.* New York: Oxford University Press, 1990.

Friend, Craig Thompson, ed. *Along the Maysville Road: The Early American Republic in the Trans-Appalachian West,* Knoxville: University of Tennessee Press, 2005.

———. *The Buzzel about Kentuck: Settling the Promised Land.* Lexington: University of Kentucky Press, 1999.

———. *Kentucke's Frontiers*. Bloomington: Indiana University Press, 2010.
Garraty, John A. *The American Nation: A History of the United States to 1877*. New York: HarperCollins, 1991.
Gates, Paul. *History of Public Land Law Development Written for the Public Land Law Review Commission*. Washington, D.C.: U.S. Government Printing Office, 1968.
Gilpin, Alec. R., ed. *The War of 1812 in the Old Northwest*. East Lansing: Michigan State University Press, 1958.
Goldman, Perry M., and James S. Young. *The United States Congressional Directories:1789–1840*. New York: Columbia University Press, 1973.
Goodstein, Anita Shafer. *Nashville, 1780–1860*. Gainesville: University of Florida Press, 1989.
Grabowskii, Bessie Berry. *The DuVal Family of Virginia 1701, Descendants of Daniel DuVal, Huguenot, and Allied Families*. Richmond, VA: Dietz Printing Co., 1931.
Green, Constance McLaughlin. *Washington: Village and Capital, 1800–1878*. Princeton: Princeton University Press, 1962.
Groene, Bertram. *Antebellum Tallahassee*. Tallahassee: Heritage Foundation, 1971.
Guild, Richard L. *DuVal: The Following Information is based on Research done by the Past and Present Owners of Mt. Comfort Plantation*. Privately published, 1983.
Hall, Kermit. *Politics of Justice: Lower Federal Judicial Selection and the Second Party System, 1829–61*. Lincoln: University of Nebraska Press, 1979.
Hammack, James Wallace, Jr. *Kentucky and the Second American Revolution: The War of 1812*. Lexington: University of Kentucky Press, 1976.
Hammond, Ashby. *The Medical Profession in 19th Century Florida: A Biographical Register*. Gainesville: George A. Smathers Library, University of Florida, 1996.
Hanna, Alfred Jackson. *A Prince in Their Midst: The Adventurous Life of Achille Murat on the American Frontier*. Norman: University of Oklahoma Press, 1946.
Hanna, Kathryn Abbey. *Florida: Land of Change*. Chapel Hill: University of North Carolina Press, 1948.
Harrison, Lowell H., and James C. Klotter. *A New History of Kentucky*. Lexington: University of Kentucky Press, 1997.
Haycraft, Samuel. *Haycraft's History of Elizabethtown, [Kentucky]*. Serialized in Elizabethtown paper, 1869; republished by Hardin County Historical Society, 1960.
Heidler, David S., and Jeanne T. *Andrew Jackson and the Quest for American Empire,* Mechanicsburg, Pa.: Stackpole Books, 1996.
———. *Henry Clay: The Essential American*. New York: Random House, 2010.
———. *Old Hickory's War: Andrew Jackson and the Quest for Empire*. Mechanicsburg: Stockpole, 1996.
Heidler, David S., and Jeanne T., eds. *Encyclopedia of the War of 1812*. Annapolis, Md.: Naval Institute Press, 2004.
Heller, J. Roderick, III. *Democracy's Lawyer: Felix Grundy of the Old Southwest*. Baton Rouge: Louisiana State University Press, 2010.
Herold, Amos L. *James Kirke Paulding: Versatile American*. New York: AMS Press, 1966.
Hickey, Donald. *The War of 1812: A Forgotten Conflict*. Urbana: University of Illinois Press, 1989.
Hoffman, Paul E. *Florida's Frontiers*. Bloomington: Indiana University Press, 2002.

Horsman, Reginald. *The War of 1812*. New York: Knopf, 1969.
Hurd, Charles. *Washington Cavalcade*. New York: E. P. Dutton, 1948.
Hynes, Lee Powers. *Our Heritage: A Record of Information about the Hynes, Wait, Powers, Chenault, Maxey, Brewster, Starr, and McIntosh Families*. Haddonfield, N.J.: L. P. Hynes, 1957.
Jabour, Anya. *Marriage in the Early Republic: Elizabeth and William Wirt and the Companionate Ideal*. Baltimore: Johns Hopkins University Press, 1998.
Johnston, Johanna. *The Heart That Would Not Hold: A Biography of Washington Irving*. New York: M. Evans and Co., 1971.
Jillson, Willard Rouse. *The Kentucky Land Grants: A Systematic Index to All of the Land Grants Recorded in the State Land Office at Frankfort, Kentucky, 1782–1924*. Louisville: Standard Printing Co., 1925.
———. *Old Kentucky Entries and Deeds: A Complete Index to All . . .* Louisville: Filson Club Publications Genealogical Publishing Co., 1926.
Karan, P. P., and Cotton Mather, eds. *Atlas of Kentucky*. Lexington: University of Kentucky Press, 1977.
Kirwan, Albert D. *John J. Chrittenden: The Struggle for the Union*. Lexington: University of Kentucky Press, 1962.
Kincaid, Robert L. *The Wilderness Road*. Harrogate, Tenn.: Lincoln Memorial University Press, 1955.
Klunder, Willard Carl. *Lewis Cass and the Politics of Moderation*. Kent, Ohio: Kent State University Press, 1996.
Knauss, James Owen. *Florida Territorial Journalism*. Deland: Florida State Historical Society, 1926.
Knetsch, Joe. *Faces on the Frontier: Florida Surveyors and Developers in the 19th Century*. Cocoa: Florida Historical Society Press, 2006.
Landers, Jane. *Black Society in Spanish Florida*. Urbana: University of Illinois Press, 1999.
Landers, Jane, ed. *Colonial Plantations and Economy in Florida*. Gainesville: University Press of Florida, 2000.
Little, John P. *History of Richmond*. Richmond: Dietz Printing Co., 1933.
———. *Richmond: The Capital of Virginia: Its History*. Richmond: MacFarland and Ferguson, 1851.
Lofaro, Michael, ed. *Davy Crockett: The Man, the Legend, the Legacy, 1786–1986*. Knoxville: University of Tennessee Press, 1985.
McClure, Daniel, Jr. *Two Centuries in Elizabethtown and Hardin County, Kentucky*. Elizabethtown: Hardin County Historical Society, 1979.
McChord, J. H. *The McChords of Kentucky and Some Related Families*. Louisville: Webster Field-Bronte Co., 1941.
McGrane. Reginald Charles. *The Panic of 1837: Some Financial Problems of the Jacksonian Era*. New York: Russell and Russell, 1965.
McMurtry, R. Gerald. *Elizabethtown, Kentucky, 1779–1879: The First Century of Its Existence*. Elizabethtown: Hardin County Historical Society, 1959.
McReynolds, Edwin C. *The Seminoles*. Norman: University of Oklahoma Press, 1972.
Mahon, John K. *History of the Second Seminole War, 1835–1842*. Gainesville: University Press of Florida, 1985.

———. *The War of 1812*. Gainesville: University of Florida Press, 1972.
Malone, Dumas. *Jefferson the President, Second Term, 1805–1809*. Boston: Little, Brown, 1974.
Manley, Walter., E. Canter Brown Jr. and Eric W. Rise. *The Supreme Court of Florida and Its Predecessor Courts, 1821–1917*. Gainesville: University Press of Florida, 1997.
Marten, James. *Texas Divided: Loyalty and Dissent in the Lone Star State, 1856–1874*. Lexington: University of Kentucky Press, 1990.
Martin, Sidney Walter. *Florida during the Territorial Days*. Athens: University of Georgia Press, 1944.
Marszalek, John F. *The Petticoat Affair: Manners, Mutiny, and Sex in Andrew Jackson's White House*. New York: Free Press, 1997.
Mason, Philip P., ed. *After Tippecanoe: Some Aspects of the War of 1812*. East Lansing: Michigan State University Press, 1963.
Meyer, Leland W. *The Life and Times of Colonel Richard M. Johnson of Kentucky*. New York: Columbia University Press, 1932.
Millett, Allen R., and Peter Maslowski. *For the Common Defense: A Military History of the United States*. New York: Free Press, 1984.
Missall, John, and Mary Lou Missall. *The Seminole Wars: America's Longest Indian Conflict*. Gainesville: University Press of Florida, 2004.
Monaco, C. S. *Moses Levy of Florida: Jewish Utopian and Antebellum Reformer*. Baton Rouge: Louisiana State University Press, 2005.
Mooney, Chase C. *William H. Crawford, 1772–1834*. Lexington: University of Kentucky Press, 1974.
Morgan, Robert J. *A Whig Embattled: The Presidency under John Tyler*. Lincoln: University of Nebraska Press, 1954.
Nevins, Allan. *Ordeal of the Union: Fruits of Manifest Destiny, 1847–1852*. New York: Charles Scribner's Sons, 1947.
Niven, John. *John C. Calhoun and the Price of Union*. Baton Rouge: Louisiana State University Press, 1988.
———. *Martin Van Buren and the Romantic Age of American Politics*. New York: Oxford University Press, 1983.
O' Connor, Mrs. T. P. [Betty Paschal]. *I Myself*. London: Methuen, 1910.
———. *My Beloved South*. New York: G. P. Putnam's Sons, 1913.
Patrick, Rembert. *Aristocrat in Uniform: General Duncan L. Clinch*. Gainesville: University of Florida Press, 1963.
Paisley, Clifton. *The Red Hills of Florida, 1528–1865*. Tuscaloosa: University of Alabama Press, 1989.
Parks, Joseph H. *Felix Grundy: Champion of Democracy*. Baton Rouge: Louisiana State University Press, 1940.
Parmet, Herbert S., and Marie B. Hecht. *Aaron Burr: Portrait of an Ambitious Man*. New York: Macmillan, 1967.
Parsons, Stanley B., William W. Beach, and Dan Hermann, eds. *The United States Congressional Districts, 1788–1841*. Westport, Conn.: Greenwood Press, 1978.
Peterson, Merrill D. *The Great Triumvirate: Webster, Clay, and Calhoun*. New York: Oxford University Press, 1987.

Peterson, Norma Lois. *The Presidencies of William Henry Harrison and John Tyler.* Lawrence: University Press of Kansas, 1989.
Phelps, John B., comp. *The People of Lawmaking in Florida, 1822–1993.* Tallahassee: Florida House of Representatives, 1993.
Pool, William C. *A Historical Atlas of Texas.* Austin: Encino Press, 1975.
Porter, Kenneth W. *The Black Seminoles: History of Freedom Seeking People.* Revised and edited by Alcione M. Amos and Thomas P. Senter. Gainesville: University Press of Florida, 1996.
———. *The Negro on the American Frontier.* New York: Arno Press, 1971.
Quisenbury, Anderson Chennault. *Kentucky in the War of 1812.* Frankfort: Kentucky Historical Society, 1915.
Remini, Robert. *Andrew Jackson and the Course of American Democracy, 1833–45.* New York: Harper and Row, 1981.
———. *Andrew Jackson and the Course of American Empire, 1867–1821.* New York: Harper and Row, 1977.
———. *Andrew Jackson and the Course of American Freedom, 1822–1832.* New York: Harper and Row, 1981.
———. *Andrew Jackson and His Indian Wars.* New York: Viking, 2001.
———. *Daniel Webster: The Man and His Time.* New York: Norton, 1997.
———. *Henry Clay: Statesman for the Union.* New York: Norton, 1991.
———. *The House: The History of the House of Representatives.* New York: HarperCollins, 2006.
———. *Martin Van Buren and the Making of the Democratic Party.* New York: Norton, 1970.
Richardson, James D., ed. *A Compilation of the Messages and Papers of the Presidents.* New York: Bureau of National Literature, 1897.
Reps, John W. *Washington on View: The Nation's Capital since 1790.* Chapel Hill: University of North Carolina Press, 1991.
Rivers, Larry E. *Rebels and Runaways: Slave Resistance in Nineteenth Century Florida.* Champaign-Urbana: University of Illinois Press, 2012.
———. *Slavery in Florida from Territorial Days to the Civil War.* Gainesville: University of Florida Press, 2000.
Rohrbough, Malcolm J. *The Trans-Appalachian Frontier: People, Societies and Institutions, 1775–1850.* Belmont, Calif.: Wadsworth, 1990.
Roell, Craig H. *Remember Goliad!: A History of La Bahia.* Austin: Texas State Historical Association, 1994.
Rogers, William W. *Outposts on the Gulf: Saint George Island and Apalachicola from Early Exploration to World War II.* Pensacola: University of West Florida Press, 1986.
Rogers, William W., and Erica Clark. *The Croom Family and Goodwood Plantation: Land, Litigation, and Southern Lives.* Athens: University of Georgia Press, 1999.
Rone, Wendell H. *An Historical Atlas of Kentucky and Her Counties.* Privately published, n.d.
Rothbard, Murray N. *The Panic of 1819: Reactions and Policies.* New York: Columbia University Press, 1962.
Rubin, Louis D. *Virginia: A Bicentennial History.* New York: Norton, 1977.

Satterfield, R. Beeler. *Andrew Jackson Donelson: Jackson's Confidant and Political Heir.* Bowling Green, Ky.: Hickory Tales, 2000.

Schmeckebier, Laurence F. *The Office of Indian Affairs: Its History, Activities and Organization.* Baltimore: Johns Hopkins University Press, 1927.

Schweikart, Larry. *Banking in the American South from the Age of Jackson to Reconstruction.* Baton Rouge: Louisiana State University Press, 1987.

Scott, Mary Wingfield. *Old Richmond Neighborhoods.* Richmond, Va.: William Byrd Press, 1975.

Seager, Robert, II. *And Tyler Too: A Biography of John and Julia Gardiner Tyler.* New York: McGraw-Hill, 1963.

Seale, William. *The President's House: A History.* Baltimore: Johns Hopkins University Press, 2008.

Share, Allen J. *Cities in the Commonwealth: Two Centuries of Urban Life in Kentucky.* Lexington: University of Kentucky Press, 1982.

Shofner, Jerrell H. *History of Jefferson County.* Tallahassee: Sentry Press, 1976.

Silbey, Joel H. *Storm over Texas: The Annexation Controversy and the Road to the Civil War.* New York: Oxford University Press, 2006.

Simkins, Francis Butler. *Virginia: History, Government, and Geography.* New York: Charles Scribners, 1957.

Simpson, Craig, M. *A Good Southerner: The Life of Henry Wise of Virginia.* Chapel Hill: University of North Carolina Press, 1985.

Smith, Julia Floyd. *Slavery and Plantation Growth in Antebellum Florida, 1821–1860.* Gainesville: University of Florida Press, 1973.

Smithwick, Noah. *The Evolution of a State: or Recollections of Old Texas Days.* Austin: Gammel Book Co., 1900.

Spaulding, Mattingly. *Biography of a Kentucky Town: A Historical, Cultural and Literary Study of Bardstown.* Baltimore: Mattingly Spaulding, 1942.

Stokesbury, James L. *A Short History of the American Revolution.* New York: William Morrow, 1991.

Swift, Roy A. *Civilizers: The DuVals of Texas, from Virginia through Kentucky and Florida.* Austin: Eakin Press, 1992.

Sydnor, Charles S. *The Development of Southern Sectionalism.* Baton Rouge: Louisiana State University Press, 1948.

Tachau, Mary K. Bonsteel. *Federal Courts in the Early Republic, Kentucky, 1789–1816.* Princeton: Princeton University Press, 1978.

Thompson, Arthur W. *Jacksonian Democracy on the Florida Frontier.* Gainesville: University of Florida Press, 1961.

Thomas, Samuel W. *Views of Louisville since 1766.* Louisville: Courier-Journal, 1971.

Tidwell, James N., ed. *The Lion of the West: Retitled the Kentuckian, or a Trip to New York.* Stanford, Calif.: Stanford University Press, 1954.

Tyler, Ron, ed. *New Handbook of Texas.* Austin: Texas State Historical Association, 1996.

Van Deusen, Glyndon G. *The Jacksonian Era, 1828–1845.* New York: Harper and Brothers, 1959.

Van Schreeven, William J., comp. *Revolutionary Virginia: The Road to Independence.* Charlottesville: University Press of Virginia, 1973.

Viola, Herman J. *Thomas L. McKenney, Architect of America's Indian Policy: 1816–1830.* Chicago: Sallow Press, 1974.

Wade, Richard C. *The Urban Frontier: The Rise of Western Cities, 1790–1830,* Cambridge, Mass.: Harvard University Press, 1959.

Ward, James Robertson. *Old Hickory's Town: An Illustrated History of Jacksonville.* Jacksonville: Old Hickory's Town, 1985.

Warner, Lee H. *Free Men in the Age of Servitude: Three Generations of a Black Family.* Lexington: University of Kentucky Press, 1992.

Watson, Harry L. *Liberty and Power: The Politics of Jacksonian America.* New York: Hill and Wang, 1990.

White, Leonard D. *The Jacksonians: A Study in Administrative History, 1829–1861.* New York: Macmillan, 1954.

———. *The Jeffersonians: A Study in Administrative History, 1801–1829.* New York: Free Press, 1965.

Williams, Stanley, T. *The Life of Washington Irving.* 2 vols. New York: Oxford University Press, 1935.

Willoughby, Lynn. *Fair to Middlin': the Antebellum Cotton Trade of the Apalachicola River Valley.* Tuscaloosa: University of Alabama Press, 1993.

Wiltse, Charles M. *John C. Calhoun, Nationalist, 1782–1828.* New York: Russell and Russell, 1968.

———. *John C. Calhoun, Nullifier, 1829–39.* Indianapolis: Bobbs-Merrill, 1949.

———. *John C. Calhoun, Sectionalist, 1840–1850.* New York: Russell and Russell, 1968.

Wright, J. Leitch. *Creeks and Seminoles: The Destruction and Regeneration of the Muscogulge People.* Lincoln: University of Nebraska Press, 1986.

Wyatt-Brown, Bertram. *Southern Honor: Ethics and Behavior in the Old South.* New York: Oxford University Press, 1982.

Yater, George H. *Two Hundred Years at the Falls of the Ohio: A History of Louisville and Jefferson County.* Louisville: Filson Club, 1987.

Young, James Sterling. *The Washington Community, 1800–1828.* New York: Columbia University Press, 1966.

Articles

Abbey, Kathryn, T. "The Story of the Lafayette Lands in Florida." *Florida Historical Quarterly* 10 (January 1932): 118–32.

———. "The Union Bank of Tallahassee: An Experiment in Territorial Finance." *Florida Historical Quarterly* 15 (April 1937): 207–31.

Arpad, Joseph J. "John Wesley Jarvis, James Kirke Paulding, and Colonel Nimrod Wildfire." *New York Folklore Quarterly* 21 (1965): 92–106.

Baptist, Edward E. "The Migration of Planters to Antebellum Florida: Kinship and Power." *Journal of Southern History* 62 (August 1996): 527–54.

———. "Revisiting the Political History of Territorial Florida: Factions and Ideology." Paper presented at the Florida Historical Society, May 24, 1996.

Belko, W. Steven. "John C. Calhoun and the Creation of the Bureau of Indian Affairs: An Essay on Political Rivalry, Ideology, and Policymaking in the Early Republic." *South Carolina Historical Magazine* 105 (July 2004): 56–63.

Birkner, Michael. "The General, the Secretary, and the President: An Episode in the Presidential Campaign of 1828." *Tennessee Historical Quarterly* 42 (1983): 243–53.
Blakey, George. "Rendezvous with Republicanism: John Pope vs. Henry Clay in 1816." *Indiana Magazine of History* 62 (1966): 233–50.
Boyd, Julian. "The Murder of John Wythe." *William and Mary Quarterly* 12 (October 1955): 513–42.
Boyd, Mark F. "Asi-yaholo or Osceola." *Florida Historical Quarterly* 33 (January–April 1955): 249–305.
———. "Enumeration of Florida Spanish Missions in 1675." *Florida Historical Quarterly* 27 (1948: 184–85.
———. "Horatio S. Dexter and Events Leading to the Treaty of Moultrie Creek with the Seminole Indians." *Florida Anthropologist* 11 (September 1958): 65–95.
Brown, Canter. "The Florida Crisis of 1826–1827 and the Second Seminole War." *Florida Historical Quarterly* 73 (April 1995): 419–42.
———. "Race Relations in Territorial Florida, 1821–1845." *Florida Historical Quarterly* 73 (January 1995): 287–307.
Cash, W. T. "William Pope DuVal." *Tallahassee Historical Society* 1 (February 1934).
Corner, William. "John Chrittenden DuVal: The Last Survivor of the Goliad Massacre." *Texas State Historical Association Quarterly* 1 (July 1897–April 1898): 47–67.
Davis, Horace. "Pensacola Newspapers, 1821–1900," *Florida Historical Quarterly*, 37 (January 1959): 418–45.
Davis, Mary Lamar. "Tallahassee through Territorial Days." *Apalachee* 1 (1944): 47–61.
Denham, James M. "'The Peerless Wind Cloud': Thomas Jefferson Green and the Tallahassee-Texas Land Company." *East Texas Historical Journal* 29 (Fall 1991): 3–14.
———. "The Read-Alston Duel and Politics in Territorial Florida." *Florida Historical Quarterly* 68 (April 1990): 427–46.
Dodd, Dorothy. "Old Tallahassee." *Apalachee* (1957–1962): 63–71.
Doherty, Herbert J. "Andrew Jackson's Cronies in Florida Territorial Politics." *Florida Historical Quarterly* 34 (July 1955): 3–29.
"Elizabethtown, Kentucky, 1779–1879." *Filson Club Quarterly* 12 (April 1938): 23.
Fairbanks, George R. "Early Churchmen in Florida." In *Historical Papers and Journal of Semi-Centennial of the Church in Florida, 1888.* 3–22. Jacksonville: Church Publishing Co., 1889.
Farris, Charles D. "The Courts of Territorial Florida." *Florida Historical Quarterly* 19 (April 1941): 346–67.
Feller, Daniel. "The Seminole Controversy Revisited: A New Look at Andrew Jackson's 1818 Florida Campaign." *Florida Historical Quarterly* 88 (Winter 2010): 309–25.
Fletcher, Duncan Upshaw. "Address before the Florida Historical Society." *Florida Historical Quarterly* 3 (January 1925): 22–30.
Garvin, Russell. "The Free Negro in Florida before the Civil War." *Florida Historical Quarterly* 46 (July 1967): 1–17.
Govan, Thomas P. "John M. Berrien and the Administration of Andrew Jackson." *Journal of Southern History* 5 (1939): 447–67.
Granade, Ray. "Slave Unrest in Florida." *Florida Historical Quarterly* 55 (July 1976): 18–36.

Graham, Thomas S. "Florida Politics and the Tallahassee Press, 1845–1861." *Florida Historical Quarterly* 46 (January 1968): 234–42.
Green, Edwin L. "Florida Historical Documents." *Gulf States Historical Magazine* 1 (November 1902): 199–201.
Groene, Bertram. "Lizzy Brown's Tallahassee." *Florida Historical Quarterly* 46 (October 1969): 155–75.
Hamilton, Robert. "The Expeditions of Major-General Hopkins up the Wabash, 1812." *Indiana Magazine of History* 43 (1947): 393–403.
Hanna, Alfred Jackson. "Diplomatic Missions of the United States to Cuba to Secure the Spanish Archives of Florida." In *Hispanic American Essays: A Memorial to James Alexander Robertson,* edited by Alva Curtis Wilgus, 208–33. Chapel Hill: University of North Carolina Press, 1942.
Harper, Roland. "Antebellum Census Enumerations in Florida." *Florida Historical Quarterly* 6 (July 1927): 42–52.
Hauck, Richard Boyd. "Making It All Up: Davy Crockett in the Theatre." In *Davy Crockett: The Man, the Legend, the Legacy, 1786–1986,* edited by Michael A. Lofaro, 102–24. Knoxville: University of Tennessee Press, 1985.
Haywood, Marshall de Lancey. "John Branch, Secretary of the Navy in the Cabinet of President Jackson, etc." *North Carolina Booklet* 15 (October 1915): 49–103.
Hemphill, E. Edwin. "Examination of George Wythe Swinney for Forgery and Murder: A Documentary Essay." *William and Mary Quarterly* 12 (October 1955): 543–74.
Herring, Julia. "Plantation Economy in Leon County, 1830–1840." *Florida Historical Quarterly* 33 (July 1954): 32–47.
Horn, Stanley F., ed. "Some Jackson-Overton Correspondence." *Tennessee Historical Quarterly* 6 (1947): 161–75.
Hoskins, F. W. "The St. Joseph Convention: The Making of Florida's First Constitution." *Florida Historical Quarterly* 16 (July 1937): 33–43; (October 1937): 97–109; (April 1938): 242–250; 17 (October 1938): 125–131.
———. "A St. Joseph Diary of 1839." *Florida Historical Quarterly* 17 (October 1938): 132–51.
Huhner, Leon. "Moses Levy, Florida Pioneer." *Florida Historical Quarterly* 19 (April 1941): 319–45.
Jabour, Anya. "'The Privations & Hardship of a New Country': Southern Women and Southern Hospitality on the Florida Frontier." *Florida Historical Quarterly* 75 (Winter 1997): 259–75.
Johnson, Leland R. "Aaron Burr: Treason in Kentucky?" *Filson Club Historical Quarterly* 75 (January 2001): 1–32.
Knauss, James Owens. "St. Joseph: An Episode in Economic and Political History of Florida." *Florida Historical Quarterly* 6 (July 1927): 178–95.
———. "William Pope Duval: Pioneer and State Builder." *Florida Historical Quarterly* 11 (January 1933): 95–139.
"Letters of Col. Richard M. Johnson." *Register of the Kentucky State Historical Society* 38 (October 1940): 327–28.
Lewis, Mary D. "Thomas Brown." *Apalachee* (1944): 90–95.

Martin, Sidney Walter. "The Public Domain in Territorial Florida." *Journal of Southern History* 10 (February 1944): 174–87.
Miller, Barbara. "Tallahassee and the 1841 Yellow Fever Epidemic." *Apalachee* 8 (1971–79): 21–31.
Marotti, Frank, Jr. "Edward M. Wanton and the Settling of Micanopy." *Florida Historical Quarterly* 73 (April 1995): 456–77.
Parker, Rosalind. "The Proctors–Antonio, George, and John." *Apalachee* (1946): 19–29.
Porter, Emily. "The Reception of the St. Joseph Constitution." *Florida Historical Quarterly* 17 (October 1938): 103–24.
Schafer, Daniel L. "'A Class of People Neither Freemen Nor Slaves': From Spanish to American Race Relations in Florida, 1821–1861." *Journal of Social History* 26 (Spring 1993): 587–609.
Seelye, John. "A Well-Wrought Crockett, or How the Fakelorists Passed through the Credibility Gap and Discovered Kentucky." In *Davy Crockett: The Man, the Legend, the Legacy, 1786–1986,* edited by Michael A. Lofaro, 21–45. Knoxville: University of Tennessee Press, 1985.
Shores, Venila Lovina. "The Laying Out of Tallahassee." *Apalachee* (1957–1962): 41–47.
Snyder, Frank L. "Nancy Hynes DuVal: Florida First Lady, 1822–1834." *Florida Historical Quarterly* 72 (July 1993): 19–34.
———. "William Pope DuVal: Extraordinary Folklorist." *Florida Historical Quarterly* 69 (October 1990): 195–212.
Thomas, John B. "Kentuckians in Texas: Capt. Burr H. DuVal's Company at Goliad." *Register of the Kentucky Historical Society* 81 (Summer 1983): 237–54.
Weisman, Brent R. "The Plantation System of the Florida Seminole Indians and Black Seminoles during the Colonial Era." in Jane Landers, ed. *Colonial Plantations and Economy in Florida,* edited by Jane Landers, 136–49. Gainesville: University Press of Florida, 2000.
"William Pope DuVal." *Tallahassee Historical Society Annual* 1 (1934): 10–13.
Winston, James E. "Kentucky and the Independence of Texas." *Southwestern Historical Quarterly* 16 (July 1912–April 1913): 27–62.

Notes

Page numbers in italics refer to illustrations

Abernethy, Thomas, 6, 11
Adams, John Quincy, 1, 35–37, 43, 48–49, 52, 53–58, 60–61, 68–69, 73, 76, 83, 89, 101, 104, 116, 121, 136–38, 167, 177–78, 183, 304; and WPD's appointment as governor (1822), 46, 93–94, 142; and Election of 1824, 75, 90–91; and Corrupt Bargain, 91–94; WPD's views on cabinet of, 137; and private meeting with WPD, 141–42, 167; contests David Levy's right to House seat, 286
Adams-Onis Treaty, 35, 37, 44
Adair, John, 47, 214; and controversy with Andrew Jackson regarding Battle of New Orleans, 96, 136, 198
Alachua, 40, 56, 87, 102–04, 107, 111, 113, 180
Alien and Sedition Acts, 11, 12
Allen, Richard C., 132, 189, 196, 266, 275; as land agent, 134, 162; appointed counsel in land cases, 176; as WPD's law partner, 232, 241, 244, 250; and Lake Wimico and St. Joseph Canal and Railroad company, 244, 254; elected delegate to Florida Constitutional Convention, 252; death of, 284
Alston, Augustus: and duel with Leigh Read, 270–71
Alston (Family), 134

Alston, Willis, 276–79; attack and murder of Leigh Read, 271, 281, 291
Ambrister (British Soldier) 124, 183
Anderson, Walker, 277, 312, 329
Apalachicola Indians, 83, 92, 118, 120, 144, 153, 172, 214, 217, 219–20. *See also* John Blount
Arbothnot, (Scot Indian Trader), 124, 183
Archer, Hugh, 351
Arnold, Benedict, 4
Arredondo, F. M., 45
Arredondo Tract, 107, 205, 300, 308
Austin, (Tx.), 316, 321, 324, 327, 341, 345–48; description of, 322

Bailey, William, 217, 328, 331, 337
Balch, Alfred, 274–75
Baltzell, George, 329
Baltzell, Thomas, 250–51, 281, 285, 309, 327; and duel with James Westcott, 213; joins WPD in defense of William Passmore, 275
Barbour, James, 68, 93, 97, 104, 109, 114–15, 135–37, 140–41, 144–45, 196, 201, 212
Barbour, Philip, 23, 44
Bardstown (Ky.), ix, 6, 7, 12, 13, 15, 25, 29–30, 34, 37, 47–48, 56–57, 73, 77, 93, 99, 147, 172, 201, 218–19, 224, 226–27,

Bardstown (Ky.) (continued)
231, 235–38, 246, 286; as legal center, 9;
social life in, 16–17
Bardstown *Herald*, 235
Barnburners, 332, 336. See also Hunkers
Barry, William T., 163, 218–219
Bartlett, Cosam Emir, 255
Beall, Elizabeth, 226, 327, 339–41, 344–46
Beall, Samuel, 219
Bell, John, 49
Bell, Peter Hansborough, 346–48, 350–51
Bellamy, Abram: as president of the Florida legislative council, 99, 185, 210; and Florida Constitutional Convention, 255, 260
Bellamy, John, 133; and road building, 80, 90, 99, 107, 114; as Indian contractor, 85, 90
Bellamy, Samuel, 257
Benton, Thomas Hart, 248
Berrien, John: appointed attorney general, 157; as attorney general, 179, 188, 197, 200; represents claimants of U. S. lands, 176, 178, 205, 209, 287
Bibb, George W., 9, 173, 191, 308; and Jefferson Day Dinner, 170–71
Birney, John, 310
Blackburn, E. E. 277–78
Blair, Francis, 94, 158; and Washington *Globe*, 186; WPD's description of, 306
Blount, John, 42, 53, 64–65, 79, 118, 219; complaints against WPD, 144, 157; and removal West, 214, 219–20; and molestation of 214, 217, 396n
Blunt, John, 103, 144, 214. See also John Blount.
"Blunt's Town," 59
Brackenridge, Henry M., 47, 48, 51, 52, 59; and dispute with Andrew Jackson over removal from judgeship, 209
Bradford (Family), 134, 250
Branch, Eliza: marries Leigh Read, 270
Branch, John, 134, 157, 250, 309–12, 320; WPD's rival for 1822 Florida gubernatorial appointment, 46, 164, 243, 368n; becomes U. S. senator, 46; becomes secretary of navy, 157; resigns Andrew Jackson's cabinet, 188, 192, 197, 200; settles in Tallahassee, 243; and Leigh Read, 255, 270, 273, 281, 291; becomes territorial governor of Florida, 307; Georgia-Florida Boundary Commission with WPD, 322
Branch (Family), 134
Branch, Joseph, 243, 309
Branch, O'Brien, 243
Brandywine, Battle of, 10
Broadnax, Henry, 8–9; as WPD's law teacher, 9–10
Broadnax, Lydia, 14–15
Brockenbroughs (Family), 14, 134
Brockenbrough, William, H. 309, 312, 326; law partner of WPD, 250–51, 271; becomes U. S. attorney for Apalachicola district, 275; and Union Bank of Florida, 280; WPD's description of , 306, 314, 317; and congressional race of 1845, 314–17
Bronough, John, 39, 47, 48; and delegate's race, 50–54, 183; death of, 52
Bronson, Isaac, 293, 313, 317, 326; WPD appraisal of, 301
Brooke, George, 113, 120
Brown, Canter, 118
Brown, Elizabeth "Lizzy," 242, 254, 266, 267, 287; describes WPD's homestead, 130–31
Brown, Thomas, 130, 131, 134, 145, 241, 251, 255, 264, 266, 267, 277; business activities of, 242, in legislative council, 280; Whig nominee for governor, 331; elected governor, 337–38, 338, 351
Buchanan, James, 286
Buckingham County (Va.): WPD's father in 15, 25–26, 47, 96, 290
Burch, Daniel, 58, 70, 86, 106, 122
Burns, Bobby (Robert), xii
Burr, Aaron: treason trial of, 15–16
Burt, George, 300
Butler, Robert, 38, 42, 56, 148, 173, 195; and concern over Spanish land records, 44; as surveyor general of Florida, 74, 78, 84, 86, 93, 95, 107, 132, 135

Cabell, Edward Carrington, 315, 327–28, 335, 350; congressional race against WPD, 1–2, 331–32, 334–38
Cabell, Joseph, 16
Cabell (Family), 14, 134
Calhoun, John C., ix–xi, xiv, 37, 97, 137, 143, 154, 156–57, 164, 197, 199, 293, 313–16, 319–20, 322–26, 329, 331, 342, 343, 354, 355; as War Hawk, 19, 305; in Thirteenth Congress, 28, 32–33; comforts WPD after economic reverses, 35–36; as secretary of war, 35–37, 42, 48–49, 54–56, 58–60, 64–70, 72, 75–81, 83, 90–93, 104; role in WPD's appointment as governor, 45–46; as vice president, 141, 168; and conflict with Jackson, xi, xiv, 158–61, 163, 170–75, 186, 188, 199–200, 202–03, 215; blocks Van Buren nomination, 202; as secretary of state, 302–07, 309, 312; and Florida statehood, 273–74; and presidential prospects in 1844, 301–02; and annexation of Texas, 304; and Oregon Question, 323–24; and opposition to war with Mexico, 325; and Compromise of 1850, 341–43, 346
Call, Richard Keith, x, 39, 47, 48, 52, 56, 67, 69, 85, 91, 95, 132, 135, 175, 270, 276, 312, 337; and territorial delegate race (1823), 62; (1832), 212, 217, 222; appointed receiver of public monies, 92; and marriage at Hermitage, 91; and Peggy O'Neale Timberlake, 160–163; defends WPD in the U. S. Senate, 206–07; learns from Andrew Jackson of the death of Rachel Jackson, 154; represents U. S. in land claims, 176, 205, 287, 300; appointed governor (1836), 233, (1841), 280; campaign against Seminoles, 232–34, 238–39, 242–43; and conflict with John P. DuVal, 246–47, 253, 269, 286–87, 292, 401n; and conflict with Joseph M. White, 136, 212–213, 217; and Read-Alston conflict, 270, 281; pardons Michael Ledwith, 291–92; and break with Andrew Jackson, 163, 242–43, 278; campaigns for William Henry Harrison, 278; and Tallahassee Railroad Company, 229; and conflict with Charles Sibley, 306, 309
Call, Mary, 91; Andrew Jackson on pregnancy of, 95
Call, Mary Ellinore "Ellen," 95
Campbell, John, 245
Campbell, John K., 217; marries Elizabeth DuVal and killed in duel, 219
Campbell, William: description of Tallahassee, 238–39
Cass, Lewis, ix, 1, 21, 67, 75, 343, 350, 352; as presidential candidate, 301, 332–38; as secretary of war, 169, 188, 209, 210, 213
Carr Family murders, 119–120, 123
Chaires, Benjamin, 133; and Indian contractor, 78, 90, 122, 206; and appraisal if Indian lands, 103, 113; and Union Bank of Florida, 217
Chaires, Green, 266
Chambers, Ezekiel, 203
Chambers, George, 237
Chapeze, Ben, 11
Cherokees, 75
Chickasaws, 181
Choctaws, 75, 181
Christian, Susan Brown: marriage to Major DuVal, 15, 47
Clark, George Rogers, 5, 10
Clark, James, 19, 27
Clarke, Isaac, 107
Clay, Henry, x, 5, 6, 12, 15, 19, 20, 21, 27–28, 47, 55, 75, 162, 183, 199–200, 218, 285–86, 350; and Chancellor Wythe, 5, 359n; and conflict with Felix Grundy, 12, 19; denounces Jackson's invasion of Florida, 35; and "Corrupt Bargain," 90–91, 94; as secretary of state, 93–96, 101–02, 136–37, 140–41, 167; and Election of 1844, 301, 305, 307, 309–10; and Compromise of 1850, 346–47; votes not to confirm WPD's re-appointment as governor, 208
Clinch, Duncan, 118, 120–22, 124, 230, 232–33, 236
Coffee, John, 95
Comanche Indians, 322, 347, 348, 350

Cornwallis, (George), 4
"Corrupt Bargain," x, 55, 90–91, 94
Crane, Ambrose: defends WPD before U. S. Senate, 206
Crawford, William H., 55–56, 75, 93, 140, 157–58, 162, 183; and patronage battle with Calhoun, 45–46, 67, 368n; WPD appraisal of, 67–68; and Election of 1824, 75, 90; and Jackson-Calhoun conflict, 159
Creek War, 29, 40, 113
Creeks, x, 29, 31, 34–35, 40, 51, 59, 72, 75, 78, 85, 102, 120, 122, 161, 233, 350. *See also* Seminoles
Crittenden, John, xiv, 21, 201, 218, 287, 333, 338–39, 343–44
Crockett, Davy, 234; as possible inspiration for James Kirke Paulding's Nimrod Wildfire, 357–58n
Croom, Bryan, 251
Croom (Family), 134
Croom, Hardy, 251
Crupper, Micjah: and Indian contractor, 78, 90, 92, 122, 206

Dade, Francis Langhorn: and Indian Scare of 1826–1827, 118–19, 121, 124; and death of, 232
Daveiss, Joseph, 15
Davis's Hotel in Washington, 27
De la Rua, John, 52
Dell, Bennett, 180
Desha, John, 95
Desha, Joseph, 19, 20
Dexter, Horatio, 42–43, 60; and exploration of Indian Country, 60; and "Observations on the Seminole Indians," 63–65
Dickinson, Daniel, 329, 333
Division (of Florida) Politics, 253, 263–64, 273–74, 280, 310; support for in East Florida, 253, 266–67, 307; opposition to, 271; WPD on, 263–64, 282, 307, 310; John C. Calhoun and 273
Dodd, Dorothy, 255, 260
Doherty, Herbert J., 228, 331
Donelson, Andrew Jackson, 158, 170, 172, 191, 222, 229, 234–33

Donelson, Emily, 158; and Eaton Affair, 163
Douglas, Samuel, 291, 309; on confused economic affairs in Middle Florida, 241; sentences Michael Ledwith to death, 291
Douglas, Stephen, 341, 346
Douglas, Thomas, 289, 307, 313, 317; and law cases with WPD, 289, 296–98, 300–01, 308, 315–16
Downing, Charles, 246–47, 250, 265–67, 271, 277
Drake, Frederick C. 30
Duels and Dueling, 138, 273; anti-dueling laws, 272, 282; Burr-Hamilton duel, 15; DuVal-Wilcox duel, 13; DuVal-White duel, 213; McRea-Hawkins duel, 164–65; Read-White duel, 213; Westcott-Baltzell duel, 213; Westcott duel in New Jersey, 163. *See also* Read-Alston duel and John K. Campbell.
Dunn (killed Kentuckian), 23
DuPont, Charles, 278, 309
DuVal, Anne Pope: death of, 4
DuVal, Burr Grayson, 321, 348
DuVal, Burr Harrison (WPD's son), 25, 47, 93, 128, 172, 207, 226; birth of, 16; works for father as clerk, 77, 81, 86, 101; visits Washington, D.C., 114–15; appointed justice of the peace, 201; and Texas War for Independence, xi, 230–36, 238; writes WPD of his military campaign in Texas, 234–35; killed in Goliad Massacre, 235–36
DuVal, Claiborne, 4, 6, 13
DuVal, Daniel, (DuVal's great grandfather), 3
DuVal, Daniel (DuVal's uncle): and service in American Revolution, 4
DuVal, Elizabeth Ann, 34, 93, 128, 131, 147–48, 172, 180; marriage to and death of John K. Campbell, 219; marriage to Samuel Beall, 219. *See also* Elizabeth Beall
DuVal, Florence, 321
DuVal, Florida, 172, 180, 226, 241, 286, 288, 309; birth of, 128
DuVal, Frances, 15
DuVal, John Crittenden, xi, 47, 93, 128, 172, 180, 201, 230, 231, 241, 266, 286–88, 296, 305, 321–22, 327, 345, 355: birth of,

34; and description of Tallahassee, 127; on Indians in Tallahassee area, 118; and Goliad Massacre, 236, 322; and Texas Rangers, 322, 327; in Mexican War, 327; as "First Texas Man of Letters," 353

DuVal, John P., 4, 14, 169, 173, 175, 231, 247, 286, 292, 309, 326–27, 348; and law practice of, 242, 300, and planting interests of, 129, 152, 157, 242; seeks political appointments, 76, 96, 163, 245, 287; compiles Florida statutes, 242; as Tallahassee city commissioner, 164; as territorial secretary, 245–46, 252–54, 269–70; and conflict with Richard K. Call, 246–47, 253, 269, 286–87, 292, 401n

DuVal, Laura Harrison, 35, 37, 93, 128, 131, 172, 180, 226, 241, 266, 267; and excursion to Cuba, 242; visits St. Joseph, 254; marries Arthur M. Randolph, 272. See also Laura Randolph

DuVal, Laura Peyton, 286, 321; marries Thomas DuVal, 241,

DuVal, Marcia, 16, 25, 47, 93, 128–29, 131; marriage to William D. Price, 147. See also Marcia Price

DuVal, Mary, 35, 47, 93, 128, 131, 172, 180, 226, 241, 321; marriage to James Robinson, 250; becomes a widow, 309. See also Mary Robinson

"DuVal Myth," 155–56

DuVal, Nancy; 15, 25–26, 31, 51, 56, 99, 128–29, 131, 147–48, 151–52, 201, 218, 224, 226, 236, 254, 267–68, 278–79, 281, 288–89, 300, 309; siblings of, 10; marriage and courtship of, 9–11; children and childbirth of, 16, 25, 34–35, 47, 93, 128, 172, 180, 241; death of 283–86. See also Nancy Hynes

DuVal, Nathaniel (WPD brother), 14

DuVal, Nathaniel Pope (WPD cousin): dies in duel, 13

DuVal, Philadelphia, 3

DuVal, Philip, 4

DuVal, Samuel (WPD brother), 4; migration in Kentucky with William P., 6–7; death of, 7; claims against estate of, 7, 14

DuVal Samuel (WPD cousin): migrates to Tallahassee, 129; purchases WPD's interest in Lafayette tract, 196; appointed U. S marshal, 245, 380n; house of 267; death of, 271

DuVal, Samuel (WPD grandfather), 3; and marriage to Lucy Claiborne, 3

DuVal Samuel (WPD nephew): fights duel, 213

DuVal, Samuel (WPD uncle), 4

DuVal, Sarah, 15, 47

DuVal, Susan Brown Christian, 15, 25, 47

DuVal, Susan Elizabeth, 15, 47

DuVal, Thomas Howard, 47, 93, 128, 172, 180, 201, 241, 276, 286; birth of, 25; marries Laura Peyton DuVal, 241; and law practice with WPD, 250; and law practice with Benjamin Allen, 283; in Texas, xi, 321–22, 324, 340, 348, 351; and Civil War, 353

DuVal, William (a. k. a Major DuVal), 3–9, 25, 47, 96; emancipates slaves, 15, 47, 96, 362n; and friendship with Thomas Jefferson, 3, 14–16; and friendship with George Washington, 3; and Henry Clay, 15, 47, 96, 359n; and Kentucky lands, 4–7; and marriage to Anne Pope, 3; and marriage to Susan Brown Christian, 15; and service in American Revolution, 3–4; and George Wythe, 3, 14–15; and Richmond home of, 4, 14; death of, 290

DuVal, William P. (WPD), accompanies Andrew Jackson traveling party from Washington to Nashville, 93; addresses Florida legislative council, 51–53; 86–87, 99–101, 164–65, 214–15, 219–220; advises Andrew Jackson that he may resign, 67, 139–40, 196, 222; advises Andrew Jackson on John Eaton and cabinet breakup, 196–200; advises Andrew Jackson on presidential prospects in 1824, 68, 74–75; advises Calhoun on Compromise of 1850, 341–43; advises Calhoun on Florida affairs, 306, 312–14, 319–20; advises Calhoun on Oregon Question, 323–24; advises Calhoun on annexation of Texas,

DuVal, William P. (WPD) (continued)
305–306; advises John Crittenden on Wilmot Proviso, 343–44; advisor to John Tyler, 286, 292; 347; at Alligator, 334; also in 1828, x, 148, 154; and annexation of Texas, 305–308, 310; attitudes toward the British, 219–20, 267–68; 305–308, 354–55; at Austin, (Tx), 346–48; at Bardstown, (Ky), 9–13, 16–17, 47, 55–58, 93–96, 99, 218–19, 226–27, 237–38; birth, childhood and family background of, 3–4; and claims against U. S., 275–76, 292–93, 299–300; compared with Henry Clay, 12–13; comments on old Spanish relics in Tallahassee area, 115; convenes the first meeting of the Florida legislative council in Pensacola, 51–53; courtship and marriage of Nancy Hynes, 9–10; death of, 350–52; delegate's race debacle (1832), 192–96; disputes with War Department over accounts, 76, 92, 104–05, 139–40, 141–42, 144–45, 156, 169, 275–76 ; dueling, 13, 185, 272, 282; educational theories of, 110, 164, 181–82, 214; explores St. Johns River, 43; Florida judge, x, 1, 39, 43–44; founding of Tallahassee, x, 61, 71–72, 77; gubernatorial appointments of, x, 1, 45–46, 93–94, 141–42, 192, 203, 208; homestead in Tallahassee, 72, 77, 99, 128, 130–31, 142–43; Hynes family legal disputes, 10–11, 48, 218, 361n; image of, 174, 228; and Indian affairs, 39–43, 49–50, 53, 58–60, 63–67, 72–73, 78–86, 102–05, 107–25, 161, 213–214, 220; inspiration for James Kirke Paulding's Nimrod Wildfire, xiii, 357–57n; inspiration for Washington Irving's Ralph Ringwood and other writings, xii-xiii, 1–3, 358n; invites Andrew Jackson to visit Kentucky, 95; law agent, 287, 296–301; law practice in Florida, 232–33, 241, 244, 250–51, 271, 275–76, 281, 286–87, 296–30, 316–17, 327, 340, 344–45; at Jacksonville, 297; at Jefferson County (FL), 147–48, 331; law practice in Kentucky, 11, 17–18, 223, 226–27, 250–52; legal training in Bardstown, 9–10; makes personal inspection of Indian lands (1826), 107–13, and Neamathla, 70–73, 78–80, 83–84, 374n; at Louisville (Ky), 218–19, 224–26; at Magnolia, 155–56; at Marianna, 153, 337; melancholy musings of, 153, 290, 296, 340–41, 344–45; member of Florida Constitutional Convention, xi, 1, 252–62; member of the Florida Senate, xi, 264–66, 272, 280–81; member of the Thirteenth Congress, 1, 25–34; and Mexican War, 326; migration to Kentucky, ix, xiii, 3, 6–7; migration to Texas, xi, 309, 345–46; moves family to Florida, 99; on need for court in Key West, 101; at Newnansville, 180, 276; offers Andrew Jackson an appraisal of Kentucky politics, bank war, 218–19; oratory of, xi-xii, 17–18, 182, 308, 310–11, 328, 332, 334–36, 355; at Palatka, 307–08, 313; at Palatka Democratic Convention, 308; Panic of 1819 and economic reverses, ix, 34–36; and patronage x, 44–47, 59, 138, 161–62, 245; at Pensacola, 48–54, 58–59, 69–75, 240; planting interests of, 132–33, 149–52, 157, 196, 230, 239; physical appearance of, xii, 288–89; personality of, xi-xii, 17–18, 130, 164, 223, 252, 288–89, 332, 348, 352; at Port Leon, 268; at Quincy, 327, 331, 337; race for Congress (1848), 1–2; 330–39; and Rogers pardon case, 212; at St. Augustine, 180, 276, 293–97, 299–307, 313–27, 331, 334–36; at St. Joseph, 240, 251–52, 254–62, 268, 271, 275; at St. Marks, 76–77, 86, 346; Senate investigation of, 203–09; serves on Florida-Georgia Boundary Dispute Commission, 322–23; singing of, xii, 17, 164; speculates on Florida's admission to the Union, 292; and territorial banks, 88, 165–66, 214–18, 354–55; at Tallahassee, 77–89, 99–105, 114–40, 145–47, 164–66, 173–201, 212–17, 219–22, 232–36, 241–43, 249–51, 266–68, 271–75, 276–83, 286–97,

298–316, 336, 340–49; and Tallahassee Disturbances (1841), 276–77; and Texas War for Independence, 230–32, 234–38, 399n; and Union Bank of Florida, 1, 220, 222, 230, 250–51, 264, 268, 278, 280, 315, 334; views on David Levy (Yulee), 283, 311–14; views on Martin Van Buren, 198, 227–28; 305, 335, 339; views on slavery, xiii, 151–52, 344–41; views on Spanish inhabitants of Florida, 52; views on William Brockenbrough, 306, 314, 317; at Wakahoota, 334; and War of 1812, ix, 19–26, 139, 158, 216, 261, 267, 333; at Washington, D. C, xi, 26–30, 44–47, 90–93, 141–45, 166–72, 202–12, 244–48, 284–84, 290–93, 349–52; on Wilmot Proviso, 328, 332, 343–44; *See also* John C. Calhoun, Richard Keith Call, Andrew Jackson, Joseph M. White, Samuel Southard, and James Westcott

"DuVal's Addition," 5

Dyke, Charles, 337

"The Early Experiences of Ralph Ringwood," xii-xiii, 1, 358n. *See also* Washington Irving, "Ralph Ringwood Tales."

Eaton, John, xi, 69, 95, 119, 169, 175, 186, 188, 192, 196–97, 200, 214; becomes secretary of war, 157; and marriage to Peggy Eaton, 160; becomes territorial governor of Florida, 222, 228–30, 233

"Eaton Malaria," 160, 170, 175;

Eaton, Peggy, xi, 160, 162–63, 228–29, 243, 398n. See also Peggy Eaton Affair, "Eaton Malaria"

Edwards, Ninian, ix, 9, 21, 36, 67, 75, 183, 200

Election of 1824, 55–56

Elizabethtown (Ky), 10, 17, 21, 238

Ellicott, Andrew, 322

Ely, Ezra Stiles: and Eaton affair, 162–63

Emerson, Ralph Waldo: comments on Tallahassee, 127

Eppes (Family), 134

Eppes, Francis, 135

Eustis, Abram, 49, 53, 66

Fairbanks, George, 293–94, 301, 307, 313, 316, 317, 328

Faith Bonds, 216, 222, 248, 265, 271, 280, 287, 334. *See also* Union Bank of Florida

Fillmore, Millard, 333, 336–38

Fannin, James, 231, 235, 238

Fatio, Francis, 43

Finley, Jesse, 337

First Seminole War, x, 35, 39, 366n. *See also* Andrew Jackson, "Florida Affair."

Fletcher, Duncan Upshaw, 353

"Florida Affair," 159, 170–71

"Florida Crisis of 1826–1827." *See* Indian Scare of 1826–1827

Florida Institute of Agriculture, Antiquities, and Sciences, 131

Fontane, John M., 45

Forbes Purchase, 107, 176, 178–79, 209

Forsythe, John, 246, 255, 269

Fort Brooke, 101, 232, 290; established, 65

Fort Harrison: and relief expedition, 21–23

Fort King, 219, 230, 232, 233; establishment and description of, 96–97; and murder of Wiley Thompson at, 232

Fort Mims, 29

Fort San Luis, 70, 142, 272, 281; DuVal's comments on, 115

Forward, William A., 307

Francis, William, 277

Frankfort (Ky), 7, 15, 20, 47, 224

Free Soil Party, 336; and Martin Van Buren, 336

Freylinghuyson, Theodore, 203

Fromentin (Judge), 39

Gadsden, James, 39, 50, 56, 65, 98, 131, 133, 135, 175, 188, 204, 210–11, 214, 217, 230, 279, 306; biographical sketch of, 59; and Treaty of Moultrie Creek, 59–60, 63, 69, 92, 112, 113; and territorial delegate race (1825), 95, 136, (1831), 174, 179–80, 183, 186, 188, 190, 192–95, 207; and Treaty of Payne's Landing, 213–14; defends WPD in Senate investigation, 207

Gaines, Edmund P., 102, 121–22, 233

Gaither, Greenbury A., 43

Gamble, Catherine, 148
Gamble, Elizabeth, 14. See also Elizabeth Wirt
Gamble, John Gratton, 217, 129, *130*, 264; and Union Bank of Florida, 222, 241, 254
Gamble, Mary, 251–52
Gamble, Robert, 14, 232, 251; migrates to Tallahassee, 126; observations on Duval family, 126–27
Gambles (Family), 14, 119; plantations of, 147
Gautier, Peter, 185, 280; praises WPD, 241; and WPD's settlement with War Department, 275
Gibson, Edward R., 188, 190
Giddings, Joshua, 304, 336
Gilmer, Thomas, 293, 299, 301, 302
Geiger, John, 45
Germantown, Battle of, 10
Goliad Massacre, xi, 234–38, 322
Goldsborough, Louis M.: describes Indian attacks in Middle Florida, 234; comments on Florida Constitutional Convention, 254; on James Westcott, 262
Goldsborough Family, 251
Gordon, Adam, 162
Gorman, William, 234
Gould, Elias B., 60, 168, 313
Gould, James, 307
Graham, George, 142
Green, Duff, ix, 158, 301–02; War of 1812, 21; and Washington *United States Telegraph*, 171, 186, 202
Green, Nathaniel, 77
Greenup, Catherine, 6
Greenup, Charlotte, 148
Greenup, Christopher, 6, 10, 359n
Grundy, Felix, 9, 11, 203; and conflict with Henry Clay, 12, 19; and legal dispute with WPD, 35, 48
Guthrie, James, 224

Hair, Thomas, 327
Hanner, Peter, 285
Hagner, Thomas, 250
Hall, William: defends WPD before U. S. Senate, 205–06

Hamilton, Alexander, 15
Hamilton, Alexander, Jr.,: and conflict with WPD, 62, 68, 135, 106, 163–64, 371n,
Hammack, James, 20
Hanham, James R., 47
Hannegan, Edward, 323
Hardin, Benjamin, 9, 11, 17, 34; on DuVal's deceitfulness, 18
Harrison, Burr, 10–11, 147, 218, 237–238
Harrison, William Henry, ix, xi, 1, 67, 240, 269, 278, 280, 354; and War of 1812, 20–21
Harrodsburg (Ky), 7, 95, 218
Hartford Convention, 33
Hawkins, Charles E.: murder of William Allison McRea, 164
Hawkins, George S., 275, 351
Haycraft, Samuel, 10; on DuVal's popularity in Bardstown, 17
Hayes, John, 11
Hays, Jack, 327
Hayne, Robert, 173, 175, 203; and debate with Daniel Webster, 170, 174; and Nullification Crisis, 215
Heintzelman, Samuel Peter, 242, 266–68, 276, 281; describes St. Joseph, 245; loans Willis Alston money to escape, 271; observations on Leigh Read, 279, 281; in Washington with WPD, 285–86, 293; observation on Judge Joseph Smith, 294
Helm, Ben, 17–18
Helm, Thomas, 10
Henry, Patrick, 4
Hernandez, Joseph, 43, 47, 61–62, 97, 136, 183, 313; becomes territorial delegate, 54
Hicks, John, 80, 84–85, 107–110, 153; and visit to Washington, 115–17. *See also* Tuko-see-Mathla
Hitchiti Fowl Towns, 40
Hopkins, Samuel (Galveston developer): and marriage to Mary DuVal Robinson, 327
Hopkins, Samuel (soldier), 19; and War of 1812, 21–23, 25
Horseshoe Bend, Battle of, 31
Houston, Sam, 159, 237, 321, 348; WPD introduces sons to, 231; WPD attorney of, 350

Houstin *Telegraph and Texas Register*, 236
Hubard, Edmund, 293, 295–96, 299
Hull, William, 21
Hunkers, 332. See also Barnburners.
Hunt, William Hasell: charges WPD with malfeasance, 139
Hunter, R. M. T., 293, 299, 301, 347, 350
Humphreys, Gad: as Indian Agent, 49, 52, 58–60, 64, 66, 72–73, 76–78, 80, 86, 96–98, 110–11, 113–15, 117, 120–23, 153, 162; establishes Indian Agency at Fort King, 85, 96; takes "deputation" of chiefs to Washington, 115–117; complains of Indian flogging law, 123; conflict with WPD, 102, 157, 161, 189, 191, 207, 213
Hynes and Company, 10; and legal disputes over, 11
Hynes, Abner, 10, 16
Hynes, Alfred, 10, 16; explores St. Johns River with WPD, 43–44; practices medicine with Burr Harrison, 218
Hynes, Andrew (Nancy DuVal's cousin), 10, 25, 26, 31, 51, 224, 238; WPD writes of planting interests and friendship toward, 152–53
Hynes, Andrew (Nancy DuVal's father), 9; and American Revolution, 10; forms business partnership with brother Thomas, 10; and ambivalence toward slavery, 10; disputes over estate of, 10, 218, 361n
Hynes, Elizabeth Warford, (Nancy DuVal's mother), 10
Hynes, Elizabeth Harrison (Nancy DuVal's sister), 10
Hynes, Hanna, 10
Hynes, Nancy, 9; background and family of, 10–11; See also Nancy DuVal
Hynes, Polly, 10, 16, 128, 151, 201, 321
Hynes, Thomas (Nancy DuVal's brother), 10; and Fort Harrison relief expedition, 22
Hynes, Thomas (Nancy DuVal's uncle), 10
Hynes, William (Nancy DuVal's cousin), 10–11, 361n; and antislavery views, 218
Hynes, William (Nancy DuVal's grandfather), 10

Indian Affairs, Bureau of: creation of, 75
Indian Flogging Law, 123
Indian Removal Act, 170, 172
Indian Scare of 1826–1827, 118–20
Indians: See Seminoles, Creeks
Ingham, Samuel, 163, 169, 188, 192, 197, 200; appointed secretary of treasury, 157
Irving, Washington, xii-xiii, 22, 24, 30, 156, 202, 279, 289, 352, 355, 364n; at Aaron Burr treason trial in Richmond, xii, 15–16; and "Ralph Ringwood Tales," 2–3, 11, 211, 278, 334, 355, 358n; and Achille and Catherine Murat, 223
Irving, William, 29
Issac (slave), 13

Jackson, Andrew, x, xiv, 1, 26, 36, 44–45, 47–53, 59–60, 67, 74, 76, 77, 91–96, 103, 132, 136–40, 143–48, 154, 158, 167, 177–81, 183, 188–89, 191–93, 219, 227, 240, 245, 248, 268, 274, 278, 285, 287, 333; and War of 1812, 26, 29, 33; and First Seminole War, 35, 39, 366n; as provisional governor of Florida, 38–42; and Election of 1824, 55–56, 68, 75, 90–99; and "Corrupt Bargain," 91, 94; elected president, 154; as president, 156–66, 168–75, 185–86, 188, 196–203, 205, 209, 211, 214–18, 222, 233, 236, 238, 241–44, 247; and conflict with Calhoun, xi, xiv; 158–61, 163, 170–75, 186, 188, 199–200, 202–03, 215; views on Indians in Florida, 39–42, 59–60; views on WPD, 39; advises WPD on governor's role, 51; invites WPD to visit Hermitage, 95; WPD complains of hardships as governor, 139; death of 313
Jackson County (FL): "Chipola District" in, 107; deaf and dumb asylum in, 136, 183
Jackson, Rachel, 36, 74, 93; description of Pensacola, 48; death of, 154, 160
Jefferson Day Dinner, 170, 173
Jefferson County (FL), 106, 129–30, 132, 147–48, 164, 232, 279, 337
Jefferson, Thomas, 3–5, 11, 76, 135, 146, 272; and embargo, 19, 26; and Wythe poisoning, 14–15

Jesup, Thomas, 239, 242, 269
Johnson, Joshua, 203
Johnson, Richard M., 19, 29, 47, 202, 227

Kain, William, 326–27
Kendall, Amos, 94, 158
Kentucky: confused land titles in, 5; condition after the American Revolution, 5; mass migration into, 5–8, 10; and militia in, 13; early politics in 11–13; population of in 1810, 16; War of 1812 in, 19–26; Jackson party in, 94–95; Old Court-New Court Battle in, 34, 55, 94
Kentucky Resolutions, 11
Key West, 121, 164–65; wrecking activity in, 100–01; need for court in, 101; Duval Street in, 354; need for military presence in, 143–44
Knickerbocker Magazine, 3, 278, 289, 355, 358n. *See also* Washington Irving
King Hijah (Tuski Hajo), 80, 103
Kings Mountain, Battle of, 20
Kingsley, Zephania, 189–90, 388–89n

L'Enfant, Pierre, 26
Lafayette, Marquis de., 4; and visit to Washington, 91
Lafayette Tract, 98–99, 132–33, 142, 149–50, 152, 196, 230, 239
Lake Wimico and St. Joseph Canal and Railroad Company, 244, 254, 271
La Plante (Indiana soldier), 24
Lancaster, Joseph B., 100
Ledwith, Michael: and murder of Leigh Read, 291–92
Leon County, (FL), 106, 139, 152, 164, 176, 291
Leon County Courthouse, 251, 267, 325, 331
Leon County Grand Jury, 127
Leon County Superior Court, 212, 232, 241, 275
Lexington (Ky), 6, 9, 12, 15, 20, 21, 95, 354; and manufacturing in, 26; and branch of the Second Bank of the U. S. in, 34
Levy, David, 269, 290, 309–18, 348; and Florida Constitutional Convention, 260, 262; and support of Florida statehood, 266; and selection as one of Florida's first senators, 311–14, ; as territorial delegate, 283, 286, 290, 292, 298–200; WPD and 283, 286, 299, 310–312, 318; and name change to Yulee, 317–18; John Quincy Adams contests right to House seat, 286. *See also* David Levy Yulee
Levy, Moses Elias, 308, 318; as legal client of WPD, 315–16
Lewis, Romeo, 196
Liberty Party, 310
Lion of the West, xiii. *See also* James Kirke Paulding
Little, Lucius: on riding circuit in Kentucky, 17
Livingston, Edward, 188, 192, 197
Loco-Focos, 249, 254–55, 262, 265, 283
Long, Richard, 257
Louisville, Ky., 7, 15, 21, 68, 93, 199, 218–19, 223, 225, 226–27, 237–40; description of, 224; branch of Second Bank of the U. S. established in, 34

McCarty, William: as territorial secretary, 140, 162
McIntosh, William 76
McIver, John, 71, 77, 206
McKee, John, 99
McKee, Samuel, 19, 20, 27–29
McKeowin's Hotel, 31
McKenney, Thomas L., 141, 144–45, 153, 161, 169; and establishment of the Bureau of Indian Affairs, 75; and reservation boundaries, 97; consults with WPD on Indian affairs, 92, 102–05, 119, 122–23; orders Humphreys to report number of runaways slaves living with Seminoles, 110; WPD introduces son Burr to, 114–15
McLane, Louis, 188
McQueen, Peter, 40–42
McRea, William Allison, 131, 168; as U. S. district attorney, 162; murdered in Key West, 164
Macomb, Alexander, 267
Macomb, David B., 195

Macon, Edgar, 47, 68; alcoholism and death of, 134–35
Madison County (FL), 106, 255, 279, 345
Madison (FL), 311, 328; Democratic State Convention in, 330–32
Madison, Dolley, 30
Madison Democratic Convention, 1–2, 330–31
Madison, James, 19; and War of 1812, 26–32, 34, 354; and nephew Edgar Macon, 47, 68, 134–35; and Kentucky and Virginia Resolutions, 203, 293
Magnolia (FL): WPD in, 155–56; Bank of, 215
Mahon, John K., 119
Mallory, Stephen R., 350
Marcy, William, 203
Marsh, Owen, 85, 110, 120, 122
Marshall, John, 5; and Burr Trial, 15–16
Marvin, William, 255, 260
Mason, John, 293, 299, 302, 346, 350
Maxwell, Augustus, 337
Mays, Dennett, 330
Micanopy (Seminole chief), 53, 64
Miccosukees, 40, 79, 80, 113, 117–20. See also Seminoles, Creeks, Indian Scare of 1826–1827
Middle Florida, x, 70; Indian removal in, 72, 88, 90; description of 98–99; migration into, 106–7, 132, 134, 144–45; surveying in, 107; support for statehood in, 253, 264–66; yellow fever epidemic in, 284; economic collapse, bank failures in, 263–65, 291, 300
Miller, Nicholas, 23
Milton, John, 337
Monmouth, Battle of, 4, 10
Monroe, James, 1, 39, 45, 47, 52, 55–56, 59, 66, 73, 91–92, 138, 156–59; and Andrew Jackson's Florida, 35, and appointment of WPD judge, ix, 37; and appointment of WPD governor, 45–46, 52; proclaims first sale of public lands in Tallahassee, 89, 98; and Indian boundary, 98
Mount Comfort (plantation), 3, 4, 5, 15, 358n; See also Samuel DuVal and William DuVal

Montgomery, Thomas, 19, 28
Morehead, James, 276
Morton, Jackson, 350
Moseley, William D., 312, 320, 323, 325, 326
Mulatto King, 42
Murat, Achille, 131, 149, 229; relation to Napoleon Bonaparte, 134; description of, 148; accompanies WPD to West Point, New York, 223; invests in Texas lands, 231–32
Murat, Catherine, 223, 281; and Washington Irving, 223
Murray (Captain), 234
My Beloved South, xiii. See also Betty Paschal O'Conner

Napoleon Bonaparte, 19, 134
Neamathla, 40, 53, 58, 71, 83, 143; and Moultee Creek talks, 64–65; WPD's description of, 70, 72, 84; WPD's confrontation with 70–73, 78–80, 83–84
Neighbors, Robert S., 347
"Negro Fort," 40
Nelson County (Ky), 5, 7, 9, 10, 18, 19, 99, 226, 319; militia in, 13; population (1810) in, 16,
Nelson County Colonization Society, 218. See also William Hynes
Newnansville (FL), 180, 233, 276
New Orleans, 26, 48, 57, 58, 66, 72, 84, 122, 214, 220, 224, 236, 327, 340–41, 346, 353; Battle of, 33; 59, 96, 136, 138, 143, 162
New York *Evening Post*, 60
Nicols (British soldier), 124
Noriega, Joseph, 52
Nucleus, 135–36, 143, 171, 175–76, 180, 183–84, 186, 188, 194, 199, 228, 249, 264. See also Richard Keith Call, Robert Butler, George T. Ward, Richard C. Allen and James Gadsden
Nuttall, William, 217, 230

Osceola, 233; murder of Wiley Thompson, 232
O'Conner, Betty Paschal, xiii
O'Neale's Tavern, 69
Onis, Don Luis de, 35

Ornsby, Stephen, 19
Overton, John, 50, 67

Panic of 1819, 34, 55
Panic of 1837, 248
Pakenham Letter, 304–05; John C. Calhoun and, 304; WPD on 305
Pakenham, Richard, 304
Palatka Democratic Convention, 307–08
Parkhill (Family), 134
Parkhill, John, 256, 264, 268
Parkhill, Samuel, 251, 256, 264; and Florida Constitutional Convention, 254–55; and Union Bank of Florida, 268; death of, 284
Partridge, John M., 255
Paschal, George Washington, 327; and marriage to Marcia Price, 349
Patriot War (1812–1813), 41
Paulding, James Kirke, 16, 29–30; and William P. DuVal, xiii, 357–58n
Peace of Ghent, 33, 34, 40, 94
Peggy Eaton Affair, 160–63
Pelham, Peter, 49, 66
Penieres, Jean, 49
Penrose, Charles, 297–98
Pensacola, x, 39; description of, 48; Andrew Jackson's capture of, 35; transfer of flags in, 38; free blacks in, 41; Andrew Jackson meets with Indians in, 42; and first session of Florida legislative council in, 51–52; yellow fever in, 52, 66; bank in, 215, 259, 273
Pensacola *Floridian*, 61
Pensacola *Gazette*, 84, 86, 88, 182, 184; 212, 352; and William Hasell Hunt, 139; Benjamin Wright, 223, 252
Perkins (captain), 15
Pierce, Benjamin, 239
Pierce, Franklin, 351
Pinckney Treaty, 11, 322
Peterson, Merrill, 94
Peterson, Norma, 302
Peyton's Boarding House, 350
Pindar (Indian contractor), 92
Phagan, John, 118, 161, 207, 211; named sub-agent if Indian affairs, 105; WPD praises, 120; charges against, 144, 209; accompanies chiefs to Arkansas territory, 213–14; dismissal of, 217
Pleiades Club, 11
Polk, James K., 1, 216, 311, 322, 328–29, 332, 334, 337, 341, 343; and Election of 1844, 305, 307, 309–10; asks WPD for information on Florida, 316; signs Texas annexation act, 321; and Oregon Question, 323; and war message to Congress, 325
Pope, Anne, 3, 4. See also Anne Pope DuVal.
Pope, Benjamin, 358n
Pope, John, 4, 9, 11, 20, 34, 55, 68, 94, 219, 274, 287, 358n, 363n
Pope, John W., 100
Pope, Patrick H., 218
Pope, William, 214, 217, 358n
Pope, Worden, 17, 227, 359n; views on John C. Calhoun's role in Jackson's cabinet breakup, 199–200
Price, Marcia, 148, 172, 226, 240, 268, 286; moves to Galveston, Texas, 309; death of husband William Price, 327, 341; marries George W. Paschal, 349. *See also* Marcia DuVal
Price, William D.: migrates to Tallahassee, 129; marries Marcia DuVal, 147; appointed Apalachicola port inspector, 172; in St. Joseph, 251, 268; moves to Galveston, Texas, 309; death of, 327
"Principles of 98," 11, 170–171, 203, 293, 312, 315, 319, 354
Proctor, George, xiii, 134, 152
Proctor, Toney (Antonio), xiii, 41, 64, 134, 152, 371n
Putnam, B. A., 307

"Ralph Ringwood Tales," xiii, 1–3, 11, 211, 278, 334, 358n. *See also* "Early Experiences of Ralph Ringwood," Washington Irving
"Ralph Ringwood Myth," 3, 358n
Randall, Laura Wirt, 234; description of Tallahassee, 127–28; uncomplimentary description of DuVals, 128–30; entertains DuVal daughters at Belmont, 148

Randall, Thomas, 130, 142, 148, 157, 250, 267, 274, 285; appointed judge of the Middle District of Florida, 129, 380n; and land speculation, 148, 157; and Rogers case, 212; and Belmont plantation, 130, 147–48, 234, 267
Randolph, Arthur M., 242, 267, 272, 309; marries Laura DuVal, 272; and surveying, 309
Randolph (Family), 14, 135, 251, 272
Randolph, John, 272
Randolph, Laura, 286, 309, 310. See also Laura Harrison DuVal
Randolph Plantation, 287
Randolph, Thomas Easton, 242, 272
Read-Alston Duel, 270–72
Read, Leigh, 255, 277, 279–80; and duel with Oscar White, 213; and duel with Augustus Alston, 270–72; and attack and murder by Willis Alston, 271, 281, 291; and Second Seminole War, 234, 236; WPD opposes appointment of as U. S. marshal, 273
Red Sticks, 40, 41, 65 See also Creeks
Reflections on the Law of 1813, 28
Reid, Robert Raymond, 266, 259; opinion of legislative council, 215; opinion of WPD, 215; opposition to banks, 215–16; on divided nature of Florida territory, 230; at Florida Constitutional Convention, 255, 258–59, 262; as territorial governor of Florida, 269–73, 277, 279–81; death of, 284
Remini, Robert, 6
Reubin (slave), 13
Richards, Stephen, 58–59, 144
Richmond (Va), ix, xii, 3–9; description of, 13–16
Ringgold, James, 176
Ritchies (Family), 14
Road building, 50, 58, 70, 86, 106–07, 113
Robinson, James, 255, 262, 267, 268, 271, 280, 286, 317; and marriage to Mary DuVal, 250; death of, 294, 296, 300
Robinson, Jonathon, 71
Robinson, Judge, 79
Robinson, Maria, 309–10, 317

Robinson, Mary, 268, 286, 288, 309, 310, 316–17, 321, 353; and marriage to Samuel Hopkins, 327 See also Mary DuVal
Rodman, John, 117, 135, 163
Rogers, David, S.,: WPD and desperation pardon appeal of, 212
Rowan, John, 117
Russell, William, 22

St. Augustine, xiii; 294; description of, 293–94; free blacks in, 41; WPD resides in, 292, 294–97, 300–01
St. Augustine East Florida Herald, 112–13, 147, 253; and Elias Gould, 168
St. Augustine Florida Herald, 54; and Joseph Smith, 139
St. Joseph (FL), 240, 244–45, 250–51; WPD's law office in, 232; description of, 245; rivalry with Apalachicola, 244; constitutional convention in 252, 254–62; yellow fever epidemic in, 283–85; decline of, 300
St. Joseph's College, 9, 172, 210, 218, 226
St. Marks (FL): capture of by Andrew Jackson, 35; and Indian talks in, 52, 54, 58–59, 75–80, 83–86, 206; troops in, 70, 79; lighthouse and improvements for 143, 220; railroad and, 185, 229
Sanchez (Family), 180
Sanchez, Francis, 43, 45
Sanchez, Joseph, 43, 45, 147, 180, 313
Scott, Charles, 20
Scott, Winfield, 144, 233–34, 333
Searcy, Isham: defends WPD before Senate, 205
Second Bank of the United States, 34, 166, 202, 248, 254; WPD on 216–19
Second Seminole War, 231–34, 338–39, 242, 273, 276
Sequi, Bernardo, 45, 47, 59
Seminoles, 65–66, 73, 102–03, 106, 111, 118, 122, 144–45, 157, 161, 182, 209–11, 220, 267, 270; origins of, x; disposition of when Florida became American territory, 39–43; and black slaves (vassals), 40–41, 63–65, 110–12, ; and contact with

Seminoles (continued)
  English and Spanish, 13, 40, 42, 64–65, 69, 97, 101, 124; delegation to Washington, 115–17. *See also* Creeks, Treaty of Moultrie Creek, Payne's Landing, First Seminole War and Second Seminole War
Sharp, Solomon P., 19; assassination of, 55
Shawnee Prophet, 20
Shelby, Isaac, 20, 21, 31, 33
Sibley, Charles, 306, 309
Sibley, Samuel, 266, 276–77, 337
Simmons, William, 134, 213, 307; and selection of site for capital, 61, 70, 72
Simpson, Craig, 293
Slavery: and Seminoles, 41, 111–12
Slaughter, Gabriel, 34
Smith, Joseph L., 46, 53, 57, 100; animosity toward WPD, 68, 135, 139, 162–63; and adjudicating cases involving runaway slaves among Indians, 111–12; Samuel Heintzelman's description of, 294
Snyder, Frank, xiv, 7
"South Carolina Exposition and Protest," 159–60
Southard, Samuel, xiv, 73, 81, , 141, 145, 154, 201, 222, 244, 309, 351; practices law in Richmond, 14; and land purchases and planting interests with WPD, 132–33, 149–52, 157, 196, 230, 239; WPD complains of his situation in Florida, 57, 62, 81–83, 113, 121, 137, 139; WPD describes family to, 128; and confrontation with Andrew Jackson, 138; WPD expresses views to on Adams cabinet, 137–38, 145
Specie Circular, 248
Speed, Thomas, 9
Steele, William, 59
Stower, John G. 168
Sydnor, Charles, 160
Sweeney, George: and poisoning of George Wythe, 14–15

Tallahassee, x, xiii, *100*, *116*, *128*, 229; selection of site for capital, 70–72; WPD's homestead in, 72, 77, 99, 130–31; description of, 82–83, 86, 99, 127–28, *167*, 238–29, 241

Tallahassee Disturbances (1841), 276–77
Tallahassee *Florida Courier*, 186, 194; Edward Gibson and, 188, 190–91
Tallahassee *Floridian*, 242, 274, 278, 337
Tallahassee *Floridian and Advocate*, 166, 182, 185, 190, 194, 203, 208, 212
Tallahassee *Floridian and Journal*, 352
Tallahassee Railroad Company, 229
Taney, Roger, 188, 247
Tappen, Benjamin, 304
Tariff of 1828, 159
Taylor, Zachary: and War of 1812, 21–23; and Mexican War, 325, 327, 333; as presidential candidate, 333–38; as president, 343–47
Tecumseh, 19, 20, 29
Texas-New Mexico Boundary Dispute, 346–48
Thomas, David: defends WPD before U. S. Senate, 206
Thompson, Arthur, 249
Thompson, Leslie, 255, 260
Thompson, Wiley, 219–220; appointed Indian agent, 217; murder of, 232
Thruston, A. S., 321
Tiger Tail (Thlocklo Tustenuggee), 234; description of 119; visits DuVal house, 129
Timberlake, Margaret O'Neale, 69, 160. See also Peggy Eaton
Tippecanoe, Battle of, 20
Treaty of Fort Gibson, 213
Treaty of Indians Springs, 76
Treaty of Fort Jackson, 33, 40
Treaty of Moultrie Creek, 59–60, 63–64, 69, 70, 77, 103, 112–13, 124, 210, 213; and dispute over reservation boundary of, 69, 91–92, 98, 112, 113
Treaty of Payne's Landing, 213–14
Troup (Georgia Governor) , 120
Tuko-see-Mathla, 80, *116*. See also John Hicks
Tyler, John, xiv, 1, *285*, 290–91, 293, 298, 301, 306–10, 354; becomes president; 285; conflict with Henry Clay, 285–86; appoints WPD law agent, 287; and annexation of Texas, 302, 304, 310; and

explosion of *Princeton*, 302–03; signs Florida admission bill, 310

Union Bank of Florida: 248–49, 254, 273–75, 315; signed into law by WPD, 216; operations of, 217, 241, 248; WPD and, 1, 220, 222, 230, 250–51, 264, 268, 278, 280, 315, 334, 354–55; and Florida Constitutional Convention, 241, 248–51, 254, 260, 262. See also Faith Bonds
United States vs. William P. DuVal, 275
Upshur, Abel, 286, 296–97 301–02; killed in explosion of *Princeton*, 302

Valley Forge, 10
Van Buren, Martin, xi, xii, 1, 14, 202, 207, 227, 245, 249, 250, 255, 259, 265, 267, 269, 271, 273–75, 277–79, 285–86, 301, 305, 313, 315, 332, 334–36, 339, 354; and Andrew Jackson's cabinet, 186, 192, 196; WPD's appraisal of, 198, 227–28, 335, 339; and Eaton Affair, 160, 199–200; Calhoun blocks appointment of, 202; as vice president, 202, 211; elected president, 240; falling out with Richard Keith Call, 243; inauguration of, 247–48; WPD praises handling of financial crisis, 249; Free Soil Party nominee, 336, 339; assists Andrew Jackson preparation of bank veto message, 211
Vass, Ellen Vass, 267
Vincennes (In), 5, 21
Virginia Resolutions, 11
Von Steuben (Baron), 4

Wabash River Campaign, 21–21, 32
Walter, George K., 242, 245, 276; appointed territorial secretary, 229
Walton, George: as territorial secretary, 48, 54, 57–58, 61, 66–67, 84, 86, 92, 96, 98–100, 104, 121
Walker, Minor, 281
Wanton, Edward, 42–43
Wanton's (Micanopy), 107
War of 1812, 19–26
Ward, George T., 132, 173, 230, 251, 264, 284, 337

Ward, George, W., 93
Washington, D. C., x; view of, 204, 221, 349; description of, 26–27, 349
Washington, George, 3, 6, 21, 77, 143
Washington *Globe*, 202, 246, 306; Francis Blair and, 186
Washington *National Intelligencer*, 31, 91, 98, 352
Washington *United States Telegraph*, 202, 204; and Duff Green, 171, 186
Waukeenah Plantation, 147
Wayne, Anthony, 77
Webb, James, 321, 322, 324
Webster, Daniel, 171, 203, 205, 240, 278, 281, 287, 291, 301, 346
Webster-Hayne Debate, 170, 173
Welaunee Planation, 147–48
West, DuVal, 353–54
Westcott, James D., 217, 219, 222, 229, 238, 245, 250–51, 258, 265, 271, 287, 309, 324, 350; appointed territorial secretary, 163; WPD praises, 176, 193; and delegate race debacle, 194–96, 209; as acting governor, 209–11, 217; and duel with Thomas Baltzell, 213; as leader of anti-bank movement, 249, 254; conflict with WPD at Florida Constitutional Convention, 255–62; description of, 213, 262; conflict with WPD, 266–71, 278, 292, 311–20; denounces WPD as "political harlot," 315; at Madison Democratic convention, 311–12
White, Ellen Adair "Florida," 48
White, Hugh Lawson, 227, 240
White, Joseph M., 47–48, 95, 104, 121, 124, 136, 138, 143–44, 167–68, 213, 217, 229, 244, 251, 287; appointed land commissioner, 51; and father-in-law John Adair, 96, 136, 214; and WPD's early recommendation of, 369n; and conflict with Richard Keith Call, 136, 213, 217; and conflict with WPD, 138–40, 146, 162–63, 170–72, 175–80, 183–86, 188–201, 203–09, 212, 222; and 1831 delegate race, 186, 190, 192–96
White, Oscar: and duel with Leigh Read, 213

White, Philip: and duel with Samuel DuVal, 213
Wickliffe, Charles, A. 9, 11, 191, 286–87, 292, 302, 319; clashes with Joseph White over appointment of law agent, 208
Wilcox (colonel), 23
Wilcox (duelist): kills Nathaniel DuVal, 13
Wilderness Road, 6, map of, 8
Wilson, Woodrow, 354
Williams, John Lee, 309; and selection of site for capital, 60, 70, 72
Williams, Robert: defends WPD before U. S. Senate, 205
Willis, Bird, 131
Willis (Family), 134
Winthrop, Robert, C., 328, 332
Wilmot, David, 325, 328–33, 336, 341, 343
Wirt, Catherine, 251
Wirt, Elizabeth, 234
Wirt (family), 134
Wirt, William, 14, 129, 138, 141, *150*, 154, 157, 201, 205, 222, 134, 287; and Aaron Burr Trial, 15; and purchase of Major DuVal's House, 14
Wirtland Planation, 234
Wise, Henry, 293, 299, 301–02
Woodbury, Levi, 188, 197
Woodward, Alfred, 255
Woodward, Augustus, 77, 131; appraisal of WPD's organization of Florida Territory, 89; rules in favor of WPD's homestead claim, 142; death of, 38on
Worthington, William, 42–45, 52
Wright, Benjamin D., 329, 351; appraisal of WPD's governorship and future political prospects, 223, 252;
Wright, Leitch, 40
Wyatt, William, 77, 267, 277–78; conflict with WPD, 170–76, 179, 182–92, 203–09, 212; and Michael Ledwith case, 291
Wythe, George, 4, 5, 359n; poisoning death of 14–15; and teacher of William DuVal and Thomas Jefferson, 3, 14–15;

Ximenez, Jose, 45

Yellow Jackets: WPD captain of, 21
Yonge, Chandler C., 326, 329
Yorktown, Battle of, 4
Yulee, David Levy, *318*, 319, 324, 331, 350; marries Annie Wickliffe, 319; contests Wilmot Proviso, 329–30; opposes Compromise of 1850, 349. *See also* David Levy